Global Issues in Antitrust and Competition Law

Third Edition

Eleanor M. Fox
Walter J. Derenberg Professor of Trade Regulation Emerita
New York University School of Law

Daniel A. Crane
Richard W. Pogue Professor of Law
University of Michigan Law School

Damien Gerard
Adjunct Professor of EU Competition Law
University of Louvain and College of Europe

Thomas K. Cheng
Professor of Law
University of Hong Kong Faculty of Law

Derek Lotter
Co-Head, Competition Practice
Bowmans (Africa)

GLOBAL ISSUES SERIES®

WEST ACADEMIC

860 Blue Gentian Road, Suite 350
Eagan, MN 55121
1-877-888-1330

Published in the United States of America

ISBN: 978-1-68561-512-3

Acknowledgments

The authors thank Hiroaki Matsunaga, Gabriel Orazi, Kurt Rajpal, Felipe Serrano Pinilla, Holden A. Steinhauer, Yusuke Takamiya and Michael Watts for excellent research assistance and Cheri Fidh, Brendan L. Heldenfels and Linda Smalls for excellent assistance in preparing the manuscript. The Filomen D'Agostino and Max E. Greenberg Foundation provided generous research support to Eleanor Fox.

Foreword to the First Edition

Eleanor Fox has frequently reminded us that while markets are global, antitrust laws—the rules that undergird effectively functioning markets—are national. She would be first to recognise that each of the key elements of this insight require a degree of qualification. In fact, surprisingly few markets are seamlessly global. And increasingly the practice of antitrust law is already in the process of becoming international, although it is certainly true that the instruments of antitrust enforcement and merger regulation are overwhelmingly national, notwithstanding their extraterritorial reach.

This monumental volume is focused on the critical interplay between the national and the global elements of antitrust. It does so through the medium of national jurisprudence, through the reproduction of key speeches, through an analysis of commissions and treaties and the efforts of antitrust enforcers to align their practice, or, at the very least, to understand the bases of divergent national practices.

Few are better qualified to undertake this task than the two authors. Eleanor Fox is the scholar most closely associated with describing, understanding and analysing international antitrust, as evidenced by her truly massive output in this area alone, and by no means her only area of contribution to antitrust scholarship. But even more than her scholarship, for those of us whose work in antitrust started at its geographical margins—that is to say, beyond the borders of the United States and the European Union—Eleanor is distinguished by her empathy with and her deep interest in these efforts. She has been a voice of the new antitrust authorities and as they have grown in stature and importance, so has she expanded her already vast horizons by incorporating the work of these new agencies into the corpus of international antitrust law and practice. The range of experiences drawn upon to produce this volume is testament not only to the centrality of the international markets/national antitrust insight, but to Eleanor's intellectual curiosity and willingness to embrace the experiences and insights of those who are not used to making an appearance in the scholarly antitrust tomes emanating from the US and Europe.

My introduction to Daniel Crane's work comes by way of his seminal historical accounts of the ups and downs, the ebbs and flows, of US antitrust. Just as I would insist that economic historians, rather than plain and simple economists, are best placed to understand contemporary economic phenomenon and even predict their future paths, so are legal historians best placed to understand the place to which decades of antitrust law has evolved and where it is likely to go. Historians are, per definition, sensitive to the often determinative force and power of context—politics, economics, stages of development, state-business relations, even wars all, as Daniel's work reminds us, influence the character and course of antitrust. This is the canvas of history and Daniel's regard for history permeates this volume.

We are at an important cusp in the development of international antitrust. Effective public international institutions are working precisely in those interstices between global markets and national antitrust that are the concern of this volume. The International Competition Network has brought together the vast majority of the world's national antitrust authorities. The ICN has developed best practices, not only in antitrust rules and approaches, but also in the building of effective antitrust authorities. And at least, as important, it has, largely through the active participation of precisely those of its members who used to be on the antitrust margins, that the ICN is beginning to appreciate "informed divergence", essentially an appreciation of why historical and other contexts may necessitate divergence rather than convergence. The OECD continues to produce applied scholarship of high quality and to embrace participation from way beyond its membership. UNCTAD continues to support those antitrust authorities from nations whose resource endowment and history most constrains their ability to develop into effective members of the international community of national antitrust authorities. And if the WTO is the avowed and self-proclaimed agent of a globalised world, for how long can antitrust remain on the periphery of its agenda.

Forewords traditionally extol the timeliness of the volumes that they are introducing. This volume is a majestic survey of an issue whose time has truly come. It will not only be a building block in the enterprise of aligning global markets and national antitrust, it is a veritable world tour of the rules and practices that already propel that world further and map out its future direction.

In their introduction to the volume the authors note that this volume on global antitrust issues may be used "to supplement domestic antitrust casebooks". They then immediately identify the oddity implicit in treating a volume on global antitrust as a supplement to national antitrust scholarship precisely because markets—the very stuff of antitrust—are global. As markets become ever more global—and even that inexorable development will experience ebbs and flows—so will this volume come to occupy a central place on the bookshelves of antitrust scholars and in the reading lists of their students.

DAVID LEWIS
GORDON INSTITUTE OF BUSINESS SCIENCE
JOHANNESBURG, SOUTH AFRICA
IMMEDIATE PAST CHAIRPERSON, SOUTH AFRICA COMPETITION TRIBUNAL

March 2010

Summary of Contents

Table of Contents

Table of Cases

The principal cases are in bold type.

Global Issues in Antitrust and Competition Law

Third Edition

Chapter 1

GOALS AND PERSPECTIVE

A. INTRODUCTION

If you were to do a comparative study in many areas of law, you would likely find that different legal systems purport to be pursuing similar objectives. Tort systems are generally about compensating injured persons for wrongs done to them, and deterring potentially harmful acts. Environmental law systems are generally about protecting natural resources while striking some balance with the need for exploitation of those resources. While different legal systems may have very different means of pursuing common objectives and give weight to different considerations as they do, there is often a fair degree of convergence on goals and purposes.

In competition law, be prepared for a wider than usual range of goals and purposes. While competition law officials around the globe often like to speak about agreement on goals, review of different countries' histories, policies, and practices often reveals very significant divergences on goals. There is broad consensus that competition law should advance efficiency and consumer welfare as at least one set of goals, but many regimes embrace a variety of other objectives as well: protecting economic opportunity, protecting small business, limiting economic concentration, protecting workers, facilitating economic development, promoting foreign investment, limiting foreign investment,; redistributing wealth and opportunity, disbursing political power, protecting democracy, preventing unfair exploitation, diminishing the need for sectoral regulation; ensuring that the state retains control over the economy; restricting the state's control over the economy. And the list goes on.

One thing that is clear from any comprehensive list of the all of the possible goals of competition law is that conflicts over the objectives of competition policy may sometimes arise. While it may be good public relations for competition policy to list a broad set of objectives, there will necessarily be trade-offs among some potential objectives at times. For example, while there could be competition law interventions that help both consumers and workers, that will not always be the case. What happens if a particular intervention might help consumers but harm workers, or vice versa? Competition law statutes usually are not very good at telling agencies or courts what to do in the event of such conflicts.

History is important here. While it may be easiest to study competition law comparatively by asking "what does country A do that is like or unlike country B," in reality the story of competition policy is dynamic. Countries A and B may have been through, or be on the verge of going through, significant shifts in policy. In the United States, antitrust law has gone through a number of different phases where different goals, objectives, and approaches were given priority. The same may be true of Europe. There was period in the early 2000s when there was a push for Europe to adopt a "more economic" approach to competition law akin to that what was perceived to be the norm in the United States. In the last several years, there has been a push for U.S. antitrust law to adopt a "more European" approach, particularly on issues of dominance. Could it be that the U.S. and Europe will reverse positions? The story is of course not so simple, but this example illustrates the importance of not only comparing countries to other countries at a fixed point in time, but in also understanding comparative work as involving some assessment of how different jurisdictions evolve over time. Given the number of jurisdictions with established or emerging competition laws—over 140 at last count—that may seem like a tall order.

Even as competition policy evolves in different countries, courts, agencies, and commentators often refer back to the "origin stories" of that particular country's competition laws. Each country or regime has its own unique competition law origins story that may shape the development of its laws. Sometimes, the telling of these stories may be quite contestable and driven by the desire to reach particular outcomes. In the section below, we present some selections from articles, speeches, or reports that tell "origins stories" as to the competition laws of the European Union, South Africa, China, Chile, India, Russia, and a country with a very new competition law—Uganda. As you read these vignettes, pay attention to the identity of the speaker, the context of their claims, and the likely audience.

B. ORIGINS STORIES

Mario Monti, European Commissioner for Competition Policy, *Antitrust in the U.S. and Europe: A History of Convergence* (2001)

I will present to you a review of the main areas of EU competition policy and attempt to identify the main respects in which our enforcement practice and that of the US antitrust agencies converge, and the main respects in which they diverge. The result of this review, as you will see, is encouraging. Despite all the noise created by what has indeed been one major divergence—the General Electric/Honeywell merger cleared by the Justice Department and prohibited by the European Commission—a silent process of convergence in competition law and practice has been going on for a number of years and has recently intensified. Of course, further efforts are needed and on both sides of the Atlantic we are deeply committed to this process. Our motivation in this endeavour is enhanced by a common awareness: besides being important in itself, US-EU convergence is a key building bloc for a multilateral co-operation in antitrust towards which our agencies are working closely together.

This trend toward convergence can be traced back to the very origins of EU competition law, and indeed of the EU itself. In his Memoires, Jean Monnet (one of the founding fathers of today's Europe) recalls the role played by then Secretary of State Dean Acheson in introducing a competition culture to Europe. He had a marked influence on the discussions that led to the "Schumann Declaration" of 9 May 1950, which lay the groundwork for the European Coal and Steel Community (the precursor of today's European Union), and which clearly stated that such an organisation of markets was to be construed as "the opposite of an international cartel designed to segment and exploit national markets by means of restrictive practices."

The influence of US antitrust law was profound during the early years of the development of competition policy in Europe and has continued ever since. This influence has helped to ensure that today, after almost 50 years of application and development of antitrust rules in Europe, we can confidently say that we share the same goals and pursue the same results on both sides of the Atlantic: namely to ensure effective competition between enterprises, by conducting a competition policy which is based on sound economics and which has the protection of consumer interest as its primary concern.

Eleanor M. Fox, US and EU Competition Law: A Comparison, in GLOBAL COMPETITION POLICY 339 (Edward M. Graham & J. David Richardson eds., Peterson Institute for International Economics 1997)

On the surface, there appears to be much in common between competition law in the United States and competition law in the European Union. Article [101 of the Treaty on the Functioning of the European Union], which prohibits agreements that distort competition and, accordingly, agreements that fix prices, is roughly comparable to section one of the US Sherman Act, which prohibits agreements in restraint of trade. Article [102] prohibits abuse of a dominant position and seems roughly comparable to Section 2 the Sherman Act, which prohibits monopolization and attempts or combinations to monopolize.

US and EC competition systems also have common objectives. Both seek to advance the interests of consumers and protect the free flow of goods in a competitive economy. Both seek to protect competitors' access to markets and protect to some extent consumer freedom of choice and seller freedom from coercion.

The respective competitive systems of the two areas have developed, however, out of different histories and different concerns, and upon closer examination significant variations in law, policy, and enforcement become apparent.

US competition policy derives from statutes enacted at different times in US history, and therefore the goals of the statutes are not identical. Overall, US antitrust policy is primarily designed to protect consumer welfare (i.e., produce a variety of products at reasonable prices), with modest elements of fairness (right of firms to be free from coercion) and of hostility to vast concentrations of economic power. Through much of its history, US enforcement agencies and courts were not very sensitive to claims of efficiency; they assumed that a robust competitive market would automatically be efficient. However, many contemporary commentators believe that efficiency claims are likely to be given more weight in the future.

Sophisticated economic analysis is a centerpiece of American antitrust enforcement. "Industrial policy," defined here as overt efforts to strengthen domestic firms to serve goals other than competition and efficiency, such as successfully competing in global markets, has not had much influence on US antitrust law. Occasionally, industrial policy concerns such as promoting research and development, influence competition rules, but these concerns rarely trump antitrust policy entirely. Fundamentally, competition has been the industrial policy of the United States.

In the European Union, economic integration of the various member nations is a dominant objective of competition policy. The common market evolved from the perceived need to break down trade barriers between western European nations, and community policy, therefore, reflects as a cardinal principle the desirability of free movement of goods and people across member state lines. By contrast, the free movement of goods in the United States was achieved through a sympathetic interpretation of the commerce clause provisions of the US constitution that effectively demolished local or regional preferences, and state barriers.

Trudi Hartzenberg, Executive Director: Trade Law Centre for Southern Africa, *Competition Policy and Practice in South Africa: Promoting Competition for Development*, 26 Nw. J. Int'l L. & Bus. 667 (2006)[1]

South Africa's new competition policy and law were drafted during the early years of South Africa's new democracy, a period characterized by important domestic policy and regulatory reform. These reforms were not only part of the comprehensive program for the country's economic, social, and political transformation, but also its integration into the global economy after decades of isolation under the apartheid regime. In the case of competition policy, however, concerns about specific development challenges entrenched by the previous era of political and economic control had to be explicitly reflected in the new South Africa's law and policy. It was clear that a robust competition law would only be politically possible if the law specifically addressed public interest concerns. The core focus of economic efficiency had to be tempered by a strong emphasis on development.

In the end, the new competition law, even with the broad sweep of its objectives, puts economic efficiency center-stage.[2] Public interest objectives are articulated alongside the goal of economic efficiency. Only as the jurisprudence develops will the nature of the trade-offs within this nexus of objectives become clear.

. . .

A key criticism by the new democratic government of the existing South Africa's competition legislation before 1998 was that it did not address the high levels of concentration in the economy—both in terms of ownership and market share. Development concerns featured strongly in the debates on the role of competition policy in addressing both structural features of the economy as well as corporate behavior, especially of the large conglomerates. The challenges of addressing poverty and unemployment were as much a part of the policy discussion as was the promotion of competition and economic efficiency.

---

1 This excerpt was first published in Trudi Hartzenberg, "Competition Policy and Practice in South Africa: Promoting Competition for Development," 26 Northwestern Journal of International Law & Business 667 (2006). Copyright 2006 Northwestern University and the Northwestern Pritzker School of Law. Reprinted by special permission of the author, Northwestern University Pritzker School of Law, and the Northwestern Journal of International Law & Business.

2 Editor's note: But see Competition Commission of South Africa v Mediclinic Southern Africa (Pty) Ltd and Another (CCT 31/20) [2021] ZACC 35 (South Africa Constitutional Court 15 October 2021), paras. 2–8.

. . .

The 1998 Competition Act covers all economic activity in South Africa and has extra-territorial reach to the extent that the Act applies to "all economic activity within, or having an effect within, the Republic." The purpose of the Competition Act's emphasis, in addition to the promotion of "efficiency, adaptability and development of the economy," is the promotion of small business development, greater participation in the economy (especially by previously disadvantaged individuals), and the promotion of a greater spread of ownership. The Act thus attempts to balance efficiency concerns and broader development priorities within the competition framework.

Small and medium-sized enterprise ("SME") development is important because of the structure of the South African economy. High levels of concentration and the conglomerate structure of business in many sectors, from mining to manufacturing to services, are important challenges for small business development in South Africa that are above and beyond the common challenges that SMEs face. The conglomerate structure of business in South Africa and the strong vertical linkages that exist in many industries can prove to be effective barriers to entry for smaller enterprises.

Promoting a broader spread of ownership, especially among historically disadvantaged persons, reflects concerns about the skewed distribution of income and wealth in South Africa. For many decades South Africa had one of the most unequal distributions of income in the world, with strong racial fault lines through the distribution. Black economic empowerment is now an important cross-cutting policy issue. A more even spread of ownership and SME promotion are important to ensure long-term, balanced, and sustainable development. These specific development challenges are articulated in the public interest issues included in the Competition Act.

Lester Ross, Partner-in-Charge of Wilmer Cutler Pickering Hale and Dorr LLP's Beijing office, *China's Antimonopoly Law*, 22-SPG ANTITR 66 (2008)

History of the AML

The People's Republic of China with its Marxist-Leninist-Maoist heritage was generally hostile to the concept of a market economy for decades after its founding in 1949. There were repeated episodes of hostility toward the emergence of market forces, most notably during the Great Leap Forward (1958–1961) and Great Proletarian Cultural Revolution (1966–1976). The state retained control of the commanding heights of the economy even during periods of economic liberalization through the exercise of monopoly control by state-owned enterprises in the banking, insurance, foreign trade, and other sectors.

The economic reform policies led by Deng Xiaoping beginning in 1978 after the Cultural Revolution accelerated in 1992 following his inspection tour to the south of the country to outmaneuver more conservative leaders.

This in turn led to the enactment of statutes with provisions regulating competition, but none of them constituted a full-fledged competition law. The Law Against Unfair Competition (1993), administered by the State Administration for Industry & Commerce (SAIC), is primarily a consumer protection statute but also prohibits abuses of authority by utilities to eliminate competition, certain tying conduct, administrative restrictions on competition from enterprises in other jurisdictions, setting prices below cost to exclude competition, and certain other anticompetitive conduct.

The Consumer Rights and Interests Protection Law (1993), also administered by the SAIC, provides that consumers have the right to choose among venders with respect to purchases and the right to reject compulsory transactions.

The Price Law (1997), administered by the National Development and Reform Commission (NDRC) and its predecessors, is intended to promote fair, open, and lawful market competition by standardizing and safeguarding normal price order and prohibiting price collusion, false or misleading pricing methods, price discrimination and other unlawful pricing conduct. It also reserves the government's right to control prices (by fixing prices or setting price guidelines) under specified circumstances: commodities with a material impact on economic development or people's livelihood, commodities in extremely short supply, commodities subject to a natural monopoly, and prices for major public utilities or welfare services.

The process of drafting the AML began in 1994. During the long, drawn-out process of finalizing the AML, China in 2003, and again in 2006, promulgated merger control regulations, both of which applied only to acquisitions by foreign investors, not to acquisitions by domestic parties. Their promulgation was hastened by China's admission to the World Trade Organization, which required China to make significant market-opening commitments with respect to foreign trade and investment.[3]

OECD: Chile—Accession Report on Competition Law and Policy 2010

Development of basic competition law

The history of the competition system in Chile began in 1959, with the enactment of the first competition act (Law No. 13.305). The competition provisions were part of an economic and industrial statute that responded to policy recommendations made by an international mission of specialists, whose main purpose was to address macroeconomic instability issues. One of the statute's chapters created the Antimonopoly Commission, whose function was to punish harmful conduct and control industrial and commercial activities. In 1963, the position of the Fiscalía Nacional Económica (National Economic Prosecutor, or "FNE") was created to investigate and prosecute anticompetitive conduct. These institutions dealt with few cases. Between 1959 and 1973, most decisions were recommendations to prevent infringements in the future. When much of the economy was planned, many products and services were subject to price regulation and many firms were owned or managed by the government, competition policy and law did not play a significant role.

After the military coup d'etat of 1973, changes in competition policy were part of a programme to roll back the previous government's steps towards a state-planned economy. The Competition Act (Decree Law No. 211 of 1973) created new institutions, the Competition Commission (also known as Comisión Resolutiva) and central and regional Consultative Commissions (the Comisiones Preventivas, central and regional). Members of the Competition Commission and the Consultative Commissions were unpaid and served part-time. These bodies could impose sanctions and issue injunctions and recommendations, while the FNE continued in its functions of investigation and prosecution. In the first two decades of work (1973–1993), the Competition Commission tended to focus on market foreclosures such as vertical restraints. Its formal, legalistic approach was founded on the 1980 Constitution's protection of economic rights. Competition policy did not seek to promote consumer welfare, but rather to protect economic freedom. Enforcement resources were low. Competition policy was overshadowed by macroeconomic reforms. Competition law

[3] Editor's note: China's competition law institutions have now been consolidated into the State Administration for Market Regulation ("SAMR").

enforcement was a less important part of Chile's reform programme, which emphasised trade liberalisation, privatisation and deregulation.

After democracy was restored in 1989, Chile undertook a major progrowth agenda, developed by the government and the private sector. This agenda stressed reform of regulation in telecoms and electricity and in areas such as capital markets that could also improve competition and efficiency. Making this kind of regulatory reform a priority created necessary conditions and prepared the way for invigorated competition enforcement. But the predominantly consultative competition law system, implemented by institutions with limited enforcement powers, could not deal effectively with significant cases in Chile's increasingly developed economic conditions. The FNE's investigative powers had been increased some by a reform in 1999, but the institutional structure needed a more thorough overhaul. The institutions were revamped in November 2003. The Competition Act of 2003 (Law No. 19.911) created the Tribunal de Defensa de la Libre Competencia ("TDLC") to replace the Competition Commission and the Consultative Commissions. Under the current system, the FNE submits complaints to the TDLC for adjudication and decision. The 2003 law also granted some new powers to the FNE. The judiciary-based nature of Chile's competition enforcement is unique among Latin American countries. The TDLC is a court, subject to the supervision of the Supreme Court of Justice, but its members include two economists as well as three lawyers. The TDLC has applied more sophisticated economic analysis, in contrast to the formal legal standards found in the administrative decisions of the old Commissions. Enforcement has stepped up markedly since these changes. Notably, sanctions are dramatically higher. Since 2004, the average fine imposed by the TDLC has been about USD 840 000. By comparison, during the period 1974–2002, the average fine, after review by the Supreme Court, was about USD 13 500. Amendments adopted in 2009 have strengthened enforcement further. Among other things, the changes authorise a leniency programme to detect and prevent cartels, add to the FNE's investigation powers and increase the penalties for infringement.

Vinod Dhall, Member of the Competition Commission of India, *Competition Law in India*, 21-SPG ANTITR 73 (2007)

For years after independence, India followed the strategy of planned economic development. The broad policy objectives were achieving self-reliance and promoting social justice. Self-reliance, over time, came to mean import substitution. There were government-imposed controls over entry and exit in the market. Plant and firm size were subject to statutory limitations, and imports and foreign investment were restricted. Government-owned businesses enjoyed protections and preferences and dominated the "commanding heights of the economy" in various sectors. These policies were reflected in many of the state's economic policies, including its industrial, trade, labor, exchange controls, financial sector, and several other policies. In this system, there was little place for competition policy.

While the above economic strategy helped in many ways, including the growth of basic industries, in the 1980s it began to be realized that it was severely constraining entrepreneurial growth. Policy reform followed more particularly since 1991 with the liberalization of industrial and trade policies, foreign investment rules, exchange rates, capital controls, reservations for the public sector, and in many other areas.

The new economic policies progressively widened the space for market forces and reduced the role for government in business. It was recognized that a new competition law was also called for because the existing Monopolies & Restrictive Trade Practices Act, 1969 (MRTPA) had become obsolete in certain respects and there was a need to shift the focus from curbing monopolies to promoting competition. A high level committee was appointed in 1999 to suggest a modern competition law in line with international developments to suit Indian conditions. The committee recommended enactment of a new competition law, called the Competition Act, and the establishment of a competition authority, the Competition Commission of India, along with the repealing of the MRTPA and the winding up of the MRTP Commission. It also recommended further reforms in government policies as the foundation over which the edifice of the competition policy and law would be built.

The Competition Act, 2002, came into existence in January 2003, and the Competition Commission of India was established in October 2003. The Act states that "it shall be the duty of the Commission to eliminate practices having adverse effect on competition, to promote and sustain competition, protect the interests of consumers and ensure freedom of trade carried on by other participants, in markets in India." Thus, it gives the Commission a heavy mandate. The Act prohibits anticompetitive agreements (section 3) and abuse of dominant position (section 4), and regulates mergers, amalgamations and acquisitions (sections 5 and 6).

OECD: *Competition Law & Policy in the Russian Federation* (2008)

Foundations and History of Competition Policy

The Russian Federation created a competition authority early in its transition period and has embodied strong support for competition in law, but competition has not always been an immediate priority in practice. In addition to core competition issues, the competition authority has been assigned a broad variety of tasks related to market activity, including the creation of legal institutions to regulate market behaviour, regulation of natural monopoly tariffs, and the development of market infrastructure and new enterprises. There have been rapid shifts in its priority areas of activity and in its authorities, as well as regular amendment of the competition law and related legislation. Current priorities include participation in the restructuring of natural monopoly areas and creation of the associated legislation and new enforcement patterns and a focus on the role of state bodies and officials in the economy. Authorities continue to be shifted into and out of the competition body and drafting work on a completely new competition law is beginning.

Context and early history

When the Soviet Union began to plan a path toward a market economy in the late 1980s, the initial transition policies of the central government focused on stimulation of the creation of small businesses and new enterprises. A gradual reduction of the amount of planned activity was to allow state enterprises to move at a measured pace into market behaviour patterns, while newer forms of business enterprise would speed increases in the provision of consumer goods and services and spur the formation of the market infrastructure needed to support broader market reform. Enterprises and activities that were considered strategic or key to basic economic stability were to be left in state hands and/or regulated until other parts of the economy had moved into more market-oriented structures. Significant concerns were expressed about the starting levels of monopolisation of both productive industry and distribution channels, and this concern led to expectations of a relatively strict regulation of dominant enterprises during a potentially long transition period, to be combined with very substantial "demonopolisation" or deconcentration of larger enterprises and associations before privatisation. Special provisions allowing state control of monopoly behaviour began appearing in legislative acts concerning reform.

In 1990, the first Russian competition authority was created—the State Committee for Antimonopoly Policy and the Support of New

Economic Structures—and the Law "On Competition and the Restriction of Monopolistic Activity on Goods Markets" (hereinafter the Law on Competition) was passed in 1991. The law contained relatively mild sanctions for most violations, preferring cease and desist orders and disgorgement of improperly received income to direct fines or the punishment of individuals. This was consistent with expectations that the worst potential problems would be controlled by regulation and also reflected fairness concerns about the complete unfamiliarity of competition law concepts and a desire to allow the new rules to become known before severe sanctions were applied. A long history of planning and coordination, as well as a lack of familiarity with methods used to govern and regulate markets, led to expectations that state bodies of various kinds would attempt to continue to control economic activity. To counter this, the Law on Competition included provisions prohibiting such behaviour. Likewise, the expectation of a need to divide large enterprises or associations was reflected in the inclusion of an article specifically authorising such division after repeated violation of the law. Many enterprises had been deliberately created by planners to be dominant or even monopolists within specific geographic areas or in specialised products and activities and transportation and distribution functions were likewise deliberately concentrated under planning. This situation contributed to fears of a massive, inflationary price explosion and wide-spread abusive behaviour as liberalisation reduced legal controls on enterprise behaviour. One of the chief tasks of the new competition authority was expected to be prevention and control of this problem and accordingly one of its first acts was the creation of a register of enterprise monopolists. It was expected that supervision would be exercised over the business decisions of those enterprises included in the register, especially over their pricing patterns.

A significant amount of energy was expended by the competition authority during the earliest part of its existence in the compilation of the register, creation of reporting forms for enterprises listed in it, verification of their activities and reports, and participation in disputes concerning the removal of enterprises from the register. At the same time, the competition authority worked to develop guidelines for the enforcement of the new law and materials for the education both of new staff and of a public almost completely unfamiliar with market mechanisms and competition concerns after several generations of state planning. As its name suggested, the State Committee's mandate was not limited to competition issues. The new State Committee was made generally responsible for the support of "new economic structures"—i.e. markets. The tasks that would be involved were not specified and it was anticipated that the

State Committee itself would take some responsibility for defining the necessary programs and legislation, as well as being assigned responsibilities by the Government. In practice, it included measures to encourage the formation of new businesses and proposals concerning the development of necessary market infrastructure. It also included the control of not only anticompetitive actions, but of all kinds of undesirable or 'uncivilised' behaviour that might be engaged in by economic actors in a market setting. As a part of this broader mandate, the new body expended substantial effort during its first years on the production of a law on consumer protection appropriate to market conditions. It was also necessary to develop the legislation, regulations and other legal acts necessary for the organisation and functioning of the authority itself and for the creation of "territorial administrations"—branch offices of the new body in the territorial units that form the Russian Federation.

Joel Basoga, H&G Chambers, Kampala, Uganda

Uganda recently enacted its first comprehensive competition law—The Competition Act 2024—on 19 April 2024.[4] This is the latest competition law in the world.[5] However, it must be understood in the context of Uganda's recent history. In the late 1980's Uganda's economy was liberalized as part of the conditions precedent—Structured Adjustment Programs—to receiving credit from several multilateral development institutions.[6] This reduced the Uganda government's involvement as a participant in the local economy and led to massive privatisation and growth of local businesses to support the new country that had emerged out of a six year civil war. At the same time, there were several multinational entities entering the Uganda market to take a piece of the Ugandan pie.

Historically, certain sectors in Uganda operate as duopolies, for instance the mobile telecommunications sector has two dominant entities—MTN Uganda and Airtel Uganda.[7] They also double as the largest payment systems providers for mobile money transactions in Uganda, controlling several aspects of the financial sector. Other sectors like the petroleum supply chain, manufacturing and communications digital infrastructure are dominated by a handful of multi national entities whose unilateral actions affect the pricing and structure of the relevant markets. Within the Uganda public

[4] The Competition Act No. 5 of 2024.

[5] Editor's note: Guatemala adopted a new competition law in December of 2024.

[6] "Policy Framework Paper—Uganda: Enhanced Structural Adjustment Facility and Policy Framework Paper 1998/99-2000/01—Text." Accessed February 10, 2025. https://www.imf.org/external/np/pfp/uganda/102998.htm.

[7] New Vision. "Duopoly Uncertainty Hurts Telecom Firms." Accessed February 10, 2025. https://allafrica.com/stories/200508100823.html.

transport market, which is heavily reliant on taxis ("*matatus*") and buses, there has been uniform price increments during festive periods. This has been termed by most Uganda's unfair and exploitative pricing. Further, the growing presence of several foreign companies has raised eyebrows over the meaningful participation of Ugandans in their economy. These instances triggered the necessity for detailed competition law in Uganda.

Prior to the passing of the Competition Act, the President of Uganda refused to assent the first Competition Bill and sent it back to Parliament for reconsideration.[8] The President reasoned that as part of government rationalisation, the proposed creation of a competition agency—The Competition Consumer Protection Commission was not economically feasible for Uganda; instead, he proposed the Ministry of Trade Industry and Cooperatives to be included as the principal competition regulator.[9] Under Uganda's Constitution, when Parliament passes a law, it must be signed by the president before it takes effect[10] The Uganda Parliament reconsidered the President's request, and The Competition Act was published in the national Gazette on 19 April 2024. This was a significant milestone, as it is the first law specifically regulating competition in Uganda.

Before the passing of the Competition Act, there was no comprehensive competition law framework in Uganda. Instead, certain sectors, such as; telecommunications[11], banking[12], and at the regional level, the Common Market for Eastern and Southern Africa (COMESA) Competition Regulations,[13] constituted the segmented framework of competition regulations in Uganda. Before enacting its legislation, Uganda was an outcast in East Africa—Kenya, Tanzania and Rwanda had all enacted competition specific laws for over a decade.[14]

---

[8] "Uganda: President Returns the Competition Act 2023 to Parliament." Accessed February 6, 2025. https://www.ensafrica.com/news/detail/7510/uganda-president-returns-the-competition-act-.

[9] "Uganda: President Returns the Competition Act 2023 to Parliament." Accessed February 6, 2025. https://www.ensafrica.com/news/detail/7510/uganda-president-returns-the-competition-act-.

[10] Article 91(3) of the Constitution of the Republic of Uganda

[11] The Uganda Communications (Competition) Regulations, 2019, S.I. 93 of 2019.

[12] The Bank of Uganda Financial Consumer Protection Guidelines.

[13] These were made pursuant to Article 55 of the Treaty establishing the Common Market for Eastern and Southern Africa

[14] See the Kenya Competition Act No. 12 of 2010, the Tanzania Fair Competition Act of 2003 and Rwanda's Law relating to Competition and Consumer Protection Law 36 of 2012.

Uganda's new Competition Act seeks to achieve five main objectives; (1) to promote efficiency, adaptability and development of the Uganda economy.[15] (2) to provide consumers and producers with competitive prices and product choices.[16] (3) to promote employment and advance the socio-economic welfare of Ugandans.[17] (4) to provide opportunities for the participation of Ugandans in the world market and recognize the role of foreign competition in Uganda.[18] (5) To guarantee that all persons have an equitable opportunity to participate in the economy.[19] Uganda's competition law must be understood in the context of National Objective XIV(a) concerning social and economic objectives, and Article 40 of the Constitution which provides for economic rights.

The Act establishes the Ministry responsible for trade as the administrator of the Act—competition regulator.[20] This is a stark contrast to the approaches taken by Uganda's East African counterparts. Tanzania, Kenya and Rwanda all establish independent statutory agencies to regulate the competition. Uganda's Competition Act applies to anti-competitive practices, anti-competitive agreements, abuse of dominant positions and effects of mergers and joint ventures on competition.[21] It seeks to protect consumers. A consumer is defined as person who buys goods or services, or who intends to buy goods or services, as the end-user of the goods or services.[22] The Act prohibits cartels as concerted practices. Concerted practices are defined as actions which involve communication or coordination between competitors which replaces the competitor's independent action and restricts or lessens competition between competitors.[23] The Act creates a framework of mandatory pre-merger notification.[24] Appeal from the decisions by the Ministry lay to the High Court of Uganda.

The Uganda Competition Act is ambitious and sets out to achieve diverse objectives including advancing the participation of Ugandans in the world market and advancing the socio-economic

15 Section 2(a) of the Competition Act No. 5 of 2024.

16 Section 2(b) of the Competition Act No. 5 of 2024.

17 Section 2(c) of the Competition Act No. 5 of 2024.

18 Ibid Section 2 (d) of the Competition Act No. 5 of 2024.

19 Ibid Section 2(e) of the Competition Act No. 5 of 2024.

20 Section 4 of the Competition Act No. 5 of 2024.

21 Section 1 of the Competition Act No. 5 of 2024.

22 Section 3 of the Competition Act No. 5 of 2024.

23 Section 9 of the Competition Act No. 5 of 2024.

24 Section 15 of the Competition Act No. 5 of 2024.

welfare of Ugandans. It remains to be seen how this can be achieved while promoting market efficiency and development.

Notes and Questions

1. Commissioner Monti suggests that U.S. and EU competition law share common origins and common purposes. As you read the coming chapters, ask yourself whether Commissioner Monti is correct in claiming that the U.S. and EU are both primarily concerned with protecting consumer interests. As Professor Fox points out, the original goals and purposes of EU law are quite different from those of U.S. antitrust law.

2. South Africa's competition statute is a product of the post-apartheid era and is intended to address "the skewed distribution of income and wealth in South Africa" and to promote Black economic empowerment. Do you expect that South African competition law will look significantly different from, say, U.S. or EU competition law given these objectives? In the coming chapters, you will encounter a number of cases and other materials from South Africa, including some that include more recent amendments to South Africa's competition laws. Ask yourself how well South Africa is doing in this daunting project and what challenges it faces in the current geopolitical environment.

3. The story of China's 2007 anti-monopoly law is framed by China's "Marxist-Leninist-Maoist heritage," on the one hand, and its accession to the Western-led WTO, on the other. Does competition law presuppose a market economy? Do the objectives and operations of competition law necessarily have to look different in a country like China where 30–40% of the economy remains state-owned?

4. Chile's competition law regimes were significantly affected by the dramatic changes in political regimes, from the Socialist Allende government, to the coup d'etat and military dictatorship from 1973–1989, and then the restoration of democracy in 1989. How should we understand the claim that the Pinochet dictatorship "did not seek to promote consumer welfare, but rather to protect economic freedom?" Is competition law about protecting "economic freedom?" In what sense might a totalitarian government be interested in protecting "economic freedom" through competition law?

5. For many decades after its independence from Britain in 1947, India pursued a planned economy as a means of decolonization and self-reliance. The 2002 competition act reflected a desire to move away from a planned economy and, following international best practices and to become more integrated into the world economy, move toward a more competitive economy. India, of course, is not the only country with a history of colonialism. This is the story of most of the African countries and many countries in the Americas. How do you think a history of

colonialism affects a country's path toward competitive markets and effective competition law?

6. The Russian Federation represents the quintessential shift from a Communist centrally planned economy to one based more on market competition, and it may therefore seem natural that competition policy has been a component of post-Soviet Russia. But, as the OECD reading suggests, a powerful state has always been a feature of the Russian polity and economy. Today, it is common to hear Russia described as an "oligarchy" (to be fair, a complaint that is sometimes made about the United States as well). What would you expect to find if you looked "under the hood" of Russian competition law?

7. One of the world's newest competition regimes, Uganda, opted for competition law enforcement to be vested in the Ministry of Trade rather than an independent commission, in contrast to its East African neighbors Tanzania, Kenya and Rwanda. A single man, Yoweri Museveni, has been in power in Uganda since he won a guerilla war in 1986 and was then elected President in 2011, 2016, and 2021. Do you think that competition law may be more effective in Uganda given the proximity of its administration to the country's longstanding leader, or do you worry that the Ministry of Trade will lack sufficient independence to enforce the laws according to neutral principles? As you think ahead to these questions and others of institutional design, keep in mind that the United States vests antitrust enforcement authority in both an independent commission (the Federal Trade Commission) and the Justice Department, which is part of the executive branch.

8. A good deal of the divergences in goals in competition law stems from whether the jurisdiction embraces only or principally allocative efficiency, often applied through an interpretation of "consumer welfare," or whether the jurisdiction also embraces distributional goals. Look back at the goals identified in the second paragraph of this chapter. Which of the goals would you identify as distributional? As you study the competition caselaw of various jurisdictions in this book, consider whether distributional, or purely allocative, goals underlie the decisions, and whether and when you detect any tradeoffs between efficiency and equity.

Chapter 2

CARTELS

A. INTRODUCTION

Cartels are a logical substantive starting point for this global reader, for five reasons. First, while 50 years ago there was basic divergence in attitudes towards cartels as a form of business activity, today there is enormous agreement around the world; cartels are bad; they undermine the market. Second, even so, there is constant pressure to allow some exceptions from the rules against cartels. Export cartels are largely exempted or not covered, usually on grounds that the nation's jurisdiction does not extend so far. Crisis cartels are a different matter. Arguments are made for crisis cartel exemptions, especially in times of financial crisis. This is a subject on which nations disagree; thus, a fruitful basis to explore comparative treatment. Third, a large percentage of contemporary cartels are international; as a result cartels have become a laboratory for enforcement cooperation among national competition authorities as well as for sharing methodologies for detection and punishment. Fourth, since many cartel conspiracies take place off the shores of victim nations, cartels have become the main subject for development of the principles of extraterritorial jurisdiction. Fifth, given the shared condemnation of cartels, the high degree of harm they inflict, and the frequency with which they occur, cartels have become the centerpiece for considering a world competition law regime, possibly in the World Trade Organization. Although such a development is not currently foreseeable, the study of an international competition law necessarily includes contours of a world framework.

Indeed, enforcement against world cartels continues to occupy the spotlight of antitrust. World fines in 2016 increased by 20% over the previous year and totaled \$6.7 billion. Fine level has since dropped slightly. Global fines imposed on cartel members were \$1.9 billion in 2023 and \$2.1 billion in 2022. More countries ordered behavioral restrictions, such as bans on cartel leaders' future board memberships, as imposed in the UK, Australia, and Sweden. In 2021, the Mexican authority for the first time in its history imposed an administrative penalty on ten individuals barring them from serving as directors, officers, and managers of a company.

In 2016 the EU posted record fines of US $4.1 billion, including Europe's highest-ever cartel fine—2.93 billion euros—on five truck makers who had, by agreement, passed on the costs of environmental compliance to their customers. In 2016 and 2017, the European Commission imposed large fines in the financial services industry attributable to rigging the LIBOR (London interbank) exchange rate. The financial service sector has remained an enforcement focus ever since. The Commission imposed fines of $32.9 million in five decisions concerning the financial services sector in 2023. In keeping with the global trend, however, overall cartel fine level in the EU has dropped significantly from the heyday of 2016. The Commission imposed fines of only $95.8 million in 2023.

In 2016, Mexico imposed $11 million in fines, including actions against sugar producers, automotive air condition compressors, and ferry operators. In 2023, it only imposed fines of $120,700. Japan and Korea have bucked this trend of shrinking fines. In 2022, the Korea Fair Trade Commission imposed fines of $666.6 million on cartels involving transportation, intermediate goods, and infrastructure. In 2023, the Japan Fair Trade Commission imposed fines of $766.1 million. Most of that was accounted for by one case involving three utilities, which received fines of $754.7 million. Just one company, Chugoku Electric Power Co., was responsible for 70% of this amount. If one discounts this anomalous case in Japan, which alone accounted for one-third of the global total cartel fines, however, only the United States exceeded the $100 million mark in cartel fines in 2023.

B. LAW AND ATTITUDE TOWARDS CARTELS

Hard core cartels—agreements of competitors to lessen competition among them—are generally illegal on their face or presumptively illegal under national law, except when they are subject to a specific exemption. In the United States, cartels are illegal per se under Section 1 of the Sherman Act. No justification is allowed, as you will have seen, for example, in *Socony Vacuum*, 310 U.S. 150 (1940).

In the European Union, agreements are treated under the competition law as set forth in the Treaty on the Functioning of the European Union ("TFEU"), Article 101. This revised version of the Treaty of Rome establishing the European Communities ("Treaty of Rome" or "EC Treaty") became effective December 1, 2009. Article 101 TFEU (formerly Article 81 EC Treaty) prohibits agreements "which have as their object or effect the prevention, restriction or distortion of competition within the common market." It singles out in particular agreements that (among other things) fix buying or selling prices or other trading conditions, limit production, or share markets. As to any particular agreement that prevents, restricts or distorts competition, the prohibition of Article 101 may be declared inapplicable if the agreement improves production, distribution or technical or economic progress, allows a fair share of the benefits to consumers, contains no unnecessary restrictions on competition, and does not create the possibility of eliminating competition in a substantial part of the market. See the text of Article 101 in Appendix 1. Under the case law interpreting Article 101, cartels by definition have as their object distortion of competition.

In 1980 the United Nations Conference on Trade and Development (UNCTAD), which caters particularly to developing nations, promulgated a set of principles and rules for the control of restrictive business practices. These principles were adopted as a voluntary code by members of the United Nations. The UNCTAD Set states, in Part D (see Chapter 10), that enterprises "should refrain from practices such as the following" when they unduly restrain competition and harm international trade, particularly harming economic development of developing countries:

> "(a) Agreements fixing prices, including as to exports and imports;
>
> (b) Collusive tendering;
>
> (c) Market or customer allocation agreements;
>
> (d) Allocation by quota as to sales and production . . . ."

UNCTAD has also published a model law on competition, and a commentary on the Model Law. The commentary describes the above quoted section as a "prohibition in principle." This means that, in general, for cartel agreements, purpose and effect need not be shown.

Some countries do not, or did not, have a per se or presumptive approach to cartels. Cartel agreements may be illegal only if it is shown that, for example, they restrict or substantially restrict competition. The competition law of Chile, Decree Law No. 211/1973 as amended, forbids agreements attempting to restrain free competition. Article 1. The Chilean law was interpreted to require proof of market power until it was overturned by a legislative amendment in 2016. Article 3(a) of Decree Law No. 211 now deems cartels to be illegal per se. In Brazil, Law No. 12529/2011, Article 36, prohibits agreements for fixing prices or sales conditions. In the opinion of officials of CADE—the Administrative Council for Economic Defense—there is no per se treatment of cartel conduct under Brazilian competition law. According to Brazilian case law, however, evidence of collusion established a rebuttable presumption of illegality. Similarly, Japan does not recognize the existence of "per se" antitrust offenses; hence greater proof may be necessary to hold a cartel illegal than would be required in jurisdictions with a categorical approach to cartel illegality. Although the Japan Fair Trade Commission ("JFTC") is technically required to prove restrictive effects of a cartel on competition, this is rarely a meaningful hurdle in reality because the JFTC is given much leeway in defining a very narrow market in cartel cases, which allows restrictive effects to be easily demonstrated.

The generally accepted rule against cartels is embedded in the 1998 Recommendation of the Organization for Economic Cooperation and Development ("OECD") Against Hard Core Cartels, which we examine further in Chapter 10, Global Governance.

Although many jurisdictions have had laws prohibiting cartel activity on their books for some time, many of these jurisdictions have only begun to impose serious fines on cartels relatively recently. A study by Professor John Connor, a leading authority on anti-cartel enforcement, identifies the following dates for the first major cartel fine in the following significant jurisdictions: India (1996), Mexico (1998), Australia (1998), South Korea (1999), Japan (1999), Taiwan (2000), Israel (2003), Kazakhstan (2005), Argentina (2005), New Zealand (2006), Brazil (2007), Colombia (2007), Indonesia (2007), Egypt (2008), Pakistan (2008), Russia (2008), Saudi Arabia (2010), Vietnam (2010), Nigeria (2012), Turkey (2012), Singapore (2013), China (2014). Vigorous anti-cartel enforcement remains in its early stages in much of the world.

Several questions recur across jurisdictions. First, proof of agreement: Has the plaintiff presented sufficient evidence to allow the fact finder to infer that the defendants agreed with one another? Second, characterization: Is this agreement a cartel, or is it a joint venture or other presumptively efficient agreement? Third, effects: Is it necessary that the plaintiff prove the agreement's effect in harming competition? Fourth, public interest: Is crisis a defense (are crisis cartels permitted)? Is there any other "public interest" justification? Fifth, state blessing: When is encouragement by the state, act of state, foreign sovereign compulsion, or political question a defense? Does comity ever require or justify deference to a home jurisdiction's permissive law?

We present two European cases on proof of agreement, *Quinine* and *Wood pulp*. Students of US antitrust law can compare these cases with *Interstate Circuit* (306 U.S. 208, 1939) and *Matsushita* (475 U.S. 574, 1986). For characterization, we refer you to *Appalachian Coals* (288 U.S. 344, 1933)—the American depression era case that looks very much like a cartel but was characterized as a joint sales arrangement. Regarding need to prove effect, we refer back to *Quinine*, and also note the US case of *Nippon*, an offshore cartel. Next, we look at justifications and defenses, including public interests—an inquiry that takes us to a recent European case involving the financially-troubled Irish beef industry. Then we turn to the state and the significance of its support for and involvement in cartels. We include an excerpt from the US international enforcement guidelines, an opinion dismissing a suit against four Chinese vitamin cartelists in which the Chinese government argued that the cartel was ordered by the government, and court opinions on legality under US law of the OPEC oil cartel. Finally, the materials note the high degree of cooperation among antitrust authorities. We leave the details about cooperation and the debate about a possible world regime for the last chapter.

C. PROOF OF A CARTEL AGREEMENT

Many cartel cases are lost for lack of proof admissible in court or attainable at trial. This is especially so when the case is prosecuted criminally, as the United States does in the case of hard core cartels. Famously, the United States lost its case against General Electric/De Beers for an industrial diamond cartel for failure to procure a key witness and obtain evidence from abroad. See Anne K. Bingman, U.S. International Antitrust Enforcement: The Past Three Years and the Future, Chap. 2 in 1996 Fordham Corporate Law Institute, INTERNATIONAL ANTITRUST LAW & POLICY (B. Hawk ed. 1977).

Since the United States and then many other nations adopted leniency policies to induce cartel members to defect and to be the first to reveal all details, enforcement against cartels has reached new heights. Although it should be noted that the number of leniency applications has dropped noticeably across the globe in recent years. The authorities now typically receive much valuable direct evidence of particular cartels. The process usually results in guilty pleas, imprisonments, and settlements. But direct evidence is not always available. A cartel might be proved, also, by circumstantial evidence; but circumstantial evidence might not satisfy the fact-finder, especially for criminal conviction.

At the time of the adoption of the Treaty of Rome establishing the European Economic Community (EC Treaty) in 1957, there were high trade barriers isolating each of the European countries. Predictably, monopolies and oligopolies developed within each. A major motivation of the EC Treaty was to break down the border barriers and to integrate Europe—in order to anchor peace in Europe. Thus, the Treaty required its Member States (six at the start) to remove their trade barriers in the internal market. As soon as the Member States complied, firms that had been insulated began to feel competitive pressures from across the borders. They co-opted the competition by entering cross-border agreements. The agreements typically divided markets along national border, re-cementing the old, insular patterns of trade. Europe did not then have a culture against cartels, but it had a mission of market integration for a higher value—peace. The European Commission detected and enjoined a large number of cartels—including sugar, cement, dyestuffs, and quinine. The quinine cartel may be the earliest example of trans-Atlantic agency cooperation in prosecuting a cross-border cartel, as you will read below.

Consider, as you read the *Quinine* case, what tools the firms used to form a cartel, to make it work, and to make it stable. What characteristics about the market and its structure made it more or less likely for a quinine cartel to work? Consider also: What evidence was the give-away that the cartel continued to operate after 1962, when the European competition enforcement system went into effect and the firms insisted to the Competition Directorate that they had called their cartel to an end.

We include the *Quinine* case to reflect on the questions above and to introduce case law on: What evidence is sufficient to prove "agreement" or "understanding"? Since the time of *Quinine*, courts in general have become more rigorous in requiring evidence that defendants' parallel actions were conspiratorial rather than independent. We follow *Quinine* with the European *Wood Pulp* case and notes on the U.S. *Twombly* case, both examining sufficiency of proof of agreement by circumstantial evidence.

Quinine

ACF CHEMIEFARMA v. COMMISSION (*QUININE*)

Case 41/69, ECLI:EU:C:1970:71 (Court of Justice of the European Union 1970)

[Nedchem and five other Dutch firms, and Boehringer and Buchler, both German firms, produced quinine and quinidine, ingredients used to manufacture drugs to treat malaria and heart disease. In 1958 they entered into a series of agreements to reserve their home markets for themselves and to fix prices and quotas for exports to all other countries. After the German Federal Cartel Office discovered the cartel, Nedchem and Boehringer concluded a new agreement that excluded deliveries within the EU from the arrangement. In March 1960 Nedchem, the two German firms, and French and British producers of quinine and quinidine concluded a new export cartel agreement. The new agreement excluded sales into EU Member States, set quotas for exports to non-member nations, and reserved certain markets outside of the common market for specified cartel members. It also provided for equalization of quantities to be sold by members if quotas were exceeded or not reached and provided that no cartel member could cooperate in the production or sale of quinine or quinidine outside of the common market with firms not participating in the agreement. Each party agreed to supply the others with information about where, to whom, and how much they sold, on the basis of which Nedchem would equalize the quantities to be sold by each.

In April 1960, two gentlemen's agreements were drawn up among the parties—though never signed—which extended the provisions of the export agreements to sales within the common market and reserved home markets. The French parties agreed not to manufacture synthetic quinidine, and all parties agreed that noncompliance with the gentlemen's agreement would terminate the written export agreement and vice versa. The agreements were supplemented by a pool agreement for bark to make quinine. The parties would jointly purchase this critical raw material through Nedchem. Nedchem would buy stockpile surpluses of bark from the United States' General Services Administration, allocate the bark among the cartel members, and receive a two percent commission from the members.

In 1962, Regulation 17 went into effect, giving the Commission the powers necessary to enforce Article [101].* Also in 1962, a dispute arose regarding the bark pool, and the parties claimed that they abandoned their gentlemen's agreement shortly thereafter.

In 1963–64 the United States, needing quinine to save the lives of sick American soldiers in Viet Nam, became suspicious of the existence of an international quinine cartel as a result of Nedchem's purchases of large quantities of the United States bark stockpile. The Department of Justice conducted extensive investigations (eventually resulting in civil and criminal cases under the US Sherman Act), and in 1967 it shared information with the EC Commission. See 1 W. Fugate, Foreign Commerce and the Antitrust Laws § 4.2 (5th ed. 1996). The Commission and national authorities began investigations into whether and to what extent the gentlemen's agreements were being applied in the common market after 1962. The Commission found that violations continued until February 1965, and imposed fines.]

---

* Editors' note: We use the current Treaty number. The Article was then numbered 85, and later 81.

115 The defendant bases its view that the gentlemen's agreement was continued until February 1965 on documents and declarations emanating from the parties to the agreement the tenor of which is indistinct and indeed contradictory so that it is impossible to conclude whether those undertakings intended to terminate the gentlemen's agreement at their meeting on 29 October 1962.

116 The conduct of the undertakings in the Common Market after 29 October 1962 must therefore be considered in relation to the following four points: sharing out of domestic markets, fixing of common prices, determination of sales quotas and prohibition against manufacturing synthetic quinidine.

Protection of the Producers' Domestic Markets

117 The gentlemen's agreement guaranteed protection of each domestic market for the producers in the various Member States.

118 After October 1962 when significant supplies were delivered on one of those markets by producers who were not nationals, as for example in the case of sales of quinine and quinidine in France, there was a substantial alignment of prices conforming to French domestic prices which were higher than the export prices to third countries.

119 It does not appear that there were alterations in the insignificant volume of trade between the other Member States referred to by the clause relating to domestic protection in spite of considerable differences in the prices prevailing in each of those States.

120 The divergences between the domestic legislation of those States cannot by itself explain those differences in price or the substantial absence of trade.

121 Obstacles which might arise in the trade in quinine and quinidine from differences between national legislation governing pharmaceutical products under trademark cannot relevantly be invoked to explain those facts.

122 The correspondence exchanged in October and November 1963 between the parties to the export agreement with regard to the protection of domestic markets merely confirmed the intention of those undertakings to allow this state of affairs to remain unchanged.

123 This intention was subsequently confirmed by Nedchem during the meeting of the undertakings concerned in Brussels on 14 March 1964.

124 From those circumstances it is clear that with regard to the restriction on competition arising from the protection of the producers' domestic markets the producers continued after the

meeting on 29 October 1962 to abide by the gentlemen's agreement of 1960 and confirmed their common intention to do so.

125 The applicant maintains that owing in particular to the shortage of raw materials the sharing out of domestic markets, as emerges from the exchange of letters of October and November 1963, had no effect on competition in the Common Market.

126 Despite the scarcity of raw materials and an increase in the demand for the products in question, as the contested decision finds, a serious threat of shortage nevertheless emerged only in 1964 as a result of the interruption of Nedchem's supplies from the American General Service Administration.

127 On the other hand such a situation cannot render lawful an agreement the object of which is to restrict competition in the Common Market and which affects trade between the Member States.

128 The sharing out of domestic markets has as its object the restriction of competition and trade within the Common Market.

129 The fact that, if there were a threatened shortage of raw materials, such an agreement might in practice have had less influence on competition and on international trade than in a normal period in no way alters the fact that the parties did not terminate their activities.

130 Furthermore the applicant has furnished no conclusive evidence capable of proving that it had ceased to act in accordance with the agreement before the date of expiry of the export agreement.

131 Consequently, the submissions concerning that part of the decision relating to the continuation of the agreement on the protection of the producers' domestic markets until the beginning of February 1965 are unfounded.

Joint Fixing of Sales Prices

132 With regard to the joint fixing of sales prices for the markets which were not shared out, that is to say, the Belgo-Luxembourg Economic Union and Italy, the gentlemen's agreement provided for the application to such sales of the current prices for exports to third countries fixed by mutual agreement, in accordance with the export agreement. * * *

134 If, as the defendant maintains, the parties to the export agreement continued until February 1965 to apply their current export prices to supplies to the above-mentioned Member States, it

would follow that they continued to abide by that part of the gentlemen's agreement relating to the joint fixing of sales prices.

135 With regard to the period from November 1962 to April 1964, the figures supplied by the defendant show a substantial and constant identity between the current prices fixed for export within the framework of the agreement and the prices maintained by the undertakings concerned, including the applicant, for their sales in unprotected domestic markets in the Community.

136 Where such prices deviate from the scale of export prices they do so in terms of rebates or increases corresponding generally to those agreed on under the gentlemen's agreement.

137 The applicant had supplied no evidence capable of proving that this argument is unfounded.

138 Moreover the increase in prices of 15%, which was jointly decided upon on 12 March 1964 under the export agreement which led Nedchem to withdraw its opposition, was uniformly applied—although that undertaking would have preferred to continue to fix lower prices—with regard to supplies to Italy, Belgium and Luxembourg also.

139 These circumstances show that with regard to sales prices the parties to the export agreement continued after October 1962 to act in the Common Market as if the gentlemen's agreement of 1960 were still in force. * * *

141 It is clear from the oral procedure, taking into account the information supplied by the parties, that during 1964 and in particular from May onwards, a party to the agreement applied prices which in an increasing number of cases deviated from the current export prices, and that the defendant has been unable to give a convincing explanation as to how this might be reconciled with the continuation in force of the agreement in question.

142 The failure to communicate to the undertakings concerned the results of the investigations carried out in Italy and Belgium, which excluded any possibility of clarification and discussion at the stage of the administrative procedure, may have contributed to leaving unexplained facts which ought to have been clarified.

143 In these circumstances proof has not been sufficiently established in law that the applicant by mutual agreement with the other producers maintained uniform prices for its sales in the Belgo-Luxembourg Economic Union and Italy after May 1964.

144 Consequently the period from May 1964 to February 1965 must be omitted from the infringement. * * *

Restrictions on the Manufacture of Synthetic Quinidine

154 The gentlemen's agreement prohibited the group of French undertakings from manufacturing synthetic quinidine. * * *

156 The fact relied upon that, when the gentlemen's agreement was concluded, the French undertakings were not in a position to manufacture synthetic quinidine does not render lawful such a restriction which entirely precluded them from taking up this activity.

157 That the French undertakings should accede to this restriction of their freedom of action is explicable in terms of their interest—owing to the particularly high prices which they maintained for their products in France—in preserving the territorial protection which they enjoyed on their domestic market.

158 Taking into account the connexion thus existing between those two restrictions on competition, it may reasonably be concluded that the prohibition on production lasted as long as the territorial protection. * * *

160 Although it is possible that, owing to the scarcity of raw materials which [w]as established by the contested decision (No 29, last paragraph), in its ultimate period protection of the domestic markets did not have important effects on competition and trade between Member States, this cartel nevertheless lasted until February 1965.

161 In the absence of any indication to the contrary and having regard to the above-mentioned connexions between the two aspects of the cartel, it must be considered that the agreement restricting the French undertakings' freedom to manufacture was of the same duration.

162 Consequently the applicant's complaints in this respect are unfounded.

General Appraisal of the Agreement Within the Common Market

163 It is clear from the foregoing that the applicant participated with other producers of quinine and quinidine in an agreement prohibited by Article [101] of the [TFEU].

164 This agreement continued in most of its forms even after the meeting on 29 October 1962.

165 Serious doubts as to the continuation of the agreement after 1962 exist only with regard to the application of sales quotas.

166 Nevertheless, the fact that the undertakings did not continue to apply the system of quotas does not seem perceptibly to have

improved the conditions of competition, since they continued jointly to fix prices, to apply uniformly to their deliveries in the Common Market joint price increases arranged in March and October 1964 and decided within the framework of the export agreement and finally to maintain protection of their respective domestic markets and the prohibition on the French undertakings' production of synthetic quinidine.

167 However, the application of uniform prices for deliveries to Italy, Belgium and Luxembourg has only been proved to exist up to April 1964.

* * *

Notes and Questions

1. In *Quinine*, consider the evidence (esp. paras. 118–124)—which was only circumstantial—from which the Court concluded that the gentlemen's agreements continued after 1962. Did the facts raise an inference that the agreements continued in force? How strong was the alternative inference that, after 1962, the parties had no agreement with respect to sales in the Community; that each one simply chose to follow past patterns of behavior and hoped that its export partners would do so too? Does the latter scenario constitute concerted action under *Quinine*? By implication, under *Twombly*? See Bell Atlantic Corp. v. Twombly, 550 U.S. 544 (2007) (interdependence is not concert).

2. Note how the quinine export cartel tended to facilitate a domestic (European) cartel. Note also how the parties used various devices that helped to make the cartel work. For example, by pooling raw material purchases in the early years of the agreement and by designating one of their members—Nedchem—to be their purchasing agent and to allocate the raw material in accordance with assigned quotas, the firms could police their own cartel agreement and be sure that no one cheated by producing too much. Likewise, as a result of sharing extensive information with one another, cheating would become obvious, and cheating was explicitly punishable by expulsion from both cartels. Finally, the agreement not to produce synthetic quinine by the French, who were selling at a particularly high price in France, tended to keep off the market a substitute product that could have undermined the cartel by driving down the cartel price.

3. Why was the quinine export agreement as such of no interest to the Court? What is the scope of EU law with respect to export cartels selling to destinations outside of the Community? Consult the language of the Treaty on the Functioning of the European Union, Article 101. US antitrust law also excludes from its scope export cartels that hurt foreigners only. See Chapter 9 *infra*.

Wood Pulp

United States, Canadian, Finnish, Swedish and Norwegian firms shipped wood pulp to the European Community. The Commission alleged and found that the US, Canadian and Finnish firms agreed on prices, and it imposed large fines. The companies sought annulment of the Commission decision before the Court of Justice. They asserted lack of jurisdiction by reason of extraterritoriality. Also, they claimed that there was not sufficient evidence from which the Commission could find concert of action. Below are excerpts from the case on proof of agreement. Before this aspect of the case came before the Court of Justice, the Court held that the alleged cartel, while not illegal under US law because it was an export cartel filed under the Webb-Pomerene Act,[1] was properly subject to EU law. We deal with the jurisdictional aspects in Chapter 9.

Å. ÅHLŠTRÖM OSAKEYHTIÖ v. COMMISSION (*WOOD PULP*)

(proof of agreement)

Cases C–89/85, C–104/85, C–114/85, C–116/85, C–117/185, C–125–129/85, ECLI:EU:C:1993:120 (Court of Justice of the European Union 1993)

[The Commission brought proceedings against 40 wood pulp producers from the United States, Canada and Finland and three of their trade associations for concerting on price announcements and on price. The producers made quarterly price announcements sometimes simultaneously and sometimes nearly so. Prices were almost always quoted in dollars, a practice that both increased the transparency of the producers' intentions to one another and assured that shifts in exchange rates in the various Member States would have no impact. Prices and price changes tended to be uniform. The Commission determined that the pulp producers had engaged in concerted conduct in violation of Article [101].

The Court annulled most of the Commission's decision.]

---

1 The Webb-Pomerene Act provides that nothing in the Sherman Act shall be construed as declaring export associations illegal, as long as they do not enhance or depress prices in the United States or restrain the export trade of a domestic competitor, and as long as they are filed with the Federal Trade Commission. 15 US Code § 61–66.

Moreover, export agreements that do not harm US commerce are jurisdictionally beyond reach of the Sherman Act, as codified in the Foreign Trade Antitrust Improvement Act of 1982. See Chapter 8. Finally, for yet further protection from application of US antitrust law, exporters can get an "export trade certificate of review" under the Export Trading Company Act of 1982. For the text of all three statutes, see Appendix 3.

55 The Finnish, US and Canadian applicants have sought the annulment of art. 1(1) of the decision, according to which they, and other Swedish, US and Norwegian producers, concerted "on prices for bleached sulphate wood pulp announced for deliveries to the European Economic Community" during the whole or part of the period from 1975 to 1981.

* * *

A. Quarterly price announcements as the infringement

59 According to the Commission's first hypothesis, it is the system of quarterly price announcements in itself which constitutes the infringement of art. [101] of the Treaty.

60 First, the Commission considers that that system was deliberately introduced by the pulp producers in order to enable them to ascertain the prices that would be charged by their competitors in the following quarters. The disclosure of prices to third parties, especially to the press and agents working for several producers, well before their application at the beginning of a new quarter, gave the other producers sufficient time to announce their own, corresponding, new prices before that quarter and to apply them from the commencement of that quarter.

61 Secondly, the Commission considers that the implementation of that mechanism had the effect of making the market artificially transparent by enabling producers to obtain a rapid and accurate picture of the prices quoted by their competitors. * * *

64 In this case, the communications arise from the price announcements made to users. They constitute in themselves market behavior which does not lessen each undertaking's uncertainty as to the future attitude of its competitors. At the time when each undertaking engages in such behavior, it cannot be sure of the future conduct of the others.

65 Accordingly, the system of quarterly price announcements on the pulp market is not to be regarded as constituting in itself an infringement of art. [101](1) of the Treaty.

B. Concertation on announced prices as the infringement

66 In the second hypothesis, the Commission considers that the system of price announcements constitutes evidence of concertation at an earlier stage. . . . [T]he Commission states that, as proof of such concertation, it relied on the parallel conduct of the pulp producers in the period from 1975 to 1981 and on different kinds of direct or indirect exchange of information. * * *

70 Since the Commission has no documents which directly establish the existence of concertation between the producers concerned, it is necessary to ascertain whether the system of quarterly price announcements, the simultaneity or near-simultaneity of the price announcements and the parallelism of price announcements as found during the period from 1975 to 1981 constitute a firm, precise and consistent body of evidence of prior concertation.

71 In determining the probative value of those different factors, it must be noted that parallel conduct cannot be regarded as furnishing proof of concertation unless concertation constitutes the only plausible explanation for such conduct. It is necessary to bear in mind that, although art. [101] of the Treaty prohibits any form of collusion which distorts competition, it does not deprive economic operators of the right to adapt themselves intelligently to the existing and anticipated conduct of their competitors.

72 Accordingly, it is necessary in this case to ascertain whether the parallel conduct alleged by the Commission cannot, taking account of the nature of the products, the size and the number of the undertakings and the volume of the market in question, be explained otherwise than by concertation.

(a) System of price announcements

* * *

74 In their pleadings, on the other hand, the applicants maintain that the system is ascribable to the particular commercial requirements of the pulp market. * * *

76 The experts [appointed by the Court] observe first that the system of announcements at issue must be viewed in the context of the long-term relationships which existed between producers and their customers and which were a result both of the method of manufacturing the pulp and of the cyclical nature of the market. In view of the fact that each type of paper was the result of a particular mixture of pulps having their own characteristics and that the mixture was difficult to change, a relationship based on close co-operation was established between the pulp producers and the paper manufacturers. Such relations were all the closer since they also had the advantage of protecting both sides against the uncertainties inherent in the cyclical nature of the market: they guaranteed security of supply to buyers and at the same time security of demand to producers.

77 The experts point out that it is in the context of those long-term relationships that, after the Second World War, purchasers demanded the introduction of that system of announcements. Since

pulp accounts for between 50–75 per cent of the cost of paper, those purchasers wished to ascertain as soon as possible the prices which they might be charged in order to estimate their costs and to fix the prices of their own products. However, as those purchasers did not wish to be bound by a high fixed price in the event of the market weakening, the announced price was regarded as a ceiling price below which the transaction price could always be renegotiated.

78 The explanation given for the use of a quarterly cycle is that it is the result of a compromise between the paper manufacturers' desire for a degree of foreseeability as regards the price of pulp and the producers' desire not to miss any opportunities to make a profit in the event of a strengthening of the market.

79 The US dollar was, according to the experts, introduced on the market by the North American producers during the 1960s. That development was generally welcomed by purchasers who regarded it as a means of ensuring that they did not pay a higher price than their competitors.

(b) Simultaneity or near-simultaneity of announcements

80 . . . [T]he Commission claims that the close succession or even simultaneity of price announcements would not have been possible without a constant flow of information between the undertakings concerned.

81 According to the applicants, the simultaneity or near-simultaneity of the announcements—even if it were established—must instead be regarded as a direct result of the very high degree of transparency of the market. Such transparency, far from being artificial, can be explained by the extremely well-developed network of relations which, in view of the nature and the structure of the market, have been established between the various traders. * * *

83 First, . . . a buyer was always in contact with several pulp producers. One reason for that was connected with the paper-making process, but another was that, in order to avoid becoming overdependent on one producer, pulp buyers took the precaution of diversifying their sources of supply. With a view to obtaining the lowest possible prices, they were in the habit, especially in times of falling prices, of disclosing to their suppliers the prices announced by their competitors.

84 Secondly, it should be noted that most of the pulp was sold to a relatively small number of large paper manufacturers. Those few buyers maintained very close links with each other and exchanged information on changes in prices of which they were aware.

85 Thirdly, several producers who made paper themselves purchased pulp from other producers and were thus informed, in times of both rising prices and falling prices, of the prices charged by their competitors. That information was also accessible to producers who did not themselves manufacture paper but were linked to groups that did.

86 Fourthly, that high degree of transparency in the pulp market resulting from the links between traders or groups of traders was further reinforced by the existence of agents established in the Community who worked for several producers and by the existence of a very dynamic trade press. * * *

88 Finally, it is necessary to add that the use of rapid means of communications, such as the telephone and telex, and the very frequent recourse by the paper manufacturers to very well-informed trade buyers meant that, notwithstanding the number of stages involved—producer, agent, buyer, agent, producer—information on the level of the announced prices spreads within a matter of days, if not within a matter of hours on the pulp market. * * *

Conclusions

126 Following that analysis, it must be stated that, in this case, concertation is not the only plausible explanation for the parallel conduct. To begin with, the system of price announcements may be regarded as constituting a rational response to the fact that the pulp market constituted a long-term market and to the need felt by both buyers and sellers to limit commercial risks. Further, the similarity in the dates of price announcements may be regarded as a direct result of the high degree of market transparency, which does not have to be described as artificial. Finally, the parallelism of prices and the price trends may be satisfactorily explained by the oligopolistic tendencies of the market and by the specific circumstances prevailing in certain periods. Accordingly, the parallel conduct established by the Commission does not constitute evidence of concertation.

Notes and Questions

1. In paragraph 71 the Court declares that parallel conduct cannot furnish proof of concertation "unless concertation constitutes the only plausible explanation for such conduct." Why such a heavy burden? If agreement was the most probable explanation of the parallel price moves, should the Court have drawn an inference of a concerted practice?

2. The buyers desired advance price information. Does that explain the quarterly price announcements? Does it explain the virtual

simultaneity of the price announcements? Does it explain the uniform price rises?

3. Did evidence suggest that the behavior was not competitive but was nonetheless not conspiratorial?

4. In *Wood pulp*, the European Court moved from an elastic definition of "concertation" to a focused and demanding one. In the United States, the Supreme Court similarly moved from a soft test for proof of "combination" or "concert" to a demanding standard. Compare Interstate Circuit, 306 U.S. 208, 1939 with Matsushita, 475 U.S. 574, 1986. What are the policy reasons for the modern approach?

5. Observe the conundrum of oligopoly behavior. A few firms in a high-barrier market may be able to mimic the effects of a cartel without an explicit agreement or even an understanding. Should this phenomenon be relevant to a judicial construction of the word "concert"? Should it make proof of concertation harder or easier?

6. "Smoking gun" evidence of an agreement is often lacking, sometimes because it is adroitly concealed and other times because the parties were able to coordinate their behavior without any overt agreement. In a 2003 enforcement decision against Toshiba Corp. and NEC Corp, the Japan Fair Trade Commission found sufficient evidence of coordination on bidding to supply the postal authority's letter-sorting machines, even though there was no explicit evidence of agreement. The JFTC considered the following factors sufficient: (1) a duopoly market structure; (2) a pattern of past business conduct before the postal service opened up for competitive bidding; (3) a meeting in which the parties contemplated limiting bidding competition; (4) the continuation of exclusive bidding even after the authority opened up competitive bidding; (5) the absence of competitive bidding was economically irrational absent coordination; and (6) prices fell dramatically once competitive bidding began.

7. Conspiracy by algorithm. Online booking platforms and algorithms to determine prices can make cartels easier to form and cheating easier to detect and punish. It can also make participants in online booking systems more vulnerable to cartel accusations. In Lithuania, travel agents used a common online booking system. The system administrator asked the travel agents, by email, for a vote on whether to cap discounts for online bookings at 3%. After an affirmative vote of those who voted, the administrator declared the 3% maximum and set the system for an automatic 3% maximum, although individual agents were not blocked from offering a higher discount if they took the trouble to maneuver around the setting. When the Lithuanian Competition Council opened proceedings, some of the agents claimed not to have received the relevant emails. The Competition Council found infringements by all of the agents who were members of the system. The

national court to which the allegedly innocent agents appealed posed a question to the Court of Justice. The Court answered:

"Article 101(1) TFEU must be interpreted as meaning that, where the administrator of an information system, intended to enable travel agencies to sell travel packages on their websites using a uniform booking method, sends to those economic operators, via a personal electronic mailbox, a message informing them that the discounts on products sold through that system will henceforth be capped and, following the dissemination of that message, the system in question undergoes the technical modifications necessary to implement that measure, those economic operators may—if they were aware of that message—be presumed to have participated in a concerted practice within the meaning of that provision, unless they publicly distanced themselves from that practice, reported it to the administrative authorities or adduced other evidence to rebut that presumption, such as evidence of a systematic application of a discount exceeding the cap in question.

It is for the referring court to examine—on the basis of the national rules governing the assessment of evidence and the standard of proof—whether, in view of all the circumstances before it, the dispatch of a message, such as that at issue in the main proceedings, may constitute sufficient evidence to establish that the addressees of that message were aware of its content. The presumption of innocence precludes the referring court from considering that the mere dispatch of that message constitutes sufficient evidence to establish that its addressees ought to have been aware of its content." Eturas, Case C–74/14, EU:C:2016:42.

EU Competition Commissioner Margrethe Vestager cited *Eturas* in cautioning that algorithms and other automated systems can make cartels more effective, and noting the opening of investigations in consumer electronics markets.

Algorithmic collusion first received widespread attention within the global competition law community following the publication in 2016 of Virtual Competition by Ariel Ezrachi and Maurice Stucke. While there was general awareness of and some theorizing about the phenomenon, enforcement effort was lagging behind. Things changed in 2024 when the U.S. Department of Justice filed a case against six of the nation's largest landlord for participating in algorithmic pricing schemes that resulted in higher rent for tenants. The allegations included: (1) use of common anticompetitive pricing algorithms; (2) directly communicating with competitors' senior managers about rents, occupancy, and other competitively sensitive information; (3) engaging in regular "market survey" calls and emails among competitors to share competitively sensitive information; (4) sharing information with competitors about their choice of parameters on the common pricing algorithm, which supposedly promoted price alignment. Although the alleged collusive scheme in the case was not solely the result of algorithmic coordination, the use of a common pricing algorithm among competitors played a pivotal role in the scheme.

8. When does competitors' exchange of sensitive information spill over into a price-fixing cartel? In China, exchange of sensitive information, plus, for example, meetings followed by a similar price rise, can be interpreted as a concerted practice. In 2016 the NDRC, the agency in charge of price conduct, found a price cartel compromising two pharmaceutical companies. A third firm, Chang Zhou No. 4 Pharmaceutical Ltd., was not a party to this cartel but had communicated with the two cartelists and raised its prices in rhythm with them. It was fined for a concerted practice. Estazolam Raw Materials and Pills Case, July 27, 2016. https://nysba.org/wp-content/uploads/2019/02/Antitrust-Compliance-2017-03-02.pdf.

The European Union, too, is more likely than the United States to draw an inference of a cartel from exchange of confidential information and surrounding circumstances. It did so in the case of smart card chips, where it determined that the exchange was aimed at slowing down price decreases. 758/14, Infineon Technologies v. Commission, EU:T:2016:737.

9. An important threshold question in jurisdictions that allow private anti-cartel enforcement is what evidence a private plaintiff must have of cartel behavior at the time of filing the complaint. In Bell Atlantic Corp. v. Twombly, 550 U.S. 544 (2007), the telephone companies had been regulated; they had legal monopolies, each for its own territory. When the regulation was lifted, each one still stayed in its historical territory and did not go across the border to compete. Plaintiff thought this must mean that they had an agreement to divide territories, and so alleged.

The US Supreme Court dismissed the complaint. Not going across the border was entirely consistent with independent, and interdependent, action. Each one liked it the way it was; they did not want competition to break out and were not going to trigger it; they hoped that each other telecom firm would do the same thing (not compete). The Court dismissed the complaint. It held that a plaintiff must allege concrete facts plausibly evidencing a conspiracy before it can proceed to discovery. This holding arguably creates a chicken-and-egg problem, since plaintiffs may need access to discovery in order to uncover the facts evidencing the alleged conspiracy. Nonetheless, some plaintiff's' lawyers report that *Twombly* has not significantly deterred the filing of private antitrust cases—only made them more careful in their pleading.

D. ARE EFFECTS NECESSARY?

In the United States, *Socony-Vacuum* (310 U.S. 150, 1940) established in dictum in famous footnote 59 that a cartel agreement is illegal on its face. A plea of "We tried to raise prices but could not do it because the market overwhelmed us" does not work.

The quinine producers tried the same tack. They argued: We tried to run a cartel but our agreement had no effect because quinine bark became scarce. What did the Court of Justice say about this defense? In what paragraph?

In the 1990s, the US authorities sued Nippon Paper Industries for a conspiracy with other Japanese manufacturers for fixing the price of thermal fax paper for export into the United States. Nippon argued that, for the time period not blocked by the statute of limitations, the conditions of supply and demand had so changed that the agreement had no effect, and also that it had already withdrawn from the conspiracy. The court held that, for purposes of subject matter jurisdiction, the United States had to prove intended and substantial effects in the US market within the statute of limitations period. The government had failed to carry this burden. United States v. Nippon Paper Indus., 62 F. Supp. 2d 173 (D. Mass. 1999).

E. CRISIS CARTELS

Are all cartels illegal? Are "good" cartels exempted? Some jurisdictions allow public interest defenses (but not the United States). Some jurisdictions allow a crisis cartel defense. Also, not the United States. Whole industries may fall into crises of overcapacity. Should they be allowed to combine in order to lift themselves out of the crisis?

The Irish beef industry faced such a crisis. The Irish government requested the industry to agree to a plan of rationalization, and, in response, all of the principal Irish beef processors, accounting for 93% of the Irish industry, formed an association and entered into a rationalization agreement. The Irish Competition Authority challenged the agreement. The Irish court sided with the Irish government and the industry, finding that the industry was in survival mode and it needed to be rationalized; the rationalization would save costs and help to restore the industry to efficiency and competitiveness; and that no credible evidence had been adduced to show that the agreement would restrict or distort competition or hurt consumers.

The Irish court made a reference to the European Court of Justice for a ruling on the interpretation of the Treaty of Rome.

COMPETITION AUTHORITY v. BEEF INDUSTRY DEVELOPMENT SOCIETY LTD.

Case C–209/07, ECLI: EU:C:2008:643 (Court of Justice of the European Union 2008)

1 This reference for a preliminary ruling concerns the interpretation of Article 81(1) EC [now 101(1) TFEU].

2 The reference was made in proceedings between the Competition Authority, on the one hand, and Beef Industry Development Society Ltd ('BIDS') and Barry Brothers (Carrigmore) Meats Ltd ('Barry Brothers'), on the other, in respect of decisions of BIDS rationalizing the beef and veal sector in Ireland.

The main proceedings and the question referred for a preliminary ruling

3 It is apparent from the decision making the reference that the dispute before the Supreme Court arises in the context of overcapacity in the beef industry in Ireland and, more particularly, in the processing sector (slaughter and de-boning of meat).

4 A study carried out in 1998 at the joint request of the Irish Government and representatives of the beef industry concluded that it was necessary to reduce the number of processors from 20 to a figure between 4 and 6. The report also recommended that the undertakings which were to remain in the sector ('the stayers') should compensate those forced to withdraw ('the goers').

5 In 1999, a task force set up by the Minister for Agriculture and Food came to similar conclusions and recommended that the processors should create a compensation fund.

6 In accordance with those conclusions, the 10 principal processors formed BIDS on May 2002. BIDS prepared a draft rationalization plan which provided, inter alia, for a reduction in processing capacity of about 25%, the equivalent of an annual volume of about 420 000 head of cattle.

7 BIDS planned to implement that objective by means of agreements between the stayers and the goers, in the terms of a standard form of contract, the principal features of which are summarized in the following paragraph.

8 That standard form of contract provides that the stayers are to compensate the goers, the amount of that compensation to be determined by the parties. BIDS is to pay the compensation to the goers. The stayers are to repay BIDS by means of a levy of EUR 2 per head of cattle up to their traditional cattle kill volume and EUR 11 above that volume. In return, the goers undertake:

—to decommission or put beyond use their processing plants or sell them only to persons established outside the island of Ireland, or, if necessary, to the stayers on condition that they be used as back-up equipment or spare parts;

—not to use the land on which those plants were situated for the purposes of beef or veal processing for a period of five years;

—not to compete with the stayers in the beef and veal processing market in Ireland for two years.

9 Barry Brothers is a beef and veal processing company. It made an agreement with BIDS complying with the features described in the previous paragraph.

10 BIDS notified the Competition Authority of that agreement and the standard form of contract ('the BIDS arrangements').

11 Having informed BIDS, on 5 and 26 June 2003, that it considered the BIDS arrangements contrary to Article [101(1) TFEU], the Competition Authority applied to the High Court, on 30 June 2003, for an order restraining BIDS and Barry Brothers from giving effect to them.

12 By judgment of 27 July 2006, the High Court dismissed that application. It held that the agreement between BIDS and Barry Brothers did not fall under the prohibition laid down in Article [101(1) TFEU] but nor did it satisfy the requirements for exemption laid down in Article [101(3) TFEU].

13 The Competition Authority appealed against that decision to the Supreme Court, which decided to stay the proceedings and to refer the following question to the Court of Justice for a preliminary ruling:

'Where it is established to the satisfaction of the court that:

(a) there is overcapacity in the industry for the processing of beef which, calculated at peak throughput, would be approximately 32%;

(b) the effect of this excess capacity will have very serious consequences for the profitability of the industry as a whole over the medium term;

(c) while . . . the effects of surplus requirements have not been felt to any significant degree as yet, independent consultants have advised that, in the near term, the overcapacity is unlikely to be eliminated by normal market measures, but over time the overcapacity will lead to very significant losses and ultimately to processors and plants leaving the industry;

(d) processors of beef representing approximately 93% of the market for the supply of beef of that industry have agreed to take steps to eliminate the overcapacity and are willing to pay a levy in order to fund payments to processors willing to cease production, and

the said processors, comprising 10 companies, form a corporate body ("the society") for the purpose of implementing an arrangement with the following features:

—[goers] killing and processing 420 000 animals per annum, representing approximately 25% of active capacity would enter into an agreement with [stayers] to leave the industry and to abide by the following terms;

—goers would sign a two year non-compete clause in relation to the processing of cattle on the entire island of Ireland;

—the plants of goers would be decommissioned;

—land associated with the decommissioned plants would not be used for the purposes of beef processing for a period of five years;

—compensation would be paid to goers in staged payments by means of loans made by the stayers to the society;

—a voluntary levy would be paid to the society by all stayers at the rate of EUR 2 per head of the traditional percentage kill and EUR 11 per head on cattle kill above that figure;

—the levy would be used to repay the stayers' loans; levies would cease on repayment of the loans;

—the equipment of goers used for primary beef processing would be sold only to stayers for use as back-up equipment or spare parts or sold outside the island of Ireland;

—the freedom of the stayers in matters of production, pricing, conditions of sale, imports and exports, increase in capacity and otherwise would not be affected, and that it is agreed that such an agreement is liable, for the purpose of application of Article [101(1) TFEU], to have an appreciable effect on trade between Member States, is such arrangement to be regarded as having as its object, as distinct from effect, the prevention, restriction or distortion of competition within the common market and therefore, incompatible with Article [101](1) of the Treaty [on the Functioning of the European Union]?'

The question referred for a preliminary ruling

14 By its question, the national court asks, in essence, whether agreements with features such as those of the BIDS arrangements are to be regarded, by reason of their object alone, as being anti-competitive and prohibited by Article [101(1) TFEU] EC or whether, on the other hand, it is necessary, in order to reach such a conclusion, first to demonstrate that such agreements have had anti-competitive effects.

15 It must be recalled that, to come within the prohibition laid down in Article [101(1) TFEU], an agreement must have 'as [its] object or effect the prevention, restriction or distortion of competition within the common market'. It has, since the judgment in Case 56/65 *LTM* [1966] ECR 235, 249, been settled case-law that the alternative nature of that requirement, indicated by the conjunction 'or', leads, first, to the need to consider the precise purpose of the agreement, in the economic context in which it is to be applied. Where, however, an analysis of the clauses of that agreement does not reveal the effect on competition to be sufficiently deleterious, its consequences should then be considered and for it to be caught by the prohibition it is necessary to find that those factors are present which show that competition has in fact been prevented or restricted or distorted to an appreciable extent.

16 In deciding whether an agreement is prohibited by Article [101(1) TFEU], there is therefore no need to take account of its actual effects once it appears that its object is to prevent, restrict or distort competition within the common market. . . .

17 The distinction between 'infringements by object' and 'infringements by effect' arises from the fact that certain forms of collusion between undertakings can be regarded, by their very nature, as being injurious to the proper functioning of normal competition.

18 In their written observations submitted to the Court, the Competition Authority, the Belgian Government and the Commission of the European Communities all submit that the object of the BIDS arrangements is obviously anti-competitive so that there is no need to analyses their actual effects and that those arrangements were concluded in breach of the prohibition laid down in Article [101(1) TFEU].

[19] On the other hand, BIDS submits that those arrangements do not come within the category of infringements by object, but should, on the contrary, be analyzed in the light of their actual effects on the market. It argues that the BIDS arrangements, first, are not anti-competitive in purpose and, second, do not entail injurious consequences for consumers or, more generally, for competition. It states that the purpose of those arrangements is not adversely to affect competition or the welfare of consumers, but to rationalize the beef industry in order to make it more competitive by reducing, but not eliminating, production overcapacity.

[20] That argument cannot be accepted.

[21] In fact, to determine whether an agreement comes within the prohibition laid down in Article [101(1) TFEU], close regard must be paid to the wording of its provisions and to the objectives which it is intended to attain. In that regard, even supposing it to be established that the parties to an agreement acted without any subjective intention of restricting competition, but with the object of remedying the effects of a crisis in their sector, such considerations are irrelevant for the purposes of applying that provision. Indeed, an agreement may be regarded as having a restrictive object even if it does not have the restriction of competition as its sole aim but also pursues other legitimate objectives. It is only in connection with Article [101(3) TFEU] that matters such as those relied upon by BIDS may, if appropriate, be taken into consideration for the purposes of obtaining an exemption from the prohibition laid down in Article [101(1) TFEU].

[22] BIDS argues, in addition, that the concept of infringement by object should be interpreted narrowly. Only agreements as to horizontal price-fixing, or to limit output or share markets, agreements whose anti-competitive effects are so obvious as not to require an economic analysis come within that category. The BIDS arrangements cannot be assimilated to that type of agreement or to other forms of complex cartels. BIDS maintains that an agreement on the reduction of excess capacity in a sector cannot be assimilated to an agreement to 'limit production' within the meaning of Article [101(1)(b) TFEU]. That concept must be understood as referring to a limitation of total market output rather than a limitation of the output of certain operators who voluntarily withdraw from the market, without causing a lowering of output.

[23] However, as the Advocate General pointed out in point 48 of her Opinion, the types of agreements covered by Article [101(1)(a) to (c) TFEU] do not constitute an exhaustive list of prohibited collusion.

24 Therefore, it must be examined whether agreements with features such as those described by the national court have as their object the restriction of competition.

25 In BIDS' submission, if an agreement does not affect the total output on a market or obstruct operators' freedom to act independently, any anti-competitive effect can be excluded. In the main proceedings, the withdrawal of certain operators from the market is irrelevant, because the stayers are in a position to satisfy demand.

26 BIDS adds that the structure of the market does not allow the processors to influence it, since up to 90% of demand is from outside Ireland. On the Irish market, the power of the processors is largely counteracted by the purchasing power of the four major retailers. Account must also be taken of the competition which new operators entering the market concerned could bring about.

27 BIDS observes that the cases in which a limitation on output has been held to be infringement by object concerned agreements supplemental to horizontal price or production-fixing agreements . . ., to which the BIDS arrangements are not comparable.

28 BIDS submits that the Commission's decision-making practice and the case-law do not permit the conclusion that there is a restriction by object. . . . * * *

30 . . . [T]he BIDS arrangements provide for neither the freezing nor the non-use of capacity, nor exchange of information, nor quotas or other measures intended to preserve the stayers' market shares.

31 In that regard, it is apparent from the documents before the Court and from the information provided by the national court that the object of the BIDS arrangements is to change, appreciably, the structure of the market through a mechanism intended to encourage the withdrawal of competitors.

32 The matters brought to the Court's attention show that the BIDS arrangements are intended to improve the overall profitability of undertakings supplying more than 90% of the beef and veal processing services on the Irish market by enabling them to approach, or even attain, their minimum efficient scale. In order to do so, those arrangements pursue two main objectives: first, to increase the degree of concentration in the sector concerned by reducing significantly the number of undertakings supplying processing services and, second, to eliminate almost 75% of excess production capacity.

[33] The BIDS arrangements are intended therefore, essentially, to enable several undertakings to implement a common policy which has as its object the encouragement of some of them to withdraw from the market and the reduction, as a consequence, of the overcapacity which affects their profitability by preventing them from achieving economies of scale.

[34] That type of arrangement conflicts patently with the concept inherent in the . . . Treaty provisions relating to competition, according to which each economic operator must determine independently the policy which it intends to adopt on the common market. Article [101(1) TFEU] is intended to prohibit any form of coordination which deliberately substitutes practical cooperation between undertakings for the risks of competition.

[35] In the context of competition, the undertakings which signed the BIDS arrangements would have, without such arrangements, no means of improving their profitability other than by intensifying their commercial rivalry or resorting to concentrations. With the BIDS arrangements it would be possible for them to avoid such a process and to share a large part of the costs involved in increasing the degree of market concentration as a result, in particular, of the levy of EUR 2 per head processed by each of the stayers.

[36] In addition, the means put in place to attain the objective of the BIDS arrangements include restrictions whose object is anti-competitive.

[37] As regards, in the first place, the levy of EUR 11 per head of cattle slaughtered beyond the usual volume of production of each of the stayers, it is, as BIDS submits, the price to be paid by the stayers to acquire the goers' clientele. However, it must be observed, as did the Advocate General . . ., that such a measure also constitutes an obstacle to the natural development of market shares as regards some of the stayers who, because of the dissuasive nature of that levy, are deterred from exceeding their usual volume of production. That measure is likely therefore to lead to certain operators freezing their production.

[38] As regards, secondly, restrictions imposed on the goers as regards the disposal and use of their processing plants, the BIDS arrangements also contain, by their very object, restrictions on competition since they seek to avoid the possible use of those plants by new operators entering the market in order to compete with the stayers. As the Competition Authority pointed out in its written observations, since the investment necessary for the construction of a new processing plant is much greater than the costs of taking over an existing plant, those restrictions are obviously intended to

dissuade any new entry of competitors throughout the island of Ireland.

39 Finally, the fact that those restrictions, as well as the non-competition clause imposed on the goers, are limited in time is not such as to put in doubt the finding as to the anti-competitive nature of the object of the BIDS arrangements. As the Advocate General observed in point 86 of her Opinion, such matters may, at the most, be relevant for the purposes of the examination of the four requirements which have to be met under Article [101(3) TFEU] in order to escape the prohibition laid down in Article [101(1) TFEU].

40 In the light of the foregoing considerations, the reply to the question referred must be that an agreement with features such as those of the standard form of contract concluded between the 10 principal beef and veal processors in Ireland, who are members of BIDS, and requiring, among other things, a reduction of the order of 25% in processing capacity, has as its object the prevention, restriction or distortion of competition within the meaning of Article [101(1) TFEU]. . . . * * *

Notes and Questions

1. What was really the purpose of the agreement? Was BIDS' purpose to address the crisis of overproduction of beef in Ireland by reducing overcapacity, thereby resuscitating the industry and making it more competitive? Assume that BIDS and the Irish government thought there was a good chance that the plan would succeed. Is such an agreement caught by Article 101(1) as a restriction of competition by object? Should it be?

2. BIDS maintained in the Irish court that, if caught by Article 101(1), the agreement should be exempted under Article 101(3). This issue came before the Irish High Court in 2010. The European Commission submitted an *amicus curiae* brief, advising the High Court on its views of how the Article 101(3) analysis should proceed. Among other points, the Commission asserted: (1) an industry rationalization plan should ensure that the factory capacity left on the market is the most efficient and that surviving firms have the practical ability to increase output following implementation of the rationalization plan; (2) "so-called 'crisis cartels' which aim to reduce industry capacity cannot be justified by economic downturns and recession-induced freefalls. As a general rule in a free market economy, market forces should reduce unnecessary capacity from a market;" spontaneous market restructuring is likely to be impeded only where (a) giving up capacity is costly for all firms, and (b) the market is structurally stable, transparent, and symmetric; and (3) consumers typically receive a fair share of the resulting benefits only when the industry rationalization results in

marginal cost savings, which is not generally characteristic of the elimination of fixed capacity such as factories or entire firms.

How much room do these standards leave for a lawful crisis cartel? Under these standards, was BIDS likely to get an exemption?

3. In Dutch brickmakers, the European Commission exempted, under Article 101(3), a rationalization agreement by brickmakers who were plagued by overcapacity. The brickmakers agreed to reduce surplus capacity over a limited period time, while not making any agreement on prices. Stichting Baksteen, Case IV/34.456, O.J. L 131/15 (May 26, 1994). This case is exceptional, and may be the last crisis cartel ever to be approved by the Commission.

The wisdom of allowing judicial or administrative authorization of crisis or restructuring cartels is much debated. United States law makes no allowance for crises, on the theory that market solutions are better than private solutions, and a crisis justification for cartels would weaken the clear rule of law. Germany and the UK once allowed authorization of crisis cartels in the public interest. They have revised their laws to mirror Article 101. Until 1999, Japanese law allowed authorization of depression and rationalization cartels. This authorization was repealed. Anti-Monopoly Law of Japan, § 24(3), Law No. 54, 1947 (amended). However the Anti-Monopoly Act of Japan prohibits "unreasonable restraint of trade" when it is "contrary to the public interest." AMA Article 2(6). In the Oil Cartel case, which arose under conditions of crisis, the Supreme Court of Japan condemned the cartel but nonetheless stated that " 'public interest' may, in 'exceptional circumstances,' override the direct objective of preservation of free competition under the AMA, from the viewpoint of the ultimate objective of consumer interests and development of the national economy." Oil Cartel, 38(4) Keishu 1287, 1311 (Sup. Ct. Feb. 24, 1984), as summarized by Toshiaki Takigawa in Competition law and policy of Japan, 54 Antitrust Bulletin 435, 440–41 (2009). The Chinese Anti-Monopoly Law allows for the exemption of an agreement made "for the purpose of mitigating a severe decrease of sales volume or excessive oversupply during economic recessions." AML Art. 20(5). To obtain an exemption the undertakings must prove that their agreement "will not substantially restrict competition . . . and can enable consumers to share the benefits." These burdens suggest that "it would be difficult for crisis cartels to be exempted in practice." Wang Xiaoye, The new Chinese Anti-Monopoly Law: A survey of a work in progress, 54 Antitrust Bul. 579, 600 (fall 2009).

In nations that do not allow a crisis cartel justification, are jurists sometimes "clever" in recasting the problem as not a cartel, or as state action or a political question? See Appalachian Coals (288 U.S. 344 (1933)). See also Hammons v. Alcan Aluminum Corp., 1997–1 (CCH) Trade Cas. ¶ 71,714 (C.D. Cal. 1996), aff'd mem., 132 F.3d 39 (9th Cir.

1997), cert. denied, 525 U.S. 948 (1998) (when Russian aluminum flooded the market, US government induced producers to limit their output; they did, but no agreement was proved). Is this flexibility necessary? inevitable?

4. See Chapter 8 for an account of the role of the European Competition Commissioner and the Competition Directorate-General in responding to the urgent public needs in the financial crisis of 2008–09. They presented competition as part of the solution, not part of the problem.

Case Study: Cartelization During the COVID-19 Pandemic

The COVID-19 pandemic that swept the world starting in late 2019 put serious strains on the antitrust systems around the world. In the United States and the EU, competition authorities issued guidelines emphasizing that competition law enforcement would continue as usual, but also suggesting that the agencies would look with sympathy on competitor collaborations necessary to combat the pandemic. *See Joint Antitrust Statement Regarding COVID-19*, https://www.justice.gov/atr/joint-antitrust-statement-regarding-covid-19. The European Commission and European Competition Network—an association of Member State competition authorities—issued a joint statement to the effect that they understood "that this extraordinary situation may trigger the need for companies to cooperate in order to ensure the supply and fair distribution of scarce products to all consumers. In the current circumstances, the ECN will not actively intervene against necessary and temporary measures put in place in order to avoid a shortage of supply." https://competition-policy.ec.europa.eu/antitrust-and-cartels/legislation/coronavirus_en.

If competition authorities were willing to tolerate some collaborations that might be necessary to fighting the pandemic, they did not abdicate their responsibility to police anticompetitive agreements. In 2019–20, the Polish Basketball League terminated the season early due to the pandemic. With the help of the league, the teams agreed among themselves not to pay their players for the remainder of season. The Polish Competition Authority found this arrangement an unlawful agreement to restrict wage competition, and fined both the league and the individual teams. While each team might have lawful contractual reasons to discontinue paying their players, for the teams to agree on this horizontally was a form of illegal price fixing. Pandemic or no pandemic, competition law remained in force.

F. CARTELIZATION AND THE DEVELOPING WORLD

There is a broad consensus in the competition law community that price-fixing cartels are what the U.S. Supreme Court has called "the supreme evil of antitrust." Verizon Communcs. Inc. v. Law Offices of Curtis V. Trinko, LLP, 540 U.S. 398, 408 (2004). But does that idea necessarily hold across all economic and political circumstances? In particular, to what extent should competition law's antipathy toward cartels hold as to the developing world?

On the one hand, there is little doubt that international cartels that sell into developing countries cause significant harm to those countries' citizens and economies. A study by Maggie Levenstein and Valerie Suslow found that, in 1997, developing countries imported $51.1 billion worth of goods from industries that had cartel activities during the 1990s. Margaret Levenstein & Valerie Y. Suslow, *Contemporary International Cartels and Developing Countries: Economic Effects and Implications for Competition Policy*, 71 Antitrust L. J. 801, 816 (2004). Another study conducted by Marc Ivaldi, Aleksandra Khimich, and Frédéric Jenny tried to estimate the economic harm caused by cartels in 12 developing or lower income countries, including Brazil, Chile, Colombia, Indonesia, Mexico, Pakistan, Peru, Russia, South Africa, South Korea, Ukraine, and Zambia *Impact of Cartels in Low-Income Countries*, https://assets.publishing.service.gov.uk/media/57a0898140f0b649740000f4/Research-Note_Impact-Cartels-Ivalid-Khimich-Jenny.pdf. Based on a dataset of information on "249 major 'hard-core' cartels that were prosecuted in more than 20 developing countries from 1995 to 2013," the authors found that cartels increased prices around 23% on average, and decreased production by 15%.

The case for policing international cartels that sell into developing countries is strong. But what about cartel-type behavior by local producers in the developing world, where small and medium enterprises ("SMEs") may enter into various forms of collaboration to survive or grow? Should the same per se rules apply when SMEs face competition from powerful foreign companies from the developed world, or even large national companies?

A group of small, regional Peruvian bakers thought that competition law should take into account the sometimes precarious position of small companies in developing markets when applying the prohibition on cartels. In 2016, Peru's competition regulator, the Competition Division of the Tribunal of Indecopi, upheld a Commission's decision finding eight smaller bakeries from three districts of Piura (a northern region in Peru), liable for fixing the price of bread. In 2013, the bakeries had agreed among themselves to raise the price of bread by about ten cents per unit. The defendants did not dispute the fact of their agreement, but argued that it should not be prohibited because the agreement had been made in response to rising distribution costs that threatened their ongoing viability and had not affected the ultimate price of bread. The Tribunal rejected these arguments categorically, holding that the agreement was per se illegal.

Despite competition law's general antipathy to cartels, some competition laws have express provisions allowing for some relaxation of competition law rules when it comes to SMEs. Article 20 of the Chinese Antimonopoly Law creates an exemption from the prohibition on monopoly agreements when necessary to increase the operating efficiency of small and medium-sized undertakings or to increase their competitiveness. In 2024, South Africa's Department of Trade, Industry and Competition issued a "Block Exemption for Small, Micro and Medium-Sized Business" that allows SME to apply for an exemption from the ordinary prohibitions on restrictive horizontal or vertical agreements in order to collaborate on a number of activities, including joint purchasing, joint selling through intermediaries, and commercialization. The Department noted that SMEs have been disproportionately affected by the COVID-19 pandemic's supply chain disruptions, and may need some relief from competition law to flourish.

Cartel agreements remain the bête noire of competition law, but some relaxation of those rules for SMEs is not a rarity.

Chapter 3

COLLABORATIONS OF COMPETITORS OTHER THAN CARTELS

A. INTRODUCTION

In Chapter 2, we studied hard-core cartels, such as price-fixing or market-division agreements, that are usually considered to be illegal without a searching inquiry into their actual economic effects in a particular case. In this chapter, we turn to agreements among competitors—horizontal agreements—that are not so obviously anticompetitive that they merit per se treatment.

Unlike cartel agreements, whose essential characteristics are usually similar from case to case, there is a great deal of variety in non-hard-core competitor collaborations. Indeed, virtually every form of business organization involves some agreement that restricts competition between its members. Think of corporations that set the terms of sale for products created by hundreds of employees or law firm partnerships that set the price for their lawyers' services. In a colloquial sense, all such arrangements among people who might otherwise be competitors "restrain trade" in the words of Section 1 of the Sherman Act or "prevent[ ], restrict[ ], or distort[ ]" competition in the words of Article 101(1) of the Treaty on the Functioning of the European Union ("TFEU") (formerly Article 81 of the Treaty of Rome). But economic activity would come to a standstill—or be relegated to a pre-industrial form of atomistic competition between individual farmers and tradespeople—if every form of agreement among actual or potential competitors were illegal. Thus, the law of non-cartel restraints of trade among competitors must sort through the myriad varieties of horizontal agreements and only scrutinize those most likely to produce net anticompetitive effects.

Different antitrust regimes employ different procedural and substantive frameworks for scrutinizing non-cartel horizontal restraints. The EU approach, reflected in Article 101(1) and (2), is to begin with a broad prohibition of all agreements that affect trade between Member States that "have as their object or effect" the "prevention, restriction or distortion of competition." Article 101(1) then lists five illustrative, but not exhaustive, prohibited kinds of agreements. Article 101(3) then declares that Article 101(1) may be declared inapplicable if the agreement (1) contributes to improving production or distribution or promoting technical or economic progress, (2) allows consumers a fair share of the benefits, (3) does not impose unnecessary restrictions (any restrictions must be "indispensable to the attainment of [the above] objectives), and (4) does not give the firms concerned the possibility eliminate to competition in a substantial part of the market.

Under EU law, the distinction between restrictions on competition "by object" and "by effect" is significant. When an agreement restricts competition by object, the Commission need not prove that it has an anticompetitive effect—that is presumed. Consten and Grundig v. Commission (56/64) [1966] E.C.R. 299, p. 342. By contrast, agreements that may restrict competition by effect but not object require a showing of such effects as part of the Commission's burden of proof.

US law, by contrast, follows a simple prohibition on "contracts, combinations, or conspiracies . . . in restraint of trade." The statute contains no catalogue of anticompetitive agreements, no broad prohibition and accompanying exemption, no statement or implication as to burdens of proof or presumptions. Nonetheless, the Supreme Court's jurisprudence on what restraints of trade are per se illegal and which come under the more tolerant rule of reason follow a similar analytical approach. Restrictions are per se illegal only when they "facially appear[ ] to be one[s] that would always or almost always tend to restrict competition and decrease output" and would almost never "increase economic efficiency and render markets more, rather than less, competitive." Broadcast Music, Inc. v. Columbia Broadcasting System, Inc., 441 U.S. 1, 19–20 (1979).

China's Anti-Monopoly Law and India's Competition Act are broadly modeled on Article 101, but contain long lists of prohibited and exempted agreements. Consider the inter-play among Articles 13, 14, and 15 of the Chinese Anti-Monopoly Law, which makes a broad set of agreements illegal and then shifts the burden onto the agreeing parties to justify their agreement on efficiencies grounds.

> **Article 16:** "Monopoly agreements" as used in this Law refers to agreements, decisions, or other concerted actions that eliminate or restrict competition.
>
> **Article 17:** Competing undertakings are prohibited from concluding the following monopoly agreements:
>
> (1) those that fix or change the price of goods;

(2) those that limit the quantity of goods manufactured or marketed;

(3) those that divide the sales markets or markets for raw materials;

(4) those that restrict the purchase of new technology or new equipment or restrict the development of new technology or new product;

(5) those that jointly boycott transactions;

(6) other monopoly agreements as determined by the State Council anti-monopoly law enforcement agency.

Article 18: Undertakings are prohibited from concluding the following monopoly agreements with trading counterparties:

(1) those that fix the price of goods resold to a third party;

(2) those that limit the lowest price of goods resold to a third party;

(3) other monopoly agreements as determined by the State Council anti-monopoly law enforcement agency.

In the case of an agreement under item (1) or (2) of the previous paragraph, where the undertaking can demonstrate that the agreement does not have the effect of eliminating or restricting competition, it is not prohibited.

Where an undertaking can demonstrate that its market share in the relevant market is below the threshold prescribed by the State Council anti-monopoly law enforcement agency, and that it meets other conditions prescribed by the State Council anti-monopoly law enforcement agency, [an agreement under paragraph 1] is not prohibited.

Article 19: Undertakings are prohibited from organizing other undertakings to conclude monopoly agreements and providing material assistance to the conclusion of monopoly agreements by other undertakings.

Article 20: Where undertakings can demonstrate that a monopoly agreement concluded has one of the following circumstances, the provisions of Article 17, Article 18, paragraph 1, and Article 19 of this Law do not apply:

(1) to improve technologies or to research and develop new products;

(2) to improve product quality, lower cost, or increase efficiency by unifying the specifications or standards of products or by implementing specialized division of labor;

(3) to increase the operating efficiency of small and medium-sized undertakings or to increase their competitiveness;

(4) to achieve energy conservation, environmental protection, disaster relief, and such other public interests;

(5) to mitigate the sharp decline in sales volume or obvious overproduction due to an economic recession;

(6) to safeguard the legitimate interests in foreign trade or in foreign economic cooperation;

(7) other circumstances prescribed by laws or the State Council.

Where the provisions of Article 17, Article 18, paragraph 1, and Article 19 of this Law do not apply in the circumstances under items (1) through (5) of the previous paragraph, the undertakings shall additionally demonstrate that the agreement concluded will not seriously restrict competition in the relevant market and that it will enable the consumers to share in the resulting benefits.

Article 21: Trade associations shall not organize undertakings in their own industries to engage in the monopolistic practices prohibited by this Chapter.

As with hard-core cartels studied in Chapter 2, there are often important issues—both substantive and evidentiary—about what constitutes an agreement or understanding. For example, various mechanisms by which competitors effectively exchange information—such as through industry associations or algorithms—may be characterized as an agreement and hence covered by concerted action provisions rather than as unilateral and hence not covered.

There are also important procedural differences between jurisdictions. Some jurisdictions use mandatory or voluntary agreement notification systems to enable early regulatory review of certain classes of horizontal agreements. Other jurisdictions rely on less formal means of regulatory policing—such as the use of informal business review letters by agencies and investigation of anticompetitive agreements upon customer complaints. We will address some of these procedural issues at the end of the chapter.

B. MARKET DEFINITION AND MARKET POWER

1. Market Definition

Most competition law cases requires definition of the relevant market and an assessment of market power. The only exception are cases involving hardcore cartel conduct subject to summary condemnation. Relevant market is a term of art in competition law and it constitutes the basket of products or services that are reasonable substitutes for the defendant's offering. Market definition is essentially an exercise of identifying these reasonable substitutes. It is important to do so in a competition case that requires a competitive effect analysis because these substitutes may constrain the defendant's exercise of market power, which in turn determines the extent of the impact of the defendant's conduct on the relevant market. Substitutes may exist in the form of similar products in the same geographical location or the same or similar products in adjacent geographical locations. Therefore, the relevant market needs to be defined both along the product and the geographic dimensions.

Traditionally, market definition is conducted through what is known as the hypothetical monopolist test or the Small but Significant, Non-Transitory Increase in Price ("SSNIP") test. This test was first proffered in the 1992 Horizontal Merger Guidelines adopted by the US Department of Justice and the Federal Trade Commission. It is a conceptual exercise that involves a succession of price increases by a hypothetical monopolist producer or supplier of the defendant's product or service. The most recent formulation of the test can be found in Section 4.3 of the 2023 Horizontal Merger Guidelines, which is excerpted here.

MERGER GUIDELINES BY U.S. DEPARTMENT OF JUSTICE AND THE FEDERAL TRADE COMMISSION

(December 18, 2023)

4.3.A. The Hypothetical Monopolist Test

This Section describes the Hypothetical Monopolist Test, which is a method by which the Agencies often define relevant antitrust markets. As outlined above, a relevant antitrust market is an area of effective competition. The Hypothetical Monopolist/Monopsonist Test ("HMT") evaluates whether a group of products is sufficiently broad to constitute a relevant antitrust market. To do so, the HMT asks whether eliminating the competition among the group of products by combining them under the control of a hypothetical monopolist likely would lead to a worsening of terms for customers. The Agencies generally focus their assessment on the constraints from competition, rather than on constraints from regulation, entry, or other market changes. The Agencies are concerned with the impact on economic incentives and assume the hypothetical monopolist would seek to maximize profits.

When evaluating a merger of sellers, the HMT asks whether a hypothetical profit-maximizing firm, not prevented by regulation from worsening terms, that was the only present and future seller of a group of products ("hypothetical monopolist") likely would undertake at least a small but significant and non-transitory increase in price ("SSNIP") or other worsening of terms ("SSNIPT") for at least one product in the group. For the purpose of analyzing this issue, the terms of sale of products outside the candidate market are held constant. Analogously, when considering a merger of buyers, the Agencies ask the equivalent question for a hypothetical monopsonist. This Section often focuses on merging sellers to simplify exposition.

4.3.B. Implementing the Hypothetical Monopolist Test

The SSNIPT. A SSNIPT may entail worsening terms along any dimension of competition, including price (SSNIP), but also other terms (broadly defined) such as quality, service, capacity investment, choice of product variety or features, or innovative effort.

Input and Labor Markets. When the competition at issue involves firms buying inputs or employing labor, the HMT considers whether the hypothetical monopsonist would undertake at least a SSNIPT, such as a decrease in the offered price or a worsening of the terms of trade offered to suppliers, or a decrease in the wage offered to workers or a worsening of their working conditions or benefits.

The Geographic Dimension of the Market. The hypothetical monopolist test is generally applied to a group of products together with a geographic region to determine a relevant market, though for ease of exposition the two dimensions are discussed separately, with geographic market definition discussed in Section 4.3.D.2.

Negotiations or Auctions. The HMT is stated in terms of a hypothetical monopolist *undertaking* a SSNIPT. This covers settings where the hypothetical monopolist sets terms and makes them worse. It also covers settings where firms bargain, and the hypothetical monopolist would have a stronger bargaining position that would likely lead it to extract a SSNIPT during negotiations, or where firms sell their products in an auction, and the bids submitted by the hypothetical monopolist would result in the purchasers of its products experiencing a SSNIPT.

Benchmark for the SSNIPT. The HMT asks whether the hypothetical monopolist likely would worsen terms relative to those that likely would prevail absent the proposed merger. In some cases, the Agencies will use as a benchmark different outcomes than those prevailing prior to the merger. For example, if outcomes are likely to change absent the merger, e.g., because of innovation, entry, exit, or exogenous trends, the Agencies may use anticipated future outcomes as the benchmark. Or, if suppliers in the market are coordinating prior to the merger, the Agencies may use a benchmark that reflects conditions that would arise if coordination were to break down. When evaluating whether a merging firm is dominant (Guideline 6), the Agencies may use terms that likely would prevail in a more competitive market as a benchmark.

Magnitude of the SSNIPT. What constitutes a "small but significant" worsening of terms depends upon the nature of the industry and the merging firms' positions in it, the ways that firms compete, and the dimension of competition at issue. When considering price, the Agencies will often use a SSNIP of five percent of the price charged by firms for the products or services to which the merging firms contribute value. The Agencies, however, may consider a different term or a price increase that is larger or smaller than five percent.

The Agencies may base a SSNIP on explicit or implicit prices for the firms' specific contribution to the value of the product sold, or an upper bound on the firms' specific contribution, where these can be identified with reasonable clarity. For example, the Agencies may derive an implicit price for the service of transporting oil over a pipeline as the difference between the price the pipeline firm paid for oil at one end and the price it sold the oil for at the other and base the SSNIP on this implicit price.

4.3.C. Evidence and Tools for Carrying Out the Hypothetical Monopolist Test

Section 4.2 describes some of the qualitative and quantitative evidence and tools the Agencies can use to assess the extent of competition among firms. The Agencies can use similar evidence and analogous tools to apply the HMT, in particular to assess whether competition among a set of firms likely leads to better terms than a hypothetical monopolist would undertake.

To assess whether the hypothetical monopolist likely would undertake at least a SSNIP on one or more products in the candidate market, the Agencies sometimes interpret the qualitative and quantitative evidence using an economic model of the profitability to the hypothetical monopolist of undertaking price increases; the Agencies may adapt these tools to apply to other forms of SSNIPTs.

One approach utilizes the concept of a "recapture rate" (the percentage of sales lost by one product in the candidate market, when its price alone rises, that is recaptured by other products in the candidate market). A price increase is profitable when the recapture rate is high enough that the incremental profits from the increased price plus the incremental profits from the recaptured sales going to other products in the candidate market exceed the profits lost when sales are diverted outside the candidate market. It is possible that a price increase is profitable even if a majority of sales are diverted outside the candidate market, for example if the profits on the lost sales are relatively low or the profits on the recaptured sales are relatively high.

Sometimes evidence is presented in the form of "critical loss analysis" which can be used to assess whether undertaking at least a SSNIPT on one or more products in a candidate market would raise or lower the hypothetical monopolist's profits. Critical loss analysis compares the magnitude of the two offsetting effects resulting from the worsening of terms. The "critical loss" is defined as the number of lost unit sales that would leave profits unchanged. The "predicted loss" is defined as the number of unit sales that the hypothetical monopolist is predicted to lose due to the worsening of terms. The worsening of terms raises the hypothetical monopolist's profits if the predicted loss is less than the critical loss. While this "breakeven" analysis differs somewhat from the profit-maximizing analysis called for by the HMT, it can sometimes be informative.

The Agencies require that estimates of the predicted loss be consistent with other evidence, including the pre-merger margins of products in the candidate market used to calculate the critical loss. Unless the firms are engaging in coordinated interaction, high pre-merger margins normally indicate that each firm's product individually faces demand that is not highly sensitive to price. Higher pre-merger margins thus indicate a smaller predicted loss as well as a smaller critical loss. The higher the pre-merger margin, the smaller the recapture rate necessary for the candidate market to satisfy the hypothetical monopolist test. Similar considerations inform other analyses of the profitability of a price increase.

Notes and Questions

1. The hypothetical monopolist test or the SSNIP test was originally conceived in the context of merger review, where the prevailing pre-merger market price is more likely to be a competitive one. If the SSNIP test is applied to a prevailing monopolist price in an abuse of dominance case, it could end up overestimating the size of the market and underestimating the extent of the defendant's market power. As the Agencies note in footnote 83 of the Guidelines: "In the entrenchment context, if the inquiry is being conducted after market or monopoly power has already been exercised, using prevailing prices can lead to defining markets too broadly and thus inferring that dominance does not exist when, in fact, it does. The problem with using prevailing prices to define the market when a firm is already dominant is known as the "Cellophane Fallacy".

2. The name of the fallacy came from the Cellophane case decided by the US Supreme Court in 1956. United States v. E.I. du Pont de Nemours & Co. (Cellophane), 351 U.S. 377 (1956). The Court did not apply the SSNIP test in the case. What it did instead was to calculate the cross elasticity of demand between the defendant's product of cellophane and other flexible packaging materials using the prevailing market price for cellophane, which was already a monopolist price. The Court ended up overestimating the degree of substitutability between cellophane and competing products and settled on the erroneous relevant market of flexible packaging materials when it should have constituted of cellophane only. The overly generous market definition underestimated du Pont's market power, allowing du Pont to escape the monopolization claim against it. The Court's mistake in the case has come to be known as the Cellophane fallacy.

3. With the increasing number of cases in the digital economy, where the product is often offered with an overt charge, the SSNIP test has had to go through some modification. A test that is premised on price increases would not work when the price is zero. It is thus sometimes suggested that users of digital services such as online search or social media do pay in some way. They do not pay a fee for the service, but instead pay with their data. A price increase can thus be reconceptualized as a deterioration of service quality in terms of data privacy. The service provider enacts a "price increase" by collecting more data from users.

4. The Guidelines provides for this possibility by stating that "A SSNIPT may entail worsening terms along any dimension of competition, including price (SSNIP), but also other terms (broadly defined) such as quality, service, capacity investment, choice of product variety or features, or innovative effort." The idea is that just like a price increase will drive consumers to substitutes, a deterioration in data privacy should do the same. This presumes that consumers have the

same sensitivity toward a price increase and a deterioration in quality, which is not necessarily the case. Some digital platforms bury their data privacy policy deep in the platform, making it difficult for users to find and change. Some users simply do not have a strong preference regarding data privacy. To the extent that a SSNIPT is not a good substitute for SSNIP, the SSNIP may not produce the desired result in a zero-price market.

5. Applying the SSNIP test in real life requires pricing data that is not always available in every case. This is more likely in non-merger cases. In cases where the SSNIP test cannot be applied, courts tend to conduct a qualitative assessment and determine the substitutability between products one by one. The Microsoft case in the US is an apt illustration of this approach.

UNITED STATES v. MICROSOFT CORP.

253 F.3d 34 (United States Court of Appeals for the D.C. Circuit 2001)

A. Monopoly Power

While merely possessing monopoly power is not itself an antitrust violation. The Supreme Court defines monopoly power as "the power to control prices or exclude competition." United States v. E.I. du Pont de Nemours & Co., 351 U.S. 377, 391, 76 S.Ct. 994, 100 L.Ed. 1264 (1956). More precisely, a firm is a monopolist if it can profitably raise prices substantially above the competitive level. Where evidence indicates that a firm has in fact profitably done so, the existence of monopoly power is clear. Because such direct proof is only rarely available, courts more typically examine market structure in search of circumstantial evidence of monopoly power. Under this structural approach, monopoly power may be inferred from a firm's possession of a dominant share of a relevant market that is protected by entry barriers.

The District Court considered these structural factors and concluded that Microsoft possesses monopoly power in a relevant market. Defining the market as Intel-compatible PC operating systems, the District Court found that Microsoft has a greater than 95% share. It also found the company's market position protected by a substantial entry barrier. * * *

1. Market Structure

a. Market definition

"Because the ability of consumers to turn to other suppliers restrains a firm from raising prices above the competitive level," Rothery Storage & Van Co. v. Atlas Van Lines, Inc., 792 F.2d 210, 218 (D.C.Cir.1986), the relevant market must include all products " reasonably interchangeable by consumers for the same purposes." *du Pont,* 351 U.S. at 395, 76 S.Ct. 994. In this case, the District Court defined the market as "the licensing of all Intel-compatible PC operating systems worldwide," finding that there are "currently no products—and . . . there are not likely to be any in the near future—that a significant percentage of computer users worldwide could substitute for [these operating systems] without incurring substantial costs." Calling this market definition "far too narrow," Microsoft argues that the District Court improperly excluded three types of products: non-Intel compatible operating systems (primarily Apple's Macintosh operating system, Mac OS), operating systems for non-PC devices (such as handheld computers and portal websites), and "middleware" products, which are not operating systems at all.

We begin with Mac OS. Microsoft's argument that Mac OS should have been included in the relevant market suffers from a flaw that infects many of the company's monopoly power claims: the company fails to challenge the District Court's factual findings, or to argue that these findings do not support the court's conclusions. The District Court found that consumers would not switch from Windows to Mac OS in response to a substantial price increase because of the costs of acquiring the new hardware needed to run Mac OS (an Apple computer and peripherals) and compatible software applications, as well as because of the effort involved in learning the new system and transferring files to its format. The court also found the Apple system less appealing to consumers because it costs considerably more and supports fewer applications. Microsoft responds only by saying: "the district court's market definition is so narrow that it excludes Apple's Mac OS, which has competed with Windows for years, simply because the Mac OS runs on a different microprocessor." This general, conclusory statement falls far short of what is required to challenge findings as clearly erroneous. Microsoft neither points to evidence contradicting the District Court's findings nor alleges that supporting record evidence is insufficient. And since Microsoft does not argue that even if we accept these findings, they do not support the District Court's conclusion, we have no basis for upsetting the court's decision to exclude Mac OS from the relevant market.

Microsoft's challenge to the District Court's exclusion of non-PC based competitors, such as information appliances (handheld devices, etc.) and portal websites that host server-based software applications, suffers from the same defect: the company fails to challenge the District Court's key factual findings. In particular, the District Court found that because information appliances fall far short of performing all of the functions of a PC, most consumers will buy them only as a supplement to their PCs. The District Court also found that portal websites do not presently host enough applications to induce consumers to switch, nor are they likely to do so in the near future. . . . [W]e adhere to that conclusion.

This brings us to Microsoft's main challenge to the District Court's market definition: the exclusion of middleware. Because of the importance of middleware to this case, we pause to explain what it is and how it relates to the issue before us.

Operating systems perform many functions, including allocating computer memory and controlling peripherals such as printers and keyboards. Operating systems also function as platforms for software applications. They do this by "exposing"—*i.e.,* making available to software developers—routines or protocols that perform certain widely-used functions. These are known as Application Programming Interfaces, or "APIs." For example, Windows contains an API that enables users to draw a box on the screen. Software developers wishing to include that function in an application need not duplicate it in their own code. Instead, they can "call"—*i.e.*, use—the Windows API. Windows contains thousands of APIs, controlling everything from data storage to font display.

Every operating system has different APIs. Accordingly, a developer who writes an application for one operating system and wishes to sell the application to users of another must modify, or "port," the application to the second operating system. This process is both time-consuming and expensive.

"Middleware" refers to software products that expose their own APIs. Because of this, a middleware product written for Windows could take over some or all of Windows's valuable platform functions—that is, developers might begin to rely upon APIs exposed by the middleware for basic routines rather than relying upon the API set included in Windows. If middleware were written for multiple operating systems, its impact could be even greater. The more developers could rely upon APIs exposed by such middleware, the less expensive porting to different operating systems would be. Ultimately, if developers could write applications relying exclusively on APIs exposed by middleware, their applications would run on any operating system on which the middleware was also present. Netscape Navigator and Java—both at issue in this case—are middleware products written for multiple operating systems.

Microsoft argues that, because middleware could usurp the operating system's platform function and might eventually take over other operating system functions (for instance, by controlling peripherals), the District Court erred in excluding Navigator and Java from the relevant market. The District Court found, however, that neither Navigator, Java, nor any other middleware product could now, or would soon, expose enough APIs to serve as a platform for popular applications, much less take over all operating system functions. Again, Microsoft fails to challenge these findings, instead simply asserting middleware's "potential" as a competitor. Appellant's Opening Br. at 86. The test of reasonable interchangeability, however, required the District Court to consider only substitutes that constrain pricing in the reasonably foreseeable future, and only products that can enter the market in a relatively short time can perform this function. Whatever middleware's ultimate potential, the District Court found that consumers could not now abandon their operating systems and switch to middleware in response to a sustained price for Windows above the competitive level. Nor is middleware likely to overtake the operating system as the primary platform for software development any time in the near future.

Alternatively, Microsoft argues that the District Court should not have excluded middleware from the relevant market because the primary focus of the plaintiffs' charge is on Microsoft's attempts to suppress middleware's threat to its operating system monopoly. According to Microsoft, it is "contradict[ory]," to define the relevant market to exclude the "very competitive threats that gave rise" to the action. The purported contradiction lies between plaintiffs' theory, under which Microsoft preserved its monopoly against middleware technologies that threatened to become viable substitutes for Windows, and its theory of the relevant market, under which middleware is not presently a viable substitute for Windows. Because middleware's threat is only nascent, however, no contradiction exists. Nothing in of the Sherman Act limits its prohibition to actions taken against threats that are already well-developed enough to serve as present substitutes. Because market definition is meant to identify products "reasonably interchangeable by consumers," *du Pont,* 351 U.S. at 395, 76 S.Ct. 994, and because middleware is not now interchangeable with Windows, the District Court had good reason for excluding middleware from the relevant market.

Notes and Questions

1. The US courts are not the only ones that consider possible substitutes in a qualitative manner when defining the relevant market. The Chinese courts have also done the same. In the first anti-monopoly case to reach the Supreme People's Court ("SPC"), Qihoo v. Tencent, the Court considered possible alternatives for the defendant's desktop chat application when defining the relevant market.

QIHOO v. TENCENT

A Summary of the Judgment

(Supreme People's Court of the People's Republic of China 2014)

The case arose out of a dispute between Qihoo, the largest provider of anti-virus software, called 360, in China at the time, and Tencent, which operated the dominant desktop chat application QQ at the moment at issue in the case and is now better known for WeChat, its smartphone super app, and its gaming operations. In October 2010, Qihoo introduced a safeguard software which rendered its antivirus software incompatible with QQ. Soon after, Tencent retaliated by making Qihoo's software incompatible with QQ, practically forcing users to choose between QQ and Qihoo's software. This policy lasted for one day. Four days later, Qihoo recalled the software and QQ became compatible with Qihoo's product. Eventually, the Ministry of Industry and Information Technology intervened and forced the two companies to resolve all the incompatibility issues.

The Court considered a variety of possible substitutes for QQ one by one, including: (1) integrated instant messaging services such as QQ and MSN; (2) cross-platform instant messaging services such as China Mobile's "Fei Xun"; (3) cross-network instant messaging services such as Skype; (4) text-based instant messaging services; (5) voice-based instant messaging services; (6) video-based instant messaging services; and (7) instant messaging services provided by microblog websites such as Weibo. The Court considered these to belong to the relevant market.

The SPC proclaimed that market definition is not an end in itself. Even if the relevant market cannot be clearly defined, direct evidence of anticompetitive effects are relevant. The Court noted that the SSNIP test is more suitable for markets for homogeneous products where competition is mostly on price. Application of the SSNIP test is more difficult if the product is differentiated or if the price is zero. Modification is needed to focus on quality. The Court agreed with the lower court that text-based, voice-based, and video-based instant messaging services belong to the relevant market.

The Court argued that the key issue is the substitutability between desktop-based IM services and mobile-based IM services. It insisted that the cost of purchasing a smartphone and phone data subscription should be irrelevant. In particular, Wifi services are prevalent. A mobile-based IM service user need not have a data subscription plan. On this basis, the Court held that mobile-based IM services such as iMessage and Line should also be included in the relevant market, despite the fact that this issue was not raised at the lower court. The court affirmed that the IM services provided by Weibo and social network services should be included in the relevant market. However, the court overturned the lower court's conclusion that the Weibo service and social media sites themselves should be included in the relevant market.

The Court upheld the lower court's finding that SMS does not belong to the relevant market. First, SMS does not allow users to find about other users' online status. Second, SMS is not free. It also agreed with the lower court that email does not belong to the relevant market, largely because email lacks the instantaneity of IM services. Lastly, the court overturned the lower court's geographic market definition. The court mentioned that that only 3% of IM service users in China use non-domestic services. Moreover, IM service providers need to comply with a slew of administrative requirements imposed by the Chinese government. Foreign service providers can only provide service in China through a Sino-foreign JV. Therefore, the market is quite domestic.

Notes and Questions

1. The relevant geographic market can be determined by economic factors such as distance and transportation costs and a variety of non-economic factors such as language, customs, and regulatory requirements. Qihoo v. Tencent is a perfect illustration of that. As the SPC acknowledged, China has stringent restrictions on online services and there is little direct interaction between its domestic service providers and their overseas counterparts. For instance, many online chat applications such as WhatsApp and Line are not available in China. It would hence be difficult to argue that there is a global market including China for online services.

2. Market Power

Following market definition, the next step in the analysis is the assessment of market power. In economic terms, market power is understood to be the power to raise and sustain prices above the competitive level profitably or to suppress output below the competitive level profitably.

In cases involving non-cartel horizontal agreements, anticompetitive effects are unlikely absent market power. In the US, these agreements are subject to the Rule of Reason, which requires a showing of market power in order to establish competitive harm. In the EU, an effects-based analysis, which apply to all cases where the conduct is not deemed to be a restriction by object, would also require market power. In the vertical context, all agreements benefit from the Rule of Reason after the Supreme Court decision in *Leegin*.

Following that seminal case, the lower courts in the US have effectively turned a showing of market power a requirement in every resale price maintenance case. The same is true of other vertical agreement cases. Assessment of market power plays an even more pivotal role in unilateral conduct cases. A case would not even fall within the scope of the unilateral conduct rules at all if the defendant was not shown to possess monopoly power in the US and a dominant position in the EU and most of the rest of the world.

Market power is everywhere in the economy. Every time there is a certain degree of product differentiation, market power exists. The inquiry therefore is not whether market power exists, but how much. Although it is difficult to give a clearcut answer, the general sense is that in effects-based restrictive agreement cases or Rule of Reason cases in the US, quite a bit of market power is necessary. The market power requirement would be even higher in unilateral conduct cases.

Assessment of market power refers to a host of factors, the most of which is market share. The US Supreme Court has never laid a clear numerical threshold for monopoly power. The most famous pronouncement by the courts on this point is probably Judge Learned Hand's observation in the famous *Alcoa* case that ninety percent "is enough to constitute a monopoly; it is doubtful whether sixty or sixty-hour per cent would be enough; and certainly thirty-three per cent is not." In the EU, *Hoffman-La Roche* and *AKZO* are generally interpreted as creating a rebuttable presumption of dominance with fifty percent market share, although dominance was found in the *British Airways* case with a market share of 39.7 percent. The Court's somewhat surprising holding can be at least partly explained by the fact that British Airways' market share was seven times greater than that of its nearest rival. In China, the Anti-Monopoly Law provides more guidance on both the factors to be considered in assessing market power and the market share needed to establish dominance:

> **Article 23:** A determination that an undertaking holds a dominant market position shall be based on the following factors:
>
> (1) the undertaking's market share in the relevant market and the level of competition in the relevant market;
>
> (2) the undertaking's ability to control the sales markets or the procurement markets for raw materials;
>
> (3) the undertaking's financial resources and technical capabilities;

(4) the extent to which other undertakings rely on the undertaking for trading;

(5) the level of difficulty for other undertakings to enter the relevant market;

(6) other factors relevant to determining the undertaking's dominant market position.

Article 24: In any of the following circumstances, it may be presumed that undertakings hold dominant market positions:

(1) where one undertaking's market share amounts to one-half of a relevant market;

(2) where two undertakings' joint market share amounts to two-thirds of a relevant market;

(3) where three undertakings' joint market share amounts to third-fourths of a relevant market.

In the circumstances provided in item (2) or (3) of the previous paragraph, if one of the undertakings has a market share of less than one-tenth, it shall not be presumed that said undertaking holds a dominant market position.

Where an undertaking that is presumed to hold a dominant market position has evidence that it does not hold a dominant market position, it shall be not determined to hold a dominant market position.

Two comments are in order. First, assessment of market power takes into account a multitude of factors. In addition to those listed in Article 23 of the Anti-Monopoly Law, barriers to entry and countervailing buyer power would also be important factors to consider. Second, China recognizes the concept of collective dominance, whereby two or three firms can be deemed to possess a dominant position collectively. This concept originated from EU law and has been taken up by China. However, it has been applied sparingly by the European Commission in recent years. Even in its adopted homeland of China, collective dominance has not featured prominently in the jurisprudence.

UNITED STATES v. MICROSOFT CORP.

253 F.3d 34 (United States Court of Appeals for the D.C. Circuit 2001)

b. Market power

Having thus properly defined the relevant market, the District Court found that Windows accounts for a greater than 95% share. The court also found that even if Mac OS were included, Microsoft's share would exceed 80%. Microsoft challenges neither finding, nor does it argue that such a market share is not predominant.

Instead, Microsoft claims that even a predominant market share does not by itself indicate monopoly power. Although the "existence of [monopoly] power ordinarily may be inferred from the predominant share of the market," *Grinnell,* 384 U.S. at 571, 86 S.Ct. 1698, we agree with Microsoft that because of the possibility of competition from new entrants, *see Ball Mem'l Hosp., Inc.,* 784 F.2d at 1336, looking to current market share alone can be "misleading." Hunt-Wesson Foods, Inc. v. Ragu Foods, Inc., 627 F.2d 919, 924 (9th Cir.1980). In this case, however, the District Court was not misled. Considering the possibility of new rivals, the court focused not only on Microsoft's present market share, but also on the structural barrier that protects the company's future position. That barrier—the "applications barrier to entry"—stems from two characteristics of the software market: (1) most consumers prefer operating systems for which a large number of applications have already been written; and (2) most developers prefer to write for operating systems that already have a substantial consumer base. This "chicken-and-egg" situation ensures that applications will continue to be written for the already dominant Windows, which in turn ensures that consumers will continue to prefer it over other operating systems.

Challenging the existence of the applications barrier to entry, Microsoft observes that software developers do write applications for other operating systems, pointing out that at its peak IBM's OS/2 supported approximately 2,500 applications. This misses the point. That some developers write applications for other operating systems is not at all inconsistent with the finding that the applications barrier to entry discourages many from writing for these less popular platforms. Indeed, the District Court found that IBM's difficulty in attracting a larger number of software developers to write for its platform seriously impeded OS/2's success.

Microsoft does not dispute that Windows supports many more applications than any other operating system. It argues instead that "[i]t defies common sense" to suggest that an operating system must support as many applications as Windows does (more than 70,000, according to the District Court) to be competitive. Consumers, Microsoft points out, can only use a very small percentage of these applications. As the District Court explained, however, the applications barrier to entry gives consumers reason to prefer the dominant operating system even if they have no need to use all applications written for it:

> The consumer wants an operating system that runs not only types of applications that he knows he will want to use, but also those types in which he might develop an interest later. Also, the consumer knows that if he chooses an operating system with enough demand to support multiple applications in each product category, he will be less likely to find himself straitened later by having to use an application whose features disappoint him. Finally, the average user knows that, generally speaking, applications improve through successive versions. He thus wants an operating system for which successive generations of his favorite applications will be released—promptly at that. The fact that a vastly larger number of applications are written for Windows than for other PC operating systems attracts consumers to Windows, because it reassures them that their interests will be met as long as they use Microsoft's product.

Thus, despite the limited success of its rivals, Microsoft benefits from the applications barrier to entry.

Of course, were middleware to succeed, it would erode the applications barrier to entry. Because applications written for multiple operating systems could run on any operating system on which the middleware product was present with little, if any, porting, the operating system market would become competitive. But as the District Court found, middleware will not expose a sufficient number of APIs to erode the applications barrier to entry in the foreseeable future.

Microsoft next argues that the applications barrier to entry is not an entry barrier at all, but a reflection of Windows' popularity. It is certainly true that Windows may have gained its initial dominance in the operating system market competitively—through superior foresight or quality. But this case is not about Microsoft's initial acquisition of monopoly power. It is about Microsoft's efforts to maintain this position through means other than competition on the merits. Because the applications barrier to entry protects a dominant operating system irrespective of quality, it gives Microsoft power to stave off even superior new rivals. The barrier is thus a characteristic of the operating system market, not of Microsoft's popularity, or, as asserted by a Microsoft witness, the company's efficiency.

Finally, Microsoft argues that the District Court should not have considered the applications barrier to entry because it reflects not a cost borne disproportionately by new entrants, but one borne by all participants in the operating system market. According to Microsoft, it had to make major investments to convince software developers to write for its new operating system, and it continues to "evangelize" the Windows platform today. Whether costs borne by all market participants should be considered entry barriers is the subject of much debate. We need not resolve this issue, however, for even under the more narrow definition it is clear that there are barriers. When Microsoft entered the operating system market with MS-DOS and the first version of Windows, it did not confront a dominant rival operating system with as massive an installed base and as vast an existing array of applications as the Windows operating systems have since enjoyed. Moreover, when Microsoft introduced Windows 95 and 98, it was able to bypass the applications barrier to entry that protected the incumbent Windows by including APIs from the earlier version in the new operating systems. This made porting existing Windows applications to the new version of Windows much less costly than porting them to the operating systems of other entrants who could not freely include APIs from the incumbent Windows with their own.

2. Direct Proof

Having sustained the District Court's conclusion that circumstantial evidence proves that Microsoft possesses monopoly power, we turn to Microsoft's alternative argument that it does not behave like a monopolist. Claiming that software competition is uniquely "dynamic," the company suggests a new rule: that monopoly power in the software industry should be proven directly, that is, by examining a company's actual behavior to determine if it reveals the existence of monopoly power. According to Microsoft, not only does no such proof of its power exist, but record evidence demonstrates the absence of monopoly power. The company claims that it invests heavily in research and development, and charges a low price for Windows (a small percentage of the price of an Intel-compatible PC system and less than the price of its rivals.

Microsoft's argument fails because, even assuming that the software market is uniquely dynamic in the long term, the District Court correctly applied the structural approach to determine if the company faces competition in the short term. Structural market power analyses are meant to determine whether potential substitutes constrain a firm's ability to raise prices above the competitive level; only threats that are likely to materialize in the relatively near future perform this function to any significant degree.

The District Court expressly considered and rejected Microsoft's claims that innovations such as handheld devices and portal websites would soon expand the relevant market beyond Intel-compatible PC operating systems. Because the company does not challenge these findings, we have no reason to believe that prompt substitutes are available. The structural approach, as applied by the District Court, is thus capable of fulfilling its purpose even in a changing market. Microsoft cites no case, nor are we aware of one, requiring direct evidence to show monopoly power in any market. We decline to adopt such a rule now.

Even if we were to require direct proof, moreover, Microsoft's behavior may well be sufficient to show the existence of monopoly power. Certainly, none of the conduct Microsoft points to—its investment in R&D and the relatively low price of Windows—is inconsistent with the possession of such power. The R&D expenditures Microsoft points to are not simply for Windows, but for its entire company, which most likely does not possess a monopoly for all of its products. Moreover, because innovation can increase an already dominant market share and further delay the emergence of competition, even monopolists have reason to invest in R&D. Microsoft's pricing behavior is similarly equivocal. The company claims only that it never charged the short-term profit-maximizing price for Windows. Faced with conflicting expert testimony, the District Court found that it could not accurately determine what this price would be. In any event, the court found, a price lower than the short-term profit-maximizing price is not inconsistent with possession or improper use of monopoly power. Microsoft never claims that it did not charge the long-term monopoly price. Microsoft does argue that the price of Windows is a fraction of the price of an Intel-compatible PC system and lower than that of rival operating systems, but these facts are not inconsistent with the District Court's finding that Microsoft has monopoly power.

More telling, the District Court found that some aspects of Microsoft's behavior are difficult to explain unless Windows is a monopoly product. For instance, according to the District Court, the company set the price of Windows without considering rivals' prices, something a firm without a monopoly would have been unable to do. The District Court also found that Microsoft's pattern of exclusionary conduct could only be rational "if the firm knew that it possessed monopoly power." It is to that conduct that we now turn.

Notes and Questions

1. The US Supreme Court has proclaimed in the *Indiana Federation of Dentists* case that where direct proof of anticompetitive

effects is available, there is no need for an inquiry into market power. A market power inquiry is only meant to indicate the likelihood of anticompetitive effects. The Court, however, did not impose direct proof as a requirement. It only proposed it as an alternative to the structural approach to market power. Microsoft attempted to push the Court's statement, knowing that direct evidence of anticompetitive effects is often unavailable.

QIHOO v. TENCENT

A Summary of the Judgment
(Supreme People's Court of the People's Republic of China 2014)

The SPC concluded that QQ was not dominant in the relevant market, despite its very high market share. Qihoo provided statistics that showed that QQ's market share in desktop-based IM services was between 80% and 89% while that of its nearest competitor was at 4.4% to 6.8%. QQ's market share in mobile-based IM services was over 90%. The Court, however, was unmoved by these statistics and concluded that QQ was not dominant in the relevant market for a variety of reasons. First, there were tens of service providers in the relevant market in China. Second, users are very sensitive to the quality of the service. Users would defect to other services if QQ's service quality deteriorated. Third, Tencent's rivals are all well-resourced. Fourth, the Court rejected the argument that IM services are characterized by high network effects and customer stickiness. Fifth, the Court noted that entry barriers are low. Sixth, the Court rejected the Qihoo's argument that the coercive conduct by Tencent was evidence of market power. The Court concluded that market share is not determinative. There are other factors to consider, such as actual power to raise price or reduce output and ease of market entry

As mentioned earlier, the SPC rejected Qihoo's argument that IM services are characterized by network effects on various grounds. First, the Court noted that most users only use IM services to communicate with their "core group" of family and close friends. The barrier to migrating such a core group is thus not insurmountable. Second, the Court further referred to the European Commission's decision in the Skype/Microsoft merger in which the Commission noted that users hopped between different types of IM services. Third, the Court noted QQ's own success in overtaking MSN as evidence that barriers to entry and competition are not strong in this market. In addition, the Court opined access to capital is not an issue for rivals. Tencent did not hold an advantage in terms of financial resources over rivals such as China Mobile, China Unicom, China Telecom, Alibaba, and Baidu, which are some of the largest enterprises in China. There was also plenty of venture capital in the market.

Notes and Questions

1. It may seem remarkable for a court to hold that a firm with more than 80% market share lacks a dominant position. This case highlights the crucial point that market share is not determinative in the assessment of market power. In the absence of barriers to entry by potential entrants and to expansion by current market participants, a high market share can be quickly eroded, suggesting a lack of market power. This is especially the case in a volatile market where market shares have been fluid. This would apply to the market for desktop chat applications in China. QQ itself had displaced MSN recently when the case was brought. Even though this was the SPC's first anti-monopoly case, it can be said to demonstrate a sophisticated understanding of the competition economics.

3. Two-Sided Markets

Although two-sided markets have been around for years, newspapers, television and credit cards are prime examples, they have received heightened attention in recent years with the emergence of the digital economy, which is replete with two-sided platforms. Two-sided markets could present thorny issues both in terms of market definition and analysis of competitive effects, as is evident in the *Ohio* v. *American Express* case in the US. In these markets, companies or "platforms" facilitate the interactions between two distinct groups of customers. The greater the number of users on one side of the platform, the more valuable is the platform to users on the other side of the platform. This dynamic creates network externalities, or indirect network effects, for both groups of customers. For instance, a credit card is more valuable to merchants the more users there are. It is also more useful to credit card users the more merchants accept it.

A critical issue for these platforms is to attract enough users on both sides in a balanced way. If only one group joins, no meaningful interactions will take place. If one group is harder to attract, platforms might adjust their pricing, potentially charging one group less or even offering incentives for them to join. A market is considered two-sided if the volume of interactions depends on how the platform sets prices between the two sides and on the overall pricing strategy. The degree of two-sidedness can vary. In some markets, the interactions between the groups are so crucial that they must be considered in economic analysis. As far as market definition goes, in some cases, it is not necessary to take two sides of the platform into account when defining the relevant market. For example, in defining the relevant market for television advertising, it is probably not necessary to consider television viewers. However, both the merchant and the card user sides of the platform will need to be taken into account when defining the relevant market for credit card payment systems. One reason is that credit card networks constitute transaction platforms, which require simultaneous transactions on both sides of the platform. The General Court considers market definition for a two-sided market in the Google Shopping case.

GOOGLE LLC v. COMMISSION (GOOGLE SHOPPING)

Case T–612/17, ECLI:EU:T:2021:763 (General Court of the European Union 2021)

473 At issue . . . is a two-sided market, that is to say, a market in which suppliers simultaneously respond to two distinct demands from different types of service user: on the one hand, the demand of internet users wishing to compare features and prices of products before ultimately making a purchase, and, on the other, the demand of those wishing to sell their products who feed information about those products into suppliers' databases for the purposes of such comparisons with a view to their products being purchased by internet users, although any transaction between buyer and seller will take place, if at all, on a different market. In the present case, the suppliers in respect of whom a determination must be made as to whether they are participants in the same comparison shopping services market fall into two categories, that of 'pure' comparison shopping services and that of merchant platforms, while those who seek their services are, on one side of the two-sided market, internet users, and, on the other side of that market, online sellers.

474 The Court notes that . . . the Commission did not reduce the relevant market for comparison shopping services to the side that is of interest to internet users only. . . . The Commission's arguments in defining the contours of that market include . . . not only an analysis in the contested decision of the characteristics of demand from the point of view of internet users, but also an analysis of the characteristics of demand from the point of view of online sellers.

475 For example, . . . when the Commission considers whether comparison shopping services and other specialised search services are substitutable, it refers to the commercial workforce necessary in order to enter into agreements with online sellers of the products or services that will ultimately be sold, which shows that it is also taking account of that side of the market on which those specialised search services are the suppliers, and online sellers represent the demand for their services. Similarly, . . . when the Commission

considers whether comparison shopping services and advertising services are substitutable, it explains that those services are not substitutable, from the perspective of both internet users and online sellers. As regards the substitutability of comparison shopping services and merchant platforms, the Commission first examines substitutability from the point of view of demand from internet users, then of demand from online sellers. Next, it analyses the characteristics of the service offered by comparison shopping services and merchant platforms to internet users and to online sellers. Lastly, the Commission rejects Google's arguments in favour of the substitutability of comparison shopping services and merchant platforms, which concern the side of the market that is of interest to internet users as well as the side that is of interest to online sellers.

476 Both sides of the market at issue were therefore examined by the Commission, leading it in particular to conclude that merchant platforms were not participating in the same market for comparison shopping services as comparison shopping service providers. Consequently, the Commission did not reduce the market to just one of its sides.

477 Yet, . . . the fact that, in order to meet demand on one side of a two-sided market, the services of two categories of supplier may be largely interchangeable does not necessarily mean that that is the case on the other side of that market with regard to the other demand that is expressed there. On a two-sided market, since demand does not emanate from the same source on each side of the market, it cannot be assumed that the issue of the substitutability of services will be resolved in the same way for each side.

478 It is therefore necessary to ascertain whether, in respect of one or other of the two sides of the market for comparison shopping services, the Commission demonstrated to the requisite standard . . . that the services offered by comparison shopping service providers had particular characteristics that so differentiate them from the comparison shopping services offered by merchant platforms, or vice versa, that they are only to a small degree interchangeable with each other and competition between them is insignificant.

479 In the contested decision the Commission indicated . . . that while comparison shopping service providers and merchant platforms both offered comparison shopping services, they served a different purpose for internet users and for online sellers.

480 As regards demand from internet users, the Commission noted . . . that comparison shopping services acted as intermediaries between internet users and individual sellers or merchant platforms, allowing users to compare different product offers; that they did not offer

internet users the possibility of making purchases on their own websites, but referred them to sellers' websites; that they did not offer after-sales support or product return options; and that they listed offers only for new products. Merchant platforms, on the other hand, allowed purchases to be made on their own websites, including of third-party products, and sometimes of second-hand products sold by non-professionals; were perceived as multi-brand retailers, that is to say, as places where users can buy products; and offered after-sales support, product return and even, in some cases, indemnification against a problem. The Commission relied in that regard on numerous statements from undertakings that participated in the procedure, and stated moreover, . . . that a majority of the comparison shopping services questioned considered merchant platforms to be business partners, not competitors, and vice versa. . . . [T]he contested decision indicate[s] that internal Google documents show that Google does not equate one category of player with the other.

481 Admittedly, as Google submits, the fact that merchant platforms provide far more functions than comparison shopping services and are their customers does not in itself prove that, in relation only to comparison shopping services offered to internet users, the services offered by both categories of player are only to a small degree interchangeable with each other and competition between them is insignificant, in other words, that they serve different purposes.

482 Nevertheless, the contested decision contains other material that substantiates this.

483 It is apparent from the information set out in paragraph 480 above that, for internet users, merchant platforms appear primarily to be places where goods can be purchased and which provide all the traditional sales functions, including in some cases operating as a sales counter for non-professionals, while the primary function of comparison shopping services is to provide information.

484 In that regard, the Commission states . . . that comparison shopping services generally display a wider range of offers than merchant platforms, which specifically includes offers from merchant platforms. Therefore, while there is a certain overlap between the databases of merchant platforms and those of comparison shopping services, the latter appear to be a much more powerful search tool in terms of search range than the comparison shopping services of merchant platforms, which are limited to their own offers and those of only those sellers that have decided to entrust the marketing of all or some of their products to a merchant platform.

485 The only specific evidence put forward by Google to counter the finding in recital 228 of the contested decision, namely that . . . in 2014 more than two million internet sellers sold more than two billion products on that platform worldwide, is insufficient to affect that finding. It concerns just one operator and the figures put forward are aggregated globally, which does not allow any assessment to be made in relation to comparison shopping services operating in any of the 13 countries covered by the contested decision.

486 The use of one search tool or another, from the perspective of internet users, appears to differ therefore. Users would consult a comparison shopping service in order to obtain a selection of product offers from the entire market, but would consult the comparison shopping service of a merchant platform only in order to obtain a selection of offers from that platform alone, albeit with the option of proceeding immediately, within that selection, to purchase the product sought.

487 In addition, . . . the Commission comments on a report by the United Kingdom Competition and Markets Authority produced by Google, which pointed out that that authority had indicated that internet users' use of either of the two types of search tool did not preclude their use of the other, and that some might use one and then the other in the same product search. The extract from that report that is quoted in the contested decision does show that a product search may start on either of those tools and be refined or supplemented on the other, but also indicates that internet users would consult the merchant platform for reviews of the quality of a particular product, whereas they would consult the comparison shopping service to find the best price for a product on the market, which confirms that each tool is used differently from the point of view of internet users. That report cannot therefore reasonably be relied on by Google to demonstrate that merchant platforms and comparison shopping services are interchangeable for internet users.

488 Lastly, it is necessary to take into consideration . . . that a majority of comparison shopping services and merchant platforms questioned by the Commission during the administrative procedure do not consider themselves to be direct competitors, even though Google drew attention to other replies to the effect that their comparison shopping services are substitutable and even though there are nuanced replies.

489 In that regard, the relationship between merchant platforms and comparison shopping services is not a simple customer-supplier relationship for the supply of a product or service, which would not rule out downstream competition; rather, it involves comparison

shopping services bringing to the attention of all internet users, usually in the form of advertising, the offers of merchant platforms, a situation which would be unlikely to arise if both categories of player were in direct competition with each other.

490 The finding, on the basis of those factors, that, from the point of view of internet users, comparison shopping services and merchant platforms serve different purposes and are therefore on different markets cannot be called into question by Google's stance . . . in relation to the characteristics of demand from the point of view of online sellers, even if it were to be accepted. In those recitals, the Commission points to the factors from which it may be inferred that sellers appearing in comparison shopping results tend to be larger retailers while those appearing in the comparison shopping results on merchant platforms tend to be small and medium-sized retailers. Even if merchant platforms and comparison shopping services were generally to offer products from the same categories of seller, as Google maintains, that would not change the fact that internet users use the comparison shopping services of each of them differently, as is apparent from paragraphs 486 and 487 above.

491 Consequently, the arguments put forward by Google do not permit the inference that the Commission made an error of assessment in finding that, for internet users, the services offered by comparison shopping services and those offered by merchant platforms were interchangeable only to a small degree and that competition between them was insignificant, that is to say, that those two categories of internet operator were not participating in that respect in the same product market.

492 As regards the side of the market of interest to online sellers, . . . the Commission explained, as is recounted in paragraph 490 above, that comparison shopping services tended to list offers from larger online retailers who wanted to retain control over the marketing of their products, whereas merchant platforms tended to list offers from small and medium-sized retailers, and possibly non-professional sellers, who were unwilling or unable to engage in online selling themselves. That shows in essence that comparison shopping services and merchant platforms have broadly different customer bases and are therefore in different markets with regard to online sellers. The Commission substantiates that assertion with the replies of comparison shopping services and merchant platforms to its questions . . . .

493 It must be noted that, in its action, as it confirmed moreover at the hearing, Google does not dispute the Commission's analysis in relation to the side of the market of interest to online sellers, since it

claims, albeit wrongly . . . that the Commission did not concern itself with that side of the market. It is significant in that respect that Google does not repeat the argument which it had advanced during the administrative procedure, according to which the Commission should have carried out an 'SSNIP' (small but significant and non-transitory increase in price) test with online sellers in order to satisfy itself as to the extent of the market. The only information put forward by Google to challenge the proposition that comparison shopping services and merchant platforms offer their services to different types of seller . . . relates, as has previously been indicated, to the discussion concerning the substitutability of services from the point of view of internet users. Furthermore, on the assumption that those statements from merchant platforms are indeed largely verified, they do not necessarily mean that online sellers view the services of comparison shopping services and those of merchant platforms as being interchangeable. In particular, the Commission stated in the contested decision that, by using one or other of those channels, the sales models were very different so far as the online seller's commercial autonomy was concerned, which means, unless there is evidence to the contrary which has not been produced in this case, that sellers will use either channel depending on their own characteristics or commercial choices, and that, while some use both channels simultaneously, they do so on a complementary basis to expand their means of selling, precisely because they are using two distinct models at the same time.

494 The Commission must therefore be considered to have demonstrated that, for those sellers, the services of comparison shopping services and those of merchant platforms were also only to a small degree interchangeable and that competition between them was insignificant.

Notes and Questions

1. If the relevant market cannot be defined in a two-sided market without regard to both sides of the market, do competitive effects also need to be considered on both sides as well? Does that mean that the plaintiff must demonstrate that certain conduct harms users on both sides of the market, or would competitive harm on one side of the market suffice? The US Supreme Court suggests the former in the American Express case mentioned earlier.

C. CLASSIFYING COMPETITOR COLLABORATIONS AS PER SE ILLEGAL, PRESUMPTIVELY ILLEGAL, OR SUBJECT TO FULLER RULE OF REASON ANALYSIS

As noted in the previous section, a threshold issue as to competitor collaborations is often whether they will be treated as "hard core" offenses like price-fixing cartels subject to some version of per se illegality, or whether instead they will be analyzed under a more expansive rule of reason. Under the TFEU, this distinction turns on whether the restriction on competition is one "by object" or "by effect," with the former receiving something akin to per se treatment and the latter something closer to rule of reason treatment.

For many years, there has been an active controversy among European competition law experts as to what constitutes an agreement by object within the meaning of Article 101 of the TFEU. As we have seen, an agreement among competitors to limit output is classically an agreement by object, even if the parties could credibly claim that their purpose was to save a collapsing industry for the good of the country. *See BIDS*, supra Chapter 2. Beyond hard core cartels, what agreements are restraints by object? Does intent play a role? Are agreements by object ones that always harm competition, or is it enough that they pose a potential threat to competition?

The Court's 2014 *Cartes Bancaires* decision addressed this question, and significantly narrowed the potential scope of the "restrictions by object" category.

GROUPEMENT DES CARTES BANCAIRES (CB) v. COMMISSION

Case C–67/13 P, ECLI:EU:C:2014:2204 (Court of Justice of the European Union 2014)

[CB was an economic interest group created in 1984 by the principal French banks in order to achieve interoperability of the systems for payment and withdrawal of banking cards. That interoperability enabled a CB-issued card to make payments or automated teller machine ("ATM") withdrawals from any member of the consortium. In 2002, CB adopted three new measures that the Commission challenged as violations of Articles 101 and 102 of the TFEU. They were: (1) a "mechanism for regulating the acquiring function," which effectively imposed a tax on banks that were disproportionately issuers of bank cards rather than acquirers of financial transactions (i.e., banks setting up ATM machines); (2) a supplementary fee per issued card imposed on banks that issued triple or more of the number of CB cards at the end of their sixth year of membership compared to at the end of their third year of membership; and (3) a "dormant member 'wake up' " per card fee imposed on members who were not very active before the implementation of new pricing measures in 2002 and subsequently became significantly more active. The Commission challenged these practices as alleged restrictions of competition by object—deliberate mechanisms to exclude new competition. The European Court of Justice thought otherwise.]

—Examination of whether there is a restriction of competition by 'object' within the meaning of Article 81(1) EC

48 It must be recalled that, to come within the prohibition laid down in Article 81(1) EC, an agreement, a decision by an association of undertakings or a concerted practice must have 'as [its] object or effect' the prevention, restriction or distortion of competition in the internal market.

49 In that regard, it is apparent from the Court's case-law that certain types of coordination between undertakings reveal a sufficient degree of harm to competition that it may be found that there is no need to examine their effects.

50 That case-law arises from the fact that certain types of coordination between undertakings can be regarded, by their very nature, as being harmful to the proper functioning of normal competition.

51 Consequently, it is established that certain collusive behaviour, such as that leading to horizontal price-fixing by cartels, may be considered so likely to have negative effects, in particular on the price, quantity or quality of the goods and services, that it may be considered redundant, for the purposes of applying Article 81(1) EC, to prove that they have actual effects on the market. Experience shows that such behaviour leads to falls in production and price increases, resulting in poor allocation of resources to the detriment, in particular, of consumers.

52 Where the analysis of a type of coordination between undertakings does not reveal a sufficient degree of harm to competition, the effects of the coordination should, on the other hand, be considered and, for it to be caught by the prohibition, it is necessary to find that factors are present which show that competition has in fact been prevented, restricted or distorted to an appreciable extent.

53 According to the case-law of the Court, in order to determine whether an agreement between undertakings or a decision by an association of undertakings reveals a sufficient degree of harm to

competition that it may be considered a restriction of competition 'by object' within the meaning of Article 81(1) EC, regard must be had to the content of its provisions, its objectives and the economic and legal context of which it forms a part. When determining that context, it is also necessary to take into consideration the nature of the goods or services affected, as well as the real conditions of the functioning and structure of the market or markets in question.

54 In addition, although the parties' intention is not a necessary factor in determining whether an agreement between undertakings is restrictive, there is nothing prohibiting the competition authorities, the national courts or the Courts of the European Union from taking that factor into account.

55 In the present case, it must be noted that, when the General Court defined in the judgment under appeal the relevant legal criteria to be taken into account in order to ascertain whether there was, in the present case, a restriction of competition by 'object' within the meaning of Article 81(1) EC, it reasoned as follows . . .

> According to the case-law, the types of agreement covered by Article 81(1)(a) to (e) EC do not constitute an exhaustive list of prohibited collusion and, accordingly, the concept of infringement by object should not be given a strict interpretation.
>
> In order to assess the anti-competitive nature of an agreement or a decision by an association of undertakings, regard must be had *inter alia* to the content of its provisions, its objectives and the economic and legal context of which it forms a part. In that regard, it is sufficient that the agreement or the decision of an association of undertakings has the potential to have a negative impact on competition. In other words, the agreement or decision must simply be capable in the particular case, having regard to the specific legal and economic context, of preventing, restricting or distorting competition within the common market. It is not necessary for there to be actual prevention, restriction or distortion of competition or a direct link between [that agreement or decision] and consumer prices. In addition, although the parties' intention is not a necessary factor in determining whether an agreement is restrictive, there is nothing prohibiting the Commission or the Community judicature from taking it into account.

56 It must be held that, in so reasoning, the General Court in part failed to have regard to the case-law of the Court of Justice and,

therefore, erred in law with regard to the definition of the relevant legal criteria in order to assess whether there was a restriction of competition by 'object' within the meaning of Article 81(1) EC.

57 First, . . . when the General Court defined the concept of the restriction of competition 'by object' within the meaning of that provision, it did not refer to the settled case-law of the Court of Justice mentioned in paragraphs 49 to 52 of the present judgment, thereby failing to have regard to the fact that the essential legal criterion for ascertaining whether coordination between undertakings involves such a restriction of competition 'by object' is the finding that such coordination reveals in itself a sufficient degree of harm to competition.

58 Secondly, in the light of that case-law, the General Court erred in finding . . . that the concept of restriction of competition by 'object' must not be interpreted 'restrictively'. The concept of restriction of competition 'by object' can be applied only to certain types of coordination between undertakings which reveal a sufficient degree of harm to competition that it may be found that there is no need to examine their effects, otherwise the Commission would be exempted from the obligation to prove the actual effects on the market of agreements which are in no way established to be, by their very nature, harmful to the proper functioning of normal competition. The fact that the types of agreements covered by Article 81(1) EC do not constitute an exhaustive list of prohibited collusion is, in that regard, irrelevant.

59 It is, however, necessary to examine whether those errors of law were capable of vitiating the General Court's analysis as regards the characterisation of the measures at issue in the light of Article 81(1) EC.

60 In that regard, it must be noted . . . that the General Court found that the measures at issue have as their object the restriction of competition within the meaning of Article 81(1) EC in that, essentially, they hinder the competition of new entrants on the market for the issue of payment cards in France.

61 . . . [T]he General Court found, after reproducing . . . the content of several recitals of the decision at issue, that that anti-competitive object stemmed from the very calculation formulas which were provided for the measures at issue.

62 In those circumstances, the General Court held . . . that the fact that the measures at issue pursue a legitimate objective of combating free-riding of the CB system did not preclude their being considered to have an object restrictive of competition, all the more so since that

object, as was apparent form the very formulas provided for the measures at issue, ran counter to the stated objectives of the Grouping.

63 The General Court also held . . . that the requirements of balance between the issuing and acquisition activities within the CB system did not have to be examined in the context of Article 81(1) EC, since the only market taken into account was the downstream market for the issue of payment cards.

64 Lastly, the General Court also held . . . that it was only on the basis of 'additional confirmation' that, in the decision at issue, the Commission relied on the Grouping's intention, as evidenced by the documents gathered during the inspections, containing the comments of the main members at the preparatory stage of the measures at issue.

65 Although it is apparent from the judgment under appeal that the General Court took the view that the restrictive object of the measures at issue could be inferred from their wording alone, the fact remains that it did not at any point explain, in the context of its review of the lawfulness of the decision at issue, in what respect that wording could be considered to reveal the existence of a restriction of competition 'by object' within the meaning of Article 81(1) EC.

66 In that regard, the General Court did indeed observe . . . that the Commission found, 'in the light of the formulas provided for the measures at issue and because of the difficulty of developing acquisition activity, that those measures required the members of the Grouping which were subject to them either to limit the issue of cards or to bear costs (linked to issuing) which were not borne by other members of the Grouping, including the main members. Those formulas therefore limited the possibility for the members subject to those measures to compete (on prices), on the issue market, with the members of the Grouping not subject to them'.

67 In addition, the General Court pointed out . . . that the Commission had stated that the function attributed by the Grouping to MERFA, namely an incentive to expand acquisition, 'was inconsistent with the existence of interchange fees which encouraged issue . . . and by the fact that the supplementary membership fee and the [dormant] member fee penalised banks that had not issued a sufficient number of cards in the recent past'.

68 The General Court inferred from this . . . that the object of the measures at issue, like those at issue in the *BIDS* judgment, is to impede the competition of new entrants on the market for the issue

of payment cards in France, since they require the banks subject to them either to pay a fee or to limit their issuing activities.

69 However, although the General Court thereby set out the reasons why the measures at issue, in view of their formulas, are capable of restricting competition and, consequently, of falling within the scope of the prohibition laid down in Article 81(1) EC, it in no way explained—contrary to the requirements of the case-law referred to in paragraphs 49 and 50 above—in what respect that restriction of competition reveals a sufficient degree of harm in order to be characterised as a restriction 'by object' within the meaning of that provision, there being no analysis of that point in the judgment under appeal.

70 Although, as the General Court correctly found . . . , the fact that the measures at issue pursue the legitimate objective of combatting free-riding does not preclude their being regarded as having an object restrictive of competition, the fact remains that that restrictive object must be established.

71 It follows that the General Court, in its characterisation of the measures at issue, not only vitiated the judgment under appeal by defective reasoning, but also misinterpreted and misapplied Article 81(1) EC.

72 It is indeed clear . . . that the General Court rejected on several occasions the appellant's claim that it was apparent from formulas prescribed for the measures at issue that the latter sought to develop the acquisition activities of the members in order to achieve an optimal rate of balance between issuing and acquisition activities. On the other hand, it is not disputed . . . that those formulas encouraged the members of the Grouping, in order to avoid the payment of fees introduced by those measures, not to exceed a certain volume of CB card issuing that enabled them to achieve a given ratio between the issuing and acquisition activities of the Grouping.

73 After stating . . . that the Grouping is active on the 'payment systems market', the General Court found . . . in its assessment of the facts—which is not subject to appeal and is not challenged in these proceedings—that, in the present case, in a card payment system that is by nature two-sided, such as that of the Grouping, the issuing and acquisition activities are 'essential' to one another and to the operation of that system: first, traders would not agree to join the CB card payment system if the number of cardholders was insufficient and, secondly, consumers would not wish to hold a card if it could not be used with a sufficient number of traders.

74 Having therefore found . . . that there were 'interactions' between the issuing and acquisition activities of a payment system and that those activities produced 'indirect network effects', since the extent of merchants' acceptance of cards and the number of cards in circulation each affects the other, the General Court could not, without erring in law, conclude that the measures at issue had as their object the restriction of competition within the meaning of Article 81(1) EC.

75 Having acknowledged that the formulas for those measures sought to establish a certain ratio between the issuing and acquisition activities of the members of the Grouping, the General Court was entitled at the most to infer from this that those measures had as their object the imposition of a financial contribution on the members of the Grouping which benefit from the efforts of other members for the purposes of developing the acquisition activities of the system. Such an object cannot be regarded as being, by its very nature, harmful to the proper functioning of normal competition, the General Court itself moreover having found . . . that combatting free-riding in the CB system was a legitimate objective.

76 In that regard, as the Advocate General observed . . . , the General Court wrongly held . . . that the analysis of the requirements of balance between issuing and acquisition activities within the payment system could not be carried out in the context of Article 81(1) EC on the ground that the relevant market was not that of payment systems in France but the market, situated downstream for the issue of payment cards in that Member State.

77 In so doing, the General Court confused the issue of the definition of the relevant market and that of the context which must be taken into account in order to ascertain whether the content of an agreement or a decision by an association of undertakings reveals the existence of a restriction of competition 'by object' within the meaning of Article 81(1) EC.

78 In order to assess whether coordination between undertakings is by nature harmful to the proper functioning of normal competition, it is necessary, in accordance with the case-law referred to in paragraph 53 above, to take into consideration all relevant aspects—having regard, in particular, to the nature of the services at issue, as well as the real conditions of the functioning and structure of the markets—of the economic or legal context in which that coordination takes place, it being immaterial whether or not such an aspect relates to the relevant market.

79 That must be the case, in particular, when that aspect is the taking into account of interactions between the relevant market and a

different related market and, all the more so, when, as in the present case, there are interactions between the two facets of a two-sided system.

80 Admittedly, it cannot be ruled out that the measures at issue . . . hinder competition from new entrants—in the light of the difficulty which those measures create for the expansion of their acquisition activity—and even lead to their exclusion from the system, on the basis, as BPCE argued at the hearing, of the level of fees charged pursuant to those measures.

81 However, . . . such a finding falls within the examination of the effects of those measures on competition and not of their object.

82 It must therefore be found that, while purporting to examine . . . the 'options' left open to the members of the Grouping by the measures at issue—at the end of which it concluded . . . that 'in practice MERFA left two options open to the banks subject to it: payment of a fee or limiting the issue of CB cards'—the General Court in fact assessed the potential effects of those measures, analysing the difficulties for the banks of developing acquisition activity on the basis of market data, statements made by certain banks and documents seized during the inspections, and thereby indicating itself that the measures at issue cannot be considered 'by their very nature' harmful to the proper functioning of normal competition.

83 In that regard, the General Court erred . . . in finding that the measures at issue could be regarded as being analogous to those examined by the Court of Justice in the *BIDS* judgment, in which the Court of Justice held that the arrangements referred to ('the BIDS arrangements'), concluded between the ten principal beef and veal processors in Ireland, members of BIDS [Beef Industry Development Society Ltd], had as their object the restriction of competition within the meaning of Article 81(1) EC.

84 By providing for a reduction of the order of 25% in processing capacity, the BIDS arrangements were intended, essentially, as their own wording makes clear, to enable several undertakings to implement a common policy which had as its object the encouragement of some of them to withdraw from the market and the reduction, as a consequence, of the overcapacity which affects their profitability by preventing them from achieving economies of scale. The object of the BIDS arrangements was therefore to change, appreciably, the structure of the market through a mechanism intended to encourage the withdrawal of competitors in order, first, to increase the degree of concentration in the sector concerned by reducing significantly the number of undertakings supplying

processing services and, secondly, to eliminate almost 75% of excess production capacity.

85 In the judgment under appeal, the General Court made no such finding, nor indeed was it argued before it that the measures at issue, like the BIDS arrangements, were intended to change appreciably the structure of the market concerned through a mechanism intended to encourage the withdrawal of competitors and, accordingly, that those measures revealed a degree of harm such as that of the BIDS arrangements.

86 Although the General Court found . . . that the measures at issue encouraged the members of the Grouping not to exceed a certain volume of CB card issuing, the objective of such encouragement was, according to its own findings . . . , not to reduce possible overcapacity on the market for the issue of payment cards in France, but to achieve a given ratio between the issuing and acquisition activities of the members of the Grouping in order to develop the CB system further.

87 It follows that the General Court could not, without erring in law, characterise the measures at issue as restrictions of competition 'by object' within the meaning of Article 81(1) EC.

88 Since the intentions of the Grouping could not in themselves, in accordance with the case-law referred to in paragraph 54 above, be sufficient to establish the existence of an anti-competitive object and the General Court moreover itself stated . . . that those intentions had been analysed as additional confirmation only, its findings in that regard . . . cannot justify such a characterisation and there is no need to examine the arguments put forward by the appellant on that point.

89 Taken together, the errors of law committed by the General Court with regard to (i) the relevant legal criteria in order to assess the existence of a restriction of competition 'by object', (ii) the grounds of the judgment under appeal and (iii) the characterisation of the measures at issue with regard to Article 81(1) EC indicate, in addition, a general failure of analysis by the General Court and therefore reveal the lack of a full and detailed examination of the arguments of the appellant and of the parties which sought the annulment of the decision at issue.

90 By simply reproducing on a number of occasions . . . the contents of the decision at issue, the General Court failed to review, even though required to do so, whether the evidence used by the Commission in the decision at issue enabled it correctly to conclude that the measures at issue, in the light of their wording, objectives and context, displayed a sufficient degree of harm to competition to

be regarded as having as their object a restriction of competition within the meaning of Article 81(1) EC and, consequently, whether that evidence constituted all the relevant data which had to be taken into consideration for that purpose.

91 In those circumstances, it is apparent that the General Court failed to fulfil its obligation to observe the standard of review required under the case-law, as set out in paragraphs 42 to 46 above.

92 In the light of all the foregoing, it must be found that, in holding that the measures at issue had as their object a restriction of competition within the meaning of Article 81(1) EC, the General Court erred in law and failed to observe the standard of review required under the case-law.

Notes and Questions

1. In *Cartes Bancaires,* the CJEU cautioned against over-expanding the category of restrictions by object, holding that the criterion is satisfied only where the restrictions "reveal a sufficient degree of harm to competition that it may be found that there is no need to examine their actual effects." In others words, the category of restrictions by object seems to be limited to those that either are hard core or generally cause significant anticompetitive harm. How does this framework differ in practice from the treatment of restraints of trade under Section 1 of the Sherman Act?

2. The Court's analysis suggests that arrangements in complex or novel economic settings may not lend themselves to "by object" analysis, since the actual effects on competition may be too unpredictable for categorical treatment. Does this mean that all "new economy" arrangements that are not hard core cartels are not restraints by object?

D. INFORMATION EXCHANGE AND LOOSE COLLABORATIONS

Competitive information exchange and loose competitor collaborations—loose, because they do not involve economic integration between the collaborating parties—are a standard problem in antitrust analysis. You might consider these agreements to fall closer on the spectrum to cartel agreements than do agreements involving significant degrees of economic integration—such as joint venture agreements. Nonetheless, information exchanges and loose collaborations can be efficiency-enhancing, and have not received as hostile a reception as naked price-fixing agreements.

ASNEF-EQUIFAX v. ASOCIACIÓN DE USUARIOS DE SERVICIOS BANCARIOS (AUSBANC)

Case C–238/05, ECLI:EU:C:2006:734 (Court of Justice of the European Union 2006)

[Financial institutions in Spain agreed to exchange information about solvency of customers and lateness of payment. They planned to establish a register for such information. The Spanish competition authority authorized the register for five years on condition that the register be available to all financial institutions on a non-discriminatory basis and that it not disclose the information it contained on lenders. Ausbanc, an association of bank users, sought an annulment in a Spanish court. It alleged that the register would facilitate a boycott against poor credit risks. The Spanish court made an Article [267] reference to the CJEU regarding applicability and treatment under Article [101]. The CJEU identified the various questions of fact regarding economic and legal context that the national court would have to decide, and it gave considerable guidance both as to when Article [101(1)]) would apply and when the Article [101(3)] criteria would be satisfied. See the Article 101(3) criteria at A. above.]

55 . . . [R]egisters such as the one at issue in the main proceedings, by reducing the rate of borrower default, are in principle capable of improving the functioning of the supply of credit. As the Advocate General observed, . . . if, owing to a lack of information on the risk of borrower default, financial institutions are unable to distinguish those borrowers who are more likely to default, the risk thereby borne by such institutions will necessarily be increased and they will tend to factor it in when calculating the cost of credit for all borrowers, including those less likely to default, who will then have to bear a higher cost than they would if the institutions were in a position to evaluate the probability of repayment more precisely. In principle, registers such as that mentioned above are capable of reducing such a tendency.

56 Furthermore, by reducing the significance of the information held by financial institutions regarding their own customers, such registers appear, in principle, to be capable of increasing the mobility of consumers of credit. In addition, those registers are apt to make it easier for new competitors to enter the market.

57 None the less, whether or not there is in the main proceedings a restriction of competition within the meaning of Article [101(1)] EC depends on the economic and legal context in which the register exists, and in particular on the economic conditions of the market as well as the particular characteristics of the register.

58 In that regard, first of all, if supply on a market is highly concentrated, the exchange of certain information may, according in particular to the type of information exchanged, be liable to enable undertakings to be aware of the market position and commercial strategy of their competitors, thus distorting rivalry on the market and increasing the probability of collusion, or even facilitating it. On the other hand, if supply is fragmented, the dissemination and exchange of information between competitors may be neutral, or even positive, for the competitive nature of the market. In the present case, it is common ground, . . . that the referring court premised its reference for a preliminary ruling on the existence of 'a fragmented market', which it is for that court to verify.

59 Secondly, in order that registers such as that at issue in the main proceedings are not capable of revealing the market position or the commercial strategy of competitors, it is important that the identity of lenders is not revealed, directly or indirectly. In the present case, it is apparent from the decision for referral that the Tribunal de Defensa de la Competencia imposed on Asnef-Equifax, which accepted it, a condition that the information relating to lenders contained in the register not be disclosed.

60 Thirdly, it is also important that such registers be accessible in a non-discriminatory manner, in law and in fact, to all operators active in the relevant sphere. If such accessibility were not guaranteed, some of those operators would be placed at a disadvantage, since they would have less information for the purpose of risk assessment, which would also not facilitate the entry of new operators on to the market.

61 It follows that, provided that the relevant market or markets are not highly concentrated, that the system does not permit lenders to be identified and that the conditions of access and use by financial institutions are not discriminatory, an information exchange system such as the register is not, in principle, liable to have the effect of restricting competition within the meaning of Article [101(1)] EC.

62 While in those conditions such systems are capable of reducing uncertainty as to the risk that applicants for credit will default, they are not, however, liable to reduce uncertainty as to the risks of competition. Thus, each operator could be expected to act independently and autonomously when adopting a given course of conduct, regard being had to the risks presented by applicants. Contrary to Ausbanc's contention, it cannot be inferred solely from the existence of such a credit information exchange that it might lead to collective anti-competitive conduct, such as a boycott of certain potential borrowers.

63 Furthermore, since, as the Advocate General observed, . . . any possible issues relating to the sensitivity of personal data are not, as such, a matter for competition law, they may be resolved on the basis of the relevant provisions governing data protection. In the main proceedings, it is apparent from the documents before the Court that, under the rules applicable to the register, affected consumers may, in accordance with the Spanish legislation, check the information concerning them and, where necessary, have it corrected, or indeed deleted.

The applicability of Article [101(3)] EC

64 Only if the referring court finds, in the light of the considerations set out at paragraphs 58 to 62 of this judgment, that there is indeed in the dispute before it a restriction of competition within the meaning of Article [101(1)] EC will it be necessary for that court to carry out an analysis by reference to Article [101(3)] EC in order to resolve that dispute.

65 The applicability of the exemption provided for in Article [101(3)] EC is subject to the four cumulative conditions laid down in that provision. First, the arrangement concerned must contribute to improving the production or distribution of the goods or services in question, or to promoting technical or economic progress; secondly, consumers must be allowed a fair share of the resulting benefit; thirdly, it must not impose any non-essential restrictions on the participating undertakings; and, fourthly, it must not afford them the possibility of eliminating competition in respect of a substantial part of the products or services in question.

66 It is clear from the documents before the Court, and in particular from the second question referred by the national court, that that court seeks an answer from the Court in respect of, in particular, the second of those conditions, which provides that consumers are to be allowed a fair share of the profit resulting from the agreement, decision or practice in question. The national court asks, in essence, whether, where all consumers do not derive a benefit from the register, the register might none the less benefit from the exemption provided for in Article [101(1)] EC.

67 Apart from the potential effects described at paragraphs 55 and 56 of this judgment, registers such as the one at issue in the main proceedings are capable of helping to prevent situations of overindebtedness for consumers of credit as well as, in principle, of leading to a greater overall availability of credit. In the event that the register restricted competition within the meaning of Article [101(1)] EC, those objective economic advantages might be such as to

offset the disadvantages of such a possible restriction. It would be for the national court, if necessary, to verify that.

68 Admittedly, in principle it is not inconceivable that, as Ausbanc suggests, certain applicants for credit will, owing to the existence of such registers, be faced with increased interest rates, or even be refused credit.

69 However, without its being necessary to decide whether such applicants would none the less benefit from a possible credit discipline effect or from protection against overindebtedness, that circumstance cannot in itself prevent the condition that consumers be allowed a fair share of the benefit from being satisfied.

70 Under Article [101(3)] EC, it is the beneficial nature of the effect on all consumers in the relevant markets that must be taken into consideration, not the effect on each member of that category of consumers.

71 Moreover, as follows from paragraphs 55 and 67 of this judgment, registers such as the one at issue in the main proceedings are, under favourable conditions, capable of leading to a greater overall availability of credit, including for applicants for whom interest rates might be excessive if lenders did not have appropriate knowledge of their personal situation.

DOLE FOOD COMPANY, INC. v. COMMISSION

Case C–286/13 P, ECLI:EU:C:2015:184 (Court of Justice of the European Union 2015)

[A group of banana producers importing into northern Europe, including Dole, Fresh Del Monte, Chiquita, and Weichert, "engaged in bilateral pre-pricing communications during which they discussed banana price-setting factors, that is to say, factors relevant to the setting of quotation prices for the forthcoming week, or discussed or disclosed price trends or gave indications of quotation prices for the forthcoming week." The Commission charged that these communications served as devices to reduce uncertainty about the prices the companies then quoted to the market. Among other things, Dole argued on appeal to the European Court of Justice that the General Court erred in treating this information exchange as a restriction of competition by object in violation of TFEU Article 101 and in failing to require proof of actual effects on banana prices.]

105 By the fifth part of their third ground of appeal, the Dole companies submit that, by finding that the pre-pricing communications constitute a restriction of competition by object, the General Court erred in its legal characterisation of the facts.

According to those companies, the exchange of information which took place cannot be regarded as capable of removing uncertainty as to the intended conduct of the participating undertakings as regards the setting of actual prices.

106 First, the pre-pricing communications were carried out by employees who were not responsible for setting quotation prices. Second, as those communications concerned quotation price trends, they were not capable of removing uncertainty as to actual prices. In that regard, all the market participants involved in the Commission's investigation stated that quotation prices were far removed from actual prices. Moreover, the Commission did not find there had been a restriction of competition by object in relation to the same type of information exchange involving two other undertakings.

107 [T]he General Court rejected those arguments, imposing, incorrectly, the burden of proving that the exchange of information was not capable of removing uncertainty as to the development of actual prices on the Dole companies. However, it was for the Commission to prove that the exchange of information was unlawful. According to the Dole companies, it is apparent from case-law that the mere fact that an exchange of information might have a certain influence on prices is not sufficient to establish the existence of a restriction of competition by object. The Commission was unable to put forward such evidence, however, in view of the fact that there is no reliable connection between quotation price movements and those of actual prices.

108 Furthermore, in so far as the General Court dismissed the Dole companies' argument based on statements made by another undertaking by stating . . . that 'the statements of that undertaking must be assessed in the light of their context, namely that of an undertaking which was an addressee of the statement of objections and which contested the anticompetitive conduct alleged', those companies contend that the General Court failed to have regard to the principle of the presumption of innocence and to fact that the burden of proof lies with the Commission.

109 Lastly, the Dole companies maintain that the pre-pricing communications relating to price-setting factors were not capable of removing uncertainty as to the intended conduct of the undertakings concerned. In particular, they point out that the General Court concluded that the exchanges concerning the industry in general were 'innocuous', that the contested decision did not include information on volume as part of the infringement and that the General Court took the view that weather conditions constituted public information that could be obtained from other sources.

110 In so far as the General Court considered that the pre-pricing communications none the less revealed the competitors' views on those factors, the Dole companies submit that, in the light of the relevant case-law, it is not possible to characterise the exchange of views on weather conditions as a restriction of competition by object, as such discussions are so far removed from the setting of actual price that they cannot reduce uncertainty and facilitate coordination of the prices of the products in question.

—*Findings of the Court*

111 It should be noted that, contrary to what is claimed by the Commission, the Dole companies do not merely seek from the Court a fresh assessment of the facts but put forward errors of law which, they claim, were committed by the General Court. The present part of the third ground of appeal is, therefore, admissible.

112 As regards the substance, it must be recalled that, to come within the prohibition laid down in Article 81(1) EC, an agreement, a decision by an association of undertakings or a concerted practice must have 'as [its] object or effect' the prevention, restriction or distortion of competition in the internal market.

113 In that regard, it is apparent from the Court's case-law that certain types of coordination between undertakings reveal a sufficient degree of harm to competition that it may be found that there is no need to examine their effects.

114 That case-law arises from the fact that certain types of coordination between undertakings can be regarded, by their very nature, as being harmful to the proper functioning of normal competition.

115 Consequently, it is established that certain collusive behaviour, such as that leading to horizontal price-fixing by cartels, may be considered so likely to have negative effects, in particular on the price, quantity or quality of the goods and services, that it may be considered redundant, for the purposes of applying Article 81(1) EC, to prove that they have actual effects on the market. Experience shows that such behaviour leads to falls in production and price increases, resulting in poor allocation of resources to the detriment, in particular, of consumers.

116 Where the analysis of a type of coordination between undertakings does not reveal a sufficient degree of harm to competition, the effects of the coordination should, on the other hand, be considered and, for the purpose of determining whether such conduct is covered by that defined in Article 81(1)) EC, it is necessary to find that factors are

present which show that competition has in fact been prevented, restricted or distorted to an appreciable extent.

117 According to the case-law of the Court, in order to determine whether a type of coordination between undertakings reveals a sufficient degree of harm to competition that it may be considered a restriction of competition 'by object' within the meaning of Article 81(1) EC, regard must be had, inter alia, to its objectives and the economic and legal context of which it forms a part. When determining that context, it is also necessary to take into consideration the nature of the goods or services affected, as well as the real conditions of the functioning and structure of the market or markets in question.

118 In addition, although the parties' intention is not a necessary factor in determining whether a type of coordination between undertakings is restrictive, there is nothing prohibiting the competition authorities, the national courts or the Courts of the European Union from taking that factor into account.

119 In so far as concerns, in particular, the exchange of information between competitors, it should be recalled that the criteria of coordination and cooperation necessary for determining the existence of a concerted practice are to be understood in the light of the notion inherent in the Treaty provisions on competition, according to which each economic operator must determine independently the policy which he intends to adopt on the common market.

120 While it is correct to say that this requirement of independence does not deprive economic operators of the right to adapt themselves intelligently to the existing or anticipated conduct of their competitors, it does, none the less, strictly preclude any direct or indirect contact between such operators by which an undertaking may influence the conduct on the market of its actual or potential competitors or disclose to them its decisions or intentions concerning its own conduct on the market where the object or effect of such contact is to create conditions of competition which do not correspond to the normal conditions of the market in question, regard being had to the nature of the products or services offered, the size and number of the undertakings involved and the volume of that market.

121 The Court has therefore held that the exchange of information between competitors is liable to be incompatible with the competition rules if it reduces or removes the degree of uncertainty as to the operation of the market in question, with the result that competition between undertakings is restricted.

122 In particular, an exchange of information which is capable of removing uncertainty between participants as regards the timing, extent and details of the modifications to be adopted by the undertakings concerned in their conduct on the market must be regarded as pursuing an anticompetitive object.

123 Moreover, a concerted practice may have an anticompetitive object even though there is no direct connection between that practice and consumer prices. Indeed, it is not possible on the basis of the wording of Article 81(1) EC to conclude that only concerted practices which have a direct effect on the prices paid by end users are prohibited.

124 On the contrary, it is apparent from Article 81(1)(a) EC that concerted practices may have an anticompetitive object if they 'directly or indirectly fix purchase or selling prices or any other trading conditions'.

125 In any event, Article 81 EC, like the other competition rules of the Treaty, is designed to protect not only the immediate interests of individual competitors or consumers but also to protect the structure of the market and thus competition as such. Therefore, in order to find that a concerted practice has an anticompetitive object, there does not need to be a direct link between that practice and consumer prices.

126 Lastly, it should be pointed out that the concept of a concerted practice, as it derives from the actual terms of Article 81(1) EC, implies, in addition to the participating undertakings concerting with each other, subsequent conduct on the market and a relationship of cause and effect between the two.

127 In that regard, the Court has held that, subject to proof to the contrary, which the economic operators concerned must adduce, it must be presumed that the undertakings taking part in the concerted action and remaining active on the market take account of the information exchanged with their competitors in determining their conduct on that market. In particular, the Court has concluded that such a concerted practice is caught by Article 81(1) EC, even in the absence of anticompetitive effects on the market.

128 In the present case, the General Court examined . . . the Dole companies' arguments concerning the relevance of quotation prices in the banana sector and the responsibility of the Dole Food employees involved in the pre-pricing communications.

129 As observed by the Advocate General . . . it is apparent from the extremely detailed findings of the General Court, first, that bilateral pre-pricing communications were exchanged between the Dole companies and other undertakings in the banana sector and, as part

of those communications, the undertakings discussed their own quotation prices and certain price trends. Moreover, the Dole companies do not contest that finding.

130 Second, the General Court found . . . that quotation prices were relevant to the market concerned, since, on the one hand, market signals, market trends or indications as to the intended development of banana prices could be inferred from those quotation prices, which were important for the banana trade and the prices obtained and, on the other, in some transactions the actual prices were directly linked to the quotation prices.

131 Third, . . . the General Court found that the Dole employees involved in the pre-pricing communications participated in the internal pricing meetings.

132 Furthermore, those findings of the General Court are to a large extent based on statements made by Dole Food and the Dole companies have not alleged any form of distortion in that regard.

133 Accordingly, the General Court was entitled to take the view, without erring in law, that the conditions for the application of the presumption referred to at paragraph 127 above were fulfilled in the present case, with the result that the Dole companies' claims that that court infringed the principle governing the burden of proof and the presumption of innocence are unfounded.

134 It also follows that the General Court was entitled to take the view . . . , without erring in law, that it was permissible for the Commission to conclude that, as they made it possible to reduce uncertainty for each of the participants as to the foreseeable conduct of competitors, the pre-pricing communications had the object of creating conditions of competition that do not correspond to the normal conditions on the market and therefore gave rise to a concerted practice having as its object the restriction of competition within the meaning of Article 81 EC.

A Note on Trade Associations

In *The Wealth of Nations*, Adam Smith wrote that "[p]eople of the same trade seldom meet together, even for merriment and diversion, but the conversation ends in a conspiracy against the public, or in some contrivance to raise prices." Smith's comments have proven prescient time and time again, as trade associations have become fora for collusion. Although trade associations can serve many positive functions, formal or informal information exchange that begins there often spills over into full-blown price fixing.

China's Anti-Monopoly Law suggests some degree of ambivalence around trade associations. The former Article 16 provides that "[i]ndustry associations shall not organize the business operators in their industry to engage in the monopolistic conducts prohibited by this Chapter." But, as though to counterbalance Article 16, the former Article 11 provides that "trade associations shall strengthen self-discipline of the industries, provide guidance for enterprises in their industries to compete lawfully, and protect the order of market competition." Article 11 survived the amendment of the Law in 2022. The 2022 Amendments have also endeavored to send a stronger message against collusive conduct by trade associations by raising the possible sanctions from RMB500,000 to RMB3 million. This move is more than justified given that many of the cartel cases in China in the first fifteen years of Anti-Monopoly Law enforcement have involved trade associations or even been orchestrated by such associations.

Competition authorities around the world closely scrutinize the practices of trade associations. The Competition Commission of India has published a report on its monitoring of trade associations, noting that "[c]ompetition enforcement is getting increasingly focussed on trade associations' practices that facilitate collusion among the members." http://164.100.58.95/sites/default/files/Newsletter_document/Newsletter_Sept.pdf#:~:text=Trade%20associations%20have, Penalises%20Chemists%20%26%20Druggists%20Association%2C. In 2015, the UK Competition and Markets Authority ("CMA") fined a real estate trade association for organizing an anticompetitive restriction on fee advertisements and discounts by the members of the association. https://www.gov.uk/government/news/companies-fined-over-775000-in-cma-investigation-into-advertising-of-agents-fees. The Hong Kong Competition Commission also spent much of its early days on educating trade associations, launching what was known as the "trade association project". Prior to the Competition Ordinance entering into effect in December 2015, there was extensive engagement with local trade associations through public seminars to raise awareness about the potential legal implications of many customary practices by trade associations. In addition, the Hong Kong Competition Commission proactively reviewed many fee schedules and price recommendations by trade associations and urged these associations to abolish them.

Competition authorities have generally been more inclined to police excesses by trade associations than to disband them altogether, but sometimes only a drastic remedy will suffice. In 2015, the Supreme Court of Chile affirmed a 2011 decision of the Chilean National Economic Prosecutor to disband a poultry trade association after the country's three major poultry producers had used the association as a forum for market allocation. See Press Release, Fiscalia Nacional Economica, Chilean Supreme Court Upholds Fines for Collusion Against Agrosuper, Ariztía and Don Pollo and Hardens Sanction Against the Trade

Association (2015), available at http://www.fne.gob.cl/english/2015/10/29/chilean-supreme-court-upholds-fines-for-collusion-against-agro super-ariztia-and-don-pollo-and-hardens-sanction-against-the-trade-association/.

Notes and Questions

1. The EU's 2011 Guidelines on the Applicability of Article 101 TFEU to Horizontal Cooperation Agreements, http://eur-lex.europa.eu/legal-content/EN/TXT/PDF/?uri=CELEX:52011XC0114(04)&from=EN, provides guidance on information exchanges by competitors. It recognizes that information exchange may sometimes benefit consumers, but that in other circumstances, it may serve to cartelize a market. The guidelines also note that information exchange among a select group of competitors may foreclose competition by unaffiliated companies who are denied access to the shared information.

2. Many cartel cases hinge on evidence that competitors exchanged data about prices, output levels, or other competitively sensitive information. Certainly, information exchange is necessary to keep cartels functioning smoothly. But information exchange need not be anticompetitive or illegal. Indeed, it may have perfectly innocent explanations. Competitors may need good information on what their rivals are doing in order to prevent waste and make efficient planning decisions about production levels. Exchange of information on prices can even lead a seller to lower its price, realizing the market price is somewhat beneath its previously established price.

3. Some relatively early US decisions seemed to condemn information exchanges as per se illegal, while others tolerated what may have been anticompetitive information exchanges. Since the 1970s, however, several fairly consistent principles have emerged from Supreme Coot and lower court decisions. First, an agreement to share information, standing alone, is never per se illegal as a price-fixing agreement. United States v. U.S. Gypsum Co., 438 U.S. 422 (1978). Second, information exchange may in some cases be treated as a "plus factor," evidencing the existence of an illegal price fix (which is per se illegal). Thirdly, to the extent that a plaintiff challenges an agreement to exchange information as an unreasonable restraint of trade under the rule of reason, several factors are relevant. The more that the information shared related to past prices, was presented in aggregate rather than customer-specific form, was made publicly available, and was unaccompanied by meetings or other interactions between the rivals, the less likely it is that a court will condemn it as anticompetitive. Conversely, the more that the information exchange related to present or future prices, provided customer-specific information, was only made available to the competitors, and was accompanied by other meetings, the more likely a court is to conclude that the information exchange

unlawfully restrained price competition. Todd v. Exxon Corp., 275 F.3d 191 (2d Cir. 2001).

4. In reading information exchange cases, it is important to ask whether the information exchange is being used as evidence of a cartel agreement or is challenged on its own as an anticompetitive concerted practice. The Seoul High Court (South Korea) had the following to say about the use of information exchanges to prove collusion in its 2012 *Dairy Cartel Case:* "Although collusion may not be conclusively found based merely on the fact of information exchange among competitors, the exchange of pricing and production information among competitors may be used as a means of facilitating collusion through increased transparency in the market which allows observation of, and response to, competitors' strategies. In this regard, such information exchange may serve as strong circumstantial evidence of collusion depending on factors such as the structure and characteristics of the relevant market, subject of the information, nature of the information, timing and method of information exchange, identity of parties exchanging information."

5. In December of 2015, the Mexican Federal Economic Competition Commission ("COFECE") issued guidelines on the exchange of information between economic agents that provide some clarity on the sorts of information exchanges that threaten competition and those that are more competitively benign. The guidelines begin by stating that information exchange in the following categories is most likely to trigger concerns: (1) prices and discounts; (2) costs; (3) inputs; (4) production and commercialization strategies; (5) client or supplier lists; (6) market share; and (7) investments for expansion. They further note that information exchange is most competitively risky in the following contexts: (1) trade associations and chambers of commerce; (2) discussions about mergers; (3) joint ventures and cooperation agreements; and (4) sharing of directories. Finally, the guidelines discuss the importance of the following information attributes: (1) strategic importance; (2) aggregation (the more aggregated, the less concerning); (3) age (historical information is less concerning; present or future information is more concerning); (4) frequency (the more frequent, the more concerning); (5) public availability (the more publicly available, the less concerning); (6) use of protocols on access (strict protocols limiting access may help mitigate the risk); and (7) purpose (is there a legitimate commercial reason for the information exchange?). These state-of-the-art guidelines reflect a broad consensus among competition experts on the sorts of questions to be posed in information exchange cases.

E. LOOSE COLLABORATIONS IN CONSUMER FINANCIAL SERVICES

One area involving loose competitor collaborations that has seen a significant amount of activity in recent years is consumer financial services or payment systems—particular credit or debit card services and retail banking. Banks and other financial service companies often need to collaborate in various ways in order to allow financial transactions between consumers, merchants, and other banks flow freely. These collaborations frequently entail complex competition law questions involving rival access, discrimination, and collusion.

Until their Initial Public Offerings ("IPOs") in the mid-2000s, Visa and MasterCard were joint ventures between competitor banks, and hence classic joint venture organizations. One set of issues was whether the Visa and MasterCard networks could prohibit their member banks from issuing Discover or American Express (or other) credit cards. In 2003, the US Court of Appeals for the Second Circuit held that Visa U.S.A.'s and MasterCard's so-called "exclusionary" or "exclusivity" rules, which prohibited members of their networks from issuing Amex and Discover cards, were unlawful restraints of trade under the rule of reason. United States v. Visa U.S.A., Inc., 344 F.3d 229 (2d Cir. 2003). This ruling broke Visa and MasterCard's deadlock on the banks.

The court did not, however, determine what kinds of rules the networks could employ within their respective systems. This has been a fertile subject of controversy on both sides of the Atlantic.

On January 31, 2007, the European Commission issued a report on the financial services. The Commission 'found widespread competition barriers which unnecessarily raise the cost of retail banking services for European firms and consumers," and vowed to "make full use of its powers under competition law to tackle these barriers, in the market for payment cards and elsewhere when they result from anticompetitive behaviour." In particular, the report identified the following conditions as problematic:

- **highly concentrated markets** in many Member States, particularly for payment card acquiring, may enable incumbent banks to restrict new entry and charge high card fees

- **large variations in merchant fees** across the EU. For example, firms in Member States with high fees have to pay banks three or four times more of their revenue from card sales than firms in Member States with low fees

- **large variations in interchange fees** between banks across the EU, which may not be passed on fully in lower fees for cardholders. The Commission is not arguing for zero interchange fees; however, their operation in some payment networks raises concerns

- **high and sustained profitability**—particularly in card issuing—suggests that banks in some Member States enjoy significant market power and could impose high card fees on firms and consumers
- **rules and practises** which weaken competition at the retailer level; for example blending of merchant fees and prohibition of surcharging and
- **divergent technical standards** across the EU prevent many service providers from operating efficiently on a pan-EU scale.

See COMMISSION OF THE EUROPEAN COMMUNITIES, SECTOR INQUIRY UNDER ARTICLE 17 OF REGULATION (EC) NO 1/2003 ON RETAIL BANKING (2007); European Commission Press Release, IP/07/114 (Jan. 31, 2007).

In response to these concerns, the European Commission has been putting pressure on banks to modify their payment card practices. In at least Austria, Finland, and Portugal, the Commission succeeded in persuading (perhaps with some implicit threat of action) banks to modify their practices in a way that satisfied the Commission's concerns.

Although the European Commission's preference has been to persuade banks and other industry participants to alter their competitively questionable practices, not all of the Commission's activities have been in the arena of gentle persuasion. In December 19, 2007, the Commission issued a decision prohibiting MasterCard from establishing intra-European Economic Area ("EEA") Multilateral Interchange Fees ("MIF"). Interchange fees are the charges that a cardholder's bank (the "issuing" bank) charges a merchant's bank (the "acquiring" bank) for each transaction at merchant outlet with a payment card. When a cardholder uses a payment card to make a purchase, the merchant receives from the acquiring bank the retail price less a merchant service charge, a large part of which is determined by the interchange fee. This merchant service charge is the price a merchant pays its bank for accepting payment cards. The issuing bank, in turn, pays the acquiring bank the retail price minus the MIF.

The Commission found that, by establishing the EEA-wide MIF, MasterCard inflated the price for intra-EEA payment transactions, "effectively determin[ing] a floor under the merchant service charge and merchants are unable to negotiate a price." The Commission found that the effect of the MasterCard establishing the MIF, instead of them being bargained over, was that MasterCard determined the minimum price merchants must pay for accepted credit cards. It enjoined MasterCard from continuing to establish MIFs. See European Commission Press Release, IP/07/1959 (Dec. 19, 2007).

In December 2010, the Commission accepted legally binding commitments from Visa Europe to reduce its MIFs for debit card transactions. As part of the commitments, the maximum weighted average MIF for both cross-border and domestic debit card transactions in countries where MIFs are directly set by Visa Europe will be lowered to 0.2% of the transaction value, amounting to an average reduction of about 60% for domestic MIFs and 30% for cross-border MIFs. In February 2014, the Commission further accepted legally binding commitments from Visa Europe to reduce its MIFs for cross-border and domestic credit card transactions to 3% of the value of transactions, amounting to an average reduction of 40% to 60% for MIFs. Visa Europe agreed also to reform its rules in order to facilitate cross-border competition, including simplifying its inter-bank fee structure and rendering the invoicing of card acceptance services more transparent to merchants. This followed statement of objections sent by the Commission to Visa Europe in July 2012 regarding Visa's inter-bank fees.

In 2015, the EU adopted Regulation 2015/751, otherwise known as the Interchange Fee Regulation (IFR) that capped interchange fees for debit cards at 0.2% and those for credit cards at 0.3% for intra-EEA transactions (where both the issuer and acquirer are located in the EEA) and for domestic transactions in EEA Member States (where both the issuer and the acquirer are located in the same Member State). The overarching goal is to increase transparency and increase competition in the payment cards market. The hope is that by increasing transparency on the level of fees paid by retailers, retailers will be better able to choose which cards to accept, thereby enhancing competition. The IFR allows the Member States to set a cap of lower than 0.3% for credit card transactions. It also permits Member States to impose a dual cap of 0.2% and 0.5 eurocent per transaction for debit or prepaid card transactions. The IFR provides limited exemptions, for example, for business cards used only for business expenses being charged directly to the account of the company.

The IFR does not cover what are known as inter-regional transactions (where at least either the issuer or acquirer is not located in the EEA). This gaping hole in the regulatory regime for MIFs was plugged in April 2019, when the Commission adopted two commitment decisions involving both Visa Europe and Mastercard

Europe. The decisions capped interchange fees for debit cards at 0.2% and those for credit cards at 0.3% for inter-regional transactions. These were supposed to amount to a 40% reduction in the level of fees. With these two commitment decisions, the Commission has achieved complete alignment of interchange fees at 0.2% for debit cards and 0.3% for credit cards for all kind transactions, domestic, intra-EEA, and inter-regional. These two decisions marked the end of EU enforcement against Visa and Mastercard concerning their interchange fees that began in 2002.

Notes and Questions

1. The *Cartes Bancaires* decision, studied in the previous section, raises a number of difficult questions regarding what economists call "two-sided markets"—platforms that bring together users on two different sides of the platform, such as merchants and customers in the case of credit cards or card holders, and banks in the case of banking cards. Competition law interventions on only one side of the market—for example, lifting the tax on bank card issuers who fail to meet a particular volume level for acquiring bank withdrawals—may destabilize the entire platform by preventing it from achieving equilibrium between the two sides of the market. On the other hand, it is often difficult for competition enforcers or courts to solve competition problems on both sides of the market simultaneously. Does this suggest that antitrust enforcers—who usually have to decide antitrust matters on a case-by-case basis—are not the best regulators to deal with the payment systems industry? Should a financial regulator with a broader regulatory mandate take charge instead? *See* David Evans, *Essays on the Economics of Two-Sided Markets*, https://www.competitionpolicyinternational.com/assets/Hot-Tubs/Evans-Two-Sided-Market-Essays-Final.pdf.

2. In 2010, the United States Department of Justice and 17 States brought an antitrust case under Section 1 of the Sherman Act against MasterCard, Visa, and American Express, alleging that these companies' "anti-steering rules," rules that prohibited merchants from "steering" customers to particular credit cards, anticompetitively limited competition among credit cards. Visa and MasterCard quickly settled, but American Express fought the case up to the federal court of appeals for the Second Circuit, which ruled in its favor in 2016. In 2018, the U.S. Supreme Court sided with American Express, holding that, at least as to two-sided markets involving a simultaneous transaction, the plaintiff bears the burden of proving anticompetitive effects across the platform as a whole, taking into account both sides of the market. Ohio v. American Express Co., 585 U.S. 529 (2018).

F. STANDARD-SETTING ORGANIZATIONS, PATENT POOLS, AND RELATED PATENT PRACTICES

In order for the benefits of technological innovation to reach consumers, it is often necessary for the firms manufacturing the new products to agree on common interoperability or other technological standards. For example, imagine a world in which each DVD manufacturer created a unique product incompatible with its rivals' DVD players. Consumers would have to own many different DVD players in order to watch all of their DVDs.

Inventors and manufacturers in high technology industries often solve their coordination problems by forming standard-setting organizations ("SSOs"), which decide on standards for particular products or industries. While SSOs are often indispensable to technological progress, they also create serious dangers of anticompetitive abuse.

Consider, for example, what happened in Allied Tube v. Indian Head, 486 U.S. 492 (1988). Indian Head, a manufacturer of polyvinyl electrical conduit sought approval from the National Fire Protective Association in its National Electrical Code. Allied and other makers of steel electrical conduit perceived the new vinyl conduit as a competitive threat and allegedly packed the SSO's meetings to ensure that Allied's efforts to become part of the standard were voted down.

Often, SSOs not only set a standard, but also attempt to solve "patent thicket" problems—problems occasioned by the fact that practicing a particular standard will often require using many different patented technologies—by providing for the pooling and blanket licensing of patents necessary to practice the standard. To return to the DVD example, in the late 1990s and early 2000s, several different consortia of DVD manufacturers sought and received approval from both the US Justice Department and the European Commission to implement pools to issue a blanket license to use all of their patents necessary to manufacture DVDs. The European Commission's "comfort letter" found that "this patent pool would help promote technical and economic progress by allowing quick and efficient introduction of the DVD technology" and noted that the pool committed to license on a non-exclusive and non-discriminatory basis. See European Commission Press Release, IP/00/1135 (Oct. 9, 2000).

Patent pooling can also have anticompetitive consequences. For example, in the old cracking patents case, three of the Standard Oil

Company's successor companies (the regional Standard companies created by the divestiture required by the 1911 Supreme Court decision) were able to cartelize much of the gasoline industry by cross-licensing to one another, and then licensing to 46 gasoline manufacturers, patents for the process of "cracking" gasoline. *See* George L. Priest, *Cartels and Patent License Arrangements*, 20 J. L. & Econ. 309 (1977). In Chapter 5, we reviewed the US and EU approaches to *Rambus*—a case involving the intersection of SSOs and patent rights in the computer memory business.

Around the globe, many jurisdictions—particularly those whose economies are heavily dependent on technology transfer—are becoming active in policing standard setting and patent pooling. Canada, the EU, Japan, and South Korea have all promulgated new guidelines on concerted patent practices since 2014. (For a useful summary, see Hartmut Schneider, Sarah H. Licht & Nicole Callan, *Antitrust and Intellectual Property Guidelines: The "Common Core" and Beyond*, ABA Section of Antitrust Law May 2016). Principles common to most or all of these guidelines include:

- Rule of reason or similar treatment for patent pooling arrangements;
- Provision of non-discriminatory access to pooled patents or the patent pooling process;
- Allowance, under most circumstances, of cross-licensing and grant-back arrangements;
- Restrictions on participants in standardization activities seeking to enforce their intellectual property rights injunctively against alleged infringers.

On November 4, 2024, the State Administration for Market Regulation of the People's Republic of China ("SAMR") released its Provisions Prohibiting Abuse of Intellectual Property Rights to Eliminate or Restrict Competition, which update the Rules on the Prohibition of Abuses of Intellectual Property Rights to Eliminate or Restrict Competition, which had been promulgated by the State Administration for Industry and Commerce in 2015. Among other things, the Guidelines contain prohibitions on the following conduct on competitor participation in patent pools:

- exchanging competitively sensitive information;
- imposing unfairly high royalty rate;
- restricting members of the patent pool from independently licensing their patents;

- restricting members or licensees from researching and developing technologies that compete with the pooled patents;
- forcing licensees to grant back on an exclusive basis to the patent pool management organization or a member of the patent pool any technologies that licensees have developed or improved;
- prohibiting licensees from challenging the validity or effectiveness of the pooled patents; and
- treating pool members or licensees differently with respect to licensing terms than similarly-situated pool members or licensees that operate in the same relevant market.

Provisions Prohibiting Abuse of Intellectual Property Rights to Eliminate and Restrict Competition (promulgated by the State Admin. for Market Reg., Jun. 25, 2023, effective Aug. 1, 2023), Order No. 79 (China).

The general movement in global antitrust law in recent years has been toward facilitation of technological standardization and patent pooling, subject to antitrust vigilance with regard to potential abuses. One might ask whether the pendulum might swing against standardization and patent pooling at some future point. Despite the many obvious benefits of standardization and patent, there is also some benefit in competition over technological standards (think VHS vs. Betamax) and patent licensing. There may also turn out to be important regional differences in perspective as among jurisdictions that are net technology exporters and those that are net technology importers. And, always lurking in the background of these doctrinal and policy questions are the foundational questions regarding dynamic efficiency and static efficiency—should antitrust policy tolerate measures that increase short-run market power but also incentivize long-run innovation? One should not expect uniform answers to such questions around the globe.

G. LEARNED PROFESSIONS

Although we often think of monopoly power arising from large corporations, some of the most pernicious restrictions on competition arise in the so called "learned professions" like medicine, law, and engineering. Consider, for example, an ethical rule promulgated by an engineers' association that prohibits the engineers from engaging in competitive bidding. The ostensible justification for such a prohibition might be that competitive bidding leads to a reduction in the quality of engineering work and ultimately a threat to public safety, since the engineers who have to accept low prices for their services are likely to cut corners. However, allowing such a rule to remain in place would effectively suppress all price competition for engineering services. *See* National Society of Professional Engineers v. United States, 435 U.S. 679 (1978) (invalidating such a restriction).

Antitrust regimes that wish to allow some space for self-regulation by learned professions must make such decisions about how much deference antitrust law should give the professions when they suppress competition.

WOUTERS ET CIE

Case C–309/99, ECLI:EU:C:2002:98 (Court of Justice of the European Union 2002)

[This judgment arises out of the request for a preliminary ruling referred to the Court by the Netherlands Council of State in the framework of proceedings initiated by Wouters and other members of the Bar seeking to set aside the decisions of the Amsterdam and Rotterdam Bar prohibiting them from practicing law in full partnership with accountants. Those decisions were adopted pursuant to the Regulation on Joint Professional Activity adopted by the Bar of the Nederland in 1993 ("the 1993 Regulation"). The 1993 Regulation prohibits members of the Bar to "assume or maintain any obligations which might jeopardize the free and independent exercise of their profession, including . . . the relationship of trust between lawyer and client" and to "enter into or maintain any professional partnership unless the primary purpose of each partner's respective profession is the practice of the law." Wouters and his colleagues claimed that the decisions of the Amsterdam and Rotterdam Bar, as well as the 1993 Regulation, were incompatible with the Treaty provisions on competition, right of establishment and freedom to provide services.]

Question 1(a) * * *

56 The question to be determined is whether, when it adopts a regulation such as the 1993 Regulation, a professional body is to be treated as an association of undertakings or, on the contrary, as a public authority.

[The Court answered that the bar is to be treated as an association of undertakings.] * * *

Question 2

73 By its second question the national court seeks, essentially, to ascertain whether a regulation such as the 1993 Regulation which,

in order to guarantee the independence and loyalty to the client of members of the Bar who provide legal assistance in conjunction with members of other liberal professions, adopts universally binding rules governing the formation of multi-disciplinary partnerships, has the object or effect of restricting competition within the common market and is likely to affect trade between Member States. * * *

[84] The prohibition at issue in the main proceedings prohibits all contractual arrangements between members of the Bar and accountants which provide in any way for shared decision-making, profit-sharing or for the use of a common name, and this makes any form of effective partnership difficult. * * *

[86] It appears to the Court that the national legislation in issue in the main proceedings has an adverse effect on competition and may affect trade between Member States.

[87] As regards the adverse effect on competition, the areas of expertise of members of the Bar and of accountants may be complementary. Since legal services, especially in business law, more and more frequently require recourse to an accountant, a multi-disciplinary partnership of members of the Bar and accountants would make it possible to offer a wider range of services, and indeed to propose new ones. Clients would thus be able to turn to a single structure for a large part of the services necessary for the organisation, management and operation of their business (the 'one-stop shop' advantage).

[88] Furthermore, a multi-disciplinary partnership of members of the Bar and accountants would be capable of satisfying the needs created by the increasing interpenetration of national markets and the consequent necessity for continuous adaptation to national and international legislation.

[89] Nor, finally, is it inconceivable that the economies of scale resulting from such multi-disciplinary partnerships might have positive effects on the cost of services.

[90] A prohibition of multi-disciplinary partnerships of members of the Bar and accountants, such as that laid down in the 1993 Regulation, is therefore liable to limit production and technical development within the meaning of Article [101(1)(b)] of the Treaty. * * *

[97] However, not every agreement between undertakings or every decision of an association of undertakings which restricts the freedom of action of the parties or of one of them necessarily falls within the prohibition laid down in Article [101(1)] of the Treaty. For the purposes of application of that provision to a particular case, account must first of all be taken of the overall context in which the

decision of the association of undertakings was taken or produces its effects. More particularly, account must be taken of its objectives, which are here connected with the need to make rules relating to organisation, qualifications, professional ethics, supervision and liability, in order to ensure that the ultimate consumers of legal services and the sound administration of justice are provided with the necessary guarantees in relation to integrity and experience. . . . It has then to be considered whether the consequential effects restrictive of competition are inherent in the pursuit of those objectives.

98 Account must be taken of the legal framework applicable in the Netherlands, on the one hand, to members of the Bar and to the Bar of the Netherlands, which comprises all the registered members of the Bar in that Member State, and on the other hand, to accountants. * * *

102 [The members of the Bar] should be in a situation of independence vis-à-vis the public authorities, other operators and third parties, by whom they must never be influenced. They must furnish, in that respect, guarantees that all steps taken in a case are taken in the sole interest of the client.

103 By contrast, the profession of accountant is not subject, in general, and more particularly, in the Netherlands, to comparable requirements of professional conduct. * * *

105 . . . The Bar of the Netherlands was entitled to consider that members of the Bar might no longer be in a position to advise and represent their clients independently and in the observance of strict professional secrecy if they belonged to an organisation which is also responsible for producing an account of the financial results of the transactions in respect of which their services were called upon and for certifying those accounts. * * *

107 A regulation such as the 1993 Regulation could therefore reasonably be considered to be necessary in order to ensure the proper practice of the legal profession, as it is organised in the Member State concerned. * * *

In 2006, the CJEU revisited the issue of fee-setting for legal services in a case that arose in Italy. Judgment of 12 May 2006, *Cipolla*, C–94/04, EU:C:2006:758. A statute dating from 1933 provided that the National Lawyers' Council shall set a fee schedule, to be approved by the Minister of Justice after consultation with the Interministerial Committee on Prices and the Council of State. Any agreement derogating from the minimum fees set by the scale for lawyers' services is legally void.

The CJEU held that the TFEU's antitrust provisions did not apply because the Italian minimum fee system was not the result of an agreement between undertakings. Since the Italian State and not the Bar Association ultimately exercised the power to make decisions on lawyers' minimum fees, the fee-setting could not be considered a private agreement and the Italian State did not require or encourage the adoption of private anticompetitive agreements.

Turning to the Treaty provision relating to the free movement of services, the Court held that the minimum fee arrangement could be caught by Article 49 because it rendered access to the Italian legal services market more difficult for lawyers established outside of Italy. However, the Court held that the system could potentially be justified based on the protection of consumers and the proper administration of justice, a decision ultimately to be made by the national court.

For many years, many US courts and commentators believed that the learned professions were beyond the reach of antitrust law. In 1975, however, the Supreme Court discarded the "learned professions" exception that many lower courts had recognized for self-regulated professions. Goldfarb v. Virginia State Bar Ass'n, 421 U.S. 773 (1975). The Court reasoned:

> The County Bar argues that Congress never intended to include the learned professions within the terms "trade or commerce" in [Section] 1 of the Sherman Act, and therefore the sale of professional services is exempt from the Act. No explicit exemption or legislative history is provided to support this contention; rather, the existence of state regulation seems to be its primary basis. Also, the County Bar maintains that competition is inconsistent with the practice of a profession because enhancing profit is not the goal of professional activities; the goal is to provide services necessary to the community. That, indeed, is the classic basis traditionally advanced to distinguish professions from trades, businesses, and other occupations, but it loses some of its force when used to support the fee control activities involved here.
>
> In arguing that learned professions are not "trade or commerce" the County Bar seeks a total exclusion from antitrust regulation. Whether state regulation is active or dormant, real or theoretical, lawyers would be able to adopt anticompetitive practices with impunity. We cannot find

> support for the proposition that Congress intended any such sweeping exclusion. The nature of an occupation, standing alone, does not provide sanctuary from the Sherman Act, nor is the public-service aspect of professional practice controlling in determining whether [Section] 1 includes professions. Congress intended to strike as broadly as it could in [Section] 1 of the Sherman Act, and to read into it so wide an exemption as that urged on us would be at odds with that purpose.
>
> The language of [Section] 1 of the Sherman Act, of course, contains no exception. "Language more comprehensive is difficult to conceive." United States v. South-Eastern Underwriters Assn., 322 U.S. 533, 553 (1944). And our cases have repeatedly established that there is a heavy presumption against implicit exemptions. Indeed, our cases have specifically included the sale of services within s 1. Whatever else it may be, the examination of a land title is a service; the exchange of such a service for money is "commerce" in the most common usage of that word. It is no disparagement of the practice of law as a profession to acknowledge that it has this business aspect, and s 1 of the Sherman Act.
>
> The fact that a restraint operates upon a profession as distinguished from a business is, of course, relevant in determining whether that particular restraint violates the Sherman Act. It would be unrealistic to view the practice of professions as interchangeable with other business activities, and automatically to apply to the professions antitrust concepts which originated in other areas. The public service aspect, and other features of the professions, may require that a particular practice, which could properly be viewed as a violation of the Sherman Act in another context, be treated differently. We intimate no view on any other situation than the one with which we are confronted today.

Although the US Court has scrutinized anticompetitive restraints by learned professions, it has granted self-regulated professions some limited deference, usually refusing to apply the rule of per se illegality to their activities but instead scrutinizing them under the rule of reason. *See*, e.g., FTC v. Indiana Federation of Dentists, 476 U.S. 447 (1986). In the last several decades, the FTC has made a high priority of attacking anticompetitive "ethics rules" of doctors, dentists, lawyers, engineers, and other professional groups. Although sometimes rebuffed in the courts, e.g. California

Dental Ass'n v. FTC, 526 U.S. 756 (1999), the Commission has had some success in ensuring that professional association ethical rules do not suppress competition without some valid ethical or regulatory justification. In its most recent victory, the Commission persuaded the US Supreme Court that a North Carolina statute delegating regulatory power over the practice of dentistry to a Board constituted of interested dental professionals did not qualify for state action immunity. North Carolina State Board of Dental Examiners v. FTC, 574 U.S. 494 (2015).

Although the US is often thought to be more permissive in its treatment of competitor collaborations than other antitrust regimes, it may play a more active role in scrutinizing professional associations than many other regimes. Some regimes explicitly allow for self-regulatory exemptions for professional associations. For example, the South African Competition Act authorizes the Competition Commission to exempt professional rules that are reasonably required:

> (1) A professional association whose rules contain a restriction that has the effect of substantially preventing or lessening competition in a market may apply in the prescribed manner to the Competition Commission for an exemption in terms of item 2.
>
> (2) The Competition Commission may exempt all or part of the rules of a professional association from the provisions of Part A of Chapter 2 of this Act for a specified period if, having regard to internationally applied norms, any restriction contained in those rules that has the effect of substantially preventing or lessening competition in a market is reasonably required to maintain—
>
> (a) professional standards; or
>
> (b) the ordinary function of the profession.

Parts (3)–(8) of the statute specify the procedures for applying for and obtaining self-regulatory authority from the Commission. Part B then lists the professions generally eligible for self-regulatory exemption: Accountants and Auditors; Architects; Engineering; Estate Agents; Attorneys and Advocates; Natural sciences; Quantity Surveyors; Surveyors; Town and Regional Planners; Valuers; Medical; Miscellaneous.

H. COLLABORATIONS IN THE NEW ECONOMY

The Internet has fundamentally disrupted economic relationships and traditional economic categories. On the one hand, the Internet radically reduces consumers' search costs, and hence intensifies competition and facilitates retail participation by many smaller businesses. On the other hand, by lowering coordination costs, the Internet also provides new opportunities for sellers of goods and services to restrict competition. As with much technological change, the Internet brings both risks and opportunities from a competition perspective.

For sellers concerned that online sales risk their profit margins by intensifying competition, one strategy is to try to limit online sales and force customers into conventional brick and mortar sales environments. Consider, for example, the *Pierre Fabre* case, involving the sale of pharmaceutical products in France. Case C–439/09 Pierre Fabre Dermo-Cosmetique SAS v. President de l'Autorite de la Concurrence and Others, judgment of 13 October 2011. Pierre Fabre sold pharmaceutical products that were not considered "medicines" under French law, and thus were not restricted by law to sales in brick and mortar pharmacies. Nonetheless, Pierre Fabre implemented distribution agreements that effectively limited sales to physical stores in the presence of a qualified pharmacist. The European Court of Justice found that the restriction was susceptible to being justified under TFEU Article 101(3), but that Pierre Fabre had failed to present sufficient evidence to justify the restriction.

Similarly, the German Bundeskartellamt has been active in investigating agreements that restrict or deny Internet competition. In 2015, it investigated agreements between online portals, car dealerships, and car manufacturers that allegedly restricted online sales, only dropping its investigation once the offending restrictions were deleted. Bundeskartellamt Case B9–28/15. It also required the shoe company Asics to remove various restrictions on online sales of its shoes, which could have limited sales on online platforms such as eBay and/or cross-border sales. Bundeskartellamt Case B 2–98/11.

These restrictions on Internet sales were mostly vertical insofar as they operated as between an upstream manufacturer and downstream distributors. But the Internet is also disrupting the traditional "vertical" and "horizontal" categories. A restriction may be nominally vertical insofar as it expresses contractual terms only between an upstream and downstream firm, and yet have the effect of softening competition horizontally by reducing the incentives of competitors to lower prices. The downstream firm may therefore play a role in coordinating role in reducing upstream competition.

Such concerns have been raised particularly with respect to the use of Most Favored Nations ("MFN"), "parity," "best price," or meeting competition clauses by online platforms that aggregate sales of multiple different sellers' products. For example, suppose an online platform requires every vendor listed on its site to make its best price available on that site. While such a restriction sounds nominally pro-consumer insofar as it ostensibly brings lower prices to that platform, its actual effect may be to homogenize prices across all platforms selling that vendor's product and hence to establish a price floor rather than a price ceiling.

In 2015, the International Competition Network issued a Special Project Report on Online Vertical Restraints. ICN2015 Special Project Report on Online Vertical Restraints, available at: https://centrocedec.wordpress.com/wp-content/uploads/2015/07/special-project_online-vertical-restraints-2015.pdf. It found that 47% of national competition authorities considered online MFNs concerning and identified a number of investigations opened by national competition authorities. Reflecting the perspective of these competition authorities, the ICN identified the following potential problems with the use of MFNs in online vertical agreements:

- disincentivising new market entry as potential new entrants are restricted from accessing lower prices with which to grow market share;
- artificially protecting a platform acting as an intermediary from direct selling by the supplier;
- softening competition between platforms, which can lead to higher fees imposed upon retailers and consequently higher prices paid by consumers; and
- facilitating collusion between platforms by reducing incentives to deviate from a collusive agreement on platform fees.

The hotel industry in Europe has been a particular focus of these enforcement actions. In December of 2014, the European Commission announced the launch of market tests in antitrust investigations by the French, Swedish and Italian competition authorities in the online hotel booking sector. The three national competition authorities expressed concerns that so-called "parity clauses" in contracts between the online travel agent Booking.com and hotels had anticompetitive effects. The parity clauses—often referred to as MFN or most favored nation clauses—obliged the hotel to offer Booking.com the same or better room prices as the hotel made available on all other online and offline distribution channels. The national authorities worried that these clauses might restrict competition between Booking.com and other online travel agents

('OTAs') and hinder new booking platforms from entering the market.

To alleviate these concerns, Booking.com offered commitments that were market tested and subsequently approved by the three national competition agencies. The commitments prevented Booking.com from requiring hotels to offer better or equal room prices via Booking.com than they do via competing OTAs. In addition, under the commitments Booking.com cannot prevent hotels from offering discounted room prices provided that these are not marketed or made available to the general public online. The discounted prices can be offered online to members of a hotel's loyalty scheme and/or via offline channels (e g direct emails, telephone and walk-in bookings).

Booking.com was a case in which the European Commission allowed national competition authorities to take the lead in resolving an arguably pan-European competition problem, because of the peculiarity of local effects. Most often, however, issues of competition in cyberspace overlap national boundaries. See European Commission Press Release, MEX/15/4819 (Apr. 21, 2015).

Some national authorities have gone even further in curtailing vertical restrictions in hotel booking. The German Bundeskartellamt has been particularly active in this area. In 2013, it led the way by prohibiting HRS, an OTA competitor of Booking.com, from enforcing any of its MFN clauses. Bundeskartellamt Case B9–66/10 of 20 December 2013. Then, following the European Commission's acceptance of Booking.com's commitments following the French, Swedish, and Italian investigations, the Bundeskartellamt went further and prohibited Booking.com from preventing hotels from offering their own rooms more cheaply on the hotel's own website than on Booking.com. Andreas Mundt, President of the Bundeskartellamt, explained the decision as follows:

> These so-called narrow best price clauses also restrict both competition between the existing portals and competition between the hotels themselves. Firstly they infringe the hotels' freedom to set prices on their own online sales channels. There is little incentive for a hotel to reduce its prices on a hotel booking portal if at the same time it has to display higher prices for its own online sales. Secondly, it still makes the market entry of new platform providers considerably difficult. The 'best price' clauses barely provide an incentive for the hotels to offer their rooms on a new portal cheaper if they cannot implement these price

reductions on their own websites as well. There is no apparent benefit for the consumer.

Narrow "best price" clauses of Booking.com also anticompetitive, http://www.bundeskartellamt.de/SharedDocs/Meldung/EN/Pressemitteilungen/2015/23_12_2015_Booking.com.html.

In May 2016, the Dusseldorf Higher Regional Court rejected Booking.com's application for an interim injunction, thus preserving the Bundeskartellamt's decision pending litigation. As of this writing, the Bundeskartellamt's decision remains subject to appellate review. There is little doubt, however, that European competition authorities will continue to challenge aggressive use of MFNs to limit online competition.

Following enforcement action by the competition authorities, a number of legislation was adopted in EU Member States to outlaw MFN clauses. Belgium and France banned both narrow and wide MFN clauses through specific legislation. Narrow MFNs only prohibit lower prices on the hotel's ow website while wide MFNs suppress discounts on all sales channels. Italy adopted a ban that only applied to hotels and accommodation providers. Article 3(5) of the EU Digital Markets Act also bans the use of MFN clauses or price parity clauses by firms designated as gatekeepers, of which Booking is one. Booking is the only online hotel booking portal to have been designated a gatekeeper by the European Commission.

Competition authorities outside of the EU have jumped on the bandwagon and brought enforcement action with respect to MFN clauses. Expedia, Booking.com, and Trip.com, which is a hotel booking portal from China, have offered commitments to the Hong Kong Competition Commission to abandon their wide MFN clauses and to undertake not to enforce them.

I. SUSTAINABILITY ISSUES

Sustainability has rightly become a topic of global importance in recent years. Many areas of law have had to confront their interface with sustainability issues. Competition law is no exception. In the last few years, it has become increasingly common for businesses to collaborate to put forward sustainability initiatives, for example, to reduce the carbon footprint of one's product. These initiatives often increase costs, which may inflate prices, and reduce output, at least of the more polluting or carbon-intensive variety. The pursuit of sustainability benefits is said to create first-mover disadvantage in the sense that the first firm to embrace higher environmental standards suffers cost disadvantages. In other words, these are agreements among competitors that increase prices and reduce output, often the archetypal anticompetitive agreements in competition law. In order for competition law not to become a stumbling block in the pursuit of sustainability goals, there is a need to reconcile the objectives of competition law, whatever they may be depending on the jurisdiction, and sustainability goals.

Assessment of the legality of such an agreement traditionally would require a balancing of the expected consumer harm and the expected procompetitive benefits. The difficulty with horizontal restrictive agreements with sustainability goals, or sustainability agreements for short, is that the benefits are diffused and distant, and most likely not confined to the consumers who are most likely to bear the competitive harm.

If an agreement is meant to reduce the carbon intensity of a product or the carbon emission of the production process, one of its main benefits would be reduced carbon emission, which by definition would be negligible in the global scheme of things. The benefit would be global in scale while the harm would be localized in the relevant market. The benefit would be highly diffuse and difficult to quantify. The benefit would also be long term, as opposed to the immediate consumer harm of a price increase or output reduction. Balancing a distant and diffuse benefit, which will probably need to be discounted, against an immediate harm is fraught with difficulty to say the least. The difficulty in the quantification of benefit, the balancing between immediate, in-the-market harm against distant, out-of-market benefit, and the most fundamental issue of whether to count reduced carbon emission as a cognizable benefit at all are some of the greatest challenges for those trying to reconcile sustainability benefits within the traditional framework of competition law.

Every discussion about the interface between competition law and environmental law needs to start with the Commission decision in the *CECED* case. In this 2000 decision, the Commission approved an agreement among leading washing machine manufacturers in Europe to stop the production and import of washing machines with the lowest energy efficiency rating under the aegis of their trade association European Council of Domestic Appliance Manufacturers (CECED). The manufacturers involved accounted for more than 95% of the market for washing machines, and the implicated washing machines amounted to about 10% of the overall sales of washing machines in Europe.

The Commission granted an exemption of less than one year under Article 101(3) TFEU. The Commission concluded that all the four conditions under Article 101(3) were met. First, the agreement contributed to technical and economic progress. The agreement facilitated the transition to the production of more energy efficient washing machines, which would have taken longer to come about otherwise. Second, the Commission recognized both benefits to individual consumers and overall benefits to Europe's economic welfare. For individual consumers, the higher initial purchase cost would be offset by lower subsequent electricity bills. The Commission acknowledged that individual consumers may not derive sufficient financial benefits from the agreement, but the overall environment benefits for Europe as a whole would still outweigh the costs. Third, the Commission opined that the restriction of competition is indispensable to the attainment of the environmental objective. There is a market failure in that the negative externality of energy inefficient washing machines is not taken into account by consumers. The agreement would help to mitigate this market failure. Finally, the agreement does not eliminate competition. Competition remains on important dimensions such as price, technical effectiveness, and brand. In any case, 90% of the washing machines in the market are unaffected.

This decision is important not only because it was the first time the Commission has allowed an otherwise anticompetitive agreement to be justified by environmental benefits, it was also remarkable in the Commission's acknowledgement that such an agreement is still exempted even though individual consumers are not fully compensated for their harm. The Commission did not try to translate environmental benefits into economic or efficiency terms. They are given due consideration in their own right. The next decade or so would witness a shift in the Commission's attitude toward environmental protection to a more circumspect approach.

There was no mention of environmental benefits in the entire 2004 then-Article 81(3) at all. Any discussion of environmental benefits was couched in economic terms, presented in the form of better production efficiency and more efficient allocation of resources. The 2011 Horizontal Cooperation Agreement Guidelines eliminated the specific section on environmental agreements that had existed in the previous guidelines. Instead, these agreements were discussed in the R&D and standard setting chapters. The *CECED* decision was also reinterpreted in economic terms. The decision was now solely justified on the cost savings for consumers. Reference to the reduction in carbon emission that had featured in the original decision was all but gone.

With the signing of the Paris Climate Agreement in 2015 and the announcement of the European Green Deal in 2019, things began to change. The EU has made combating climate change one of its top priorities. This culminated in the 2023 Horizontal Cooperation

Agreement Guidelines, which give much greater prominence to sustainability agreements.

GUIDELINES ON THE APPLICABILITY OF ARTICLE 101 OF THE TREATY ON THE FUNCTIONING OF THE EUROPEAN UNION TO HORIZONTAL COOPERATION AGREEMENTS

(2023/C 259/01)

532 Where sustainability agreements negatively affect one or more parameters of competition, they have to be assessed under Article 101(1).

533 Where a cooperation agreement between competitors (whether or not it is covered by any of the preceding Chapters of these Guidelines) pursues a sustainability objective, this must be taken into account for the purpose of determining whether the agreement restricts competition by object within the meaning of Article 101(1).

534 Where the parties to an agreement substantiate that the main object of an agreement is the pursuit of a sustainability objective, and where this casts reasonable doubt on whether the agreement reveals by its very nature, having regard to the content of its provisions, its objectives, and the economic and legal context, a sufficient degree of harm to competition to be considered a by object restriction, the agreement's effects on competition will have to be assessed. This is not the case where the agreement is used to disguise a by object restriction of competition such as price fixing, market sharing or customer allocation, or limitation of output or innovation.

535 Any effects assessment is carried out according to the principles set out in Section 1.2.5 and in the Sections on 'Restrictive effects on competition' of the preceding Chapter of these Guidelines corresponding to the particular type of horizontal agreement. The following factors should in particular be taken into account when assessing the effects of a sustainability agreement: the market power of the parties participating in the agreement; the degree to which the agreement limits the decision-making independence of the parties in relation to the main parameters of competition; the market coverage of the agreement; the extent to which commercially sensitive information is exchanged in the context of the agreement; and whether the agreement results in an appreciable increase in price or an appreciable reduction in output, variety, quality or innovation.

536 Sustainability agreements that restrict competition within the meaning of Article 101(1), either by object or by effect, can still benefit from the exception provided by Article 101(3) if the parties

are able to demonstrate that the four cumulative conditions of that provision are fulfilled (see Section 9.4).

537 Sustainability standardisation agreements are a sub-category of sustainability agreements. Their compliance with Article 101 is to be assessed according to the following principles.

9.3.2.1. *Definition and characteristics*

538 In order to contribute to sustainable development, competitors may wish to agree to phase out, withdraw, or, in some cases, replace non-sustainable products (for example, plastics or fossil fuels, such as oil and coal) and processes (for example, coal-fired steel production) with sustainable ones. Competitors may also wish to agree to harmonise packaging materials in order to facilitate recycling or harmonise packaging sizes (and hence product content) to reduce waste. They may wish to agree to purchase only production inputs that have been manufactured in a sustainable manner. Similarly, they may wish to agree on certain standards to improve animal welfare (e.g. standards to provide animals with more space and better living conditions). For these purposes, competitors may agree to adopt and comply with certain sustainability standards. In this Chapter, such agreements are referred to as 'sustainability standardisation agreements' or 'sustainability standards'. However, for the purposes of these Guidelines, agreements between competitors that limit the participating undertakings' output of the products concerned by the agreement do not qualify as sustainability standardisation agreements.

539 Sustainability standardisation agreements are used to specify requirements that producers, processors, distributors, retailers or service providers in a supply chain have to meet in relation to a wide range of sustainability metrics, such as the environmental impacts of production. Sustainability standardisation agreements usually provide rules, guidelines or characteristics for products and processes in relation to such sustainability metrics and are sometimes referred to as sustainability systems. They are often private initiatives and can range from codes of conduct adopted by undertakings, to standards driven by civil society organisations and multi-stakeholder initiatives that involve undertakings across the value chain. These Guidelines only cover sustainability standards developed by competitors or in which competitors participate, including quality marks or labels.

540 Sustainability standardisation agreements have similarities with the standardisation agreements addressed in Chapter 7, and the guidance provided in that Chapter contains further explanations of some of the conditions set out in Section 9.3.2.4. However,

sustainability standardisation agreements also have specific features.

541 First, the adoption of a sustainability standard may lead to the creation of a label, logo or brand name for products that meet certain minimum requirements. The use of such labels, logos or brand names in principle obliges the adopters to comply with those requirements and if they cease to do so, they lose the right to use the label, logo or brand name.

542 Second, the cost of adhering to and complying with a sustainability standard can be high, particularly if this requires changes to existing production or distribution processes. Therefore, adhering to a sustainability standard may lead to an increase in production or distribution costs and consequently to an increase in the price of the products sold by the parties.

543 Third, unlike technical standards, which ensure interoperability and encourage competition between technologies developed by different undertakings in the standard development process, questions of interoperability and compatibility between technologies are generally less relevant for sustainability standards.

544 Fourth, many sustainability standards are process-, management- or performance-based. This means that, unlike many technical standards, sustainability standards often simply specify a goal to be met, without imposing a specific technology or production method to achieve that goal. Adopters of such sustainability standards may commit to the target but remain free to decide on the use of a particular technology or production method to attain the target.

9.3.2.2. *Main competition concerns*

545 Sustainability standardisation agreements often have positive effects on competition. They may contribute to sustainable development by enabling the development of new products or markets, increasing product quality or improving conditions of supply or distribution. In particular, by providing information about sustainability matters (e.g. via labels), sustainability standards empower consumers to make informed purchase decisions and therefore play a role in the development of markets for sustainable products. Lastly, sustainability standards can also level the playing field between producers that are subject to different regulatory requirements.

546 In some circumstances, however, sustainability standards may restrict competition. This can occur in three ways in particular: through price coordination, foreclosure of alternative standards, and the exclusion of, or discrimination against certain competitors.

9.3.2.3. *Restriction of competition by object*

547 Sustainability standards that are used to disguise price fixing, market or customer allocation, limitations of output or limitations of quality or innovation restrict competition by object.

548 In particular, an agreement between competitors on how to pass on to customers increased costs resulting from the adoption of a sustainability standard in the form of increased sale prices or to fix the prices of products incorporating the standard restricts competition by object. Similarly, an agreement between the parties to a sustainability standard to put pressure directly on competing third parties to refrain from marketing products that do not comply with the standard restricts competition by object. The same applies to agreements between competitors to limit technological development to the minimum sustainability standards required by law, instead of cooperating to achieve more ambitious environmental goals.

9.3.2.4. *Restrictive effects on competition*

(a) *Soft safe harbour*

549 Sustainability standardisation agreements are unlikely to produce appreciable negative effects on competition as long as the following six cumulative conditions are met:

First, the procedure for developing the sustainability standard must be transparent, and all interested competitors must be able to participate in the process leading to the selection of the standard.

Second, the sustainability standard must not impose on undertakings that do not wish to participate in the standard any direct or indirect obligation to comply with the standard.

Third, in order to ensure compliance with the standard, binding requirements can be imposed on the participating undertakings, but they must remain free to apply higher sustainability standards.

Fourth, the parties to the sustainability standard must not exchange commercially sensitive information that is not objectively necessary and proportionate for the development, implementation, adoption or modification of the standard.

Fifth, effective and non-discriminatory access to the outcome of the standard-setting process must be ensured.

This includes allowing effective and non-discriminatory access to the requirements and conditions for using the agreed label, logo or brand name, and allowing undertakings that have not participated in the process of developing the standard to adopt the standard at a later stage.

Sixth, the sustainability standard must satisfy at least one of the following two conditions:

(a) The standard must not lead to a significant increase in the price or a significant reduction in the quality of the products concerned;

(b) The combined market share of the participating undertakings must not exceed 20 % on any relevant market affected by the standard.

550 These conditions ensure that the sustainability standard does not lead to an appreciable restriction of competition (for example, by eliminating less expensive product variants from the market). Moreover, the conditions ensure that the standard does not foreclose alternative standards, or exclude or discriminate against other undertakings, and they ensure effective access to the standard. The condition not to exchange unnecessary commercially sensitive information ensures that information exchanges are limited to what is necessary and proportionate to the standard-setting procedure and that they are not used to facilitate collusion or restrict competition between the parties.

551 As mentioned in paragraph 542, sustainability standards often lead to price increases. However, where the standard is adopted by undertakings representing a significant share of the market, it may allow undertakings to preserve the previous price level or to apply only an insignificant price increase. This will be particularly relevant where the product covered by the sustainability standard represents only a small input cost for the product.

552 Failure to comply with one or more of the conditions of the soft safe harbour does not create a presumption that the sustainability standardisation agreement restricts competition within the meaning of Article 101(1). However, if one or more of these conditions are not met, it is necessary to carry out an individual assessment of the agreement under Article 101. There are different models for standard setting, and undertakings are free to agree rules and procedures that do not infringe the competition rules, even though they may differ from those described in paragraph 549 above.

553 A sustainability standardisation agreement is more likely to promote the attainment of a sustainability objective if it provides for a mechanism or monitoring system to ensure that undertakings adopting the sustainability standard comply with the requirements of the standard.

(b) *Assessment under Article 101(1) outside the soft safe harbour*

554 To assess the effects of sustainability standardisation agreements that do not fulfil the conditions of the soft safe harbour, the factors listed in paragraph 549 should be taken into account as well as the ability for third parties to participate in the agreement.

555 The sustainability standard may still lack appreciable anti-competitive effects because there exists sufficient competition from alternative sustainability labels or standards and/or from products produced and distributed outside any sustainability label or standard. Even if the market coverage of the sustainability standardisation agreement is significant, the constraint exerted by potential competition may still be sufficient, in particular in cases where the sustainability standardisation agreement is limited to establishing a label, leaving the participating firms free to also operate outside the label. In that case, consumers have the choice of buying products that bear the label or other products, possibly produced by the same undertakings, that do not comply with the label, and hence competition is unlikely to be restricted. In cases where a sustainability standardisation agreement is likely to lead to a significant increase in price or reduction in output, product variety, quality or innovation, the agreement may nonetheless fulfil the conditions of Article 101(3)

9.4. **Assessment of sustainability agreements under Article 101(3)**

556 A sustainability agreement that restricts competition within the meaning of Article 101(1) can benefit from the exception provided by Article 101(3) if the parties to the agreement are able to show that the four cumulative conditions of that provision are satisfied.

9.4.1. *Efficiency gains*

557 The first condition of Article 101(3) requires that the agreement contributes to improving the production or distribution of goods or contributes to promoting technical or economic progress. In essence, it requires that the agreement contributes to objective efficiencies, understood in broad terms, encompassing not only reductions in production and distribution costs but also increases in product variety and quality, improvements in production or distribution processes, and increases in innovation. It therefore allows for a broad

range of sustainability benefits resulting from the use of particular ingredients, technologies and production processes to be taken into account.

558 Examples of efficiencies that can be generated by sustainability agreements include the use of less polluting production or distribution technologies, improved conditions of production and distribution, more resilient infrastructure, better quality products. Sustainability agreements can also reduce supply chain disruptions, shorten the time it takes to bring sustainable products to the market and enable consumers to make informed purchasing decisions by facilitating the comparison of products. These efficiency gains can contribute to a resilient internal market.

559 Such efficiencies cannot simply be assumed; they must be capable of being substantiated. They also need to be objective, concrete and verifiable. For instance, if the claimed efficiency consists of a product improvement, the parties must be able to demonstrate the exact characteristics of the product improvement. If the claimed efficiency is the reduction of water contamination, the parties must be able to explain how exactly the agreement contributes to the reduction of water contamination and provide an estimate of the magnitude of the claimed benefit.

9.4.2. *Indispensability*

560 For the purpose of these Guidelines, it is appropriate to deal with the third condition of Article 101(3) (indispensability), before the second condition (the fair share for consumers). This is because the analysis of consumer fair share should not include the effects of any restrictions that do not meet the indispensability condition and that are therefore prohibited by Article 101.

561 According to the third condition of Article 101(3), the restrictive agreement must not impose restrictions of competition that are not indispensable to the attainment of the benefits generated by the agreement. To satisfy this condition, the parties must be able to demonstrate that their agreement as such, and each of the restrictions of competition that it entails, are reasonably necessary for the claimed sustainability benefits to materialise, and that there are no other economically practicable and less restrictive means of achieving those benefits.

562 In principle, each undertaking should decide for itself how to achieve sustainability benefits, and insofar as consumers value such benefits, the market will reward good decisions and sanction bad ones. Where there is demand for sustainable products, cooperation agreements are in general not indispensable for the attainment of

sustainability benefits. However, they may be indispensable in order to reach a sustainability goal in a more cost-efficient or quicker way.

563 A sustainability agreement may be indispensable in cases where the parties can show that the consumers in the relevant market find it difficult, for example due to lack of sufficient knowledge or information about the product or the consequences of its use, to objectively assess whether the benefits that they will obtain from the sustainability agreement outweigh the harm that they will suffer from the agreement and that, as a result, they overestimate the magnitude of the immediate negative effects. For example, fast-moving consumer goods manufacturers often use large packaging because consumers perceive big as better. If the manufacturers reduce the excess packaging while maintaining the same contents, consumers will not suffer any harm, however they may perceive the smaller package as a reduction in quantity (see Example 1 at paragraph 599). Similarly, consumers may not appreciate the value of future benefits in the form of improved quality or innovation where the immediate effect of the agreement is an increase in the price of the product.

564 Negative externalities or other market failures are often addressed through public policy and regulation. These public measures typically require action by all involved, in order to ensure efficient market outcomes by making citizens and undertakings responsible for the sustainability consequences of their individual choices/actions. Therefore, where EU or national law requires undertakings to comply with specific obligations that have a sustainability objective, cooperation agreements and the restrictions they entail cannot be considered to be indispensable to ensure compliance with the obligation imposed, given that the legislator has already decided that each undertaking must individually comply with the obligation in question.

565 However, even in the presence of regulation, agreements may still be indispensable for the achievement of sustainability benefits in specific situations. First, this may be the case if not all aspects of a market failure are addressed by regulation, leaving residual scope for cooperation agreements. For instance, where undertakings enter into a sustainability agreement in order to achieve a substantially higher sustainability standard than the one set by regulation. Second, cooperation agreements may be indispensable to reach the goal in a more cost-efficient way or more quickly, provided that the relevant regulation leaves room for companies to agree on this and, when doing so, they respect all the requirements of the regulation.

566 There may be other instances where, due to negative externalities or other market failures, sustainability benefits cannot be achieved through the free interplay of market forces, or can be achieved more cost-efficiently through cooperation between undertakings. For example, a sustainability agreement may be necessary—in an initial phase—to avoid free-riding on the investments required to promote a sustainable product and to provide information to consumers (overcoming the so-called 'first mover disadvantage').

567 In this context, a restrictive agreement may also be necessary to achieve economies of scale, in particular to reach a sufficient scale to cover the fixed costs of setting up, operating and monitoring a sustainability label or standard. Restrictions may also be indispensable in order to align the incentives of the parties and ensure that they concentrate their efforts on the implementation of the agreement. If the agreement obliges the parties not to operate outside the label or standard, they must be able to show why merely establishing a label or standard is not sufficient to attain the efficiencies. In general, it is sufficient that the agreement defines the sustainability standard as a common minimum standard, thereby leaving the participating undertakings free to individually apply higher sustainability standards.

539 As a general rule, the obligations imposed by sustainability agreements must not go beyond what is necessary to achieve the objective of the agreement.

9.4.3. *Pass-on to consumers*

569 The second condition of Article 101(3) requires that consumers receive a fair share of the claimed benefits. The concept of 'consumers' encompasses all direct and indirect customers of the products covered by the agreement. Consumers receive a fair share of the benefits when the benefits deriving from the agreement outweigh the harm caused by the agreement, so that the overall effect on consumers in the relevant market is at least neutral. Therefore, the sustainability benefits that result from an agreement must accrue to the consumers of the products covered by that agreement.

570 There may be instances where the competitive harm is clearly insignificant compared to the potential benefits for the consumers in the relevant market, obviating the need for a detailed assessment. Conversely, in many instances, it may be obvious either that the claimed sustainability benefits do not accrue to the consumers in the relevant market or that they would not be significant enough to compensate for the harm suffered by those consumers. However,

there may also be cases in which a detailed assessment cannot be avoided.

9.4.3.1. *Individual use value benefits*

571 Consumer benefits typically derive from the consumption or the use of the products covered by the agreement under assessment. These benefits may take the form of improved product quality or product variety resulting from qualitative efficiencies, or take the form of a price decrease as a result of cost efficiencies. Such benefits may also result from the consumption of a sustainable product in the same way as they result from the consumption of any other product. These benefits can be referred to as 'individual use value benefits', as they result from the use of the product and directly improve the consumer's experience of the product in question.

572 For example, vegetables that are cultivated using organic fertilizers may have better taste and/or be healthier for consumers than vegetables produced with non-organic fertilizers. Similarly, replacing plastic in certain products with more durable materials may increase the longevity of the products in question. In these circumstances, consumers enjoy greater quality simply by consuming the product in question. These are typical qualitative efficiencies that may be brought about by a restrictive agreement and may outweigh the harm caused by a price increase (for example, due to the agreed use of more expensive sustainable materials), or by a reduction in choice (for example, due to an agreement not to use a non-sustainable input). If the benefits are significant enough to outweigh the harm caused by the price increase or reduced choice, they will compensate the consumers harmed by the agreement and will thus fulfil the second condition of Article 101(3).

573 In the examples above, in addition to the individual use value benefits, the agreements in question may generate positive effects that are external to the consumers (positive externalities). Positive externalities are present when negative externalities, such as pollution, soil erosion, etc. are reduced. These positive externalities, which may benefit society today or in the future, may not have been possible in the absence of the restrictive agreement in question. Such positive externalities are distinct from the individual use value benefits enjoyed by the consumers in the relevant market (see Section 9.4.3.3).

574 Agreements to reduce packaging may also reduce production and distribution costs and ultimately the price of the product. For example, an agreement between competitors to supply detergent liquid in a concentrated form in smaller bottles may reduce the costs of materials, transport and storage. Similarly, agreements to share

infrastructure or distribution transport services between competitors may reduce the parties' costs and thus the price of the final product. The harm resulting from such agreements may consist in reduced choice for consumers or reduced product quality, but the benefit of the lower price may outweigh such harm. The same agreements may also have positive externalities consisting of a reduced negative impact on the environment (see Section 9.4.3.3 below).

9.4.3.2. *Individual non-use value benefits*

575 Consumer benefits from sustainability agreements may consist not only of direct benefits from the use of a sustainable product but also indirect benefits resulting from consumers' appreciation of the impact of their sustainable consumption on others. In particular, some consumers may value their consumption of a sustainable product more highly than the consumption of a non-sustainable product because the sustainable product has less negative impact on others.

576 For example, consumers may opt for a particular washing liquid not because it cleans better but because it contaminates the water less. Similarly, consumers may be willing to pay a higher price for furniture made from wood that is grown sustainably, not because of the better quality of the furniture but because they want to stop de-forestation and the loss of natural habitats. Likewise, drivers may opt to use more expensive fuel not because it is of higher quality and better for their vehicles, but because it pollutes less.

577 In these cases, the consumer's experience of the product is not directly improved. Nevertheless, consumers may be willing to pay a higher price for a sustainable product or to limit their choice of products (by not buying non-sustainable variants) in order to benefit society or future generations. Hence, indirect, non-use value benefits accrue to consumers within the relevant market via their individual valuation of the effect on others, including on non-users outside the relevant market.

578 Consumers who are willing to pay more for such products may perceive them to be of a higher quality precisely because of the benefits accruing to others. From an economic perspective, such indirect qualitative benefits are no different from the quality-enhancing benefits that increase the direct use value of a product, as discussed in Section 9.4.3.1. Such indirect, non-use value benefits can in some cases be measured by investigating consumers' willingness to pay, for instance, through customer surveys.

579 There may be a difference between what consumers declare to be their preferences and what their purchasing behaviour shows to be

their actual preferences. This may indicate that consumers' declared preferences either over-estimate or under-estimate their true preferences. To mitigate such biases, which often result from hypothetical questions in consumer surveys, such surveys should provide appropriate context. In addition, the questions posed should take into account societal norms, consumer knowledge and habits, and expectations about the behaviour of others.

580 More generally, to discharge their burden of proof under Article 101(3), the parties to an agreement have to be able to provide evidence of the actual preferences of consumers. Parties should avoid projecting their own preferences onto consumers.

581 For the purpose of assessing consumers' willingness to pay, it is not necessary to assess the willingness to pay of each and every consumer in the relevant market. It is sufficient that the assessment is based on the overall effect on consumers in the relevant market.

9.4.3.3. *Collective benefits*

582 Section 9.4.3.2 refers to individual non-use value benefits that are limited to voluntary (altruistic) choices by individual consumers. However, not all negative externalities can be cured through voluntary, individual consumer actions. As the sustainability impact from individual consumption accrues not necessarily to the consuming individual but to a larger group, a joint initiative, such as a cooperation agreement, may be needed to internalise negative externalities and bring about sustainability benefits for a wider section of society. For example, consumers may be unwilling to pay a higher price for a product produced with a green but costly technology. To ensure that the benefits derived from the use of that technology materialise, an agreement to phase out the polluting technology may be necessary. These benefits are referred to as 'collective benefits', as they occur irrespective of the consumers' individual appreciation of the product and accrue to a wider section of society than just consumers in the relevant market.

583 Although the weighing of the positive and negative effects of the restrictive agreements is normally done within the relevant market to which the agreement relates, where two markets are related, efficiencies generated on separate markets can be taken into account, provided that the group of consumers that is affected by the restriction and that benefits from the efficiencies is substantially the same.

584 By analogy, where consumers in the relevant market substantially overlap with, or form part of the group of beneficiaries outside the relevant market, the collective benefits to the consumers

in the relevant market that occur outside that market can be taken into account if they are significant enough to compensate the consumers in the relevant market for the harm that they suffer.

585 For example, drivers purchasing less polluting fuel are also citizens who would benefit from cleaner air, if less polluting fuel were used. To the extent that a substantial overlap of consumers (the drivers in this example) and the wider beneficiaries (citizens) can be established, the sustainability benefits of cleaner air can be taken into account, provided that they compensate the consumers in the relevant market for the harm suffered. Conversely, consumers may buy clothing made of sustainable cotton that reduces the use of fertilisers and water on the land where the cotton is cultivated. Such environmental benefits could in principle be taken into account as collective benefits. However, in this case there is unlikely to be any substantial overlap between the consumers of the clothing and the beneficiaries of the environmental benefits, as these occur only in the area where the cotton is grown. Therefore, it is unlikely that these collective benefits would accrue to the consumers in the relevant market. They could therefore only be taken into account if and to the extent that consumers of the clothing are willing to pay more for clothing that is made of sustainably grown cotton (individual non-value benefit, see Section 9.4.3.2).

586 For collective benefits to materialise, the market coverage of the agreement will often need to be significant. If, for example, only two out of ten washing machine producers agree to abandon their more polluting models, then it is unlikely that the agreement will be able to prevent free-riding (by washing machine producers continuing to offer more polluting models) and hence will be unlikely to sufficiently reduce pollution, since self-interested consumers could switch to polluting models produced by the remaining suppliers.

587 For collective benefits to be taken into account, the parties to the agreement must be able to:

(a) describe clearly the claimed benefits and provide evidence that they have already occurred or are likely to occur;

(b) define clearly the beneficiaries;

(c) demonstrate that the consumers in the relevant market substantially overlap with the beneficiaries or form part of them; and

(d) demonstrate that the share of the collective benefits that accrues to the consumers in the relevant market, possibly together with individual use and non-use value benefits accruing to those consumers, outweighs the harm suffered by those consumers as a result of the restriction.

588 Evidence for collective benefits contained in public authorities' reports or in reports prepared by recognized academic organisations may be of particular value for this assessment.

589 Where there is no available data that allows for a quantitative analysis of the benefits of the agreement, other evidence may be considered, provided that it shows a clearly identifiable positive impact on consumers in the relevant market, not a marginal one. As there is currently little experience with measuring and quantifying collective benefits, the Commission aims to provide more guidance on this issue when it has gained sufficient experience of dealing with concrete cases, which may enable it to develop methodologies of assessment.

9.4.3.4. *Any or all types of benefits*

590 Parties to sustainability agreements may rely on any or all of the three types of consumer benefits to justify their agreement under Article 101(3). The choice of benefits relied upon may depend on the facts of the case and the robustness of the available evidence. In some cases, demonstrating only individual use value benefits may be enough to satisfy the conditions of Article 101(3). In other cases, evidence of individual non-use value benefits or of collective benefits may suffice. And in some cases the parties may be able to show a combination of two or all three types of benefits.

591 In some cases a certain period of time may be needed before the benefits materialise. Until such time, the agreement may have only negative effects. The fact that pass-on to consumers occurs with a certain time lag does not in itself exclude the application of Article 101(3). However, the greater the time lag, the greater must be the efficiencies to compensate also for the loss to consumers during the period preceding the pass-on. In making this assessment, the value of future benefits must be appropriately discounted.

9.4.4. *No elimination of competition*

592 According to the fourth condition of Article 101(3), the agreement must not allow the parties the possibility to eliminate competition in respect of a substantial part of the products in question. In essence, this condition ensures that there remains a degree of residual competition on the relevant market(s), regardless of the extent of the benefits.

593 This last condition may be satisfied even if the agreement restricting competition covers the entire industry, as long as the

parties to the agreement continue to compete vigorously on at least one important parameter of competition. For instance, if the agreement eliminates competition on quality or variety, but price is also an important parameter of competition in the industry concerned, and prices are not restricted, this condition may still be fulfilled.

594 Moreover, if competitors compete with a range of differentiated products, all in the same relevant market, the elimination of competition for one or more of the variants of the product does not necessarily mean that competition in the relevant market is eliminated.

595 Similarly, if competitors decide not to use a particular polluting technology or a particular non-sustainable ingredient in the production of their products, competition will not be eliminated if they continue to compete on the price and/or quality of the final product.

596 Finally, the elimination of competition for a limited period of time, where this has no impact on the development of competition after that period elapses, is not an obstacle to meeting this condition. For example, an agreement between competitors to temporarily limit the production of one variant of a product, containing a non-sustainable ingredient, in order to introduce to the market a sustainable substitute for the product, with the aim of raising consumer awareness about the characteristics of the new product, will, in general, fulfil the last condition of Article 101(3).

9.5. Involvement of public authorities

597 The involvement of national or local public authorities in the process of conclusion of sustainability agreements, or knowledge by those authorities of the existence of such agreements, does not in itself preclude the application of Article 101 to such agreements. Similarly, if acts by public authorities merely encourage, or make it easier for undertakings to engage in anti-competitive sustainability agreements, without depriving undertakings of their autonomy, such agreements remain subject to Article 101.

598 However, the parties to an anti-competitive sustainability agreement will not be liable under Article 101 if they have been compelled or required by public authorities to conclude the agreement or where the public authorities reinforce the effect of the agreement.

Notes and Questions

1. Did the 2023 Guidelines come up with a credible way to balance in a quantitative manner diffuse and distant sustainability benefits with immediate and concrete consumer harm? If this problem is insurmountable, what are the options for competition authorities? What about the soft safe harbor approach in the Guidelines? It arguably amounts to a qualitative balancing approach, whereby if a benefit falls within a certain category and is produced by a sustainability that meets certain criteria, it is deemed to outweigh possible consumer harm. This is tantamount to the Commission deciding that balancing is not necessary for these standards.

2. For agreements that do not benefit from the soft safe harbor and require individual assessments, the Commission requires the benefits to offset the costs such that there is net neutrality under rubric of the fair share criterion for consumers. Is this a realistic requirement? Is the impracticality of this requirement exacerbated by the fact that the Guidelines explicitly recognize collective sustainability benefits such as the elimination of greenhouse gases?

3. The EU is not the only jurisdiction that has promulgated guidelines on sustainability agreements. The Japan Fair Trade Commission released its Guidelines Concerning Activities of Enterprises, etc. Toward the Realization of a Green Society under the Antimonopoly Act on April 24, 2024. In the same year, the Korea Fair Trade Commission ("KFTC") issued its Guidelines for Self-Compliance with the Fair Trade Law regarding Environmental Sustainability on December 5, 2024.

4. The KFTC Guidelines apply to agreements that pursue sustainability benefits in the form of reduction in carbon emissions, waste minimization, pollution mitigation, and promotion of recycling. The general principle is that the efficiency enhancing effects from sustainability benefits must outweigh the consumer harm for the agreement to be upheld. By way of example, the Guidelines explain that for a voluntary standard to be deemed to raise few competitive concerns, it must be certain requirements, including: (1) there is no exchange of competitively sensitive information such as price; (2) the adoption process must be transparent and open to all to participate; (3) standard certification must be available to non-participants in the standard setting activity; (4) compliance is voluntary; (5) application of the standard is uniform and non-discriminatory; (6) competing standards are not excluded; and (7) the increase in cost from standard compliance does not constitute a significant proportion of the total cost of the product or service.

5. To learn more about this increasingly important area of law, see Julian Nowag, Environmental Integration in Competition and Free-

Movement Laws (2017); Julian Nowag (ed.), Research Handbook on Sustainability and Competition Law (2024)

J. PAY-FOR-DELAY SETTLEMENTS IN THE PHARMACEUTICAL INDUSTRY

Many complex issues arise at the intersection of competition law and intellectual property law—patent law in particular, although copyright, trademark, and trade secrecy law are sometimes implicated as well. An important current example, which has received intensive scrutiny in various jurisdictions, involves allegedly collusive "pay-for-delay" agreements between branded and generic pharmaceutical companies that keep the generic off the market for some period of time.

The legal issues are complicated, involving the interaction of patent law, food and drug regulatory law, and antitrust law, but the basic antitrust theory is simple. When a generic enters the market, the branded firm loses large sums of money in two ways. First, it loses many sales to the generic rival. Second, the price of the generic drug will be significantly lower than the price of the branded drug, so the branded firm may have to sell its own drugs at a significantly lower price.[1] The branded firm would obviously rather avoid generic competition, so if it could lawfully pay the generic not to enter, it would have a clear incentive to do so. The generic would be happy not to enter if the payment from the branded firm were greater than the profits the generic would make by entering. Since the branded firm would make monopoly profits if it did not face competition and lose those profits if it did, both the branded and generic firm could be better off if the branded firms shared some of its monopoly profits with the generic in exchange for the generic's agreement not to enter. Consumers, of course, would lose.

On the other hand, if the branded company has valid patent rights, the generic arguably should not be in the market and the branded company's monopoly profits are the unavoidable cost of stimulating innovation. Also, the law generally wants to encourage settlements and avoid protracted and costly litigation. Finally, there is some literature suggesting that "pay for delay" settlements may actually encourage more generic entry in the long run.

---

1 This is a simplification of the actual economics. Upon generic entry, the price of the branded drug may actually increase, since only brand-sensitive buyers, who have less elastic demand, may continue to buy the branded version. So, upon generic entry, many branded firms begin to offer an "authorized generic" that competes with their own branded drug.

Beginning in 2008, the European Commission began to take an active interest in pay-for-delay agreements, issuing a series of reports on the practice and actively monitoring any pay-for-delay agreements affecting the European market. In 2010, the Commission opened an investigation of the Danish pharmaceutical firm Lundbeck for allegedly paying rival generic companies to delay production of generic versions of the anti-depressant medication Citalopram. In 2012, it issued a Statement of Objections, eventually resulting in a €93.8 million fine on Lundbeck and fines totaling €52.2 million against several generic manufacturers.

While the *Lundbeck* case was being appealed to the General Court, in 2013 and 2014, the Commission fined companies in two other pay-for-delay investigations—one concerning fentanyl, a pain-killer and the other concerning perindopril, a cardiovascular medicine. The Fentanyl Decision was not appealed. Several appeals concerning the perindopril decision (*Servier*) are pending before the General Court as of this writing. They are likely to be influenced by the General Court's decision in *Lundbeck,* rendered on September 8, 2016.

H. LUNDBECK A/S

Case C–591/16 P, ECLI:EU:C:2021:243 (Court of Justice of the European Union 2021)

[Citalopram is a blockbuster antidepressant medicine and was Lundbeck's best-selling product at the relevant time. After Lundbeck's underlying patent for the citalopram molecule expired, it only held a number of related process patents which provided a more limited protection. Producers of cheaper, generic versions of citalopram were preparing for market entry. One of them had actually started selling its own generic version of citalopram and several other producers had made serious preparations to do so. Prices of generic citalopram dropped on average by 90% in the UK compared to Lundbeck's previous price level following wide-spread generic market entry.

In 2002, the generic producers agreed with Lundbeck not to enter the market in return for substantial payments and other inducements from Lundbeck amounting to tens of millions of euros. The Commission found particularly significant internal documents referring to a "club" being formed and "a pile of $$$" to be shared among the participants. It held these pay-for-delay agreements to be restrictions of competition by object within the meaning of Article 101(1) of the TFEU. The Commission's decision was upheld by the General Court. Lundbeck appealed the General Court's decision to the European Court of Justice].

52 If the conduct of undertakings is to be subject to the prohibition in principle laid down in Article 101(1) TFEU, that conduct must not only reveal the existence of coordination between them—in other words, an agreement between undertakings, a decision by an association of undertakings or a concerted practice—but that coordination must also have a negative and appreciable effect on competition within the internal market [citation omitted].

53 The latter requirement means, with respect to horizontal cooperation agreements entered into by undertakings that operate at the same level of the production or distribution chain, that the coordination involves undertakings who are in competition with each other, if not in reality, then at least potentially [citation omitted].

* * *

54 In order to assess whether an undertaking that is not present in a market is a potential competitor of one or more other undertakings that are already present in that market, it must be determined whether there are real and concrete possibilities of the former joining that market and competing with one or more of the latter [citation omitted].

55 When the agreements in question are ones which have the effect of temporarily keeping several undertakings outside a market, such as the agreements at issue, it must be determined, having regard to the structure of the market and the economic and legal context within which it operates, whether there would have existed, in the absence of those agreements, real and concrete possibilities for those undertakings to enter that market and compete with the undertakings established in that market [citation omitted].

56 Specifically, with regard to such agreements occurring in the context of the opening of the market, for a medicine containing an active ingredient that has recently entered the public domain, to the manufacturers of generic medicines, it should be established, by taking due account of the regulatory constraints that are characteristic of the medicine sector and of the intellectual property rights and, in particular, the patents held by the manufacturers of originator medicines relating to one or more processes for the manufacture of an active ingredient that is in the public domain [citation omitted], whether the manufacturer of generic medicines has in fact a firm intention and an inherent ability to enter the market, and does not meet barriers to entry that are insurmountable [citation omitted].

57 In order to do so, it is necessary to assess, first, whether, at the time when those agreements were concluded, that manufacturer had taken sufficient preparatory steps to enable it to enter the market

concerned within such a period of time as would impose competitive pressure on the manufacturer of originator medicines. Second, it must be determined that the market entry of such a manufacturer of generic medicines does not meet barriers to entry that are insurmountable [citation omitted]. Furthermore, a finding of potential competition between a manufacturer of generic medicines and a manufacturer of originator medicines can be confirmed by additional factors, such as the conclusion of an agreement between them at a time when the former was not present on the market concerned [citation omitted].

58 Specifically, with regard to the assessment of whether there are barriers to entry into the market concerned which are insurmountable, the Court has held that the existence of a patent which protects the manufacturing process of an active ingredient that is in the public domain cannot, as such, be regarded as such an insurmountable barrier, regardless of the presumption of validity attached to that patent, since that presumption sheds no light, for the purposes of applying Articles 101 and 102 TFEU, on the outcome of any dispute in relation to the validity of that patent [citation omitted].

59 Consequently, the existence of such a patent does not, as such, mean that a manufacturer of generic medicines who has in fact a firm intention and an inherent ability to enter the market, and who, by the steps taken, shows a readiness to challenge the validity of that patent and to take the risk, upon entering the market, of being subject to infringement proceedings brought by the patent holder, cannot be characterised as a 'potential competitor' of the manufacturer of originator medicines concerned [citation omitted].

60 Furthermore, the Court has also held that it is not for the competition authority concerned to carry out a review of the strength of the patent at issue or of the probability of a dispute between the patent holder and a manufacturer of generic medicines being brought to an end with a finding that that patent is valid and has been infringed [citation omitted].

61 It follows that, in the present case, and contrary to what Lundbeck maintains, the General Court did not make any error of law and, in particular, did not infringe either the presumption of validity attached, inter alia, to Lundbeck's new process patents or the rules applicable to the burden of proof in respect of the practices referred to in Article 101 TFEU, when it ruled, in essence, in paragraphs 117 to 132, 157 to 167 and 195 of the judgment under appeal that it was not for the Commission to provide definite proof that the citalopram which the manufacturers of generic medicines intended to market

did not infringe Lundbeck's new process patents, and that the fact that Lundbeck held such patents did not preclude a finding that there was potential competition between Lundbeck and those manufacturers.

62 The General Court, taking due account, in paragraphs 117, 119 and 129 of the judgment under appeal, of the fundamental characteristics both of the patents and of the competitive relationships specific to the relevant market as well as the situation in the present case in which, first, Lundbeck's original patents, relating to both the citalopram API and the alkylation and cyanation production processes, had expired and, second, there were other processes for the production of generic citalopram which were not found to infringe other Lundbeck patents, held, in paragraph 124 of that judgment, that the Commission had not erred in considering that Lundbeck's new process patents did not necessarily constitute insurmountable barriers for the manufacturers of generic medicines, which were both willing and ready to enter the citalopram market, and which had already made considerable investments to that end at the time the agreements at issue were concluded.

63 In addition, in paragraph 159 of the same judgment, the General Court was fully entitled to find that, unless it were to be held that there is no distinction between actual and potential competition, it is not necessary to demonstrate with certainty that the manufacturers of generic medicines would have entered the market and that that entry would inevitably have been successful, but only that those manufacturers had real and concrete possibilities in that respect.

64 Furthermore, the conclusion that the General Court did not err in finding that the manufacturers of generic medicines were potential competitors of Lundbeck is not called into question by the 2014 Guidelines, in particular point 29 thereof. First, that point applies exclusively to technology transfer agreements, to which the agreements at issue cannot be compared. Second, it is clear from that point that the Commission's finding that there is no competitive relationship between undertakings that find themselves in a blocking position arising from an exclusive technology right is valid only 'in principle' and is therefore subject to exceptions, which is also alluded to in that same point when it mentions situations in which 'there is no certainty whether a particular technology right is valid and infringed'.

65 Therefore, the first part of the fourth ground of appeal must be rejected as being unfounded. * * *

81 Finally, with regard to the fourth to seventh parts of the fourth ground, in which Lundbeck submits that the General Court wrongly

held that it was at least a potential competitor of Merck (GUK) in the United Kingdom and other EEA countries, a potential competitor of Arrow in the United Kingdom and Denmark and a potential competitor of Alpharma and Ranbaxy in the EEA, it should be noted that those allegations are inadmissible in part, as was found in paragraphs 49 and 50 of the present judgment, since they seek to obtain a re-examination by the Court of Justice of all or part of the evidence assessed by the General Court.

82 To the extent that they do not seek to do so, those allegations by Lundbeck, first, repeat the criticisms of methodology which were held to be unfounded in the context of the first to third parts of the present ground, and, second, seek to criticise, in essence, the General Court for having found there to be potential competition, or at least potential competition, between Lundbeck and the manufacturers of generic medicines, even though the latter did not have an MA for their respective generic medicines when the agreements at issue were concluded.

83 In that respect, although it is indeed necessary for a manufacturer of generic medicines to hold a valid MA when it enters the market and it can, therefore, be found that there is currently competition between that manufacturer of generic medicines and a manufacturer of originator medicines that correspond to those generic medicines only if the manufacturer of generic medicines does hold a valid MA, it nevertheless remains the case that the fact that a manufacturer of generic medicines does not hold such an MA when it concludes an agreement with a manufacturer of originator medicines cannot, as Lundbeck maintains, preclude, as such, all potential competition between those two manufacturers of medicines.

84 As was pointed out, in essence, in paragraph 57 of the present judgment, in the absence of an insurmountable barrier to market entry, the existence of potential competition between a manufacturer of generic medicines and a manufacturer of originator medicines presupposes only that the manufacturer of generic medicines has taken sufficient preparatory steps to enable it to enter the market concerned within a period of time capable of putting competitive pressure on the manufacturer of originator medicines, it being of no relevance whether those steps will in fact be finalised in due time or will be successful, as the General Court rightly points out in paragraphs 313 and 314 of the judgment under appeal.

85 Indeed, the Court has previously had the opportunity to find, to that effect, that, in the pharmaceutical sector, potential competition may be exerted before the expiry of a compound patent protecting an originator medicine, since the manufacturers of generic medicines

want to be ready to enter the market as soon as that patent expires (judgment of 30 January 2020, *Generics (UK) and Others*, C–307/18, EU:C:2020:52, paragraph 51).

86 Such preparatory steps which make it possible to establish the firm intention and inherent ability of a manufacturer of generic medicines to enter the market for a medicine containing an active ingredient that is in the public domain include, inter alia, steps taken to put it in a position to obtain the MAs or equivalent authorisations necessary for the marketing of its generic medicine, which, the General Court established, in the present case, in paragraphs 171 to 179, 230, 231, 246, 249, 269, 290 and 312 to 326 of the judgment under appeal, had been taken by each of the manufacturers of generic medicines concerned and were sufficient to exert competitive pressure on Lundbeck (see, by analogy, judgment of 30 January 2020, *Generics (UK) and Others*, C–307/18, EU:C:2020:52, paragraph 134).

87 Consequently, the General Court did not err in law when it found, in paragraph 171 of the judgment under appeal, that the steps taken by each of the manufacturers of generic medicines concerned with a view to obtaining an MA for the medicines concerned constituted relevant indications in establishing the existence of potential competition between them and Lundbeck.

88 In addition, the findings that there was potential competition between Lundbeck and each of the manufacturers of generic medicines at issue are based on a consistent body of evidence (see, to that effect, judgment of 30 January 2020, *Generics (UK) and Others*, C–307/18, EU:C:2020:52, paragraph 44) which reflect the fact that the General Court took into consideration not only the real and concrete possibilities for each of those manufacturers to obtain MAs or equivalent authorisations but also, as is apparent from paragraph 181 of the judgment under appeal, a number of factors relating to the specific situation of each manufacturer of generic medicines at the time when the agreements at issue were concluded and the fact that Lundbeck entered into agreements with manufacturers of generic medicines that were not yet present on the market (see, to that effect, judgment of 30 January 2020, *Generics (UK) and Others*, C–307/18, EU:C:2020:52, paragraphs 55 to 57). * * *

110 As a preliminary point, it should be noted that Lundbeck's criticisms are of two kinds: the first, second and fourth parts of the first ground challenge the characterisation of the agreements at issue as 'restrictions by object', and the third part of that ground challenges the methodology used to arrive at that conclusion and, specifically, the failure of the General Court to examine the 'counterfactual scenario'.

[111] It is therefore appropriate to start by examining the first, second and fourth parts of the first ground, taken together, and then to move on to examine the third part of that ground.

[112] As regards, in the first place, the first, second and fourth parts of the first ground, the Court of Justice has previously held, as the General Court pointed out in paragraph 343 of the judgment under appeal, that the concept of restriction of competition 'by object' must be interpreted strictly and can be applied only to some agreements between undertakings which reveal, in themselves and having regard to the content of their provisions, their objectives, and the economic and legal context of which they form part, a sufficient degree of harm to competition for the view to be taken that it is not necessary to assess their effects, since some forms of coordination between undertakings can be regarded, by their very nature, as being harmful to the proper functioning of normal competition (judgment of 30 January 2020, *Generics (UK) and Others*, C–307/18, EU:C:2020:52, paragraph 67 and the case-law cited).

[113] With regard to similar settlement agreements that cover disputes over a process patent for the manufacture of an active ingredient that is in the public domain which have been concluded between a manufacturer of originator medicines and several manufacturers of generic medicines and have the effect of delaying the market entry of generic medicines in exchange for monetary or non-monetary transfers of value from the former to the latter, the Court of Justice has held that such agreements cannot be considered to be 'restrictions by object' in all cases for the purpose of Article 101(1) TFEU (judgment of 30 January 2020, *Generics (UK) and Others*, C–307/18, EU:C:2020:52, paragraphs 84 and 85.

[114] However, such characterisation as a 'restriction by object' must be adopted when it is plain from the examination of the settlement agreement concerned that the transfers of value provided for by it cannot have any explanation other than the commercial interest of both the holder of the patent at issue and the party allegedly infringing the patent not to engage in competition on the merits, since agreements whereby competitors deliberately substitute practical cooperation between them for the risks of competition can clearly be characterised as 'restrictions by object' (see, to that effect, judgment of 30 January 2020, *Generics (UK) and Others*, C–307/18, EU:C:2020:52, paragraphs 83 and 87).

[115] For the purpose of that examination, it is appropriate to assess on a case-by-case basis whether the net gain of the transfers of value from the manufacturer of originator medicines to the manufacturer of generic medicines was sufficiently significant actually to act as an

incentive to the manufacturer of generic medicines to refrain from entering the market concerned and, consequently, not to compete on the merits with the manufacturer of originator medicines; however, there is no requirement that the net gain should necessarily be greater than the profits which that manufacturer of generic medicines would have made if it had been successful in the patent proceedings (see, to that effect, judgment of 30 January 2020, *Generics (UK) and Others*, C–307/18, EU:C:2020:52, paragraphs 93 and 94).

116 In the present case, it is apparent from the judgment under appeal that the effects of the agreements at issue were to keep the manufacturers of generic medicines outside the markets concerned and to lead one of them—namely Merck (GUK)—to stop supplying a reseller operating on the Swedish market with the generic medicines concerned and to exit the UK market, as is apparent from paragraph 131 of the judgment under appeal.

117 In addition, paragraphs 361 to 363 and paragraph 366 of the judgment under appeal, which are not contested by Lundbeck in the context of its appeal, highlight, first, the fact that the parties to the agreements at issue were, prior to the conclusion of those agreements, in dispute over whether Lundbeck's new process patents were sufficiently strong to prevent the market entry of generic citalopram which means that those patents could not have constituted the decisive basis of the commitment by the manufacturers of generic medicines not to enter the market. Second, it is also apparent from those paragraphs that Lundbeck does not dispute that the amounts which it paid to those manufacturers could have been calculated by taking into consideration the profit or turnover which the latter expected to make during the term of the agreements at issue if they had entered the market. Third, those paragraphs also indicate that the evidence relating to the period preceding the conclusion of the agreements at issue shows that the manufacturers of generic medicines had made considerable efforts to prepare for their market entry and that they did not intend to desist from those efforts on account of Lundbeck's new process patents and, consequently, that it is principally the size of the reverse payments to the manufacturers of generic medicines which had induced them to accept the limitations governing their behaviour.

118 In the light of those findings of fact, and there being no need to determine whether the General Court was entitled to treat the agreements at issue, in paragraphs 435 and 476 of the judgment under appeal, as market exclusion agreements or even as market-sharing agreements, it concluded, without committing any error of law, that the agreements at issue should be characterised as

'restrictions by object' for the purpose of Article 101(1) TFEU, especially since Lundbeck has not in any way argued, in particular in its reply to the question to be answered in writing of 6 February 2020, that the transfers of value which are associated with the agreements at issue could be justified by the existence of possible consideration or proven and legitimate commitments by one or other of the manufacturers of generic medicines to refrain from taking action.

119 That conclusion cannot be called into question by the arguments put forward by Lundbeck.

The General Court in the *Lundbeck case* relied on the US Supreme Court's decision in FTC v. Actavis, 570 U.S. 136 (2013), in holding that the structure of a reverse payment settlement—particularly the presence of a large and otherwise unexplained reverse payment—could be instructive in determining whether the reverse payment was intended to quash competition or instead served some legitimate purpose. *Actavis* resolved a longstanding dispute in the US as to the appropriate treatment of reverse payment settlements. A few lower courts viewed such agreements as akin to naked market division agreements and held them *per se* illegal under Section 1 of the Sherman Act. Another line of cases, which before *Actavis* acquired majority status in the lower courts, held pay-for-delay settlements lawful so long as they fell within the exclusionary scope of the patent. In 2013, the US Supreme Court finally weighed into the controversy, rejecting both per se illegality and the scope of the patent test and holding reverse payment settlements subject to rule of reason analysis. The Court held:

> In sum, a reverse payment, where large and unjustified, can bring with it the risk of significant anticompetitive effects; one who makes such a payment may be unable to explain and to justify it; such a firm or individual may well possess market power derived from the patent; a court, by examining the size of the payment, may well be able to assess its likely anticompetitive effects along with its potential justifications without litigating the validity of the patent; and parties may well find ways to settle patent disputes without the use of reverse payments.

Despite holding rule of reason analysis applicable, the Court provided relatively few signals as to how such analysis should be conducted. For example, although suggesting that courts need not conduct a detailed review of the strength of the branded firm's patent infringement claim that precipitated the settlement, the Court recognized that some direct or indirect inquiry into "the patent's weakness" might be required. In light of *Actavis,* lower courts are sorting through the methodological questions that both per se illegality and the scope of the patent test had avoided.

Notes and Questions

1. *Lundbeck* and *Actavis* differ insofar as *Lundbeck* treats pay-for-delay settlements as restrictions of competition "by object," whereas *Actavis* holds them subject to rule of reason analysis. Despite these apparent differences in juridical classification, one might ask whether the form of the analysis differs considerably between the two opinions. Further exposition of the legal tests in coming years may tell.

2. Although certain aspects of "pay-for-delay" are jurisdiction-specific due to differing pharmaceutical regulations and patent laws, the core issue resonates around the world. In 2014, there were media reports that Competition Commission of India had opened an investigation of "pay-for-delay" patent settlements between US and India pharmaceutical companies engaged in litigation in India. Do you think that competition law can provide a general framework for addressing pay-for-delay issues, or are the issues so bound up in other facets of a jurisdiction's regulatory and economic practices that general answers are unavailing?

K. JOINT VENTURES

1. Substantive Rules and Analysis

Joint ventures ("JVs"), like mergers, raise important questions of competition law because of their tendency to create efficiencies and market power simultaneously. Imagine, for example, that two competitors create a research and development joint venture that permits the two companies to pool personnel, patents, and economic resources to create a better product. At the same time, however, the fact of the joint venture reduces competition between the two firms, and perhaps even creates market power—the power to charge a higher price. How should competition law assess the joint venture? Ordinarily, competition law analysis of joint ventures asks two sorts of questions: (1) should the joint venture be permitted at all, or should it rather be prohibited because any efficiencies are overshadowed by anticompetitive effects; and (2) assuming that the joint venture is permitted, are any restrictions it places on competition among the joint venturers more restrictive than necessary to allow the JV to function?

a. *Should the JV Be Permitted?*

Although regulators often decline to challenge *the fact* of joint ventures, preferring to challenge their structure or bylaws, in some instances joint ventures themselves are unlawful because they unduly restrict competition. In November of 2008, Yahoo! And Google were forced to abandon an advertising joint venture after the Justice Department made clear that it would challenge the joint venture as monopolistic. Then, on July 29, 2009, Yahoo! and Microsoft announced their plan to form a 10-year joint venture. Under the terms of the deal, Yahoo! licensed Microsoft its existing search engine technology but relied on Microsoft for future software development in the search engine business, even while retaining its own distinctive customer basis. Yahoo manages search-related advertising for both companies. Yahoo! keeps 88% of search and ad revenues from its own websites (subject to re-pricing after five years) and Microsoft keeps 100% of corresponding revenues from Microsoft websites.

Microsoft and Yahoo! justified their proposed joint venture as combining the forces of two struggling search engine companies to keep pace with Google, the industry leader. Google had a 65% share of the search-ad market, whereas Yahoo! and Microsoft together had only a combined 28% share. Regulators in Washington and Brussels ultimately chose not to challenge the deal, apparently finding the prospect of a Microsoft-Yahoo alliance a procompetitive counterweight to the growing power of Google.

A proposed 2010 joint venture for iron ore production in Western Australia between BHP Billiton and Rio Tinto's raised big issues around the globe. With an estimated value of approximately $116 billion, the parties estimated that the JV would generated synergies that would have helped cut costs by about $10 billion. But competition authorities in the European Commission, Australian Competition and Consumer Commission, Japan Fair Trade Commission, Korea Fair Trade Commission, and the German Bundeskartellamt all voiced concerns, leading the parties to abandon the deal.

The analysis of the Japan Fair Trade Commission ("JFTC") was typical. The JFTC notified the parties that the JV would substantially restrain competition in the field of the production and sale of lumps and fines of iron ores in the worldwide seaborne market. The JFTC applied Article 10 of the AMA. This article applies to stock acquisition and usually comes into play as to full mergers. However, once Article 10 is applied to a case, the difference between full merger and a JV is not significant because the ultimate standard, in either case, is whether the challenged activity "substantially restrains competition in the field." Like its peer authorities in Asia and Europe, the JFTC found that the joint venture would substantially restrain competition in the market for iron ore production.

Sometimes, authorities around the world differ as to whether a JV should be permitted to operate. In 2014, three of the major shipping companies—MSC, CMA CGM, and Maersk Line—entered into a long-term operational vessel sharing agreement, the so-called "P3 Alliance." The purported aim of the joint venture was to make container shipment more efficient and improve service quality for the shippers due to more frequent and reliable services. The putative joint venturers announced the following expected benefits of the collaboration:

- Operational efficiencies due to improved port productivity, network optimization and cargo consolidation
- More direct services due to more port pair connections
- Increased flexibility due to the combined capacity of P3 making it easier to increase or move capacity to meet short-term, sudden changes in demand
- Cost savings and environmental benefits

Nonetheless, the shipping companies had a history of collusive or collusive-like behavior, including making regular, simultaneous, and close to identical price increase announcements, which led to an investigation by the European Commission. Antitrust: Commission opens proceedings against container liner shipping companies, http://europa.eu/rapid/press-release_IP-13-1144_en.htm. Some observers viewed the P3 alliance as little more than a cover for collusive behavior.

After reviewing the JV, the US Maritime Commission and the European Commission decided not to challenge the arrangement. But, on June of 2014, the Chinese Ministry of Commerce ("MOFCOM") surprised many observers by informing the parties that it would oppose the JV based on merger provisions in China's Anti-Monopoly Law. The parties subsequently abandoned plans for the 3P Alliance.

Although some observers criticized MOFCOM's decision as out of step with competition law globally, the shipping trade has remained subject to antitrust concerns even in light of the 3P Alliance's failure. In 2016, the European Commission reached a settlement with the shipping industry in which the companies agreed to discontinue their practice of advance rate publication. And, in March of 2017, the United States Department of Justice announced that it had issued subpoenas to the executives of five leading container lines on apparent suspicion of collusion. Was MOFCOM correct to see the 3P Alliance as another industry measure to facilitate collusion?

b. Are the JV's Restrictions on Competition Excessive?

Even if a JV is lawful in essence, there remains the question of whether its bylaws, terms, and other contractual provisions or understandings unduly restrict competition. Many cases have been brought challenging JV practices as unnecessarily anticompetitive.

An initial juridical question concerns the mode of analysis to be applied. In the US, all activities within the scope of an otherwise lawful joint venture are subject to the rule of reason. Texaco, Inc. v. Dagher, 547 U.S. 1 (2006). But, in some cases, that begs the question of what it means for activities to be within scope of a lawful joint venture.

Take, for example, the U.S. FTC's enforcement action against Polygram and Warner Communications concerning the two music labels' agreement to jointly distribute "The Three Tenors III" in 1998. Warner had distributed Three Tenors I in 1994, and Polygram had distributed Three Tenors II in 1990. (The concerts were set to coincide with the World Cup). Warner and Polygram entered into a separate agreement to suspend, for ten weeks, advertising and discounting on the two earlier Three Tenors materials. The FTC challenged this arrangement as something akin to per se illegal. Polygram Holding, Inc. v. FTC, 416 F.3d 29 (2005). Polygram and Warner protested that the agreement to discontinue promotion of Three Tenors I and II was not a "naked" price fixing agreement but rather reasonably ancillary to the promotion of Three Tenors III, since absent that restriction, the joint venturers would have faced incentives to free ride on one another's investments in the promotion of Three Tenors III. The US Court of Appeals for the D.C. Circuit found this justification unconvincing, holding that "a restraint cannot be justified solely on the ground that it increases the profitability of the enterprise that introduces the new product, regardless whether that enterprise is a joint venture or a solo undertaking." Id. at 38.

The South African Competition Tribunal took a similar approach in 2015 when it found that two shipping companies in a joint venture, Nison Yupen Kaisha Shipping Logistics and BLG Logistics, had used to the JV to exchange competitively significant information on matters outside the scope of the JV. Acknowledging that it is "difficult to divorce the conduct of the Parties outside the Joint Venture, with their conduct within the Joint Venture," the Tribunal nonetheless found that the parties had colluded on information exchange outside the scope of the joint venture and imposed a fine of 3.5% of the JV's turnover in the prior year.

India's Competition Act approaches the analysis of restraints by joint ventures as follows. Section 3(3) of the Act states that a specified list of horizontal agreements are "presumed to have an appreciable effect on competition." The list includes those "directly or indirectly determin[ing] purchase or sale price," "limit[ing] or control[ling] production, supply, markets, technical development, investment or provision of service," "shar[ing] the market or source of production or provision of services," and "directly or indirectly result[ing] in bid rigging or collusive bidding." These descriptions literally apply to most joint ventures, therefore Section 3(3) adds the following caveat: "Provided that nothing contained in this sub-section shall apply to any agreement entered into by way of joint ventures if such agreement increases efficiency in production, supply, distribution, storage, acquisition or control of goods or provision of services." The effect of the statute is that efficiency-enhancing joint ventures are lawful.

Joint ventures sometimes raise issues of collusion (the joint venture might be a cover for a cartel or induce cartel-like behavior) and sometimes raise issue of exclusion (the joint venture anticompetitively excludes rivals). In the latter set of cases, the joint venture's activities may be analyzed under "abuse of dominance" or "abuse of joint dominance" principles in addition to or instead of restraint of trade principles. Consider, for example, the consent order entered in the Canadian *Interac* case, The Director of Investigation and Research v. Bank of Montreal, CT–85/2 (1995). Interac Association was an electronic network created by nine of Canada's leading banks. The association provided financial services to the member banks, such as shared cash dispensing (i.e., ATM) services and electronic funds transfers at point of sale outlet that allowed consumers to make purchases at participating retail outlets using Interac branded debit cards. The Canadian Competition Bureau charged the nine banks and Interac with abuses of a joint dominant position for putting in place a structure and membership criteria that discriminated against non-financial institutions, imposed excessively high fees for new members wanting to join Interac, and unnecessarily limiting the services that could be provided through the network. The Bureau and the defendants entered into a consent order whereby Interac would become available to other market participants on a non-discriminatory basis and would agree to cease engaging in a list of anticompetitive practices.

2. Procedural Rules

Should competition authorities seek to screen the thousands of horizontal agreements that will arise every year to catch those that are anticompetitive? One approach is to require that all parties to horizontal agreements file their agreements with the competition authorities for a determination whether they are anticompetitive or not. There are some obvious downsides to such an approach, illustrated by Europe's history with "block exemptions" under Article 101.

The institutional and federalism issues with the notification system are discussed in greater detail in Chapter 7, so we will provide just a brief sketch here. As previously noted, the structure of Article 101 provides a broad prohibition on competition-limiting horizontal agreements in Articles 101(1), subject to an exemption for competition and efficiency-enhancing agreements in Article 101(3). In 1962, the European Council promulgated Regulation 17, which required that agreements within the scope of now Article 101(1) had to be notified to the Commission; no Article 101(3) exemptions could be granted until notification was filed. Parties to agreements that did not infringe Article 101(1) were entitled to "negative clearance," a statement by the Commission that the agreements did not violate the Treaty.

The obvious problem with such a system is that the filing and individual review of tens of thousands of commercial contracts would clog the system. So the Commission proceeded under a "block exemption" system. The Commission issued "block exemptions" for certain categories of generally benign contractual provisions, and parties that limited themselves to these clauses were automatically exempt from the filing requirement and Article 101 liability.

Still, notification was required as to many rather routine business contracts, and by the late 1990s competition officials were worried that the notification and prior approval system was becoming too cumbersome and time-intensive to manage. The result—described in greater detail in Chapter 8—was Regulation 1/2003, printed in Appendix 2, which radically altered the procedures for regulatory review of competition-restricting agreements and granted a far greater role to the competition authorities and courts of the Member States. In a nutshell, effective May 2004, Regulation 1 abolished the notification requirement and made Article 101(3) directly effective, so that national competition authorities and courts, as well as the Commission, may decide whether agreements fulfill the requirements of Article 101(3).

A number of other jurisdictions have experimented with mandatory notification rules, often having copied the European system. Block exemptions still exist for many transactions; they have been liberalized, so that it is easier to receive their benefits.

Some jurisdictions are experimenting with a form of voluntary notification that may provide some interesting possibilities for orderly review of joint venture agreements. Take, for example, Singapore 2006 Competition Act. In addition to a pre-Regulation 1 EU-style exemption procedure, the Competition Act allows voluntary submission to the Competition Commission by parties who are concerned that their agreement could be deemed to violate Section 34 of the Competition Act, which prohibits agreements prohibiting or distorting competition. The parties may seek either "guidance" under Section 43 or "decision" under Section 44. In either case, the parties are relieved of the possibility of penalties between the date they file their petition with the Commission and the date specified in the Commission's "guidance" or "decision." The difference between guidance and decision is that in guidance cases the Commission merely specifies a view as to whether the agreement probably infringes Section 34 and in a decision case it actually makes a decision with legal effect.

The Commission's first Section 44 decision came on February 13, 2007 on an application from Qantas Airways and British Airways. Notification for Decision by Qantas Airways and British Airways of their Restated Joint Services Agreement, No. CCS 400/002/06 (Feb. 13, 2007). The parties entered into a Joint Services Agreement that provided for coordination of their business activities in relation to routing, fares, frequencies, aircraft types, production specifications, aircraft configurations, connection requirements, and other aspects of operations, sales, and marketing. The parties submitted that their joint venture was necessary for them to remain competitive on the "Kangaroo route" between Australia and Europe, via Asia or the Middle East. After extensive review of the facts, the Commission found that the agreement fell within the ambit of Section 34, as an agreement that potentially prohibited or distorted competition, but nonetheless brought about net economic benefits to Singapore and hence was "excluded from the Act." It therefore stated that it would take no action against the agreement, but cautioned that it might change if its position if the market facts materially changed or it learned that the information on which it had relied was incorrect, false, or misleading.

Both the US and the EU have informal procedures for seeking agency input into the legality of joint venture agreements. In the US, the primary method is through the process of seeking a business review letter from the Antitrust Division. 28 C.F.R. ¶ 50.6. Parties seeking a business review on a joint venture must supply information in a long list of categories, including documents discussing the competitive state of the market and lists of the top ten customers for any products that the joint venture may offer. The Division attempts to answer requests within sixty to ninety days. Its review letters do not offer immunity from suit, "approve" the joint venture, or have any formal effect on the ability of private parties to sue. Still, receipt of a business review letter provides a significant layer of comfort to the joint venturers.

The European Commission follows a more limited procedure in issuing guidance letters in response to request for the Commission's opinion about case-specific application of Articles 101 or 102. Commission Notice on informal guidance relating to novel questions concerning Articles [101 and 102] of the EC Treaty that raise in individual cases. O.J. C 101 (April 27, 2004).

Both the US and the EU have adopted special provisions to encourage research and development joint ventures, which have the potential to encourage quicker, cheaper, and higher quality innovation. In the US, the National Cooperative Research Act ("NCRA") of 1984, amended in 1993, 15 U.S.C. § 4301, states that research and development joint ventures are to be adjudged under the rule of reason and not as per se illegal. That much is not terribly significant in the modern era, since joint ventures are not judged under the per se rule. A provision with perhaps more importance is that any joint venture notified under the Act cannot subject the parties to treble damages liability—but only single damages—even if the agreement is later found anticompetitive. For its part, the European Commission has adopted a block exemption for research and development joint ventures. Commission Regulation 2659/2000, O.J. L 304/7 (Dec. 5, 2000). Article 1 of the Regulation declares exempt joint R&D and joint exploitation of the results of such R&D, and necessary ancillary restraints, as long as the parties market share does not exceed 25% and does not include any blacklisted clauses. Moreover, to qualify for block exemption, several additional conditions must be satisfied: (1) each party must have access to the results in order to further its research; (2) the supplying partner, in the event of specialisation not entailing joint distribution, must fulfill orders for suppliers from other partners; and (3) in the event of joint exploitation the results must be IP-protected and substantially contribute to technical or economic progress and be decisive for the manufacture of the contract products or the application of contract processes.

Notes and Questions

1. How are the competition authorities likely to address cases like Yahoo/Microsoft in the future? In a market increasingly dominated by one larger player like Google, should any joint venture between the market's smaller firms that has the potential of creating a counterweight to the dominant firm be viewed with approval? Does it matter that the Internet is uniquely dynamic in terms of the development of the relevant technology, social practices, and economic structures (*i.e.*, advertising-driven versus subscription driven models)? In dynamic markets, is it better to insist on technological competition among even the smaller firms, on the theory that technological advances created by the spur of competition may allow even smaller firms to break out quickly and overtake the industry leader?

2. In view of the fact that a notification system can be cumbersome, what are the advantages of a voluntary notification system that allows parties to seek review of their joint venture agreements on a prospective basis? Should such systems be formal and determinative, as in Singapore's example, or informal and qualified, as with the U.S. example?

Chapter 4

VERTICAL RESTRAINTS

A. INTRODUCTION

Vertical restraints are restraints in the course of distributing a product or service, or in the course of bringing technology and its commercial applications to market. They involve arrangements entered into between two or more undertakings each of which operates, for the purposes of the arrangements, at a different level of the production or distribution chain, and relating to the conditions under which the parties may purchase, sell or resell certain goods or services. Their assessment typically entails a trade-off between their effects on intrabrand competition (i.e., competition in the sale of products of the same make) and interbrand competition (i.e., competition between suppliers of products of different makes), respectively.

Vertical restraints can harm competition by blocking (or "foreclosing") access to inputs or outlets, by increasing barriers to entry and facilitating cooperative behavior among competitors at a horizontal level, and by increasing unilateral power to exploit. There are some recurrent differences among jurisdictions in addressing vertical restraints. Principal among these are: 1) Goals—Is the jurisdiction concerned about market integration, as is Europe, and therefore worried about restraints that impair the flow of goods across borders? Is the jurisdiction worried about chilling opportunities of firms to compete on the merits or to get a fair deal, as in many Asian and developing countries? 2) Tests, evidence and burdens, including different default presumptions.

The United States approaches vertical restraints with a permissive stance: if a restraint is vertical it is probably efficient and good for the market because all actors in the value chain are incentivize to maximize output (it is assumed); vertical restraints are often explained as attempts by producers to protect them and their distributors from free riding discounters who undermine investments in service. Hence, US law is referred throughout this chapter as a comparative benchmark when discussing the assessment of vertical restraints in the European Union, Japan and South Korea, as well as developing countries, respectively.

The European Union, while recognizing possible efficiency properties of vertical restraints, is less permissive. It fears that such restraints may impede free (cross-border) trade within the EU and thereby hurt the market (including consumers). It is less confident that inefficient free riding exists to any worrisome extent. Hence, it has developed a large body of cases and guidance assessing vertical restraints, which is presented extensively in section B.

Vertical restraints can also have a special importance in jurisdictions such as Japan, whose vertical restraint rules include the rhetoric of equality of opportunity and correction of unequal bargaining power (see section C). Moreover, developing countries can be particularly concerned with buyer power, exercised along the vertical chain, which is used to exploit powerless farmers and other small producers (see section D). In many developing countries, business firms' efficient access to inputs and to final markets is already impaired by corruption, privilege, and the scarcity of capital, and often the authorities are suspicious that vertical restraints will exploit the country's small suppliers or clog the path to mobility and growth.

Therefore, as you approach the materials on vertical restraints from various jurisdictions, you should ask yourself: What does this jurisdiction mean by harm to competition? What does it mean when it says that a restraint forecloses the market, or a part of the market, to outsiders? If the restraint is an exclusionary restraint: When is foreclosure significant, and when is it anticompetitive? When does significant foreclosure shift the burden to the firm imposing the restraint, and can that firm argue that the foreclosure was not anticompetitive or only that the restraint was justified, and justified by what? Which jurisdictions pay attention to these questions, and which jurisdictions are likely to apply a very broad brush, quickly concluding, for example, that a restraint forecloses competitors and it anticompetitive?

Exclusionary vertical restraints may also constitute monopolistic abuses. We will study exclusive dealing by dominant firms in Chapter 5. Conceptually, the same forms of analysis are applicable.

B. EUROPEAN UNION

1. Introduction

Article 101(1) of the Treaty on the Functioning of the European Union (TFEU), ex Article 81(1) of the Treaty of Rome, prohibits restraints that distort competition. Distortion is broadly construed. Under Article 101(2), agreements that distort competition are null and void. Under Article 101(3), subparagraph (1) can be declared inapplicable if (in inexact summary) the agreement is on balance procompetitive or efficient.

Enforcement of the competition provisions of the Treaty had to await an implementing regulation, which was adopted in 1962. The first implementing regulation (17/62, or Regulation 17) effectively required all agreements within now Article 101(1) to be notified to the European Commission. The Commission would then determine whether indeed the agreement fell within 101(1). If not it would get a negative clearance. If so the Commission would determine whether the agreement was entitled to an "exemption" under 101(3), which would normally be granted, if at all, with conditions and for a period of years.

In the first several years of competition law enforcement, so many thousands of agreements were filed with the European Commission that the workload and backlog became untenable, and the Commission began to adopt "block exemptions" for agreements of certain sorts that were not problematic. If the agreement fell within a block exemption, it would not be necessary for the parties to file; the block exemption regulation gave them their exemption from the date of the agreement. Most of the block exemptions were tailored for common forms of vertical agreement; for example, automobile dealership agreements. The block exemption regulation specified necessary clauses, permissible clauses, and forbidden clauses, and if the agreement incorporated all necessary and permissible clauses, and no impermissible clauses, it was entitled automatically to the benefits of the block exemption. Block exemptions were adopted for exclusive distribution, exclusive purchasing, motor vehicle distribution, and technology licensing agreement, among others. Successive block exemption regulations became more and more regulatory, with more and more mandates as to what the parties must do and must not do to get the benefit of the exemption. If an agreement did not come within a block exemption, the parties could still apply for an individual exemption, but that process was a long one and the benefits of the block exemption were so attractive that parties often simply molded their agreement to fit what became known as "a straight jacket."

In the 1990s, the Competition Directorate of the Commission began to rethink the institutional design. Vertical restraints began to be recognized as less harmful and more helpful to competition and efficiency than originally perceived. Economic learning was pointing the way to a more liberal approach. The Commission embarked on a process of "modernisation" to reduce regulatory burdens and introduce a more economic approach. The process began with vertical restraints. The vertical block exemptions were simplified, with fewer mandatory and prohibitory clauses, and guidelines for analysis were adopted. The requirement for notification in order to obtain an exemption was abolished for vertical agreements in 1999. The Commission issued a general vertical block exemption regulation and guidelines for the assessment of vertical restraints first in 2000 and again in 2010.

A new general vertical distribution block exemption and guidelines became effective in 2022, with a term of twelve years. The Commission's Competition Directorate also amended the specific regulation and guidelines for motor vehicle distribution in 2023 and launched a process of reassessment for the technology licensing agreement package in 2022.

Meanwhile, effective since 2004, the Commission adopted even more thorough-going reform, applicable to both agreements and abuse of dominance. It adopted Regulation 1/2003, printed in Appendix 3, which totally abolished the notification and exemption system (for horizontal as well as vertical restraints), and devolved powers to the Member States to apply (now) Article 101 TFEU in its entirety. Pursuant to the reform, national courts and national competition authorities, as well as the Commission, can decide that an agreement fulfills the requirements of Article 101(3) and that therefore the prohibition of 101(1) does not apply. Over the past twenty years, a large majority of the cases involving the prosecution of vertical restraints under Article 101 have been handled by national competition authorities.

Given the system of block exemptions and of individual exemptions imposing conditions that were usually consented to, relatively few vertical cases have gone to the courts. But several have done so.

We present here cases on tight territorial restraints, parallel imports and exports and dual pricing across borders, resale price maintenance, tying and other foreclosures, and materials on block exemptions and guidelines. Also referenced are technology transfer agreements, which are the subject of a 2014 block exemption (in the process of being updated).

2. Territorial Restraints, Parallel Imports and Exports, and Dual Pricing

The first important competition law case to reach the Court of Justice is the case of *Consten and Grundig*, wherein Grundig, a German manufacturer of electronics products, tried unsuccessfully to defend its distribution system. Grundig had appointed a distributor for each Member State. Each distributor was forbidden to sell Grundig product outside of its territory, and each was empowered to defend its territory from Grundig products coming in from the outside (parallel imports). The Commission took a strict approach in assessing the existence of a restriction of competition in this case, very much influenced by the market integration objective of the EU (then EEC) Treaty. Market integration was still in its infancy at the time, and the Court of Justice upheld the Commission's view. As market integration became a reality, the assessment framework was progressively relaxed even though it continues to these days to reflect the complementarity of free trade and competition principles in the European Union.

Consten and Grundig

Grundig, a manufacturer of radios, television sets, tape recorders, and dictating machines, appointed Consten to be its exclusive distributor in France. Consten and Grundig wanted Consten to be the only distributor of the Grundig products in France; thus, they wanted Consten to be able to exclude from France Grundig products put on the market in other Member States. To achieve this result they relied on the French trademark law as well as the distribution contract. Since French case law held that only the owner of a trademark was entitled to enforce the trademark, the parties agreed that Consten should apply for and own the trademark GINT (Grundig International). Consten and Grundig agreed that if Consten should cease to be the distributor for Grundig in France, Consten would assign the mark to Grundig. Grundig made similar exclusive distribution and trademark arrangements with each of its distributors in the other countries.

Before the EU Treaty was adopted, the Western European nations had high tariffs and low quotas. Quotas would prevent goods from moving across national borders. The EU Treaty required the Member States to remove the quotas and tariffs in the internal market. In the spring of 1961 when French quotas ended, the French discounter UNEF began purchasing GINT television sets, tape recorders, dictaphones and other electronic equipment from German wholesalers (who had also accepted export bans) and selling them in competition with Consten's dealers in France. Consten sued UNEF under French law for unfair competition and trademark infringement, alleging that UNEF knew that the sales to it were in breach of contract and that the sales by UNEF undermined Consten's contract. Thereupon, UNEF petitioned the Commission to declare the agreement between Consten and Grundig void under Article [101](2). Meanwhile, Regulation 17 came into effect, and Grundig filed a notification of its distribution agreement and sought an exemption under Article [101](3).

In justification of the territorial division, Grundig argued that German buyers were familiar with its product and French buyers were not, and that the French market demanded a higher level of service and promotion than the German market. Moreover, it noted that Consten was responsible for guarantees, repair, customer service, accepting advance orders, maintaining stocks, and advertising in France. Grundig argued that cheap imports from Germany would undercut Consten's incentives to fulfill these duties, and that Consten's failure to fulfill its duties would undercut the brand's reputation and frustrate sales. Grundig depicted the market for electronics products as highly competitive, with prices dropping steadily even before UNEF's appearance on the French market.

The Commission refused to consider evidence of (inter-brand) competition from competitors of Grundig, and denied Grundig's request for an exemption under Article [101](3). It observed that prices for Grundig products in France were substantially higher than prices for Grundig products in Germany. Consten and Grundig sued the Commission, seeking annulment of its decision.

Consten and Grundig appealed to the Court of Justice. (The EU General Court had not yet been established.) In most appeals to the Court of Justice, an advocate general is appointed. The advocate general reads all submissions, hears the argument, and writes an advisory opinion for the benefit of the Court. Karl Roemer was the advocate general in *Consten and Grundig*.

Advocate General Karl Roemer criticized the Commission for considering only competition among distributors of Grundig's products (i.e., intra-brand competition) and not competition from competing brands (i.e., inter-brand competition). He said:

> [I]t is not proper if the Commission proceeds in such a manner that from the very outset it considers *exclusively* the last-mentioned internal competition [intraband competition] and completely neglects in its considerations the competition with similar products [interbrand competition]. In fact, it is conceivable that the competition between different products or, to be more precise, between different producers is so severe as not to leave any room worth mentioning for what was called internal competition in a product (possibly with regard to price and service). . . . Rightfully, it was . . . therefore incumbent on the Commission to make a survey of the entire competition situation. . . . Such a survey of the effects on the market

> would possibly have led to a result favorable for the plaintiffs. . . . Such more favorable result might have been possible in view of the relatively small share of Grundig in the French market for tape recorders and dictating machines (roughly 17 percent)—as far as we know, the Commission has not conducted any investigations concerning other products—or in view of the plaintiffs' allegation that the markets for television sets . . . and for transistor sets showed so severe a competition of various, and sometimes very strong producers of the Community and of third countries that it repeatedly became necessary to reduce the prices of Grundig sets considerably.
>
> Because of the Commission's narrow concept of the term "restraint of competition," no such survey was made, and the Court of Justice in its proceeding cannot be obligated to make the survey itself belatedly. The only thing we can do in this situation is to find that the results which the Commission arrived at in the investigation of the criterion "restraint of competition" must be deemed to lack a sufficient foundation and must for that reason be rejected.

The Court of Justice disagreed. Here are excerpts from its judgment.

CONSTEN AND GRUNDIG v. COMMISSION

Cases C–56, 58/64, ECLI:EU:C:1966:41 (Court of Justice of the European Union 1966)

. . . [A]n agreement between producer and distributor which might tend to restore the national divisions in trade between Member States might be such as to frustrate the most fundamental objectives of the Community. The Treaty, whose preamble and content aim at abolishing the barriers between States, and which in several provisions gives evidence of a stern attitude with regard to their reappearance, could not allow undertakings to reconstruct such barriers. Article [101](1) is designed to pursue this aim, even in the case of agreements between undertakings placed at different levels in the economic process. . . .

The applicants and the German Government maintain that since the Commission restricted its examination solely to Grundig products the decision was based upon a false concept of competition and of the rules on prohibition contained in Article [101](1), since this concept applies particularly to competition between similar products of different makes. . . .

The principle of freedom of competition concerns the various stages and manifestations of competition. Although competition between producers is generally more noticeable than that between distributors of products of the same make, it does not thereby follow that an agreement tending to restrict the latter kind of competition should escape the prohibition of Article [101](1) merely because it might increase the former.

Besides, for the purpose of applying Article [101](1), there is no need to take account of the concrete effects of an agreement once it appears that it has as its object the prevention, restriction or distortion of competition.

Therefore the absence in the contested decision of any analysis of the effects of the agreement on competition between similar products of different makes does not, of itself, constitute a defect in the decision.

It thus remains to consider whether the contested decision was right in founding the prohibition of the disputed agreement under Article [101](1) on the restriction on competition created by the agreement in the sphere of the distribution of Grundig products alone. The infringement which was found to exist by the contested decision results from the absolute territorial protection created [by] the said contract in favour of Consten on the basis of French law. The applicants thus wished to eliminate any possibility of competition at the wholesale level in Grundig products in the territory specified in the contract essentially by two methods.

First, Grundig undertook not to deliver even indirectly to third parties products intended for the area covered by the contract. The restrictive nature of that undertaking is obvious if it is considered in the light of the prohibition on exporting which was imposed not only on Consten but also on all the other sole concessionnaires of Grundig, as well as the German wholesalers. Secondly, the registration in France by Consten of the GINT trade mark, which Grundig affixes to all its products, is intended to increase the protection inherent in the disputed agreement, against the risk of parallel imports into France of Grundig products, by adding the protection deriving from the law on industrial property rights. Thus no third party could import Grundig products from other Member States of the Community for resale in France without running serious risks. . . .

The situation as ascertained above results in the isolation of the French market and makes it possible to charge for the products in question prices which are sheltered from all effective competition. In addition, the more producers succeed in their efforts to render their own makes of product individually distinct in the eyes of the consumer, the more the effectiveness of competition between producers tends to diminish. Because of the considerable impact of distribution costs on the aggregate cost price, it seems important that competition between dealers should also be stimulated. The efforts of the dealer are stimulated by competition between distributors of products of the same make. Since the agreement thus aims at isolating the French market for Grundig products and maintaining artificially, for products of a very well-known brand, separate national markets within the Community, it is therefore such as to distort competition in the Common Market.

It was therefore proper for the contested decision to hold that the agreement constitutes an infringement of Article [101](1). No further considerations, whether of economic data (price differences between France and Germany, representative character of the type of appliance considered, level of overheads borne by Consten) or of the corrections of the criteria upon which the Commission relied in its comparisons between the situations of the French and German markets, and no possible favourable effects of the agreement in other respects, can in any way lead, in the face of abovementioned restrictions, to a different solution under Article [101](1). . . .

The applicants maintain more particularly that the criticized effect on competition is due not to the agreement but to the registration of the trade-mark in accordance with French law, which gives rise to an original inherent right of the holder of the trade-mark from which the absolute territorial protection derives under national law.

Consten's right under the contract to the exclusive use in France of the GINT trade-mark, which may be used in a similar manner in other countries, is intended to make it possible to keep under surveillance and to place an obstacle in the way of parallel imports. Thus, the agreement by which Grundig, as the holder of the trade-mark by virtue of an international registration, authorized Consten to register it in France in its own name tends to restrict competition. . . .

That agreement therefore is one which may be caught by the prohibition in Article [101](1). The prohibition would be ineffective if Consten could continue to use the trade-mark to achieve the same object as that pursued by the agreement which has been held to be unlawful.

[The Court did not interfere with the Commission's decision to deny an exemption under Article [101](3). It acknowledged that Consten, as Grundig's distributor in France, was required to perform various obligations such as to accept advance orders and to provide warranty and after-sales service. The Court stated that territorial protection would give the parties to the agreement an advantage in *their* production and distribution activities. But, it said, to qualify for exemption the "improvement must in particular show appreciable objective advantages of such a character as to compensate for the disadvantages which they cause in the field of competition," and must be indispensable. The argument that every "improvement as conceived by the parties to the agreement must be maintained intact" . . . "not only tends to weaken the requirement of indispensability but also among other consequences to confuse solicitude for the specific interests of the parties with the objective improvements contemplated by the Treaty."]

Notes and Questions

1. In designing the distribution system that became the subject of this case, Grundig appointed an exclusive distributor for each territory. Grundig agreed that it, itself, would not distribute GINT-brand product in the assigned territory; and each distributor agreed with Grundig to sell the GINT product in its territory (and more, as we note below). These obligations are the essence of an exclusive distribution agreement. The producer says to the distributor: I appoint you and you alone to distribute my product in this territory.

The Commission does not regard such an agreement as falling necessarily within Article 101(1). Why?

2. The additional obligations on both Consten and Grundig are the key obligations in the case. What were these additional obligations and why were they of particular concern? Did they lessen competition? Clearly by definition, they lessened intrabrand competition. Did they lessen interbrand competition?

3. How does the rule of *Consten and Grundig* increase market integration? Be specific; state more than: More GINT product will move across Member State lines.

4. Why do you suppose that German prices were lower than French prices for the GINT product? Why might you want to know? Is the answer relevant to (a) whether the restraint is caught by Article 101(1)? (b) whether the restraint is entitled to an exemption under Article 101(3)?

5. Note the relationship between French trademark law and EU competition law. Which has the upper hand? Is the Court's answer consistent with Article 345 TFEU, ex 295 ECT, preserving for the Member States the right to define property within their states? Did the Court properly resolve the tension between free movement/competition principles, and the right to exclusive control over one's intellectual property?

6. In the light of *Consten and Grundig,* can an agreement that absolutely eliminates parallel imports ever be justified in the EU as essential for improvement of production or distribution?

7. *Consten and Grundig* may remind you of United States v. Arnold, Schwinn & Co., 388 U.S. 365 (1967) (overruled in 1977). In *Schwinn,* a manufacturer's imposition of absolute territorial restrictions on its distributors was held to be illegal on its face. The Court held that a manufacturer could not lawfully assign an exclusive territory to a distributor, require the distributor to stay within the territory, and agree to keep parallel imports out of the territory. The *Schwinn* decision protected the autonomy of distributors to sell where they wished. The existence of robust interbrand competition was irrelevant. The US Supreme Court overruled *Schwinn* in Sylvania. Continental T.V., Inc. v. GTE Sylvania Inc., 433 U.S. 36 (1977). In *Sylvania* the Supreme Court observed that non-price restraints imposed by a manufacturer on its own distributors can improve the efficiency of the manufacturer and stimulate competition among brands, and it held that improvements in interbrand competition (e.g., competition between Sylvania and Sony TVs) can outweigh harm from the decrease in intrabrand competition (i.e., competition among Sylvania's own distributors). In Leegin Creative Leather Products v. PSKS, 551 U.S. 877 (2007), considered in greater detail below, the US Court went further. Overruling the *per se* rule against resale price maintenance agreements, the Court held that protecting interbrand competition is "the primary purpose of the antitrust laws." According to the Court, competition among producers (interbrand competition) is likely to force manufacturers to behave competitively and to assure that vertical restraints on distributors are efficient and procompetitive. Can *Consten and Grundig* be reconciled with this perspective? Is the difference justified by context? Consider that the European judicature might value intrabrand competition more than the American judicature, and also that market integration is not a goal of US antitrust. We will consider below how *Consten and Grundig* might have been affected by the European program of modernisation.

Volkswagen

In the 1990s, when the Italian lire was depressed, Volkswagen, maker of Volkswagens and Audis, tried to protect the German and Austrian dealers in its network from a shift of buyers to Italy. It entered into agreements with its subsidiaries and Italian dealers, imposing supply quotas and a bonus system designed to induce the Italian dealers to sell at least 85% of their available vehicles to customers located in Italy. The Commission severely fined Volkswagen for partitioning national markets. The Commission describes the case as follows, in the 1998 Competition Policy Report:

Opening-up of markets

68 The Commission has always kept a close eye on distribution agreements and their restrictive effects in so far as they hindered intra-Community trade. Some exclusive distribution agreements lead to the setting-up of watertight national distribution networks. In particular, clauses which prohibit distributors from supplying customers based outside the contract territory. In this way, national markets are artificially isolated from one another. The Commission considers that measures should be taken to combat this situation, not just in order to re-establish effective competition between economic operators but also in order to promote market integration. In practice, the compartmentalisation of national markets prevents price convergence within the Union and restricts access by consumers to the markets with the lowest prices. With the creation of the single currency, price differentials will be obvious because they will be expressed in euro. They will be increasingly viewed as unjustified by ordinary people, who will want to derive full benefit from economic and monetary union.

69 In 1998 the Commission clearly demonstrated its determination to promote the opening-up of markets, a prime example of this being the *Volkswagen* case [O.J. L 124, 23/4/98]. Since 1995 the Commission had received numerous complaints from European consumers, particularly from Germany and Austria, who had been confronted with various difficulties when attempting to buy new Volkswagen and Audi cars in Italy. These consumers wanted to benefit from the price differentials between their Member State and Italy, where prices were particularly advantageous. Following a series of inspections at the offices of Volkswagen AG, Audi AG and Autogerma SpA, which is a subsidiary of Volkswagen and the official importer for both makes in Italy, and at the offices of a number of Italian dealers, the Commission concluded that Europe's largest motor-manufacturing group had been pursuing a market-partitioning policy in the Union for about 10 years. Volkswagen AG had systematically forced its dealers in Italy to refuse to sell Volkswagen and Audi cars to foreign buyers, especially from Germany and Austria. The Commission fined Volkswagen ECU 102 million, the largest fine ever imposed on a single company."

COMMISSION OF THE EUROPEAN COMMUNITIES, XXVIIIST REPORT ON COMPETITION POLICY 1998, ¶¶ 68–69 (1999).

The Court of First Instance confirmed the existence and gravity of the infringements. It reduced the fine to 90 million euros since the Commission had overstated the time period of the infringement; still the fine set a record at the time. Volkswagen AG v. Commission, Case T–62/98, EU:T:2000:180.

In what sense did the system of quotas and of bonuses based on sales in Italy "partition markets"? Should Volkswagen have been able to protect its German and Austrian dealers from the siphoning off of sales as a result of a bad exchange rate?

Volkswagen is one of several car brands that continued to be sold at widely varying prices in different Member States even after the introduction of the Euro. Fines have been imposed, also, on Opel, DaimlerChrysler, and Peugeot for employing distribution systems that deprived consumers of their "single-market right" to buy a car wherever the price is lowest.

In the *Peugeot* case, Peugeot employed two strategies:

> "Firstly, part of the remuneration of Peugeot's Dutch dealers was made dependent on the final destination of the vehicle, and discriminated against sales to foreign consumers. In particular, performance bonuses were refused if dealers sold cars to non-Dutch citizens. Secondly, Automobiles Peugeot SA exercised, through Peugeot Nederland N.V., direct pressure on those dealers who were identified as having developed significant export activities, for example by threatening to reduce the number of cars supplied to them." See European Commission Press Release, MEMO/09/328 (July 9, 2009).

The infringement led to a fine of 44.55 million euros.

* * *

Consten and Grundig established that air-tight territorial distribution restraints at Member States borders are prohibited by Article 101(1). Did it say or imply anything about treatment under Article 101(3)? After *Consten and Grundig,* such tight territorial restraints have been treated as 'hard core' restraints. The successive block exemptions have retained the hard-core treatment, and an agreement cannot get the benefit of a block exemption if it contains a hard core restriction. Also after *Consten and Grundig,* rules were developed to allow manufacturers to assign territories to distributors and to allow the manufacturer to prohibit the distributor's active solicitation outside of its territory, but the manufacturer may not prohibit the distributor from making "passive sales" (accepting unsolicited bids from outside of the territory). See the block exemption and guidelines, discussed below. Are these wise rules? Do they differ from US law? Do they sufficiently recognize the procompetitive and efficiency properties of distribution restraints?

Might a manufacturer need to prevent passive Internet sales in order to prevent destructive free riding on services provided by store-based sellers?

As crystallized in the block exemption regulation and its guidelines (see supra point 5), much of the law on territorial restrictions has narrowed down over time to a distinction between active sales to a particular territory or a customer group allocated to another distributor or reserved to the supplier, which may be constrained under certain conditions, and passive sales in response to unsolicited request from individual customers, which may not. With the advent of e-commerce, the distinction between active and passive sales has been transposed to the online world. In particular, the use of a website by a distributor has been considered a form of passive selling, which cannot be restricted. Conversely, specific restrictions on the use of the internet by distributors have been considered compatible with the block exemption regulation to the extent that they would lead to active selling into, for instance, other distributors' exclusive territories or customer groups. In recent years, the Commission has repeatedly enforced the law against restrictions of passive sales, including in online trade (see cases involving, e.g., Guess, Nike or Steam). There is a companion to the *Consten and Grundig* rule as applied to exclusive territories. This is the rule against restraints on parallel (intrabrand) imports and exports (illustrated in *Volkswagen*). The rule against restraints on parallel imports and exports implies that the seller may not charge more for goods to be resold as exports than for the same product that is sold domestically. This rule against dual pricing poses challenges especially for pharmaceutical companies faced with capped prices in the domestic market and willing buyers at higher prices in neighboring markets. The unwavering rule against restraints on parallel imports was tested by GlaxoSmithKline.

GLAXOSMITHKLINE SERVICES UNLIMITED v. COMMISSION

Case T–168/01, ECLI:EU:T:2006:265 (General Court of the European Union 2006), CFI appeals dismissed, 6 Oct. 2009 (see CJEU judgment immediately below)

[Spanish legislation capped the price of pharmaceuticals sold to pharmacies and hospitals and covered by Spanish reimbursement rules. GlaxoSmithKline, a major pharmaceutical producer, made agreements with its wholesalers that for all other products (essentially, pharmaceuticals not for the domestic market), GSK would charge a price set by objective economic factors, and that this would be the price that GSK had initially proposed to the Spanish government as the reimbursement price plus a cost-of-living adjustment. These terms were specified in Clause 4 of the General Sales Conditions. The Commission found that the clause fell within Article 101(1) as a restriction by object, and that, despite GSK's efficiency and innovation justifications, the agreement was not entitled to an Article 101(3) exemption. In particular, the Commission discounted GSK's arguments and evidence as to the virtues and advantages of Clause 4. GSK asked the General Court to annul the Commission's decision. The General Court did so, on grounds of the Commission's "lack of serious examination" of GSK's efficiency and innovation arguments. The General Court held also that Clause 4 was not a restriction by object, for it could not be taken for granted, in this unusual market, that parallel trade would reduce prices and increase consumer welfare. Both parties appealed aspects of the judgment to the Court of Justice. We set forth below excerpts from the General Court judgment related to GSK's efficiency and innovation claims, which the Court of Justice upheld, and then we set forth excerpts from the CJEU judgment, largely confined to the CJEU holding that the restraint on parallel imports was a restraint by object even if it did not harm consumers.]

295 In the light of the structure of GSK's arguments and also of the discussion of that point during the administrative procedure, the Decision could not avoid examining, first of all, whether parallel trade led to a loss in efficiency for the pharmaceutical industry in general, and for GSK in particular. . . .

296 However, a comparison of the evidence provided by GSK with the other evidence invoked by the Commission in the Decision clearly reveals that in the medicines sector the effect of parallel trade on competition is ambiguous, since the gain in efficiency to which it is likely to give rise for intrabrand competition, the role of which is limited by the applicable regulatory framework, must be compared with the loss in efficiency to which it is likely to give rise for interbrand competition, the role of which is central.

297 In those circumstances, the Commission could not refrain from examining, second, whether Clause 4 of the General Sales Conditions could enable GSK's capacity for innovation to be reinstated and thus could give rise to a gain in efficiency for interbrand competition.

298 That, moreover, formed the very core of the prospective analysis which the Commission was under a duty to carry out in order to respond to GSK's request for an exemption. According to the consistent case-law cited . . ., it is necessary to determine whether the agreement prohibited on account of the disadvantage which it represents for competition (Article [101](1) [TFEU] presents an

advantage of such a kind as to offset that disadvantage (Article [101](3) [TFEU].

299 The Commission was therefore still required to examine GSK's arguments relating to the advantages expected of Clause 4 of the General Sales Conditions. In that regard, recital 156 to the Decision, the only recital susceptible of attesting to an examination on that point, indicates essentially:

> '[I]t is a matter of discretion for pharmaceutical companies to decide how much they wish to invest in R & D. Any savings they might hypothetically make by preventing parallel trade would therefore not automatically lead to higher R & D investments. It is conceivable that these savings might merely be added to the companies' profits. Obviously, the generation of extra profits alone cannot justify an exemption. In this regard, GSK's argument would mean that the first condition for [the application of Article 101(3) TFEU] would be fulfilled for every agreement that could be said to contribute to an increase in the revenues of a firm engaged in R & D. The condition would in any case be meaningless, since it is in the nature of any agreement restricting competition to be likely to increase a firm's earnings.'

300 However, GSK did not claim that the creation of additional profits would in itself justify an exemption. On the contrary, it maintained that parallel trade prevented it from making the profits necessary for the optimum financing of its R & D, that Clause 4 of the General Sales Conditions would enable it to increase its revenues and that it would have every interest, in the light of the fierce interbrand competition, of the central role played by innovation in that competition and of the methods of financing R & D, in investing a part of this surplus in R & D in order to overtake its competitors or to ensure that it would not be overtaken by them. In other words, it claimed that its General Sales Conditions should be exempted because they would have not merely the immediate effect of increasing its revenues, but above all the secondary effect of increasing its capacity for innovation. Furthermore, it maintained that that advantage must be compared with the fact that, when it was obtained by parallel traders, that surplus did not constitute an advantage, because, not being obliged to engage in genuine competition among themselves, the parallel traders reduced prices only to the extent necessary to attract retailers and therefore kept most of that surplus for themselves, as GSK again submitted at the hearing.

301 The Commission could not merely reject those arguments outright on the ground that the advantage described by GSK would not necessarily be achieved, as it did at recital 156 to the Decision, but was required, in accordance with the case-law, also to examine, as specifically as possible, in the context of a prospective analysis, whether, in the particular circumstances of the case and in the light of the evidence submitted to it, it seemed more likely that the advantages described by GSK would be achieved or, on the contrary, that they would not. It was not entitled to consider, in a peremptory manner and without providing proper arguments, that the factual arguments and the evidence submitted by GSK must be regarded as hypothetical, as it maintained most recently at the hearing. * * *

303 It follows from the foregoing that the Decision is vitiated by a failure to carry out a proper examination, as the Commission did not validly take into account all the factual arguments and the evidence pertinently submitted by GSK, did not refute certain of those arguments even though they were sufficiently relevant and substantiated to require a response, and did not substantiate to the requisite legal standard its conclusion that it was not proved, first, that parallel trade was apt to lead to a loss in efficiency by appreciably altering GSK's capacity for innovation and, second, that Clause 4 of the General Sales Conditions was apt to enable a gain in efficiency to be achieved by improving innovation.

The balancing exercise * * *

306 . . . [T]he Commission's finding that Clause 4 of the General Sales Conditions restricts competition is well founded only in so far as it finds that Clause 4 has the effect of depriving final consumers of medicines reimbursed by a national sickness insurance scheme of the advantage which they would have derived, in regard to prices and costs, from the participation of the Spanish wholesalers in intrabrand competition on the markets of destination of the parallel trade from Spain.

307 Consequently, the Commission's conclusion that there is no need to carry out a balancing exercise, which would show in any event that the advantage associated with Clause 4 does not offset the disadvantage which it represents for competition, cannot be upheld. The Commission was required, first, to conduct an appropriate examination of GSK's factual arguments and evidence, in order to be in a position to carry out, second, the complex assessment necessary in order to weigh up the disadvantage and the advantage associated with Clause 4 of the General Sales Conditions.

Conclusion

308 It follows from the foregoing that the Commission could not lawfully conclude that, as regards the existence of a contribution to the promotion of technical progress, GSK had not demonstrated that the first condition for the application of Article [101](3) [TFEU] was satisfied. In those circumstances, there is no need to examine GSK's arguments relating to a contribution to the improvement of the distribution of medicines.

c) Evidence of the advantage being passed on to the consumer, of the indispensability of Clause 4 of the General Sales Conditions and of the absence of the elimination of competition

309 As stated previously, it follows from the Decision and from the oral argument presented at the hearing that the summary conclusions which the Commission reached concerning the existence of a passing-on to consumers, the indispensability of Clause 4 of the General Sales Conditions and the absence of elimination of competition rest on the conclusion relating to the existence of a gain in efficiency.

310 In so far as that conclusion is vitiated by illegality, in that it concerns the existence of a contribution towards the promotion of technical progress, those conclusions are themselves invalid.

311 In so far as, when it examined whether Clause 4 of the General Sales Conditions would or would not eliminate competition for a substantial part of the products, the Commission further stated . . . that, in any event, for several of the leading products affected by the General Sales Conditions, GSK held substantial market shares (for example, for Zofran, Flixonase, Zovirax and Imigran) in one or more Member States, it remains necessary to review that assessment.

312 In that regard, it must be observed that the Commission acknowledged at the hearing that it had not really resolved the question of GSK's market power and further stated that it would have had to continue with the analysis in order to determine that point.

313 In fact, owing to the particular legal and economic context of the sector under consideration, the fact of holding substantial market shares, which, moreover, is limited to certain of the relevant products, of which the Commission provided only four examples, clearly does not in itself make it possible to conclude, in a convincing manner, that competition would be eliminated for a substantial part of the relevant products.

314 In effect, irrespective of the question of the definition of the relevant products market, which has been debated by the parties, a number of elements relied on by GSK during the administrative procedure, and then in its written submissions, prevent such a conclusion from being reached automatically.

315 In particular, GSK's argument . . .was not so irrelevant that the Commission could refrain from making it the subject of a specific assessment under the fourth condition for the application of Article [101](3) [TFEU]. In effect, the fact that Clause 4 of the General Sales Conditions prevents the limited pressure which might exist, owing to parallel trade from Spain, on the price and the cost of medicines in the geographic markets of destination must be related to the facts, put forward by GSK and not disputed by the Commission, that competition by innovation is very fierce in the sector and that competition on price exists in another form, although by law it emerges only when, upon expiry of the patent, manufacturers of generic medicines are able to enter the market. In those circumstances, it was still necessary . . . to assess what form of competition must be given priority with a view to ensuring the maintenance of effective competition sought by Article 3(1)(g) EU [removed from Treaty to become Protocol 27] and Article [101 TFEU].

4. Conclusion * * *

317 Accordingly, the Decision must be annulled in so far as, in Article 2, it rejects GSK's request for an exemption.

GLAXOSMITHKLINE SERVICES UNLIMITED v. COMMISSION

Cases C–501/06 P, C–513/06 P, C–15/06 P, C–519/06 P, ECLI:EU:C:2009:610
(Court of Justice of the European Union 2009)

* * *

46 . . . [T]he Court of First Instance . . . ruled that the principal conclusion reached by the Commission, namely that Clause 4 of the agreement must be considered to be prohibited by Article [101(1) TFEU] in so far it has as its object the restriction of parallel trade, cannot be upheld. As the prices of the medicines concerned are to a large extent shielded from the free play of supply and demand owing to the applicable regulations and are set or controlled by the public authorities, it cannot be taken for granted at the outset that parallel trade tends to reduce those prices and thus to increase the welfare of final consumers. An analysis of the terms of Clause 4 of the agreement, carried out in that context, therefore does not permit the presumption that that provision, which seeks to limit parallel trade, thus tends to diminish the welfare of final consumers. In this largely

unprecedented situation, it cannot be inferred merely from a reading of the terms of that agreement, in its context, that the agreement is restrictive of competition, and it is necessary to consider the effects of the agreement, if only to ascertain what the regulatory authority was able to apprehend on the basis of such a reading. * * *

55 First of all, it must be borne in mind that the anti-competitive object and effect of an agreement are not cumulative but alternative conditions for assessing whether such an agreement comes within the scope of the prohibition laid down in Article [101(1) TFEU]. According to settled case-law . . ., the alternative nature of that condition, indicated by the conjunction 'or', leads first to the need to consider the precise purpose of the agreement, in the economic context in which it is to be applied. Where, however, the analysis of the content of the agreement does not reveal a sufficient degree of harm to competition, the consequences of the agreement should then be considered and for it to be caught by the prohibition it is necessary to find that those factors are present which show that competition has in fact been prevented, restricted or distorted to an appreciable extent. It is also apparent from the case-law that it is not necessary to examine the effects of an agreement once its anti-competitive object has been established. . . .* * *

58 According to settled case-law, in order to assess the anti-competitive nature of an agreement, regard must be had inter alia to the content of its provisions, the objectives it seeks to attain and the economic and legal context of which it forms a part. . . . In addition, although the parties' intention is not a necessary factor in determining whether an agreement is restrictive, there is nothing prohibiting the Commission or the Community judicature from taking that aspect into account.

59 With respect to parallel trade, the Court has already held that, in principle, agreements aimed at prohibiting or limiting parallel trade have as their object the prevention of competition. * * *

61 The Court has, moreover, held in that regard, in relation to the application of Article [101 TFEU] and in a case involving the pharmaceuticals sector, that an agreement between producer and distributor which might tend to restore the national divisions in trade between Member States might be such as to frustrate the Treaty's objective of achieving the integration of national markets through the establishment of a single market. Thus on a number of occasions the Court has held agreements aimed at partitioning national markets according to national borders or making the interpenetration of national markets more difficult, in particular those aimed at preventing or restricting parallel exports, to be

agreements whose object is to restrict competition within the meaning of that article of the Treaty.

62 With respect to the Court of First Instance's statement that, while it is accepted that an agreement intended to limit parallel trade must in principle be considered to have as its object the restriction of competition, that applies in so far as it may be presumed to deprive final consumers of the advantages of effective competition in terms of supply or price, the Court notes that neither the wording of Article [101(1) TFEU] nor the case-law lend support to such a position.

63 First of all, there is nothing in that provision to indicate that only those agreements which deprive consumers of certain advantages may have an anti-competitive object. Secondly, it must be borne in mind that the Court has held that, like other competition rules laid down in the Treaty, Article [101 TFEU] aims to protect not only the interests of competitors or of consumers, but also the structure of the market and, in so doing, competition as such. Consequently, for a finding that an agreement has an anti-competitive object, it is not necessary that final consumers be deprived of the advantages of effective competition in terms of supply or price.

64 It follows that, by requiring proof that the agreement entails disadvantages for final consumers as a prerequisite for a finding of anti-competitive object and by not finding that that agreement had such an object, the Court of First Instance committed an error of law.

[The Court proceeded to find that the CFI's error was harmless, since the CFI had found that the agreement fell within Article 101(1), albeit by reason of its effect. The Court of Justice then reviewed the Commission's claims of CFI error regarding the Article 101(3) analysis, and found them unfounded. The Commission had examined the inefficiency from loss of parallel trade "without deeming it necessary to examine whether it had also been demonstrated that Clause 4 of the agreement entailed a gain in efficiency." para. 156.]

Notes and Questions

1. Explain why and how Clause 4 was a restriction by object even if it did not harm consumers. Does your answer reflect a major difference between US and EU competition law?

2. When the Commission reconsidered the matter, what did GSK have to establish to entitle it to an exemption? What evidence should and must GSK introduce to show that it will be more inventive if it has the freedom to obtain higher prices on sales for export? In response, how can and should the Commission quantify the harm to competition that must be balanced against the gains in innovation? Is the Commission well placed to conduct the balancing exercise?

3. Resale Price Maintenance

United States antitrust law long took a skeptical stance towards vertical restraints. The case law was based on the premise that vertical restraints impair the give-and-take of the competition process and harm powerless market actors and consumers. US antitrust law condemned, *per se*, agreements between a manufacturer and a distributor as to the price, customers or territories at which, to whom, or where the distributor must sell.

But perspectives changed. Beginning in the 1970s, the Chicago School of economic analysis was ascendant in the courts. Chicago School scholars generally argued that resale price maintenance (known as 'RPM') was often procompetitive and efficient. By 2007, the Supreme Court came around to this point of view, but over the strong dissent of four Justices.

LEEGIN CREATIVE LEATHER PRODUCTS, INC. v. PSKS, INC.

551 U.S. 877 (United States Supreme Court 2007)

KENNEDY, J.:

* * *

A

Though each side of the debate can find sources to support its position, it suffices to say here that economics literature is replete with procompetitive justifications for a manufacturer's use of resale price maintenance. Even those more skeptical of resale price maintenance acknowledge it can have procompetitive effects.

The few recent studies documenting the competitive effects of resale price maintenance also cast doubt on the conclusion that the practice meets the criteria for a ***per se*** rule.

The justifications for vertical price restraints are similar to those for other vertical restraints. Minimum resale price maintenance can stimulate interbrand competition—the competition among manufacturers selling different brands of the same type of product—by reducing intrabrand competition—the competition among retailers selling the same brand. The promotion of interbrand competition is important because "the primary purpose of the antitrust laws is to protect [this type of] competition." A single manufacturer's use of vertical price restraints tends to eliminate intrabrand price competition; this in turn encourages retailers to invest in tangible or intangible services or promotional efforts that aid the manufacturer's position as against rival manufacturers.

Resale price maintenance also has the potential to give consumers more options so that they can choose among low-price, low-service brands; high-price, high-service brands; and brands that fall in between.

Absent vertical price restraints, the retail services that enhance interbrand competition might be underprovided. This is because discounting retailers can free ride on retailers who furnish services and then capture some of the increased demand those services generate. Consumers might learn, for example, about the benefits of a manufacturer's product from a retailer that invests in fine showrooms, offers product demonstrations, or hires and trains knowledgeable employees. Or consumers might decide to buy the product because they see it in a retail establishment that has a reputation for selling high-quality merchandise. If the consumer can then buy the product from a retailer that discounts because it has not spent capital providing services or developing a quality reputation, the high-service retailer will lose sales to the discounter, forcing it to cut back its services to a level lower than consumers would otherwise prefer. Minimum resale price maintenance alleviates the problem because it prevents the discounter from undercutting the service provider. With price competition decreased, the manufacturer's retailers compete among themselves over services.

Resale price maintenance, in addition, can increase interbrand competition by facilitating market entry for new firms and brands. "[N]ew manufacturers and manufacturers entering new markets can use the restrictions in order to induce competent and aggressive retailers to make the kind of investment of capital and labor that is often required in the distribution of products unknown to the consumer." New products and new brands are essential to a dynamic economy, and if markets can be penetrated by using resale price maintenance there is a procompetitive effect.

Resale price maintenance can also increase interbrand competition by encouraging retailer services that would not be provided even absent free riding. It may be difficult and inefficient for a manufacturer to make and enforce a contract with a retailer specifying the different services the retailer must perform. Offering the retailer a guaranteed margin and threatening termination if it does not live up to expectations may be the most efficient way to expand the manufacturer's market share by inducing the retailer's performance and allowing it to use its own initiative and experience in providing valuable services.

B

While vertical agreements setting minimum resale prices can have procompetitive justifications, they may have anticompetitive effects in other cases; and unlawful price fixing, designed solely to obtain monopoly profits, is an ever-present temptation. Resale price maintenance may, for example, facilitate a manufacturer cartel. An unlawful cartel will seek to discover if some manufacturers are undercutting the cartel's fixed prices. Resale price maintenance could assist the cartel in identifying price-cutting manufacturers who benefit from the lower prices they offer. Resale price maintenance, furthermore, could discourage a manufacturer from cutting prices to retailers with the concomitant benefit of cheaper prices to consumers.

Vertical price restraints also "might be used to organize cartels at the retailer level." A group of retailers might collude to fix prices to consumers and then compel a manufacturer to aid the unlawful arrangement with resale price maintenance. In that instance the manufacturer does not establish the practice to stimulate services or to promote its brand but to give inefficient retailers higher profits. Retailers with better distribution systems and lower cost structures would be prevented from charging lower prices by the agreement

A horizontal cartel among competing manufacturers or competing retailers that decreases output or reduces competition in order to increase price is, and ought to be, ***per se*** unlawful. To the extent a vertical agreement setting minimum resale prices is entered upon to facilitate either type of cartel, it, too, would need to be held unlawful under the rule of reason. This type of agreement may also be useful evidence for a plaintiff attempting to prove the existence of a horizontal cartel.

Resale price maintenance, furthermore, can be abused by a powerful manufacturer or retailer. A dominant retailer, for example, might request resale price maintenance to forestall innovation in distribution that decreases costs. A manufacturer might consider it has little choice but to accommodate the retailer's demands for vertical price restraints if the manufacturer believes it needs access to the retailer's distribution network A manufacturer with market power, by comparison, might use resale price maintenance to give retailers an incentive not to sell the products of smaller rivals or new entrants. As should be evident, the potential anticompetitive consequences of vertical price restraints must not be ignored or underestimated.

[Having found both procompetitive and anticompetitive explanations for RPM, the Court concluded that rule of reason analysis was warranted. In an opinion by Justice Breyer, four

Justices dissented. They argued *stare decisis*, the tendency of RPM to increase consumer prices, and judicial administrability counselled in favor of maintaining per se illegality for RPM].

Meanwhile, Europe continued to condemn RPM agreements as falling categorically into Article 101(1) because they have the object to restrict competition, that is intrabrand competition, in the first place, but also interbrand competition inasmuch as they may, e.g., facilitate collusion or raise barriers to entry. RPM agreements are designated as a hard core violation by the vertical block exemption regulation and vertical guidelines insofar as they entail "the restriction of the buyer's ability to determine its sale price, without prejudice to the possibility of the supplier to impose a maximum sale price or recommend a sale price, provided that they do not amount to a fixed or minimum sale price as a result of pressure from, or incentives offered by, any of the parties." They may be entitled to an Article 101(3) exemption only in rare instances, as in the case of newspaper and periodical distribution where RPM constitutes "the sole means of supporting the financial burden resulting from the taking back of unsold copies . . . if the latter practice constitutes the sole method by which a wide selection of newspapers and periodicals can be made available to readers. . . ." The decision-maker "must take account of those factors. . . ." SA Binon & Cie v. SA Agence et Messageries de la Presse, Case 243/83, EU:C:1985:284, paras. 44–46.

Coincidentally with the decision in *Leegin*, the European Commission embarked on a process to reexamine its legislation on vertical restraints. The legislation takes the form of a regulation adopting a block exemption, and accompanying guidelines. The block exemption exempts (automatically unless the exemption is withdrawn) vertical agreements where the parties have 30% or less of the market, subject to certain other conditions, unless the agreement contains a "hard core restriction." Minimum RPM is a hard core restriction. Commission Regulation 2022/720, art. 4(a), 2022 O.J. (L 134), https://eur-lex.europa.eu/eli/reg/2022/720/oj/eng. An agreement containing a hard core restriction does not get the benefit of a block exemption. Recently, in the Super Bock case, the Court of justice clarified that a minimum resale price clause is not illegal per se but needs to be assessed under the main test for "by object" restrictions, i.e. assessment of the content, context and objective of the agreement or clause in question (Super Bock Bebidas, C–211/22, EU:C:2023:529).

RPM remains an important issue in Europe, including in the digital economy. In May 2017, the Commission released the final report on its sector inquiry into e-commerce business practices. (Final report on the E-commerce Sector Inquiry, 10 May 2017, COM (2017) 229 final.) That final report revealed that resale-price related restrictions are by far the most widespread restrictions of competition in e-commerce markets. Subsequently, on 24 July 2018, the European Commission found consumer electronics manufacturers Asus, Denon & Marantz, Philips and Pioneer guilty of imposing fixed or minimum resale prices on their online retailers in breach of Article 101 TFEU, and imposed fines totaling €111 million.

Asus, Denon & Marantz, Philips and Pioneer restricted the ability of their online retailers to set their own retail prices for widely used consumer electronics products such as kitchen appliances, notebooks and hi-fi products. If those retailers did not follow the prices requested by manufacturers, they faced threats or sanctions such as blocking of supplies. Many, including the biggest online retailers, use pricing algorithms which automatically adapt retail prices to those of competitors. In this way, the pricing restrictions imposed on low pricing online retailers typically had a broader impact on overall online prices for the respective consumer electronics products. Moreover, the use of sophisticated monitoring tools allowed the manufacturers to effectively track resale price setting in the distribution network and to intervene swiftly in case of price decreases. The Commission found that the practices in question limited effective price competition between retailers and led to higher prices with an immediate effect on consumers. (Case AT.40181—Philips; Case AT.40182—Pioneer; Case AT.40465—Asus; Case AT.40469—Denon & Marantz.) The vertical guidelines accompanying the draft block exemption would now give the following guidance on resale price restrictions, minimum and maximum.

EUROPEAN COMMISSION NOTICE GUIDELINES ON VERTICAL RESTRAINTS (2022)

available at http://ec.europa.eu/competition/antitrust/legislation/vertical.html (resale price maintenance)

* * *

6.1.1. Resale price maintenance

(185) The hardcore restriction set out in Article 4, point (a) of Regulation (EU) 2022/720 concerns resale price maintenance ('RPM'), that is, agreements which, directly or indirectly, have the object of restricting the buyer's ability to determine its sale price, including those which establish a fixed or minimum sale price to be

observed by the buyer (103). A requirement for the buyer to set its sale price within a certain range is RPM within the meaning of Article 4, point (a) of the Regulation.

(186) RPM can be applied through direct means. This is the case for contractual provisions or concerted practices that directly set the price that the buyer must charge to its customers (104), or which allow the supplier to set the resale price, or which prohibit the buyer from selling below a certain price level. The restriction is also clear-cut where the supplier requests a price increase and the buyer complies with the request.

(187) RPM can also be applied through indirect means, including incentives to observe a minimum price or disincentives to deviate from a minimum price. The following examples provide a non-exhaustive list of such indirect means:

(a) fixing the resale margin;

(b) fixing the maximum level of discount that the distributor can grant from a prescribed price level;

(c) making the grant of rebates or the reimbursement of promotional costs by the supplier subject to the observance of a given price level;

(d) imposing minimum advertised prices ('MAPs'), which prohibit the distributor from advertising prices below a level set by the supplier;

(e) linking the prescribed resale price to the resale prices of competitors;

(f) threats, intimidations, warnings, penalties, delay or suspension of deliveries or contract terminations in relation to the observance of a given price level.

(188) Pursuant to Article 4, point (a) of Regulation (EU) 2022/720, the imposition by the supplier of a maximum resale price or the recommendation of a resale price is not a hardcore restriction. However, if the supplier combines such a maximum price or resale price recommendation with incentives to apply a certain price level or disincentives to lower the sale price, this can amount to RPM. This would be the case, for example, where the supplier reimburses promotional costs incurred by the buyer subject to the condition the buyer does not deviate from the maximum resale price or the recommended resale price. An example of a disincentive to lower the sale price would be where the supplier threatens to cut further supplies in response to a deviation by the buyer from the maximum or recommended resale price.

(189) Although in principle MAPs leave the distributor free to sell at a price that is lower than the advertised price, they disincentivise the distributor from setting a lower sale price by restricting its ability to inform potential customers about available discounts. A key parameter for price competition between retailers is thereby removed. For the purpose of applying Article 4, point (a) of Regulation (EU) 2022/720, MAPs will therefore be treated as an indirect means of applying RPM.

(190) Direct or indirect means of applying RPM can be made more effective when combined with measures aimed at identifying price-cutting distributors, such as implementing a price monitoring system, or obliging retailers to report other members of the distribution network that deviate from the standard price level.

(191) Price monitoring is increasingly used in e-commerce, where both suppliers and retailers often use price monitoring software (105). This software increases price transparency in the market and allows manufacturers to effectively track the resale prices in their distribution network (106). It also allows retailers to track the prices of their competitors. However, on their own, price monitoring and price reporting are not RPM.

. . .

(194) Article 4, point (a) of Regulation (EU) 2022/720 is fully applicable in the online platform economy. In particular, where an undertaking provides online intermediation services within the meaning of Article 1(1), point (e) of the Regulation, it is a supplier in respect of those services and therefore Article 4, point (a) of the Regulation applies to restrictions imposed by the undertaking on buyers of the online intermediation services relating to the sale price of goods or services that are sold via the online intermediation services. While this does not prevent a provider of online intermediation services from incentivising users of the services to sell their goods or services at a competitive price or to reduce their prices, the imposition by the provider of online intermediation services of a fixed or minimum sale price for the transactions that it intermediates is a hardcore restriction within the meaning of Article 4, point (a) of Regulation (EU) 2022/720.

(195) The Court of Justice of the European Union has held on several occasions that RPM is a restriction of competition by object within the meaning of Article 101(1) of the Treaty (110). However, as stated in paragraphs (179) to (181), the qualification of a restriction as a hardcore restriction or as a by object restriction does not mean that it is a per se infringement of Article 101 of the Treaty. Where undertakings consider RPM to be efficiency-enhancing in an

individual case, they may rely on efficiency justifications under Article 101(3) of the Treaty.

(196) RPM can restrict intra-brand and/or inter-brand competition in various ways:

(a) RPM may facilitate collusion between suppliers, by enhancing price transparency in the market, thereby making it easier to detect whether a supplier is deviating from the collusive equilibrium by cutting its price. This negative effect is more likely in markets prone to collusive outcomes, for example, where suppliers form a tight oligopoly and a significant share of the market is covered by RPM agreements;

(b) RPM may facilitate collusion between buyers at the distribution level, in particular where it is driven by the buyers. Strong or well organised buyers may be able to force or convince one or more of their suppliers to fix their resale price above the competitive level, thereby helping the buyers reach or stabilise a collusive equilibrium. RPM serves as a commitment device for retailers not to deviate from the collusive equilibrium through discounting prices;

(c) in some cases, RPM may also soften competition between manufacturers and/or between retailers, in particular when manufacturers use the same distributors to distribute their products and RPM is applied by all or many of them;

(d) RPM may reduce the pressure on the supplier's margin, in particular where a manufacturer has a commitment problem, that is, where it has an interest in lowering the price charged to subsequent distributors. In that situation, the manufacturer may prefer to agree to RPM, to help it to commit not to lower the price for subsequent distributors, and to reduce the pressure on its own margin;

(e) by preventing price competition between distributors, RPM may prevent or hinder the entry and expansion of new or more efficient distribution formats, thus reducing innovation at the distribution level;

(f) RPM may be implemented by a supplier with market power to foreclose smaller rivals. The increased margin that RPM may offer distributors may incentivise them to favour the supplier's brand over rival brands when advising customers, even where such advice is not in the customer's interest, or not to sell the rival brands at all;

(g) the direct effect of RPM is the elimination of intra-brand price competition, by preventing some or all distributors from lowering their sale price for the brand concerned, thus resulting in a price increase for that brand.

(197) However, RPM may also lead to efficiencies, in particular where it is supplier driven. Where undertakings rely on an efficiency defence for RPM, they must be able to substantiate this with concrete evidence and show that all the conditions of Article 101(3) are fulfilled in the individual case (111). Four examples of such efficiencies are set out below.

(a) When a manufacturer introduces a new product, RPM may be an efficient means to induce distributors to better take into account the manufacturer's interest in promoting that product. Article 101(3) of the Treaty also requires that there are no realistic and less restrictive alternative means of incentivising the distributors to promote the product. To meet that requirement, suppliers may, for example, demonstrate that it is not feasible in practice to impose on all buyers effective promotion obligations by contract. In such circumstances, the imposition of fixed or minimum retail prices for a limited period of time in order to facilitate the introduction of the new product may be considered on balance pro-competitive.

(b) Fixed resale prices, and not just maximum resale prices, may be necessary to organise a coordinated short-term low price campaign (of 2 to 6 weeks in most cases), in particular in a distribution system where the supplier applies a uniform distribution format, such as a franchise system. In such a case, given its temporary character, the imposition of fixed retail prices may be considered on balance pro-competitive.

(c) A minimum resale price or MAP can be used to prevent a particular distributor from using the product of a supplier as a loss leader. Where a distributor regularly resells a product below the wholesale price, this can damage the brand image of the product and, over time, reduce overall demand for the product and undermine the supplier's incentives to invest in quality and brand image. In that case, preventing that distributor from selling below the wholesale price, by imposing on it a targeted minimum resale price or MAP may be considered on balance pro-competitive.

(d) In some situations, the extra margin provided by RPM may allow retailers to provide additional pre-sales services, in particular in the case of complex products. If enough customers take advantage of such services in order to choose a product but subsequently purchase at a lower price with retailers that do not provide such services (and hence do not incur those costs), high-service retailers may reduce or stop providing pre-sales services, which enhance the demand for the supplier's product. The supplier must demonstrate that there is a risk of free riding at the distribution level, that fixed or minimum resale prices provide sufficient incentives for investments in pre-sale services and that there is no realistic and less restrictive alternative means of overcoming such free riding. In this situation, the likelihood that RPM will be considered as pro-competitive is higher when competition between suppliers is fierce and the supplier has limited market power.

(198) The use of recommended resale prices or maximum resale prices can benefit from the exemption provided by Article 2(1) of Regulation (EU) 2022/720 where the market share of each of the parties to the agreement does not exceed the 30 % threshold and provided that this does not amount to the imposition of a minimum or fixed sale price as a result of pressure or incentives from any of the parties, as set out in paragraphs (187) and (188). Paragraphs (199) to (201) provide guidance for the assessment of recommended or maximum resale prices above the market share threshold.

(199) The risks to competition associated with recommended and maximum resale prices are, first, that they may act as a focal point for resellers and may be followed by most or all of them. Second, they may soften competition or facilitate collusion between suppliers.

(200) An important factor for assessing possible anti-competitive effects of recommended or maximum resale prices is the market position of the supplier. The stronger the market position of the supplier, the higher the risk that a recommended or maximum resale price will lead to a more or less uniform application of that price level by the resellers, because they may find it difficult to deviate from what they perceive to be the preferred resale price proposed by such an important supplier.

(201) Where recommended or maximum resale prices produce appreciable anti-competitive effects, it is necessary to assess whether they fulfil the conditions of the exception provided by Article 101(3)

of the Treaty. As regards maximum resale prices, the avoidance of 'double marginalisation' (112) may be particularly relevant. A maximum resale price may also help to ensure that the supplier's brand competes more fiercely with other brands distributed by the same distributor, including private label products.

Notes and Questions

1. Compare the European block exemption and guidelines with the US *Leegin* case. What different perceptions do you observe about the possible harms and possible benefits of RPM? Is the structure of analysis, including burdens of proof, likely to lead to different results? What would be the outcome of the *Leegin* case (agreement not to discount a minor brand of five belts) in each jurisdiction? Is one approach more likely to benefit consumers than the others?

2. Although some commentators believe that *Leegin* killed off the possibility of a successful challenge to RPM in the US, a few post-*Leegin* challenges have been successful. In 2015, the retailer Cosco brought a challenge to Johnson & Johnson's RPM policies with respect to contact lenses. The case was voluntarily dismissed in 2016, but only after J&J agreed to abandon the practice.

3. *Leegin* creates a natural experiment for economists: Does RPM in fact increase consumer prices? One of the first large scale post-*Leegin* empirical studies—undertaken, perhaps ironically, by economists at the University of Chicago, found that RPM increased consumer prices and reduced sales output. Alexander MacKay & David Aron Smith, *The Empirical Effects of Resale Price Maintenance,* https://papers.ssrn.com/sol3/papers.cfm?abstract_id=2513533. Should findings like these motivate courts, agencies, or legislatures to prohibit RPM categorically? Or are such results consistent with RPM incentivizing greater quality, including more service, and hence not necessarily anti-consumer?

4. Although *Leegin* articulates the federal antitrust standard making RPM subject to rule of reason rather than *per se* treatment, not all US states follow that precedent under their state antitrust laws. The Attorneys General of New York, Illinois, and Michigan have taken the view that RPM remains illegal in those states, and precedent in Maryland and California suggests that it may be unlawful per se in those states as well. The Kansas Supreme Court applied per se illegality to RPM, O'Brien v. Leegin Creative Leather Products, Inc., 294 Kan. 318 (2012), but that result was subsequently overturned by Kansas legislation. K.S.A. § 50–163. Does it make sense for states to experiment with a different rule than *Leegin*, or is a uniform national rule important?

5. On August 1, 2013, the Shanghai High People's Court delivered a much-anticipated decision concerning RPM in China in the case of Rainbow v. Johnson & Johnson (J&J). J&J sells medical

equipment, including suture threads for surgeries. Beijing Ruibang Yonghe Science & Technology Company ("Rainbow") distributed J&J's sutures for 15 years. In 2008, however, Rainbow sold below the minimum distribution price stipulated in the parties' distribution agreement, and J&J thereafter terminated Rainbow as a distributor. Article 14 of the Chinese Anti-Monopoly Law prohibits undertakings from fixing the prices of products resold to third parties, and hence appeared to prohibit RPM categorically. Nonetheless, the High Court held that RPM agreements are not categorically illegal but subject to rule of reason analysis including inquiry into: (1) the competitiveness of the relevant market; (2) the defendant's market power; (3) the defendant's purpose in implementing the RPM; and (4) the competitive effect of the RPM. Applying this test, the High Court found the RPM unlawful. For a helpful analysis of the case, see Hao Zhan, *The Chinese Shanghai Higher Court decides on the first private antitrust action involving vertical agreements (Rainbow/Johnson & Johnson)*, e-Competitions August 2013, Art. N 66633. Since then, the Chinese competition authorities have adopted a number of decisions in RPM cases considering it inherently illegal, whereas courts have shown an openness towards the consideration of their effects and the thereto related efficiencies following an amendment to China's Anti-Monopoly Law in 2022. For an overview, see Heng Ju and Meitong Li, *Object and Effects Tests in Resale Price Maintenance Cases in China*, Journal of Competition law & Economics (2025).

6. In other jurisdictions, RPM is often prohibited, either categorically or with limited exceptions. Section 76 of Canada's competition statute prohibits RPM where it is likely to have "an adverse effect on competition." According to the 2014 Guidelines of the Canadian Competition Bureau, suppliers should not engage in behavior that discourages price cutting by retailers. The Brazilian Conselho Administrativo de Defesa Econômica ("CADE") has a long-standing practice of considering minimum RPM as presumptively unlawful while being more lenient on maximum or recommended RPM. (see, originally, the SKF case, no. 08012.001271/2001–44). By contrast, the Indian statute treats RPM as subject to the rule of reason and the Competition Commission of India ("CCI") has consistently assessed the effects of RPM on the market rather than adopting a per se approach, including in e-commerce cases, thereby putting the onus on the CCI to determine whether RPM arrangements cause or are likely to cause an appreciable adverse effect on competition.

4. Tying and Exclusive Dealing

For many years, US law focused on negative aspects of tying: competitors were fenced out of segments of the market to which they could no longer sell their products on the merits. US law also focused on negative aspects of exclusive dealing, which meant that the firm saddled with the exclusive dealing obligation could not deal with competitors of its supplier, even if they offered a better or cheaper product. The inefficiencies and the unfairness of the fencing out led to enactment of Clayton Act Section 3 in 1914. Ultimately, however, it was recognized that these practices may have procompetitive aspects. In general, the presumptions are reversed in the US today. Exclusive dealing is recognized as normally efficient, and it is usually lawful; but it can be illegal if it is a device to keep rivals from needed access to scarce inputs or outlets, is not justified by efficiencies, and is likely to increase or maintain economic power. Tying—although technically still subject to a rule of modified per se illegality with need to prove market power, two products and forcing but no need to prove anticompetitive effects—is now regarded as often efficient or competitively neutral. The fencing out effect in itself is no longer considered a competitive harm. The modified per se rule may be en route to elimination.

Some jurisdictions still have concerns with the fencing-out effect, especially where it results from tying and especially where the share of the market foreclosed is significant. These concerns are underscored where tying is (still) regarded as most likely to be undertaken in order to exploit leverage and not to serve consumers. See, for example, the law of Japan, at C below.

The United Nations Set of Multilaterally Agreed Equitable Principles and Rules singles out, as conduct to be avoided by dominant firms, exclusive dealing and tying. (The Set, D(f)(ii) and (iv).) The UNCTAD Model Law on Competition sums up one view of the usual motivation for tying:

> Tying arrangements are normally imposed in order to promote the sale of slower moving products and in particular those subject to greater competition from substitute products. (para. 90.)

The Set allows as a justification "ensuring the achievement of legitimate business purposes, such as quality, safety, adequate distribution or service".

In Europe, most tying and other foreclosing restraints are treated under Article 102 as possible abuses of dominance. Tying and exclusive dealing by a dominant firm that forecloses significant parts of an adjoining market are treated as suspect and illegal unless justified. E.g., Hoffmann-La Roche, Case 85/76, EU:C:1979:36; *Tetra Pak*, Case C–333/94 P, EU:C:1996:436; Hilti, Case C–53/92 P, EU:C:1994:77; Google Android, Case C–738/22 P, forthcoming 2025). See Chapter 5. For proof of tying, it is necessary that there be two separate products. Objective justifications may include efficiencies but not safety. When Hilti, dominant in the market for nail guns, defended its tying of nails to the cartridge strips on grounds that its competitors' products might be dangerous, the court replied that safety is a matter for regulation; it is not the job of the dominant firm.

For some time, the EU Court of Justice's case law on tying has not kept step with the increasing sophistication of analysis within the Competition Directorate and evidenced in case selection and Commission decisions. Since approximately 2003, the Commission has followed a welfare economics approach, essentially asking whether the business practice increases or maintains market power. Meanwhile, the European case law progressively began to also ask whether the firm with substantial market power is using its power or leverage to obtain competitive advantages over rivals. E.g., British Airways PLC v. Commission, Case C–95/04 P, EU:C:2007:166; Microsoft Corp. v. Commission, Case T–201/04, EU:T:2007:289.

We present a small selection of EU cases below, and then reflect the analysis used by the Commission as reflected in the draft vertical guidelines.

The next case, *Delimitis*, delineates when tying and 'single branding' are sufficiently significant to be caught by Article 101(1); and the following case, *Schöller Lebensmittal*, delineates when exclusive dealing significantly blocks access and the undertaking cannot prove appreciable objective advantages that compensate for the disadvantages.

STERGIOS DELIMITIS v. HENNINGER BRÄU AG

Case C–234/89, ECLI:EU:C:1991:91 (Court of Justice of the European Union 1991)

[Stergios Delimitis rented a pub from Henninger Bräu, agreeing to sell only Henninger Bräu beer in the pub. Asserting that the contract violated Article 101 and was void, Delimitis failed to pay rent, and Henninger deducted the rent from Delimitis' rental deposit. Delimitis sued for return of the rent. Henninger relied on the contract, which presumably was not intended to harm competition but reflected the brewery's desire for an assured outlet for its beer and Delimitis' desire for the premises and an assured supply.

The national court sought a preliminary ruling on whether the contract was caught by Article 101(1) and if so whether it fell within the then block exemption on exclusive purchasing. The Court of Justice set forth the following framework for determining whether exclusive contracts that are part of a network of similar contracts have the effect, if not the object, of "preventing, restricting or distorting competition":]

15 . . . [I]t is necessary to analyse the effects of a beer supply agreement, taken together with other contracts of the same type, on the opportunities of national competitors or those from other Member States, to gain access to the market for beer consumption or to increase their market share and, accordingly, the effects on the range of products offered to consumers. * * *

18 [The relevant market is] the national market for beer distribution in premises for the sale and consumption of drinks.

19 In order to assess whether the existence of several beer supply agreements impedes access to the market as so defined, it is further necessary to examine the nature and extent of those agreements in their totality, comprising all similar contracts tying a large number of points of sale to several national producers. The effect of those networks of contracts on access to the market depends specifically on the number of outlets thus tied to national producers in relation to the number of public houses which are not so tied, the duration of the commitments entered into, the quantities of beer to which those commitments relate, and on the proportion between those quantities and the quantities sold by free distributors.

20 The existence of a bundle of similar contracts, even if it has a considerable effect on the opportunities for gaining access to the market, is not, however, sufficient in itself to support a finding that the relevant market is inaccessible, inasmuch as it is only one factor, amongst others, pertaining to the economic and legal context in which an agreement must be appraised. The other factors to be taken into account are, in the first instance, those also relating to opportunities for access.

21 In that connection it is necessary to examine whether there are real concrete possibilities for a new competitor to penetrate the bundle of contracts by acquiring a brewery already established on the market together with its network of sales outlets, or to circumvent the bundle of contracts by opening new public houses. For that purpose it is necessary to have regard to the legal rules and agreements on the acquisition of companies and the establishment of outlets, and to the minimum number of outlets necessary for the economic operation of a distribution system. The presence of beer wholesalers not tied to producers who are active on the market is also a factor capable of facilitating a new producer's access to that market since he can make use of those wholesaler's sales networks to distribute his own beer.

22 Secondly, account must be taken of the conditions under which competitive forces operate on the relevant market. In that connection it is necessary to know not only the number and the size of producers

present on the market, but also the degree of saturation of that market and customer fidelity to existing brands, for it is generally more difficult to penetrate a saturated market in which customers are loyal to a small number of large producers than a market in full expansion in which a large number of small producers are operating without any strong brand names. . . .

23 If an examination of all similar contracts entered into on the relevant market and the other factors relevant to the economic and legal context in which the contract must be examined shows that those agreements do not have the cumulative effect of denying access to that market to new national and foreign competitors, the individual agreements comprising the bundle of agreements cannot be held to restrict competition within the meaning of Article [101](1) of the Treaty. They do not, therefore, fall under the prohibition laid down in that provision.

24 If, on the other hand, such examination reveals that it is difficult to gain access to the relevant market, it is necessary to assess the extent to which the agreements entered into by the brewery in question contribute to the cumulative effect produced in that respect by the totality of the similar contracts found on that market. Under the Community rules on competition, responsibility for such an effect of closing off the market must be attributed to the breweries which make an appreciable contribution thereto. Beer supply agreements entered into by breweries whose contribution to the cumulative effect is insignificant do not therefore fall under the prohibition under Article [101](1). * * *

27 The reply to be given to the first three questions is therefore that a beer supply agreement is prohibited by Article [101](1) of the [ ] Treaty, if two cumulative conditions are met. The first is that, having regard to the economic and legal context of the agreement at issue, it is difficult for competitors who could enter the market or increase their market share to gain access to the national market for the distribution of beer in premises for the sale and consumption of drinks. The fact that, in that market, the agreement in issue is one of a number of similar agreements having a cumulative effect on competition constitutes only one factor amongst others in assessing whether access to that market is indeed difficult. The second condition is that the agreement in question must make a significant contribution to the sealing-off effect brought about by the totality of those agreements in their economic and legal context. The extent of the contribution made by the individual agreement depends on the position of the contracting parties in the relevant market and on the duration of the agreement.

Notes and Questions

1. *Delimitis* was considered a break-through judgment. Prior to *Delimitis*, single-branding contracts ("I will sell only your brand") with significant producers were deemed almost automatically caught by Article 101(1) and thus were illegal unless justified.

2. What would have been Delimitis' theory of antitrust harm?

3. Duration of exclusive contracts is a factor to be considered. Long duration, the Court has said, can contribute to the "sealing off effect." In *Neste Markkinointi Oy*, Neste, the leading petrol supplier in Finland, sued former service station proprietors for abandoning their service stations without giving the contractually required one-year notice. The proprietors defended that the contract was void because it contained an exclusivity clause (for one year), that Neste's network of agreements, or its network combined with those of other suppliers, significantly foreclosed access of new oil companies, and that the network ran afoul of Article 101(1). The national court posed to the Court of Justice the question whether the contracts allowing termination on short notice could be separated from contracts of long duration in considering compatibility of the plaintiffs' contracts with the Treaty. The Court noted that all gas stations carry only one brand of motor fuels; the supplier must invest in adapting the sales point to the brand image, so that exclusivity as such was not in question; rather "duration is the decisive factor in the market-sealing effect." (para. 32) A one-year period is reasonably necessary to protect the interests of the parties. The one-year contracts in effect at any given time represented a very small portion of the exclusive purchasing agreements of any particular supplier; therefore they made no significant contribution to any cumulative effect; therefore they were not caught by Article 101(1). Case C–214/99, EU:C:2000:679.

4. Why did the gas station proprietors in *Neste* (who breached their agreement to give proper notice) and the beer house tenant in Delimitis (who owed rent) have standing to claim that their commitment to purchase goods only from their supplier, combined with a network of similar contracts, amounted to an anticompetitive sealing off of the market for those goods?

Note that European cases are seldom dismissed for lack of standing. Under the Treaty, persons directly and individually concerned have a right to sue. Art. 263 TFEU, ex 230 ECT.

SCHÖLLER LEBENSMITTEL v. COMMISSION

Case T–9/93, ECLI:EU:T:1995:99 (General Court of the European Union 1995)

[Langnese-Iglo, a subsidiary of Unilever, and Schöller Lebensmittel were the leading firms in Germany in the sale of ice cream; particularly impulse-buying ice cream. Each, separately, had a network of agreements with the sellers requiring that the retailers purchase ice cream only from it, or supplying freezers "free" and requiring that the retailer use the freezer only for the supplier's ice cream and not for the ice cream of competitors.

Mars, a French manufacturer of ice cream bars, was trying to pierce the German impulse ice cream market. Finding the two firms' supply contracts to be road blocks to market access, Mars complained to the Commission. The Commission brought proceedings against each. The Commission withdrew a comfort letter that it had previously given to Schöller and decided both the question of applicability of Article 81(1) and the question of entitlement of the applicants to an individual exemption.

In *Schöller*, the court first examined whether the contested supply agreements had an appreciable effect on competition. It found "that the applicant holds a strong position in the relevant market"; it held "more than 25 per cent" in the traditional trade, and, by its agreements, tied more than 10% of the sales outlets. Combined with Langnese's contracts, the tied portion of the market exceeded 30%.]

83 With respect to [other] factors, the Commission has drawn attention to the existence of additional substantial barriers to access to the market, both in the grocery trade and in the traditional trade. . . . [A]ccess to the market for new competitors is made more difficult by the existence of a system under which a large number of freezer cabinets are lent by the applicant to retailers both in the grocery trade and in the traditional trade . . ., the retailers being obliged to use them exclusively for the applicant's products.

84 The Court considers that the Commission was right to treat that factor as contributing to making access to the market more difficult. The necessary consequence of that situation is that any new competitor entering the market must either persuade the retailer to exchange the freezer cabinet installed by the applicant for another, which involves giving up the turnover in the products from the previous supplier, or to persuade the retailer to install an additional freezer cabinet, which may prove impossible, particularly because of lack of space in small sales outlets. Moreover, if the new competitor is able to offer only a limited range of products, as in the case of the intervener, it may prove difficult for it to persuade the retailer to terminate its agreement with the previous supplier.

85 It is also apparent from the documents before the Court that, in the traditional trade, there are numerous individual retailers whose average turnover is rather low. The establishment of a profitable distribution system therefore presupposes that a new competitor must have a large number of retailers concentrated within a specified

geographical area which can be supplied through regional or central warehouses. The fact that there are no independent intermediaries means that this fragmentation of demand constitutes an additional barrier to access to the market. Finally, the Commission rightly took into account the fact that the applicant's product brands are very well known.

86 In those circumstances, the Court considers that examination of all the similar agreements concluded on the market and of other aspects of the economic and legal context in which they operate . . . shows that the exclusive purchasing agreements concluded by the applicant are liable appreciably to affect competition within the meaning of Article [101](1) of the Treaty.

87 In view of the strong position occupied by the applicant in the relevant market and, in particular, its market share, the Court considers that the agreements contribute significantly to the closing-off of the market.

88 In view of all the foregoing, the Court considers that the Commission was right to conclude that the contested agreements give rise to an appreciable restriction of competition in the relevant market. * * *

139 In considering whether the Commission was right to refuse to grant an individual exemption, it must first be borne in mind that an individual exemption decision may be granted only if, in particular, the four conditions laid down by Article [81](3) of the Treaty are all met by the agreement in question, with the result that an exemption must be refused if any of the four conditions is not met. * * *

142 As regards the first of the four conditions laid down by Article [101](3) of the Treaty, the Court points out that, according to that provision, the agreements capable of being exempted are those which contribute "to improving the production or distribution of goods or to promoting technical or economic progress". It is settled law that the improvement cannot be identified with all the advantages which the parties obtain from the agreement in their production or distribution activities. The improvement must in particular display appreciable objective advantages of such a character as to compensate for the disadvantages which they cause in the field of competition.

143 . . . Although it is apparent . . . that exclusive purchasing agreements lead in general to an improvement in distribution, in that they enable the supplier to plan the sale of his goods with greater precision and for a longer period and ensure that the reseller's requirements will be met on a regular basis for the duration of the agreement, and even if it is assumed that it would be necessary

for the applicant, for reasons of cost, to terminate supplies to certain small sales outlets if it were obliged to give up supplies to them on an exclusive basis, the Commission considers nevertheless that the contested agreements do not give rise to objective and specific advantages for the public interest such as to compensate for the disadvantages which they cause in the field of competition.

144 In support of that argument, the Commission states, first, that, in view of the strong position on the market held by the applicant, the contested agreements do not . . . have the effect of intensifying competition between different brands of products. The Commission rightly took the view that the network of agreements at issue constitutes a major barrier to access to the market, with the result that competition is restricted.

145 . . . [It is clear] that the Commission considered that supplies to any small sales outlets abandoned by the applicant, for reasons of costs, would be taken over either by other suppliers, for example small local producers, or by independent dealers selling several ranges of products. Moreover, the Commission points out that the applicant itself recognised that it continues to supply even very small sales outlets, whose annual turnover hovers around 300 German marks, in those cases where their geographical situation is favourable.

146 Against that background, it must be borne in mind that the intervener, Mars, stated that it is wholly exceptional for impulse products to be distributed using a transport system owned by the producers. The parties agree that it is only in Germany, Denmark and Italy that undertakings in the Unilever group, including Langnese, have concluded exclusive agreements covering sales outlets.

147 Although the applicant claims that it would be obliged, for reasons of cost, to cease supplying a number of small sales outlets if it had to give up its exclusive purchasing agreements, the Court considers that it has not provided any evidence to show that such a situation would be liable to jeopardise regular supplies of impulse ice-cream to the territory as a whole and, in particular, that the small sales outlets concerned would not subsequently be supplied by other suppliers or wholesalers, simply as a consequence of the unrestricted competition which would then prevail. Nor has the applicant produced any convincing evidence of the special conditions in Germany which made it necessary to create an ice-cream distribution system belonging to the producers. The Court therefore considers that the applicant has not shown that the Commission committed a manifest error of assessment in considering that the contested

agreements did not fulfil the first condition laid down by Article [101](3) of the Treaty. . . . * * *

Notes and Questions

1. Did Schöller have market power? Is market power a necessary condition for a violation? Should it be?

2. What were the effects of the exclusivity and freezer clauses on competitors? on potential competitors? on consumers? Which effects are most important?

3. What were the efficiencies of the exclusive supply contracts? of the "free" freezer arrangements? How would you balance the efficiencies against the anticompetitive aspects of the agreements? Did the court agree?

4. What was the strongest case for granting the exemption? Was the Commission right to deny it? Note that the case arose before modernisation measures abolished the notification/exemption process. Still, given the Treaty language, agreements caught by Article 101(1) must fulfill the four conditions of 101(3).

5. If you were Mars and if you could not expect the European Commission to grant you relief from your competitors' exclusivity and freezer clauses, what strategies would you adopt?

6. If Schöller and Langnese withdrew the exclusivity obligation and offered retailers the choice of a) freezers for sale at market price, b) freezers for rent at market price, or c) freezers "free" with an obligation to use only the supplier's ice cream in the freezer, would the new arrangement be permissible? What if virtually all of the retailers chose option (c)? See Van den Bergh Foods Ltd. (subsidiary of Unilever), Cases IV/34.073, 34.395, 35.436, Commission Decision 98/531, O.J. L 246/1 (Sept. 4, 1998). Langnese-Iglo GmbH v. Commission, Case T–7/93, the companion case to *Schöller*, is reported at EU:T:1995:98, aff'd, Case C–279/95 P, EU:C:1998:447.

7. The Irish court took an entirely different view of the freezer arrangement and its effects, even when the freezer clause was imposed by a dominant firm. Masterfoods (Mars) had been enlisting numerous retailers in Ireland to stock and display Mars bars in their freezers. HB Ice-cream (of the Unilever family), the dominant impulse ice cream seller in Ireland, sought to enforce its exclusive contracts with the retailers. In 1992 it persuaded an Irish court to permanently restrain Masterfoods from inducing breach of HB's contracts. The Irish court, by Judge Lynch, analyzed the contracts as follows:

> I think that a breach of paragraph (e) [distorting competition by imposing unrelated obligations] does not arise at all in this case. The contracts in question are bailments of freezers

> whether they be on loan or hire. The terms objected to relate to the very basis of the contract of bailment, namely, the purpose for which the goods (the freezers) are bailed to the bailee (the retailer). The freezers are bailed to the bailees for the purpose of storing, selling and advertising HB ice cream products only. Those terms are not supplementary obligations nor by their nature or according to commercial usage do they not have an essential connection with the contracts of bailment. They do. It would seem that none of the particular breaches set out in paragraphs (a) to (e) of Article [101](1) apply: certainly, none clearly apply to the facts of Article [101] if it was reasonably clear that there was a contravention of the general intention of the article. Is it reasonably likely that these contracts of bailment of freezers may affect trade between member states of the European Community and may prevent, restrict or distort competition within the common market? I am not satisfied that Mars has made out a sufficient prima facie or serious case to that effect.

H.B. Ice-cream Ltd. v. Masterfoods Ltd. (trading as Mars Ireland), [1990] 2 IR 463.

Masterfoods complained to the European Commission about the exclusivity clauses and the Irish court injunction. The Commission, after finding that 40% of sales outlets in Ireland were tied up by the exclusivity clause, held:

> [T]he exclusivity provision in the freezer-cabinet agreement concluded between HB and retailers in Ireland, for the placement of cabinets in retail outlets which have only one or more freezer cabinets supplied by HB for the stocking of single-wrapped items of impulse ice cream, and not having a freezer cabinet either procured by themselves or provided by another ice-cream manufacturer constitutes an infringement of Article [101](1) of the Treaty. * * *
>
> HB's inducement to retailers in Ireland to enter into freezer-cabinet agreements subject to a condition of exclusivity by offering to supply them with one or more freezer cabinets for the stocking of single-wrapped items of impulse ice cream and to maintain the cabinets, free of any direct charge, constitutes an infringement of Article [102] of the Treaty.

Van den Bergh Foods Ltd., Cases IV/34.073, IV/34.395 and IV/35.436, Commission Decision 98/531 of 11 March 1998, O.J. L 246/1 (Sept. 4, 1998), Arts. 1, 3.

Meanwhile, the Irish Supreme Court stayed the Irish appeal and asked the European Court of Justice whether its obligation of sincere cooperation (Art. 4 Treaty on European Union (TEU), ex 10 ECT) required it to stay the Irish case pending the disposition of Van den Bergh's appeal. The Court of Justice responded in the affirmative, holding that Ireland could not maintain a judgment inconsistent with the Community disposition of the same issue. Masterfoods Ltd. (Mars Ireland), Case C–344/98, EU:C:2000:689.

On its appeal from the Commission decision, Van den Bergh stressed that the retailers were free to terminate their contract with HB or to install freezers not belonging to HB; and it argued that their freedom to do so meant that there was no foreclosure. The Court of First Instance responded that the retailers had little incentive to exercise this freedom, and seldom did. It noted also the unique circumstances of the market, including the limited space in the retail stores and the popularity of HB's ice cream, and concluded that the Commission did not err in finding that the clause produced a sufficiently high degree of foreclosure to constitute an infringement. Van den Bergh Foods v. Commission, Case T–65/98, EU:T:2003:281.

8. US law tends to examine more skeptically, first, the market power of the seller, and second, the practical ability of outsiders to reach the market efficiently notwithstanding exclusivity clauses. Also, US courts would take account of the fact that a "free" freezer is a good deal for the retailer. But if the undertaking had significant market power and if its exclusive contract requirements excluded efficient outsiders, causing the price of impulse ice cream to rise, would the clause be likely to offend US law also? See, e.g., United States v. Dentsply Int'l Inc., 399 F.3d 181 (3d Cir. 2005).

5. Block Exemptions and Guidelines

In early days of operations, under its system requiring parties to notify potentially anticompetitive agreements and requiring the Commission to clear or exempt the notified agreements, the Commission was flooded with more notifications than it could handle. The largest part of these notifications were vertical distribution agreements. The Commission began the practice of adopting block exemption regulations. Agreements that fell within the block exemptions would get the benefit of an automatic Article 101(3) exemption. The block exemption regulations specified clauses that must be in the agreement, clauses that could not be in the agreement, and clauses that might be in the agreement (white, black, and grey clauses). These block exemption regulations were at first highly detailed. Moreover, firms were induced to bring their deals within the terms of the exemption, for comfort and certainty. Eventually, the block exemption regulations were recognized as straight-jacketing business. Some were withdrawn. The remaining ones were liberalized and modernized and published with guidelines, to announce policy and to give business a degree of certainty.

The most important set of block exemption regulations and guidelines are the general set on distribution. Also adopted are important vertical block exemption regulations and guidelines for the motor vehicle sector and for technology licensing.

Below we include the most important provisions of the vertical block exemption regulation. We then provide excerpts from the accompanying guidelines.

a. Vertical (Distribution and Supply) Block Exemption and Guidelines

The European Commission has a block exemption and guidelines for the regulation of distribution and supply arrangements. In general, the scheme of the block exemption and guidelines is to provide a safe harbor for vertical agreements involving a seller and a buyer both of whom have market shares not exceeding 30%. The buyer's market share is assessed on the upstream market, to take account of buyer power. In addition, to get advantage of the safe harbor (block exemption), there must be no "hard core" restriction—a category that includes resale price maintenance, tight territorial agreements, and certain Internet restrictions such as terminating Internet customers' transactions if their credit card reveals an address outside of the territory. For agreements not accorded a block exemption, an analysis is performed to consider the net economic effect. Guidelines provide general principles for analysis and then specify the analysis appropriate to various kinds of restraints, such as exclusive supplying, selective distribution and tying. Hard core restraints are presumed illegal and will seldom be allowed, but still, it is possible for the parties to bring forward evidence to show that efficiencies outweigh negative effects.

In recent years, digitization and sustainability have influenced the enforcement of Article 101 in relation to vertical restrains. The enforcement of Article 101 has reflected the impact of the growth of online sales and online platforms on distribution models. Notably, consumers' expectations to have a continuous experience across a variety of different channels ('omni-channel') such as offline and online shops, marketplaces and other online platforms has led suppliers to increase the number of sales channels used to promote and distribute their products and services. New or more prevalent types of distribution arrangements (such as online intermediation services or dual distribution) or contractual provisions (such as MFN or price parity clauses) have emerged as a result and become the focus of enforcement actions. Sustainability objectives also impacted the enforcement of Article 101 in relation to vertical restraints. For example, a supplier in a selective distribution system could require the use of ecological means for delivery. Hence, the main innovations brought about by the 2022 block exemption regulation and vertical restraints guidelines relate to these areas.

The block exemption follows.

COMMISSION REGULATION ON THE APPLICATION OF ARTICLE 101(3) OF THE TREATY ON THE FUNCTIONING OF THE EUROPEAN UNION TO CATEGORIES OF VERTICAL AGREEMENTS AND CONCERTED PRACTICES (2022)

available at https://competition-policy.ec.europa.eu/antitrust-and-cartels_en

(1) Regulation No 19/65/EEC empowers the Commission to apply Article 101(3) of the Treaty by regulation to certain categories of vertical agreements and corresponding concerted practices falling within Article 101(1) of the Treaty.

(2) Commission Regulation (EU) No 330/2010 (3) defines a category of vertical agreements that the Commission regarded as normally satisfying the conditions laid down in Article 101(3) of the Treaty. Experience with the application of Regulation (EU) No 330/2010, which expires on 31 May 2022, has been positive overall, as shown by the evaluation of that Regulation. Taking into account that experience as well as new market developments, such as the growth of e-commerce, and new or more prevalent types of vertical agreements, it is appropriate to adopt a new block exemption regulation.

(3) The category of agreements which can be regarded as normally satisfying the conditions laid down in Article 101(3) of the Treaty includes vertical agreements for the purchase or sale of goods or services where those agreements are concluded between non-competing undertakings, between certain competitors or by certain associations of retailers of goods. It also includes vertical agreements containing ancillary provisions on the assignment or use of intellectual property rights. The term 'vertical agreements' should be understood to include the corresponding concerted practices.

(4) For the application of Article 101(3) of the Treaty by regulation, it is not necessary to define those vertical agreements which are capable of falling within Article 101(1) of the Treaty. In the individual assessment of agreements under Article 101(1) of the

Treaty, account has to be taken of several factors, in particular the market structure on the supply and purchase side.

(5) The benefit of the block exemption established by this Regulation should be limited to vertical agreements for which it can be assumed with sufficient certainty that they satisfy the conditions of Article 101(3) of the Treaty.

(6) Certain types of vertical agreements can improve economic efficiency within a chain of production or distribution by facilitating better coordination between the participating undertakings. In particular, they can lead to a reduction in the transaction and distribution costs of the parties and to an optimisation of their sales and investment levels.

(7) The likelihood that such efficiency-enhancing effects will outweigh any anti-competitive effects due to restrictions contained in vertical agreements depends on the degree of market power of the parties to the agreement and, in particular, on the extent to which those undertakings face competition from other suppliers of goods or services regarded by their customers as interchangeable or substitutable for one another, by reason of the products' characteristics, their prices and their intended use.

(8) It can be presumed that, where the market share held by each of the undertakings party to the agreement on the relevant market does not exceed 30%, vertical agreements which do not contain certain types of severe restrictions of competition generally lead to an improvement in production or distribution and allow consumers a fair share of the resulting benefits.

(9) Above the market share threshold of 30 %, there can be no presumption that vertical agreements falling within the scope of Article 101(1) of the Treaty will usually give rise to objective advantages of such a character and size as to compensate for the disadvantages that they create for competition. At the same time, there is no presumption that those vertical agreements are either caught by Article 101(1) of the Treaty or that they fail to satisfy the conditions of Article 101(3) of the Treaty.

(10) The online platform economy plays an increasingly important role in the distribution of goods and services. Undertakings active in the online platform economy make it possible to do business in new ways, some of which are not easy to categorise using concepts associated with vertical agreements in the traditional economy. In particular, online intermediation services allow undertakings to offer goods or services to other undertakings or to final consumers, with a view to facilitating the initiation of direct transactions between

undertakings or between undertakings and final consumers. Agreements relating to the provision of online intermediation services are vertical agreements and should therefore be able to benefit from the block exemption established by this Regulation, subject to the conditions set out in this Regulation.

(11) The definition of online intermediation services used in Regulation (EU) 2019/1150 of the European Parliament and of the Council (4) should be adapted for the purpose of the present Regulation. In particular, to reflect the scope of Article 101 of the Treaty, the definition used in the present Regulation should refer to undertakings. It should also include online intermediation services that facilitate the initiation of direct transactions between undertakings, as well as those that facilitate the initiation of direct transactions between undertakings and final consumers.

(12) Dual distribution refers to the scenario where a supplier sells goods or services not only at the upstream level but also at the downstream level, thereby competing with its independent distributors. In that scenario, in the absence of hardcore restrictions, and provided that the buyer does not compete with the supplier at the upstream level, the potential negative impact of the vertical agreement on the competitive relationship between the supplier and buyer at the downstream level is less important than the potential positive impact of the vertical agreement on competition in general at the upstream or downstream level. This Regulation should therefore exempt vertical agreements entered into in such scenarios of dual distribution.

(13) The exchange of information between a supplier and buyer can contribute to the pro-competitive effects of vertical agreements, in particular the optimisation of production and distribution processes. However, in dual distribution, the exchange of certain types of information may raise horizontal concerns. Therefore, this Regulation should only exempt information exchange between a supplier and a buyer in a dual distribution scenario where the information exchange is both directly related to the implementation of the vertical agreement and necessary to improve the production or distribution of the contract goods or services.

(14) The rationale for exempting vertical agreements in scenarios of dual distribution does not apply to vertical agreements relating to the provision of online intermediation services where the provider of the online intermediation services is also a competing undertaking on the relevant market for the sale of the intermediated goods or services. Providers of online intermediation services that have such a hybrid function may have the ability and the incentive to influence

the outcome of competition on the relevant market for the sale of the intermediated goods or services. This Regulation should therefore not exempt such vertical agreements.

(15) This Regulation should not exempt vertical agreements containing restrictions which are likely to restrict competition and harm consumers or which are not indispensable to the attainment of the efficiency-enhancing effects. In particular, the benefit of the block exemption established by this Regulation should not apply to vertical agreements containing certain types of severe restrictions of competition, such as minimum and fixed resale prices and certain types of territorial protection, including the prevention of the effective use of the internet to sell or certain restrictions of online advertising. Accordingly, restrictions of online sales and online advertising should benefit from the block exemption established by this Regulation, provided that they do not, directly or indirectly, in isolation or in combination with other factors controlled by the parties, have the object of preventing the effective use of the internet by the buyer or its customers to sell the contract goods or services to particular territories or customers, or of preventing the use of an entire online advertising channel, such as price comparison services or search engine advertising. For instance, online sales restrictions should not benefit from the block exemption established by this Regulation where their objective is to significantly diminish the aggregate volume of online sales of the contract goods or services in the relevant market or the possibility for consumers to buy the contract goods or services online. The categorisation of a restriction as hardcore within the meaning of Article 4, point (e) may take into account the content and context of the restriction, but should not depend on market-specific circumstances or the individual characteristics of the parties.

(16) This Regulation should not exempt restrictions for which it cannot be assumed with sufficient certainty that they satisfy the conditions of Article 101(3) of the Treaty. In particular, to ensure access to and to prevent collusion on the relevant market, certain conditions should be attached to the block exemption. To this end, the exemption of non-compete obligations should be limited to obligations which do not exceed a duration of five years. Obligations causing the members of a selective distribution system not to sell the brands of particular competing suppliers should likewise be excluded from the benefit of this Regulation. The benefit of this Regulation should not apply to retail parity obligations causing buyers of online intermediation services not to offer, sell or resell goods or services to end users under more favourable conditions via competing online intermediation services.

(17) The market share limitation, the non-exemption of certain vertical agreements and the conditions provided for in this Regulation generally ensure that the agreements to which the block exemption applies do not enable the participating undertakings to eliminate competition in respect of a substantial part of the goods or services in question.

(18) The Commission may withdraw the benefit of this Regulation, pursuant to Article 29(1) of Council Regulation (EC) No 1/2003 (5), where it finds in a particular case that an agreement to which the block exemption established by this Regulation applies nevertheless has effects which are incompatible with Article 101(3) of the Treaty. The competition authority of a Member State may withdraw the benefit of this Regulation where the conditions of Article 29(2) of Regulation (EC) No 1/2003 are fulfilled.

(19) Where the Commission or the competition authority of a Member State withdraws the benefit of this Regulation, it has the burden of proving that the vertical agreement in question falls within the scope of Article 101(1) of the Treaty, and that the agreement fails to fulfil at least one of the four conditions of Article 101(3) of the Treaty.

(20) In determining whether the benefit of this Regulation should be withdrawn pursuant to Article 29 of Regulation (EC) No 1/2003, the anti-competitive effects that may derive from the existence of parallel networks of vertical agreements that have similar effects, which significantly restrict access to a relevant market or competition therein, are of particular importance. Such cumulative effects may in particular arise in the case of exclusive distribution, exclusive supply, selective distribution, parity obligations or non-compete obligations.

(21) In order to strengthen the supervision of parallel networks of vertical agreements which have similar anti-competitive effects and which cover more than 50% of a given market, the Commission may by regulation declare this Regulation inapplicable to vertical agreements containing specific restraints relating to the market concerned, thereby restoring the full application of Article 101 of the Treaty to such agreements,

HAS ADOPTED THIS REGULATION:

Article 1

Definitions [omitted]

Article 2

Exemption

1. Pursuant to Article 101(3) of the Treaty and subject to the provisions of this Regulation, it is hereby declared that Article 101(1) of the Treaty shall not apply to vertical agreements. This exemption shall apply to the extent that such agreements contain vertical restraints.

2. The exemption provided for in paragraph 1 shall apply to vertical agreements entered into between an association of undertakings and an individual member, or between such an association and an individual supplier, only if all the members of the association are retailers of goods and if no individual member of the association, together with its connected undertakings, has a total annual turnover exceeding EUR 50 million. Vertical agreements entered into by such associations shall be covered by this Regulation without prejudice to the application of Article 101 of the Treaty to horizontal agreements concluded between the members of the association or decisions adopted by the association.

3–7. [. . .]

Article 3

Market share threshold

1. The exemption provided for in Article 2 shall apply on condition that the market share held by the supplier does not exceed 30% of the relevant market on which it sells the contract goods or services and the market share held by the buyer does not exceed 30% of the relevant market on which it purchases the contract goods or services.

2. For the purposes of paragraph 1, where in a multi-party agreement an undertaking buys the contract goods or services from one undertaking that is a party to the agreement and sells the contract goods or services to another undertaking that is also a party to the agreement, the market share of the first undertaking must respect the market share threshold provided for in that paragraph both as a buyer and a supplier in order for the exemption provided for in Article 2 to apply.

Article 4

Restrictions that remove the benefit of the block exemption—hardcore restrictions

The exemption provided for in Article 2 shall not apply to vertical agreements which, directly or indirectly, in isolation or in combination with other factors under the control of the parties, have as their object:

(a) The restriction of the buyer's ability to determine its sale price, without prejudice to the possibility of the supplier to impose a maximum sale price or recommend a sale price, provided that they do not amount to a fixed or minimum sale price as a result of pressure from, or incentives offered by, any of the parties;

(b) Where the supplier operates an exclusive distribution system, the restriction of the territory into which, or of the customers to whom, the exclusive distributor may actively or passively sell the contract goods or services, except:

(i) the restriction of active sales by the exclusive distributor and its direct customers, into a territory or to a customer group reserved to the supplier or allocated by the supplier exclusively to a maximum of five other exclusive distributors;

(ii) the restriction of active or passive sales by the exclusive distributor and its customers to unauthorised distributors located in a territory where the supplier operates a selective distribution system for the contract goods or services;

(iii) the restriction of the exclusive distributor's place of establishment;

(iv) the restriction of active or passive sales to end users by an exclusive distributor operating at the wholesale level of trade;

(v) the restriction of the exclusive distributor's ability to actively or passively sell components, supplied for the purposes of incorporation, to customers who would use them to manufacture the same type of goods as those produced by the supplier;

(c) where the supplier operates a selective distribution system,

(i) the restriction of the territory into which, or of the customers to whom, the members of the selective distribution system may actively or passively sell the contract goods or services, except:

(1) the restriction of active sales by the members of the selective distribution system and their direct customers, into a territory or to a customer group reserved to the supplier or allocated by the supplier exclusively to a maximum of five exclusive distributors;

(2) the restriction of active or passive sales by the members of the selective distribution system and their customers to unauthorised distributors located within the territory where the selective distribution system is operated;

(3) the restriction of the place of establishment of the members of the selective distribution system;

(4) the restriction of active or passive sales to end users by members of the selective distribution system operating at the wholesale level of trade;

(5) the restriction of the ability to actively or passively sell components, supplied for the purposes of incorporation, to customers who would use them to manufacture the same type of goods as those produced by the supplier;

(ii) the restriction of cross-supplies between the members of the selective distribution system operating at the same or different levels of trade;

(iii) the restriction of active or passive sales to end users by members of the selective distribution system operating at the retail level of trade, without prejudice to points (c)(i)(1) and (3);

(d) where the supplier operates neither an exclusive distribution system nor a selective distribution system, the restriction of the territory into which, or of the customers to whom, the buyer may actively or passively sell the contract goods or services, except:

(i) the restriction of active sales by the buyer and its direct customers into a territory or to a customer group reserved to the supplier or allocated by the supplier exclusively to a maximum of five exclusive distributors;

(ii) the restriction of active or passive sales by the buyer and its customers to unauthorised distributors located in a territory where the supplier operates a selective distribution system for the contract goods or services;

(iii) the restriction of the buyer's place of establishment;

(iv) the restriction of active or passive sales to end users by a buyer operating at the wholesale level of trade;

(v) the restriction of the buyer's ability to actively or passively sell components, supplied for the purposes of incorporation, to customers who would use them to manufacture the same type of goods as those produced by the supplier;

(e) the prevention of the effective use of the internet by the buyer or its customers to sell the contract goods or services, as it restricts the territory into which or the customers to whom the contract goods or services may be sold within the meaning of points (b), (c) or (d), without prejudice to the possibility of imposing on the buyer:

(i) other restrictions of online sales; or

(ii) restrictions of online advertising that do not have the object of preventing the use of an entire online advertising channel;

(f) the restriction, agreed between a supplier of components and a buyer who incorporates those components, of the supplier's ability to sell the components as spare parts to end users or to repairers, wholesalers or other service providers not entrusted by the buyer with the repair or servicing of its goods.

Article 5

Excluded restrictions

1. The exemption provided for in Article 2 shall not apply to the following obligations contained in vertical agreements:

(a) any direct or indirect non-compete obligation, the duration of which is indefinite or exceeds 5 years;

(b) any direct or indirect obligation causing the buyer, after termination of the agreement, not to manufacture, purchase, sell or resell goods or services;

(c) any direct or indirect obligation causing the members of a selective distribution system not to sell the brands of particular competing suppliers;

(d) any direct or indirect obligation causing a buyer of online intermediation services not to offer, sell or resell goods or services to end users under more favourable conditions via competing online intermediation services;

2. By way of derogation from paragraph 1, point (a), the time limitation of five years shall not apply where the contract goods or services are sold by the buyer from premises and land owned by the supplier or leased by the supplier from third parties not connected with the buyer, provided that the duration of the non-compete obligation does not exceed the period of occupancy of the premises and land by the buyer.

3. By way of derogation from paragraph 1, point (b), the exemption provided for in Article 2 shall apply to any direct or indirect obligation causing the buyer, after termination of the agreement, not to manufacture, purchase, sell or resell goods or services where all of the following conditions are fulfilled:

(a) the obligation relates to goods or services which compete with the contract goods or services;

(b) the obligation is limited to the premises and land from which the buyer has operated during the contract period;

(c) the obligation is indispensable to protect know-how transferred by the supplier to the buyer

(d) the duration of the obligation is limited to a period of one year after termination of the agreement.

Paragraph 1, point (b) shall be without prejudice to the possibility of imposing a restriction which is unlimited in time on the use and disclosure of know-how which has not entered the public domain.

Article 6

Withdrawal in individual cases

1. The Commission may withdraw the benefit of this Regulation, pursuant to Article 29(1) of Regulation (EC) No 1/2003, where it finds in any particular case that a vertical agreement to which the exemption provided for in Article 2 of this Regulation applies nevertheless has effects which are incompatible with Article 101(3) of the Treaty. Such effects may occur, for example, where the relevant market for the supply of online intermediation services is highly concentrated and competition between the providers of such services is restricted by the cumulative effect of parallel networks of similar agreements that restrict buyers of the online intermediation services from offering, selling or reselling goods or services to end users under more favourable conditions on their direct sales channels.

2. The competition authority of a Member State may withdraw the benefit of this Regulation where the conditions of Article 29(2) of Regulation (EC) No 1/2003 are fulfilled.

Article 7

Non-application of this Regulation [omitted]

Article 8

Application of the market share threshold

For the purposes of applying the market share thresholds provided for in Article 3 the following rules shall apply:

(a) the market share of the supplier shall be calculated on the basis of market sales value data and the market share of the buyer shall be calculated on the basis of market purchase value data. If market sales value or market purchase value data are not available, estimates based on other reliable market information, including market sales and purchase volumes, may be used to establish the market share of the undertaking concerned;

(b) the market shares shall be calculated on the basis of data relating to the preceding calendar year;

(c) the market share of the supplier shall include any goods or services supplied to vertically integrated distributors for the purposes of sale;

(d) if a market share is initially not more than 30 %, but subsequently rises above that level, the exemption provided for in Article 2 shall continue to apply for a period of two consecutive calendar years following the year in which the 30 % threshold was first exceeded;

(e) the market share held by the undertakings referred to in Article 1(2), second subparagraph, point (e) shall be apportioned equally to each undertaking having the rights or the powers listed in point (a) of that subparagraph.

Article 9

Application of the turnover threshold

1. For the purpose of calculating total annual turnover within the meaning of Article 2(2), the turnover achieved during the previous financial year by the relevant party to the vertical agreement and the turnover achieved by its connected undertakings in respect of all goods and services, excluding all taxes and other duties, shall be added together. For this purpose, no account shall be taken of dealings between the party to the vertical agreement and its connected undertakings or between its connected undertakings.

2. The exemption provided for in Article 2 shall remain applicable where, for any period of two consecutive financial years, the total annual turnover threshold is exceeded by no more than 10 %.

The block exemption regulation is accompanied by guidelines. The guidelines describe vertical agreements that fall outside of Article 101(1), comment on application of the block exemption regulation, state the principles concerning withdrawal of the block exemption, treat market definition and market share calculations, and describe the framework for analysis of individual cases under Article 101(3).

The guidelines section devoted to analysis in individual cases describes the general framework for analysis and then the framework for analyzing specific restraints. Individual analysis is applied to cases that fall outside of the block exemption. These are largely cases in which either the seller's or buyer's share of the market is more than 30%. It may also include agreements that contain a hard core restriction—such as resale price maintenance—where the undertaking might possibly have a justification under Article 101(3).

The framework for analysis in general and for single-branding, exclusive distribution, exclusive supply, and tying follows.

EUROPEAN COMMISSION NOTICE GUIDELINES ON VERTICAL RESTRAINTS (2022)

(excerpts)

available http://competition-policy.ec.europa.eu

* * *

1. INTRODUCTION

1.1. Purpose and structure of these Guidelines (omitted)

*1.2. Applicability of Article **101** of the Treaty to vertical agreements*

(omitted)

(7) While there is no mandatory sequence for the assessment of vertical agreements, the assessment generally involves the following steps:

— first, the undertakings involved need to establish the market shares of the supplier and the buyer on the relevant market where they respectively sell and purchase the contract goods or services;

— if neither the market share of the supplier nor that of the buyer exceeds the 30 % market share threshold set out in Article 3 of Regulation (EU) 2022/720, the vertical agreement is covered by the safe harbour established by the Regulation, provided that the agreement does not contain hardcore restrictions within the meaning of Article 4 of the Regulation or any excluded restrictions within the meaning of Article 5 of the Regulation that cannot be severed from the rest of the agreement;

— if the relevant market share of the supplier or the buyer exceeds the 30 % threshold or the agreement contains one or more hardcore restrictions or non-severable excluded restrictions, it is necessary to assess whether the vertical agreement falls within the scope of Article 101(1) of the Treaty;

— if the vertical agreement falls within the scope of Article 101(1) of the Treaty, it is necessary to examine whether it fulfils the conditions of the exception provided by Article 101(3) of the Treaty.

(8) Sustainable development is a core principle of the Treaty and a priority objective for the policies of the Union (12), together with digitalisation and a resilient Single Market (13). The notion of sustainability includes, but is not limited to, addressing climate change (for instance, through the reduction of greenhouse gas emissions), limiting the use of natural resources, reducing waste and promoting animal welfare (14). The Union's sustainability, resilience and digital objectives are furthered by efficient supply and distribution agreements between undertakings. Vertical agreements which pursue sustainability objectives or which contribute to a digital and resilient Single Market are not a distinct category of vertical agreements under Union competition law. These agreements must therefore be assessed using the principles set out in these Guidelines, while taking into account the specific objective that they pursue. Accordingly, the exemption provided by Article 2(1) of Regulation (EU) 2022/720 applies to vertical agreements that pursue sustainability, resilience and digital objectives, provided that they meet the conditions of the Regulation. These Guidelines include examples to illustrate the assessment of vertical agreements that pursue sustainability objectives (15).

(9) Where a vertical agreement restricts competition within the meaning of Article 101(1) of the Treaty and Regulation (EU) 2022/720 does not apply, the agreement may nonetheless fulfil the conditions of the Article 101(3) exception (16). This also applies to vertical agreements which pursue sustainability objectives or which contribute to a digital and resilient Single Market. While section 8 includes guidance on the assessment of such vertical agreements in individual cases, other Commission guidelines may also be relevant. That includes the Article 101(3) Guidelines, the Horizontal Guidelines (17) and any guidance that may be provided in future versions of those Guidelines. Those Guidelines may, in particular, provide guidance on the circumstances under which sustainability, digital or resilience benefits can be taken into account as qualitative or quantitative efficiencies under Article 101(3) of the Treaty.

2. EFFECTS OF VERTICAL AGREEMENTS

[omitted]

2.1. Positive effects

(12) Vertical agreements may produce positive effects, including lower prices, the promotion of non-price competition and improved quality of services. Simple contractual arrangements between a

supplier and a buyer which determine only the price and the quantity of a transaction can often lead to sub-optimal levels of investments and sales, as they do not take into account externalities arising from the complementary nature of the activities of the supplier and its distributors. These externalities fall into two categories: vertical externalities and horizontal externalities.

(13) Vertical externalities arise because the decisions and actions taken at different levels of the production or distribution chain determine aspects of the sale of goods or services, such as price, quality, related services and marketing, which affect not only the undertaking making the decisions but also other undertakings at other levels of the production or distribution chain. For instance, a distributor may not gain all the benefits of its efforts to increase sales, as some of those benefits may go to the supplier. This is because, for every extra unit that a distributor sells by lowering its resale price or by increasing its sales efforts, the supplier benefits if its wholesale price exceeds its marginal production costs. This represents a positive externality bestowed on the supplier by the distributor's sales-enhancing actions. Conversely, there may be situations where, from the supplier's perspective, the distributor may be pricing too high (20), making insufficient sales efforts or both.

(14) Horizontal externalities may arise in particular between distributors of the same goods or services where a distributor is unable to fully appropriate the benefits of its sales efforts. For example, where demand-enhancing pre-sales services are provided by one distributor, such as personalised advice in relation to particular goods or services, this may lead to higher sales by competing distributors offering the same goods or services and thus create incentives among distributors to free-ride on costly services provided by others. In an omni-channel distribution environment, free riding can occur between the online and offline sales channels, and in both directions (21). For example, customers may visit a brick and mortar shop to test goods or services or to obtain other useful information on which they base their decision to purchase, but then order the product online from a different distributor. Conversely, customers may gather information in the pre-purchase phase from an online store and then visit a brick and mortar shop, use the information they have gathered online to select and test particular goods or services, and ultimately purchase offline in a brick and mortar shop. Where such free riding is possible and where the distributor that provides pre-sales services is unable to fully appropriate the benefits, this may lead to sub-optimal provision of such pre-sales services in terms of quantity or quality.

(15) In the presence of such externalities, suppliers may have an incentive to control certain aspects of their distributors' operations and vice versa. In particular, vertical agreements may be used to internalise such externalities, increase the joint profit of the vertical supply and distribution chain, and, under certain circumstances, consumer welfare.

(16) Although these Guidelines seek to give an overview of the various justifications for vertical restraints, they do not claim to be complete or exhaustive. The reasons that may justify the application of particular vertical restraints include the following:

(a) to address the vertical externality issue. The setting of too high a price by the distributor, not taking into account the effect of its decisions on the supplier, can be avoided by the supplier imposing a maximum resale price on the distributor. Similarly, to increase the distributor's sales efforts, the supplier may use selective or exclusive distribution;

(b) to address the free-rider problem. Free riding between buyers may occur at the wholesale or retail level, in particular where it is not possible for the supplier to impose effective promotion or service requirements on all buyers. Free riding between buyers can only occur on pre-sales services and other promotional activities, but not on after-sales services for which the distributor can charge its customers individually. Pre-sales efforts on which free riding can occur may be important, for example, where the goods or services are relatively new, technically complex or of high value, or where the reputation of the goods or services is an important determinant of their demand (22). Restrictions in exclusive or selective distribution systems, or other restrictions may be helpful in avoiding or reducing such free riding. Free riding can also occur between suppliers, for instance where one manufacturer invests in promotion at the buyer's premises that also attracts customers for the competitors of that manufacturer. Non-compete type restrictions can help to overcome free riding between suppliers (23);

(c) to open up or enter new markets. Where a supplier wishes to enter a new geographic market, for instance by exporting to another country, this may involve special sunk investments by the distributor to establish the brand on the market. In order to persuade a local distributor to make these investments, it may be necessary to provide territorial protection so that the distributor can recoup its investments. This may justify restricting distributors located in other geographic markets from selling on the new market (see also paragraphs (118), (136) and (137)). This is a special case related to the free-rider problem set out in point (b);

(d) to address the certification free-rider issue. In some sectors, certain distributors have a reputation for stocking only quality goods or providing quality services (so-called 'premium distributors'). In such a case, selling through those distributors may be crucial, in particular for the successful launch of a new product. If the supplier cannot ensure that the distribution of its products is limited to such premium distributors, it runs the risk of not being listed by such distributors. In that scenario, the use of exclusive or selective distribution may be justified;

(e) to address the hold-up problem. Either the supplier or the buyer may need to make relationship-specific investments (for example in specific equipment or training) which are sunk investments and have little or no value outside the specific vertical relationship. For instance, a component manufacturer may have to build specific machines to satisfy the requirements of one of its customers, but the machines may be unsuitable for use with other customers and it may be impossible to resell them. In the absence of an agreement, the investing party will find itself in a weak bargaining position once it has made the relationship-specific investment, as it risks being 'held up' during negotiations with its trading partner. The threat of such opportunistic hold-up may lead to sub-optimal investments by the investing party. Vertical agreements can eliminate the scope for hold-up (in particular when the investment can be fully contracted and all future contingencies can be foreseen) or they can reduce the scope for hold-up. For example, non-compete obligations, quantity forcing, or exclusive sourcing can lessen the hold-up problem when the relationship-specific investment is made by the supplier, whereas exclusive distribution, exclusive customer allocation or exclusive supply can lessen the hold-up problem when the investment is made by the buyer;

(f) to address the specific hold-up problem that may arise where there is a transfer of substantial know-how. The provider of know-how may not wish the know-how to be used by or for the benefit of its competitors, for example in franchising. Insofar as the know-how was not readily available to the buyer, and it is substantial and indispensable for the implementation of the agreement, such a transfer may justify a non-compete restriction, which would generally fall outside Article 101(1) of the Treaty in such cases;

(g) to achieve economies of scale in distribution. To have scale economies exploited and thereby see a lower retail price for its goods or services, the manufacturer may want to concentrate the resale of its goods or services on a limited number of distributors. To do so, the manufacturer could use exclusive distribution, quantity forcing in the form of a minimum purchasing requirement, selective distribution containing a minimum purchasing requirement or exclusive sourcing;

(h) to ensure uniformity and quality standardisation. A vertical restraint can help to create or promote a brand image, by imposing a certain measure of uniformity and quality standardisation on the distributors. This can protect the reputation of the brand, increase the attractiveness of the goods or services concerned for end users and increase sales. Such standardisation can, for instance, be achieved through selective distribution or franchising;

(i) to address capital market imperfections. Providers of capital such as banks and equity markets may provide capital sub-optimally when they have imperfect information on the solvency of the borrower or where there is an inadequate basis to secure the loan. The buyer or supplier may have better information and may be able, through an exclusive relationship, to obtain extra security for its investment. Where the supplier provides the loan to the buyer, this may lead to the imposition of a non-compete obligation or quantity forcing on the buyer. Where the buyer provides the loan to the supplier, this may be the reason for imposing exclusive supply or quantity forcing on the supplier.

(17) There is a large degree of substitutability between the various vertical restraints, meaning that the same inefficiency problem can be addressed using different vertical restraints. For instance, it may be possible to achieve economies of scale in distribution by using exclusive distribution, selective distribution, quantity forcing or exclusive sourcing. However, the negative effects on competition may differ between the various vertical restraints. This is taken into account when indispensability is assessed under Article 101(3) of the Treaty.

2.2. Negative effects

(18) The negative effects on the market which can result from vertical restraints and which Union competition law aims to prevent are, in particular, the following:

(a) anti-competitive foreclosure of other suppliers or other buyers, by raising barriers to entry or expansion;

(b) softening of competition between the supplier and its competitors and/or the facilitation of explicit or tacit collusion between competing suppliers, often referred to as the reduction of inter-brand competition;

(c) softening of competition between the buyer and its competitors or the facilitation of explicit or tacit collusion between competing buyers, often referred to as the reduction of intra-brand competition where it concerns distributors of the goods or services of the same supplier (24);

(d) the creation of obstacles to market integration, including, in particular, limitations on the consumer's choice to purchase goods or services in any Member State.

(19) Foreclosure, softening of competition and collusion at the supplier level may harm consumers, in particular by:

(a) increasing the prices charged to buyers of goods or services, which may in turn lead to higher retail prices;

(b) limiting the choice of goods or services;

(c) lowering the quality of goods or services;

(d) reducing innovation or service at the supplier level.

(20) Foreclosure, softening of competition and collusion at the distributor level may harm consumers, in particular by:

(a) increasing the retail prices of goods or services;

(b) limiting the choice of price-service combinations and distribution formats;

(c) lowering the availability and quality of retail services;

(d) reducing the level of innovation at the distribution level.

(21) A reduction of intra-brand competition (i.e. competition between distributors of the goods or services of the same supplier) is by itself unlikely to lead to negative effects for consumers if inter-brand competition (i.e. competition between distributors of the goods or services of different suppliers) is strong (25). In particular, in markets where individual retailers distribute the brand(s) of only one supplier, a reduction of competition between the distributors of the same brand will lead to a reduction of intra-brand competition between these distributors, but may not have a negative effect on competition between distributors in general.

(22) The possible negative effects of vertical restraints are reinforced where several suppliers and their buyers organise their trade in a similar way, leading to so-called cumulative effects (26).

[omitted]

4.6. Specific types of distribution systems

[omitted]

4.6.1. Exclusive distribution systems

4.6.1.1. Definition of exclusive distribution systems

(117) In an exclusive distribution system, as defined in Article 1(1), point (h) of Regulation (EU) 2022/720, the supplier allocates a territory or a group of customers exclusively to one or a limited number of buyers, while restricting all its other buyers within the Union from actively selling into the exclusive territory or to the exclusive customer group (80).

(omitted)

*4.6.1.2. Application of Article **101** of the Treaty to exclusive distribution systems*

(119) In a distribution system where the supplier allocates a territory or customer group exclusively to one or more buyers, the main possible competition risks are market partitioning, which may

facilitate price discrimination, and reduced intra-brand competition. When most or all of the strongest suppliers active in a market operate an exclusive distribution system, this may also soften inter-brand competition and/or facilitate collusion, at both the supplier and the distributor levels. Lastly, exclusive distribution may lead to the foreclosure of other distributors and thereby reduce both inter-brand and intra-brand competition at the distributor level.

(120) Exclusive distribution agreements can benefit from the exemption provided by Article 2(1) of Regulation (EU) 2022/720, provided that the supplier's and the buyer's market share do not exceed 30 %, the agreement does not contain any hardcore restrictions within the meaning of Article 4 of Regulation (EU) 2022/720, and the number of distributors appointed per exclusive territory or customer group does not exceed five. An exclusive distribution agreement can still benefit from the safe harbour provided by Regulation (EU) 2022/720 if it is combined with other non-hardcore vertical restraints, such as a non-compete obligation not exceeding five years, quantity forcing or exclusive purchasing. [The Guidelines then discuss various factors as significant, including the market position of the supplier, the position of competitors, entry barriers, conditions of foreclosure, buyer power, maturity of trade, level of the market].

8. ENFORCEMENT POLICY IN INDIVIDUAL CASES

8.1. The framework of analysis

(275) Where the block exemption provided by Regulation (EU) 2022/720 does not apply to a vertical agreement, it is necessary to assess whether, in the individual case, the vertical agreement falls within the scope of Article 101(1) of the Treaty and, if so, whether the conditions of Article 101(3) of the Treaty are fulfilled. Provided that they do not contain restrictions of competition by object and in particular hardcore restrictions within the meaning of Article 4 of Regulation (EU) 2022/720, there is no presumption that vertical agreements that fall outside the scope of Regulation (EU) 2022/720 fall within the scope of Article 101(1) of the Treaty or fail to satisfy the conditions of Article 101(3) of the Treaty. Such agreements require an individual assessment. Agreements that either do not restrict competition within the meaning of Article 101(1) of the Treaty or which fulfil the conditions of Article 101(3) of the Treaty are valid and enforceable.

(276) Pursuant to Article 1(2) of Regulation (EC) No 1/2003, undertakings do not need to notify their vertical agreements to benefit from an individual exemption under Article 101(3) of the Treaty. In the case of an individual examination by the Commission,

it is the Commission which bears the burden of proof that the vertical agreement in question restricts competition within the meaning of Article 101(1) of the Treaty. Undertakings which claim the benefit of Article 101(3) of the Treaty bear the burden of proving that the conditions of that provision are fulfilled. Where likely anti-competitive effects are demonstrated, undertakings may substantiate efficiency claims and explain why a particular distribution arrangement is indispensable to bring likely benefits to consumers without eliminating competition. The Commission will then decide whether the agreement satisfies the conditions of Article 101(3) of the Treaty.

(277) The assessment of whether a vertical agreement has the effect of restricting competition is made by comparing the situation on the relevant market with the vertical restraints in place with the situation that would prevail in the absence of the vertical restraints in the vertical agreement. In the assessment of individual cases, the Commission may take both actual and likely effects into account. For vertical agreements to be restrictive of competition by effect, they must affect actual or potential competition to such an extent that on the relevant market negative effects on prices, output, innovation, or the variety or quality of the goods or services can be expected with a reasonable degree of probability. The negative effects on competition must be appreciable (159). Appreciable anti-competitive effects are more likely to occur when at least one of the parties to the agreement has or obtains some degree of market power and the agreement contributes to the creation, maintenance or strengthening of that market power, or allows the parties to the agreement to exploit such market power. Market power is the ability to maintain prices above competitive levels or to maintain output in terms of product quantities, product quality and variety or innovation below competitive levels for a not insignificant period of time. The degree of market power generally required for a finding of a restriction of competition within the meaning of Article 101(1) of the Treaty is less than the degree of market power required for a finding of dominance under Article 102 of the Treaty.

8.1.1. Relevant factors for the assessment under Article 101(1) of the Treaty (omitted)

8.1.1. Relevant factors for the assessment under Article 101(3) of the Treaty (omitted)

8.2. Analysis of specific vertical restraints

(297) Whereas section 6 includes guidance on the assessment of vertical restraints that amount to hardcore restrictions within the meaning of Article 4 of Regulation (EU) 2022/720, or to excluded

restrictions within the meaning of Article 5 of the Regulation, the following paragraphs provide guidance on other specific vertical restraints. As regards vertical restraints that are not specifically addressed in these Guidelines, the Commission will assess them vertical restraints in accordance with the same principles taking into account the relevant factors, as set out in this section 8.

8.2.1. Single branding

(298) Under the heading of 'single branding' fall those agreements which have as their main element the fact that the buyer is obliged or induced to concentrate its orders for a particular type of product with one supplier. That requirement can be found amongst others in non-compete and quantity forcing clauses agreed with the buyer. A non-compete arrangement is based on an obligation or incentive scheme which causes the buyer to purchase more than 80 % of its requirements on a particular market from only one supplier. This does not mean that the buyer must buy directly from the supplier, but that the buyer must de facto not buy, sell or incorporate competing goods or services. Quantity forcing on the buyer is a weaker form of non-compete, where incentives or obligations agreed between the supplier and the buyer result in the latter concentrating its purchases to a large extent with one supplier. Quantity forcing may, for example, take the form of minimum purchase requirements, stocking requirements or non-linear pricing, such as conditional rebate schemes or a two-part tariff (fixed fee plus a price per unit). A so-called English clause, requiring the buyer to report any better offer and allowing the buyer to accept such an offer only if the supplier does not match it, can be expected to have the same effect as a single branding obligation, especially when the buyer has to reveal who makes the better offer.

(299) The possible competition risks of single branding are foreclosure of the market to competing suppliers and potential suppliers, softening of competition and facilitation of collusion between suppliers in the case of cumulative use and, where the buyer is a retailer, a loss of in-store inter-brand competition. Such restrictive effects have a direct impact on inter-brand competition.

(300) Single branding agreements can benefit from the exemption provided by Article 2(1) of Regulation (EU) 2022/720 where neither the supplier's nor the buyer's market share exceeds 30 % and the non-compete obligation does not exceed five years. As set out in paragraph (248), single branding agreements that are tacitly renewable beyond a period of five years can benefit from the block exemption, provided that the buyer can effectively renegotiate or terminate the single branding agreement by giving a reasonable

period of notice and at a reasonable cost, thus allowing the buyer to effectively switch its supplier after the expiry of the 5-year period. If those conditions are not satisfied, the single branding agreement must be individually assessed.

(301) The potential for single branding obligations to result in anti-competitive foreclosure arises in particular where, without the obligations, an important competitive constraint would be exercised by competitors that are either not yet present on the market at the time the obligations are concluded, or are not in a position to compete for the full supply of the customers. Competitors may not be able to compete for an individual customer's entire demand because the supplier in question is an unavoidable trading partner for at least part of the demand on the market, for instance because its brand is a 'must stock item' preferred by many consumers, or because the capacity constraints on the other suppliers are such that a part of the demand can only be provided by the supplier in question (168). The market position of the supplier is thus of primary importance when assessing the possible anti-competitive effects of single branding obligations.

(302) If competitors can compete on equal terms for each individual customer's entire demand, single branding obligations imposed by a single supplier are generally unlikely to restrict competition appreciably unless the ability of customers to switch between suppliers is rendered difficult by the duration and market coverage of the single branding obligations. The higher the proportion of its market share that a supplier sells under a single branding obligation and the longer the duration of the single branding obligations, the more significant foreclosure is likely to be. Single branding obligations are more likely to result in anti-competitive foreclosure when entered into by dominant undertakings.

(303) When assessing the supplier's market power, the market position of its competitors is important. As long as the competitors are sufficiently numerous and strong, no appreciable anti-competitive effects can be expected. Foreclosure of competitors is not very likely where they hold similar market positions and can offer similarly attractive products. However, in such a case, foreclosure may occur for potential entrants where a number of major suppliers enter into single branding agreements with a significant number of buyers on the relevant market (cumulative effect situation). This is also a situation where single branding agreements may facilitate collusion between competing suppliers. Where those agreements individually benefit from the exemption provided by Regulation (EU) 2022/720, a withdrawal of the benefit of the block exemption may be

necessary to deal with such a negative cumulative anti-competitive effect. A tied market share of less than 5 % is generally not considered to contribute significantly to such a cumulative effect.

(304) In cases where the market share of the largest supplier is below 30 % and the combined market share of the five largest suppliers is below 50 %, there is unlikely to be a single or a cumulative anti-competitive effect. In such cases, where a potential entrant cannot penetrate the market profitably, it is likely to be due to factors other than single branding obligations, such as consumer preferences.

(305) To determine whether anti-competitive foreclosure is likely, it is necessary to assess the scale of entry barriers. Where it is relatively easy for competing suppliers to create their own integrated distribution network or find alternative distributors for their product, foreclosure is unlikely to be a real problem.

(306) Countervailing buyer power is relevant, as powerful buyers will not easily allow themselves to be cut off from the supply of competing goods or services. More generally, in order to convince customers to accept single branding, the supplier may have to compensate them, in whole or in part, for the loss in competition resulting from the exclusivity. Where such compensation is given, it may be in the individual interest of a customer to enter into a single branding obligation with the supplier. However, it would be wrong to conclude from this that all single branding obligations, taken together, are overall beneficial for customers in that market and for the consumers. It is, in particular, unlikely that consumers as a whole will benefit if the single branding obligations, taken together, have the effect of preventing the entry or expansion of competing undertakings.

(307) Lastly, the level in the production or distribution chain is relevant. Foreclosure is less likely in the case of an intermediate product. Where the supplier of an intermediate product is not dominant, the competing suppliers still have a substantial share of demand that is free. However, single branding may lead to anti-competitive foreclosure effects below the level of dominance in cases where there is a cumulative effect situation. A cumulative anti-competitive effect is unlikely to arise as long as less than 50 % of the market is tied.

* * *

8.2.2. Exclusive supply

(321) Exclusive supply refers to restrictions that oblige or induce the supplier to sell the contract products only or mainly to one buyer,

in general or for a particular use. Such restrictions may take the form of an exclusive supply obligation, obliging the supplier to sell to only one buyer for the purposes of resale or a particular use. They may also for instance take the form of quantity forcing on the supplier, where incentives are agreed between a supplier and a buyer which make the former concentrate its sales mainly with that buyer. For intermediate goods or services, exclusive supply is often referred to as industrial supply.

(322) Exclusive supply agreement can benefit from the block exemption provided by Regulation (EU) 2022/720 where neither the supplier's nor the buyer's market share exceeds 30 %, even if combined with other non-hardcore vertical restraints, such as non-compete obligations. The remainder of this section 8.2.2. provides guidance for the assessment of exclusive supply agreements in individual cases above the market share threshold.

(323) The main competition risk of exclusive supply is anti-competitive foreclosure of other buyers. There is a similarity with the possible effects of exclusive distribution, in particular where the exclusive distributor becomes the exclusive buyer for a whole market (see in particular paragraph (130). The market share of the buyer on the upstream purchase market is obviously important for assessing the ability of the buyer to impose exclusive supply which forecloses other buyers from access to supplies. However, the importance of the buyer's position on the downstream market is the most significant factor to determine whether a competition problem may arise. If the buyer does not have market power downstream, then no appreciable negative effects for consumers can be expected. Negative effects may arise when the market share of the buyer on the downstream supply market as well as the upstream purchase market exceeds 30 %. Where the market share of the buyer on the upstream market does not exceed 30 %, significant foreclosure effects may still arise, especially where the market share of the buyer on its downstream market exceeds 30 % and the exclusive supply relates to a particular use of the contract products. Where a buyer is dominant on the downstream market, any obligation to supply the products only or mainly to the dominant buyer may easily have significant anti-competitive effects.

* * *

8.2.8. Tying

(389) Tying refers to situations where customers that purchase one product (the tying product) are required also to purchase another distinct product (the tied product) from the same supplier or someone designated by the latter. Tying may constitute an abuse within the

meaning of Article 102 of the Treaty (183). Tying may also constitute a vertical restraint within the meaning of Article 101 of the Treaty where it results in a single branding type of obligation for the tied product (see paragraphs (298) to (318). Only the latter situation is dealt with in these Guidelines.

(390) Whether products will be considered as distinct depends on customer demand. Two products are distinct where, in the absence of the tying, a substantial number of customers would purchase or would have purchased the tying product without also buying the tied product from the same supplier, thereby allowing stand-alone production for both the tying and the tied product (184). Evidence that two products are distinct could include direct evidence that, when given a choice, customers purchase the tying and the tied products separately from different sources of supply, or indirect evidence, such as the presence on the market of undertakings specialised in the manufacture or sale of the tied product without the tying product (185), or evidence indicating that undertakings with little market power, particularly on competitive markets, tend not to tie or not to bundle such products. For instance, since customers want to buy shoes with laces and it is not practicable for distributors to lace new shoes with the laces of their choice, it has become commercial usage for shoe manufacturers to supply shoes with laces. Therefore, the sale of shoes with laces is not a tying practice.

(391) Tying may lead to anti-competitive foreclosure effects on the tied market, the tying market, or both at the same time. The foreclosure effect depends on the tied percentage of total sales on the market of the tied product. As regards the question of what can be considered appreciable foreclosure under Article 101(1) of the Treaty, the analysis for single branding can be applied. Tying means that there is at least a form of quantity forcing on the buyer in respect of the tied product. Where, in addition, a non-compete obligation is agreed in respect of the tied product, this increases the possible foreclosure effect on the market of the tied product. The tying may lead to less competition for customers interested in buying the tied product, but not the tying product. If there is not a sufficient number of customers that will buy the tied product alone to sustain competitors of the supplier on the tied market, the tying can lead to those customers facing higher prices. If the tied product is an important complementary product for customers of the tying product, a reduction of alternative suppliers of the tied product and hence a reduced availability of that product can make entry onto the tying market alone more difficult.

(392) Tying may also directly lead to prices that are above the competitive level, especially in three situations. First, if the tying and

the tied product can be used in variable proportions as inputs to a production process, customers may react to an increase in price for the tying product by increasing their demand for the tied product while decreasing their demand for the tying product. By tying the two products, the supplier may seek to avoid this substitution and as a result be able to raise its prices. Second, the tying may allow price discrimination according to the use the customer makes of the tying product, for example the tying of ink cartridges to the sale of photocopying machines (metering). Third, in the case of long-term contracts or in the case of after-markets with original equipment with a long replacement time, it may be difficult for customers to calculate the consequences of the tying.

(393) Tying can benefit from the exemption provided by Article 2(1) of Regulation (EU) 2022/720 where the market share of the supplier, on both the market of the tied product and the market of the tying product, and the market share of the buyer, on the relevant upstream markets, do not exceed 30 %. It may be combined with other vertical restraints that are not hardcore restrictions within the meaning of the Regulation, such as non-compete obligations or quantity forcing in respect of the tying product, or exclusive sourcing. The remainder of this section 8.2.8 provides guidance for the assessment of tying in individual cases above the market share threshold.

(394) The market position of the supplier on the market of the tying product is obviously of central importance for the assessment of possible anti-competitive effects. In general, this type of agreement is imposed by the supplier. The importance of the supplier on the market of the tying product is the main reason why a buyer may find it difficult to refuse a tying obligation.

(395) The market position of the supplier's competitors on the market of the tying product is important in assessing the supplier's market power. As long as its competitors are sufficiently numerous and strong, no anti-competitive effects can be expected, as buyers have sufficient alternatives to purchase the tying product without the tied product, unless other suppliers are applying similar tying. In addition, entry barriers on the market of the tying product are relevant to establish the market position of the supplier. When tying is combined with a non-compete obligation in respect of the tying product, this considerably strengthens the position of the supplier.

(396) Buying power is relevant, as important buyers will not easily be forced to accept tying without obtaining at least part of the possible efficiencies. Tying not based on efficiency is therefore mainly a risk where buyers do not have significant buying power.

(397) Where appreciable anti-competitive effects are established, it is necessary to assess whether the conditions of Article 101(3) of the Treaty are fulfilled. Tying obligations may help to produce efficiencies arising from joint production or joint distribution. Where the tied product is not produced by the supplier, an efficiency may also arise from the supplier buying large quantities of the tied product. For tying to fulfil the conditions of Article 101(3) of the Treaty, it must, however, be shown that at least part of those cost reductions are passed on to the consumer, which is normally not the case where the retailer is able to obtain, on a regular basis, supplies of the same or equivalent products on the same or better conditions than those offered by the supplier which applies the tying practice. Another efficiency may exist where tying helps to ensure a certain uniformity and quality standardisation (see paragraph (16), point (h)). However, it needs to be demonstrated that the positive effects cannot be realised equally efficiently by requiring the buyer to use or resell products satisfying minimum quality standards, without requiring the buyer to purchase them from the supplier or someone designated by the latter. The requirements concerning minimum quality standards would not normally fall within the scope of Article 101(1) of the Treaty. Where the supplier of the tying product requires the buyer to purchase the tied product from designated suppliers, for instance because the formulation of minimum quality standards is not possible, this may also fall outside the scope of Article 101(1) of the Treaty, especially where the supplier of the tying product does not derive a direct (financial) benefit from designating the suppliers of the tied product.

Notes and Questions

1. The 2022 block exemption and guidelines introduce limited changes compared to the legislation that was in effect for the previous 10 years. The most significant evolutions include: (i) a greater focus on the consequences of the growth in e-commerce, including on restraints associated with multi-channels distribution, such as dual distribution, and on contractual provisions favored by online intermediation platforms, such as price parity clauses); and (ii) the treatment of sustainability objectives as efficiencies in the assessment of vertical restraints such as single branding or selective distribution.

2. Internet sales: In the last two decades, Internet sales have become much more significant. The guidelines address this phenomenon, especially in the context of what is a passive sale (a producer may not restrict its exclusive distributor from making merely passive sales that come in from outside of the territory) and what is an active sale (the producer may restrict its exclusive distributor from making active sales outside of its territory).

Take a look at the guidelines' treatment of Internet freedoms and restrictions. See Guidelines paragraphs 202–210 (not included in the printed excerpt). Are the lines drawn in the appropriate place? Consider, for example, that sending unsolicited e-mails to specified customers outside of the territory is an active sale. The agreement may prohibit such a practice and still qualify for the block exemption. Requiring exclusive distributors to reroute web customers to the distributor in their territory would involve a lost opportunity for a passive sale, and would be prohibited. But sellers (often brand owners) can restrict sales to distributors with brick-and-mortar outlets (who then can sell on the Internet), and the brand sellers can block on-line sales of their goods by distributors without brick-and-mortar outlets. Are the Internet provisions appropriately protective of brand owners' needs to guard against free riders? or too restrictive of the freedom of eBay and its ilk to give good deals to consumers?

3. What is your assessment of both the form and the substance of the block exemption? Has the Commission succeeded in moving away from rigid forms to effects-based analysis? Does the block exemption give sufficient guidance? How well does it maneuver between the goals of giving more certainty to business and elucidating the line between clauses that are procompetitive and those that are anticompetitive?

4. Where the relevant market shares are 30% or below, which system—US or EU—fulfills these goals better?

Note that no firm is forced to come within the strictures of a block exemption, but that firms tend to do so if it is possible and not too inconvenient, for simplicity and business certainty. Moreover, clauses that are singled out as disqualifying are likely to fare badly at the stage of individual scrutiny.

5. How helpful is the guidance for individual assessments? In terms of predictors of anticompetitive effects, how accurate and sound is the guidance for exclusive purchasing? exclusive selling? tying? Are the guidelines sufficiently clear to give guidance on what is anticompetitive foreclosure? If not, what more should be stated?

6. Compare the guidelines' analysis with US case law. Is it essentially the same? Are there important respects in which the analysis is different—either in substance or burdens?

7. Describe the major differences in approach between US and EU law on vertical restraints. Are the differences formalistic or substantive? Are they driven by different values and goals, or the same ones? How significant is the goal of achieving EU market integration in explaining the differences?

The current Block Exemption Regulation and Guidelines are available on the Europa website at https://competition-policy.ec.europa.eu/antitrust-and-cartels/legislation.

b. Technology Transfer Licensing Block Exemption and Guidelines

Agreements for the licensing of technology have been the subject of a block exemption for many years. This regulation, too, has been liberalized.

A revised technology transfer block exemption became effective May 1, 2014. The regulation covers patents, knowhow, design rights, and software copyrights. The regulation contains a list of hardcore prohibitions. For example, prohibited clauses in licensing between competitors include price fixing and limitation of output where the restriction is reciprocal; allocation of markets or customers, with exceptions where the restriction is not reciprocal; and restriction on the licensee's using its own technology.

The block exemption regulation imposes a cap of 20% market share for licensing between competitors and a 30% market share for licensing between non-competitors. Outside of the exemption, a rule of reason applies, as explained in accompanying guidelines. The ceilings are low for firms that are significant players in technology-based markets, and for that reason alone licenses may not be able to get the benefit of the block exemption. The block exemption regulation and guidelines are available at https://competition-policy.ec.europa.eu/antitrust-and-cartels/legislation. In anticipation of their expiry in 2026, the Commission launched a revision process of the regulation and guidelines to assess the need and scope for an update.

The European regime might be compared with the US Department of Justice and Federal Trade Commission Antitrust Guidelines for the Licensing of Intellectual Property, April 1995, updated January 2017, available at https://www.justice.gov/atr/guidelines-and-policy-statements-0/2017-update-antitrust-guidelines-licensing-intellectual-property.

APPLE, AMAZON, AND E-BOOKS: A CASE STUDY

In Chapter 4, we saw that restraints sometimes can be characterized as either horizontal or vertical, and that the characterization can be legally significant. The growing market for distribution of e-books has raised many such questions in recent years, with technology giants like Apple and Amazon in alternatively friendly and antagonistic arrangements with book publishers that have led to important antitrust actions in the US and EU.

The immediate history of this story began with the introduction of Amazon's Kindle in 2007. From then until the introduction of Barnes & Noble's Nook in 2009 and Apple's iPad in 2010, Amazon was the juggernaut in the e-book and e-reader market. In the US, Amazon strategically priced premium e-books at $9.99 to stimulate demand for the Kindle and, in the view of some industry players, to entrench its market position in advance of competitive technologies reaching the market.

The book publishers felt that Amazon was devaluing the e-book market in order to promote its proprietary systems and technology. They feared that Amazon's low e-book pricing would condition consumers to expect low e-book prices forever for premium books. Because Amazon was initially the only game in town for e-book distribution, the publishers had little power to resist Amazon's demands. The advent of the iPad and the Nook emboldened the publishers to demand different terms of dealing.

According to the Justice Department and the European Commission, in late 2008 the publishers began to conspire with one another, and eventually with Apple, to force Amazon's hand. The conspiracy allegedly began as a deal between Apple and the publishers. Under the terms of the deal, the publishers would set the ultimate retail price, which would be capped in several tiers based on the hard-copy list price. Further, the publishers would agree to a most-favored nation (MFN) contract with Apple, providing that the publisher would guarantee to lower the retail price of each e-book in Apple's iBookstore to match the lowest price offered by any other retailer.

Having agreed to these terms with Apple, the publishers were allegedly able to force Amazon into the same type of arrangement. Because allowing Amazon to continue to undercut prices in iBookstore would quickly erode the whole deal, the publishers collectively forced Amazon to adhere to the new e-book pricing plan and agency model.

Following a Justice Department antitrust lawsuit in 2012, the publishers quickly accepted consent decrees terminating the allegedly offensive practices. The publishers and Apple also quickly offered commitments to settled the EU investigation, terminating on-going agency agreements and excluding certain clauses in their agency agreements during the next five years. The publishers also offered to give retailers freedom to discount e-books, subject to certain conditions, during a two-year period. *Commission accepts legally binding commitments from Simon & Schuster, Harper Collins, Hachette, Holtzbrinck and Apple for sale of e-books*

(December 13, 2012), http://europa.eu/rapid/press-release_IP-12-1367_en.htm.

Apple, however, decided to take its chances with a trial in the US, where the law on vertical restraints is generally more lenient than in the EU. As the sole defendant at trial, Apple argued that its contracts with the book publishers were all vertical not horizontal, that the shift from the wholesale to agency model was procompetitive, and that it had resulted in new entry, expanded output, and average lower prices. After trial, however, the district court found that Apple had joined the conspiracy among the book publishers and hence that it had committed a per se violation of Section 1 of the Sherman Act. In 2–1 opinion, the US Court of Appeals for the Second Circuit affirmed the district court opinion, finding that district court's decision that "Apple orchestrated a horizontal conspiracy among the Publisher Defendants to raise e-book prices is amply supported and well-reasoned, and that the agreement unreasonably restrained trade in violation of § 1 of the Sherman Act." United States v. Apple, Inc., 791 F.3d 290, 297 (2d 2015). A dissenting judge identified Amazon as the true villain of the story.

Although getting some vindication out of Apple's upbraiding, Amazon faced troubles of its own on the e-book front. On June 11, 2015, the European Commission announced that it had opened a formal antitrust investigation into certain business practices by Amazon in the distribution of electronic books ("e-books"). The Commission investigated contractual clauses requiring publishers to inform Amazon about more favorable or alternative terms offered to Amazon's competitors and/or offer Amazon similar terms and conditions than to its competitors, or through other means ensure that Amazon is offered terms at least as good as those for its competitors. The Commission stated concerns that such clauses might make it more difficult for other e-book distributors to compete with Amazon by developing new and innovative products and services. *Antitrust: Commission Opens Formal Investigation into Amazon's E-Book Distribution Arrangements,* (June 11, 2015) http://europa.eu/rapid/press-release_IP-15-5166_en.htm. In May of 2017, Amazon agreed to abandon its MFN clauses for a five-year period in order to settle the EU case.

In 2023, the U.S. Federal Trade Commission (FTC) and 17 U.S. states filed a lawsuit denouncing Amazon's abuse of its dominant position, including by means of parity clauses. The trial is set to take place in 2026.

C. JAPAN AND SOUTH KOREA

Japan

Japan's Antimonopoly Law prohibits conduct in three categories: private monopolization, unreasonable restraints of trade (both within Article 3), and unfair trade practices (Article 19). Article 19 provides: "An enterprise must not employ unfair trade practices." Market power is not a necessary element of the violation, and the market need not be defined. Article 3 violations may be punished criminally by large fines and even jail. For Article 19 violations, cease and desist orders are common, and 2009 amendments introduced fines for certain categories of conduct.

The Japan Fair Trade Commission (JFTC) is charged with designating the acts that constitute unfair trade practices, but sometimes the Japanese Parliament updates the list of prohibitions in the statute itself. For example, the JFTC has designated resale price maintenance an unfair trade practice, but after 2009 statutory amendments, RPM is directly covered in the Act. Minimum RPM is treated as virtually per se illegal. Suggested resale prices are not caught if they are merely reference prices.

Other JFTC designation prohibit:

— Tying: "Unjustly causing another party to purchase goods or services from oneself or from an entrepreneur designated by oneself by tying it to the supply of other goods or services, or otherwise coercing the said party to trade with oneself or with an entrepreneur designated by oneself." (Section 10)

— Exclusive dealing: "Unjustly dealing with the another party on condition that said party shall not trade with a competitor, thereby tending to reduce trading opportunities for the said competitor." (Section 11)

— Vertical territorial and customer restrictions: ". . . trading with the another party on conditions which unjustly restrict any transaction between said party and its other transacting party or other business activities of said party." (Section 12)

In practice, most vertical territorial, customer, and exclusive dealing restrictions that have been held illegal under these sections have been restrictions in support of resale price maintenance such as restrictions regarding price advertisement.

Other unfair practices include abuse of a dominant bargaining position. The JFTC published "Guidelines Concerning Abuse of Superior Bargaining Position under the Antimonopoly Act" on November 30, 2010, and has since evidenced the will to enforce the regulation. On June 22, 2011, the JFTC imposed an administrative fine of 222,160,000 yen (about $2 million) on a supermarket that allegedly forced its distributors provide employees to help with supermarket renovations without any compensation. The case received wide attention in the Japanese business community and signaled a more aggressive enforcement attitude by the Commission.

In 2019, the JFTC also published specific "Guidelines Concerning Abuse of a Superior Bargaining Position in Transactions between Digital Platform Operators and Consumers that Provide Personal Information", pertaining to the acquisition and use of personal data by digital platform operators. These guidelines clarify that the notion of abuse of a superior bargaining position can also apply to transactions between businesses and consumers (B2C) and not only in a business-to-business (B2B) context.

However, the main document governing the assessment of vertical restraints in Japan is the JFTC "Guidelines Concerning Distribution Systems and Business Practices", which may be found at https://www.jftc.go.jp/en/legislation_gls/imonopoly_guidelines.html. These guidelines were adopted in 1991 and regularly updated thereafter. They originate in the conclusion of talks held between the US and Japan in the 1980 on "structural impediments" to trade and competition. This was called the Structural Impediments Initiative, or SII. During these talks, the United States alleged that Fuji Film, enabled by Japanese law, used distribution restraints to marginalize Kodak in Japan's consumer film market. Selected excerpts follow.

GUIDELINES CONCERNING DISTRIBUTION SYSTEMS AND BUSINESS PRACTICES UNDER THE ANTIMONOPOLY ACT

Secretary General, Fair Trade Commission

Issued: July 11, 1991
revised: November 1, 2005,
January 1, 2010,
June 23, 2011,
March 30, 2015
March 27, 2016
June 16, 2017

Table of Contents

Introduction

1. Distribution systems and business practices have been formed with various historical and social backgrounds, and they differ from one country to another. There is the need to review them from time to time in order to change them for the better. In Japan, distribution systems and business practices are rapidly changing in accordance with the increasing globalization of economic activities, technological innovations, and other factors. Under these circumstances, for the purpose of enabling enterprises to exert their originality and ingenuity and further protecting consumers' interests, it is important to promote fair and free competition and enable the market mechanism to fully perform its functions: more specifically, it is essential to make sure that (a) enterprises are not prevented from freely entering markets, (b) each enterprise can freely and independently select its trading partners, (c) each enterprise can set prices and other transaction terms in its free and independent business discretion, and (d) competition is engaged in by fair means on the basis of prices, quality and services.

   These Guidelines are intended to contribute to prevention of enterprises and trade associations from violating the Antimonopoly Act and helping in the pursuit of their appropriate activities, by specifically describing, with respect to Japanese distribution systems and business practices, what types of conduct may impede fair and free competition and violate the Antimonopoly Act.

2. Part I of these Guidelines gives guidance under the Antimonopoly Act concerning enterprises' restrictions on their trading partners' business activities (for example, finished product manufacturers' restrictions on parts manufacturers' business activities or vice versa, and manufacturers' restrictions on wholesalers' and/or retailers' business activities or vice versa). Throughout these Guidelines, the term "trading partners" mean direct and/or indirect trade partners, unless otherwise specifically indicated. Part II contains guidance under the Antimonopoly Act concerning enterprises' selection of their own business partners. Part III provides guidance under the Antimonopoly Act concerning sole distributorship for the entire domestic market.

   In addition, although these Guidelines provide guidance mainly with respect to transactions of goods, in principle the same guidance also applies to transactions of services.

3. These Guidelines provide guidance on major types of distribution systems and business practices which may present problems under the Antimonopoly Act. These Guidelines, however, do not cover all types of practices which may present problems. For example, price-fixing cartels, purchasing volume cartels, and bid riggings, which are not covered in the Guidelines, in principle constitute violations of the Antimonopoly Act. Accordingly, it is to be judged on a case-by-case basis whether other types of practices not provided in these Guidelines may present problems under the Antimonopoly Act.

PART I. Restrictions on trading partners' business activities

1. Scope of These Guidelines

   (1) In cases where as a part of marketing activities an enterprise interferes with or influences sales prices of distributors (such as wholesalers and retailers), the kind of products they sell, their sales territories, their customers, etc., it may reduce or eliminate inter-brand or intra-brand competition. For the purpose of these Guidelines, the term "inter-brand competition" means competition among suppliers including manufacturers or among distributors, etc. who deal in different brand products, and the term "intra-brand competition" means competition among distributors, etc. who deal in the same brand products.

   This Part I provides guidance on approaches to be followed under the Antimonopoly Act with respect to the following types of conduct, from the view point of regulation of unfair trade practices: enterprises' restrictions on sales prices, handling of products, sales territories, customers, etc. of their trading partners and enterprises' provision of rebates and allowances to their trading partners (Note 1).

With the development and expansion of e-commerce, various business models have been created and enterprises actively use the Internet in their advertising and publicity as well as in their distribution channels. In especial, transactions through the Internet are effective means for enterprises and their customers. For example, in those transactions, enterprises can reach wider areas and more diversified customers than in traditional transactions in brick-and-mortar stores. The basic approaches described in the following sections apply commonly to transactions through the Internet and that in brick-and-mortar stores.

In addition, the basic approaches described below also apply to any platformer's actions toward users of its platform. For the purpose of these Guidelines, the term "platformer" means an enterprise that operates and offers a so-called platform which serves two or more user groups (such as consumers and enterprises offering products to them) and in which a level of its use by one user group influences a level of its use by another user group and vice versa. Such platforms include shopping malls, online marketplaces, online travel booking services and video game consoles.

(2) As seen in a relationship between a large-scale retailer and its supplier, if a party who has superior bargaining position against the other transacting party makes use of such position to impose a disadvantage on the transacting party, unjustly in light of normal business practices, such act would impede transactions based on the free and independently select of the said transacting party, and put the said transacting party in a disadvantageous competitive position against its competitors, while putting the party having superior bargaining position in an advantageous competitive position against its competitors. Since such act poses the risk of impeding fair competition, it is regulated under the Antimonopoly Act as "abuse of superior bargaining position," which constitutes a category of unfair trade practices. Approaches to regulation of such conduct are specifically described in the Guidelines Concerning Abuse of a Superior Bargaining Position under the Antimonopoly Act published on November 30, 2010.

As to unjust low price sales and related discriminatory pricing, the Japan Fair Trade Commission has given guidance on regulation of those practices in the Guidelines Concerning Unjust Low Price Sales under the Antimonopoly Act published on December 18, 2009 (Note 1).

(Note 1) As to in what cases these practices cause a substantial restraint of competition in markets and are illegal as private monopolization, the Japan Fair Trade Commission has given guidance on this issue in, for example, the Guidelines for Exclusionary Private Monopolization under the Antimonopoly Act published on October 28, 2009 (hereinafter referred to as "Exclusionary Private Monopolization Guidelines").

2. Basic Principles concerning Effects of Vertical Restraints on Competition

The purpose of the Antimonopoly Act is, by prohibiting unfair trade practices and encouraging fair and free competition, to assure the interests of general consumers and promote the democratic and wholesome development of the national economy. Enterprises' business practices which restrain sales prices, handling of products, sales territory, customers, etc. of their trading partners (hereinafter referred to as "vertical restraints") have various effects on competition depending on their degree, manners and other factors. Vertical restraints include not only restraints imposed under contracts or agreements but also virtual restraints implied by enterprises' direct or indirect requirements or requests (Note 2).

In some cases, vertical restraints may have anti-competitive effects: for example, such restraints may prevent innovative business activities, reduce or eliminate inter-brand or intra-brand competition, raise entry barriers and thereby hold back new market entrants, or limit consumers' choice of products.

In other cases, vertical restraints may have pro-competitive effects: those restraints may promote launch of new products, render market entry easier, or result in improvement of quality of products and services.

Thus, when vertical restraints have effects on competition, such effects may be pro-competitive or anti-competitive.

Promotion of fair and free competition is attained through assuring fair and free competition in each and every level of commercial transactions; it cannot be accomplished simply by securing either inter-brand or intra-brand competition, as long as the other one is eliminated.

(Note 2) In some cases, vertical restraints may be imposed with background of actions, including an enterprise's acquisition or possession of stocks of a trading partner or an enterprise's involvement in management of a trading partner (An enterprise's acquisition or possession of stokes of a trading partner or an enterprise's involvement in management of a trading partner, by itself, is not problematic under the Antimonopoly Act.). Also in such cases, legality of such actions should be determined under the criteria set forth in Section 3 below and in accordance with the guidance given in Chapters 1 and 2 below. (Refer to Appendix (Transactions between Parent and Subsidiary Companies or between Fellow Subsidiaries) attached hereto, with respect to cases where a restraining enterprise is a parent company of its business partner restrained by it.)

3. Criteria for Judging Legality or Illegality of Vertical Restraints

(1) Guidance on the criteria for judging legality or illegality of vertical restraints

As mentioned in Section 2 above, vertical restraints have various effects on competition. If a vertical restraint tends to impede fair competition, such restraint is prohibited as unfair trade practices. Whether a particular vertical restraint imposed in a commercial transaction tends to impede fair competition or not should be examined by assessing the scope influenced by such transaction depending on factors such as objects, regions and manners of the conduct and transaction and then considering the following factors comprehensively.

In this examination, due consideration should be given to not only anticompetitive effects (such as reduction or elimination of inter-brand or intrabrand competition) but also pro-competitive effects (refer to Sub-Section (3) below) that result from the vertical restraint. Anti-competitive and procompetitive effects to be so examined should include effects on potential competitors in each and every transaction level. The factors to be considered are:

(i) actual conditions of inter-brand competition (such as market concentration, characteristics of products in question, the degree of product differentiation, distribution channels, difficulty of new market entry, etc.);

(ii) actual conditions of intra-brand competition (such as the degree of dispersion in prices, and business types of distributors, etc. dealing in products in question, etc.);

(iii) position in the market of an enterprise that imposes the vertical restraint (in terms of a market share, ranking, brand value, etc.);

(iv) impact of the vertical restriction on business activities carried out by the affected trading partners (such as the degree and manners of the restraint, etc.); and

(v) the number of trading partners affected by the restraint, and their positions in the market.

The importance of individual factors is different on a case-by-case basis, and therefore each of these factors should be considered depending upon a nature of business carried out by an enterprise which impose a vertical restraint. For example, assessment of effects on competition arising from a vertical restraint imposed by a platformer should take into account actual conditions of competition among the platformer and its competitors and position in the market of the platformer based on a reflection of network effects (Note 3)

(Note 3) Network effects may be direct or indirect. Network effects are direct if, for example, benefits to users arising from a particular platform and usefulness of the platform to its users are improved by increase of the number of users in the same group. On the other hand, network effects are indirect if, for example, two groups of users of a particular platform transact with each other via the platform and benefits to users in one of those groups arising from transactions via the platform and usefulness of such transactions to those users are improved by increase of the number of users in the other group.

(2) "Tend to impede fair competition"

There are 2 types of vertical restraints: resale price maintenance practices (See Chapter 1 below for details.) and vertical non-price restraints. Vertical nonprice restraints consist of an enterprise's restraints on handling products, sales territory, customers, etc. of the enterprise's trading partners.

Resale price maintenance practices reduce or eliminate price competition among distributors. Therefore, those practices usually have significant anticompetitive effects and, as a general rule, they tend to impede fair competition.

On the other hand, effects of vertical non-price restraints on competition in markets differ depending upon the types of restraints and specifics of each case. Vertical non-price restraints include the following two categories: (i) those which should not be considered illegal merely based on types of the restraints, but should be determined on a case-by-case basis whether or not tend to impede fair competition (i.e., whether or not they have foreclosure effects or price maintenance effects) taking into account, among others, a position in the market of an enterprise which imposes the restraint; and (ii) those each of which usually tends to impede price competition and is considered in principle to tend to impede fair competition, regardless of a position in market of an enterprise which imposes the restraint.

If an enterprise simultaneously imposes a vertical non-price restraint and another vertical non-price restraint or resale price maintenance, assessment as to whether or not the first-mentioned vertical non-price restraint tends to impede fair competition may take into account effects of the other vertical non-price restraint or the resale price maintenance simultaneously imposed by the enterprise.

a. Cases where vertical non-price restraints have foreclosure effects

"Cases where vertical non-price restraints have foreclosure effects" refer to cases where a vertical non-price restraint tends to cause situation that new entrants to the relevant market and the enterprise's existing competitors are excluded and/or opportunities available to them are reduced (for example, a situation where such restraint makes difficult for them to easily acquire alternative trading partners, and causes increase of their expenses for conduct of business and/or their discouragement from entering the market or developing new products).

Whether or not a particular vertical non-price restraint has foreclosure effects should be determined in accordance with the guidance on the criteria for judging legality or illegality as set forth in Sub-Section (1) above. For example, if an enterprise which impose a vertical non-price restraint holds a stronger position in a market, the restraint is more likely to have foreclosure effects. Such determination should be made also taking other enterprises' actions into consideration. For example, if two or more enterprises impose vertical non-price restraints respectively and parallel, those restraints are more likely to have foreclosure effects on the market as a whole than in the case where a single enterprise imposes a vertical non-price restraint.

When determining whether or not a particular vertical non-price restraint has foreclosure effects, the restraint is not required to cause any tangible said situation.

b. Cases where vertical non-price restraints have price maintenance effects

"Cases where vertical non-price restraints have price maintenance effects" refer to cases where a vertical non-price restraint tends to impede competition among a counterparty to the restraint and its competitors and enable the counterparty to reasonably freely control its prices in its own discretion and thus maintain or raise its prices for a product or products in question.

Whether or not a particular vertical non-price restraint has price maintenance effects should be determined in accordance with the guidance on the criteria for judging legality or illegality as set forth in Sub-Section (1) above. For example, if a strict territorial restriction (refer to Sub-Section 3 (3) of Chapter 2 below) is imposed by an influential enterprise in the market under circumstances where inter-brand competition does not work well due to oligopolistic structure of the market and/or due to brand differentiation, then price competition for products included in the enterprise's brand may be impeded, and the restriction may have price maintenance effects. Such determination should be made also taking other enterprises' actions into consideration. For example, if two or more enterprises impose vertical non-price restraints respectively and parallel, those restraints are more likely to have price maintenance effects on the market as a whole than in the case where a single enterprise imposes a vertical non-price restraint.

When determining whether or not a particular vertical non-price restraint has price maintenance effects, the restraint is not required to cause any tangible said situation.

(3) Pro-competitive effects which may result from vertical restraints

In the case where vertical restraints actually promote sales of new products, ease new entrants, improve quality and services and so on, pro-competitive effects can be recognized. The followings are typical and non-exhaustive examples:

a. Distributors may sell any enterprises' product without their own promotional activities if other distributors have already implemented promotional activities for the product as pre-sales efforts, which thus have actually boosted demand for the product. In such a case, distributors may refrain from actively implementing voluntary promotional activities on their own expenses, resulting in a situation where consumers who would otherwise have purchased the product do not purchase it. This type of situation is called the "free-rider" problem. One situation in which the free-rider problem is likely to occur is when consumers have limited information on the products. For example, in case of relatively new or technically complex products for consumers, consumers tend to have insufficient information so distributors may have to provide enough information or implement through promotional activities. In addition, consumers must have a sufficient cost-saving effect on purchasing products when purchasing the products from a distributor that does not implement such promotional activities instead of purchasing from one which actually does so. Generally, consumers will have a profound effect when the price of products is relatively high. When these conditions are met and therefore the free-rider problem occurs, making it highly likely that distributors will not provide consumers with sufficient information on a product of the enterprise and that consequently the product will not be sufficiently supplied, then the enterprise's allocation of one sales area to one distributor may be an efficient restriction to avoid such free-riding. However, pro-competitive effects are recognized, for one thing, only if such promotional activities can benefit many new customers who do not yet have enough information and therefore increase of amount of purchase can be expected and so on. Also, such promotional activities may be unique for the product, and the cost of the promotional activities cannot be recouped (so-called "sunk-cost").

b. In some cases, in order to build a reputation for high quality of its new product, it may be vital in an enterprise's marketing strategy to supply the new product to retailers which have established reputation for sale of high-quality products. In such a case, it may be helpful for the enterprise's building-up of reputation for high quality of the new product if the enterprise permits its distributors to sell the enterprise's products only to those retailers.

c. In order to release a new product, an enterprise may request its distributors to make special investments such as installation of special equipment. In such a case, the distributors may not recoup these investments if other distributors are permitted to sell the same product without making such investments. As a result, all distributors may refrain from making such investments. Under said circumstances, the enterprise's allocation of one distribution territory to one distributor may be helpful for the enterprise's encouragement of its distributors to make special investments.

d. In the event that a parts manufacturer has to make special investments (such as installation of special machinery and/or equipment) in order to manufacture parts that satisfy specific requirements of a finished product manufacturer, it may be helpful inducement for the special investment by the parts manufacturer if the parts manufacturer obligates the finished product manufacturer to purchase the specified quantity of the parts from the parts manufacturer, etc.

e. An enterprise may try to create uniform sales services and/or standardize the quality of sales services in order to build a reputation among its customers (so-called "brand image") for its products. In such a case, it will be helpful for the enterprise's building-up of reputation among its customers for the products if the enterprise permits its distributors to sell the products only to those retailers who can meet certain criteria or if the enterprise restricts retailers' sales methods.

(4) An influential enterprise in a market

Some vertical non-price restraints may be illegal as unfair trade practices if such restraints are imposed by "an influential enterprise in a market." Examples of such restraints are described in Section 2 (Restriction on Dealings with Competitors, etc.), Sub-Section 3(3) (Strict territorial restriction) and Section 7 (Tie-in Sales) of Chapter 2 below.

Whether or not "an enterprise is influential in a market" is in the first instance judged by a market share of the manufacturer, that is, whether or not it has a share exceeding 20% in the market. (meaning a product market which consists of a group of products with the same or similar functions and utility as the product covered by the conduct, and competing with each other judging from geographical conditions, transactional relations and other factors, and which is determined, in principle, in terms of substitutability for users and also, when necessary, substitutability for suppliers). Nevertheless, even if an enterprise falls under this criterion, a restriction by the enterprise is not always illegal. Such restriction is illegal if it has "foreclosure effects" or "price maintenance effects."

In cases an enterprise which has a market share of 20% or less or a new entrant commits any said action, it does not usually tend to impede fair competition and therefore is not illegal.

Chapter 1. Resale Price Maintenance

1. Viewpoint

(1) It is one of the most basic matters in an enterprise's business activities that it independently determines its own sales price, in keeping with conditions in a market, and moreover this secures competition among enterprises and consumer choice.

In cases where, as one aspect of marketing activities or upon a distributor's request, an enterprise restricts sales price of distributors, it is in principle illegal as unfair trade practices, because it reduces or eliminates price competition among distributors.

(2) In cases where an enterprise's suggested retail price or quotation is indicated to distributors as a reference price, such conduct itself is not problematic. However, in cases where the enterprise goes beyond notifying a price merely as a reference one and seeks to restrict resale prices of its distributors by, for example, causing them to keep the price indicated by the enterprise, such conduct falls under the conduct described in Sub-Section (1) above, and is in principle illegal (Note 4).

(Note 4) In cases where an enterprise sets a suggested retail price, such conduct is not usually problematic unless it does not constitute restriction of resale prices. (Whether or not a particular price setting constitutes restriction of resale prices should be determined based upon the guidance given in Section 2 below.) From a viewpoint of prevention of violation of the Antimonopoly Act, it is desirable that, if an enterprise notifies a suggested retail price of its product to its distributors, the enterprise should refrain from using the expression "True Price" (Seika), "Set Price" (Teika) or merely indicating the value of the price and should use non-binding expressions such as "Reference Price" (Sanko Kakaku) or "manufacturer's suggested retail price" and that the enterprise should clearly state in a written notice that the suggested retail price is given solely for reference purposes and that each distributor is free to set its resale price independently.

2. Restriction of Resale Prices

(1) Any enterprise's restrictions of sales prices of its distributors (i.e., resale prices) are in principle illegal as unfair trade practices (Article 2, Paragraph (9), Item (iv) (Resale Price Restriction) of the Antimonopoly Act) (Note 5). That is to say, since resale price maintenance (RPM) reduces or eliminates price competition among distributors, generally RPM has serious anti-competitive effects and so tends to impede fair competition in principle. Therefore, the Antimonopoly Act stipulates that any RPM imposed by an enterprise on distributors without "justifiable grounds" is illegal as unfair trade practices. In other words, RPM is not

illegal on an exceptional basis on the condition that it has "justifiable grounds."

(Note 5) Any enterprise's restriction of prices of its distributors for any service falls under Paragraph 12 (Trading on Restrictive Terms) of the General Designation. Basic approach is the same as that which applies to cases which fall under Article 2, Paragraph (9), Item (iv) of the Antimonopoly Act.

(2) "Justifiable grounds" might be granted only within a reasonable scope and only for a reasonable period, in the case where RPM by an enterprise with respect to its product results in actual pro-competitive effects, promotes inter-brand competition, and increases demand for the product thus benefiting consumers, and these pro-competitive effects would not have resulted from less restrictive alternatives other than the RPM.

For example, when an enterprise engages in RPM with respect to a product, such RPM is deemed to have "justifiable grounds" if the RPM actually has procompetitive effects through avoiding the "free-rider" problem mentioned in Sub-section 3(3)a of Part 1 above, promotes inter-brand competition, and increases demand of the product, thus benefiting consumers, and pro-competitive effects would not have resulted from less restrictive alternatives other than the RPM.

(3) Whether or not resale prices are restricted by an enterprise is to be determined with reference to whether or not the enterprise has taken artificial means to secure the effectiveness in attaining its distributors' sales at a price indicated by the enterprise.

In the following cases, it should be determined that the effectiveness in attaining distributors' sales at a price indicated by the enterprise is secured:

(i) in case where a written or oral agreement between an enterprise and its distributor causes the distributor to sell the enterprise's product at a price indicated by the enterprise, including the cases where:

(a) a written or oral contact between an enterprise and its distributor provides that the distributor should sell the enterprise's product at a price indicated by the enterprise;

(b) a distributor is required to pledge in writing to sell at a price indicted by an enterprise;

(c) an enterprise proposes to a distributor the condition that the distributor should sell the enterprise's product at a price indicated by the enterprise, and the enterprise starts dealing with the distributor only if it accepts such condition; or

(d) an enterprise deals with a distributor on the condition that the distributor should sell the enterprise's product at a price indicated by the enterprise and that unsold units of the product should not be sold at any discounted price but repurchased by the enterprise.

(Example) Company X has established the following sales regulation (hereinafter referred to as the "Sales Regulation") applicable to retailers' sale of Company X's camping equipment products in the next season:

- retailers' sales prices for each of those products should be equal to or higher than the minimum price set by Company X; and
- each retailer will be permitted to sell those products at discounted prices only if the retailer does the discount sale covering all products including other brands or if the retailer does the discount sale for the purpose of selling out its inventory at its brick-and-mortar stores, without issuing advertisement leaflets, and not earlier than the day designated by Company X.

Company X caused retailers to sell its camping equipment products in compliance with the Sales Regulations as follows: Company X by itself or through wholesalers:

- in negotiations for transactions to be done in the next season with each retailer that is Company X's current trading partner, requests the retailer to sell those products in compliance with the Sales Regulations in such a way as to present a quotation in which the minimum price set by Company X is written; and

- at commencement of transactions between Company X and each retailer that is Company X's new trading partner, requests the retailer to sell those products in compliance with the Sales Regulation, and under the condition that Company X should cause other retailers to sell those products in compliance with the Sales Regulation, obtained from each retailer an agreement to sell those products in compliance with the Sales Regulation.

  This action done by Company X was found to fall under Article 2, Paragraph (9), Items (iv) (a) and (iv) (b) of the Antimonopoly Act and therefore to breach the provision of Article 19 of the Act. (Cease and Desist Order of June 15, 2016; JFTC Disposition No. 7 of 2016.)

(ii) In case where an enterprise, through any artificial means (such as an enterprise's imposing or suggesting to impose economic disadvantage on its distributors if the distributors do not sell the enterprise's product at a price indicated by the enterprise), causes the distributors to sell at the indicated price, including the cases where:

(a) curtailment of shipments or any other economic disadvantage (including reduction of quantities shipped, raising of a shipment price, reduction of rebates, and refusal to supply other products: hereinafter the same) is imposed by an enterprise on its distributor if the distributor does not sell the enterprise's product at a price indicated by the enterprise, or an enterprise's intention to do so is notified or suggested by the enterprise to its distributor;

(b) rebates or other economic rewards (including lowering of a shipment price and supply of other products; hereinafter the same) are provided by an enterprise to its distributor if the distributor sells the enterprise's product at a price indicated by the enterprise, or an enterprise's intention to do so is notified or suggested by the enterprise to its distributor;

(c) an enterprise compels its distributor to sell the enterprise's product at a price indicated by the enterprise, by collecting sales price reports, patrolling the distributor's retail establishments, conducting price supervision by salespersons dispatched to the distributor's shops, examining the distributor's ledgers or records and/or taking similar measures in order to ascertain whether or not the distributor sells the product at the indicated price;

(d) an enterprise compels its distributors to sell the enterprise's product at a price indicated by the enterprise, by detecting distribution channels through which the product is supplied to price-cutting distributors (through, for example making use of secret marks) and requesting distributors who make supply to such price-cutting distributors not to sell the product to them;

(e) an enterprise compels its distributors to sell the enterprise's product at a price indicated by the enterprise, by buying the product from a pricecutting distributor and causing such price-cutting distributor or a distributor who supplied the product to the distributor to buy the product from the enterprise or pay the enterprise's cost of purchase of the product; or

(f) an enterprise compels its distributors to sell the enterprise's product at a price indicated by the enterprise, by transmitting complaints to a price cutting distributor which the enterprise receives from other distributors with regard to the price-cutting distributor's low-price sales, and requesting the price-cutting distributors to end such sales.

(4) In cases where discriminatory treatment in the form of refusals to deal or provision of rebates, and so on, has been used to secure the effectiveness of restrictions on resale price, such conduct itself is illegal as unfair trade practices (Paragraph 2 (Other Refusal to Deal) or 4 (Discriminatory Treatment on Trade Terms, etc.) of the General Designation).

(5) For the purpose of Sub-Section (3) above, prices indicated by enterprises to distributors include both specific prices and any of the following types of prices:

a. a price within x% discount from the enterprise's suggested retail price;

b. a price within a specific range (i.e., not less than JPY Y and not more than JPY Z);

c. a price approved in advance by the enterprise;

d. a price not less than that charged by nearby stores; or

e. a price suggested by the enterprise to distributors as the lowest limit by, for example, warning the distributors if they sell the product in question at any price lower than such suggested price.

(6) The guidance given in Sub-Sections (3), (4) and (5) above applies not only to an enterprise's restriction on its direct trading partners (for example, a manufacturer's restriction on wholesalers) but also to an enterprise's restriction imposed on its indirect trading partners (for example, a manufacturer's restriction on retailers or secondary wholesalers) either directly or indirectly via the enterprise's direct trading partners (Article 2, Paragraph (9), Item (iv) of the Antimonopoly Act; Paragraph 2 or 4 of the General Designation).

(7) In cases where, in the following kinds of transactions, an enterprise's direct trading partner only functions as a commission agent and it is deemed that in substance a sale is done by the enterprise, then the sale is usually not illegal even if the enterprise instructs a resale price to the direct trading partner.

(i) in the case of consignment sales, and if the transaction is made with a consignor on its own risks and account so that a consignee bears no risk beyond that associated with its obligation to exercise the care of a good manager in storage of products, collection of payments, and so on, i.e., is not liable for loss of products, damage to them, or for unsold products; or

(ii) in the case of transactions where a supply price is negotiated and decided directly between a manufacturer and a retailer (or user), and the manufacturer instructs a wholesaler to deliver products to the retailer (or the user), and if the manufacturer is deemed, in substance, to sell the products to the retailers (or the user), under such circumstances that the wholesaler is charged only with responsibility for physical delivery of the products and collection of payment, and a fee is paid for such work.

(Examples)

(i) Content Provider A engages in an online music distribution business. Content Provider A is planning to execute a consignment sales contract with Platformer B (an enterprise which runs a portal site), and the contract provides that Platformer B should provide online music distribution services at prices indicated by Content Provider A. Under the contract, Content Provider A engages Platformer B merely to upload music contents provided by Content Provider A to Platformer B's servers and to collect prices of such music contents on behalf of Content Provider A, so providing music contents held by Content Provider A is deemed to in substance be done by Content Provider A directly to its users. Therefore, execution of the contract does not immediately constitute a problem under the Antimonopoly Act. ("3. Content provider's designation of prices for music content services," 2004 Consultation Cases)

(ii) Company X is a manufacturer of Industrial Component A. Company X set its selling price of Industrial Component A charged to Customer Z through negotiations with Customer Z. Company X is planning to instruct its Agent Y to supply Industrial Component A to Customer Z at such price. (More specifically, Agent Y is responsible for physical delivery of Industrial Component A to Customer Z, collection of the payment from Customer Z and storage of Industrial Component A. A commission payable by Company X to Agent Y is the difference between Agent Y's sales price of Industrial Component A to Customer Z and Agent Y's purchase price of Industrial Component A from Company X.) Company X is deemed to in substance sell Industrial Component A directly to Customer Z because Agent Y is considered to bear minimal risks arising from its storage of Industrial Component A although, as stated above, Agent Y is responsible for delivery of Industrial Component A, collection of the payment and storage. In addition,

Company X is deemed to exert few influence on price competition for Industrial Component A because Company X instructs only a price for Agent Y's supply of Industrial Component A to Customer Z and does not instruct prices applicable to Agent Y's sale of Industrial Component A to any customers other than Company Z or sale of Industrial Component A by any other agents other than Agent Y. Therefore, the said instruction by Company X to Agent Y does not immediately constitute a problem under the Antimonopoly Act. ("2. Restriction on an agent's resale price," 2009 Consultation Cases)

3. Distribution Research When an enterprise carries out a research on actual sales prices, customers, etc. of distributors handling the enterprise's products ("distribution research"), such research itself is generally not illegal, unless the research is accompanied by restrictions of sales prices of distributors such as imposing, notifying or suggesting imposition of curtailment of shipments or other economic disadvantage (including reduction of quantity shipped, raising of shipment price, reduction of rebate, refusal to supply other products) in the event that sales are not made at the enterprise's indicated price.

Chapter 2. Vertical Non-Price Restraints

1. Viewpoint

   (1) As mentioned in Section 3 of Part I above, whether or not an enterprise's vertical non-price restraint constitutes a violation of the Antimonopoly Act should be determined with reference to a type of such restraint on a case-by-case basis, analyzing its effect on competition in a market. Principles underlying the criteria for judging legality or illegality of major types of vertical non-price restraints are described in the following sections.

   (2) As to whether or not a vertical non-price restraint is imposed by an enterprise, as is the case with restrictions on resale prices described in Section 2 of Chapter 1 above, it should be found that the enterprise imposes a vertical nonprice restraint not only in cases where the enterprise imposes such restraint on its trading partners under a contract or by other means, but also in cases where the enterprise has taken any artificial means (such as imposing economic disadvantage on trading partners who do not comply with the enterprises' requests) to secure the effectiveness of the restraint.

2. Restrictions on Dealings with Competitors, etc.

(1) Restriction on trading partners' dealing with competitors and/or trading partners' handling of competing products

a. In cases where as a part of marketing activities, an enterprise may restrict its trading partners from dealing with its competitors. It is said that such restriction has managerial benefits. However, any such restriction may possibly impede current competitors' business activities and/or raise entry barriers, depending upon the enterprise's position in the market.

b. In cases where any below-listed conduct done by an influential enterprise in a market has foreclosure effects, such conduct is illegal as unfair trade practices (Paragraph 2 (Other Refusal to Trade), 11 (Trading on Exclusive Terms) or 12 (Trading on Restrictive Terms) of the General Designation): enterprise's engaging in transactions with its trading partners on the condition that the trading partners should not deal with competitors of the enterprise or another enterprise having close relations with the enterprise (Note 6); the enterprise's causing its trading partners to refuse to deal with competitors of the enterprise or another enterprise having close relations with the enterprise; or the enterprise's engaging in transactions with its trading partners on the condition that the trading partners should limit their handling of products that compete with products of the enterprise or another enterprise having close relations with the enterprise (hereinafter referred to as "competing products").

Whether or not a particular vertical non-price restraint has foreclosure effects should be determined in accordance with the guidance given in Part I, Sub-Section 3(1) above and Part I, Sub-Section 3(2)a above. For example, if products of an enterprise which imposes a vertical non-price restraint have a stronger brand value or the excess supply capacity of such enterprise's competitors is smaller as a whole, the vertical non-price restraint is more likely to have foreclosure effects, because availability of the enterprise's products is more important to its competitors and effectiveness of the restriction is greater. In addition, if a vertical non-price restraint is imposed for a longer period or on a larger number of competitors or if commercial transactions between an enterprise and its trading partner on which the enterprise imposes a vertical non-price restraint is more important to such trading partner, the vertical nonprice restraint is more likely to have foreclosure effects. If two or more enterprises impose vertical non-price restraints respectively and parallel, those restraints are more likely to have foreclosure effects on the market as a whole than in the case where a single enterprise imposes a vertical non-price restraint.

(i) An influential material manufacturer in a market, by notifying or suggesting to a customer (which is a finished product manufacturer) that it intends to discontinue supply of its materials to the customer if the customer purchases corresponding parts from other parts manufacturers, requests the customer not to do so (Paragraph 11 of the General Designation);

(ii) an influential finished product manufacturer in a market requests an influential parts manufacturer in a market to refrain from selling its parts to the finished product manufacturer's competitors or to restrict such supply, and obtains the supplier's consent to do (Paragraph 11 or 12 of the General Designation);

(iii) an influential manufacturer deals with a distributor on the condition that the manufacturer makes it mandatory for the distributor to handle only the manufacturer's products (Paragraph 11 of the General Designation);

(iv) an influential manufacturer in a market does business with a distributor under any condition which restricts the distributor from handling specific products (such as competing imported products) or from handling a specific enterprise's products (Paragraph 12 of the General Designation);

(v) an influential manufacturer deals with a distributor on the condition that the manufacturer restricts the distributor's handling of competing products by means of requiring the distributor to sell such a large volume of the manufacturer's products as is close to the distributor's selling capacity (Paragraph 12 of the General Designation); or

(vi) an influential manufacturer in a market causes distributors not to accept any offers of transactions from a specific manufacturer attempting to enter the market (Paragraph 2 of the General Designation).

(Note 6) A enterprise "having close relations with the enterprise" means one having common interests with the other. Whether or not an enterprise means one having common interests with another enterprise is to be judged on a case-by-case basis, taking comprehensively into consideration such factors as stockholding relationship, interlocking or dispatching of directorates, trading and financing relationship, and common membership of so-called corporate groups. The same applies throughout in these Guidelines.

c. In case where there is proper justification under the Antimonopoly Act for any enterprise's restriction on its trading partner's transactions with the enterprise's competitors or its trading partner's handling of competing products, the restriction is not illegal. For example;

(i) the case where a finished product manufacturer engages a parts manufacturer to manufacture parts for the former's product by making use of materials supplied by the former to the latter and the former requires the latter to sell those products exclusively to the former

(ii) the case where a finished product manufacturer engages a parts manufacturer to manufacture parts for the former's product, the former provides know-how (meaning and limited to know-how related to industrial technologies, and excluding any know-how that is not secret in nature) to the latter for the purpose of such manufacture, and the former requires the latter to sell those parts exclusively to the former, to the extent that such restriction is deemed necessary for keeping the knowhow confidential or for preventing its unauthorized diversion.

d. The guidance given in Sub-Sections a, b and c above also applies to cases where an enterprise causes its direct trading partners to restrict their counterparties' (e.g., a manufacturer causes wholesalers to restrict retailers') dealing with the enterprise's competitors and/or handling of competing products (Paragraph 2 or 12 of the General Designation).

(2) Restrictions on Dealing with Competitors by Price Matching

a. Any enterprise's reducing prices of its products in accordance with market conditions is indeed a manifestation of competition, and should be positively evaluated from a viewpoint of competition policies. However, in cases where the enterprise causes its customer to agree to continue business with the enterprise if it reduces its price to the extent that, as mentioned in Sub-Section b below, such price reduction is in response to lower prices offered by the enterprise's competitors, then such conduct may reduce business opportunities available to the enterprise's competitors.

b. In cases where an influential enterprise in a market causes its trading partner to agree to continue business with the enterprise on the condition that terms of any proposal, if any, made by the enterprise's competitors to the trading partner should be made known to the enterprise, and that if the enterprise reduces its sales price to the same level as or to a more attractive level than prices quoted by the competitors, the trading partner should not deal with the competitors or should maintain the volume of transaction with the enterprise at the same level as before, and if such conduct has foreclosure effects, then such conduct is illegal as unfair trade practices (Paragraph 11 or 12 of the General Designation).

The guidance given in Sub-Section (1) (Enterprises' restriction on trading partners' dealing with competitors and/or trading partners' handling of competing products) of this Section 2 applies to determination of whether or not a particular restriction has foreclosure effects.

3. Restrictions on Sales Territories

(1) In cases where as a part of marketing activities, enterprises may impose restrictions on distributors in terms of their sales territories. Such restrictions include the followings:

(i) an enterprise's assigns a specific territory to each distributor as the area of the distributor's primary responsibility, and imposes on the distributor the requirement that the distributor should carry out active marketing and sales activities within its own territory (i.e., establishment of an area of the distributor's primary responsibility, not involving restrictions mentioned in (iii) or (iv) below; hereinafter referred to as "area-of responsibility system");

(ii) an enterprise limits areas where a distributor may establish outlets such as stores, or an enterprise designates a place where such outlets are to be established (i.e., restriction of locations of distributors' outlets, not involving restrictions mentioned in Clause (iii) or (iv) below; hereinafter referred to as "location system");

(iii) an enterprise assigns a specific area to each distributor and restricts the distributor's sale of the enterprise's products outside the assigned area (hereinafter referred to as "strict territorial restriction"); and

(iv) an enterprise assigns a specific area to each distributor and restricts the distributor's sale of the enterprise's products to customers outside the assigned area upon such customers' request (hereinafter referred to as "restriction on passive sales to outside customers"); and

(2) Area-of-responsibility system and location system. It is not illegal for an enterprise to adopt an area-of-responsibility system or a location system for the purpose of developing effective outlets for the products or securing a better system for provision of after-sales services for the products, unless such restriction falls under the category "strict territorial restriction" or "restriction on passive sales to outside customers". The said restriction is not illegal because it does not usually have price maintenance effects.

For example in sales through the Internet, it is usually not illegal for an enterprise to obligate distributors to engage in active marketing activities in specific areas and/or toward specific customer groups, such as publication of advertisements on websites of the distributors or third parties (including platformers) and issuance of mail magazines. However, if an enterprise's restriction falls under the category "strict territorial restriction" or "restriction on passive sales to outside customers" (including the case where an enterprise restricts distributors' sales to any areas or customers other than the specific ones), illegality of such restriction should be determined in accordance with the guidance given in Sub-Section (3) or (4) below.

(3) Strict territorial restriction

In cases where an influential enterprise in a market imposes a strict territorial restriction on distributors and such restriction has price maintenance effects, the restriction is illegal as unfair trade practices (Paragraph 12 (Trading on Restrictive Terms) of the General Designation) (Note 7).

Whether or not a particular strict territorial restriction imposed by an enterprise has price maintenance effects should be determined in accordance with the guidance given in Part I, Sub-Section 3(1) above and Part I, Sub-Section 3(2)b above. For example, if a strict territorial restriction is imposed by an influential enterprise in the market under circumstances where inter-brand competition does not work well due to oligopolistic structure of the market and/or due to brand differentiation, then price competition for products included in the enterprise's brand may be impeded, and the restriction may have price maintenance effects. If two or more enterprises impose strict territorial restrictions respectively and parallel, those restrictions are more likely to have price maintenance effects on the market as a whole than in the case where a single enterprise imposes a strict territorial restriction.

(Note 7) If, in test marketing of a new product or in sale of local souvenirs, distribution areas of such products or souvenirs are restricted, such restriction usually does not have price maintenance effects and is not illegal.

(4) Restriction on passive sales to outside customers

In cases where an enterprise imposes a restriction on a distributor's passive sales to outside customers and such restriction has price maintenance effects, the restriction is illegal as unfair trade practices (Paragraph 12 of the General Designation).

Because restrictions on passive sales to outside customers even make it impossible for distributors to sell the products in response to outside customers' request, such restrictions have more effect of restricting intra-brand competition than strict territorial restrictions.

For example, in sales through the Internet, if a customer visits a website of a distributor and contacts the distributor and if such contact leads to a sale, then that is considered passive sales. The same is true if a customer chooses to continuously receive information such as mail magazines from the distributor, the customer places a purchase order with the distributor based upon the information and the purchase order leads to a sale. Under such circumstances, in the event that an enterprise assigns a specific area to the distributor and the customer's shipping address or another similar information reveal the address that is not within the distributor's territory, it constitutes a restriction on passive sales to an outside customer for the enterprise to cause the distributor to discontinue its dealings through the Internet with the customer. If such conduct has price maintenance effects, it is illegal as unfair trade practices.

(5) The guidance given in Sub-Sections (2), (3) and (4) above of this Section 3 also applies to cases where an enterprise causes its direct trading partners to restrict sales territories of their counterparties (for example, the case where a manufacturer causes wholesalers to restrict sales territories of retailers) (Paragraph 12 of the General Designation).

4. Restrictions on Distributors' Trading Partners

(1) An enterprise may requires and causes distributors to do business only with specified trading partners and to distribute the enterprise's products only to those partners. Examples of such restriction include the following cases:

(i) an enterprise's requiring each wholesaler to identify retailers that are the wholesaler's customers, so that each of the retailers can buy the enterprise's products only from that wholesaler (hereinafter referred to as "requirement of designated accounts");

(ii) an enterprise's prohibition of distributors from buying and selling the enterprise's products among themselves (hereinafter referred to as "prohibition of sales among distributors"); and

(iii) an enterprise's prohibition of wholesalers' sale of the enterprise's products to price-cutting retailers.

(2) Requirement of designated accounts

If an enterprise imposes requirement of designated accounts on distributors and such requirement has price maintenance effects, the restriction is illegal as unfair trade practices (Paragraph 12 (Trading on Restrictive Terms) of the General Designation).

Under a scenario of requirement of designated accounts, an enterprise assigns particular retailers to each wholesaler as the wholesaler's trading partners and prohibits the wholesaler from accepting any offer, if any, made to the wholesaler by any retailer that has been assigned by the enterprise to any other wholesaler. This conduct by the enterprise is same as that the enterprise assigns a specific area to each distributor and restricts the distributor's sale of the enterprise's products to customers outside the assigned area upon such customers' request. Therefore, the guidance given in Part I, Chapter 2, Subsection 3(4) above "Restriction on passive sales to outside customers" applies to determination of whether or not a particular requirement of designated accounts has price maintenance effects.

(3) Prohibition of sales among distributors

Because prohibition of sales among distributors imposes restrictions on selection of trading partners which is an essential element of transactions, the prohibition may lead to restrictions on distribution competition, depending upon a manner of the restrictions. If it has price maintenance effects, it is illegal as unfair trade practices (Paragraph 12 of the General Designation).

In cases where an enterprise prohibits sales among distributors for the purpose of prohibition of wholesalers' sale of the enterprise's products to price-cutting retailers described in Sub-Section (4) below, such prohibition of sales among distributors usually tends to impede price competition, and therefore, in principle, such prohibition is illegal as unfair trade practices (Paragraph 12 of the General Designation).

(4) Prohibition of sales to price-cutting retailers

When an enterprise prohibits wholesalers from selling the enterprise's products to a retailer on account of the retailer's price-cutting (Note 8), such prohibition is an action involved in one of the most basic matters in an enterprise's business activities that it independently determines its own sales price, in keeping with conditions in a market. Therefore, in light of the guidance given in Chapter I "Resale Price Maintenance" of this Part I, such prohibition usually tends to impede price competition, and is in principle illegal as unfair trade practices (Paragraph 2 (Other Refusal to Trade) or 12 of the General Designation).

An enterprise's discontinuance of shipments to a distributor that is its current direct customer, on account of the distributor's price-cutting

(Note 8), also usually tends to impede price competition, and such conduct is in principle illegal as unfair trade practices (Paragraph 2 of the General Designation). (Note 8) Whether or not such restriction is "on account of the distributor's price-cutting" is to be objectively judged based on actual conditions of the transactions (including the enterprise's response to other distributors, and related circumstances).

5. Selective Distribution

An enterprise may set up certain criteria to limit distributors that handle its products to those who meet the criteria. In such a case, the enterprise may prohibit distributors from reselling its product to other distributors who do not meet the criteria. This is called "selective distribution" and may result in such pro-competitive effects as described in Sub-Section 3(3) of Chapter 1 above. It is generally not problematic in itself even if, as a result of any enterprise's adoption of the selective distribution, certain price-cutters (and/or other distributors) that do not satisfy the enterprise's criteria are prevented from handling the enterprise's product, to the extent that such criteria are deemed to have plausibly rational reasons from the viewpoint of the consumers' interests such as preservation of quality of the product and/or assurance of appropriate use of the product and that such criteria are equally applied to other distributors who want to deal in the product.

Chapter 3. Provision of Rebates and Allowances [Omitted]

PART II Selection of trading partners

1. Through fair and free competition, each enterprise selects its trading partners on its own independent judgment based on their superiority in prices, quality, services and other transaction terms. Furthermore, there may be a case where an enterprise, in selecting its trading partners, takes account of overall business capability of suppliers in terms of, such as steady supply, technological development capability and flexibility in response to the enterprise's requests, in addition to prices, quality, services and other terms of individual transactions. If an enterprise selects its trading partner from the viewpoint mentioned above and such selection results in continuous a transaction relationship between the enterprise and the trading partner, there are no problems under the Antimonopoly Act.

   If, however, for example, any enterprise consults with another enterprise on mutual respect of and priority to the existing business relations to maintain such relations, or engages in such conduct as concertedly with another enterprise excluding competitors, competition to win customers in a market is to be restrained and entries of new competitors hindered, which result in restraining competition in the market.

(omitted)

Chapter 1. Customer Allocation [Omitted]

Chapter 2. Boycotts [Omitted]

Chapter 3. Primary Refusals to Deal by a Single Enterprise

1. Viewpoint

   Basically speaking, it is a matter of freedom of choice of trading partners for an enterprise to decide which enterprise it does business with. Even if an enterprise, considering such factors as price, quality and service, decides not to deal with a certain enterprise at its own judgment, there would be fundamentally no problem under the Antimonopoly Act.

   However, exceptionally, even a refusal to deal by a single enterprise is illegal in cases where the enterprise refuses to deal as a means to secure the effectiveness of its illegal conduct under the Antimonopoly Act. A refusal to deal by a single enterprise may also present a problem in cases where the enterprise refuses to deal as a means to achieve to achieve such unjust purposes under the Antimonopoly Act as excluding its competitors from a market (Note 4).

(Note 4) As to in what cases these practices substantially restrict competition in markets and are illegal as private monopolization, the Japan Fair Trade Commission has given guidance on this issue in Exclusionary Private Monopolization Guidelines.

2. Cases Where There are Problems under the Antimonopoly Act

In cases where an enterprise engages in, for example, the conduct mentioned in Sub-Section (i) below as a means to secure the effectiveness of its illegal practice under the Antimonopoly Act, such conduct is illegal as unfair trade practices (Paragraph 2 (Other Refusal to Trade) of the General Designation).

Moreover, in cases where an influential enterprise in a market (Note 5) engages in, for example, the conduct mentioned in Sub-Section (ii) or (iii) below as a means to achieve unjust purposes under the Antimonopoly Act (such as exclusion of its competitor from a market), and if such conduct tends to make it difficult for the refused competitor to carry on normal business activities, such conduct is illegal as unfair trade practices (Paragraph 2 of the General Designation):

(i) an influential manufacturer in a market, by causing distributors not to deal with its competitor, reduces the competitor's business opportunities and prevents the competitor from easily finding alternative trading partners, and, with a view to ensure the effectiveness of such conduct, refuses to deal with distributors not complying with this request (this conduct also falls under Paragraph 11 (Trading on Exclusive Terms) of the General Designation);

(ii) an influential material manufacturer in a market, in an attempt to prevent a finished product manufacturer from manufacturing by itself some of materials supplied by the material manufacturer to it, stops its supply to the finished product manufacturer of main materials which have been being supplied by the material manufacturer to the finished product manufacturers; or

(iii) an influential material manufacturer in a market, in an attempt to exclude competitors of its customer (more specifically, an enterprise which has a close relation with the material manufacturer and which manufactures a finished product by making use of materials supplied by the manufacturer) from a market for the said finished product, stops its supply to those competitors of materials which have been being supplied by the material manufacturer to them.

(Note 5) The guidance given in Sub-Section 3 (4) of Part I above applies to a definition of "an influential enterprise in a market."

* * *

South Korea

South Korea's law on vertical restraints is similar to Japan's, notably as it emphasizes the concept of "fair trade" and includes provisions on the abuse of superior bargaining position. Explaining the fairness content of the Korean competition law (known as the MRFTA for "Monopoly, Regulation and Fair Trade Act," last updated in 2020), Eun Hye Kim and Mel Marquis write:

> the proper conception of competition law's goal is value-laden and socially construed. In the case of Korea, competition law aims at efficiency but also supports equity and freedom for all. (. . .) Based on art. 1 [of the Monopoly, Regulation and Fair Trade Act], two types of goals emerge: (i) those focusing on traditional efficiency concerns; and (ii) those focusing on greater fairness and freedom. (. . .) Among these objectives, the goal of fairness in a competition statute is particularly striking. The MRFTA is sometimes referred to as Korea's 'economic constitution'. Its symbolic foundation is art. 119(2) of the Constitution, the 'economic democratization' clause. The aim of art. 119(2), (. . .), is to ensure that economic benefits are spread among not only powerful businesses but also weaker parties such as consumers and employees." *Eun Hye Kim, Mel Marquis,* A new competition law for Korea: political, economic and legal context, E.C.L.R., 649 (2021).

Unfair Trade Practices (UTP) are generally governed by Chapter VI of the MRFTA (available at https://www.ftc.go.kr, under Laws & Guidelines). Interestingly, though, following the 2020 revision, RPM practices in South Korea became subject to a rule of reason analysis. Indeed, Article 46(1) MRFTA now carves out an exception to the prohibition of RPM: "Where there is good cause for practices of resale price maintenance, such as when the effect of increasing consumer welfare due to the increase in efficiency is greater than the negative effect of restricting competition". For an overview of South Korea's competition law as revised in 2020, see also *Hwang Lee,* South Korea: Pouring old wine into new wineskins—

Competition law as fully revised in 2020, Concurrences N°3–2025, Art. N°123979, www.concurrences.com.

Notes and Questions

1. Note the center of gravity of harms to be prevented by the Guidelines: reducing business opportunities of competitors and making it difficult for them to find alternative trading partners, and harm to consumers. Comment on these objectives. To what extent is the business opportunity goal consistent or inconsistent with consumer goals?

2. Part 1, on vertical non-price restraints, contains a safe harbor for manufacturers with a market share less than 20%. This figure was increased in 2016 from the prior figure of 10%, suggesting some liberalization in the treatment of non-price restraints by smaller manufacturers.

3. Consistent with US law, the JFTC Guidelines recognize that prevention of free-riding may be a procompetitive reason for certain vertical restraints. Some US critics of the Supreme Court's Chicago School era jurisprudence have argued that the free-rider justification for vertical restraints has been unrealistically and uncritically expanded to justify anticompetitive restraints that could not plausibly serve to prevent free-riding. *See generally* HOW THE CHICAGO SCHOOL OVERSHOT THE MARK: THE EFFECT OF CONSERVATIVE ECONOMIC ANALYSIS ON U.S. ANTITRUST (Robert Pitofsky, ed. 2008) (especially essays in Part 5). If the US has gone too far in accepting a free rider explanation, do the JFTC Guidelines provide a more realistic and balanced approach to assessing free-rider justifications?

4. Compare the Japanese distribution guidelines with the law and guidelines of the EU and the law of the US in form, goals, and substance. What are the main divergences? Comment on the wisdom of each approach, given its context.

D. DEVELOPING COUNTRIES: SPECIAL CONCERNS

Developing countries have special concerns, given extreme poverty, high concentration, often high barriers to entry, often a culture of statism and special privilege, and characteristics of their economies including the importance of farming and commodities for a source of livelihood and large, informal economies.

These factors may produce rules for vertical restraints that differ from the rules in the developed world in two regards. First, vertical restraints in the form of backward integration or tie-ups may create buying power that squeezes farmers and transfers a larger and larger part of the value chain to multinational firms. The story is told graphically about cocoa bean growing in Ivory Coast, Africa, and the value added chain from cocoa bean to dark chocolate bars, by Bruno Dorin, *From Ivorian Cocoa Bean to French Dark Chocolate Tablet*, in THE EFFECTS OF ANTI-COMPETITIVE BUSINESS PRACTICES ON DEVELOPING COUNTRIES AND THEIR DEVELOPMENT PROSPECTS (H. Qaqaya and G. Lipimile, eds., UNCTAD 2008), 237 (excerpts below).

Second, one or a few large firms often dominate the most important markets. The dominant firms establish strong distribution systems, from production to the ultimate consumer. Beer is an example. The dominant beer company "gives" refrigerators to the small retailer establishments, all of which need to carry the dominant firm's beer, need a refrigerator, and have no room for a second one. If the dominant firm's agents find other brands in the refrigerator, they may toss them out. Entry is difficult. You have read the European *Schöller Lebensmittel* case and the reference to the *Van den Bergh (Unilever)* case, in which the European Court ordered that rivals' brands must have access to the ice cream freezers. The European cases have been criticized for insufficient analysis of harm to competition, and US law is even more reluctant than EU law to impose a duty to give access. In poor developing countries, the foreclosure effects are likely to be magnified. Should these factors affect the choice of legal rule?

Consider the developing practice of the Competition Commission of the Common Market for Eastern and Southern Africa (COMESA), which groups 21 African countries. The Comesa Competition Commission issued Guidelines on Restrictive Business Practices in 2019, and its early practice included cases pertaining to the distribution agreements of large producers of beer, such as AB Inbev, Castel, Diageo and Heineken (territorial restrictions), and of other beverages, such as Coca-Cola (RPM and other restraints). The Comesa Guidelines deal with a variety of vertical restraints, including resale price maintenance, single branding, exclusive distribution and supply arrangements, selective distribution, franchise agreements.

To illustrate the above discussion, review the following excerpt from the article by Bruno Dorin, preceded by an excerpt from the editors' introductory essay. Dorin's analysis includes and goes beyond vertical restraints. It has implications for abuse of dominance and mergers.

QAQAYA AND LIPIMILE, IN THE EFFECTS OF ANTI-COMPETITIVE BUSINESS PRACTICES ON DEVELOPING COUNTRIES AND THEIR DEVELOPMENT PROSPECTS (UNCTAD 2008)

(Executive Summary, v, xiii–xiv)

. . . [D]evelopments in commodity sectors have implications for poverty reduction.

There are certain competition problems in commodity markets, which are usually characterized by a high degree of concentration as well as vertical integration between various stages of the value chain. [The Dorin article] provides the developments and problems encountered in the cocoa market in the Ivory Coast, which supplies 40 per cent of the world demand for cocoa. The analysis of the value chain from Ivorian farm gate to a bar of dark chocolate on the shelves of French supermarkets reveals that chocolate makers and/or distributors have been gaining more and more from a bar of dark chocolate between 1992 and 2001. . . .

The trend following the liberalization of cocoa markets has been the elimination of small local traders through tough competition with large multinational firms. Over time, the remaining local exporting and processing companies became subsidiaries of large multinational firms. On the other hand, cocoa markets have been experiencing increased horizontal concentration through mergers of large multinational companies, such as those between large chocolate companies and cocoa processing firms, or through takeovers by large international companies of smaller companies operating at the national market. As a result of these developments, small local cocoa producers have to contend with a strong purchasing power held by several large multinational companies.

The existence of an oligopolistic market structure with high concentration and market power points to competition law enforcement as a potential instrument to curb anti-competitive practices. Nonetheless, it is difficult to gather evidence on anti-competitive behaviour, such as collusive agreements and other concerted practices, in oligopolistic markets. Another policy option is merger control, which ensures that mergers and acquisitions likely to increase market concentration and reduce potential competition are either prevented or approved with conditions. As for abuse of market power in commodity markets local farmers do not have enough bargaining power and are in a disadvantaged position to negotiate fair prices for their products *vis-à-vis* large international cocoa traders. The approach to competition law implementation in commodity markets should be on how to protect producers from the purchasing power of international traders and processors rather than how to protect consumers from market power. . . .

Bruno Dorin, on the Ivorian cocoa bean market[1]

More and more agricultural producers are currently being held by a few major firms in a pincer movement (Marette et Raynaud, 2003), with the major world seed and agrochemical suppliers upstream (AstraZeneca/Norvatis, Bayer-Aventis, Monsanto, etc.) and, downstream, the emergence of major distributors operating over vast consumer zones, such as the French Carrefour or American Wal-Mart (the world's leading company in terms of turnover for 2001 according to *Fortune* magazine). In both cases, competition policies—at least in Europe and the USA—are not failing to monitor the phenomenon, which is amplified in the distribution field by purchasing platforms set up by the major distributors to ensure collective supplies. However, this last point has not received all the attention it deserves, insofar as—more generally and in slightly overstating things—the aim of such checking of concentrations is to protect consumers from market powers, and not producers from purchasing powers. Yet, as already clearly pointed out in the report by the Conseil d'Analyse Economique (Rey et Tirole, 2000), producers also need to be protected, notably in cases where they are led to make specific investments[16] which they would ultimately be unable to amortize if distributors subsequently imposed inadequate prices on them[17]. . . .

Why such pronounced concern for consumers? Probably because competition policies are based on an economic theory presenting the same bias. As indeed suggested by Alain and Chambolle (2003), traditional microeconomic analysis tends to neglect upstream oligopsony powers since it automatically models producer-distributor relations by a principal-agent relation in which the dominant role is

---

[1] From Bruno Dorin, From Ivorian Cocoa Bean To French Dark Chocolate Tablet: Price Transmission, Value Sharing and North/South Competition Policy, in Qaqaya and Lipimile, eds., supra, pp. 265, 309–311.

[16] Like setting up a cocoa plantation.

[17] To solve this problem, the solution would then consist, according to the authors, in rebalancing contracts, and stepping up sanctions in cases of violation of the commitments. This is perfectly realistic for the particular case of French fruit and vegetable producers, but barely so for the more universal case we are examining: agricultural producers far from major distributors, not only vertically (numerous processes and numerous middlemen before the end product) but also horizontally (production in developing countries of foodstuffs consumed in industrialized countries), i.e. a case in which the possibilities of contractualization, and applying sanctions are severely limited, or even ruled out.

assigned to the producer (i.e. power to impose his conditions on distributors). Likewise, since Spengler revealed the inefficiency of double marginalization in 1950, that same literature has focused on the effect of vertical contracts on efficiency and total profit of vertical structures, but virtually ignores its impact on profit sharing within those structures. Yet an imbalance in profit sharing can be harmful to long-term social well-being, by threatening the survival of certain producers and reducing the variety or quality of products available to consumers. . . . Some . . . recent work seems to corroborate theoretically what we observe empirically in the cocoa-chocolate commodity chain. But as Allain and Chambolle (2003) concluded, whilst several questions omitted from the vertical analysis are at last starting to be explored today, the work still required remains considerable.

Once this work has made some headway, competition policies may then perhaps speak more of producers than consumers, of monopsonies and oligopsonies than monopolies and oligopolies, of a "hypothetical monopsonist test" rather than a "hypothetical monopolist test".

Notes and Questions

1. From Dorin's formulation, what implications do you draw regarding competition rules that advance efficient development? Does Dorin want to protect competitors? Or does he suggest that analysis focused on efficient *development* may differ from an analytical framework designed to serve consumers in developed economies?

2. In the developed world, it is easy to take for granted the availability of certain basic services, such as financial transactions, that are that vital to the welfare of low-income people in developing countries. Competition law can play an important role in increasing access to such services. In 2014, the Competition Authority of Kenya launched an investigation into potentially anticompetitive vertical restrictions imposed by Safaricom, a leading mobile network operator in Kenya. In 2007, Safaricom launched the M-Pesa mobile money system that allows users to pay for goods and services, access loans, and exchange money on a cash-free basis. The service has become a huge success, with over 30 million users in ten African countries, and plans to expand throughout the African continent. However, the Kenyan Competition Authority became concerned about exclusivity clauses in Safaricom's contracts with financial agents that restricted those agents' ability to work for rival mobile money providers. The Authority and Safaricom reached an official settlement in 2014, with Safaricom agreeing to expunge the exclusivity clauses from its agency contracts. If you were the head of competition agency in the developing world, how would you prioritize

your scarce agency resources? What industry sectors or practices deserve the most attention?

Chapter 5

MONOPOLIES AND ABUSE OF DOMINANCE

A. INTRODUCTION

Abuse of monopoly or dominant firm power is a major feature of competition laws. While cartels harm competition through competitor cooperation, dominant firms may harm competition through unilateral exclusionary or exploitative behavior. Despite agreement in principle that competition law should rein in misbehavior by dominant firms, the views on what is misbehavior are widely divergent. For convenience, we can group the issues into two categories.

First, jurisdictions may disagree on the goals of monopolization or abuse of dominance law. Articulation of goals varies, but three main perspectives are: 1) the law should protect allocative efficiency usually defined as or encapsulated in consumer welfare, 2) the law should protect the functioning of the market processes, including access, opportunity, and contestability, and including regard for farmers, suppliers, and workers, but all within the framework of making markets work better, and 3) the law should protect fairness in the marketplace in addition to consumer welfare and market processes, including preventing abuses of a superior bargaining position.

US courts tend to take a narrow perspective—mostly limiting monopolization law to harms that threaten consumer welfare while acknowledging that there may be harms to upstream players by use of monopsony power. The narrow view protects freedom of even dominant business firms on the theory that freedom to act produces the most efficient, innovative, and competitive results. In the United States, antitrust is not about business fairness, or ethics, or achieving a level playing field. The US Supreme Court has stated that "even an act of pure malice by one business competitor against another does not, without more, state a claim under the federal antitrust laws." Brooke Group v. Brown & Williamson, 509 U.S. 209, 225 (1993). US courts and antitrust agencies often repeat the mantra that antitrust law protects competition, not competitors.

EU law is closer to the second perspective, while keeping consumers in its sight. The Court of Justice defines the purpose of the abuse of dominance provision as: "to prevent competition from being restricted to the detriment of the public interest, individual undertakings and consumers, by sanctioning the conduct of undertakings in a dominant position that has the effect of hindering competition on the merits and is thus likely to cause direct harm to consumers, or which causes them harm indirectly by hindering or distorting that competition . . . ." European Superleague, Case C-333/21, ECLI:EU:C:2023:1011 (Grand Chamber), para. 124.

Other jurisdictions go further by including as a goal fairness to people and firms excluded and exploited by uses of disparate bargaining power, especially, but not only, historically ingrained severe and persistent disparities as in South Africa.

Abuses by Big Tech firms have called attention to the limits of some competition laws, and several jurisdictions have adopted special statutes to address unfair practices (many of which are also inefficient, and many of which are not immediately connected to consumer harm) to fill the gap. The EU Digital Markets Act is the prime example.

A second difference of perspective concerns prior beliefs about how well markets work and how effective is government intervention compared with the market to produce efficient results. The US Supreme Court has expressed skepticism that anticompetitive exclusionary conduct happens very often or that it will succeed in increasing monopoly power. It has opined that when exclusionary conduct does occur, markets tend to correct the monopolistic distortions quickly. It has viewed monopolization litigation itself as a potential source of anticompetitive restraint, chilling procompetitive conduct.

Enforcers and courts elsewhere reveal different perspectives. And indeed often their markets are different and work less well. They may observe that abusive conduct by dominant firms is frequent and that markets are not quick to correct their imperfections. They may have confidence that antitrust agencies and reviewing courts can effectively improve the market. Their courts are also less concerned about frivolous lawsuits as private action accounts for proportionately far less of the overall competition law cases in these jurisdictions than in the U.S. Their courts need not worry as much about competitors using competition law to hide their relative inefficiency.

In this chapter, we survey some of the leading issues in monopolization and abuse of dominance law. For market definition and proof of dominance or monopoly power, which are preliminary elements of the case, we refer you to the curriculum videos of the International Competition Network (ICN); one for market definition: https://www.internationalcompetitionnetwork.org/training/market-definition/ and one for market power (which includes the notion of dominance and monopoly power: https://www.internationalcompetitionnetwork.org/training/market-power/.

The statutes and case law of various jurisdictions reflect wide differences in what it takes to prove the threshold question of dominance. Jurisdictions vary in how much weight they give to market share, and indeed how large a market share must be to suggest dominance. The South African statute states that if a firm has 45% or more of a market it is dominant, and at market shares between 35% and 45%, the firm is dominant unless it can show that it does not have market power. The German statute provides that a firm is presumed dominant, subject to rebuttal, if it has a market share of 40% or more. In the United States, the plaintiff must prove monopoly power. Large market share is usually the starting point. Courts generally will infer market power, subject to rebuttal, if the firm has a share of about 70% or more and barriers to entry and expansion are significant.

In our treatment of exclusionary practices we include refusals to deal and discriminatory dealing, predatory pricing, margin squeezes, loyalty rebates, and exclusive dealing, among others. For exploitative practices we cover excessive pricing and the high price prong of price discrimination, and certain exploitation of intellectual property.

Abuses in the digital economy have amplified the differences. We deal specially with digital cases at B.7. below.

B. EXCLUSIONARY OFFENSES

This section is about exclusionary practices by dominant firms or firms with monopoly power. In the United States the offense is monopolization under Section 2 of the Sherman Act. In the European Union and the many countries that adopt its language, the offense is abuse of dominance, which in the EU is illegal under Article 102 of the Treaty on the Functioning of the European Union (TFEU). Read Section 2 of the Sherman Act and Article 102 TFEU in Appendix 1 now.

Exclusionary offenses are practices that exclude competitors by anticompetitive means. What qualifies as "anticompetitive" is the key inquiry. The statutory law and the case law of various jurisdictions differ, both in terms of goals and in terms of how to assess the evidence of market harm. Some jurisdictions, such as the

United States, focus on consumer welfare and efficiency and take a narrow view of the offense, preferring to give a wide range of freedom to (even) dominant firms to decide on their business strategies, expecting that this freedom will produce the most competitive and innovative results. Some other jurisdictions, worried that firms without power might get squeezed out or marginalized by strategies of dominant firms, focus on harm to the "competitive process" and take a more copious view of the offense. To some extent, the differences are based on different market facts. Where markets work less well, capital markets are poor, barriers are high, and especially where the market leaders are or were state-owned and have been privileged by the state, there is a stronger case for more antitrust intervention to help make the market work. To some extent the differences are goal-based and ideological. Some jurisdictions' laws mean to advance small enterprises and ease the way of outsiders into the market; and in some jurisdictions there is more trust in the antitrust intervention than in dominant firms' behavior.

Despite the differences, there is a common core. When a firm uses its power to keep out competitors or push them back by means that have no benefits for consumers, when the acts are against consumer interests, and when they increase or maintain the dominant firms' power, these acts constitute monopolization and abuse of dominance. In Europe a number of port cases paradigmatically fit this description. A state owned or licensed firm runs a port and operates a ferry service. The firm refuses to allow access to a would-be ferry competitor. The refusal is illegal. Port of Rødby, 94/119/EC, Commission Decision 1993, OJ L 0052. A US example may be found in the litigation against AT&T beginning in the 1970s when AT&T was the monopoly supplier of all telecom services, including long distance and local, and all related hardware, including telephones and wires, in the United States. For many years AT&T performed great service for the people and was lovingly called Ma Bell. But when MCI appeared on the horizon with microwave technology for long distance service, AT&T erected all possible roadblocks to keep MCI from connecting to the local service structure. See United States v. American Telephone & Telegraph Co., 524 F. Supp. 1336 (D.D.C. 1981). The case was settled by consent decree breaking up AT&T.

Exclusionary practices come in many forms, and we cover a sampling of them. We start with refusals to deal and proceed to predatory pricing, margin squeezes, rebates including loyalty rebates, and cutting edge issues of abuse of intellectual property and Internet technology. To telescope the cutting edge issues, we mention in advance that competition authorities around the world are challenging acts of Google (search engine dominance and owner of Android smartphone technology) and Qualcomm (owner of essential IP in smartphones). We return to these pending issues after setting the stage for abuse of dominance/monopoly law generally.

1. Refusals to Deal

In the US antitrust law of monopolization, three areas have been separated out for protected treatment: low pricing, even low pricing targeted to stave off a competitive threat, and innovation. In these three areas, there is a very strong presumption that can amount almost to a per se legal rule. For refusals to deal, the leading case is Verizon v. Trinko, 540 U.S. 398 (2004). In *Trinko*, the incumbent telecom degraded the service of new competitors from the local loop (controlled by the incumbent). The Court characterized the conduct as a refusal to give sufficient assistance to rivals, and as a refusal to deal. It declared that refusals to deal are lawful unless they fit within one of two exceptions: 1) a profit-sacrifice strategy to enhance market power as in *Aspen Skiing,* 472 U.S. 585 (1985), and possibly 2) a violation of essential facility duties if such duties exist (and, the Court said, they rarely do). The Court stressed the importance of firms' freedom to deal or not as necessary to provide incentives to invest and invent. The Court labeled duties to deal as "forced sharing," which undercuts incentives to invent, leads to the "supreme [antitrust] evil"—cartels, and imposes on courts supervision duties that they are ill prepared to bear. In contrast, the European courts have expressed concerns in the *Microsoft* case, which is excerpted below, for the impact of a dominant firm's refusal to deal on its competitors' incentive to invest, which tends to be overlooked by the U.S. courts.

European Union law has a different history and evolution. While it too presumes that firms, even dominant firms, can deal with whom they choose, the presumption is weaker and can be countered by the special responsibility of the dominant firm not to distort competition.

The line of EU jurisprudence includes *Commercial Solvents, Magill*, and *Bronner*. The cases are well summarized in *Bronner,* which denied a small local newspaper the right to avail itself of the distribution system of its large, dominant rival. Here is an excerpt from *Bronner*:

OSCAR BRONNER GMBH & CO. KG AND MEDIAPRINT ZEITUNGS-UND ZEITSCHRIFTENVERLAG GMBH & CO. KG

ECLI:EU:C:1998:56

* * *

Although in *Commercial Solvents v Commission* and *CBEM*, . . . the Court of Justice held the refusal by an undertaking holding a dominant position in a given market to supply an undertaking with which it was in competition in a neighbouring market with raw materials (*Commercial Solvents v Commission*, paragraph 25) and services (*CBEM*, paragraph 26) respectively, which were indispensable to carrying on the rival's business, to constitute an abuse, it should be noted, first, that the Court did so to the extent that the conduct in question was likely to eliminate all competition on the part of that undertaking.

39 Secondly, in *Magill*, at paragraphs 49 and 50, the Court held that refusal by the owner of an intellectual property right to grant a licence, even if it is the act of an undertaking holding a dominant position, cannot in itself constitute abuse of a dominant position, but that the exercise of an exclusive right by the proprietor may, in exceptional circumstances, involve an abuse.

40 In *Magill*, the Court found such exceptional circumstances in the fact that the refusal in question concerned a product (information on the weekly schedules of certain television channels) the supply of which was indispensable for carrying on the business in question (the publishing of a general television guide), in that, without that information, the person wishing to produce such a guide would find it impossible to publish it and offer it for sale (paragraph 53), the fact that such refusal prevented the appearance of a new product for which there was a potential consumer demand (paragraph 54), the fact that it was not justified by objective considerations (paragraph 55), and that it was likely to exclude all competition in the secondary market of television guides (paragraph 56).

41 Therefore, even if that case-law on the exercise of an intellectual property right were applicable to the exercise of any property right whatever, it would still be necessary, for the *Magill* judgment to be effectively relied upon in order to plead the existence of an abuse within the meaning of Article 86 of the Treaty [now Article 102 TFEU] in a situation such as that which forms the subject-matter of the first question, not only that the refusal of the service comprised in home delivery be likely to eliminate all competition in the daily newspaper market on the part of the person requesting the service

and that such refusal be incapable of being objectively justified, but also that the service in itself be indispensable to carrying on that person's business, inasmuch as there is no actual or potential substitute in existence for that home-delivery scheme.

42 That is certainly not the case even if, as in the case which is the subject of the main proceedings, there is only one nationwide home-delivery scheme in the territory of a Member State and, moreover, the owner of that scheme holds a dominant position in the market for services constituted by that scheme or of which it forms part.

43 In the first place, it is undisputed that other methods of distributing daily newspapers, such as by post and through sale in shops and at kiosks, even though they may be less advantageous for the distribution of certain newspapers, exist and are used by the publishers of those daily newspapers.

44 Moreover, it does not appear that there are any technical, legal or even economic obstacles capable of making it impossible, or even unreasonably difficult, for any other publisher of daily newspapers to establish, alone or in cooperation with other publishers, its own nationwide home-delivery scheme and use it to distribute its own daily newspapers.

45 It should be emphasised in that respect that, in order to demonstrate that the creation of such a system is not a realistic potential alternative and that access to the existing system is therefore indispensable, it is not enough to argue that it is not economically viable by reason of the small circulation of the daily newspaper or newspapers to be distributed.

46 For such access to be capable of being regarded as indispensable, it would be necessary at the very least to establish . . . that it is not economically viable to create a second home-delivery scheme for the distribution of daily newspapers with a circulation comparable to that of the daily newspapers distributed by the existing scheme.

47 In the light of the foregoing considerations, the answer to the first question must be that the refusal by a press undertaking which holds a very large share of the daily newspaper market in a Member State and operates the only nationwide newspaper home-delivery scheme in that Member State to allow the publisher of a rival newspaper, which by reason of its small circulation is unable either alone or in cooperation with other publishers to set up and operate its own home-delivery scheme in economically reasonable conditions, to have access to that scheme for appropriate remuneration does not constitute abuse of a dominant position within the meaning of Article 86 of the Treaty.

* * *

In a subsequent decision discussed below (*Alphabet*) the court qualified the requirement of indispensability in cases where the undertaking developed the infrastructure not solely for its own business needs but to enable third-party usage.

After *Bronner*, the Court of Justice found the duty-to-deal requirements satisfied in *IMS Health*, Case C–418/01, EU:C:2004:257, where a pharmaceutical research company was allowed to use the grid structure [geographic neighborhoods] drawn by its dominant competitor as the metric for selling marketing data to pharmaceutical companies, where all of the users were attached to the structure and did not want a deviating format.

Not long thereafter, both the EU and the US brought cases against Microsoft for illegal exclusionary practices that built moats around Microsoft's dominant personal computer operating system. Both antitrust authorities won their cases, but not on the same grounds. For United States v. Microsoft, see 253 F. 3d 34 (D.C. Cir. 2001) (condemning exclusionary practices that closed off all efficient routes for operating system potential competitors to gain a foothold). The practices condemned were not refusals to deal. The European cases targeted refusals to deal and bundling.

MICROSOFT CORP. v. COMMISSION

(interoperability)

Case T–201/04, ECLI:EU:T:2007:289 (General Court of the European Union 2007)

[The European Commission brought proceedings against Microsoft, a "super-dominant" firm with more than 90% of the PC operating systems market, for abusing its dominant position in violation of Article 102. The Commission found two sets of Microsoft's practices to be illegal: 1) Bundling its media player with its operating system (Windows), which had become the standard in the market. RealNetworks had pioneered the media player and RealNetworks' player was popularly used with Windows. Thereafter Microsoft made its own media player and bundled it with Windows, foreclosing media player rivals from the most efficient channels to the market. 2) Refusal to deal, in the form of refusing to provide workgroup server software rivals with full interoperability information to connect with Windows and with Microsoft's workgroup server software. Workgroup servers are servers used by small enterprises to interconnect file, printing, document-sharing and management functions of all PCs within the enterprise. Novell and others had pioneered workgroup server software. Before Microsoft developed such software of its own, it gave full interoperability information to the workgroup server software providers. Then Microsoft made its own workgroup server software and withheld from its rivals the full information they needed for seamless interoperability. Microsoft noted that it provided a good deal of interoperability information and claiming that it had no legal duty to help its rivals.

The Commission found violations in both cases. It ordered Microsoft to supply the full interoperability protocols, to offer an unbundled version of Windows without the media player, and to pay a fine of € 497 million for the two violations.

On appeal, on the interoperability (duty to deal) issue, Microsoft contended that disclosure of the interface protocols would entail disclosure of intellectual property. The Commission disputed this claim and also argued that the circumstances satisfied the criteria of *Magill/IMS*: (1) access [here, to the complete interoperability information] must be indispensable, (2) the refusal must exclude any effective competition on a neighboring market, and (3) the refusal must prevent the appearance of a new product for which there is a potential consumer demand. (4) If the criteria are satisfied, it then falls to the dominant firm to prove an objective justification.]

(1) Indispensability

369 . . . [T]he Commission adopted a two-stage approach in determining whether the information at issue was indispensable, in that, first of all, it considered what degree of interoperability with the Windows domain architecture non-Microsoft work group server operating systems must achieve in order for its competitors to be able to remain viably on the market and, second, it appraised whether the interoperability that Microsoft refused to disclose was indispensable to the attainment of that degree of interoperability. * * *

[The Commission established, and the Court accepted, that users value interoperability; that a lesser degree of interoperability "will have an impact on the efficiency with which that work group server delivers its services to the users of the networks" (para. 413). As a first example, "if a work group server does not interoperate sufficiently with the 'security architecture' of the Windows work group network, the user might be required to log on twice." para. 415.] * * * [Other examples omitted.]

421 It follows from all of the foregoing considerations that Microsoft has not established that the Commission made a manifest error when it considered that non-Microsoft work group server operating systems must be capable of interoperating with the Windows domain architecture on an equal footing with Windows work group server operating systems if they were to be marketed viably on the market.

422 The Court also concludes . . . that the absence of such interoperability with the Windows domain architecture has the effect of reinforcing Microsoft's competitive position on the work group server operating systems market, particularly because it induces consumers to use its work group server operating system in preference to its competitors', although its competitors' operating systems offer features to which consumers attach great importance. * * *

560 In the contested decision, the Commission considered whether the refusal at issue gave rise to a 'risk' of the elimination of competition on the work group server operating systems market. Microsoft contends that [the refusal must have a high probability of eliminating all competition on the market.] . . .

561 The Court finds that Microsoft's complaint is purely one of terminology and is wholly irrelevant. The expressions 'risk of elimination of competition' and 'likely to eliminate competition' are used without distinction by the Community judicature to reflect the same idea, namely that Article [102] does not apply only from the time when there is no more, or practically no more, competition on the market. If the Commission were required to wait until competitors were eliminated from the market, or until their elimination was sufficiently imminent, before being able to take action under Article [102], that would clearly run counter to the objective of that provision, which is to maintain undistorted competition in the common market and, in particular, to safeguard the competition that still exists on the relevant market.

562 In this case, the Commission had all the more reason to apply Article [102] before the elimination of competition on the work group server operating systems market had become a reality because that market is characterized by significant network effects and because the elimination of competition would therefore be difficult to reverse.

563 Nor is it necessary to demonstrate that all competition on the market would be eliminated. What matters, for the purpose of establishing an infringement of Article [102], is that the refusal at issue is liable to, or is likely to, eliminate all effective competition on the market. It must be made clear that the fact that the competitors of the dominant undertaking retain a marginal presence in certain niches on the market cannot suffice to substantiate the existence of such competition.

[The Court then summarized the evidence showing the sharp rise of Microsoft's share of workgroup server software, to more than 60%, and the decline of the competitors' shares, as soon as Microsoft stopped providing full interoperability information. It also gave examples of how Microsoft killed off two of competitors' products, NDS for NT developed by Novell, and PC NetLink developed by Sun Microsystems, by withholding interoperability information. See facts at para. 654 below]. * * *

(3) The new product * * *

646 In *IMS Health*, the Court of Justice, when assessing the circumstance relating to the appearance of a new product, also placed that circumstance in the context of the damage to the interests of consumers.... [T]he Court emphasized ... that that circumstance related to the consideration that, in the balancing of the interest in protection of the intellectual property right and the economic freedom of its owner against the interest in protection of free competition, the latter can prevail only where refusal to grant a license prevents the development of the secondary market, to the detriment of consumers.

647 The circumstance relating to the appearance of a new product, as envisaged in *Magill* and *IMS Health*, cannot be the only parameter which determines whether a refusal to license an intellectual property right is capable of causing prejudice to consumers within the meaning of Article [102](b). As that provision states, such prejudice may arise where there is a limitation not only of production or markets, but also of technical development.

648 It was on that last hypothesis that the Commission based its finding in the contested decision....

649 The Court finds that the Commission's findings at the recitals referred to in the preceding paragraph are not manifestly incorrect.

650 Thus, in the first place, the Commission was correct to observe that '[owing] to the lack of interoperability that competing work group server operating system products can achieve with the Windows domain architecture, an increasing number of consumers are locked into a homogeneous Windows solution at the level of work group server operating systems'.

651 It must be borne in mind that it has already been stated that Microsoft's refusal prevented its competitors from developing work group server operating systems capable of attaining a sufficient degree of interoperability with the Windows domain architecture, with the consequence that consumers' purchasing decisions in respect of work group server operating systems were channeled towards Microsoft's products. The Court has also already observed that it was apparent from a number of documents in the file that the technologies of the Windows 2000 range, in particular Active Directory, were increasingly being taken up by organizations. As

interoperability problems arise more acutely with work group server operating systems in that range of products than with those of the preceding generation, the increasing uptake of those systems merely reinforces the 'lock-in' effect referred to in the preceding paragraph.

652 The limitation thus placed on consumer choice is all the more damaging to consumers because, as already observed, they consider that non-Microsoft work group server operating systems are better than Windows work group server operating systems with respect to a series of features to which they attach great importance, such as 'reliability/availability of the . . . system' and 'security included with the server operating system'.

653 In the second place, the Commission was correct to consider that the artificial advantage in terms of interoperability that Microsoft retained by its refusal discouraged its competitors from developing and marketing work group server operating systems with innovative features, to the prejudice, notably, of consumers. That refusal has the consequence that those competitors are placed at a disadvantage by comparison with Microsoft so far as the merits of their products are concerned, particularly with regard to parameters such as security, reliability, ease of use or operating performance speed.

654 The Commission's finding that '[i]f Microsoft's competitors had access to the interoperability information that Microsoft refuses to supply, they could use the disclosures to make the advanced features of their own products available in the framework of the web of interoperability relationships that underpin the Windows domain architecture' is corroborated by the conduct which those competitors had adopted in the past, when they had access to certain information concerning Microsoft's products. The two examples which the Commission gives at recital 696 to the contested decision, 'PC NetLink' and 'NDS for NT', speak volumes in that regard. PC NetLink is software developed by Sun on the basis of AS/U, which had been developed by AT&T using source code which Microsoft had licensed to it in the 1990s. A document submitted by Microsoft during the administrative procedure shows that the innovative features and added value that PC NetLink brought to Windows work group networks was used as a selling point for that product. Likewise, in its marketing material, Novell highlighted the new features which NDS for NT—software which it had developed using reverse engineering—brought to the Windows domain architecture (in this instance Windows NT).

655 The Commission was careful to emphasize, in that context, that there was 'ample scope for differentiation and innovation beyond the design of interface specifications'. In other words, the same

specification can be implemented in numerous different and innovative ways by software designers.

656 Thus, the contested decision rests on the concept that, once the obstacle represented for Microsoft's competitors by the insufficient degree of interoperability with the Windows domain architecture has been removed, those competitors will be able to offer work group server operating systems which, far from merely reproducing the Windows systems already on the market, will be distinguished from those systems with respect to parameters which consumers consider important.

657 It must be borne in mind, in that regard, that Microsoft's competitors would not be able to clone or reproduce its products solely by having access to the interoperability information covered by the contested decision. . . . * * *

659 Last, Microsoft's argument that it will have less incentive to develop a given technology if it is required to make that technology available to its competitors is of no relevance to the examination of the circumstance relating to the new product, where the issue to be decided is the impact of the refusal to supply on the incentive for Microsoft's competitors to innovate and not on Microsoft's incentives to innovate. That is an issue which will be decided when the Court examines the circumstance relating to the absence of objective justification.

660 In the third place, the Commission is also correct to reject as unfounded Microsoft's assertion during the administrative procedure that it was not demonstrated that its refusal caused prejudice to consumers.

661 First of all, as has already been observed, the results of the third Mercer survey show that, contrary to Microsoft's contention, consumers consider non-Microsoft work group server operating systems to be better than Windows work group server operating systems on a number of features to which they attach great importance.

662 Next, Microsoft cannot rely on the fact that consumers never claimed at any time during the administrative procedure that they had been forced to adopt a Windows work group server operating system as a consequence of its refusal to disclose interoperability information to its competitors. . . . [T]he Commission states '[w]hen confronted with a "choice" between putting up with interoperability problems that render their business processes cumbersome, inefficient and costly, and embracing a homogeneous Windows solution for their work group network, customers will tend to opt for

the latter proposition' and that '[o]nce they have standardized on Windows, they are unlikely to report interoperability problems between their client PCs and the work group servers'. * * *

664 Last, it must be borne in mind that it is settled case-law that Article [102] covers not only practices which may prejudice consumers directly but also those which indirectly prejudice them by impairing an effective competitive structure. In this case, Microsoft impaired the effective competitive structure on the work group server operating systems market by acquiring a significant market share on that market. * * *

(4) The absence of objective justification

* * *

697 The Court finds that, as the Commission correctly submits, Microsoft, which bore the initial burden of proof, did not sufficiently establish that if it were required to disclose the interoperability information that would have a significant negative impact on its incentives to innovate.

698 Microsoft merely put forward vague, general and theoretical arguments on that point. . . . Microsoft merely stated that '[d]isclosure would . . . eliminate future incentives to invest in the creation of more intellectual property', without specifying the technologies or products to which it thus referred. * * *

701 It follows that it has not been demonstrated that the disclosure of the information to which that remedy relates will significantly reduce—still less eliminate—Microsoft's incentives to innovate.

702 In that context, the Court observes that it is normal practice for operators in the industry to disclose to third parties the information which will facilitate interoperability with their products and Microsoft itself had followed that practice until it was sufficiently established on the work group server operating systems market. Such disclosure allows the operators concerned to make their own products more attractive and therefore more valuable. In fact, none of the parties has claimed in the present case that such disclosure had had any negative impact on those operators' incentives to innovate. * * *

710 The Commission came to a negative conclusion [Microsoft failed to prove an objective justification] but not by balancing the negative impact which the imposition of a requirement to supply the information at issue might have on Microsoft's incentives to innovate against the positive impact of that obligation on innovation in the industry as a whole, but after refuting Microsoft's arguments

relating to the fear that its products might be cloned, establishing that the disclosure of interoperability was widespread in the industry concerned and showing that IBM's commitment to the Commission in 1984 was not substantially different from what Microsoft was ordered to do in the contested decision and that its approach was consistent with Directive 91/250 [on the legal protection of computer programs, which considers disclosure of interoperability information beneficial to innovation].

711 It follows from all of the foregoing considerations that Microsoft has not demonstrated the existence of any objective justification for its refusal to disclose the interoperability at issue. * * *

The European General Court affirmed the Commission order that Microsoft provide the competitors with the full interoperability information.

Virtually the same case arose in the US courts some years later—and the US courts gave a different answer. Novell invented WordPerfect, which became a popular word processing program. Microsoft gave Novell the code it needed to operate WordPerfect seamlessly on the Microsoft operating system, Windows. In the months leading up to the release of Windows 95, Microsoft shared its code with WordPerfect and others to help them be prepared for compatibility with the newest version of Windows. WordPerfect, however, had begun developing a new, innovative idea to use the code to harness what became known as "the cloud," and the cloud could commoditize operating systems. Microsoft learned about the research, pulled the code from Novell, and introduced Windows 95, with its own word processing program Microsoft Word en suite, before Novell could figure out the interconnectivity protocols. Users predictably shifted from WordPerfect to Word, despite superior qualities of WordPerfect. This was the beginning of the decline of WordPerfect. Novell sued Microsoft. At trial, 11 of the 12 jurors voted to find a violation, but one holdout hung the jury and the district court granted Microsoft's motion to dismiss. The Court of Appeals for the 10th Circuit affirmed, in an opinion written by Judge (now Supreme Court Justice) Neil Gorsuch that reads as a reprise to Justice Scalia's opinion in *Trinko*. Thus:

> If the law were to make a habit of forcing monopolists to help competitors by keeping prices high, sharing their property, or declining to expand their own operations,

> courts would paradoxically risk encouraging collusion between rivals and dampened price competition—themselves paradigmatic antitrust wrongs, injuries to consumers and the competitive process alike. Forcing firms to help one another would also risk reducing the incentive both sides have to innovate, invest, and expand—again results inconsistent with the goals of antitrust. The monopolist might be deterred from investing, innovating, or expanding (or even entering a market in the first place) with the knowledge anything it creates it could be forced to share; the smaller company might be deterred, too, knowing it could just demand the right to piggyback on its larger rival.

Novell v. Microsoft, 731 F.3d 1064 (10th Cir. 2013).

Notes and Questions

1. Comment on the European court's treatment of Microsoft's refusal to give its rivals full interoperability information, and the relation of this refusal to Microsoft's IP rights. How does this compare with the US jurisprudence against "forced sharing," as in *Trinko*? How important was, and should have been, the Commission's evidence that Microsoft's cut-off of information squelched rivals' innovations?

2. In *Novell v. Microsoft*, did the court think Novell should have made its own operating system? Would it have mattered to the outcome if the plaintiff were the US government? While not included in the excerpt above, the court expressed concern that if Novell were successful in establishing antitrust injury from a deception claim, this would "turn private parties into bounty hunters entitled to a windfall every time they can ferret out anti-competitive conduct lurking somewhere in the marketplace." Was this a legitimate fear?

3. What are the differences in premises and assumptions in the two cases—*Microsoft* Europe and *Novell*? Can the differences be resolved empirically; that is, can empirical analysis answer which set of rules, in view of the incentives they promote, is better for consumers and robust markets? Or is the choice more fundamentally philosophical?

4. A number of the current refusal to deal cases come up in Big Tech litigation, and the refusal to deal claims have been dismissed. See FTC v. Facebook, 560 F. Supp. 3d 1 (D.D.C. 2021). For example, Facebook cut off data from Vine when Vine developed an innovative video app. The court said:

"These decisions, to be clear, "are not premised on the view that [monopolist refusals to deal] are incapable of harming competition"; obviously, "refusals to aid new entrants can indeed" have that effect. See Daniel A. Crane, Does Monopoly Broth Make Bad Soup?, 76 Antitrust

L.J. 663, 669 (2010). Rather, the rule declaring unilateral refusals to deal essentially "per se lawful," id. at 666, or "presumptive[ly] legal[ ]," Novell, 731 F.3d at 1073, rests on three overriding considerations of antitrust policy. First, and most importantly, "[f]irms may acquire monopoly power by establishing an infrastructure that renders them uniquely suited to serve their customers. Compelling such firms to share the source of their advantage is in some tension with the underlying purpose of antitrust law, since it may lessen the incentive for the monopolist, the rival, or both to invest in those economically beneficial facilities.? Trinko, 540 U.S. at 407–08, 124 S.Ct. 872. Put another way, already large and successful firms "might be deterred from investing, innovating, or expanding . . . with the knowledge [that] anything [they] creat[e] [they] could be forced to share," while "smaller [competitors] might be [similarly] deterred, knowing [they] could just demand the right to piggyback on [their] larger rival." Novell, 731 F.3d at 1073. That equilibrium would hinder, rather than advance, consumer welfare. See Olympia Equip. Leasing, 797 F.2d at 379 ("Consumers would be worse off if a firm with monopoly power had a duty to extend positive assistance to new entrants, or having extended it voluntarily a duty to continue it indefinitely."). Second, "compelled sharing puts federal courts in the role of central planners," requiring them to pick and choose the applicable terms and conditions of the forced sharing they would order "despite their being ill-equipped to assume this role." Aerotec, 836 F.3d at 1183. Finally, "compelled sharing may actually provide opportunities for collusion" between the monopolist and its rival or rivals. Id. Collusion is "the supreme evil of antitrust," Trinko, 540 U.S. at 408, 124 S.Ct. 872, and itself quite "injuri[ous] to consumers and the competitive process alike." Novell, 731 F.3d at 1073."

Meanwhile, the European Court of Justice has gone in the opposite direction. In *Alphabet Inc.*, the Court of Justice made a preliminary ruling in response to a question by an Italian court in a case by a small firm that had designed an app to service electronic vehicles and had repeatedly requested to be admitted to the Google Android Auto platform. Google repeatedly refused, saying that it had no template for interoperability with the small firm. The Court of Justice held that Google had a duty to provide a template if it otherwise would be obstructing competition on the merits and is capable of harming consumers; and Google could charge an appropriate fee for the cost of the template. Case C–233/23, Feb. 25, 2025, ECLI:EU:C:2025:110.

In its judgment, the Court qualified *Bronner*. Access to the platform need not be indispensable where the undertaking developed the infrastructure not solely for its own business needs but to enable third-party usage. In that case, neither freedom of contract nor of property nor incentives to invest justify limiting access. Para. 45.

To establish a duty the plaintiff must show that the refusal "has the actual or potential effect of excluding, obstructing or delaying the development on the market of a product or service which is at least potentially in competition with a product or service supplied or capable of being supplied by the undertaking in a dominant position and constitutes conduct which restricts competition on the merits, and is thereby capable of causing harm to consumers."

The dominant firm can justify its refusal on grounds that the refusal is objectively necessary by reason of efficiency advantages to it "which also benefit the consumer . . . ." (para. 71), as where interoperability would "compromise the integrity or security of the platform concerned, or where it would be impossible for other technical reasons to ensure that interoperability by developing such a template." Para. 73. "By contrast, outside such situations, the fact that there is no template for the category of apps concerned or the difficulties involved in its development which the undertaking in a dominant position may face cannot in themselves constitute an objective justification for that undertaking's refusal to grant access." Para. 74.

The dominant firm is entitled to "appropriate financial consideration, taking into account the needs of the [requesting] party . . ., the actual cost . . . , and the right of the dominant . . . [firm] to derive an appropriate benefit from it." Para. 81.

Unless one can fit within the narrow exception under *Aspen Skiing* or rely on the essential facilities doctrine, upon which the *Trinko* court cast some doubt, the general presumption is that U.S. antitrust law imposes no duty to deal with a rival, even on a monopolist or dominant firm. In the EU, the right to refuse to deal is accorded greater protection under competition law when the facility in question is reserved for own use, such as in the *Oscar Bronner* case. In that case, the party seeking access needs to demonstrate that the dominant firm's facility is indispensable to the party's operation. But if the facility at issue is in fact made available to other third-party users, the dominant firm's right to refuse to grant access is much more circumscribed.

In the view of the EU courts, if the dominant firm has never shared its facility with rivals, it is entitled to preserve its competitive advantage absent exceptional circumstances. But if the dominant firm has already granted access to some rivals, the refusal to deal with one particular rival raises a concern about discrimination, which is absent when access has never been granted to anyone. When a dominant firm is only picking and choosing rivals with whom it will share access, there is a greater possibility that the choice is motivated by an exclusionary motive. The dominant firm may refuse to grant access to a rival who poses the greatest threat to the rest of its business.

EU competition law has always evinced greater concerns for discrimination than U.S. antitrust law. Aside from the Robinson-Patman Act, discrimination is not generally considered an issue under the rest of

U.S. antitrust law. The *Trinko* court probably would have argued that the monopolist's right to refuse to deal extends to picking and choosing the party with whom it will deal. This is consistent with what is known as the *Colgate* doctrine promulgated in the *Colgate* case in 1919, in which the Supreme Court declared that "[i]n the absence of any purpose to create or maintain a monopoly, the act does not restrict the long recognized right of trader or manufacturer engaged in an entirely private business, freely to exercise his own independent discretion as to parties with whom he will deal."[1] In contrast, Article 102(c) prohibits "applying dissimilar conditions to equivalent transactions with other trading parties, thereby placing them at a competitive disadvantage", even though this provision arguably has not been interpreted and enforced literally. The EU courts essentially believe that while a dominant firm is entitled to keep the use of its facility entirely to itself unless the facility is indispensable to rivals, once it has opened its facility to use by rivals, it is not entitled to withhold access from rivals when such denial can have competitive consequences.

The EU courts arguably strike a more appropriate balance between protecting private property rights and promoting competition. But the EU approach may cause a dominant firm to be doubly cautious about opening its facility to rival access for the first time, which could also end up hurting rivals in the long run.

2. Exclusionary Practices in General

We have just examined refusals to deal, which comprise one of the most commonly alleged offenses by dominant firms. We shall proceed to several other categories. Before we do, we note that there are multiple varieties of unilateral acts, practices and strategies that many be contested as anticompetitive and unlawful. They might fit a category, but they might not. The US government's *Microsoft* case comprised various exclusionary practices that were held illegal. The case is generally considered a sound case, applying good analysis; and at least with respect to the practices found unlawful, most jurisdictions would agree.

Microsoft is an example of applying a standard, not rules, to determine whether conduct is anticompetitive and should be prohibited. The standard is: Is the conduct likely to put costs on competitors and thereby to create, increase, or maintain market power, rather than conduct designed to increase efficiency, responsiveness to consumers, and innovation?

When rules are derived for particular categories of conduct, they are generally meant to be an application of this standard, customized

---

[1] United States v. Colgate Co., 250 U.S. 300, 307 (1919).

to particular conduct, and customized in a way likely to promote incentives of firms to be more responsive to consumers and the market. Rules that focus on incentives recognize, for example, that freedom to price low and freedom to invent are of the essence of the market system.

Here, then, is a brief selective summary of the acts found illegal in the US government *Microsoft* case.

Microsoft had a monopoly in the desktop computer operating system. The biggest barrier to entry was the applications: Users need applications to do their work on the computer, and applications were written specifically to an operating system. Because of network effects, applications writers would prefer to write to the Microsoft code than to any other operating system. But Microsoft saw a serious challenge looming on the horizon: Netscape, which had invented the browser (Navigator) and was teaming up with Sun Microsystems' Java language to create a new language that would be portable. It would figuratively "sit on top" of Windows as "middleware." Applications makers could write to it, and the middleware could port to any other operating system. Netscape needed a critical mass of Navigator users to make its innovation work, and thus it needed to be visible on Windows. Microsoft adopted a strategy to try to make sure that the Netscape/Java challenge would never happen. The strategy included many acts, some of which were dropped during the government's investigation. These included: If anyone loaded a non-Microsoft browser on Windows, a caution notice would pop up threatening a computer crash. Acts that were litigated and held illegal included blocking all efficient routes for Navigator to get on the Windows screen and thus become popular. Thus, in its contracts with Internet service providers such as AOL, Microsoft imposed the condition that they not distribute Navigator on their service. In its contracts with original equipment manufacturers, Microsoft imposed the condition that they not preinstall any browser other than its own, Internet Explorer (IE). In providing IE on Windows, Microsoft bound IE to Windows code so that IE could not be removed without crippling Windows. (These were the days when it was not easy, or was perceived as not easy, to download another browser, and it was perceived as costly to have more than one browser.) Microsoft took a license from Sun for Java language, which was meant to be cross-platform, and deceptively and against the terms of the license converted Java language to Microsoft-only Java language, effectively destroying its cross-platform properties. Microsoft had research joint ventures with a number of firms including Intel and required the partner as a condition of the joint venture not to participate in creating cross-platform interfaces. United States v. Microsoft Corp., 253 F.3d 34 (D.C. Cir. 2001), cert. denied.

* * *

In 2009, the European Commission gave general guidance regarding exclusionary practices under (now) TFEU Article 102 in its Guidance Paper: Communication from the Commission—Guidance on the Commission's enforcement priorities in Article 82 of the EC Treaty to abusive exclusionary conduct by dominant undertakings, 2009/C 45/02. This Guidance was amended in 2023. In parallel with this amendment, the European Commission launched the process for the adoption of its first Guidelines on exclusionary abuses of dominance. The Commission published a draft of these Guidelines on August 1, 2024 and a three-month public consultation process ensued. On February 13, 2025, the Commission hosted an interactive stakeholder workshop to further gather views on different key aspects of the draft Guidelines and to discuss the practical implications of their application. The Commission currently is in the process of finalizing these Guidelines. The 2009 Guidance will be withdrawn once the Guidelines are adopted.

There is a sense among commentators that the draft Guidelines signaled a retreat by the Commission from a more economic approach to the enforcement of Article 102 and a move toward relying on presumptions. One of the issues touched on in the draft Guidelines is the application of the As Efficient Competitor test ("the AEC test"). The AEC test essentially asks whether the exclusionary conduct at issue, which in many instances concern rebates, is capable of foreclosing a rival that is as efficient as the dominant firm. The case law suggests that when a dominant undertaking submits evidence on the AEC test, the Commission must assess it. And when the Commission applies the AEC test, it must do so rigorously. The draft Guidelines indicate an attempt by the Commission to limit the application of the AEC test to cases involving exclusionary pricing conduct such as predatory pricing, marginal squeeze and rebates. The Commission declares as a matter of general principle that the assessment of exclusionary effects generally is not premised on the application of the AEC test. Whether the Commission's effort to cabin the application of the AEC test and limit it to exclusionary pricing conduct cases remains to be seen.

With these anchors in place, we proceed to other selected specific categories.

3. Digital Economy Issues

a. *Introduction*

If there is one area of competition law that has risen in importance above all else in recent years, it is digital economy issues. An argument can be made that competition law was slow to catch on to the competitive significance of the emergence of the Big Tech and the giant digital platforms such as Google, Meta, Apple, and Amazon. For much of the 2000s most commentators were focused on the technological benefits brought by these tech giants, while being largely oblivious to their burgeoning market power.

Things began to change in the early 2010s when the European Commission began to investigate these Big Tech companies. One of the earliest cases was the *Google Shopping* case, which was launched by the European Commission in November 2010. In its proceedings, the European Commission alleged that Google engaged in what has subsequently been termed in the literature as "self-preferencing", whereby Google was said to have given a "more favourable positioning and display, in Google's general results pages, of its own comparison shopping service compared to competing comparison shopping services." Self-preferencing sits uncomfortably in the intersection of various anticompetitive conduct, such as tying and unilateral refusal to deal, while not falling squarely within the scope of any of them. While Google can be said to tie its general search service with its comparison shopping service, the act of promoting the comparison shopping service in the general search results probably does not constitute sufficient coercion to support a tying claim.

Google, in its appeal to the ECJ, strenuously argued that self-preferencing should be analyzed as unilateral refusal to deal under the so-called Bronner criteria from the famous *Oscar Bronner* case. The restrictive nature of these criteria, in particular the indispensability requirement, mean that Google's conduct would be unlikely to have infringed Article 102 if the Bronner criteria were to apply to Google's conduct. It would be difficult to argue that priority in search results on Google is indispensable to competing comparison shopping websites. Thus one of the first issues the ECJ was confronted with in its consideration of Google's appeal was whether the Bronner criteria applied to Google's conduct, and if not, what should be relevant legal test for assessing the legality of Google's conduct.

The ECJ refused to apply the Bronner criteria in the case and instead argued that Google's conduct should be analyzed as a *sui generis* conduct of self-preferencing. Importantly, the Court also held that the AEC [as efficient competitor] test, which was vigorously applied in the *Intel* case, has no application in self-preferencing cases. Given the difficulty in satisfying the AEC test, a further extension of the test to non-price related conduct would erect a significant hurdle to the European Commission's enforcement of Article 102. The European Commission's championing of self-preferencing as a new kind of exclusionary conduct and the subsequent endorsement of the argument by the European courts provided the basis for the inclusion of self-preferencing as an instance of proscribed conduct by a designated gatekeeper under the Digital Markets Act, a new legal instrument adopted by the European Parliament and the Council in 2022 to regulate the digital platforms.

b. Self-Preferencing—the Google Shopping Case

GOOGLE LLC v. COMMISSION (*GOOGLE SHOPPING*)

Case C–48/22 P, ECLI:EU:C:2024:726 (Court of Justice of the European Union 2024)

[The Court of Justice rejected Google's appeal and refused to apply the *Bronner* criteria to Google's conduct. Instead, the Court analyzed Google's conduct as a sui generis exclusionary conduct of self-preferencing. The Court said:]

109 . . . [T]he the Commission was not required to establish that the conditions laid down in the judgment of 26 November 1998, *Bronner* (C–7/97, EU:C:1998:569), recalled in paragraph 89 of the present judgment, were satisfied, in order to make a finding of infringement on the basis of the practices found, since those practices can be distinguished in their constituent elements from the refusal of access at issue in the case that gave rise to that judgment in *Bronner* and constitute an independent form of leveraging abuse. * * *

110 . . . [T]he the imposition of the conditions referred to in paragraph 41 of that judgment [the Bronner criteria] was justified by the particular circumstances of the case which gave rise to that judgment, which consisted in a refusal by a dominant undertaking to give a competitor access to an infrastructure that it had developed for the purposes of its own business, to the exclusion of any other conduct. . . .

111 By contrast, where a dominant undertaking gives access to its infrastructure but makes that access, provision of services or sale of products subject to unfair conditions, [the Bronner criteria] do not apply. It is true that where access to such an infrastructure—or service or input—is indispensable in order to allow competitors of the dominant undertaking to operate profitably in a downstream

market, this increases the likelihood that unfair practices on that market will have at least potentially anticompetitive effects and will constitute abuse within the meaning of Article 102 TFEU. However, as regards practices other than a refusal of access, the absence of such an indispensability is not in itself decisive for the purposes of examining potentially abusive conduct on the part of a dominant undertaking [citations omitted].

112 While such practices can constitute a form of abuse where they are able to give rise to at least potentially anticompetitive effects, or exclusionary effects, on the markets concerned, they cannot be equated to a simple refusal to allow a competitor access to the infrastructure, since the competent competition authority or national court will not have to force the dominant undertaking to give access to its infrastructure, as that access has already been granted. The measures that would be taken in such a context will thus be less detrimental to the freedom of contract of the dominant undertaking and to its right to property than forcing it to give access to its infrastructure where it has reserved that infrastructure for the needs of its own business [citations omitted].

113 Since, . . . Google gives competing comparison shopping services access to its general search service and to the general results pages, but makes that access subject to discriminatory conditions, [the Bronner criteria] do not apply to the conduct at issue. * * *

183 [T]he the conduct at issue consisted in treating results from comparison shopping services differently depending on whether they originated from Google's comparison shopping service or from competing comparison shopping services, in terms of display and positioning on the general results pages, and led to a difference in treatment in the form of Google's favouring its own comparison shopping service.

184 Next, the General Court pointed out that, on account of the three specific circumstances to which it had referred, the Commission had considered that that favouring was liable to lead to a weakening of competition on the market and that it could be classified in law as a matter of conduct which did not fall within the scope of competition on the merits.

185 Lastly, the General Court held that the conduct at issue was implemented through leveraging, consisting in Google's exploiting its dominant position on the upstream market for online general search services, characterised by high barriers to entry, in order to gain competitive advantages on the downstream market for specialised product search services, on which it did not hold such a position, and by favouring its own comparison shopping service.

186 It is important to add that it cannot be considered that, as a general rule, a dominant undertaking which treats its own products or services more favourably than it treats those of its competitors is engaging in conduct which departs from competition on the merits irrespective of the circumstances of the case.

187 However, in the present case, the General Court, in upholding the Commission's analysis, did not merely note the existence of such more favourable treatment by Google of its own comparison shopping service, but established that, having regard to the characteristics of the upstream market and the specific circumstances identified, the conduct at issue, with its two components, namely the highlighted presentation of its own results and the demotion of those of competing operators, was discriminatory and did not fall within the scope of competition on the merits. * * *

265 The assessment of the capability of the conduct at issue to foreclose an as-efficient competitor, referred to by Google as the principle underlying the application of Article 102 TFEU, appears, in particular, to be relevant, where the dominant undertaking submitted, during the administrative procedure, on the basis of supporting evidence, that its conduct was not capable of restricting competition and, in particular, of producing the alleged foreclosure effects. In such a case, the Commission is not only required to analyse the extent of the undertaking's dominant position on the relevant market, but it is also required to assess the possible existence of a strategy aiming to exclude competitors that are at least as efficient as the dominant undertaking from the market [citations omitted].

266 Furthermore, since the Commission is required to demonstrate the infringement of Article 102 TFEU, it must establish the existence of an abuse of a dominant position in the light of various criteria, by applying, inter alia, the as-efficient competitor test, where that test is relevant, its assessment of the relevance of such a test being, where appropriate, subject to review by the EU judicature.

267 In the present case, it must be observed that, as is apparent, in particular, from paragraphs 54 to 63 of the judgment under appeal, the abuse identified by the Commission consisted in the more favourable positioning and display which Google reserved, in the pages of its general search engine, for its own comparison shopping service as opposed to competing comparison shopping services. Thus, the Commission found, given that a comparison shopping service's ability to compete depended on traffic, that this discriminatory conduct on Google's part had had a significant impact on competition in that it had enabled Google to redirect, in favour of its own comparison shopping service, a large proportion of traffic previously

existing between Google's general results pages and comparison shopping services belonging to its competitors, without the latter being able to compensate for that loss of traffic by using other sources of traffic, since increased investment in alternative sources was not an 'economically viable' solution.

268 The General Court was therefore right, . . . to state, without that finding being invalidated by the appellants, which merely make allegations in principle, that it would not have been possible for the Commission to obtain objective and reliable results concerning the efficiency of Google's competitors in the light of the specific conditions of the market in question.

269 It follows that the General Court did not err in law in holding, first, that such a test was not mandatory in the context of the application of Article 102 TFEU and, second, that, in the circumstances of the present case, that test was not relevant.

Notes and Questions

1. What is the basis for prohibiting self-preferencing? Is self-preferencing always exclusionary? Can we prohibit self-preferencing by a digital platform without implicitly imposing public utility-like obligations of neutrality or fair dealing on it? Should self-preferencing be considered exclusionary when undertaken by other types of business? What if an airline prefers to use its own subsidiary for catering services? Did the ECJ expressly limit its ruling to digital platforms or gatekeepers? Is there something unique about digital platforms that justify the imposition of a unique obligation of neutrality on them? Consider paragraph 186 of the judgment and how much light it has shed on the issue.

2. Did the ECJ lay down a clear legal test for determining the legality of self-preferencing? What else beyond leveraging of a dominant position in an upstream market to gain a competitive advantage in a downstream market is required? Does self-preferencing amount to a general leveraging offense? If it does, how can we effectively limit its scope? Again, is it limited to digital platforms and gatekeepers? If it is, are we not better off adopting a sector-specific legislation to regulate them directly?

3. Other jurisdictions such as Korea have also confronted self-preferencing by digital platforms. In KFTC, self-preferencing can be pursued both as an abuse of market dominance under Article 5 and an unfair trade practice under Article 45 of the Monopoly Regulation and Fair Trade Act ("MRFTA"). The KFTC has brought enforcement action against Naver, a search engine dominant in Korea, and Kakao, a leading digital platform in Korea that provides messenger, banking,

entertainment and shopping services. The actions were brought under both Article 5 and Article 45 of the MRFTA.

4. In the *Naver* case, the KFTC defined two relevant markets of online comparison shopping service and open marketplace. The KFTC alleged that Naver had favored merchants operating on its marketplace platform called Smart Store through its comparison shopping service, which the KFTC alleged Naver held a 70% market share. This conduct constituted the unfair trade practice of unfairly inducing customers of competitors by providing consumers distorted information that hindered consumers' rational choice and the fair distribution of resources. The KFTC imposed a fine of USD23 million on Naver. The decision was upheld by the Seoul High Court and is pending in front of the Supreme Court of Korea at the time of writing.

5. In the *Kakao Mobility* case, the KFTC alleged that Kakao Mobility, which can be thought of as the Uber of Korea, favored its affiliated taxi drivers on its ride hailing platform. In addition to operating a mobility platform, Kakao Mobility also has taxi drivers affiliated with it through franchise agreements. Under Korean law, a taxi driver is limited to one franchise agreement, which means these affiliated taxi drivers are essentially exclusive to Kakao. The KFTC alleged that Kakao had manipulated its algorithms to favor its own affiliated drivers in the allocation of rides. The KFTC defined two relevant markets of general ride hailing service and franchise taxi service. The KFTC argued that by favoring its own affiliated drivers, Kakao improved the competitive position of these drivers, which may induce the taxi drivers of other franchises to defect to Kakao's franchise service. Such conduct infringed both Article 5 and Article 45 of the MRFTA by interfering with other undertakings' business conduct and by imposing discriminatory and disadvantages that amounted to an abuse of superior bargaining position. Kakao has appealed the KFTC's decision to the Seoul High Court. For more details about these two cases, *see* Yo Sop Choi, *Self-Preferencing in Korea and Japan*, 47 World Competition 495 (2024)

6. The availability of a wider toolkit to the KFTC renders the regulation of self-preferencing more flexible and feasible in Korea. The KFTC need not establish a dominant market position. The requirements of the proof of an unfair trade practice also tend to less stringent than those of the proof of an abuse of market dominance.

7. By taking the lead in enforcement against self-preferencing by Google, the EU seems to have established it in the international competition law community as a new kind of competition law violation. The US courts have yet to recognize self-preferencing as an antitrust violation. The future development of the law on self-preferencing remains to be seen. It could turn out to be another area of trans-Atlantic divergence in competition law.

c. *Digital Markets Act*

Adopting sector-specific regulation is precisely what the European Union eventually did with the Digital Markets Act, which was adopted and came into effect in 2022. The Act adopts a sector-specific approach and singles out gatekeeper digital platforms for regulation.

The Act imposes special obligations on a designated gatekeeper, which is defined in Article 1 as an undertaking if "(a) it has a significant impact on the internal market; (b) it provides a core platform service which is an important gateway for business users to reach end users; and (c) it enjoys an entrenched and durable position, in its operations, or it is foreseeable that it will enjoy such a position in the near future." Criterion (a) is considered met if an undertaking "achieves an annual Union turnover equal to or above EUR 7,5 billion in each of the last three financial years, or where its average market capitalisation or its equivalent fair market value amounted to at least EUR 75 billion in the last financial year, and it provides the same core platform service in at least three Member States". Criterion (b) is deemed satisfied where an undertaking "provides a core platform service that in the last financial year has at least 45 million monthly active end users established or located in the Union and at least 10 000yearly active business users established in the Union". Criterion (c) is fulfilled if "the thresholds in point (b) of this paragraph were met in each of the last three financial years."

On September 6, 2023, the European Commission announced the designation of six digital platforms as gatekeepers, including Google, Amazon, Apple, Booking, Bytedance, Meta, and Microsoft. Designation is not by entity but is instead by platform service. These six companies were designated for the following services respectively: Google (Google Play, Google Maps, Google Shopping, Google Search, YouTube, Android Mobile, online advertising service, Google Chrome); Amazon (Amazon Marketplace, Amazon Advertising); Apple (Appstore, iOS, Safari, iPadOS); Booking (online intermediation services); Bytedance (TikTok); Meta (Facebook Marketplace, Instagram, WhatsApp, Messenger, Meta Ads); Microsoft (Linkedin, Windows PC OS).

Apple, Meta and Bytedance contested their designation as gatekeepers. Meta challenged the designation of Messenger and Marketplace. Apple argued that its core platform services should be segregated according to their device-specific functionalities. Bytedance disputed the classification of TikTok as a gatekeeper on multiple grounds, including the fact that it faces competitive pressure from competing products in the market which have imitated its product experience.

The General Court dismissed Bytedance's challenge in June 2024. The Court reversed the burden of proof in DMA gatekeeper designation decisions, holding that once the European Commission demonstrated the presumptive quantitative thresholds based on user number, turnover, and market capitalization under Article 3(2) are met, the burden shifts to the undertaking to adduce sufficient evidence to "manifestly call into question" these presumptions.

The DMA imposes a whole host of obligations and prohibitions on designated gatekeepers. These include an obligation to provide data portability; a prohibition on using a third party seller's business data when competing with such seller on its platform, conduct which Amazon reportedly has engaged in in the past; a ban on price parity clauses; a prohibition of self-preferencing conduct; an obligation to enable interoperability of number-independent interpersonal communication services, among others.

Enforcement of the DMA is still in its early days. It remains to be seen whether it will boost competition against the entrenched digital platforms. One of the most significant impact of the passage of the DMA is arguably the Brussels effect, where other jurisdictions follow the lead of the EU in adopting, or at least considering adopting, regulation. Since 2022, a number of jurisdictions have considered adopting DMA-like legislation. For much of 2024, the Korean government kept wavering on following the EU's lead toward sector-specific digital economy regulation. In September 2024, the Korean government officially scrapped the DMA-style bill and announced that it will amend existing legislation instead. The Indian government proposed the Digital Competition Bill in 2024, which is still under consideration as of the time of writing. The Indian government is reportedly considering revision of the Bill in the face of vociferous opposition by technological companies.

A number of jurisdictions have gone further and adopted legislation of varying scopes. In June 2024, Japan adopted the Act on the Promotion of Competition in Relation to Specified Software Used in Smartphones, otherwise known as the Smartphone Act. The Act will come into effect in 2025. It has a more limited scope than the DMA in that it only applies to the operating system, app stores, browsers, and search engines on a smartphone. It is also sometimes known as the AppStore Act as many of its provisions concern app stores. For example, tying of payment processing services to app stores is prohibited. As are unfair treatment of app developers and certain limitations with respect to third-party app stores. Self-preferencing and tying of browser to operating system are also banned.

In May 2024, the United Kingdom promulgated the Digital Markets, Competition and Consumers ("DMCC") Act. The DMCC Act is similar to the DMA in that it also contains a designation process. Under the DMCC Act, a company must have: (a) a position of strategic significance in respect of a digital activity; (b) substantial and entrenched market power; and (c) UK turnover of more than GBP 1 billion or global turnover of more than GBP 25 billion in the previous 12 months in order to be designated as having a strategic market status ("SMS"). Contrary to the DMA, the DMCC Act does not impose a set of obligations on SMS firms. Instead, the DMCC Act empowers the Competition and Markets Authority ("CMA") to impose bespoke conduct requirements on each SMS firm. The DMCC Act requires the conduct requirement imposed to be proportionate, to satisfy the trio of objectives of fair dealing, open choices, and transparency. The general perception is that the UK government would like the CMA to adopt a more light-touch approach as compared to the DMA.

d. The Apple AppStore and Google Play Cases

In addition to Google Shopping and the self-preferencing conduct with which it is concerned, one digital economy issue has featured prominently across a number of jurisdictions. It pertains to app stores on Android and Apple iOS and the requirement that app developers use the app store payment system for in-app purchases and the related issue of the 30% commission that Google and Apple charge many app developers for in-app purchases.

The opening act in this long-running saga can be said to have begun with the litigation between Apple and Epic Games, a prominent game developer that counts Fortnite as one of its most successful products. Epic Games sued Apple in the District Court for the Northern District of California, alleging that Apple violated Section 1 and Section 2 of the Sherman Act by requiring app developers to use the App Store to distribute their apps on iOS devices, by requiring in-app purchases on iOS devices to be processed through the App Store's in-app payment system, and limiting the ability of app developers to notify iOS device users of the availability of alternative payment options. The District Court rejected the Sherman Act claims with respect to the first two restrictions largely on the ground that Epic Games failed to provide a less restrictive alternative that would allow Apple to achieve its objectives. The District Court upheld Epic Games' claim with respect to the third restriction under California state law and enjoined Apple from enforcing it against app developers. Epic Games appealed.

On appeal, the Ninth Circuit largely upheld the District Court's determination of the Sherman Act claims, refusing to condemn Apple's restrictions under the antitrust law. The Ninth Circuit held that Epic Games had failed to substantiate its proposed market definition. Moreover, it held that Epic Games made an adequate showing that Apple's restrictions had anticompetitive effects on mobile game transactions, upon which Apple generally proffered adequate procompetitive justifications for its restrictions. Epic Games then failed to provide less restrictive means to accomplish Apple's procompetitive justifications under its walled-garden approach to iOS devices.

EPIC GAMES, INC. v. APPLE, INC.

67 F.4th 946 (United States Court of Appeals for the Ninth Circuit 2023)

We now turn to the main thrust of Epic's market-definition argument: that it is entitled, as a factual matter, to a finding in favor of its proposed aftermarkets. Though Epic attempts to avoid the clear-error label, its argument requires it to carry the heavy of burden on appeal of showing that the district court clearly erred in finding that (1) Epic failed to show a lack of general consumer awareness regarding Apple's restrictions on iOS distribution and payment processing, (2) Epic failed to show significant switching costs, and (3) the empirical evidence in the record and the *Brown Shoe* practical indicia support a market of mobile-game transactions, not Epic's iOS-specific aftermarkets.

Beginning with the first prong, Epic had the burden of showing a lack of consumer awareness—whether through a change in policy or otherwise. Epic identified a purported change in policy, contrasting the App Store's now-immense profitability with a pre-launch statement from Steve Jobs that Apple did not "intend to make money off the App Store['s]" 30% commission. The district court reasonably found this statement to simply reflect Jobs's "initial expectation" about the App Store's performance, not an announcement of Apple policy. Especially in light of the district court's finding that Apple has "maintained the same general rules" for distribution and payment processing since the App Store's early days, it did not clearly err in concluding that Epic failed to prove a lack of consumer awareness through a change of policy.

Nor did the district court clearly err in finding that Epic otherwise failed to establish a lack of awareness. Indeed, the district court squarely found: "[T]here is ***no evidence*** in the record demonstrating that consumers are unaware that the App Store is the sole means of digital distribution on the iOS platform" (emphasis added). And on appeal, Epic fails to cite any evidence that would undermine the district court's characterization of the record.

Because of this failure of proof on the first prong of Epic's *Kodak/Newcal* showing, we need not reach—and do not express any view regarding—the other factual grounds on which the district court rejected Epic's single-brand markets: (1) that Epic did not show significant switching costs, and (2) that empirical evidence and the *Brown Shoe* factors rebut Epic's proposed aftermarkets.

. . . .

Epic proposes access to competing payment processors as an LRA to Apple's IAP requirement. Like the distribution requirement LRA, this LRA suffers from a failure of proof on how it would achieve Apple's IP-compensation rationale. As the district court noted, in a world where Apple maintains its distribution restriction but payment processing is opened up, Apple would still be contractually entitled to its 30% commission on in-app purchasers. Apart from any argument by Epic, the district court "presume[d]" that Apple could "utilize[e] a contractual right to audit developers . . . to ensure compliance with its commissions." But the court then rejected such audits as an LRA because they "would seemingly impose both increased monetary and time costs."

Notes and Questions

1. One of the thorniest issues regarding app stores cases is market definition. Is there an independent for iOS App Store? From whose perspective do we look at the market definition issue? The app developers or the smartphone users? From the app developers' perspective, there would seem to be genuine choice between the iOS App Store and Google Play, even though in reality no one can afford to ignore either one. But there is at least a plausible argument that there is a general app store market. From the smartphone users' perspective, once the user has bought the phone, they are essentially locked into the operating system and the app store on their phones. The operating system and the app store are essentially aftermarkets. Which perspective did the Court to establish market definition? Was the Court correct to hold that a failure to demonstrate consumers' lack of awareness of Apple's restrictions is fatal to Epic Games' attempt to define a single-brand app store aftermarket?

2. Was the Court correct to ask Epic Games to proffer less restrictive means? Under a standard Rule of Reason analysis, does the an analysis usually proceed to a balancing of anticompetitive effects and procompetitive justifications after both parties have satisfied their

burden? Does the requirement of a showing of less restrictive means not erect an artificial hurdle for plaintiffs?

3. Epic Games filed essentially the same claims against Google over the restrictions Google imposes over Google Play also in the District Court for the Northern District of California. In re Google Play Store Antitrust Litigation, 2024 WL 3302068. Epic Games had better luck this time convincing the jury of the anticompetitive nature of Google's conduct. The jury found in favor of Epic Games on market definition, agreeing that Epic Games had demonstrated "(1) an "Android app distribution market," and (2) a market for "Android in-app billing services for digital goods and services transactions." Google attempted to rely on Epic Games v. Apple to overturn this market definition, which the Court rejected on two grounds. First, while the iOS app store does constitute a single-brand aftermarket, the Android app store market does not. Android is an operating system and not a brand and there are many brands that manufacture and sell Android devices. Second, while the iOS App Store is the only app store on iOS devices, multiple app stores have been allowed to exist on Android. The Court further found that the various agreements Google had entered into to protect Google Play's competitive position were anticompetitive and that Google had unlawfully tied the use of Google Play Store with Google Play Billing. The Court was also more sympathetic toward Epic Games regarding the less restrictive means argument, arguing that jury might have rejected Google's procompetitive justifications, in which no demonstration of less restrictive means needs to be made. The U.S. Court of Appeals for the Ninth Circuit affirmed, finding significant differences between the Apple and Google cases. In re Google Play Store Antitrust Litig., 147 F.4th 917 (9th Cir. 2025).

4. While the fight between app developers on the one hand and Google and Apple on the other hand continue to roar on, other jurisdictions have chosen to settle the issue through legislation. In August 2021, the Korea Parliament adopted amendments to the Telecommunications Business Act that ban Apple and Google from forcing app developers to use their in-app payment systems. In response to the passage of the amendments, Apple and Google lowered their commission from 30% to 15% for certain app developers. These actions did not stop the Korea Communications Commission ("KCC") from pursuing enforcement action, alleging that Apple and Google still force app developers to use specific payment methods and have caused undue delay in app reviews. The KCC called for corrective action and threatened fines of up to $50.5 million.

5. The European Commission launched an antitrust investigation in June 2020 against Apple for the mandatory use of Apple's own proprietary in-app purchase system and restrictions on the ability of developers to inform iPhone and iPad users of alternative purchasing possibilities and an investigation under the DMA in June

2024 for preventing app developers from freely steering consumers to alternative channels for offers and content.

4. Predatory Pricing

US antitrust jurisprudence strongly favors low pricing. In a succession of cases since the mid-1980s, the US Supreme Court has expressed reluctance to punish dominant firms for unilateral decisions, particularly those relating to prices. In the relatively simple case of single-product price discounting, the Supreme Court requires, for a violation, a showing that the defendant priced below its cost (although the Supreme Court has yet to decide what is the appropriate measure of cost) and that its below-cost pricing created a dangerous probability that defendant would be able to exclude others from the market and thereafter raise its price and recoup all of the costs of predation. Brooke Group Ltd. v. Brown & Williamson Tobacco Corp., 509 U.S. 209 (1993). The Supreme Court has extended its approach to below-cost pricing to other pricing-related claims, including predatory overbidding and price squeezes. See Weyerhaeuser Co. v. Ross-Simmons Hardwood Lumber Co., Inc., 549 U.S. 312 (2007) (predatory overbidding) and Pacific Bell Tel. Co. v. LinkLine Commun., Inc., 555 U.S. 438 (2009) (price squeezes).

Not all other jurisdictions follow the US in condemning low and below-cost pricing only if recoupment is provable.

AKZO CHEMIE BV v. COMMISSION

Case C–62/86, ECLI:EU:C:1991:286 (Court of Justice of the European Union 1991)

[AKZO, a large Dutch multinational firm, and ECS (Engineering and Chemical Supplies Ltd.), a small UK firm, both manufactured organic peroxides. AKZO had a market share of 50%. Benzoyl peroxide is the most important organic peroxide. Benzoyl peroxide is a bleaching agent for flour and is also used in plastics as an initiator of the polymer production process. ECS was engaged in the flour segment of the market. For a decade, ECS was content with its sales for the flour business, but in 1979 it developed excess capacity and started to sell to plastics makers, soliciting and selling to some of AKZO's customers. An AKZO official told ECS's manager Sullivan "that AKZO would take aggressive commercial action on the milling products unless [Sullivan] refrained from supplying his products to the plastics industry." The AKZO official told Sullivan AKZO would pry away ECS's flour customers at prices far below prevailing prices. When ECS ignored AKZO's threats, AKZO implemented selective, low prices, with the intent to damage the business of ECS.

From the end of 1980 for about four years, AKZO targeted ECS's customers in the flour segment, selling to them at prices that were below its average total cost and that were much lower than the previously prevailing rates. Meanwhile, AKZO charged its own loyal customers (whose business was not at risk) about sixty percent more than the targeted customers of ECS. As part of its strategy, AKZO sold these customers flour milling complements they needed at prices below AKZO's average variable cost, and it sold them some vitamin mixes (which it bought specifically for resale to these customers) below its own purchase price. ECS's business declined by about seventy percent in four years, and its profit margins fell.

The Commission initiated proceedings and obtained an interim order enjoining AKZO's conduct. In its decision on the merits, the Commission noted AKZO's "clear predatory intent" as well as its scheme of price discrimination. However, perhaps because of the interim order, the predatory campaign had little affect on ECS. ECS's share in the flour additive sector went from 35% to 30%, and AKZO's share went from 52% to 55%.

Placing much weight on AKZO's intent to eliminate its competitor, the Commission found an infringement and levied a fine of 10 million ECUs on AKZO.]

A. Dominant position

60 With regard to market shares the Court has held that very large shares are in themselves, and save in exceptional circumstances, evidence of the existence of a dominant position (judgment in Case 85/76 *Hoffmann-La Roche v Commission* [1979] ECR 461, paragraph 41). That is the situation where there is a market share of 50% such as that found to exist in this case.

61 Moreover, the Commission rightly pointed out that other factors confirmed AKZO's predominance in the market. In addition to the fact that AKZO regards itself as the world leader in the peroxides market, it should be observed that, as AKZO itself admits, it has the most highly developed marketing organization, both commercially and technically, and wider knowledge than that of their competitors with regard to safety and toxicology. . . .

62 The pleas put forward by AKZO in order to deny that it had a dominant position within the organic peroxides market as a whole must therefore be rejected.

B. Abuse of a dominant position

63 According to the contested decision (point 75) AKZO had abusively exploited its dominant position by endeavoring to eliminate ECS from the organic peroxides market mainly by massive and prolonged price-cutting in the flour additives sector. * * *

[69] It should be observed that . . . the concept of abuse is an objective concept relating to the behavior of an undertaking in a dominant position which is such as to influence the structure of a market where, as a result of the very presence of the undertaking in question, the degree of competition is weakened and through recourse to methods which, different from those which condition normal competition in products or services on the basis of the transactions of commercial operators, has the effect of hindering the maintenance of the degree of competition still existing in the market or the growth of that competition.

[70] It follows that Article [102] prohibits a dominant undertaking from eliminating a competitor and thereby strengthening its position by using methods other than those which come within the scope of competition on the basis of quality. From that point of view, however, not all competition by means of price can be regarded as legitimate.

[71] Prices below average variable costs (that is to say, those which vary depending on the quantities produced) by means of which a dominant undertaking seeks to eliminate a competitor must be regarded as abusive. A dominant undertaking has no interest in applying such prices except that of eliminating competitors so as to enable it subsequently to raise its prices by taking advantage of its monopolistic position, since each sale generates a loss, namely the total amount of the fixed costs (that is to say, those which remain constant regardless of the quantities produced) and, at least, part of the variable costs relating to the unit produced.

[72] Moreover, prices below average total costs, that is to say, fixed costs plus variable costs, but above average variable costs, must be regarded as abusive if they are determined as part of a plan for eliminating a competitor. Such prices can drive from the market undertakings which are perhaps as efficient as the dominant undertaking but which, because of their smaller financial resources, are incapable of withstanding the competition waged against them.

[73] These are the criteria that must be applied to the situation in the present case. * * *

[114] The prices charged by AKZO to its own customers were above its average total costs, whereas those offered to customers of ECS were below its average total costs.

[115] AKZO is thus able, at least partly, to set off losses resulting from the sales to customers of ECS against profits made on the sales to the 'large independents' which were among its customers. This behavior shows that AKZO's intention was not to pursue a general policy of

favorable prices, but to adopt a strategy that could damage ECS. The complaint is therefore substantiated. * * *

140 By maintaining prices below its average total costs over a prolonged period, without any objective justification, AKZO was thus able to damage ECS by dissuading it from making inroads into its customers. * * *

[The Court concluded that AKZO, at various times, offered customers of ECS prices lower than AKZO's total or average variable costs, and did so as part of its threat to obtain ECS's withdrawal from the plastics sector.

162 . . . [I]t must be observed that the infringement committed by AKZO is particularly serious, since the behavior complained of was intended to prevent a competitor from extending its activity into a market in which AKZO held a dominant position.

[The Court reduced the fine to 7.5 million ECUs—predecessor to the Euro—on grounds that the controlling law had not previously been specified and the infraction did not have a significant effect on market shares.]

POST DANMARK A/S v. KONKURRENCERÅDET

Case C–209/10, ECLI:EU:C:2012:172 (Court of Justice of the European Union 2012)

[Post Danmark had a statutory monopoly over the market for addressed mail under a certain weight. The market for unaddressed mail, which consisted mostly of commercial promotional materials, had been liberalized in Danmark. Post Danmark operated a nationwide delivery network for its addressed mail business, which it also used for the unaddressed mail business. Post Danmark was accused by a competitor of trying to steal some of the latter's largest customers through selective price cuts. The Danish Competition Authority, Konkurrencerådet, launched an investigation but could not find any evidence of an intent to eliminate competition. The Konkurrencerådet found that in two instances, Post Danmark's prices were above ATC, and in one instance, the price was below ATC but above average incremental cost, which was a short-run variable cost concept that takes into account the cost of the delivery network. Applying the AKZO framework, the Konkurrencerådet concluded that Post Danmark had not engaged in predatory pricing. However, it held that Post Danmark had abused its dominance through its selective price cuts.]

35 When that estimation [cost attribution] was completed, it was found, among other things, that the price offered to the Coop group did not enable Post Danmark to cover the average total costs

attributed to the activity of unaddressed mail distribution taken as a whole, but did enable it to cover the average incremental costs pertaining to that activity, as estimated by the Danish competition authorities.

36 Moreover, it is common ground that, in the present case, the prices offered to the Spar and SuperBest groups were assessed as being at a higher level than those average total costs, as estimated by those authorities. In those circumstances, it cannot be considered that such prices have anti-competitive effects.

37 As regards the prices charged the Coop group, a pricing policy such as that in issue in the main proceedings cannot be considered to amount to an exclusionary abuse simply because the price charged to a single customer by a dominant undertaking is lower than the average total costs attributed to the activity concerned, but higher than the average incremental costs pertaining to the latter, as respectively estimated in the case in the main proceedings.

38 Indeed, to the extent that a dominant undertaking sets its prices at a level covering the great bulk of the costs attributable to the supply of the goods or services in question, it will, as a general rule, be possible for a competitor as efficient as that undertaking to compete with those prices without suffering losses that are unsustainable in the long term.

39 It is for the court making the reference to assess the relevant circumstances of the case in the main proceedings in the light of the finding made in the previous paragraph. In any event, it is worth noting that it appears from the documents before the Court that Forbruger-Kontakt managed to maintain its distribution network despite losing the volume of mail related to the three customers involved and managed, in 2007, to win back the Coop group's custom and, since then, that of the Spar group.

40 If the court making the reference, after carrying out that assessment, should nevertheless make a finding of anti-competitive effects due to Post Danmark's actions, it should be recalled that it is open to a dominant undertaking to provide justification for behaviour that is liable to be caught by the prohibition under Article 82 EC (see, to this effect, Case 27/76 *United Brands and United Brands Continentaal* v *Commission* [1978] ECR 207, paragraph 184; Joined Cases C–241/91 P and C–242/91 P *RTE and ITP* v *Commission* [1995] ECR I–743, paragraphs 54 and 55; and *TeliaSonera Sverige*, paragraphs 31 and 75).

41 In particular, such an undertaking may demonstrate, for that purpose, either that its conduct is objectively necessary (see, to that

effect, Case 311/84 *CBEM* [1985] ECR 3261, paragraph 27), or that the exclusionary effect produced may be counterbalanced, outweighed even, by advantages in terms of efficiency that also benefit consumers (Case C–95/04 P *British Airways* v *Commission* [2007] ECR I–2331, paragraph 86, and *TeliaSonera Sverige*, paragraph 76).

42 In that last regard, it is for the dominant undertaking to show that the efficiency gains likely to result from the conduct under consideration counteract any likely negative effects on competition and consumer welfare in the affected markets, that those gains have been, or are likely to be, brought about as a result of that conduct, that such conduct is necessary for the achievement of those gains in efficiency and that it does not eliminate effective competition, by removing all or most existing sources of actual or potential competition.

43 In the present case, it is enough to state, with regard to the considerations set out at paragraph 11 above, that the mere fact that a criterion explicitly based on gains in efficiency was not one of the factors appearing in the schedules of prices charged by Post Danmark cannot justify a refusal to take into account, where necessary, such gains in efficiency, provided that that their actual existence and their extent have been established in accordance with the requirements set out in paragraph 42 above.

44 Having regard to all the foregoing considerations, the answer to be given to the questions referred is that Article 82 EC must be interpreted as meaning that a policy by which a dominant undertaking charges low prices to certain major customers of a competitor may not be considered to amount to an exclusionary abuse merely because the price that undertaking charges one of those customers is lower than the average total costs attributed to the activity concerned, but higher than the average incremental costs pertaining to that activity, as estimated in the procedure giving rise to the case in the main proceedings. In order to assess the existence of anti-competitive effects in circumstances such as those of that case, it is necessary to consider whether that pricing policy, without objective justification, produces an actual or likely exclusionary effect, to the detriment of competition and, thereby, of consumers' interests.

Notes and Questions

1. The *AKZO* court allowed a below-cost price coupled with evidence of predatory intent—intent to eliminate a competitor—to suffice for a violation. Can one reconcile the US insistence on probable recoupment with the *AKZO* test by saying that a dominant firm would

not engage in below-cost pricing to eliminate a competitor unless it expected to be able recoup the costs of predation through later supracompetitive pricing? If so, why insist on proof of recoupment? Would a dominant firm ever invest in below-cost pricing to drive out a competitor if it only expected to obtain a greater share of the market at competitive prices?

2. The Post Danmark case arguably did not concern predatory pricing at all, unless the Court defined the relevant market as consisting of only those three big customers. Otherwise, it would have made no sense to measure cost only with respect to the three customers. Cost would have to be ascertained with respect to the entire unaddressed mail market or at least the market for unaddressed mail delivered for large commercial establishments. Given that the price cuts were only offered to the three customers, it is highly unlikely that the price for the market overall would have fallen by much and would have been below ATC.

3. What would have been the implications if the Court had found that selective price cuts that fall below some measure of short-run incremental cost by a dominant firm amounted to an abuse under Article 102, even absent any evidence of an intent to eliminate competition? Would that greatly hamper a dominant firm's ability to offer selective price cuts?

4. It is obvious from paragraphs 38 and 39 that the Court was greatly comforted by the fact that the competitor was able to withstand the price cuts and even to win back some of the lost customers. How does this compare with the AKZO case, where the analysis seemed to focus on the relationship between the dominant firm's price and costs and profitability of the price cuts for the dominant firm? There was hardly any mention in AKZO about the competitors' response to the price cuts? Is this a new consideration in predatory pricing cases? Should it be? If it were a consideration, how should a Court rule if the price was clearly shown to be below AVC but nonetheless the competitor was able to withstand it?

5. The Post Danmark I case has been much praised by economically-minded analysts, who have touted the case as adopting a consumer welfare standard and as adopting an "as efficient competitor" litmus test for exclusionary acts; but later judgments, particularly Post Danmark II (loyalty rebates), Case C–23/14, ECLI:EU:C:2015:651, do not bear out the prediction of retrenchment of EU competition law.

5. Margin Squeezes

In margin squeeze cases, the dominant firm with power over an input prices the input so high and its own integrated product so low that unintegrated downstream rivals cannot profitably sell their product. Typically, the industry involves sector regulation, and the cases may discuss the relationship between antitrust rules and sector regulation. How should antitrust authorities or jurists decide monopolization or abuse of dominance questions where sectoral regulators are also involved in policing the conduct? Should antitrust authorities find it less necessary to police regulated industries since the sectoral regulators are better situated to control abuses of dominance? Or is antitrust enforcement especially needed in heavily regulated sectors where entry barriers are likely to be pervasive, high, and durable and the regulators might be captured by the regulated? We observe a significant divide between the US and the EU on the issue of margin squeezes.

The European Commission accused Deutsche Telekom of violating Article [102 TFEU]. The European Commission eventually found a violation, and imposed a fine. Deutsche Telekom brought suit against the Commission in the General Court—the intermediate appellate court—and later in the Court of Justice to annul the Commission's decision.

DEUTSCHE TELEKOM AG v. COMMISSION

Case C–280/08 P, ECLI:EU:C:2010:603 (Court of Justice of the European Union 2010)

[Deutsche Telekom (DT) was the dominant provider of telecommunications services in Germany and had sole access to the local loop. DT was regulated by the German Regulatory Authority, which imposed price ceilings. DT charged new entrants into the local telecom service market higher fees for wholesale access to the local loop than it charged its customers for services including DSL for fast-speed Internet connection. The competing providers of DSL service complained to the European Commission. The Commission found a margin squeeze in violation of Article 102. The General Court affirmed, and the Court of Justice affirmed. DT had a duty to provide competitors access to the local loop. It therefore had a duty not to create a margin squeeze. DT had sufficient scope to eliminate the margin squeeze on terms consistent with the regulation, and could go back to the German regulator (RegTP) if it needed an adjustment in price. The Court said:]

* * *

80 According to the case-law of the Court of Justice, it is only if anti-competitive conduct is required of undertakings by national legislation, or if the latter creates a legal framework which itself eliminates any possibility of competitive activity on their part, that Articles [101] and [102] do not apply. In such a situation, the restriction of competition is not attributable, as those provisions implicitly require, to the autonomous conduct of the undertakings.

Articles [101] and [102] may apply, however, if it is found that the national legislation leaves open the possibility of competition which may be prevented, restricted or distorted by the autonomous conduct of undertakings.

81 The possibility of excluding anti-competitive conduct from the scope of Articles [101] and [102] on the ground that it has been required of the undertakings in question by existing national legislation or that the legislation has precluded all scope for any competitive conduct on their part has thus been accepted only to a limited extent by the Court of Justice.

82 Thus, the Court has held that if a national law merely encourages or makes it easier for undertakings to engage in autonomous anti-competitive conduct, those undertakings remain subject to Articles [101] and [102].

83 According to the case-law of the Court, dominant undertakings have a special responsibility not to allow their conduct to impair genuine undistorted competition on the common market.

84 It follows from this that the mere fact that the appellant was encouraged by the intervention of a national regulatory authority such as RegTP to maintain the pricing practices which led to the margin squeeze of competitors who are at least as efficient as the appellant cannot, as such, in any way absolve the appellant from responsibility under Article [102].*

85 Since, notwithstanding such interventions, the appellant had scope to adjust its retail prices for end-user access services, the General Court was entitled to find, on that ground alone, that the margin squeeze at issue was attributable to the appellant.

86 . . . [A]ppellant does not challenge the General Court's findings . . . that, in essence, the appellant was able to make applications to RegTP for authorization to adjust its retail prices for end-user access services, specifically retail prices for narrowband access services for the period between 1 January 1998 and 31 December 2001, and retail prices for broadband access services for the period from 1 January 2002.

* * *

159 It is clear . . . that, according to the General Court, it is not the level of the wholesale prices for local loop access services—which . . . cannot be challenged in the present appeal—or the level of retail

* Editors' addition: "RegTP took the view in each case that other operators should be able to offer their end users competitive prices by resorting to cross subsidization of access services and call services." General Court, paragraph 267.

prices for end-user access services which is contrary to Article [102], but the spread between them.

* * *

172 As regards the abusive nature of the appellant's pricing practices, it must be noted that subparagraph (a) of the second paragraph of Article [102] expressly prohibits a dominant undertaking from directly or indirectly imposing unfair prices.

* * *

177 It follows from this [special responsibility] that Article [102] prohibits a dominant undertaking from, inter alia, adopting pricing practices which have an exclusionary effect on its equally efficient actual or potential competitors, that is to say practices which are capable of making market entry very difficult or impossible for such competitors, and of making it more difficult or impossible for its co-contractors to choose between various sources of supply or commercial partners, thereby strengthening its dominant position by using methods other than those which come within the scope of competition on the merits. From that point of view, therefore, not all competition by means of price can be regarded as legitimate.

178 In the present case, it must be noted that the appellant does not deny that, even on the assumption that it does not have the scope to adjust its wholesale prices for local loop access services, the spread between those prices and its retail prices for end-user access services is capable of having an exclusionary effect on its equally efficient actual or potential competitors, since their access to the relevant service markets is, at the very least, made more difficult as a result of the margin squeeze which such a spread can entail for them.

179 At the hearing the appellant submitted, however, that the test applied in the judgment under appeal for the purpose of establishing an abuse within the meaning of Article [102] required it, in the circumstances of the case, to increase its retail prices for end-user access services to the detriment of its own end-users, given the national regulatory authorities' regulation of its wholesale prices for local loop access services.

180 It is true . . . that Article [102] aims, in particular, to protect consumers by means of undistorted competition.

181 However, the mere fact that the appellant would have to increase its retail prices for end-user access services in order to avoid the margin squeeze of its competitors who are as efficient as the appellant cannot in any way, in itself, render irrelevant the test

which the General Court applied in the present case for the purpose of establishing an abuse under Article [102].

182 By further reducing the degree of competition existing on a market—the end-user access services market—already weakened precisely because of the presence of the appellant, thereby strengthening its dominant position on that market, the margin squeeze also has the effect that consumers suffer detriment as a result of the limitation of the choices available to them and, therefore, of the prospect of a longer-term reduction of retail prices as a result of competition exerted by competitors who are at least as efficient in that market.

183 In those circumstances, in so far as the appellant has scope to reduce or end such a margin squeeze . . . by increasing its retail prices for end-user access services, the General Court correctly held . . . that that margin squeeze is capable, in itself, of constituting an abuse within the meaning of Article [102] in view of the exclusionary effect that it can create for competitors who are at least as efficient as the appellant. The General Court was not, therefore, obliged to establish, additionally, that the wholesale prices for local loop access services or retail prices for end-user access services were in themselves abusive on account of their excessive or predatory nature, as the case may be.

(c) i) The complaint concerning the misapplication of the as-efficient-competitor test * * *

252 The General Court therefore held . . . , without any error of law, that the anti-competitive effect which the Commission is required to demonstrate, as regards pricing practices of a dominant undertaking resulting in a margin squeeze of its equally efficient competitors, relates to the possible barriers which the appellant's pricing practices could have created for the growth of products on the retail market in end-user access services and, therefore, on the degree of competition in that market.

253 . . . [A] pricing practice such as that at issue in the judgment under appeal that is adopted by a dominant undertaking such as the appellant constitutes an abuse within the meaning of Article [102] if it has an exclusionary effect on competitors who are at least as efficient as the dominant undertaking itself by squeezing their margins and is capable of making market entry more difficult or impossible for those competitors, and thus of strengthening its dominant position on that market to the detriment of consumers' interests.

254 Admittedly, where a dominant undertaking actually implements a pricing practice resulting in a margin squeeze of its equally efficient competitors, with the purpose of driving them from the relevant market, the fact that the desired result is not ultimately achieved does not alter its categorization as abuse within the meaning of Article [102]. However, in the absence of any effect on the competitive situation of competitors, a pricing practice such as that at issue cannot be classified as exclusionary if it does not make their market penetration any more difficult.

* * *

Note the relationship between EU competition law and Member State sector regulation. Note also that the Court of Justice might find harm to competition and consumers even if prices rise in the short term. See paragraphs 182–183.

The US Supreme Court reached a very different result in Pacific Bell Tel. Co. v. LinkLine Commun., Inc., 555 U.S. 438 (2009). The plaintiffs were four regional digital subscriber line ("DSL") providers who alleged that AT&T (and various corporate affiliates) violated Section 2 of the Sherman Act by selling their telephonic facilities and infrastructure necessary to provide DSL at too high a wholesale price and then charged too low a retail price to AT&T's own customers, thus squeezing plaintiffs out of the market. The Supreme Court held that a price squeeze claim without an allegation of below-cost pricing at retail was not cognizable. The Court found this result required by two of its precedents. In Verizon v. Trinko, 540 U.S. 398 (2004), the Court rejected monopolization liability for (almost all) unilateral refusals to deal; hence AT&T could not have had any *antitrust* duty to provide access to its infrastructure at wholesale, much less to provide such access at a reasonable price. In Brooke Group v. Brown & Williamson, 509 U.S. 209 (1993), the Court rejected predatory pricing liability absent a showing that defendant priced below cost (and could recoup losses). Hence, AT&T could not be liable for low but above-cost retail prices.

In addition to this fairly formalistic doctrinal analysis, the Court offered policy explanations for its decision.

> Institutional concerns also counsel against recognition of such claims. We have repeatedly emphasized the importance of clear rules in antitrust law. Courts are ill suited "to act as central planners, identifying the proper price, quantity, and other terms of dealing." Trinko, 540 U.S., at 408. " 'No court should impose a duty to deal that it

> cannot explain or adequately and reasonably supervise. The problem should be deemed irremedia[ble] by antitrust law when compulsory access requires the court to assume the day-to-day controls characteristic of a regulatory agency.' " * * *
>
> It is difficult enough for courts to identify and remedy an alleged anticompetitive practice at one level, such as predatory pricing in retail markets or a violation of the duty-to-deal doctrine at the wholesale level.... Recognizing price-squeeze claims would require courts simultaneously to police both the wholesale and retail prices to ensure that rival firms are not being squeezed. And courts would be aiming at a moving target, since it is the interaction between these two prices that may result in a squeeze.
>
> Perhaps most troubling, firms that seek to avoid price-squeeze liability will have no safe harbor for their pricing practices.... At least in the predatory pricing context, firms know they will not incur liability as long as their retail prices are above cost. No such guidance is available for price-squeeze claims.

Notes and Questions

1. Compare the US law with the EU law on the relationship between antitrust and sector regulation. What policy and institutional considerations seem to have driven the choice of each jurisdiction?

2. Compare US and EU law on the notion of what is harm to competition and consumers.

3. Assuming that neither jurisdiction wants to protect inefficient competitors, is one or the other approach wiser?

6. Loyalty Rebates and Exclusive Dealing

Dominant firms may reward customers for loyalty or for agreeing not to deal with competitors (in whole or in part). Typically they adopt these strategies when a younger firm is catching up, threatening the incumbent's dominance.

A number of these cases involve Intel, the dominant maker of an essential computer chip. AMD was the weak competitor for a number of years, but when it produced a desirable new chip, Intel took action to forestall its inroads during the crucial first six months of its launch. But the action was based on lower prices. Were Intel's acts anticompetitive?

In 2008, the Korea Fair Trade Commission (KFTC) fined Intel $25 million for offering rebates to the Korean computer makers Samsung and Sambo Computer in exchange for their not doing business with AMD, Intel's chief rival in the computer microprocessor (CPU) market. Among other things, the KFTC found:

- In the fourth quarter of 2001, Intel had a 100% market share at Samsung. In 2002, Samsung began buying CPUs from AMD and Intel's market share fell to about 80%. Intel then offered Samsung rebates in exchange for a commitment to purchase solely from Intel, at which point Intel's market share with Samsung reverted to 100%.
- "Economic analysis on the case showed that with Intel's rebate practice intact, AMD would not be able to viably compete against Intel, even if it supplies its CPUs to OEMs for free."
- Between 2000 and 2006, AMD's market share never exceeded 17%, and was usually no higher than 10%.
- "In the CPU sales agency market where PC consumers' preferences are directly reflected, AMD's [market share] between 2000 and 2006 was continuously on the rise, reaching around 30% at the end of 2005."

Intel's appeal was denied by the Seoul High Court (2013).

The same week that the Korean authority announced its decision, the US FTC announced its own investigation of Intel's rebating practices. (The investigation was settled by consent decree.) Then, in May of 2009, the European Commission announced its own Intel decision and an unprecedented fine of nearly $1.5 billion. The Commission found a violation by object (a category reserved for hard core or near hard core conduct), and found that the conduct was not justified. The General Court affirmed. Intel appealed to the Court of Justice. The appeal called into question whether it was proper to treat Intel's rebates as an abuse by object and thus provable without inquiry into effects; and whether it was proper to declare that, even in the case of an effects inquiry, there was no need for the Commission to prove that AMD was an equally efficient competitor. Case T–286/09 12 June 2014. The European Court of Justice disagreed on both counts.

We reproduce below some selections from the Commission's and later the General Court's press releases. Excerpts from the Court of Justice appear on page 115.

INTEL CORP. v. COMMISSION

Case C–413/14 P, ECLI:EU:C:2017:632 (Court of Justice of the European Union 2017)

[Throughout the period October 2002–December 2007, Intel had a dominant position in the worldwide x86 CPU market (at least 70% market share). The Commission found that Intel engaged in two specific forms of illegal practice [when it was challenged by the competitive new chip of its only significant competitor, AMD]. First, Intel gave wholly or partially hidden rebates to computer manufacturers on condition that they bought all, or almost all, their x86 CPUs from Intel. Intel also made direct payments to a major retailer on condition it stock only computers with Intel x86 CPUs. Such rebates and payments effectively prevented customers—and ultimately consumers—from choosing alternative products. Second, Intel made direct payments to computer manufacturers to halt or delay the launch of specific products containing competitors' x86 CPUs and to limit the sales channels available to these products. The Commission found that these practices constituted abuses of Intel's dominant position on the x86 CPU market that harmed consumers throughout the EEA [European Economic Area]. By undermining its competitors' ability to compete on the merits of their products, Intel's actions undermined competition and innovation. The General Court had upheld the Commission's decision. Intel appealed to the Court of Justice.]

[The Court of Justice set aside the judgment of the General Court and referred the case back to the General Court for review of whether the rebates were capable of restricting competition. The Court said:]

129 In the first place, by the first two parts of its first ground of appeal, Intel, supported by ACT, argues, in essence, that the General Court accepted that the practices at issue could be considered an abuse of a dominant position within the meaning of Article 102 TFEU without first examining all of the circumstances of the present case and without assessing the likelihood of that conduct restricting competition.

130 In the second place, by the third part of its first ground of appeal, Intel criticises the General Court's analysis, carried out for the sake of completeness, inter alia in paragraphs 172 to 197 of the judgment under appeal, concerning the capacity of the rebates and payments granted to Dell, HP, NEC, Lenovo and MSH to restrict competition in the circumstances of the case.

131 In that context, Intel challenges, inter alia, the General Court's assessment of the relevance of the AEC test applied by the Commission in the present case.132 It submits, in particular, that, since the Commission applied that test, the General Court should have examined Intel's line of argument alleging that the application of that test was badly flawed and that, had it been correctly applied, it would have led to the conclusion contrary to that which the Commission reached, namely that the rebates at issue were not capable of restricting competition.133 . . . [I]t must be born in mind that it is in no way the purpose of Article 102 TFEU to prevent an undertaking from acquiring, on its own merits, the dominant position on a market. Nor does that provision seek to ensure that competitors less efficient than the undertaking with the dominant position should remain on the market . . . . * * *

137 . . . [T]he Court has already held that an undertaking which is in a dominant position on a market and ties purchasers—even if it does so at their request—by an obligation or promise on their part to obtain all or most of their requirements exclusively from that undertaking abuses its dominant position within the meaning of Article 102 TFEU . . . .

138 However, that case-law must be further clarified in the case where the undertaking concerned submits, during the administrative procedure, on the basis of supporting evidence, that its conduct was not capable of restricting competition and, in particular, of producing the alleged foreclosure effects.

139 In that case, the Commission is not only required to analyse, first, the extent of the undertaking's dominant position on the relevant market and, secondly, the share of the market covered by the challenged practice, as well as the conditions and arrangements for granting the rebates in question, their duration and their amount; it is also [re]quired to assess the possible existence of a strategy aiming to exclude competitors that are at least as efficient as the dominant undertaking from the market . . . .

140 The analysis of the capacity to foreclose is also relevant in assessing whether a system of rebates which, in principle, falls within the scope of the prohibition laid down in Article 102 TFEU, may be objectively justified. It has to be determined whether the exclusionary effect arising from such a system, which is disadvantageous for competition, may be counterbalanced, or outweighed, by advantages in terms of efficiency which also benefit the consumer . . . .

Notes and Questions

1. The Court of Justice *Intel* judgment may be read as an important turn-around to put much more weight on actual competitive effects and to weaken prior holdings that adopt formalistic presumptions. Comment on this proposition and consider the judgment's effects on prior EU rulings.

2. Does the Court of Justice leave standing the analysis of the naked restraints, which it does not mention in the operative portion of its judgment? If so, what is a naked restriction, allowing no defense? When justification is possible, what satisfies an undertaking's burden to justify?

In general, when is it necessary for the plaintiff to prove harm to competition and consumers (competitive effects)? What is anticompetitive foreclosure? When must the plaintiff show that the targeted competitor was actually squeezed out of the market? When must it show that the competitor was as efficient, or potentially so? Is it correct to base foreclosure on the contestable share of the market? How is this share to be calculated?

3. These questions are difficult ones all over the world. They are not all resolved in the United States, where there is a split of the circuits on the test for loyalty rebates. A principal question in play in the United States is whether, in a loyalty rebate case, the plaintiff must prove that the rebate amounted to a predatory price using the *Brooke Group* test (thus turning on price/cost margins), or whether the question is a more open question of fact as to whether the rebates were unreasonably exclusionary.

4. Exclusive dealing, tying and bundling by dominant firms reflect all of the same considerations we have discussed. These are leveraging and foreclosure violations, when they are violations. They may be efficiency justified, but they may not be; they may be used to put costs on competitors; to preserve or entrench market power in the main market or to monopolize an adjacent one. Coercive tying by a dominant firm that forecloses a significant share of the market to rivals is often seen as presumptively illegal and in need of justification, as in the European Union. Such tying was once per se illegal in the United States but is now more likely to be examined under a rule of reason, putting plaintiff to the burden of proving probable harm to consumers. In the European Union the draft Article 102 TFEU Guidelines gives the Commission's view of how to analyze each of these issues. Communication from the Commission—Guidelines on the application of Article 102 of the Treaty on the Functioning of the European Union to abusive exclusionary conduct by dominant undertakings.

5. The *Intel* judgment left open a number of important issues. The first one concerns the tension between the Court's affirmation of the

by-objection restriction of exclusive dealing under *Hoffman-La Roche* and the effects-based analysis of loyalty rebates it mandated in *Intel.* The *Hoffman-La Roche* by-object restriction designation would be meaningless if effects-based analysis is in fact required in every case. In paragraph 138 of the judgment, the Court clarified that the *Hoffman-La Roche* presumption cannot be relied upon if the defendant argues that its conduct is not capable of restricting competition, in which case the Commission and the courts must conduct an assessment of the defendant's capacity to foreclose. What remains unclear is whether this assessment requires an examination of actual foreclosure effects or whether a reference to potential effects suffice, as seems to be the case under prior jurisprudence such as *British Airways.* A further complication is the role to be played by the AEC test in the assessment. Must the Commission demonstrate that the loyalty rebates are capable of foreclosing an as-efficient competitor? Or does it suffice to show that the rebates can foreclose any competitor?

The second one concerns the applicability of the Intel judgment, whether it extends beyond conditional rebates to exclusivity payments or even contractual exclusivity obligations. In theory, one can distinguish between the loyalty rebates at issue in *Intel* from other exclusivity practices on the grounds that the rebates are conditional in nature. Outright contractual exclusivity obligations arguably are more anticompetitive as they leave the contractual counterparty with no choice. For a while, the Commission seemed to have drawn a distinction between these obligations and other exclusivity practices such as exclusivity payments. The Court of Justice will provide an answer to both of these questions in the Unilever Italia case, which is excerpted below.

UNILEVER ITALIA MKT. OPERATIONS SRL v. AUTORITÀ GARANTE DELLA CONCORRENZA E DEL MERCATO

Case C–680/20, ECLI:EU:C:2023:33 (Court of Justice of the European Union 2023)

[Unilever Italia sold and distributed individually packaged ice cream under the trademarks of "Algida" and "Carte d'Or". Unilever imposed exclusivity obligations on sales outlets, obliging them to obtain their entire supplies of individually package ice cream products from Unilever. In return, Unilever offered a wide range of rebates and commissions, which were conditioned upon meeting the sales and turnover targets for a specific range of Unilever products.

Unilever appealed the decision by the AGCM that its exclusivity practices constituted an infringement of Article 102 TFEU. The AGCM had refuse to entertain evidence offered by Unilever that showed that Unilever's practices were not capable of foreclosing an as-efficient competitor. AGCM deemed such evidence to be wholly irrelevant for exclusivity clauses. Its appeal was rejected by the Tribunale Amministrativo Regionale per il Lazio. Unilever further appealed to the Consiglio di Stato of Italy, which made a reference to the Court of Justice for a preliminary ruling.]

46 In that context, with regard more specifically to exclusivity clauses, it is true that the Court has held that clauses by which contracting parties undertook to purchase all or a considerable part of their requirements from an undertaking in a dominant position, even if not accompanied by rebates, constituted, by their very nature, an exploitation of a dominant position and that the same was true of the loyalty rebates granted by such an undertaking . . . .

47 However, in . . . Intel v Commission . . ., the Court clarified, in the first place, that case-law in a situation where an undertaking in a dominant position submits, during the administrative procedure, with evidence in support of its claims, that its conduct was not capable of restricting competition and, in particular, of producing the alleged exclusionary effects.

48 In that regard, the Court stated that, in that situation, the competition authority is not only required to analyse, first, the extent of the undertaking's dominant position on the relevant market and, secondly, the share of the market covered by the challenged practice, as well as the conditions and arrangements for granting the rebates in question, their duration and their amount; it is also required to assess the possible existence of a strategy aiming to exclude competitors that are at least as efficient as the dominant undertaking from the market . . . .

49 The Court added, in the second place, that the analysis of the capacity to foreclose is also relevant in assessing whether a system of rebates which, in principle, falls within the scope of the prohibition laid down in Article 102 TFEU, may be objectively justified. In addition, the exclusionary effect arising from such a system, which is disadvantageous for competition, may be counterbalanced, or outweighed, by advantages in terms of efficiency which also benefit the consumer. That balancing of the favourable and unfavourable effects of the practice in question on competition can be carried out only after an analysis of the intrinsic capacity of that practice to foreclose competitors which are at least as efficient as the dominant undertaking . . . .

50 It is true that, in providing that second clarification, the Court referred only to rebate schemes. However, since both rebate practices and exclusivity clauses are capable of being objectively justified or of having the disadvantages which they generate counterbalanced, or even outweighed, by advantages in terms of efficiency which also

benefit the consumer, such a clarification must be understood as applying to both of those practices.

51 Moreover, in addition to the fact that such an interpretation appears to be consistent with the first clarification provided by the Court in . . . Intel v Commission . . . , it must be held that, although, by reason of their nature, exclusivity clauses give rise to legitimate concerns of competition, their ability to exclude competitors is not automatic, as, moreover, is illustrated by the Communication from the Commission entitled 'Guidance on the Commission's enforcement priorities in applying Article [102 TFEU] to abusive exclusionary conduct by dominant undertakings . . . .

52 It follows that, first, where a competition authority suspects that an undertaking has infringed Article 102 TFEU by using exclusivity clauses, and where that undertaking disputes, during the procedure, the specific capacity of those clauses to exclude equally efficient competitors from the market, with supporting evidence, that authority must ensure, at the stage of classifying the infringement, that those clauses were, in the circumstances of the case, actually capable of excluding competitors as efficient as that undertaking from the market.

53 Secondly, the competition authority which initiated that procedure is also required to assess, specifically, the ability of those clauses to restrict competition where, during the administrative procedure, the undertaking which is under suspicion, without formally arguing that its conduct was incapable of restricting competition, maintains that there are justifications for its conduct.

54 In any event, the submission, in the course of the procedure, of evidence capable of demonstrating the inability to produce restrictive effects gives rise to an obligation for the competition authority to examine that evidence. Respect for the right to be heard, which, according to settled case-law, is a general principle of EU law, requires competition authorities to hear the undertaking in a dominant position, which means that they must pay due attention to the observations thus submitted by that undertaking, examining carefully and impartially all the relevant aspects of the individual case, and, in particular, the evidence submitted by that undertaking . . . .

55 It follows that, where the undertaking in a dominant position has produced an economic study in order to demonstrate that the practice of which it is accused was not capable of excluding competitors, the competent competition authority cannot exclude the relevance of that study without setting out the reasons why it considers that the study does not contribute to demonstrating that the practices in question

were incapable of undermining effective competition on the relevant market and, consequently, without giving that undertaking the opportunity to determine the evidence which could be substituted for that study.

56 As regards the 'as efficient competitor' test, to which the referring court expressly referred in its request, it should be noted that that concept refers to various tests which have in common the aim of assessing the ability of a practice to produce anti-competitive exclusionary effects by reference to the ability of a hypothetical competitor of the undertaking in a dominant position, which is as efficient as the dominant undertaking in terms of cost structure, to offer customers a rate which is sufficiently advantageous to encourage them to switch supplier, despite the disadvantages caused, without that causing that competitor to incur losses. That ability is generally determined that competitor to incur losses. That ability is generally determined in the light of the cost structure of the undertaking in a dominant position itself.

57 A test of that nature may be inappropriate in particular in the case of certain non-pricing practices, such as a refusal to supply, or where the relevant market is protected by significant barriers. Moreover, such a test is only one of a number of methods for assessing whether a practice is capable of producing exclusionary effects; moreover, that method takes into consideration only price competition. In particular, the use by a undertaking in a dominant position of resources other than those governing competition on the merits may be sufficient, in certain circumstances, to establish the existence of such an abuse . . . .

58 Consequently, the competition authorities cannot be under a legal obligation to use the 'as efficient competitor test' in order to find that a practice is abusive . . . .

59 Nevertheless, even in the case of non-pricing practices, the relevance of such a test cannot be ruled out. A test of that type may prove useful where the consequences of the practice in question can be quantified. In particular, in the case of exclusivity clauses, such a test may theoretically serve to determine whether a hypothetical competitor with a cost structure similar to that of the undertaking in a dominant position would be able to offer its products or services otherwise than at a loss or with an insufficient margin if it had to bear the compensation which the distributors would have to pay in order to switch supplier, or the losses which they would suffer after such a change following the withdrawal of previously agreed discounts . . . .

60 Consequently, where an undertaking in a dominant position suspected of abuse provides a competition authority with an analysis based on an 'as efficient competitor test', that authority cannot disregard that evidence without even examining its probative value.

61 That fact is not called into question by the existence of a number of practices at issue. Even if the cumulative effects of those practices cannot be understood by such a test, the fact remains that the result of a test of that nature may nevertheless constitute an indication of the effects of some of those practices and, therefore, be relevant in order to determine whether certain classifications may be made with regard to the practices at issue.

7. Japan

The Japanese Fair Trade Commission (JFTC) promulgated Guidelines for Exclusionary Private Monopolization under the Antimonopoly Act in 2009, which were revised in 2020. They are available in English translation at https://www.jftc.go.jp/en/legislation_gls/imonopoly_guidelines.html. The Guidelines' "factors for assessing whether conduct falls under exclusionary conduct" appear on the JFTC website on a single page with graphic representations, which we reproduce below.

JFTC: Assessing Exclusionary Conduct

Under the JFTC Guidelines, only exclusionary acts that prevent competition by an equally or more efficient competitor are prohibited. The JFTC states in its Guidelines that "if such conduct would make it difficult for competitors to continue their inefficient business activities, it does not fall under Exclusionary Conduct because it is a result of fair and free competition, which the Antimonopoly Act intends to promote." Further, rebates that are conditional on minimum levels of purchases that have the effect of restraining dealing in competitors' products are treated as exclusive dealing agreements. The Guidelines do not provide information on the key issues in *Intel*, such as whether discounts or rebates given in exchange for exclusivity should be assessed across the entire range of output sold by the defendant or only across the contestable share of the market.

Moreover, in two categories—tying and refusal to supply—the harm required for anticompetitive effect is whether the conduct "may cause difficulty in the business activities of competitors who are unable to easily find alternative trade partners in the market of the tied product" and whether the conduct "may cause difficulty in the business activities in the downstream market of the trading customers who are unable to easily find an alternative supplier in the upstream market This implies a more expansive standard than the standards in the US and EU.

Notes and Questions

1. The Korean authority took pains to point out the effect that the rebates had on AMD's market share and its viability in the market. The publicly available portions of the European Commission decision contain less concrete detail on the effect on AMD and the effect on competition: "The Commission found that these payments had the potential effect of preventing products for which there was a consumer demand from coming to the market." How much evidence of an exclusionary effect on AMD should be required to find an abuse of dominance or violation of Section 2 of the Sherman Act?

2. Competition authorities around the world have taken an interest in Intel's activities. In addition to Korean, US FTC, and European decisions mentioned earlier, the Japanese Fair Trade Commission issued a warning to Intel in 2005. Intel subsequently reached a settlement with the JFTC. After a nearly three-year investigation, in December 2009, the US FTC filed an administrative complaint against Intel related to its activities with respect to AMD and also in the separate market for graphics processing units in which Intel competes with Nvidia. As noted, this was settled by consent decree.

3. Some other jurisdictions may apply an equally efficient competitor test as well. See, for example, Japan: LP Gas Discriminatory Price, 52 SHINETSHUSHU 818, 826 (Tokyo High Court, May 31, 2005); Yamato Transp. v. Japan Post, 2006 (Ne) No. 1078, LEX/DB Legal Database No. 28140088 (Tokyo High Ct., Nov. 28, 2007). However, influential scholars have argued that the test unduly insulates defendants from liability in circumstances where the entry of even a less efficient competitor could benefit consumers. *See*, e.g., Herbert Hovenkamp, *Exclusion and the Sherman Act*, 72 U. Chi. L. Rev. 147, 154–55 (2005). Do you see why?

4. The Intel/AMD saga led to an important US Supreme Court decision, although not on the substantive merits of the case. After the European Commission opened its investigation, AMD sought an order from the Federal District Court for the Northern District of California requiring Intel to produce certain documents for use in the European proceedings. In 2004, the Supreme Court ruled that AMD could potentially obtain such discovery in the US and that, on remand, the district court should consider four factors: (1) the fact that Intel was a party to the foreign proceedings and therefore could be ordered by the European Commission to produce documents; (2) "the nature of the foreign tribunal, the character of the proceedings underway abroad, and the receptivity of the foreign government or the court or agency abroad to US federal-court judicial assistance;" (3) whether the "request

conceals an attempt to circumvent foreign proof-gathering restrictions or other policies of a foreign country or the United States;" and (4) "unduly intrusive or burdensome requests may be rejected or trimmed." Intel Corp. v. Advanced Micro Devices, Inc., 542 U.S. 241 (2004). On remand, the district court found that AMD was not entitled to the discovery. Still, the Supreme Court's decision has opened up the possibility for parties to obtain the help of US courts in obtaining discovery to aid in European and other proceedings.

8. Intellectual Property Issues

a. Introduction

Some of the highest profile cutting-edge issues involve intellectual property, the digital economy, or both. Antitrust actions have been brought, and a number are still pending and evolving, against some of the most successful new-economy companies in the world, including Google, which is dominant in the search engine function in many countries, and Qualcomm, which owns intellectual property essential to smart phones. The law is in flux across nations and even within nations. Different outcomes can be a function of 1) whether the jurisdiction sees dominant firms as having special responsibilities or whether it stresses freedoms to refuse to deal, and 2) the jurisdiction's degree of deference to IP exclusivity at the IP/competition interface. We present below an excerpt on challenges to Google, followed by three IP/antitrust problems: patent ambush, IP holders' right or not to enjoin infringement of essential patents, and antitrust authorities' right or not to limit the terms of licensing crucial patents.

b. FRAND and Patent Ambush

One area of active controversy involves the interaction of high-technology, intellectual property, and the antitrust laws. In order to make sure that all of the companies working on implementations of new technologies—such as DVDs, computer chips, or cell phones—are compatible, the companies often have to get together and agree on the standards that they will follow. Standard Setting Organizations or "SSOs" are the bodies that create these new standards. New technologies often draw upon a slew of different inventions in which many different inventors have intellectual property rights. Thus, as the members of the SSOs are debating what standards to adopt, they have to be cognizant of what and whose patents they may be treading on if they write the standard in a particular way. If the SSO implements a standard that requires all users of the standardized technology to follow Path A and Company A owns a patent that will be infringed by anyone who follows Path A,

Company A has the power to force anyone who wants to practice the standard to pay a hefty royalty.

If all of the members of the SSO are aware of the patents that will be infringed by a particular standard, they presumably will consider the royalty rate to be paid to the patentee a cost of choosing any particular standard. Indeed, they may negotiate up front with the patentee on a royalty rate to be charged or require the patentee to commit to license its patent on "Reasonable and Nondiscriminatory" or RAND (also known as "Fair, Reasonable, and Nondiscriminatory" ("FRAND")—although the "Fair" does not seem to add anything) terms.

What if a patentee participates in the SSO, says nothing about its patents, and then starts sending users of the standardized technology royalty demand letters after the standard has been adopted? Is this sort of "patent ambush" an antitrust violation? The European Commission thought it was. It issued a Statement of Objections. Rambus and the Commission reached a commitment decision under which Rambus would offer licenses at specified maximum royalty rates. No fine was imposed. Case COMP/38.636–RAMBUS (9.12.2009)

* * *

The US Federal Trade Commission shared the European Commission's concern. It ruled that Rambus had violated Section 2 of the Sherman Act by deceiving the SSO JEDEC about its patents and patent applications and subsequently charging a monopoly royalty rate for use of the patents after the SSO standard was announced. A divided US FTC imposed a cap on the amount that Rambus could charge for its patents used to practice JEDEC's standards.

Rambus appealed to the US Court of Appeals for the Federal Circuit. Rambus, Inc. v. FTC, 522 F.3d 456 (D.C. Cir. 2008). The court explained its holding as follows:

> The Commission held that Rambus engaged in exclusionary conduct consisting of misrepresentations, omissions, and other practices that deceived JEDEC about the nature and scope of its patent interests while the organization standardized technologies covered by those interests. Had Rambus fully disclosed its intellectual property, "JEDEC either would have excluded Rambus's patented technologies from the JEDEC DRAM standards, or would have demanded RAND assurances, with an opportunity for ex ante licensing negotiations." But the

Commission did not determine that one or the other of these two possible outcomes was the more likely. The Commission's conclusion that Rambus's conduct was exclusionary depends, therefore, on a syllogism: Rambus avoided one of two outcomes by not disclosing its patent interests; the avoidance of either of those outcomes was anticompetitive; therefore Rambus's nondisclosure was anticompetitive.

We assume without deciding that avoidance of the first of these possible outcomes was indeed anticompetitive; that is, that if Rambus's more complete disclosure would have caused JEDEC to adopt a different (open, non-proprietary) standard, then its failure to disclose harmed competition and would support a monopolization claim. But while we can assume that Rambus's nondisclosure made the adoption of its technologies somewhat more likely than broad disclosure would have, the Commission made clear in its remedial opinion that there was insufficient evidence that JEDEC would have standardized other technologies had it known the full scope of Rambus's intellectual property. Therefore, for the Commission's syllogism to survive-and for the Commission to have carried its burden of proving that Rambus's conduct had an anticompetitive effect-we must also be convinced that if Rambus's conduct merely enabled it to avoid the other possible outcome, namely JEDEC's obtaining assurances from Rambus of RAND licensing terms, such conduct, alone, could be said to harm competition. We are not convinced.

Deceptive conduct—like any other kind—must have an anticompetitive effect in order to form the basis of a monopolization claim. "Even an act of pure malice by one business competitor against another does not, without more, state a claim under the federal antitrust laws," without proof of "a dangerous probability that [the defendant] would monopolize a particular market." *Brooke Group*, 509 US at 225. Even if deception raises the price secured by a seller, but does so without harming competition, it is beyond the antitrust laws' reach. Cases that recognize deception as exclusionary hinge, therefore, on whether the conduct impaired rivals in a manner tending to bring about or protect a defendant's monopoly power. * * *

[A]n otherwise lawful monopolist's use of deception simply to obtain higher prices normally has no particular tendency to exclude rivals and thus to diminish competition.

Despite vociferous urging from the FTC, industry and consumer groups, and law professors and scholars, the Supreme Court declined to grant a writ of *certiorari* in *Rambus*. The FTC then closed its Rambus file, giving Rambus the last word in the FTC matter.

Notes and Questions

1. In rejecting the FTC's findings in *Rambus*, the court relied on the Supreme Court's decision in NYNEX Corp. v. Discon, Inc., 525 U.S. 128 (1998), for the proposition that mere deception leading to higher prices is insufficient to state an antitrust claim without a showing that the deception impaired the market's competitive functioning. *NYNEX*, however, was a private lawsuit and not a government enforcement action. Should the FTC be treated differently from private litigants? After all, most of the concerns that have led the courts to be cautious with private antitrust lawsuits—particularly the fear of abusive or frivolous lawsuits and the chilling effect of treble damages—have little relevance to enforcement actions by the FTC. Some commentators believe that rules applicable to public enforcers like the FTC and Department of Justice have become overwhelmed by the "baggage" of private enforcement and that this has constricted the agencies' ability to win cases in the courts. Do enforcement systems that rely entirely or primarily on public enforcement have an advantage in this regard?

2. In *Rambus,* the European Commission had one advantage over the US FTC, and one disadvantage. The disadvantage was: EU has no attempt to monopolize violation and Rambus was not dominant at the time of its deception. The advantage was: EU has an excessive pricing law and the US doesn't.

c. Suits to Enjoin Infringement of Essential Patents as Antitrust Violations

A cutting edge issue today in both the United States and the European Union arises in the context of standard-setting organizations where standards are necessary to facilitate technological progress and access by each player in the market to all essential technology is necessary to produce its products. Each of several players, such as Apple, Samsung, and Microsoft, is likely to need to use the intellectual property of the others to make its product, and barring of access would take its entire product (such as the iPhone) off the market. To assure their access to essential technology, and to prevent hold-ups for excessive license fees by IP owners, the firms (all owners of technology) make FRAND commitments: Each agrees that it will disclose its relevant technology during the standard setting process, and that, if the choice of standard makes its IP essential, it will license all of its essential patents on fair, reasonable, and non-discriminatory terms. Does the holder of a standard essential patent (SEP) under FRAND commitments have an *antitrust* duty to license that patent to willing licensees, and an *antitrust* duty not to seek an injunction for infringement against willing licensees (which typically are still bargaining on the terms of the license)?

Google acquired Motorola Mobility, which gave Google a portfolio of more than 24,000 patents. Motorola Mobility had agreed, in the standard setting organization, to license its patents necessary to work the standards on fair, reasonable and non-discriminatory terms. Motorola Mobility sought or was threatening to seek injunctions against infringers such as Apple and Microsoft, who were willing licensees but had not yet made an offer that Motorola Mobility would accept.

In the US, the FTC accused Motorola Mobility and Google of violating Section 5 of the Federal Trade Commission Act by suing for injunctions. It negotiated a consent order in which Google agreed not to seek injunctions on FRAND-encumbered SEPs against willing licensees. If the parties could not reach agreement on license terms, a neutral third party would settle the terms. Motorola Mobility LLC, Docket No. C–4410, Jan. 3, 2013, issued as modified July 23, 2013, reported at 5 CCH Trade Reg. Rep. ¶ 16,876.

Commissioner Maureen Ohlhausen, later Acting Chair of the FTC, dissented from entry of the consent order. She viewed any limitation on Motorola Mobility's right to seek an injunction for infringement of a FRAND-encumbered patent a matter of contract, not an antitrust problem, and she thought an antitrust duty not to seek an injunction would be an impermissible interference with IP rights. She doubted whether the FRAND agreement was properly construed to bar such a suit, and she thought that, if antitrust were implicated, the *Noerr-Pennington* right to petition courts would be a complete defense. There is virtually no litigated US case on point, and any court would have to contend with the Ohlhausen arguments, bolstered by the *Trinko* philosophy of no duty to deal and the difficulties of proving that a patent is a monopoly.

The European view is more developed, for the European Court of Justice has ruled, in *Huawei v. ZTE*.

HUAWEI TECHNOLOGIES CO. LTD v. ZTE CORP.

Case C–170/13, ECLI:EU:C:2015:477 (Court of Justice of the European Union 2015)

* * *

44 . . . [T]he referring court asks, essentially, in what circumstances the bringing of an action for infringement, by an undertaking in a dominant position and holding an SEP, which has given an undertaking to the standardization body to grant licenses to third parties on FRAND terms, seeking an injunction prohibiting the infringement of that SEP or seeking the recall of products for the manufacture of which the SEP has been used, is to be regarded as constituting an abuse contrary to Article 102 TFEU.

45 First of all, it must be recalled that the concept of an abuse of a dominant position within the meaning of Article 102 TFEU is an objective concept relating to the conduct of a dominant undertaking which, on a market where the degree of competition is already weakened precisely because of the presence of the undertaking concerned, through recourse to methods different from those governing normal competition in products or services on the basis of the transactions of commercial operators, has the effect of hindering the maintenance of the degree of competition still existing in the market or the growth of that competition (judgments in Hoffmann-La Roche, AKZO, and Tomra).

46 It is, in this connection, settled case-law that the exercise of an exclusive right linked to an intellectual-property right—in the case in the main proceedings, namely the right to bring an action for infringement—forms part of the rights of the proprietor of an intellectual-property right, with the result that the exercise of such a right, even if it is the act of an undertaking holding a dominant position, cannot in itself constitute an abuse of a dominant position.

47 However, it is also settled case-law that the exercise of an exclusive right linked to an intellectual-property right by the proprietor may, in exceptional circumstances, involve abusive conduct for the purposes of Article 102 TFEU. * * *

49 [This case] is characterized, first, by the fact that the patent at issue is essential to a standard established by a standardization body, rendering its use indispensable to all competitors which envisage manufacturing products that comply with the standard to which it is linked.

50 That feature distinguishes SEPs from patents that are not essential to a standard and which normally allow third parties to manufacture competing products without recourse to the patent

concerned and without compromising the essential functions of the product in question.

51 Secondly, the case in the main proceedings may be distinguished by the fact . . . that the patent at issue obtained SEP status only in return for the proprietor's irrevocable undertaking, given to the standardization body in question, that it is prepared to grant licenses on FRAND terms.

52 Although the proprietor of the essential patent at issue has the right to bring an action for a prohibitory injunction or for the recall of products, the fact that that patent has obtained SEP status means that its proprietor can prevent products manufactured by competitors from appearing or remaining on the market and, thereby, reserve to itself the manufacture of the products in question.

53 In those circumstances, and having regard to the fact that an undertaking to grant licenses on FRAND terms creates legitimate expectations on the part of third parties that the proprietor of the SEP will in fact grant licenses on such terms, a refusal by the proprietor of the SEP to grant a license on those terms may, in principle, constitute an abuse within the meaning of Article 102 TFEU.

54 It follows that, having regard to the legitimate expectations created, the abusive nature of such a refusal may, in principle, be raised in defense to actions for a prohibitory injunction or for the recall of products. However, under Article 102 TFEU, the proprietor of the patent is obliged only to grant a license on FRAND terms. In the case in the main proceedings, the parties are not in agreement as to what is required by FRAND terms in the circumstances of that case.

55 In such a situation, in order to prevent an action for a prohibitory injunction or for the recall of products from being regarded as abusive, the proprietor of an SEP must comply with conditions which seek to ensure a fair balance between the interests concerned. * * *

57 Thus, the need to enforce intellectual-property rights, covered by, inter alia, Directive 2004/48, which—in accordance with Article 17(2) of the Charter [of Fundamental Rights of the European Union]—provides for a range of legal remedies aimed at ensuring a high level of protection for intellectual-property rights in the internal market, and the right to effective judicial protection guaranteed by Article 47 of the Charter, comprising various elements, including the right of access to a tribunal, must be taken into consideration.

58 This need for a high level of protection for intellectual-property rights means that, in principle, the proprietor may not be deprived of

the right to have recourse to legal proceedings to ensure effective enforcement of his exclusive rights, and that, in principle, the user of those rights, if he is not the proprietor, is required to obtain a license prior to any use.

59 Thus, although the irrevocable undertaking to grant licenses on FRAND terms given to the standardization body by the proprietor of an SEP cannot negate the substance of the rights guaranteed to that proprietor by Article 17(2) and Article 47 of the Charter, it does, none the less, justify the imposition on that proprietor of an obligation to comply with specific requirements when bringing actions against alleged infringers for a prohibitory injunction or for the recall of products.

60 Accordingly, the proprietor of an SEP which considers that that SEP is the subject of an infringement cannot, without infringing Article 102 TFEU, bring an action for a prohibitory injunction or for the recall of products against the alleged infringer without notice or prior consultation with the alleged infringer, even if the SEP has already been used by the alleged infringer.

61 Prior to such proceedings, it is thus for the proprietor of the SEP in question, first, to alert the alleged infringer of the infringement complained about by designating that SEP and specifying the way in which it has been infringed.

62 . . . [I]n view of the large number of SEPs composing a standard such as that at issue in the main proceedings, it is not certain that the infringer of one of those SEPs will necessarily be aware that it is using the teaching of an SEP that is both valid and essential to a standard.

63 Secondly, after the alleged infringer has expressed its willingness to conclude a licensing agreement on FRAND terms, it is for the proprietor of the SEP to present to that alleged infringer a specific, written offer for a license on FRAND terms, in accordance with the undertaking given to the standardization body, specifying, in particular, the amount of the royalty and the way in which that royalty is to be calculated.

64 . . . [W]here the proprietor of an SEP has given an undertaking to the standardization body to grant licenses on FRAND terms, it can be expected that it will make such an offer. Furthermore, in the absence of a public standard licensing agreement, and where licensing agreements already concluded with other competitors are not made public, the proprietor of the SEP is better placed to check whether its offer complies with the condition of non-discrimination than is the alleged infringer.

65 By contrast, it is for the alleged infringer diligently to respond to that offer, in accordance with recognized commercial practices in the field and in good faith, a point which must be established on the basis of objective factors and which implies, in particular, that there are no delaying tactics.

66 Should the alleged infringer not accept the offer made to it, it may rely on the abusive nature of an action for a prohibitory injunction or for the recall of products only if it has submitted to the proprietor of the SEP in question, promptly and in writing, a specific counter-offer that corresponds to FRAND terms.

67 Furthermore, where the alleged infringer is using the teachings of the SEP before a licensing agreement has been concluded, it is for that alleged infringer, from the point at which its counter-offer is rejected, to provide appropriate security, in accordance with recognized commercial practices in the field, for example by providing a bank guarantee or by placing the amounts necessary on deposit. The calculation of that security must include, inter alia, the number of the past acts of use of the SEP, and the alleged infringer must be able to render an account in respect of those acts of use.

68 In addition, where no agreement is reached on the details of the FRAND terms following the counter-offer by the alleged infringer, the parties may, by common agreement, request that the amount of the royalty be determined by an independent third party, by decision without delay.

69 [The alleged infringer retains the right to challenge the validity of the patent and to challenge its essentiality to the standard, which it can do in parallel with negotiations for the license fee.] * * *

71 It follows . . . that Article 102 TFEU must be interpreted as meaning that the proprietor of an SEP, which has given an irrevocable undertaking to a standardization body to grant a license to third parties on FRAND terms, does not abuse its dominant position, within the meaning of Article 102 TFEU, by bringing an action for infringement seeking an injunction prohibiting the infringement of its patent or seeking the recall of products for the manufacture of which that patent has been used, as long as:

> —prior to bringing that action, the proprietor has, first, alerted the alleged infringer of the infringement complained about by designating that patent and specifying the way in which it has been infringed, and, secondly, after the alleged infringer has expressed its willingness to conclude a licensing agreement on FRAND terms, presented to that infringer a specific, written offer for a

license on such terms, specifying, in particular, the royalty and the way in which it is to be calculated, and

—where the alleged infringer continues to use the patent in question, the alleged infringer has not diligently responded to that offer, in accordance with recognized commercial practices in the field and in good faith, this being a matter which must be established on the basis of objective factors and which implies, in particular, that there are no delaying tactics. * * *

Notes and Questions

1. Before the *Huawei* judgment came down, the European Commission found that Motorola Mobility abused its dominant position in violation of EU competition law by seeking and enforcing an injunction against Apple for using Motorola Mobility's standard essential patents in its smart phones without a license, where Motorola Mobility had made a FRAND commitment and Apple was a willing licensee. At the same time, Samsung settled a separate investigation with the Commission committing to discontinue just such conduct. European Commission—IP/14/489 (29 April 2014).

2. The *Huawei* judgment resolved divergences in approach taken by some national courts.

3. Describe the *Huawei* judgment and the steps a SEP holder must take in terms of good faith bargaining for the license fee in order to be entitled to seek an injunction. Is the judgment properly respectful of intellectual property rights, which, as it says, are protected by the Charter on Fundamental Rights as well as the Treaty?

4. Would you expect the US courts to adopt the European approach? to adopt the approach outlined by Commissioner Ohlhausen? Why? What are the relative merits of each?

d. Unfair Royalties and Other Licensing Terms as Antitrust Violations

Qualcomm is the dominant supplier in the world of baseband processors, which are chips that manage cellular communications in mobile products. It also holds patents essential to cellular connectivity. Firms in China are the principal manufacturers of mobile products that need the technology. After a long investigation in China by the National Development and Reform Commission ("NDRC"), which was one of the three authorities formerly tasked with enforcement of the AML until enforcement was centralized under the State Administration for Market Regulation, in which the NDRC often stressed its claim that the Chinese firms were paying excessive royalties to Qualcomm, Qualcomm accepted the following terms, including a fine of nearly one billion US dollars—the highest fine yet imposed by the Chinese antitrust authorities. Here is NDRC's statement, as translated by Linklater's Greater China Translation Team.

NDRC ORDERED RECTIFICATION AND FINED QUALCOMM RMB6 BILLION FOR MONOPOLISTIC CONDUCTS

10 February 2015

The National Development and Reform Commission ("**NDRC**") recently sanctioned Qualcomm Incorporated ("**Qualcomm**") according to laws for its abuse of dominant market position to eliminate or restrict competition, ordered Qualcomm to cease the relevant illegal activities and imposed on it a fine equaling to 8% of its sales in China in 2013, i.e. RMB6.088 billion.

In November 2013, NDRC initiated the anti-monopoly investigation on Qualcomm based on complaints received. In the process of the investigation, NDRC conducted in-depth investigation into dozens of domestic and international cell phone manufacturing enterprises and baseband chip manufacturers, acquired evidence on Qualcomm's price monopoly and other monopolistic conducts, fully solicited Qualcomm's statements and defenses, and analyzed and assessed on whether the relevant activities of Qualcomm constitute the abuse of market dominance under the Anti-Monopoly Law of China (the "**AML**").

Based on the investigation and the evidence obtained and through analysis and assessment as described above, it is found that Qualcomm has a dominant position in the markets of standard essential patents ("**SEPs**") licensing in respect of CDMA, WCDMA and LTE wireless communication and the market of baseband chips, and that Qualcomm has engaged in the following conducts in abuse of its dominant market position:

1. **Charged unfairly high patent licensing fees.** Qualcomm refused to provide Chinese enterprises with its patent lists when granting license to them and charged licensing fees for expired patents which are always included in its patent portfolio. In the meantime, Qualcomm requested a free cross-license of the Chinese licensees' own relevant patents, while refused to deduct the value of such cross-licensed patents from its licensing fees or offer another consideration. In addition, for Chinese licensees who have been forced to accept Qualcomm's packaged

licensing of non-SEPs, Qualcomm charged royalties on the basis of the net wholesale price of the device while imposing a relatively high royalty rate. A combination of these factors resulted in the excessively high royalties.

2. **Bundled sales of non-SEPs in relation to the wireless communication without justifications.** Qualcomm did not distinguish or offered separate licenses in respect of its SEPs and non-SEPs in relation to the wireless communication, which are of a different nature; instead, it took advantage of its dominant position in the market of licensing of SEPs in relation to the wireless communication to bundle the licensing of non-SEPs in relation to the wireless communication. Some of Chinese licensees have been forced to obtain the license of non-SEPs in relation to the wireless communication from Qualcomm.

3. **Imposed unreasonable restrictions on the sales of baseband chips.** Qualcomm conditioned its supply of baseband chips to Chinese customers on the signing without challenging a patent-license agreement by such customers. If a potential licensee did not sign the patent-license agreement including the above unreasonable terms, or the licensee disputed such patent-license agreement and brought actions, Qualcomm would refuse to supply baseband chips to it. Since Qualcomm has a dominant position in the market of baseband chips and the Chinese licensees highly relied on its baseband chip products, Qualcomm imposed unreasonable conditions on the sales of baseband chip and forced Chinese licensees to accept unfair or unreasonable patent licensing terms.

Qualcomm's above conducts have eliminated or restricted the market competition, impeded and restrained the technology innovation and development, harmed the interest of consumers, and violated the provisions under the AML in relation to the prohibition on the business operators with a dominant market position from charging unfairly high prices in the sales of products, bundling sales of products without justifications and imposing unreasonable trading conditions.

In the process of the anti-monopoly investigation, Qualcomm was cooperative and voluntarily proposed a package of rectification commitments in respect of Qualcomm's certain SEPs in relation to the wireless communication, which include: (1) to charge royalties at the rate of 65% of the net wholesale price of the cell phones sold for being used within China; (2) to provide patent lists when granting license to Chinese licensees and not to charge licensing fees for expired patents; (3) not to request a free cross-license from Chinese licensees; (4) not to bundle the non-SEPs when licensing the SEPs in relation to the wireless communication without justifications; and (5) not to request Chinese licensees to enter into a patent-license agreement including unreasonable conditions when selling baseband chips, and not to condition the supply of baseband chips to Chinese licensees on no challenging such patent-license agreement. The rectification commitments proposed by Qualcomm meet the requirements of NDRC. Qualcomm also indicated that it will continue to increase the investment and pursue a better development in China. NDRC welcomes Qualcomm's continued investment in China and supports Qualcomm in also indicated that it will continue to increase the investment and pursue a better development in China. NDRC welcomes Qualcomm's continued investment in China and supports Qualcomm in charging reasonable royalties for the use of its patented technologies.

Since Qualcomm's monopolistic conducts in the abuse of market dominance were severe in nature, implemented in a deep degree and persisted for a long time, NDRC, while ordering Qualcomm to cease its illegal activities, also imposed a fine on Qualcomm equaling to 8% of its sales in China in 2013. This instance of anti-monopoly law enforcement deters Qualcomm's monopolistic conducts, maintains the fair competition of the market and protects the interest of consumers.

Notes and Questions

1. Does the Chinese enforcement appear to be reasonable? Unreasonable? "Normal" antitrust? Discriminatory antitrust?

2. In the course of the investigation, here is what the Global Competition Review reported (in an article by Ron Knox, A red wave rising, Oct. 14, 2014) about the US perception of the Chinese investigation:

> "Midway through her speech dedicated to issues in the US, [Federal Trade Commission Chairwoman Edith] Ramirez shifted her focus to a recent spate of Chinese antitrust cases. She broached recent media reports that suggested Chinese enforcers were targeting standard-essential patent holders over competition concerns—a topic familiar to Ramirez and other enforcers in the US, Europe and elsewhere. But rather than attacking patent owners for their apparent abuses,

Ramirez said, it appeared for the all the world that the Chinese investigations were fueled instead by unhappiness with the prices charged to Chinese tech companies for access to those patents.

'I am seriously concerned by these reports, which suggest an enforcement policy focused on reducing royalty payments for local implementers as a matter of industrial policy, rather than protecting competition and long-run consumer welfare,' Ramirez told the crowd. The cutlery quietened.

Ramirez's statements—the harshest yet by one of China's international antitrust counterparts—mirror widespread Western backlash against a host of new Chinese competition cases that appear to be aimed squarely at foreign companies and the prices they charge Chinese businesses."

3. Meanwhile, challenges to practices of Qualcomm have been made by agencies around the world, including by the US FTC in early January 2017. The US FTC complaint alleges that Qualcomm maintains a monopoly by a no-license, no chips policy, by refusing to license standard essential patents, and by extracting chip exclusivity from Apple in exchange for lower royalties. Commissioner Maureen Ohlhausen dissented to the filing of the complaint. She asserts that the FTC complaint fundamentally attacks unreasonably high royalties on FRAND-encumbered patents. https://www.ftc.gov/news-events/press-releases/2017/01/ftc-charges-qualcomm-monopolizing-key-semi conductor-device-used. The debate on the IP/antitrust interface, including how much deference to give intellectual property, and when and how much antitrust intervention is appropriate continues to rage across countries and even within jurisdictions.

4. On November 8, 2024, the State Administration for Market Regulation ("SAMR") issued the Anti-Monopoly Guidelines for Standard-Essential Patents. These Guidelines impose a range of obligations and restrictions on standard-setting participants. Article 6 imposes information disclosure obligations on participants in standard-setting activities. Article 7 require standard-setting participants to accede to FRAND obligations when licensing SEPs and to ensure any future transferee of the SEP agrees to be bound by the FRAND obligation. Article 8 imposes an obligation on SEP holders and SEP implementers to negotiate in good faith in licensing negotiations. In particular, SEP holders are required to a list of SEPs, claim charts showing the relationship between the SEPs and the standard at issue, the calculation method and the basis for the royalty rate, and a reasonable time to respond. These requirements can be seen as a response to Qualcomm's conduct in the NDRC investigation. The NDRC was reportedly dissatisfied by the fact that Qualcomm had not even provided the putative licensees with a list of SEPs, let alone any claim charts

explaining how the patents implicate the standard. Regarding the legality of patent pools, Article 10 highlights the following factors in assessing the legality of patent pools: (1) whether there is exchange of commercially sensitive information; (2) whether the pool contains substitute patents; and (3) whether the pool requires exclusive licensing. The Guidelines also contain provisions regulating the imposition of unfairly high royalty rates, unilateral refusal to license, exclusive grant-backs, compulsory royalty-free grant-backs, package licenses, discriminatory licensing obligations, and no-challenge clauses, many of which featured prominently in the Qualcomm decision.

C. EXPLOITATIVE OFFENSES

1. Excessive Pricing

A quintessential economic evil of monopoly is output limitation, which causes a distortion in the flow of scarce resources. Fewer resources flow to the monopolized market than would be the case if the market were competitive. The corollary to limiting output is raising prices; higher prices means lower output. Excessive pricing would, then, seem to be an essential evil that competition law could address. But matters are complex. Antitrust is normally intended to free up the market; to remove obstructions to meritorious competition, not to control the market. Price is the central nervous system of the competition process, which is built upon freedom of pricing, up and down. Moreover, the antitrust authority is not a price regulator, at least not normally; it does not normally have functions—and corresponding powers—to decide when price is too high, much less to decide the right price level; nor regulatory powers of supervising the prices of a high-price offender.

These cautionary factors have led the United States to reject an excessive pricing violation under US antitrust law. In its 2004 decision in Verizon v. Trinko, 540 U.S. 398 (2004), the US Supreme Court even had good words to say about monopoly pricing. Thus:

> The mere possession of monopoly power, and the concomitant charging of monopoly prices, is not only not unlawful; it is an important element of the free-market system. The opportunity to charge monopoly prices—at least for a short period—is what attracts "business acumen" in the first place; it induces risk taking that produces innovation and economic growth. To safeguard the incentive to innovate, the possession of monopoly power will not be found unlawful unless it is accompanied by an element of anticompetitive conduct.

Similarly, in Pacific Bell Tel. Co. v. LinkLine Commun., Inc., 555 U.S. 438 (2009), the Supreme Court strongly reaffirmed that even monopolists "are free to choose the parties with whom they will deal, as well as the prices, terms, and conditions of that dealing." It said that "antitrust law does not forbid lawfully obtained monopolies from charging monopoly prices." In both *LinkLine* and *Trinko*, the Supreme Court justified this refusal to police monopoly prices on institutional grounds. The Court stated that "[c]ourts are ill suited 'to act as central planners, identifying the proper price, quantity, and other terms of dealing.' " Courts should thus refuse to "assume the day-to-day controls characteristic of a regulatory agency," which they could not do without "examining costs and demands" on the monopolist.

The antitrust laws of a number of other jurisdictions prohibit excessive pricing. Especially in nations with a statist background where the economy was marked by powerful state-owned firms, it seemed natural for the competition law to proscribe excessive pricing. The European Union competition law expressly prohibits dominant firms from "imposing unfair purchase or selling prices or other unfair trading conditionlinks." TFEU Article 102 (a). Numerous jurisdictions have copied this provision of the EU law, whether for efficiency or fairness.

Even in the United States the issue resurfaces from time to time, as we see rogue traders finding profit opportunities to raise the price of life-saving drugs hundreds of percentage points, as did Martin Shkreli, who bought up pharma firms in order to raise the price of drugs. The Federal Trade Commission, apparently urged on by Congress and public outrage, announced it was examining the matter, but no action resulted. Two years later, ironically following through on a complaint by Shkreli, the FTC sued and settled with Mallinckrodt for buying and shutting down its only potential competitor, creating a monopoly and enabling the monopolist to increase the price of a drug used to treat infant spasms by 85,000%. http://nypost.com/2017/01/18/complaint-from-martin-shkreli-leads-to-ftc-drug-price-suit/ Proposed Stipulated Order for Permanent Injunction and Equitable Monetary Relief, FTC v. Mallinckrodt ARD Inc. and Mallinckrodt plc, No. 1:17–cv–00120 (D.D.C. Jan. 18, 2017). But the Mallinckrodt episode was not a "mere" extraordinary price rise. It was an acquisition with accompanying conduct to shut down the only competing drug.

In some parts of the world, "mere" extraordinary price hikes of essential drugs have been met with antitrust prohibition, although rarely so. The UK Competition Marketing Authority fined Pfizer and its distributor nearly 90 million pounds for a price hike of 2400%

immediately after the drug was de-branded (genericized) and thus freed from price regulation. The National Health Service was a main buyer of the drug. https://www.gov.uk/government/news/cma-fines-pfizer-and-flynn-90-million-for-drug-price-hike-to-nhs.

Litigation of excessive pricing charges is, however, usually a complex endeavor. In the remainder of this section we discuss the leading EU case, which is now of older vintage, and more recent South African cases. South Africa has been especially plagued by extraordinarily high prices. In the early days of its modern competition law the Competition Commission successfully challenged GlaxoSmithKline and Boehringer Ingelheim for over-pricing an HIV/AIDS cocktail at the height of the AIDS epidemic in South Africa. When the Commission insisted on examining the companies' books, the companies settled, agreeing to license a generic manufacturer. See note on *Hazel Tau* by South Africa on Generic Pharmaceuticals submitted to the OECD 18–19 June 2014, DAF/COMP/WD(2014)68 at 2.1.

In jurisdictions that prohibit excessive pricing, the agencies and courts tend to exercise their powers with caution so as not to interfere with the normal give and take of the market. The challenge is to adopt standards that will allow the authority or court to identify excessive prices with some confidence and to devise relief likely to be effective without excessive supervision.

In the context of a Latvian collecting society's licenses for public performance of musical works, a Latvian national court asked the Court of Justice how to determine when a price is excessive under EU law. The Court answered that there is no single method of deciding; that the Competition Council may make the determination by reference to a sufficiently representative sample of other national markets, and that the price difference must be significant and appreciable. Latvian collection society, Case C–177/16, EU:C:2017:286.

In the first leading EU case on excessive pricing—Case 27/76, United Brands Co. v. Commission, EU:C:1978:22, the European Court of Justice reversed a finding of the European Commission that United Brands—the purveyor of the Chiquita banana brand—engaged in excessive pricing of bananas in certain EU member states. The evidence showed that United Brands made its European sales to distributors free on rail at Rotterdam or Bremerhaven and that it charged vastly different prices based on the degree of Chiquita brand recognition in each distributor's country. For example, the price charged to the distributor for Ireland—where the brand was not well known—was half of the price charged to the distributor for Denmark—where the brand was well known.

The Court first found that United Brands' pricing practices amounted to unlawful price discrimination; that they were "obstacles to the free movement of goods" within the European Union and that they distorted competition by placing certain distributors at a great competitive advantage over others. The Court then turned to the unfair pricing claim.

> The questions . . . to be determined are whether the difference between the costs actually incurred and the price actually charged is excessive, and, if the answer to this question is in the affirmative, whether a price has been imposed which is either unfair in itself or when compared to competing products.
>
> Other ways may be devised—and economic theorists have not failed to think up several—of selecting the rules for determining whether the price of a product is unfair.
>
> The Commission bases its view that prices are excessive on an analysis of the differences—in its view excessive—between the prices charged in different Member States and on the policy of discriminatory prices which has been considered above.
>
> The foundation of its argument has been the applicant's letter of 10 December 1974 which acknowledged that the margin allowed by the sale of bananas to the Irish ripeners was much smaller than in some other Member States and it concluded from this that the amount by which the actual prices f.o.r. Bremerhaven and Rotterdam exceed the delivered Rotterdam prices for bananas to be sold to Irish customers c.i.f. Dublin must represent a profit of the same order of magnitude.
>
> Having found that the prices charged to ripeners of the other Member States were considerably higher, sometimes by as much as 100%, than the prices charged to customers in Ireland it concluded that UBC was making a very substantial profit.
>
> Nevertheless the Commission has not taken into account in its reasoning . . . a confidential document . . . pointing out that the prices charged in Ireland had produced a loss.

> The applicant also states that the prices charged on the relevant market did not allow it to make any profits during the last five years, except in 1975. * * *
>
> However unreliable the particulars supplied by UBC may be (and in particular the document mentioned previously which works out the "losses" on the Irish market in 1974 without supporting evidence), the fact remains that it was for the Commission to prove that the applicant charged unfair prices.
>
> UBC's retraction, which the Commission has not effectively refuted, establishes beyond doubt that the basis for the calculation adopted by the latter to prove that UBC's prices are excessive is open to criticism and on this point in particular there is doubt which must benefit the applicant, especially as for nearly 20 years banana prices, in real terms, have not risen on the relevant market. * * *
>
> In these circumstances it appears that the Commission has not adduced adequate legal proof of the facts and evaluations which formed the foundation of its findings that UBC had infringed Article [102] of the Treaty by directly and indirectly imposing unfair selling prices for bananas.

Many competition law statutes contain prohibitions on excessive pricing, but relatively few competition authorities and courts have put these prohibitions to a serious test. One place where that has clearly happened is South Africa. Tracking the language of *United Brands*, the South African Competition Act of 1998 defined excessive pricing as a price that "bears not reasonable relation to the economic value of that good or service" and is higher than reasonable value. Implementing that standard has led to a series of complex and informative interactions between the Competition Tribunal, Competition Appeal Court, and Parliament.

In a landmark 2007 decision, Harmony Gold Mining Company Ltd. v. Mittal Steel Corp., Case No. 13/CR/Feb-04 (2007), the Competition Tribunal of South Africa found that Mittal Steel, the dominant producer of flat steel products in South Africa, had engage in unlawful excessive pricing. The Tribunal found that Mittal "set its base price for flat steel products in the domestic market by calculating the notional cost of importing those products" and then adding a "5% hassle factor, essentially a reflection of the additional costs or 'hassle' entailed in importing over the advantage of utilizing a domestic supplier." The Tribunal found that Mittal was "structurally super-dominant" and had engaged in "ancillary conduct aimed at maintaining the segmentation of differently price markets," such as "prohibiting its dealers for export from re-selling into the South African market." The Tribunal also found that there was an easily administrable remedy for the excessive pricing—enjoining enforcement of clauses that limited certain buyers to purchasing only for export. Absent these clauses, arbitrage back into the South African market would be possible, and the excessive pricing scheme disrupted.

On appeal, the Competition Appeal Court of South Africa quashed the Tribunal's decision. Case No. 70/CAC/Apr 07 (2009). It held that the evidence, as pleaded, "raised a prima facie presumption" of a contravention of the excessive pricing prohibition, but that the Tribunal's analysis did not support the conclusion that Mittal's prices had actually been objectively excessive. The court suggested that "there may be no alternative to a detailed exercise in comparative costing," including consideration of "the relevant opportunity costs of capital," in order to make a sufficient determination.

The Competition Tribunal returned to excessive pricing in Commission v. Sasol Chemical Indus. Ltd. (Case No. 131/CAC/Jun 14), where it attempted to apply the holding of *Mittal Steel* to the feedstock propylene industry. It calculated a competitive market baseline through some very complicated cost accounting, and again found liability. Again, the Competition Appeal Court reversed, disputing the Tribunal's cost computations and finding that mark-ups between 12% and 14% were not excessive.

Frustrated with the Tribunal's inability to win excessive pricing cases, the South African Parliament implemented significant revisions to the competition act's abuse of dominance provisions in 2018–19. The 2018–19 amendments deleted the 1998 definition of excessive pricing and provided a new set of criteria in Section 8(3):

Any person determining whether a price is an excessive price must determine if that price is higher than a competitive price and whether such difference is unreasonable, determined by taking into account all relevant factors, which may include—

(a) the respondent's price-cost margin, internal rate of return, return on capital invested or profit history;

(b) the respondent's prices for the goods or services—(i) in markets in which there are competing products; (ii) to customers in other geographic markets; (iii) for similar products in other markets; and (iv) historically; Competition Commission South Africa 33

(c) relevant comparator firm's prices and level of profits for the goods or services in a competitive market for those goods or services;

(d) the length of time the prices have been charged at that level;

(e) the structural characteristics of the relevant market, including the extent of the respondent's market share, the degree of contestability of the market, barriers to entry and past or current advantage that is not due to the respondent's own commercial efficiency or investment, such as direct or indirect state support for a firm or firms in the market; and

(f) any regulations made by the Minister, in terms of section 78 regarding the calculation and determination of an excessive price.

Significantly, the new statute also provides that "[i]f there is a prima facie case of abuse of dominance because the dominant firm charged an excessive price, the dominant firm must show that the price was reasonable."

Following this legislative intervention, the Tribunal returned to excessive pricing in the context of the COVID-19 pandemic in the matter of *Babelegi Workwear and Indus. Supplies CC* (No. 2020–06–01). The Tribunal found that Babelegi had engaged in excessive pricing with respect to COVID masks. After finding Babelegi dominant within the meaning of South Africa's competition statute, the Tribunal turned to the evidence of excessive pricing:

94 As indicated, the construction of section 8(3) demands as a first step the determination of whether the price charged by the firm in question is higher than a 'competitive price'.

95 As we have stressed throughout these reasons, one must have regard to the proper context including the economic conditions when assessing pricing conduct. As we have also noted, in the present case it is common cause that the increase or surge experienced in the demand for face masks is directly related to Covid-19; Babelegi offers no other explanation for the sudden increase in the demand for dust masks. Furthermore, it is common cause that Babelegi's pricing conduct takes place in a crisis period. FTI confirms this: "*The surge period is an* <u>*abnormal period*</u> *where demand was driven by panic buying.*"

* * *

99 We find that in the context of disrupted competitive conditions such as the Covid-19 health crisis, the relevant economic test for determining whether or not a firm's price charged is excessive, is a relatively simple yet instructive economic test. In such a scenario one

can determine whether the firm's price or markup or margin increased materially relative to what was previously charged or applied, and if so, whether that increase is justified by any cost increases from a supplier further up the value chain. Motta very succinctly explains what evidence can be used in a crisis situation to determine what the competitive price to be used in the assessment is: "*[u]sing the pre-crisis price as a benchmark is sensible because demand and supply conditions at that time were presumably "normal"* (emphasis added)." We agree that this is a sensible approach in the current context.

* * *

101 As indicated above, the basic test of "*whether the price charged is higher than a competitive price*" is whether the price exceeds what the firm would have obtained in the counterfactual world of normal and sufficiently effective competition. There is no reason in this case not to accept that Babelegi's pre-crisis price (and associated mark-up) i.e. its price (and mark-up) for masks in December 2019, are sensible and appropriate benchmarks for the competitive price (and mark-up) since that price (and mark-up) were determined under normal competitive conditions, as Motta puts it "*demand and supply conditions at that time were presumably 'normal'* ". Babelegi adduces no evidence that normal competitive conditions in relation to the sale of masks did not prevail in December 2019, when its admitted markup on masks was approximately 23% . . . . This approach is also consistent with section 8(3)(b)(iv) of the Act that states that the respondent's prices for the goods or services historically is a relevant factor to consider.

102 The approach taken by many USA States to price gouging also gives a reference to how and what evidence can be used to assess potential excessive pricing abuses in circumstances such as a crisis. An OECD document confirms that in a period of crisis or disaster the comparative or "normal" price for the product may be determined by having regard to the prices charged for the product in the period before the crisis or disaster. The OECD 2011 Excessive Pricing: Policy Roundtables[80] report records the approach of various States of the USA[81] to the economic test for price gouging as "*The basic methodology employed is based on a comparison of a (fictitious) "normal" price with the potentially excessive price in periods of abnormal supply disruptions. In determining the "normal" supply price a variety of definitions are used. While some US States do not define the normal price at all, others use the average price over a specified period or the price immediately prior to the supply disruption or the emergency declaration.*"

* * *

105 Whilst FTI contends that making assessments of market power and excess profits based on costs and margins is complex and requires interrogating replacement cost for assets and other economic costs,[83] this ignores the current context and the simple yet instructive economic test that can be utilised to assess conduct in a crisis period such as Covid-19. There is no evidence that Babelegi's actual supplier costs have changed during the Complaint Period (discussed below) or that the period preceding the Complaint Period would not be an appropriate benchmark for the competitive price and markup . . .

[The Tribunal went on to review the evidence that Babelegi's prices had increased dramatically—by 888%—from December 9, 2019 (when the COVID-19 pandemic was just beginning) to March 5, 2020. Then, drawing on the new burden-shifting provision, the Tribunal found liability:]

141 We conclude that Babelegi has not put up a rational and valid explanation for its successive and massive price increases during the Complaint Period since these price increases are not substantiated by any corresponding increase in cost. Although Babelegi alleges that a supplier signalled prices potentially doubling in February 2020, this does not explain the behaviour of Babelegi to increase prices during the Complaint Period successively and at levels multiple fold higher than double.

Notes and Questions

1. Babelegi was a "mom and pop" store that would not have qualified as dominant under ordinary competition law principles applicable to excessive pricing. Still, the social, political, and economic circumstances surrounding the COVID-19 pandemic set the stage for a nonconventional approach to excessive pricing. Although the Competition Tribunal's intervention was unlikely to result in lower prices for protective masks in time to make a significant difference while demand for the masks remained high, it felt that it could not sit by and allow the precipitous price increases to go unchallenged during the pandemic.

2. The *Babelegi* decision found excessive pricing based on the exogenous shock of the COVID-19 pandemic. A dramatic difference between "before and after" prices, with no cost explanation, was relatively straightforward to demonstrate. In light of South Africa's experience with excessive pricing cases, does this suggest that excessive pricing offenses will be easiest to demonstrate in circumstances similar to the "gauging" cases invoked by the Tribunal—circumstances where some natural disaster or other exogenous shock results in suddenly

increased demand for the relevant product, and prices skyrocket without some reasonable cost justification?

3. In China, competition authorities have questioned the excessiveness of royalties charged by owners of essential or highly important patents. Qualcomm makes important technology used in mobile devices including smartphones. Most of the devices are manufactured in China; they are also manufactured in Korea, the US and elsewhere. The Chinese competition authority NDRC accused Qualcomm of charging royalties that were unreasonably high, charging royalties based on a percentage of the whole end product rather than only the part licensed, charging royalties on expired patents, and requiring licensees to grant-back their improvements in technology free to Qualcomm. After a long investigation, Qualcomm agreed to pay an unprecedented fine (nearly $1 billion), to charge royalties based on no more than 65% of the end product, and to pay for grant-backs. See part 1(d) above. Was this essentially an excessive pricing violation?

4. An excessive pricing violation is usually, as you see, a complicated one. Yet excessive pricing is often perceived as one of the serious social ills emanating from great market power; one that reflects raw exploitation and widening inequality. Are antitrust institutions competent to challenge pricing as excessive? Should they do so only in egregious cases? What is egregious?

2. Discriminatory Pricing: Exploitative, Exclusionary, and Unfair

Price discrimination is a complex subject, in part because price discrimination may evidence price competition itself (thus, it may be good for competition and efficiency); in other circumstances it may impair competition and efficiency (and economists debate when, whether and to what extent this is so); and in some circumstances, whether efficient or not, price discrimination is perceived as unfair and legislatures may prescribe it.

Price discrimination is by definition compromised of two prongs: a low price to favored customers and a high price to disfavored customers. The high price might under some circumstances be regarded as excessive. Even jurisdictions, such as the US, that do not recognize an excessive pricing antitrust offense do recognize a discriminatory pricing offense. In the US, the Robinson-Patman Act prohibits price discrimination in commodities where the effect of such discrimination is "substantially to lessen competition or tend to create a monopoly or to injure, destroy, or prevent competition with any person who either grants or knowingly receives" the discriminatory price. The Robinson-Patman Act has been widely criticized as protecting small, less efficient competitors from beneficial competition and, in recent years, the Supreme Court has read the statute essentially to require a showing that the discriminatory price harmed competition at either the level of the firm giving the discriminatory price (primary line) or at the level of the firm receiving the discount (secondary line). *See,* e.g., Volvo Trucks v. Reeder-Simco, 546 U.S. 164 (2006) (observing, in secondary line price discrimination case, that the Robinson-Patman Act should be read consistently with the broader policies of the antitrust laws and that the Court "would resist interpretation geared more to the protection of existing *competitors* than to the stimulation of *competition*").

The European Union Treaty, in Article 102, prohibits dominant firms from imposing certain discriminatory terms "placing other trading parties at a competitive disadvantage." The European Union, as a common market intent on market integration, is especially concerned with acts that disfavor actors or goods from other Member States. Thus, United Brands could not lawfully charge its ripener/distributors varying prices for its unripened bananas depending on the Member State to which the bananas were destined. Case 27/76, United Brands Co. v. Commission, EU:C:1978:22. Recall, however, the earlier discussion that in *Post Danmark I,* the Court of Justice concluded that selective price cuts to a competitor's key customers to a price between the dominant firm's ATC and AIC does infringe Article 102. The Court reiterated that price discrimination on its own does not constitute an exclusionary abuse and noted that the Danish authority could not provide evidence that the defendant had deliberately sought to drive out its competitor.

Certain other jurisdictions may prohibit dominant firms from imposing discriminatory prices or terms where by some measure the terms are perceived as unfair. In some cases the competition statute itself may suggest an "unfairness" violation. In India, for example, the Competition Act (2002) says:

> Abuse of Dominant Position: (2) There shall be an abuse of dominant position . . . if an enterprise or group (a) directly or indirectly, imposes unfair or discriminatory (i) condition in purchase or sale of good or services or (ii) price in purchase or sale (including predatory price) of goods or service.

On its face, the Act contains no requirement of competitive injury. The Indian CCI has applied the act to remedy allegedly unfair bargaining by a real estate firm of questionable dominance. The CCI fined DLF Limited INR 630 crore (US $99.2 million) for abusing its dominant position by entering into one-sided agreements and imposing arbitrary, unfair and unreasonable conditions on home buyers. The targeted conditions included DLF's right to make unilateral changes in an apartment buyers' agreement without any corresponding right for the buyers, its right unilaterally to change apartment plans, and arbitrary forfeitures by apartment buyers in certain situations. https://www.cci.gov.in/images/antitrustorder/en/6720101652503709.pdf, reversed for redetermination of the market.

The South African law may have a special claim to a market value of fairness. South Africa adopted its competition act at the end of the troubled era of apartheid and, as noted in Chapter 1, South African competition law is meant to dismantle the unequal power structures left in place from the apartheid era. But, as the Competition Tribunal discovered, it is one thing to oppose price discrimination in principle, and quite another to implement that prohibition given complex market facts.

In 2003, the Tribunal entertained a price discrimination case brought by a small producer of poles for grape vines against his supplier of creosote, Sasol, alleging that the supplier had charged significantly higher prices than it had charged to four or five of his competitors. The statutory prohibition on price discrimination in place at that time required a showing that the challenged pricing substantially prevented or lessened competition. Sasol was a dominant previously state-owned firm, and it conceded that there was no cost justification for the lower prices it offered to the complainant's competitors. The complainant appeared pro se and offered no evidence of a general lessening of competition, but nonetheless believed that a pricing structure that disadvantaged him versus other pole producers violated the statute.

On these facts, the Tribunal found a violation of the statute. Recognizing that "some contemporary anti-trust scholars are highly skeptical of the negative impact of price discrimination on competition," the Tribunal observed that price discrimination prohibitions were not solely based on consumer welfare considerations, but also fairness: "There mere fact that equity considerations sit uncomfortably in competition economics orthodoxy is no warrant for ignoring our legislature's express desire that they play a role in our decision." The Tribunal found for the complainant. In re Matter Between Nationwide Poles and Sasol (Oil) PTY Ltd., 72/CR/Dec 03.

Once again, the Competition Appeal Court disagreed, finding that the evidence showed no harm to competition. That Nationwide Poles may have sustained a competitive disadvantage was not sufficient to sustain a violation of the act, since "competition law does not protect the competitor, it protects competition." 49CACApril 05.

As occurred with respect to excessive pricing, the Tribunal's enforcement efforts against price discrimination received a boost in the 2018–19 amendments to the Competition Act. The new provisions make price discrimination unlawful when a discriminatory price substantially lessens competition ***or*** "*impede[s] the ability of small and medium businesses and firms controlled or owned by historically disadvantaged persons to participate effectively.*" Under the second provision, there is no need for a complainant to show any anti-competitive or consumer harm. This appears to reverse the holding in *Nationwide Poles*.

In Competition Commission of South Africa v. Mediclinic Southern Africa (Pty) Ltd., 2022 SA (4) 232, the South African Constitutional Court held that application of the Competition Act must align with the South African Bill of Rights and that the Competition Tribunal must consider socio-economic facts, such as historical inequities, in determining the application of the Competition Act. The court observed that "South Africa is at present the land of gross economic inequalities. Its wealth or economic ownership and control is concentrated in the hands of a few." Although the predicted effects of the merger might be a comparatively low increase in prices, even a small price increase could significantly harm traditionally disadvantaged persons already facing "ever-escalating costs in the private health care services sector." In this context, there was a "constitutional imperative" for the Tribunal to protect the interests of disadvantaged health care patients. Although the particular context of that case was merger review, are there also implications for price discrimination?

D. ABUSE OF A SUPERIOR BARGAINING POSITION/RELATIONAL POWER

1. Introduction

Regulation of unilateral conduct in some jurisdictions in Asia and Europe goes beyond the traditional law on monopolization and abuse of dominance. In these jurisdictions, it is possible for unilateral conduct by firms which hold a less than dominant position in the relevant market to fall afoul of the law. Instead of monopoly power or dominance, what is required is relational power over the transactional counterparty in a long-term contractual relationship. In Japan and Korea this is referred to as a superior bargaining position. In a few EU Member States such as Germany, France, Italy, and Belgium, this is referred to as economic dependence. China is reportedly considering adopting similar provisions in its Anti-Unfair Competition Law, partly motivated by patent licensing issues and partly by digital economy issues.

Abuse of superior bargaining power or economic dependence has gained increasing salience in recent years in the digital economy. There is considerable dissatisfaction with how platform operators such as Apple, Google, and Amazon treat their contractual counterparties. Much of their conduct probably lies in the realm of abuse of buyer power, which traditionally has not been a major concern in the abuse of dominance jurisprudence. Moreover, these platform do not always possesses a dominant position, which renders the abuse provisions powerless in policing against their conduct. There have thus been calls to adopt and apply abuse of superior bargaining position provisions against them.

An example of how regulation of abuse of superior bargaining position and the digital economy have become increasingly intertwined is the Protocol to the Agreement Establishing the African Continental Free Trade Area on Competition Policy. Article 5(d) of Protocol singles out abuse of economic dependence as an anticompetitive practice. Under Article 11, an undertaking or a gatekeeper is prohibited from abusing "the relative position of economic dependence over a customer or supplier if the conduct substantially affects the functioning and structure of competition in the Market." In the same article the Protocol proceeds to impose DMA-style ex ante conduct regulation on gatekeepers such as a prohibition of self-preferencing and a prohibition of price parity clauses.

Regulation of abuses of relational power is not without controversy. Proponents of such regulation argue that it fills an important enforcement gap. While the consumer harm in some of the reported abuses in Japan and Korea may not always be apparent, few would dispute that the conduct concerned is unfair and exploitative and should require some form of legal redress. Opponents of such regulation believe that it amounts to regulatory overreach and undermines commercial freedom. These views are exemplified in the submissions by respondents that had eschewed ASBP provisions. Belgium thought that adoption of ASBP could create confusion with unilateral conduct laws, although, ironically, it eventually adopted such provisions in 2020. The UK and the US feared that such provisions could undermine efficient bargaining between contracting parties. "[C]ontracts between parties at different level of the manufacturing-distribution chain are likely to reflect an efficient allocation of risks and duties among the parties." Singapore pointed out that its competition law is concerned only with exclusionary and not exploitative offenses, as is the case in the United States also.

Even if it is decided that regulation is necessary, there is the question of the appropriate regulatory instrument, i.e., whether redress should be provided by competition law or related legislation. The reservation expressed by the Singaporean and United States authorities perhaps explains the choice of legal instrument in France. In Japan and Korea, perhaps the two jurisdictions best known for enforcement in this area of law, abuse of superior bargaining position falls under the rubric of unfair trade practices regulated in their respective competition legislation, the Japanese Anti-monopoly Act ("AMA") and the Korean Monopoly Regulation and Fair Trade Act ("MRFTA").

There is also the related concern that the enforcement authority may seek the easy way out with relational power regulation to avoid the often-arduous task of proving dominance or monopoly power. Some Korean scholars have in fact raised this concern with respect to the Korea Fair Trade Commission ("KFTC"), which brought five times as many abuse of superior bargaining position cases as abuse of dominance cases in 2021.

The reservation about relational power regulation may account for the disparate enforcement record in different jurisdictions. While some jurisdictions such as Germany have been relatively hesitant to pursue economic dependence cases, other jurisdictions such as Korea have applied their abuse of superior bargaining position provisions with fervor. Twelve percent of all the cases resolved by the KFTC in 2021 concerned abuse of superior bargaining position.

2. Abuse of Superior Bargaining Position Regulation in Japan

Article 2(5) of the AMA prohibits abuse of superior bargaining position. In 2010, the Japan Fair Trade Commission ("JFTC") issued a set of guidelines, Guidelines Concerning Abuse of Superior Bargaining Position under the Antimonopoly Act, on the application of Article 2(5). The Guidelines state that a violation requires a superior bargaining position and an abuse, which is understood to be a business practice conducted "unjustly in light of normal business practices."

Market power is not prerequisite for a finding of superior bargaining position, which is regarded as a sort of relational market power, as opposed to general market power, vis-à-vis a specific trading partner. The defendant in some of the JFTC decisions cannot be said to possess market power, at least not to the extent that it would trigger the private monopolization provisions of the AMA. It follows that market definition is not a required step in the assessment of a superior bargaining position. According to the JFTC Guidelines, a superior bargaining position exists '(i) where the supplier needs to continue transactions with the retailer, as discontinuing the transaction substantially impedes the supplier's business and (ii) thus, the supplier finds it difficult to reject the retailer's request, although it causes substantial disadvantage to the supplier'. Factors such as the supplier's degree of dependence on the commercial relationship with the retailer at issue, the retailer's position in the market, the possibility for the supplier to replace the trading partner, and other facts indicating the supplier's need to continue transactions with the retailer are considered in the JFTC's assessment. These factors are particularly relevant to the assessment of factor (i), although none of them is supposed to be necessary or sufficient. Interestingly, a retailer need not be larger than the supplier to hold a superior bargaining position. It is possible for the smaller contractual counterparty to be found to possess a superior bargaining position.

Just like in some older tying cases in the US such as *Northern Pacific*, the JFTC attaches significant weight to the supplier's acceptance of the retailer's disadvantageous request in its assessment of a superior bargaining position. The fact that a supplier has acceded to such a request indicates a high degree of importance of the trading relationship to the supplier and bolsters the case for a superior bargaining position. The assessment of a superior bargaining position and unfair or abusive conduct thus overlaps to some extent.

Conventional wisdom is that the supplier's acceptance of the retailer's disadvantageous request plus any concrete evidence indicating a need to trade on the supplier's part constitutes a superior bargaining position. The JFTC seems to consider the difficulty of replacing the retailer as a trading partner as a particularly relevant and perhaps even necessary factor. One obvious way to ascertain this difficulty or the degree of dependence on a retailer is to calculate the percentage of a supplier's sales that are made to a retailer. Despite the lack of a specified threshold, the JFTC is understood to deem 8 percent to 10 percent as sufficient to demonstrate the relevant degree of dependence.

The next question is what constitutes abusive conduct. Finding of an infringement requires a showing of 'unjustly in light of the normal business practices'. This phrase was inserted to refer to 'having the tendency to inhibit fair competition' (Article 2(9)6). The normality of a business practice is not solely an issue of prevalence in the industry in general. It entails a normative assessment in view of a fair competition system. Not every activity that is common in practice is regarded as a 'normal business practice'. A business practice such as requiring suppliers to dispatch employees to assist in the opening of new stores or refurbishment of old stores may be common, but that does not preclude a finding of 'unjust in light of the normal business practices'. In fact, prevalence of the conduct among a retailer's suppliers may count against the retailer. The fact that a particular business practice is widely employed by a retailer may render it more likely to be an enforcement target by the JFTC. In many cases brought by the JFTC the number of affected suppliers was substantial and the practice was imposed in a systematic manner over a long period of time.

The tendency to inhibit fair competition is demonstrated when the retailer imposes on the suppliers a disadvantage that is either unreasonably excessive or unforeseen by the suppliers. Unreasonable excessiveness or unforeseeability seems to be consistently applied in the JFTC Guidelines to determine whether certain conduct constitutes unjust practices. The application of these two concepts is context-specific and varies by the type of practice at issue.

Another relevant consideration is the extent of compulsion by the retailer. Evidence of voluntary compliance negates the finding of an abusive practice. The ascertainment of voluntariness of conduct can be a complex matter in the context of a supply relationship. The lack of option cannot be taken literally. The supplier can always say no and risk losing all of the retailer's business. The question is thus not whether the supplier can say no, but whether the supplier can remain viable without the retailer's business. This of course overlaps with the assessment of degree of dependence and the existence of a superior bargaining position. Therefore, the appearance of voluntariness in Ralse's request to its suppliers did not preclude a finding off compulsion by the JFTC.

Article 2(9)5 of the AMA specifically enumerates certain instances of abuse of superior bargaining position, including (i) forced purchase or use of product or service, (ii) forced contribution of expenses, (iii) forced dispatch of employees, and (iv) late payment, retrospective discounts, and return of goods.

In addition to the AMA, there are two other pieces of legislation that also regulate of abuse of superior bargaining position type behavior, the Subcontract Act and the Freelance Act. The Freelance Act applies mainly in the labor context and will not be discussed in detail here. The Subcontract Act can be applied to cases in which the retailer commissions the manufacture of the products that it sells, especially with respect to private-label products. The Subcontract Act goes beyond Article 2(9)5 by regulating companies that meet a certain size requirement. It obviates the need to demonstrate a superior bargaining position. In relation to a manufacturing subcontract, the act is applicable when the retailer, whose capital exceeds JPY300 million, commissions the manufacture of goods from a company whose capital does not exceed JPY300 million, or when the retailer, whose capital is between JPY10 million and JPY300 million, commissions the manufacture of goods from a manufacturer whose capital does not exceed JPY10 million.

The Subcontract Act prohibits the following practices: refusal to take the commissioned products, late payment, retrospective discounts, return of goods, setting the price substantially lower than that of the equivalent product or the market price, forced purchase or usage, and compelling the subcontractor to provide it with economic benefits such as contribution fee and dispatch of employees (Articles 4(1) and (2)). It stipulates that the commissioning party must pay for the goods within 60 days of receipt. It must also deliver to the subcontractor a document prescribing the details of the transaction upon the conclusion of the contract, keep transaction records for two years, and in case of a delay in payment, pay interest at a rate of 14.6%. A substantial number of the cases under this Act have involved retrospective discounts and contribution fees.

The JFTC has stepped up enforcement in abuse of superior bargaining position in recent years. The JFTC tends to settle its investigations with commitments from the party or issue cease and desist orders. Fines, which are known as surcharges in Japan, are relatively rare in abuse of superior bargaining position cases. The JFTC has historically tended to rely on cease and desist orders.

The high-profile Amazon Japan case was settled by a commitment decision on September 10, 2020. According to the JFTC decision, Amazon Japan had abused its superior bargaining position by imposing certain conditions or demands on its third-party sellers, including demanding reduction in sales price without a valid reason and returning excess goods to the suppliers without justifications. The only reason allegedly given by Amazon Japan for demanding a price reduction was to increase its profitability. Amazon Japan offered to withdraw the abovementioned demands and to pay ¥2 billion to 1,400 suppliers. These commitments were accepted by the JFTC.

In another case against a dominant retailer, the JFTC ordered Seven-Eleven Japan, one of the largest convenient store operators in Japan, to cease interfering with its franchisees' decision to offer discounts on soon-to-expire products. Apparently, it was common for Seven-Eleven franchisee store owners to offer discounts on perishable products that are close to their expiry dates. Seven-Eleven Japan was unhappy with the decision and has asked its franchisees to stop the discounting. This was despite the fact that the franchisees alone bore the loss of discarded expired products. In its cease and desist order, the JFTC required Seven-Eleven Japan to desist from interfering with the pricing decisions of its franchisees.

In March 2, 2021, the Tokyo High Court issued its decision in an abuse of superior bargaining position case against Ralse, one of the largest supermarket operators in Hokkaido, the northernmost island of Japan. The JFTC had issued a cease and desist order and a surcharge payment order of ¥12.87 billion against Ralse. Ralse requested that the JFTC cancel the order, which the JFTC refused, upon which Ralse filed a lawsuit in the Tokyo High Court seeking an annulment of the decision. The Court found that Ralse held a superior bargaining position vis-à-vis its eighty-eight suppliers and had abused this position by, inter alia, (1) demanding suppliers to dispatch employees to assist with Ralse's operations, (2) requesting sponsorship funds, and (3) demanding suppliers to purchase products from Ralse.

The Court held that when one party with a dominant position in a transaction unfairly disadvantages the other party by using that position against normal business practices, hindering the other party's free and voluntary decision-making in the transaction and putting them at a competitive disadvantage, while potentially giving the actor an advantage in competition, such actions are regulated as unfair trading practices. Specifically, the Court held that requesting a dispatch of employees and sponsorship funds constitute an abuse if the burden exceeds the reasonable range and is an unforeseen disadvantage. Both conditions are met in the case. Requesting product purchases constitutes an abuse if the requested items are unnecessary for the supplier's business operations. The Tokyo High Court interpreted the requirement of "unjustly in light of the normal business practices" as being unreasonable from the perspective of maintaining and promoting fair competition.

3. Abuse of Superior Bargaining Position Regulation in Korea

Article 45 MRFTA regulates abuse of superior bargaining position and prohibits 'trading by unjustly using a superior bargaining position'. The MRFTA provides that a superior bargaining position is to be established in light of factors such as the 'ease of securing a substitute party for trade, level of income dependency in the relationship, control or supervision involved, and characteristics of goods or services traded'. Proscribed conduct includes forced purchase, forced provision of benefit, imposition of sales target, imposition of disadvantage, and interference with business management and operations. Imposition of disadvantage is defined as an '[a]ct of causing a disadvantage in the process of carrying out the trade, setting or changing the trading condition to the disadvantage of the counterpart using methods other than [. . .] forced purchase, forced provision of benefit, and imposed sales target.'

According to the Guidelines issued by the Korean Fair Trade Commission ("KFTC"), the rationale for the prohibition of abuse of superior bargaining position is that abuses may "hurt independent growth of other undertakings and harm fair trade." The KFTC emphasizes coercion or the lack of choice and ex post revision of contractual terms as the main bases for prohibition. The KFTC states that the prohibition 'does not apply to cases in which an undertaking, at the beginning stage of a trade, was able to choose its counterparty on its own and engaged in trade in full knowledge of the terms of the agreement, and the participating parties abide by the agreed terms'. The focus on the lack of choice is reinforced by the next sentence, which states that '[t]he Act applies to cases in which an undertaking, already engaged in trade, uses its superior position, established due to reasons such as lack of substitutes, to impose disadvantage to [sic] its counterparty'. The reference to 'already engaged in trade' implies an ongoing contractual relationship between the parties, which indicates a focus on ex post revision of contractual terms. This is an important distinction as abuses of bargaining power can occur at the time the initial contract is signed as well.

According to the KFTC Guidelines, ease of securing a substitute party for trade refers to 'whether or not it is possible to find another undertaking to trade with at a low transaction cost'. Proof of absolute impossibility is not required. Instead, it only needs to be shown that a replacement cannot be found without incurring high transaction costs. Not any replacement will do. A replacement will only be deemed to be adequate if it does not reduces trading volume or prevent the counterparty from recovering its investments. Just like the JFTC, the KFTC considers the fact that the counterparty had no choice but to accept the abusive conduct to be evidence for a superior bargaining position. The Guidelines proceed to enumerate a number of scenarios of likely superior bargaining position: 'large retailer and companies doing business with the retailer', 'manufacturer and parts supplier', and 'broadcasting company and broadcasting program supplier'. The Guidelines also refer to situations where significant relation-specific investment has been made as a likely scenario in which a superior bargaining position may arise.

The KFTC has consistently applied a multi-factored test to determine the existence of a superior bargaining position, emphasizing the importance of substitutability of the defendant's business to the plaintiff. In the Korea Land and Housing Corp. case, the KFTC states that '[w]hen establishing a superior bargaining position, it is sufficient to find that the subject is in a relatively superior position or that the subject can exert significant influence on the counterparty's business activities'. The KFTC proceeds to list these factors for consideration: the market in which the parties operate, the gap between the parties' business capacities and their scope of business activities, and the characteristics of the product or service.

Unlike the JFTC, the KFTC's decisional practice suggests that it pays much attention to the defendant's market power. The KFTC usually begins each decision with a very detailed analysis of the relevant market and tries to ascertain the defendant's market share and relative position in the market. The Korean Supreme Court, however, has noted that superiority of bargaining power refers to relative superiority in relation to one's trading partner, and not an absolute superiority in terms of market monopoly. This statement clearly draws a distinction between superior bargaining power and market power. The KFTC also stresses economic power concerns. For example, in the Lotte.com case, the KFTC emphasizes that the defendant was one of the 77 companies affiliated with the Lotte conglomerate. Also relevant is the fact that the counterparty relies on the defendant in multiple markets. The KFTC occasionally focuses on the difference in size between the two parties.

The Guidelines addresses various abuses. It is important to note that in all cases, the defendant can prove an efficiency-enhancing effect which appreciably exceeds its anticompetitive effect, or other reasonable justifications, to justify its conduct.

The first type of abuse, forced purchase, is defined as 'an undertaking forcing its trading counter[party] to purchase goods or services even though the counterparty has no intention of doing so'. Proof of coercion is required, which can be by way of the existence of penalty for failure to purchase and other objective facts suggesting that the counterparty was forced to make the purchase. The Guidelines explain that if the forced purchase was 'clearly predictable or if the purchase is specified in the contract from the beginning, such forced purchase shall not be considered unfair'. This seems to suggest that at least with respect to forced purchase; the abuse of superior bargaining position only applies to ex post contractual revisions, which substantially narrows its scope.

The second type is forced provision of benefit, which is defined as 'an undertaking forcing its trading counterparty to provide financial benefits, e.g. money, goods, and services'. The legality of forced provision of benefit is assessed similarly to that of forced purchases.

The third type, imposition of sales target, is defined as 'an undertaking [. . .] forcing its trading counterparty to meet a sales target'. The main consideration here is whether there is coercion involved in the imposition of the target. The Guidelines state that coercion could be found regardless of 'whether the target was excessive, whether the counterparty actually met the target, or whether penalty was actually used when the target was not met'. The existence of a penalty for failure to meet a target is conclusive evidence of coercion. In contrast, the existence of a financial reward such as a subsidy negates the existence of coercion.

The fourth type, imposition of disadvantages, is a catch-all category. The Guidelines identify two cases: (1) imposing disadvantage through setting or changing terms of trade, and (2) imposing disadvantage through execution of trade, 'by refusing to fulfill [sic] the terms of trade or forcing its counterparty to [. . .] execute certain practices in trade'. The assessment criteria for the imposition of disadvantage are the same as those for forced purchases, which means that the counterparty's expectation is one of the factors to be considered. Imposition of disadvantages seems to feature fairly prominently in the KFTC's decisional practice, including the Sony Pictures Buena Vista case, the Lotte.com case, and the LG Electronics case. Despite the variety of the practices involved within this category, a few recurrent themes arguments emerge, such as the fact that the conduct was against the will of the counterparty, and the fact that the conduct deviated from normal industry practice.

The last category is interference with business management and operations. The Guidelines define it as 'an undertaking interfering in the management and operations of its counterparty by imposing restriction on items manufactured, scale of facilities and equipment, quantity of manufacture, and terms of trade, or by giving orders or approval for appointment or dismissal of staff and executives'. Examples include a firm demanding the appointment or dismissal of a specific executive in exchange for a loan.

Notes and Questions

1. Are ASBP rules a helpful complement to the traditional single-firm conduct rules? Are they particularly important in developing and transitional economies worried about exploitations by state and other dominant players, or worried about exploitations and exclusions by global value chains? See Ioannis Lianos and Claudio Lombardi, Superior Bargaining Power and the Global Food Value Chain: The Wuthering Heights of Holistic Competition Law?, https://discovery.ucl.ac.uk/id/eprint/10045043/.

2. Or, are ASBP provisions in tension with antitrust? Do they interfere with efficient bargaining? Should the problems they address be left to the law of contract? See Masako Wakui and Thomas K. Cheng, Regulating abuse of superior bargaining position under the Japanese competition law: an anomaly or a necessity?, 3(2) J. Antitrust Enforcement 302–333 (2015). Might the answer depend on the state of development of the nation and the availability of alternative solutions to problems of severely and persistently one-sided bargains?

E. CONCLUSION

The law of monopolization and abuse of dominance is the most divergent of all segments of antitrust law. The statutes and cases reveal the fault lines. While all systems target exclusionary conduct by firms with substantial market or monopoly power that have no purpose or effect except to entrench or extend the monopoly, jurisdictions diverge on the extent to which they insist on proof of substantial power, whether excessive pricing is ever a violation, whether low pricing can offend if it does not fall below marginal or average variable cost and plaintiff cannot prove probable recoupment, whether loyalty rebate and margin squeeze violations are merely instances of predatory pricing, the extent of primacy of intellectual property over competition law provisions, and whether access and inclusiveness are antitrust values. The fault lines can be explained by different systems, different stages of development, and different judgments and choices on the role of antitrust in society. This comparative study should help the student and the policy maker to appreciate the differences, identify the convergences, and contemplate the room for more convergence.

Chapter 6

MERGERS

A. INTRODUCTION

Global issues with respect to mergers can be divided into three parts: First, with respect to domestic mergers, how do we define markets that have a transborder dimension? Should effects on competition be seen through a wider lens—i.e., one that captures the whole market, even beyond the nation's borders? Second, comparatively, are issues framed and resolved in the same way in all parts of the world? Is the standard of prohibition the same? We know that US law does not allow for defenses based on public interest or industrial policy. How do other nations treat these concerns? Third, cooperation and conflict. Almost 100 jurisdictions have premerger notification regimes. Fifty nations or so might claim jurisdiction over the same merger. What is the state of convergence on premerger notification processes and procedures? When jurisdictions vet the same merger and reach different assessments as to anticompetitiveness or appropriate relief, how is the conflict resolved? How might it be resolved? Is there room for transnational cooperation in the process of investigating and analyzing mergers that are of interest to more than one jurisdiction?

B. DOMESTIC ISSUES IN ANALYSIS OF TRANSBORDER MERGERS

1. Market Definition, and Deciding What Sales and What Firms Are in the Market

The problem of defining the market and determining what sales or capacity to include in the market is the most straightforward of the issues. The question that the analyst wants to answer is the same as with any other merger. The analyst wants to include in the market all good constraints on pricing power. This means inclusion of all constraints that would tend to keep the post-merger price down to the premerger price. If outsiders are already selling the relevant product into the geographic market, their product is included in the geographic market. If higher domestic prices would induce an increased flow of the foreign product, this larger quantity should be included. If suppliers not already selling in the market would enter in response to a non-transitory price increase, their expected effect on the market should be assessed.

Thus in United States v. Baker Hughes, 908 F.2d 981 (D.C. Cir. 1990), a Finnish company's subsidiary, Tamrock, sought to buy the French subsidiary of a Texas firm, Secoma. Both merger partners manufactured and sold hydraulic underground drilling rigs in the highly concentrated United States and world markets. Judge (now Justice) Thomas said: "[A] number of firms competing in Canada and other countries had not penetrated the United States market, but could be expected to do so if Tamrock's acquisition of Secoma led to higher prices." "[E]ntry in the United States HHUDR market would likely avert anticompetitive effects from Tamrock's acquisition of Secoma."

In some cases markets are global. Sellers seek buyers and buyers seek sellers without regard to borders. Transportation costs are low in proportion to the size of transaction. Such was the case in the jet aircraft market, as in *Boeing/McDonnell Douglas*, which we discuss below. While in that case the United States and Europe was each concerned about its own citizens, both recognized that the market was global.

2. Effects Beyond Borders

Most jurisdictions are directed by their laws to consider only effects within their borders.

Canada has a total-Canadian-welfare standard. Competition Act, Canada, R.S.C. 1985, C–34, as revised, Sec. 96 (1) (stating the efficiency exception), and Canada's Merger Enforcement Guidelines, Sept. 1, 2004, available at https://competition-bureau.canada.ca/en/how-we-foster-competition/education-and-outreach/merger-enforcement-guidelines, and Bulletin on Efficiencies in Merger Review, March 2, 2009, available at http://www.competitionbureau.gc.ca/eic/site/cb-bc.nsf/eng/02989.html. Thus, if Canadian producers profit at the expense of foreign buyers, and the producers gain more than the Canadian consumers lose, the law recognizes a welfare gain.

However, a merger approved in Canada on total welfare grounds may run into resistance elsewhere, as two Canadian chemical manufacturers discovered in the summer of 2016. Toronto-based Superior Plus Corp., and Canexus Corp., headquartered in Alberta, are two of the three major North American producers of sodium chlorate—a commodity chemical used to bleach wood pulp that is then processed into paper, tissue, diaper liners, and other products. Their proposed merger would have left the new company and rival

AkzoNobel controlling approximately 80 percent of the total sodium chlorate production capacity in North America.

The Canadian Competition Bureau and the US FTC ran parallel and collaborative investigations, both concluding on June 27, 2016, but with different results. The Competition Bureau issued a No Action Letter, thus allowing the transaction to proceed. It acknowledged that "customers of Superior and Canexus could face materially higher prices for these chemical inputs and would have limited options for alternative supply as a result of the merger." However, it then applied the efficiency defense, finding that the merger would create significant efficiencies from the "elimination of overhead costs, freight optimization, and the elimination of duplicate corporate services." On balance, it found that the efficiencies outweighed the anticompetitive effects:

> The Bureau retained an external economic expert to model the likely effects of the proposed merger and, in particular, to estimate the deadweight loss (allocative inefficiency) that would likely result from the merger, as well as an external efficiencies expert to evaluate Superior's claims. The Bureau concluded that the anti-competitive effects of the merger would be clearly outweighed by the efficiency gains from the transaction.

Competition Bureau Statement Regarding Superior's Proposed Acquisition of Canexus, http://www.competitionbureau.gc.ca/eic/site/cb-bc.nsf/eng/04111.html.

By contrast, the FTC brought an administrative challenge against the merger, alleging that it would lead to anticompetitive reductions in output and higher prices, and that by removing Canexus as an independent sodium chlorate producer, with its large scale and low-costs, the acquisition would increase the likelihood of coordination in an already vulnerable market (Under the Justice Department and FTC's 2010 Horizontal Merger Guidelines, efficiencies must be passed onto consumers in order to offset any competitive concerns). Faced with the FTC's opposition, the parties abandoned the transaction.

Jurisdictions generally consider benefits and harms beyond their borders as not their problem. An exception is *Italimpiante*, a merger of an Italian and a German firm that created a monopoly of oil pipeline technology that was becoming obsolete in the Western world but was very much in use in China. The German cartel office declined to address the problem since no harms would fall within Germany, but the Italian Antitrust Authority recognized the harm and ordered the merged firm to grant licenses upon request to any firm within the European Union that sought to make the monopolized technology. Fiatimpresit-Mannesmann Demagtechint/ Italimpianti, Case No. 3622 (C2227), Italian Antitrust Authority (1996).

Mature jurisdictions whose citizens are hurt by an off-shore merger can normally fend for themselves and perhaps even prohibit a harmful off-shore merger. The authorities in small jurisdictions and developing economies are not so fortunate. They can usually do little to prevent world mergers that hurt them or to impose effective conditions. For example, the merger may create buying power that exploits African farmers. Should such negative effects be part of the merger calculus by American or European authorities? Would a broader view encompassing effects wherever they fall require legislative change? Would a national legislature ever vote to increase the scope of domestic law to recognize harms by their nationals to foreigners? We return to some of these issues when we treat cooperation and related global issues below.

C. COMPARATIVE ISSUES

1. Substantive Analysis

a. Market Definition

Context dictates the confines of markets. The importance of context is illustrated by the proposed merger of two South African department stores that catered to the poorest consumers.

In the large merger between JD Group Ltd. and Ellerine Holdings Ltd., Competition Tribunal, Republic of South Africa, case 78/LM/Jul00. Two of South Africa's best-known department stores proposed to merge. One of these enterprises had pioneered a marketing approach that offered generous credit to "some of South Africa's poorest consumers, many of whom do not even have access to a bank account." Because no credit had been available to black South Africans, many of these individuals had not previously been able to buy furniture and appliances. In discussing whether the market was limited to credit purchases of furniture and appliances and also whether it included more upscale sellers, the Tribunal said:

> In this case . . . the parties to the transaction are the final link with the consumers, and, at that, the poorest, least powerful of South African consumers. In other words, the interests directly affected by this merger are represented by millions of atomized, disorganized individuals incapable of defending their economic interests except to the extent that they are able to exercise a preference for one retail outlet

> over another. This evaluation will seek to assess whether the transaction has the potential to increase the power of the parties over the consumers that they serve and who are the source of their prosperity.

Rejecting defendants' argument that the market included higher end stores, the Tribunal said:

> The distinction [based on Living Standard categories] informs advertising strategy in very subtle ways as an amusing example alluded to during our proceedings shows. Ellerines in the LSM [Living Standard Measure] 3–5 market offer a free sheep worth R300 if goods above a specified amount are purchased. A graphic of a sheep is depicted in the advert. Bradlow's, the high end JD brand, also offers a free gift for customers purchasing above a specific amount. The gift, however, underlines the difference in social status of the LSM categories—Bradlow's offers not a free sheep, but a coffee table book on 101 ways to cook lamb!

The Tribunal found that the relevant market was the sale of furniture and appliances on credit to consumers in a low-end LSM category through national chains of furniture shops. It enjoined the merger.

A second issue concerns the informal economy. In many developing countries, including many in Africa and South America, there is a large informal economy. This means there are many enterprises—often unable to fulfill dense, expensive, and time-consuming licensing requirements—that operate outside of the legal system. They do not pay taxes, they risk being raided, and they cannot enforce contracts in court, but they may impose competitive pressures. Reliable data on the informal economy are hard to obtain. How should the informal economy be counted in defining markets and assessing competitive effects of firms merging in the formal economy? *See* OECD Policy Roundtable, Competition Policy and the Informal Economy 2009, available at https://www.oecd.org/daf/competition/44547855.pdf.

b. Standard of Violation

Mergers violate US law when their "effect may be substantially to lessen competition." This is sometimes referred to as the SLC standard. In fact, the modern US standard is whether the merger is likely to create, enhance or entrench market power or facilitate its exercise. See Horizontal Merger Guidelines for Public Comment, released April 20, 2010, US department of Justice and Federal Trade

Commission. For shorthand, this standard is called "enhancing market power." A merger that enhances market power is virtually always illegal. It is possible, however, that such a merger might create efficiencies that are greater than the consumer loss and that would otherwise be unattainable. If the authorities are convinced that this is the case (they seldom are), they might withhold enforcement.

Merger control in the European Union was late in coming. Concentration of business by merger was not an issue in the early days of the European Community. Markets had been bounded by national borders, business was usually smaller than efficient scale, and cross-border mergers were welcomed both to increase efficiency and to integrate the common market. Moreover, various European Member States were skeptical about centralized merger control. Germany was afraid that European standards would be too weak; France did not want to lose control over the structure of its economy; Britain generally opposed more regulation from Brussels. Eventually, however, economic power-creating mergers did become a recognized problem in Europe, and the Member States agreed to a regime of centralized control for mergers (or other concentrations) of community dimension; that is, having cross-border effects and not centrally of interest to one Member State. In 1989, effective in 1990, a European merger control regime was established. It entailed notification, as in the United States, and a one-stop-shop, unlike the United States. That is, if the merger is subject to European jurisdiction, it cannot also be enjoined or conditioned by a Member State.

The standard for violation in the original merger control regulation was: Did the merger "create[ ] or strengthen[ ] a dominant position as a result of which effective competition would be significantly impeded." This "dominance" standard predictably proved too limiting. Many mergers were anticompetitive not because they created nascent monopolies but because they entrenched oligopolies. The European courts addressed the problem by giving a flexible interpretation to "dominance," construing the word to cover "collective dominance"—which meant, essentially, coordinated effects among oligopolists. Kali und Salz, [1998] ECR I–1375.

Still, there was a gap. The prohibitory language could not be stretched further to cover unilateral effects where the merger would not create dominance. Moreover, the "collective dominance" stretch was recognized as instrumental, to cover oligopolistic mergers. Because of these limits, the merger regulation was revised. The revised merger regulation, effective in 2004, proscribes mergers "which would significantly impede effective competition, . . . in particular as a result of the creation or strengthening of a dominant position . . . ." This is called the SIEC standard.

Most jurisdictions adopt either a form of SCL (substantial lessening of competition) or a form of SIEC. Some have a dominance standard (i.e., they prohibit mergers that create or entrench dominance), and some (like Germany) have a dominance standard that covers oligopolistic dominance. Act Against Restraints of Competition, § 36, which incorporates in its merger law its definition of dominance. (§ 19). Japan not only prohibits mergers and acquisitions that may result in a "substantial restraint of competition in a particular field of trade"; it also prohibits certain mergers that create "excessive concentration of economic power" (Anti-Monopoly Act, Article 9) and it prohibits financial institutions from holding more than 5% of joint stock in a non-financial institution, with a 10% limit for holdings in insurance companies. AMA Art. 11.

There is a significant degree of substantive convergence in merger law throughout the world. The International Competition Network has produced a very useful merger workbook. See https://www.internationalcompetitionnetwork.org/wp-content/uploads/2018/05/MWG_MergerGuidelinesWorkbook.pdf. The content of the workbook confirms the high degree of similarity.

Consider the following European Commission press release explaining its decision to block a merger between two telephone companies operating in the UK market. The Commission's explanation does not sound materially different from the US Justice Department's explanation for challenging the merger between AT&T and T-Mobile in 2011.

MERGERS: COMMISSION PROHIBITS HUTCHISON'S PROPOSED ACQUISITION OF TELEFÓNICA UK

Brussels, 11 May 2016

The Commission has blocked the proposed acquisition of O2 by Hutchison under the EU Merger Regulation. It had strong concerns that UK mobile customers would have had less choice and paid higher prices as a result of the takeover, and that the deal would have harmed innovation in the mobile sector.

Today's decision follows an in-depth investigation by the Commission of the deal, which would have combined Telefónica UK's "O2" and Hutchison 3G UK's "Three", creating a new market leader in the UK mobile market. The takeover would have removed an important competitor, leaving only two mobile network operators, Vodafone and BT's Everything Everywhere (EE), to challenge the merged entity.

The significantly reduced competition in the market would likely have resulted in higher prices for mobile services in the UK and less choice for consumers than without the deal. The takeover would also likely have had a negative impact on quality of service for UK consumers by hampering the development of mobile network infrastructure in the UK. Finally, the takeover would have reduced the number of mobile network operators willing to host other mobile operators on their networks.

The remedies proposed by Hutchison failed to adequately address the serious concerns raised by the takeover.

Commissioner Margrethe Vestager, in charge of competition policy, said:

> "We want the mobile telecoms sector to be competitive, so that consumers can enjoy innovative mobile services at fair prices and high network quality. The goal of EU merger control is to ensure that tie-ups do not weaken competition at the expense of consumers and businesses.
>
> Allowing Hutchison to takeover O2 at the terms they proposed would have been bad for UK consumers and bad for the UK mobile sector. We had strong concerns that consumers would have had less choice finding a mobile package that suits their needs and paid more than without the deal. It would also have hampered innovation and the development of network infrastructure in the UK, which is a serious concern especially for fast moving markets. The remedies offered by Hutchison were not sufficient to prevent this."

The UK mobile market

The UK mobile market is currently competitive—retail mobile prices are among the lowest in the entire EU. The UK is also one of the most advanced countries in the EU in terms of roll-out of 4G technology and take-up of 4G services.

There are currently four mobile network operators in the UK—BT's mobile business EE, Telefónica's O2, Vodafone and Hutchison's Three.

EE and Three have combined their networks as "Mobile Broadband Network Limited"—MBNL. Similarly, Vodafone and O2 combined their networks to set up Beacon. This allows EE / Three, and Vodafone / O2 respectively, to share the costs of rolling out their networks but they continue to compete with each other for retail customers.

In addition to the four mobile network operators, there are a number of mobile "virtual" operators active in the UK retail mobile market, such as Virgin Media, Talk Talk and Dixons Carphone's iD. These mobile virtual operators do not own the networks they use to provide mobile services to UK consumers. Instead, they entered agreements with one of the mobile network operators to access their network at wholesale rates.

The Commission's competition concerns

The Commission had serious concerns that the takeover would have reduced competition in the market, hampered the development of the UK mobile network infrastructure as well as the ability of mobile virtual operators to compete.

1. **Less competition leads to higher prices and reduced choice and quality for consumers:** The takeover would have eliminated competition between two strong players in the UK mobile market. Three is the latest market entrant and has been an important driver of competition in the UK mobile market. O2 has a strong position with high brand value and reputation. It is the second largest mobile operator by revenues and the largest in terms of subscribers (if its share in the Tesco Mobile joint venture is included). Combined, Three and O2 would have been the market leader with a share of more than 40%. They would have had much less incentive to compete with Vodafone and EE. This would have **reduced choice and quality of service for UK consumers**. The Commission's analysis also showed that with the takeover **retail mobile prices would have been higher** for all UK operators than without.

2. **Future development of entire UK mobile network infrastructure hampered:** The merged entity would have been part of both network sharing arrangements, MBNL and Beacon. It would have had a full overview of the network plans of both remaining competitors, Vodafone and EE. Its role in both networks would have **weakened EE and Vodafone** and **hampered the future development of mobile infrastructure** in the UK, for example with respect to the roll-out of next generation technology (5G), to the detriment of UK consumers and businesses.

3. **Reduced number of mobile network operators effectively willing to host virtual operators:** The transaction would have reduced the number of mobile network operators willing to

host other mobile operators on their networks. Mobile virtual operators rely on access to the infrastructure to provide mobile services to consumers. The reduced number of host mobile networks would have left prospective and existing mobile virtual operators in a **weaker negotiating position to obtain favourable wholesale access terms**.

* * *

While convergence in merger outcomes may be true as to many cross-border mergers, the increasing number of competition law regimes with active scrutiny of mergers increases the likelihood for disparities in outcomes. And the practical effect of one significant jurisdiction saying no may be to kill a deal from happening, even if other significant authorities say yes.

Sabre Corp. and Farelogix, two companies that provide global distribution or "booking" systems for airlines, learned this the hard way in 2020 when they beat back the Justice Department's challenge to their merger in federal court in Delaware, only to see the U.K. Competition and Markets Authority ("CMA") prohibit the merger and subsequently win Sabre's appeal in the U.K.'s Competition Appeal Tribunal. We present below a brief selection from the District of Delaware and Competition Appeal Tribunal's decisions that explain the nub of their respective reasoning:

> [T]he Court concludes that DOJ failed to establish a prima facie case that the merger of Sabre and Farelogix will violate Section 7 of the Clayton Act. Specifically, DOJ has not identified a proper relevant market. As a matter of antitrust law, Sabre, a two-sided transaction platform, only competes with other two-sided platforms, but Farelogix only operates on the airline side of Sabre's platform. Even if that were not the law, DOJ's market analysis fails because it does not relate to the relevant product market or the relevant geographic market. In the alternative, even if the Court were to assume that DOJ has identified a relevant product market, and were to assume that the record at least supports a prima facie case that the effects of the merger are likely to be anticompetitive, the Court further concludes that Defendants have rebutted the government's prima facie case. After making credibility determinations, drawing the reasonable inferences the Court deems most warranted, and weighing the evidence, the Court concludes that the government has failed to prove by a preponderance of the evidence that the Sabre-

> Farelogix transaction is reasonably probable to substantially lessen competition.

United States v. Sabre Corp., 452 F. Supp. 3d 97 (United States District Court of Delaware 2020).

The Competition Appeal Tribunal recognized the factual point on which the Justice Department's challenged faltered—that Farelogix only competed on one side of the two-sided market in which Sabre competed—but found that the merger could still reduce competition:

> As regards distribution solutions in particular, competition takes place in multiple forms reflecting differentiated business models in the market. While the Parties' solutions allow airlines ultimately to distribute content to passengers, they operate different approaches which affect the ways in which they face constraints from each other and from other suppliers. While Sabre and other GDSs compete for both airlines and travel agents, Farelogix and other suppliers of distribution solutions based on the NDC API compete on the airline side only. Airlines decide how to use these solutions to connect to travel agents and passengers; these suppliers compete with GDSs and with one another by offering reliable innovative technology and lower booking fees to reduce airlines' distribution costs. The two theories of harm considered by the CMA were whether the Merger would give rise to an SLC on a worldwide basis (i) in the supply of merchandising solutions, and (ii) in the supply of distribution solutions.

Sabre Corp. v. Competition and Markets Authority, Case No: 1345/4/12/20 U.K. Competition Appeal Tribunal (May 21, 2021)

The sequence of decisions in the U.S. and UK is interesting. Sabre and Farelogix won in federal court April 7 of 2020, then two days later, on April 9, the CMA issued its final report finding the deal anticompetitive. On May 1, 2020, Sabre and Farelogix abandoned their merger and the United States Court of Appeals for the Third Circuit subsequently dismissed the Justice Department's appeal as moot. 2020 WL 4915824 (3d Cir. July 20, 2020). Sabre nonetheless appealed the CMA decision, ultimately losing before the Competition Appeal Tribunal a year later in 2021. Should the Justice Department have felt ultimately vindicated by the success of their theories across the Atlantic? In dismissing the Department's appeal as moot, the Third Circuit cautioned: "this Order should not be construed as detracting from the persuasive force of the District Court's decision, should courts and litigants find its reasoning persuasive." So the outcome of this particular merger may have been decided by the jurisdiction that took the more restrictive view, but the questions on which the respective courts disagreed may live on for another day.

If different jurisdictions sometimes diverge in horizontal merger analysis, even more divergence appears in the analysis of vertical and conglomerate mergers. The divergence is illustrated in the different treatment by the United States and the European Union of the merger of General Electric and Honeywell. General Electric was the dominant producer of engines for jet aircraft and Honeywell was the leading producer of avionic and non-avionic products (such as steering equipment) for jet aircraft. The European Commission was concerned that the combined firm would bundle its products and marginalize competitors, especially Honeywell's competitors, who would find it harder to beat Honeywell and would decrease their investments in those products. These were "conglomerate" issues. The case also raised some horizontal and vertical issues. The European Court of First Instance affirmed the Commission's prohibition of the merger, but only on horizontal issues (both companies made jet engines, albeit at different ends of the value spectrum). The court held that the Commission had not proved that the merged firm would bundle its products. [2005] ECR II–5575. See Eleanor Fox, *GE/Honeywell: The U.S. Merger that Europe Stopped—A Story of the Politics of Convergence*, in ANTITRUST STORIES, Chapter 12 E. Fox and D. Crane, eds. (2007).

The US and the EU (and other jurisdictions) may apply different default presumptions in analyzing conglomerate mergers, especially in matters involving foreclosing effects. The European Commission and European courts are more likely than US courts to find that a merger creates significant foreclosing effects that block the market, undermine rivals' ability to contest the market, and ultimately harm consumers. See the European non-horizontal merger guidelines. https://eur-lex.europa.eu/legal-content/EN/ALL/?uri=CELEX%3A 52008XC1018%2803%29. The US Courts, on the other hand, are more likely to find a merged firm's potentially exclusionary conduct, such as bundling, a stimulus to rivals to compete harder. See *GE/ Honeywell* at D. 3 below.

Developing countries often have an additional concern: buyer power. Hassan Qaqaya and George Lipimile note in the Executive Summary of their book, THE EFFECTS OF ANTI-COMPETITIVE BUSINESS PRACTICES ON DEVELOPING COUNTRIES AND THEIR DEVELOPMENT PROSPECTS (UNCTAD 2008), referencing an article by Bruce Dorin:

> . . . [C]ocoa markets have been experiencing increased horizontal concentration through mergers of large multinational companies, such as those between large chocolate companies and cocoa processing firms, or through takeovers by large international companies of smaller companies operating at the national market. As a result of these developments, small local cocoa producers have to contend with a strong purchasing power held by several large multinational companies. Id., xiii.

c. *Treatment of Efficiencies*

Differences among jurisdictions may appear in the treatment of efficiencies. The United States and the EU both consider efficiencies in connection with the competition analysis; not largely as a defense to anticompetitive mergers but as an important factor in determining whether the merger might be procompetitive. For example, in affirming a district court injunction against a merger between the Anthem and Cigna health insurance groups, the D.C. Circuit noted that the current legal status of the efficiencies defense remains unsettled, but that any cognizable efficiencies defense would need to be merger-specific, verifiable, and sufficient to offset any anticompetitive effects of the merger. U.S. v. Anthem, Inc., 855 F.3d 345 (D.C. Cir. April 28, 2017).

Some jurisdictions, however, allow an efficiencies defense to an anticompetitive merger. As noted above with respect to the Superior Plus/Canexus merger, Canada has a total welfare standard, and if the producers gain more in efficiencies than consumers lose in high prices, the merger is allowed. Also in Canada, increased exports may be a factor justifying a price-raising merger. Competition Act, Section 96. See Commissioner of Competition v. Superior Propane Inc., CT 1998/002, Aug. 30, 2000.

In Tervita Corp. v. Commissioner of Competition, CT 2015/3, March 27, 2015, the Supreme Court of Canada explained the efficiencies defense as follows in overruling a Tribunal decision to prohibit a merger between hazardous waste disposal companies operating in Northeastern British Columbia:

> As s. 92 of the Act is engaged [based on a finding that merger is prima facie anticompetitive], it is necessary to determine whether the s. 96 efficiencies defence applies to prevent the making of an order under s. 92. The defence requires an analysis of whether the efficiency gains of the merger, which result from the integration of resources, outweigh the anti-competitive effects, which result from the

> decrease in or absence of competition in the relevant geographic and product market. The Commissioner has the burden of proving the anti-competitive effects, and the merging parties bear the onus of proving the remaining elements of the defence. There are different possible methodologies for the comparative exercise under s. 96, two of which have been the subject of judicial consideration in Canada: the "total surplus standard" which involves quantifying the deadweight loss which will result from a merger, and the "balancing weights standard" under which the Tribunal weighs the effects of the merger on consumers against the effects of the merger on the shareholders of the merged entity. Because the Act does not set out which methodology should be used, the Tribunal has the flexibility to make the ultimate choice of methodology in view of the particular circumstances of each merger.
>
> The test may be framed as a two-step inquiry. First, the quantitative efficiencies of the merger should be compared against the quantitative anti-competitive effects. Where the quantitative anti-competitive effects outweigh the quantitative efficiencies, this step will in most cases be dispositive, and the defence will not apply. Under the second step, the qualitative efficiencies should be balanced against the qualitative anticompetitive effects, and a final determination must be made as to whether the total efficiencies offset the total anti-competitive effects of the merger at issue.

In small and developing economies, nations might face a trade-off. A merger might increase prices at home, but the merged firm might be more efficient and thus more competitive in world markets. (Theoretically, this can happen also in the United States and the EU, but given the size of our markets it is much less likely.) The nation might choose to sacrifice its own consumers' welfare in order to get more traction in international markets. See Michal Gal, COMPETITION POLICY FOR SMALL MARKET ECONOMIES (2003).

d. Harm to Innovation

Merger analysis often focuses on price effects—would the merger reduce competition and thus allow the merging firms, or other firms in the market, to increase their prices? However, as discussed at various points in the ICN's guidance document below, competition authorities are increasingly concerned also with innovation effects—that a merger will reduce the merging parties' incentives to innovate.

A classic version of this argument was made by Nobel Laureate Kenneth Arrow in a 1962 paper that was mostly concerned with patents. Kenneth J. Arrow, *Economic Welfare and the Allocation of Resources for Invention, in* THE RATE AND DIRECTION OF INVENTIVE ACTIVITY: ECONOMIC AND SOCIAL FACTORS 609 (Richard R. Nelson ed., 1962). Arrow noted when a monopolist has a diminished incentive to invest in research and development to create a product that will replace the monopolist's existing product, since the monopolist will simply cannibalize its own revenues with the new product. By contrast, firms that can take market share with new products have a bigger incentive to innovate. In the merger context, one of the merging firms might have had an incentive to innovate to challenge the other firm pre-merger, but post-merger the firm is better off just continuing to collect monopoly profits from its existing products.

In recent years, some empirical research has suggested that dominant firms may engage in even worse behavior—"killer acquisitions" in which the dominant firm buys a smaller firm to kill off its R&D efforts before they become a challenge to the acquiring firm's dominance. *See* Colleen Cunningham, Florian Ederer & Song Ma, *Killer Acquisitions*, 129 J. Pol. Econ. 649 (2021). The idea of "killer acquisitions" was coined by Cunningham, Ederer, and Ma in a since-published working paper in 2018, and it has quickly captured the imagination of competition authorities around the globe.

For example, in September of 2023, the Chinese State Administration for Market Regulation (SAMR) conditionally cleared a merger between Simcere Pharmaceutical and Tobishi Beijing after requiring concessions to address a "killer acquisition" concern. Simcere is a distributor of an active pharmaceutical ingredient to produce batroxobin, a drug that treats sudden hearing loss. Simcere had a contract for exclusive supply of batroxobin in China. Downstream, in the batroxobin injections market, Tobishi was the only manufacturer and supplier in China. However, Simcere was developing its own batroxobin injection product and was relatively close to putting it on the market

SAMR found that the acquisition raised a classic "killer acquisition" concern—that Simcere would discontinue its R&D toward a batroxobin injection product. To address these concerns, SAMR required Simcere to divest its batroxobin injections business, to terminate its exclusive supply agreement, and to assist in providing batroxobin to the divested asset buyer.

The Simcere/Tobishi shows how quickly new economic theories—particularly those centered on innovation—can get around in a world in which economists are reading each other's work and competition authorities are sharing theories about the potential harms of mergers.

e. ICN Recommended Practices for Merger Analysis

The International Competition Network, a network of more than 100 antitrust/competition authorities, has adopted recommended practices for merger analysis. The ICN is open to all competition authorities in the world, and its working groups are open to all members, who are assisted by non-governmental advisors (NGAs). The ICN published recommended best practices guidelines for merger analysis in 2008, with comments by the network's merger working group in 2009. In 2017, the ICN added new sections based on subsequent learning by its members:

ICN RECOMMENDED PRACTICES FOR MERGER ANALYSIS

(International Competition Network, 2008, with revisions as of 2017) available at https://www.internationalcompetitionnetwork.org/wp-content/uploads/2025/02/MWG-RPs-Merger-Analysis-2024.pdf.

These recommendations on substantive merger analysis are derived from the ICN Merger Guidelines Workbook and common practices across member jurisdictions. They are intended to complement the detailed descriptions of merger analysis in the Workbook. For a description of effective investigative techniques to develop evidence to account for particular facts presented in merger investigations, see the ICN Investigative Techniques Handbook for Merger Review.

The ICN Recommended Practices for Merger Notification and Review Procedures address the procedural aspects of notification and review. Several topics covered in those recommended practices relate to the legal framework for substantive merger analysis. In particular, the practices that address transparency, agency powers, confidentiality, and the conduct of a merger investigation are relevant to the legal framework for substantive merger review.

I. The Legal Framework for Competition Merger Analysis

A. The purpose of competition law merger analysis is to identify and prevent or remedy only those mergers that are likely to harm competition significantly.

WORKING GROUP COMMENTS
Original Comments (April 2008)

Comment 1: The legal framework for competition law merger review ("merger review law") should focus exclusively on identifying and preventing or remedying anticompetitive mergers. A merger review law should not be used to pursue other goals.

Comment 2: Most mergers do not harm competition. Many mergers enable the merged firm to reduce costs and become more efficient, leading to lower prices, higher quality products, or increased investments in innovation. Some mergers, however, may harm competition by creating or enhancing the merged firm's ability or incentives to exercise market power—either unilaterally or through coordination with rivals—resulting in price increases above competitive levels for a significant period of time, reductions in quality or a slowing of innovation.

Comment 3: Merger review laws and policies should provide competition agencies with the ability to differentiate mergers that are unlikely to have significant anticompetitive effects from those that require more analysis. The identification of those mergers that potentially threaten to harm competition and expeditious clearance of non-problematic mergers can lead to more efficient use of agency resources and more effective analysis of critical legal and economic issues.

Comment 4: A competition authority's decision to take enforcement action against a merger should not be based on expected anticompetitive effects that are insignificant or transient in duration.

Comment 5: Agencies should only intervene to prohibit or remedy a merger when it is necessary to prevent anticompetitive effects that may be caused by that merger. The appropriate goal of agency intervention to prohibit or remedy a merger is to restore or maintain competition affected by the merger, not to enhance premerger competition.

B. A jurisdiction's merger review law and policy should provide a comprehensive framework for effectively addressing mergers that are likely to harm competition significantly.

WORKING GROUP COMMENTS
Original Comments (April 2008)

Comment 1: A jurisdiction's merger law and policies should enable the competition agency to perform its competition analysis and to take appropriate and effective enforcement action.

Comment 2: A merger review law should have broad application to transactions[1] that may raise significant competitive concerns, regardless of how the transaction is structured. The legal authority to analyze a merger should not be based on the form or technicalities of a merger agreement.

Comment 3: Specific sector exceptions or exemptions to generally applicable merger review provisions, if any, should be narrowly drawn, clearly delineated, and reviewed periodically.

Comment 4: The substantive legal standard for mergers and any analytical guidelines should be based on sound and robust economic principles. Merger review laws and policies should establish a framework for analysis that can address the likely anticompetitive effects of a merger while retaining sufficient flexibility to adapt to developments in economic learning. Clear, comprehensive, and transparent legal and analytical standards, that include identifying the range of mergers subject to the law and the substantive standard for assessing whether a merger is likely to harm competition significantly, improve the predictability of enforcement actions.

Comment 5: A determination of whether a merger is likely to harm competition significantly should take place within established legal procedures, including an appropriate and transparent standard of proof.

C. An agency's merger analysis should be comprehensive in its assessment of factors affecting the determination of whether a merger is likely to harm competition significantly.

WORKING GROUP COMMENTS
Original Comments (April 2008)

Comment 1: An agency's merger analysis should not be a mechanical application of a legal standard based on rigid presumptions, structural criteria, or formulaic concentration numbers. An agency should apply its merger analysis reasonably and flexibly on a case-by-case basis, recognizing the broad range of possible factual contexts and the specific competitive effects that may arise in different transactions.

Comment 2: The substantive legal standard in a merger review law should permit intervention only where it can be established to the requisite standard of proof that any likely future anticompetitive

---

[1] A detailed discussion of the types of transactions that merger review laws cover is contained in the ICN report, "Defining 'Merger' Transactions for Purposes of Merger Review."

effects are attributable to the merger itself and not to any other factor. Central to the analysis, therefore, should be a comparison of competition in the relevant market with and without the merger. In most cases, the starting point for such analysis will be an assessment of the competitive conditions existing before the merger, but account should also be taken of any changes in those conditions likely to take place irrespective of the merger.

Comment 3: Merger analysis requires an agency to predict a merger's competitive impact to prevent any competitive problems before they materialize. Agencies should recognize that the further in the future the predicted effects (both harmful and beneficial) are projected to occur, the more difficult it is to predict confidently that they will occur.

Comment 4: The objective application of competition law standards in merger analysis promotes consistency and predictability. An agency's merger analysis practice should also include a commitment to transparency (subject to appropriate confidentiality protections) in order to achieve consistency and predictability and allow merging parties and the public to understand better how the merger laws are enforced. An agency should clearly articulate the analytical factors it uses for merger analysis.

II. Market Definition

A. Agencies generally should assess the competitive effects of a merger within economically meaningful markets. A relevant market consists of a product or group of products and a geographic area in which it is produced or sold that could be subject to an exercise of market power.

[The remaining discussion is omitted. The Recommendations generally advocate the use of the Small but Significant and Nontransitory ("SSNIP") test for defining relevant markets.]

III. Use of Market Shares: Thresholds & Presumptions

A. Market shares and measures of market concentration play an important role in merger analysis but are not determinative of possible competition concerns. Agencies should give careful consideration to market definition and the calculation of market shares and market concentration.

WORKING GROUP COMMENTS
Original Comments (April 2008)

Comment 1: Market shares are an indication of the competitive significance of each merging firm in the relevant market. They provide an indication of a firm's incentives to coordinate its actions with rivals and its ability unilaterally to exercise market power. The significance of market shares and measures of market concentration is specific to the analytical context presented in each investigation. They are not determinative of possible competition concerns in themselves, as they may, for instance, either underestimate or overestimate the future competitive significance of a firm or the impact of a merger.

Comment 2: In general, agencies should pay greater attention to a merger that significantly increases market concentration than to one that does not, or does so only marginally. Whatever the existing level of concentration, the change in concentration caused by a merger is a useful, although imperfect, indicator of the loss of direct competition between the parties and of the potential for competitive harm.

Comment 3: Market shares and measures of concentration are useful in merger analysis only when they are based on properly defined product and geographic markets. Particular caution is needed in markets involving differentiated products, as market definition itself is more complex in these cases. Market share calculations should be based on reliable data and sources and sound assumptions.

Comment 4: Market shares should be based on a measure of economic strength (e.g., sales, production, or capacity) that is appropriate to the circumstances of the market. Market share and concentration estimates used for a merger analysis should reflect the best available indication of the firms' future competitive significance. Market characteristics and changes in market conditions should be considered in interpreting market shares and market concentration data. Before drawing any conclusions from market share and concentration data, agencies should consider imminent or reasonably certain changes to the market, such as the entry or exit of a firm or the introduction of additional capacity. To gain a better insight into the competitive dynamics of some markets, it may also be relevant to analyze changes in market shares and concentration over time.

B. Market shares and measures of market concentration can provide useful initial guidance to help identify mergers that may raise competitive concerns requiring further analysis.

WORKING GROUP COMMENTS
Original Comments (April 2008)

Comment 1: The purpose of initial guidance based upon market shares or measures of concentration is to help differentiate mergers that are unlikely to have anticompetitive consequences from those that require more detailed analysis. Such guidance can enhance predictability and allow for a better allocation of agency resources.

Comment 2: The absence of high market shares or post-merger concentration ordinarily supports a conclusion that a given transaction requires no further analysis. Similarly, a transaction that does not significantly increase post-merger market shares or concentration ordinarily requires no further analysis, as the premerger competitive conditions are unlikely to be significantly altered by the merger. However, there may be exceptions. For example, when at least one party to the merger has substantial market power, even small increases in market share may be indicative of possible competition concerns. Evidence that the merged firm would have a high market share or that the market is highly concentrated can be significant to a decision to initiate an in-depth investigation.

Comment 3: Many agencies identify thresholds based on market shares and levels of concentration to give initial guidance as to the likely need for an in-depth investigation. An agency can set threshold levels of market shares and measures of concentration under which it commits itself not to, or is generally unlikely to, challenge a merger or over which it is likely to continue an in-depth analysis of the merger's effects on competition.

C. High market concentration and significant increases in market shares brought about by a merger are useful, but generally are not conclusive indicators that a merger is likely to harm competition significantly. Jurisdictions that use market concentration and/or market shares to presume competitive harm should ensure that any such presumption may be overcome or confirmed by a detailed review of market conditions.

WORKING GROUP COMMENTS
Original Comments (April 2008)

Comment 1: Mergers that lead to high market share for the merging firms and that result in significant increases to concentration levels are in general the mergers most likely to raise competition concerns.

Comment 2: In some jurisdictions, high market share or market concentration gives rise to a presumption of competitive harm, whereas in others they do not. When agencies use presumptions of competitive harm based on market shares or market concentration, the investigatory process should take into account evidence that may overcome or confirm the presumption. Agencies should be transparent about the meaning and use of any presumptions, including any quantitative standards used to evaluate market shares or concentration.

Comment 3: Agencies should not make enforcement decisions to prevent or remedy a merger solely on the basis of market shares and concentration. Thus, agencies should not automatically reach a final conclusion that a merger is likely to be anticompetitive because the merger increases concentration above a certain level or reduces the number of remaining firms below a certain level. A detailed analysis of other market factors and of theories of unilateral and/or coordinated effects should always be required before definitive conclusions are drawn regarding the likely competitive effects of a merger.

V. Entry & Expansion

A. The assessment of firm entry and/or expansion by existing competitors should be an integral part of the analysis of whether a merger is likely to harm competition significantly (e.g., the merged firm could raise prices or reduce output, quality, or innovation).

WORKING GROUP COMMENTS
Original Comments (April 2008)

Comment 1: Entry, or the threat of entry from potential competitors or from customers turning to in-house supply, can be an important competitive constraint on the conduct of the merged firm. If the merged firm is subject to competitive constraints from the threat of market entry (e.g., if barriers to entry are low and entry is likely to be profitable at premerger prices), the merger is unlikely to have anticompetitive effects.

Comment 2: The ability of rival firms to expand capacity in a timely manner, or use existing spare capacity or switch capacity from one use to another, can also constitute an important competitive constraint on the merged firm's conduct (these shorter term supply-side responses can also be assessed in the context of market definition). Many of the factors that are used to assess entry are relevant to the analysis of expansion, including competitor expansion plans, barriers to expansion, and the profitability of expansion.

Comment 3: Competition agencies should consider whether entry and/or expansion would deter or offset the likely anticompetitive effects of a merger. Competition agencies should focus on entry and/or expansion that would occur as a result of the post-merger competitive situation as well as entry and expansion that is likely to take place independent of the merger.

B. In assessing whether entry and/or expansion would effectively constrain the merged entity, competition agencies should consider whether entry and/or expansion would be: (a) likely; (b) timely; and, (c) sufficient in nature, scale and scope.

WORKING GROUP COMMENTS
Original Comments (April 2008)

Comment 1: For entry and/or expansion to be likely, it should be profitable for competitors of the merged entity to expand output and/or for potential entrants to enter the market in response to an attempt by the merged entity to profit from the potential reduction in competition brought about by the merger (e.g., a post-merger price increase). In assessing the *likelihood* of entry, competition agencies should also consider establishing, if possible, the history of entry into and/or exit from the relevant market by using available evidence including information on firms that have recently entered or exited the market, information about past and expected market growth, evidence of planned entry and/or expansion, direct observation of the costs, risks and benefits associated with entry and information from firms identified as potential entrants.

Comment 2: In assessing the *likelihood* of entry and/or expansion, competition agencies should consider the existence and significance of barriers to entry and expansion to the relevant market (i.e., the advantages enjoyed by incumbent firms over the potential entrants that may prevent or delay new firms from entering the market). When assessing ease of entry, agencies should focus on whether potential entrants would consider entry to be profitable in light of factors including but not limited to:

- economies of scope and/or scale, the availability of a scarce resource that is an essential input, technical capability or intellectual property rights;
- the reputation of incumbent firms, incumbent firms' investment in excessive capacity, or the duration, termination and renewal provisions in existing contracts;
- government regulations that might, for example, limit the number of market participants or impose substantial regulatory approval costs; and,

- sunk costs that could not be recovered if the entrant left the market including machinery that might be site specific or R & D that has not yet resulted in any marketable invention or innovation.

Comment 3: In assessing whether entry and/or expansion is timely, competition agencies should consider whether entry and/or expansion would take place within a reasonable period of time after the merger (many jurisdictions consider that entry must have a competitive impact within two years to have a sufficiently disciplining effect). The appropriate time horizon may vary according to the characteristics of the relevant market.

Comment 4: For entry and/or expansion to be sufficient, competition agencies should consider whether entry and/or expansion would be:

- sufficient in scale to compete effectively with the merged entity;
- able to counteract any specific anti-competitive effects resulting from the merger; and,
- able to counteract any localized effects of the merger (e.g., in markets differentiated by geographic areas or customer categories).

IV. Competitive Effects Analysis in Horizontal Merger Review: Overview

A. The goal of competitive effects analysis in the review of horizontal mergers is to assess whether a merger is likely to harm competition significantly by creating or enhancing the merged firm's ability or incentives to exercise market power, either unilaterally or in coordination with rivals.

WORKING GROUP COMMENTS
Original Comments (June 2009)

Comment 1: Agencies should conduct competitive effects analysis in merger review to identify those mergers likely to harm competition significantly by creating or enhancing market power. When exercised by sellers, market power is the ability profitably to raise price above competitive levels for a significant period of time, and/or to lessen competition on parameters other than price, such as quality, service, or innovation. In some cases, market power may be exercised by buyers. In such cases, market power is the ability profitably to reduce the price paid to suppliers below competitive levels for a significant period of time, which may in some cases lead to an anticompetitive reduction in supplier output.

Comment 2: Agencies generally should conduct competitive effects analysis within the context of properly defined product and geographic markets. However, market definition is not an end in itself but is a tool to assist in determining whether a merger will create or enhance market power. In some cases, evidence of competitive effects, such as price effects following a consummated merger under investigation or a prior merger in the industry, may inform the analysis of the appropriate relevant markets.

Comment 3: Agencies engaged in competitive effects analysis should conduct a forward-looking inquiry focusing on a comparison of the anticipated state of competition in the relevant market(s) with and without the merger. An agency's assessment of competition without the merger (sometimes called the "counterfactual") should be informed not only by the existing conditions of competition, but also by any significant changes in the state of competition likely to occur without the merger.

Comment 4: While changes in market share or market concentration are useful indicators of potential competitive concerns, competitive effects analysis involves a comprehensive assessment of market conditions, and provides agencies with a more reliable means to assess potential harm to competition than changes in market share or market concentration alone.

B. In conducting competitive effects analysis, agencies should consider whether a merger likely will result in anticompetitive unilateral or coordinated effects. These two theories of competitive harm provide the analytical frameworks for determining whether a horizontal merger may be expected to harm competition significantly.

WORKING GROUP COMMENTS
Original Comments (June 2009)

Comment 1: Unilateral effects, also known as non-coordinated effects, arise when, as a result of a merger, it is likely that the merged firm, without any coordination with non-merger rivals, will be able profitably to exercise market power to a materially greater degree than would have been possible for either of the merged firms before the merger.

Comment 2: Coordinated effects arise when, as a result of a merger, it is likely that firms remaining in the market after the merger will be able to coordinate (either tacitly or explicitly) their behavior or strengthen existing coordination in order to exercise market power.

Comment 3: Unilateral effects and coordinated effects are broad analytical frameworks designed to encompass the full range of anticompetitive effects that may result from horizontal mergers. While anticompetitive effects of a merger within a particular market are often best characterized as either unilateral or coordinated, a merger may result in both unilateral and coordinated effects.

C. The analysis of competitive effects under either the unilateral or coordinated effects framework should be clearly grounded in both sound economics and the facts of the particular case.

WORKING GROUP COMMENTS
Original Comments (June 2009)

Comment 1: Economic theories and models are useful in analyzing competitive effects under both unilateral and coordinated effects frameworks, but only to the extent that the theory or model used to assess the likely competitive effects of a merger is based on sound and robust economic principles and fits the factual conditions of the market to which it is applied.

Comment 2: Competitive effects analysis depends heavily on the specific facts of each case. In conducting competitive effects analysis, agencies should refine their theories or models of likely competitive harm in light of the available qualitative and quantitative evidence. Qualitative evidence often comes from documents or first-hand observations of the industry by customers or other market participants. Quantitative evidence is often derived from statistical analysis of price, quantity, or other data related to, among other things, prior market events (sometimes called "natural experiments") involving incumbent responses to prior events such as entry or exit by rivals. Competitive effects analysis should be flexible enough to adapt over time to evolving markets, business practices, and economic learning.

V. Unilateral Effects

A. In analyzing the potential for a horizontal merger to result in anticompetitive unilateral effects, agencies should assess whether the merger is likely to harm competition significantly by creating or enhancing the merged firm's ability or incentives to exercise market power independently.

WORKING GROUP COMMENTS
Original Comments (June 2009)

Comment 1: Horizontal mergers eliminate any competitive constraint that the merging parties formerly exerted upon one another. In the majority of mergers, this has no significant adverse effect on competition because there are other sufficient competitive constraints on the merged entity. In some cases, however, the elimination of competition between the merging parties in itself may create or enhance the ability of the merged firm independently to exercise market power, depending on market conditions, including the existence and effectiveness of other competitive constraints.

Comment 2: Agencies conducting unilateral effects analysis should look not only at market shares and market concentration, but should also examine the specific features of the market that affect the merged firm's ability to exercise market power. While market shares are a useful indicator of the potential for the merged firm to exercise unilateral market power, market shares alone may overstate or understate the potential for a merger to result in anticompetitive unilateral effects. Competitive constraints may preclude the exercise of market power even by firms with high market shares. On the other hand, even small changes in market share in some circumstances may increase the ability or incentives of a firm to exercise market power.

B. In conducting unilateral effects analysis, agencies should apply the economic theory or model that best fits the characteristics of the market(s) at issue.

WORKING GROUP COMMENTS
Original Comments (June 2009)

Comment 1: Mergers may increase the likelihood of the exercise of unilateral market power in a variety of settings. There are a number of unilateral effects theories and models in the economic literature that address competitive effects in specific factual settings. While the specific model or theory used will vary depending on the characteristics of the market, all are designed to assess whether there is any material increase in unilateral market power as a result of the merger. Common theories and models include, but are not limited to:

- *Merger to monopoly*: A merger that would combine the only two rivals in a properly defined market raises a high risk of significant anticompetitive unilateral effects. In examining a merger combining the only two rivals in a relevant market, agencies should assess whether any competitive constraints exist, such as ease of entry, that would preclude the unilateral exercise of market power by the merged firm.

- *Merger of competitors in differentiated product markets*: A merger that would combine competing suppliers of differentiated products may raise the potential for significant anticompetitive unilateral effects if a sufficient proportion of consumers view the products combined by the merger as their first and second choices (or closest substitutes). Commonly used sources of evidence on the degree of substitutability among differentiated products include marketing surveys, analysis of purchasing patterns, cross-price elasticities, and information contained in normal course of business documents from market participants. Agencies should assess whether the merger would allow the merged firm profitably to increase price on one or more products after the merger, or whether sufficient customers would switch to products of other competitors so as to render such a price increase unprofitable for the merged firm. Agencies should also consider whether rival sellers likely would replace any loss of competition by repositioning or extending their product lines to compete more closely with the merged firm.

- *Merger of competitors in undifferentiated product markets*: In examining a merger that would combine competing suppliers of undifferentiated products in markets in which firms are distinguished primarily by capacity, agencies should consider whether the merged firm would find it profitable to raise price by reducing output below the level that would have prevailed absent the merger. The exercise of market power in such markets is likely only if competitors of the merged firm likely would not respond to the price increase and output reduction by the merged firm with increases in their own outputs sufficient in the aggregate to make the unilateral action of the merged firm unprofitable. This may occur if non-merging firms face binding capacity constraints that could not be economically relaxed in a timely manner, or if existing excess capacity is significantly more costly to operate than capacity currently in use. In such cases, competitors may find it more profitable to raise price than expand output, resulting in additional anticompetitive unilateral effects.

- *Merger of rivals in bidding or auction markets*: A merger that would combine rival bidders in bidding or auction markets may raise the potential for significant anticompetitive unilateral effects. There are a variety of models in the economic literature addressing a wide array of bidding and auction formats involving both differentiated and undifferentiated products. For example, some models focus on whether the merger would combine the two lowest-cost or otherwise closest competitors. Other models focus on whether the merger would result in a competitively significant reduction in the number of bidders. Agencies should determine the appropriate model depending upon the circumstances of the market, and each bid or auction market should be analyzed on its own facts.

Comment 2: Merger simulation and other formal economic modeling can be useful tools in unilateral effects analysis. In order to be useful, the particular model used should be based on sound and robust economic principles, fit the facts of the market, and suitable data must exist to calibrate the model. The fit of a model should be based on the totality of the evidence.

C. In conducting unilateral effects analysis, agencies should assess the competitive constraints and other factors relevant to the ability of the merged firm to exercise market power in the relevant market(s).

WORKING GROUP COMMENTS
Original Comments (June 2009)

Comment 1: In assessing the impact of a merger on the merged firm's ability to exercise market power, agencies should draw on all available evidence, especially evidence created in the ordinary course of business. Common sources of evidence include documents, information, quantitative evidence, and economic analyses from the merging parties, customers, competitors, and other third parties; statements, representations, and testimony from representatives of the merging parties and other industry participants; and generally available industry studies, reports, and market data.

Comment 2: Agencies should assess whether competitive constraints or other market conditions that will remain in the market following the merger are adequate to prevent the creation or enhancement of unilateral market power. Factors that are often relevant in assessing the likelihood of a unilateral exercise of market power as a result of a merger include, but are not limited to:

- *Availability and Responsiveness of Alternative Suppliers*: If alternative suppliers (offering adequate substitutes and with sufficient available capacity) will remain post-merger, and a significant number of customers are willing and able to turn to these alternative suppliers in the event of an anticompetitive increase in price, the threat of losing such customers may be enough to deter the exercise of market power by the merged firm.

- *Entry, Repositioning, or Expansion*: The prospect of entry by new competitors, or expansion or repositioning by existing competitors, may be sufficient in time, scope, and likelihood to deter or defeat any attempt by the merged firm to exercise market power.[1] In some cases, however, a merger may lessen the potential for entry, expansion or repositioning to act as a competitive constraint against the exercise of market power.

- *Buyer Power*: In some circumstances, customers may have the incentive and ability to defeat the exercise of market power through their bargaining strength against the seller because of their size, commercial significance to the seller, or ability to switch to alternative sources of supply. Customers also may have the ability to encourage or sponsor competitive entry or expansion, or to produce the relevant product themselves. In such cases, even firms with very high market share may not be in a position to exercise market power post-merger. To prevent significant anticompetitive effects, however, buyer power must constrain the exercise of market power in the market and not merely protect certain individual customers.

- *Efficiencies*: Agencies should carefully assess any substantiated claims by the merging parties that a merger will generate efficiencies sufficient to prevent or mitigate anticompetitive unilateral effects from the merger. For instance, cost reductions may reduce a merged firm's incentive to raise price. Efficiencies may

---

[1] Recommended Practice for Merger Analysis III addresses the analysis of entry and expansion.

also result in benefits in the form of new or improved products, even when price is not immediately and directly affected. Agencies should consider the impact of substantiated efficiencies that are unlikely to be achieved in the absence of the merger on the merged firm's ability and incentives to compete, and whether such efficiencies may preserve or intensify competition, thereby benefiting consumers.

VI. Coordinated Effects

A. In analyzing the potential for a horizontal merger to result in coordinated effects, agencies should assess whether the merger increases the likelihood that firms in the market will successfully coordinate their behaviour or strengthen existing coordination in a manner that harms competition significantly.

WORKING GROUP COMMENTS
Original Comments (June 2009)

Comment 1: To identify those mergers that materially enhance the likelihood of coordination or strengthen existing coordination, agencies should: (a) assess whether market conditions are conducive to coordination in the relevant market(s) affected by the merger; and (b) analyse specifically whether and how the merger would affect market conditions and firms' ability or incentives that would make coordination more likely post merger.

Comment 2: The fact that a market has conditions that are conducive to coordination in itself is not sufficient to conclude that a merger is likely to further or enhance coordination. Agencies should also be able to determine whether the merger will make coordination easier or more likely, considering the specific features of the market that affect the merged firm's ability and incentives to exercise market power in coordination with rivals.

Comment 3: Changes in market concentration and market share are relevant, but not determinative, factors in assessing whether a merger is likely to further or enhance coordinated interaction. Agencies should focus on whether the merger will materially alter firms' ability or incentives to achieve and sustain coordination. An examination of the role each competitor plays in the competitive dynamics of the market may help to determine how the merger is likely to impact the likelihood of coordination post-merger.

B. In conducting coordinated effects analysis, agencies should assess whether the conditions that are generally necessary for successful coordination are present: (a) the

ability to identify terms of coordination, (b) the ability to detect deviations from the terms of coordination, and (c) the ability to punish deviations that would undermine the coordinated interaction.

WORKING GROUP COMMENTS
Original Comments (June 2009)

Comment 1: Coordinated behaviour can take many forms: it may be tacit or explicit and may or may not be lawful in itself. In some markets, firms may coordinate their behaviour on prices in order to keep them above the competitive level. In other markets, firms' coordination may aim at limiting production or the amount of new capacity brought to the market. Firms may also coordinate by dividing the market, for instance by geographic area or other customer characteristics, or by allocating contracts in bidding markets.

Comment 2: In order to coordinate, firms need to achieve an understanding as to how to do so. This need not involve explicit agreements among competitors, or any communication between them, nor need it involve all firms or perfect coordination between firms. Agencies should assess whether it is likely that participants could achieve terms of coordination that would be sufficiently successful to result in significant harm to competition. When assessing market conditions conducive to reaching terms of coordination, important factors include, but are not limited to:

- The number of firms in a market, since it is easier to coordinate among a few players than among many;
- The existence of frequent and regular orders, which make it easier to coordinate and to detect deviations from the terms of coordination;
- The homogeneity of the products, since it is easier to coordinate on terms such as price when competing products are substantially the same;
- The homogeneity of the firms, especially in terms of symmetry of market shares, similarity of cost structures, levels of vertical integration, and the impact that such homogeneity may have on their ability or incentives to coordinate;
- The degree of transparency of important information that could provide a focal for coordination, such as information concerning prices, output, capacity,

customers served, territories served, discounts, new product introductions, etc.;

- Cross-shareholdings and other links that may make it easier for competitors to exchange information on terms of coordination, and may reduce their incentives to compete; and,
- Other market conditions: for instance, it is easier to coordinate on price when demand and supply conditions are relatively stable than when they are frequently changing (e.g., because of the ease of entry by new firms or rapid, significant product innovations).

Comment 3: Firms may be able to identify terms of coordination even in markets with complex product characteristics or terms of trade. For instance, in a market with many differentiated products, firms may still be able to coordinate on prices by establishing simple pricing rules that reduce the complexity of coordinating on a large number of prices or to coordinate on terms other than prices. Moreover, coordination may not necessarily be achieved on all dimensions of competition.

Comment 4: Although coordination may be in the collective interest of participants, it is often in a firm's individual interest to deviate from the terms of coordination in order to take advantage of the profit opportunity created when other firms raise their prices or otherwise coordinate their behaviour. For coordination to be maintained, participants must have the ability to detect and respond to deviations from the terms of coordination. Agencies should assess the extent to which firms would have the ability to monitor the important terms of coordination and to detect deviations from the terms of coordination in a timely manner. When assessing the likelihood and timeliness of detection of deviations from the coordinated behaviour, important factors include, but are not limited to:

- The degree of transparency of important information necessary to verify compliance by other firms with the terms of coordination, such as information concerning other firms' pricing, output levels, or individual transactions. For instance, if orders for the relevant products are regular both in terms of frequency and size, it may be difficult for a firm to deviate (by expanding its output) without being detected. Also, if there is little fluctuation in demand or costs, deviations may be easier to detect. On the other hand, if orders for the relevant products are infrequent and large, firms may have a greater incentive to deviate to secure orders and the threat of later punishment may not serve as an effective deterrent.

- The extent to which the homogeneity or heterogeneity of the products and firms may make monitoring of compliance with the terms of coordination and detection of deviations more or less difficult.

Comment 5: In order to deter deviations from the terms of coordination, firms must have the ability to punish deviations in a manner that will ensure that coordinating firms find it more profitable to adhere to the terms of coordination than to deviate, given the cost of reprisal. Punishment may take many forms, including temporary abandonment of the terms of coordination by other firms in the market. In assessing whether there will be a sufficiently credible and severe punishment when a deviation by one of the firms is detected, important factors include, but are not limited to:

- The effectiveness of the deterrent mechanism itself: e.g., the threat of expanding output to punish a deviating firm may not be credible or effective if coordinating firms have no or little excess capacity;
- The speed with which the deterrent mechanism can be implemented, given that reprisal that manifests itself after some significant time lag is less likely to be sufficient to offset the benefits from deviating; and,
- the costs of implementing the deterrent mechanism compared to the long-term benefits of coordination.

Other factors, such as the presence of the same firms in several markets (sometimes called "multi-market contacts"), may also be of relevance in determining the likelihood of sufficiently credible and severe punishment.

C. In conducting coordinated effects analysis, agencies should assess the extent to which existing competitive constraints and other factors would likely deter or disrupt effective coordination. In making this assessment, agencies should consider all available evidence, including the pre-merger market conditions that may constrain or facilitate successful coordination, and the impact of the merger on these conditions.

WORKING GROUP COMMENTS
Original Comments (June 2009)

Comment 1: Agencies should assess whether competitive constraints or other market conditions that will remain in the market following the merger are adequate to prevent the creation or enhancement of coordinated interaction. Factors that are often relevant in making this assessment include, but are not limited to:

- *Past Coordination/Behaviour of Firms*: In assessing the likelihood of coordinated effects, agencies should take into account information on the pre-merger characteristics of the markets concerned, including the past behaviour of firms. Evidence of past coordination is important and may serve as strong evidence that all three conditions for successful coordination are present if the relevant market characteristics have not changed appreciably or are not likely to do so in the near future.

- *Entry or Expansion*: Agencies should also consider the actions of competitors not expected to participate in the coordination ("non-coordinating competitors") and potential competitors, which may be sufficient in time, scope, and likelihood to jeopardise the outcome expected from coordination.[2] For instance, the existence of non-coordinating competitors with the ability to expand capacity to take sales from coordinating firms may deter or disrupt coordination. Agencies should therefore consider the existence and significance of barriers to entry and expansion into the relevant market(s) since low barriers to entry and expansion may render successful coordination unlikely or impossible.

- *Maverick Firm*: Coordination may also be difficult to sustain in the presence of a maverick firm—a firm with a different competitive strategy and a greater economic incentive than its rivals to deviate from the terms of coordination. Particular care is needed in mergers involving the acquisition of a maverick firm because in some circumstances those mergers may eliminate a significant constraint to effective coordination and

---

2 Recommended Practice for Merger Analysis III addresses the analysis of entry and expansion.

make coordinated interaction more likely, more successful, or more complete.

- *Buyer Power*: Agencies should consider whether the actions or characteristics of customers affect the likelihood of successful coordination. In some circumstances, buyers may be able to undermine coordinated behaviour, for example by sponsoring entry or expansion. Where large buyers likely would engage in long-term contracting, so that sales covered by such contracts would be large relative to a firm's total output, firms may have a greater incentive to deviate from the terms of coordination.

- *Efficiencies*: Agencies should carefully assess any substantiated claims by the merging parties that a merger will generate efficiencies sufficient to prevent or mitigate coordinated effects from the merger. For instance, cost reductions may enhance a merged firm's incentives to lower prices, thus reducing incentives to coordinate. Efficiencies may also result in benefits in the form of a new or improved product that could undermine coordination. Agencies should consider the impact of substantiated efficiencies that are unlikely to be achieved in the absence of the merger on the merged firm's incentives to coordinate.

Comment 2: In assessing market conditions conducive to coordination, competition authorities should bear in mind that no single factor or group of factors is always determinative.

VII. Assessment of Potential Efficiencies

A. The assessment of potential efficiencies should be part of a competition agency's overall analytical framework for merger review. In specific cases where the merging parties assert that a merger is unlikely to harm competition significantly because of expected efficiencies, agencies should carefully assess appropriate efficiency claims.

Comment 1: Mergers can produce significant efficiencies for the merged firm and such efficiencies can be important business motivation for a merger. Merger efficiencies can include cost savings in production or distribution, more intensive use of existing capacity, economies of scale or scope, increased innovation leading to new or improved products, increased network size or product quality, among others. Some of these efficiencies (innovation, combination of complementary assets, etc.) may bring synergies in a potentially continuous basis, thus considerably enhancing the potential performance of the merged entity.

Comment 2: Mergers can produce efficiencies that may counteract potential anti-competitive effects. To counteract likely anticompetitive harm, efficiencies need to increase rivalry by enhancing the ability and economic incentive of the merged firm to compete. Efficiencies can have such impact if they lower costs and there is sufficient competitive pressure remaining. The benefits of some merger efficiencies can be passed on to consumers, for example, in lower prices or gains in innovation that lead to new or improved products.

Comment 3: In order to determine the impact of a merger that potentially harms competition, agencies should take into account substantiated and likely efficiencies put forward by the parties.

Agencies should not challenge a proposed merger if the demonstrated efficiencies likely would be passed through to consumers and likely would counteract the anticompetitive effects in any relevant market(s) that otherwise would be likely to result from the merger. Efficiency claims should be assessed in light of all other evidence. Efficiencies are most likely to impact merger analysis when the likely adverse competitive effects, absent the efficiencies, are not large.

Comment 4: In most cases, a merger will not raise competition concerns because there are sufficient competitive constraints in the market to prevent significant harm regardless of whether the merger will enable efficiencies. When a merger does not raise competition concerns, the assessment of efficiencies is not necessary.

Comment 5: Efficiencies can be important to merger remedy design. Where feasible, merger remedies should eliminate the anti-competitive effects of a merger in the relevant market without unnecessarily sacrificing substantiated efficiencies in other markets or aspects of the transaction.

Comment 6: Agencies should provide transparency with respect to their approach to evaluating potential efficiencies in merger control, including the weight the agency is likely to place on efficiency claims, the types of efficiencies that are likely to be taken into account, and any evidentiary requirements for substantiating efficiencies. Such guidance may be provided, for example, through public merger guidelines and other statements explaining merger analysis, as well as through decisions in specific cases in which efficiency claims are raised by the parties.

B. In assessing claims that a merger will not harm competition significantly because it will produce efficiencies, agencies should carefully review whether the claimed efficiencies are (a) merger specific, (b) sufficient enough to counteract the potential harm of the proposed merger, and (c) properly substantiated.

Merger Specificity

Comment 1: Agencies should credit only those efficiencies that are merger specific. Merger-specific efficiencies are those that are of direct consequence of the merger, unlikely to be accomplished in the absence of the merger, and cannot be achieved by less anticompetitive alternatives. In many cases, efficiencies can be achieved without the proposed merger. Efficiencies that are achievable, for instance, via internal growth, modernizing equipment, or adoption of industry best practices are not merger specific. In assessing whether efficiencies can be achieved by alternatives other than the merger, only practical business alternatives should be considered.

Sufficiency

Comment 2: Agencies should evaluate whether the claimed efficiencies are sufficient to counteract the merger's potential anticompetitive harm in the relevant market(s), e.g., by likely enhancing the merged firm's ability and incentive to lower prices or otherwise compete.

Comment 3: In many jurisdictions, this sufficiency requirement includes a showing that a sufficient share of the benefits expected to be realised from the efficiencies is likely to be passed on to consumers (or customers), usually in the form of lower prices or increased output. Efficiencies that reduce variable or marginal costs are more likely to be passed on to customers in the form of lower prices and thus more likely to be relevant to the assessment than those that reduce fixed costs. Cost reductions due to anticompetitive reductions in input prices, innovation, output, or service should not be considered. When dynamic efficiencies are important, they may benefit consumers by resulting in either improved or new products stemming from higher R&D investment or new combinations of understanding, experience or technologies.

Comment 4: Where reasonably possible, efficiencies and resulting benefits should be quantified. Efficiency claims should be assessed net of the costs to achieve the expected efficiencies. While the quantification of claimed efficiencies is often among the most speculative elements of merger review, it can better inform identifiable benefits to consumers and a comparison of the efficiencies with the likely harm to competition.

Substantiation

Comment 5: Merger-specific efficiency gains are difficult to assess and verify both for merging parties and for competition agencies. Agencies should advise merging parties to submit efficiency claims very early in the process as their verification by reasonable means typically requires a significant amount of time and resources. The merging parties typically have the best knowledge about the likely efficiencies that a merger may create as the information about the claimed efficiencies is normally solely in their possession. Therefore, the merging parties should be required to present evidence regarding the type, likelihood, size, and timing of any claimed efficiencies, including how they would be achieved, how they would enhance the firm's ability and incentive to compete, and why they are merger specific. Efficiency gains are often claimed by merging parties but not frequently supported with convincing evidence.

Comment 6: To verify efficiency claims, agencies typically review internal data and documents from the merging firms to determine how realistic the claims are. Evidence that agencies consider in evaluating efficiency claims typically includes internal documents that were used by management to decide on the merger, company statements about the expected efficiencies, business plans on how the company plans to achieve the efficiencies, examples of past efficiencies and any studies on the type and size of expected efficiency gains. Proof that similar efficiencies were achieved in the past from similar actions can be among the most convincing evidence in evaluating efficiency claims. In evaluating the information submitted to substantiate efficiency claims and any conclusions, agencies should assess the accuracy of the parties' data and information, as well as the analytical methods and assumptions used.

Comment 7: The greater the likely adverse effects on competition, the greater the need to demonstrate clear, significant, and verifiable efficiencies and their impact on competition and consumers. When the potential adverse competitive effects of a merger are likely to be substantial, significant verifiable efficiencies that are likely to benefit consumers would be necessary to prevent the merger from being anticompetitive. Likewise, the more uncertain and modest the likely harm to competition, the greater potential role for claimed efficiencies to outweigh the harm.

Comment 8: The stronger the evidence to substantiate the efficiency claims, the more confidence an agency is likely to have in relying on the claims as part of its analysis. Efficiency claims that are vague, speculative, and cannot be verified by reasonable means should not be credited.

Comment 9: The time horizon for claimed efficiencies can be an important consideration in evaluating efficiencies in light of potential anti-competitive harm. Efficiencies should have a timely impact on the merged firm's ability and incentives to compete. The more time projected for the efficiencies to be realised, the more uncertainty and difficulty there is with respect to predicting their effects.

Possible addition to A, comment 3, for consideration and comment:

The evaluation of efficiencies commonly is part of an agency's competitive assessment, focusing on whether the claimed efficiencies counteract the harm in the market in which the lessening of competition occurs. In a few jurisdictions, efficiencies also are considered after a merger is determined to be anticompetitive, as a separate assessment of the offsetting customer benefits of a merger.

[Parts VIII and IX, on entry and expansion and the failing firm defense, are omitted]

XI. Remedies

A. A remedy should address the identified competitive harm arising from the proposed transaction.

WORKING GROUP COMMENTS (2017)

Comment 1: The object of a remedy should be to maintain or restore competition otherwise lost due to the merger. A remedy should be considered only if the agency has a sound basis to believe that the proposed transaction, if implemented, would contravene the applicable merger review law. The remedy should adequately address the potential competitive harm identified, but should not have the object of improving upon premerger competition. Tailoring the remedy to the competitive harm allows competition agencies to require the least intrusive remedy and permit, if possible, the realization of the merger's benefits, without compromising effectiveness.

Comment 2: There are instances in which only an outright prohibition can adequately address the competitive concerns. The merging parties should be permitted, however, to propose alternative resolutions that permit the transaction to proceed with appropriate modifications, conditions, and/or obligations that maintain or restore competition otherwise likely to be lost due to the proposed transaction, consistent with the applicable merger review law. Before pursuing or adopting an outright prohibition, agencies should consider such alternative resolutions. In addition, the agency may take the initiative to propose alternative resolutions.

Comment 3: The proposal, discussion, and adoption of remedies should be conducted in a manner consistent with other Recommended Practices, particularly those on Conduct of Merger Investigations, Procedural Fairness, Transparency, and Interagency Coordination and informed by the Merger Remedies Guide and the Practical Guide on International Cooperation.

B. The merger review system should provide a transparent framework for the proposal, discussion, and adoption of remedies.

WORKING GROUP COMMENTS (2017)

Comment 1: Information on the jurisdiction's procedures for proposing, discussing, evaluating, and adopting remedies should be readily available to those involved in merger review proceedings. Such information may include, as applicable, when, how and to whom remedies should be proposed, the types of remedies that the agency generally prefers and in which instances, and any standard terms or implementation provisions the remedy would be expected to include.

Comment 2: In the event the competition agency identifies competitive concerns, the agency should provide the merging parties with timely and substantiated information on those concerns so the parties can consider and propose remedies to address those concerns in due time prior to the final enforcement decision. Merger review procedures should provide means to ensure that competition agencies have adequate time to discuss suitable remedies with the merging parties, evaluate the proposed remedies, and consult appropriate third parties on the effectiveness of the remedies.

C. Procedures and practices should be established to ensure that remedies are effective and easily administrable.

WORKING GROUP COMMENTS (2017)

Comment 1: Remedies should be effective in maintaining or restoring competition otherwise lost due to the proposed transaction and be easily administrable. Remedies should not require significant administrative intervention by the agency after the transaction is consummated.

Comment 2: Remedies can take two basic forms: (a) structural remedies, which help to maintain or restore the pre-merger market structure (such as commitments to divest assets), and (b) non-structural remedies, which involve modifications or constraints on the future conduct of the merged entity (such as commitments with respect to certain contractual clauses). Certain remedies, such as commitments involving licensing of intellectual property rights or access to facilities, may be characterized as structural or non-structural, depending on the circumstances. An effective package of remedies adopted with respect to a proposed transaction may consist of structural and/or non-structural components, including short-term transitional arrangements that support a structural remedy.

Comment 3: Structural remedies are generally preferred over non-structural remedies because they directly maintain or restore the competitive structure of the market that would be otherwise lost due to the proposed transaction, have a durable impact, are easier to administer and do not require medium or long-term monitoring to ensure compliance. Structural remedies can take several forms. The preferred structural remedy is typically the divestiture of an ongoing, stand-alone business unit, including the sale of all the infrastructure, components, and human resources necessary for the divested business to compete immediately after the remedy is implemented. The divestiture of less than an existing business carries more risk, and requires more agency scrutiny, but may constitute an effective remedy if, taking into account resources already owned and operated by a potential buyer, the divested assets are sufficient to allow the buyer to compete successfully in the relevant market. While short-term assistance from the merging parties can be necessary to transition assets to an independent buyer, remedies should avoid creating ongoing relationships and entanglements between the merged entity and the purchaser of divested assets that may impede competition.

Comment 4: Where structural remedies are either not possible or not appropriate to address the competitive harm, or where structural remedies may undermine significant efficiency benefits, a non-structural remedy may be appropriate to address the competition concerns. Non-structural remedies that facilitate or protect competition (such as reducing switching costs and opening up tender processes) are generally more effective than those that aim to control prices or output levels (such as price controls, service level agreements, and supply commitments). In crafting non-structural remedies, competition agencies should consider whether ongoing monitoring of the remedy is feasible and be wary of high implementation costs associated with monitoring, terms that restrain potentially pro-competitive conduct, and terms that are vulnerable to circumvention and manipulation. Competition agencies should consider other alternatives before imposing price controls as remedies, as price controls can distort market forces and harm competition, require a great deal of market insight that is not readily available, and will likely require regulatory oversight and intervention to implement and maintain.

Comment 5: The remedy's effectiveness may depend on the identity of the prospective purchaser of the assets to be divested, particularly where less than an ongoing business unit is being divested. For a remedy to be effective, it should enable the prospective purchaser to be a viable and long-term competitor in the market in which the competitive harm was identified. Competition agencies should evaluate prospective purchasers for their financial strength, managerial expertise and operational capabilities, as well as for their independence and intention to compete with the merged firm in the affected market after divestitures. The agency should retain the authority and have appropriate procedures to approve a prospective purchaser.

Comment 6: When competition agencies have concerns about the availability of a suitable purchaser or viability of the proposed remedy, they should consider requiring approval of a pre-identified buyer of the divested assets before the merger is consummated. Pre-identified buyers should also be considered when there are concerns about a lengthy divestiture process resulting in deterioration of the divested assets.

Comment 7: Market testing, either a formal or informal process by which competition agencies obtain views and comments from third-party customers, suppliers, and/or competitors, should be encouraged when it helps to determine if the proposed remedy will adequately address competitive concerns. Third party submissions or comments should be evaluated for self-interest or any motives that might attempt to influence the agencies' views.

Comment 8: Timing is a critical factor in determining whether a merger remedy is effective. Remedies should be implemented in a prompt and timely manner. Remedies should have a specified end date or termination provision.

D. Remedies should provide appropriate means to ensure implementation, monitoring of compliance, and enforcement of the remedy.

WORKING GROUP COMMENTS (2017)

Comment 1: Jurisdictions may have different terminology or mechanisms for formalizing and enforcing remedies. Regardless of the terminology used ("remedy order" or other), a formal and written form of imposing remedies should identify, provide notice, and bind the entities subject to its terms. The terms should be sufficiently clear and precise to provide the parties adequate guidance in implementing the remedy, in particular with respect to the scope of any assets to be divested and any obligations regarding the ongoing conduct of the parties. The remedy order should also include provisions which will enable the competition agency to investigate compliance and ensure the order is fully implemented.

Comment 2: As part of a structural remedy, a competition agency should require the merging parties to maintain and preserve the assets pending divestiture to ensure that there is no deterioration of the assets' competitive strength. Such requirements or "hold separate" measures can help to ensure the independence and viability of divested assets by maintaining their value and goodwill, protecting sensitive information, encouraging employees to remain with the entity until divestiture, and otherwise ensuring the divested assets are not allowed to deteriorate. In some cases, a competition agency may wish to appoint a hold separate manager who can oversee implementation of hold separate provisions.

Comment 3: In a remedy order, it may be appropriate to include terms permitting the competition agency to select one or more trustees who are independent of the parties and can oversee the divestiture process or the conduct of the merging parties over the duration of a non-structural remedy. Monitoring trustees can help to oversee implementation of remedies and provide regular reports or updates to the competition agency. A divestiture trustee may take over the divestiture process from the merging parties if they fail to sell the divested assets within the required time period.

Trustees should be independent of the merging firms, have appropriate qualifications for the role, and should not be subject to conflicts of interest. The scope and limits of the trustee's responsibilities and authority should be clearly set out in a mandate provided by the competition agency, which should also state that the trustee cannot accept instructions or be dismissed by the merging firms. Nevertheless, the parties can be required to compensate the trustee.

Comment 4: The competition agency should have the means to investigate compliance with the remedy order, including the ability to inspect and copy records, conduct reviews, and to require periodic or one-time reporting obligations by the parties and/or the trustee(s) on the implementation of the remedy. The ultimate decision regarding compliance with the remedy order should rest with the agency or court, and not with the trustee.

Comment 5: Competition agencies are unable to control or predict every factor capable of impacting the implementation of remedies. Significant and permanent changes in market conditions may impact the effectiveness of a remedy, especially in cases where a non-structural remedy continues over a long duration. Review or revision clauses, or other procedures which would permit remedies to be removed or modified upon demonstration of specified objectives or criteria, may provide flexibility to address unanticipated factors. Modifications can range from extensions of implementation deadlines to remedy substitutions or waivers to implement commitments.

Comment 6: A party's failure to comply with the terms of a remedy order should either be enforceable by the competition agency directly or through the courts. In some jurisdictions, the merger clearance may automatically lapse. To discourage non-compliance, the potential penalties should be clearly articulated. In the event of deliberate non-compliance with a remedy order by the merging parties, competition agencies should contemplate available options within their legal framework to ensure that the remedy order is properly implemented. If non-compliance results from the remedy order being impossible to implement, competition authorities can consider whether modifications or alternative remedies may be effective to address the relevant competition concerns.

2. Public Interest Defenses and Concerns

Many newer antitrust jurisdictions, and especially developing countries, allow public interest justifications for anticompetitive mergers. If many jurisdictions allow public interest justifications, why do the ICN recommended practices propose that antitrust merger analysis be confined to significant harm to competition?

a. The Public's Interest Beyond Competition and Consumer Welfare

A major design question is whether the public interest justifications, when allowed, are applied by the competition authorities themselves or by a minister after being presented with the competition analysis. The latter model (discretion of the minister) has been adopted in the UK and Germany. The former model is the one adopted in South Africa. This model has been defended by the former Chair of the South African Competition Tribunal as likely to result in greater appreciation of the competition concerns and more likely to probe whether expectations for achieving the public interest objectives are realistic. David Lewis, *The Political Economy of Antitrust*, 2001 FORDHAM CORPORATE LAW INSTITUTE, Chap. 24 (B. Hawk ed. 2002).

In South Africa a merger may be stopped or allowed on purely public interest grounds, regardless whether the merger is procompetitive or anticompetitive. Competition Act South Africa, 1998, Section 1A Empowering the previously discriminated-against majority (black South Africans or "historically disadvantaged persons" as defined in the statute) is a major public interest concern that pervades virtually all positive law—reflecting a central imperative.

In dealing with public interest justifications, one must first try to understand the public interest standard.

The South Africa Competition Law prohibits mergers likely to substantially prevent or lessen competition, except that the Commission and Tribunal must also determine whether the merger can or cannot be justified on substantial public interest grounds. The statute was amended in 2019 to say:

> When determining whether a merger can or cannot be justified on public interest grounds, the Competition Commission or the Competition Tribunal must consider the effect that the merger will have on—
>
> a) a particular industrial sector or region;
>
> b) employment;
>
> c) the ability of small and medium businesses, or firms controlled or owned by historically disadvantaged persons, to effectively enter into, participate in or expand within the market; and

d) the ability of national industries to compete in international markets. § 12 A(3);

e) the promotion of a greater spread of ownership, in particular to increase the levels of ownership by historically disadvantaged persons and workers in firms in the market.

During 2024, the Commission published Revised Public Interest Guidelines relating to Merger Control (CC_Public-Interest-Guidelines-.pdf). While not binding, they reflect the approach that the Commission will seek to adopt and generally aligned with earlier drafts of the guidelines and, for the most, with the caselaw.

Significantly, however, the Guidelines have sought to adopt the position that the provisions dealing with ownership create a positive obligation to promote a greater spread thereof. The perspective is that all mergers are required to promote these outcomes. According to the Guidelines, this means that parties to a neutral merger that raises no competition or public interest concerns are still required to demonstrate that they have promoted a greater spread of ownership. The Guidelines say that this may be demonstrated through remedial measures including the introduction of ownership interests in favour of workers or historically disadvantaged persons.

The Commission has sought to underline that its position accords with the purpose of the statute that articulates its transformational aspirations to address concentration and the racially-skewed nature of the South African economy consistent with the Constitutional Court's observations in the Mediclinic merger (Competition Commission of South Africa v Mediclinic Southern Africa (Pty) Ltd 2022 (4) SA 323 (CC)).

While laudable and justified in relation to its aspirations, the approach has attracted controversy as reflecting an implausible interpretation of the statute, not according with merger specific assessment, misapplying the observations of the Constitutional Court, amounting to unjustified appropriation and as arbitrary and misdirected—disincentivizing investment (local and foreign) to the detriment of the public interest.

While the Commission is willing to consider remedies outside ownership interests, its approach is seen as a misuse of merger regulation to address imperatives better done through other legislative and policy interventions, as well as outside appropriate holistic merger specific assessments as encouraged by the Tribunal in Epiroc Holdings SA / K2022596519 (South Africa) (Pty) Ltd and Polkadots Properties 117 (Pty) Ltd (Case No. LM148Nov2022). The view may be that the Commission's interventions may be dilatory, rather than enhancing, to the public interest in this regard and fails to appreciate the economic and commercial context of mergers and related decisions. Although predating the amendments to the statute, the debate about the nature of ownership interventions may be illustrated by considering the large merger between Shell South Africa (Pty) Ltd. and Tepco Petroleum (Pty) Ltd., Competition Tribunal, Republic of South Africa, case 66/LM/Oct01, Feb. 22, 2002. Thebe Investment Corporation was a black empowerment investment holding company established to use economic opportunities to benefit historically disadvantaged persons and communities, owned Tepco, an employer of 38 people, 80% of whom were historically disadvantaged. Tepco owned 14 gas stations country-wide, and was failing. Thebe proposed to sell Tepco to Shell South Africa, and at the same time acquire 17.5% to 25% of Shell South Africa Marketing. Shell South Africa Marketing expected to maintain Tepco as a separate brand for the foreseeable future, to develop it in the market as long as it should remain profitable, and to retain Tepco's management, which was predominantly black.

The South African oil industry had adopted a charter on empowering historically disadvantaged South Africans, aiming to bring about their 25% ownership and control within 10 years. Shell's overriding reasons for purchasing Tepco was to lay the foundation for involvement of previously disadvantaged South Africans.

The Competition Commission vetted the transaction, found that it would not harm competition, and recommended that the Tribunal approve the transaction subject to three conditions designed to further the urgent South African goal of black empowerment: 1) that Tepco continue to exist jointly controlled by Thebe and Shell S.A., 2) that Tepco be maintained as a viable brand, and 3) that any agreement between the parties be submitted to the Commission for approval.

The Tribunal agreed with the Commission that the transaction would not harm competition and proceeded to examine the "public interest" conditions:

> ***First Condition****—Tepco continue to exist in the market jointly controlled/owned by Thebe and Shell South Africa*

42 The difficulty that the Tribunal saw with this condition was that it amounted to restructuring the merger in a form that neither of the merging parties wanted. Tepco was no longer viable as a self-standing company. It appeared that its difficulties were, to some significant extent, structural as a small company isolated in a low return segment of the oil industry's value chain had little chance of

sustainable growth. The Commission's condition was not seen as a solution to this problem and adding Shell as a shareholder would not cure Tepco's ills nor was it likely that Shell would agree to a condition that kept the companies separate operationally. Empowerment not was seen as being furthered by obliging firms controlled by historically disadvantaged persons to continue to exist on a life support machine.

Second Condition*—That the Tepco brand be maintained as a viable brand in the market place*

43 Noting that the Tribunal seemed to assume firstly that this remedy was not self-standing and must be coupled to the first condition, in which case it was seen as suffering from the same defects as the first condition viz. the prolonging of a non-viable option. The parties had not said they would discontinue the Tepco brand as confirmed at the hearing—yet wanted the freedom to make this judgment call themselves. The Tribunal noted that there is no public interest served by imposing on them the compulsory continuation of a brand name.

44 * * *

49 It falls to be recognized that, while the Commission may have stated that it had no wish to prevent the transaction, the imposition of a condition on the purchaser would come with a price and Thebe, precisely the firm owned and controlled by historically disadvantaged persons, would pay that price. Further, even if Tepco had been a company in perfect health, it was noted that the Commission should be extremely careful when, in the name of supporting historically disadvantaged investors, it intervenes in a commercial decision by such an investor.

50 Consider the following eminently plausible scenario: Thebe, in its commercial wisdom, may have decided to consolidate and expand its interests in the leisure and tourism industry. In order to do this it may have elected to dispose of its assets in the oil industry. That would represent a significant and perfectly respectable mode of financing business expansion and, while the Commission may have believed that its proposed condition only constrains the acquiring firm, it constrains the seller, the target firm, to sell its assets only to a purchaser who will accept those conditions, or it is also constrained to offer its assets at a discount because the assets are accompanied by conditions specifying the post-transaction utilization of these assets.

51 To constrain the capital-raising options of firms owned by historically disadvantaged persons in this way not only condemns

these firms to the margins of the economy and the margins of those sectors in which it believes it is best able to make a significant mark, it also lays the Commission open to a charge of paternalism. The Commission's role is to promote and protect competition and a specified public interest. It is not to second-guess the commercial decisions of precisely that element of the public that it is enjoined to defend, particularly where no threat to competition is entailed.

Following the amendments, the Commission nonetheless proceeded to prohibit the acquisition between ECP Africa Fund, Burger King South Africa and Grand Foods in June 2021.

The Commission considered that, while not anticompetitive, the merger would lead to a significant reduction in the shareholding of historically disadvantaged persons in the target firm. The Commission claimed that it was therefore concerned that the proposed merger will have a substantial negative effect on the promotion of greater spread of ownership, in particular to increase the levels of ownership by historically disadvantaged persons in firms in the market as contemplated by the amendments to the statute (Section 12A(3)(e) of the Competition Act)—concluding that the proposed merger cannot be justified on substantial public interest grounds because it was seen as have a "substantial negative effect on the promotion of a greater spread of ownership, in particular the levels of ownership by historically disadvantaged persons and workers in firms in the market".

The coherence of the Commission's decision falls to be questioned on similar grounds to those described by the Tribunal in Tepco (above). While noting that merging parties typically engaged with the Commission and it appears proposed consequential remedies in this matter, the Commission appeared to adopt a myopic and unbalanced stance unwilling to consider broader factors and circumstances as required by the statute (and highlighted in Tepco)—potentially undermining the value historically disadvantaged persons may achieve for their investments and, accordingly, undermining the public interest.

Indeed, the question may now legitimately be asked whether the Commission's stance is not harming the transformation of the South African economy—however well-meaning—by causing uncertainty, inhibiting investment (local and foreign) including where historically disadvantaged shareholders decide to decrease their interests for legitimate commercial and other reasons.

The Tribunal has not pronounced definitively about the stance of the Commission in the Guidelines that a positive obligation arises to promote a greater spread of ownership. Nonetheless, in statements in 2025 in the context of the Vodacom/Maziv transaction LM148Dec21, the Tribunal appears to align with a plausible and merger specific interpretation of the law that the first step in the assessment of any public interest effects resulting from a merger (both positive and negative) is to determine if they are merger-specific, considering inter alia the relevant counterfactual(s). The Tribunal correctly notes that effects are not regarded as "merger-specific" if they are not related to or as a result of the proposed transaction and/or if they will likely occur regardless of or absent the proposed transaction.

For the remainder, the Guidelines set out approaches that broadly align with the statute and the prevailing caselaw. The Commission's general approach is: (i) to determine the likely effect of a merger on each public interest ground; (ii) to determine if the effect is substantial; (iii) where it is determined that there is an effect and the effect is substantial, the Commission will consider possible remedies to cure that effect; and (iv) where the effect cannot be remedied, the Commission may, on a case-by-case basis, consider equally weighty countervailing grounds. As noted above, however, the Commission adopted the implausible interpretation of the statute that a failure to "promote" ownership outcomes, as a positive requirement even where no competition or public interest concerns arise in a merger, may be a detrimental public interest outcome.

In this context, the Wal-Mart Stores, Inc. & Massmart merger is worth considering and which came before the Competition Appeal Court in South Africa. The decision affords insight into the nature of the assessment of the public interest and remains applicable in the context of the Guidelines.

WAL-MART STORES, INC. & MASSMART HOLDINGS LIMITED

Competition Appeal Court of South Africa, Case No: 110/CAC/Jul11 (March 2012)

On 31 May, 2011 the South African Competition Tribunal conditionally approved an acquisition by Wal-Mart of a controlling interest in Massmart, a leading South African retailer. The Tribunal found that the merger raised no competition concerns. It did find that the merger raised public interest concerns—particularly the potential loss of jobs and of opportunities for local suppliers. To alleviate these concerns, the merging parties agreed to certain commitments: (1) no non-voluntary layoffs for two years; (2) employment preferences for 503 previously laid off employees; (3) to honor existing collective bargaining agreements; and (4) committing 100 million South African Rands (about $7 million) aimed at the development of South African suppliers. Despite these commitments, various entities challenged the Tribunal's approval decision, including a number of labor unions, the Minister of Economic Development, the Minister of Trade and Industry and the Minister of Agriculture, Forestry and Fisheries ("the Ministers"), and the South African Small Medium and Micro Enterprises Forum. The Competition Appeal Court ultimately upheld the Tribunal's decision to allow the merger, but with some conditions.

The appeal

91 The trade union SACCAWU based the foundation of its appeal upon a criticism of the normative approach adopted by the Tribunal to the application of the Act. Thus, it contended that the approach adopted by the Tribunal and the merging parties ignored the express language of the Act. It argued that the South African competition regime is concerned with economic or market power, its creation, extension, distribution and (ab)use, and that the entry of a firm with the scale of operations and consequent economic power of Wal-Mart into the South African economy will disrupt the competitive equilibrium and processes in the retail sector, as well as alter competition for suppliers in the retail supply chain. SACCAWU therefore contended that the merging parties' uncritical adoption of the perspective of a consumer welfare standard ignored its "rejection" by the Act. SACCAWU suggested that s 12A enjoins the competition authorities to take account of factors which do not play a role in terms of the consumer welfare approach to competition policy. In this connection, reference was made to David Lewis *Global Competition: Law Makers and Globalisation* (2011) and the perspective which extends beyond that of a narrow consumer welfare standard as contended for by Eleanor Fox *Poverty and Markets* (March 2009). In citing these authorities, SACCAWU was not taken to be arguing in favour of a total welfare standard which would take account only of consumer and producer surplus, but rather that the Act supported a more nuanced test than that of a consumer welfare standard.* * *

98 Viewed holistically, it was considered that there was merit in the argument that the Act should be read in terms of an economic perspective that extends beyond a standard consumer welfare approach. By virtue of an embrace of the goals of a free market and effective competition together with an incorporation of uniquely South African elements, including the need to address South Africa's exclusionary past (reflected expressly in the statute), the legislature imposed ambitious goals upon the competition authorities. This ambition is further captured in section which mandates an enquiry into substantial public interest grounds.* * *

104 Much of the debate in the proceedings turned on the question, which was considered to be of importance to the merger by the Tribunal, namely would Wal-Mart post-merger be able to source goods from overseas and in particular Asia more cheaply than can Massmart and if so would it. This question was deemed to hold the key to the determination of whether the potential losses which were argued to flow from the merger, particularly when analysed in terms of public interest factors, would outweigh the proclaimed consumer advantages of the merger. The Tribunal complained about an absence of more precise evidence, commenting that 'it is highly probable that if Massmart was procuring at the prices near to those of Wal-Mart, this exercise—entirely within the knowledge of the merging parties—would have been done. Hence the Tribunal appeared sceptical of the claim that no change to procurement patterns would take place.

However, in its view,

> "The problem is that the concern raised in relation to local procurement/imports is also associated with important benefits for consumers. A possible loss of jobs in manufacturing of an uncertain extent must be weighed up against consumer interests in lower prices and job creation at Massmart. Since the evidence is that the likely consumers who will benefit most from the lower prices associated with the merger are low income consumers and those consumers without any means of support of their own, thus the poorest of South Africans, the public interest in lower prices is no less compelling."

105 The determination of the trade-off between consumer benefits and job losses caused by increased importation of goods presently obtained in South Africa, was bedevilled by the lack of precise evidence. * * *

115 The evidence in the case thus became crucial as to the proper judicial engagement with the range of enquires. The intervening parties had some difficulty in obtaining the comprehensive picture which would have included the merging parties' proposals with regard to the ratio between domestic procurement and imports. This was seen as somewhat surprising because it was expected that Wal-Mart would have developed a series of business models in order to test the extent to which the considerable investment in Massmart would prove to be profitable.

116 Nonetheless, even if that information had been available, it would not have gainsaid the conclusion, based on uncontested evidence, that prices would reduce to the benefit of consumers as a result of the

merger. The legitimate criticism about insufficient evidence notwithstanding, it was clear from the record as a whole that consumer benefits would flow from the merger.

117 It did also not appear to be disputed either that there is the potential for small and medium sized South African suppliers to gain benefit from the presence of Wal-Mart and its unique access to global value supply chains.

118 These positive factors were seen as being needed to be weighed against any losses which would be experienced by small and medium sized businesses, as well as the consequences for employment, when the transaction was viewed holistically. But, as was noted, in dealing with a standard that seeks to balance consumer and other forms of societal welfare as set out in the Act, it was seen as unlikely that, even with further information as sought by the Ministers, a set of calculations could have been produced which would ultimately have justified the conclusion based on such a standard, that the merger should not have been approved. The available evidence, together with inferences that could reasonably be drawn, particularly from uncontested evidence, was seen as supporting that conclusion. * * *

Employment rights

122 SACCAWU also sought the intervention of the court in order to protect its members against the adverse effects of what it termed 'the Wal-Mart model' on employment levels, particularly terms and conditions of employment and the organisational rights of workers within the merged firm. It conceded that the conditions imposed by the Tribunal had gone some way towards achieving the protection of workers. However, it was contended that more was required to protect the union structurally against what was termed 'Wal-Mart's anti-union stance'.

123 SACCAWU contended that there was compelling evidence relating to Wal-Mart's practice and policies concerning workers; in particular empirical evidence of the adverse impact of Wal-Mart's employment practices and policies and wages and other terms and conditions of employment. In its view, Wal-Mart had ruthlessly pursued a labour relations strategy which was designed to prevent the unionisation of its workers. It had done so successfully in that 1.3 million out of 2.1 million of its workers in the United States of America were not unionised. This had resulted in wage levels of Wal-Mart employees being 12.4% less than for workers employed by other retailers. According to SACCAWU, the merging parties, in their evidence before the Tribunal, had provided no firm and enforceable commitments regarding labour and employment issues but merely required the Tribunal to accept their 'bold denials or say-so' that

'Wal-Mart's global reputation for poor labour relations' would not be imported into South Africa through the merger. * * *

After reviewing a lengthy body of conflicting evidence on Wal-Mart's effect on labor conditions, the court held that such questions should be left to labor law rather than competition law. In summary, it is not the role of competition law to provide legal protections to potential disputes of interest which stand to be resolved by the exercise of collective power. To the extent that the merging parties would seek to erode union or employee rights guaranteed under existing law, these fell to be protected by the labor courts, which are set up to deal with disputes of rights.

The Tribunal's order

The court turned finally to the sufficiency of the commitment to invest in local suppliers. It found that the concern about Wal-Mart turning to global supply chains was insufficient to block the merger—yet the court's remedial analysis did not end there.

164 In summary, the concern that Wal-Mart's coordinated global purchasing operation and superior infrastructure for utilizing global value chains would result in the importation of consumer goods, thereby harming domestic producers, which harm would exceed the benefits of cheaper products for local consumers, could not, on the basis of the available evidence, particularly that of the intervening parties, justify the prohibition of the merger. That did not however lead to the conclusion that the statute justifies a blanket approval where the solution to the possible threats of greater imports and therefore detrimental consequences for local manufacturers was not, in the view of the court, to impose a domestic content requirement. The Tribunal had shown the difficulties which such a proposal would create. Further, a blanket procurement quota could also give rise to distortions both between the merged firm and other large firms in the market and in respect of manipulation of the product mix in order to circumvent the designated procurement levels—and may also facilitate forms of price collusion. For these reasons, the Tribunal's rejection of the proposals for import restrictions was not be disturbed on appeal.

165 The court noted a problem however with the conditions as approved by the Tribunal in that they reflected an offer made by the merging parties which were accepted by the Tribunal, without sufficient interrogation as to precisely how the programme would be implemented and the consequences for dealing with the potential difficulties which may be encountered by local manufacturers, the effects on employment and the ability of small and medium sized businesses to operate within a competitive global environment. * * *

[168] To this end, a variation of the proposal put up by the merging parties was seen as justified. The merging parties suggested that the programme could benefit from the advice given by a committee which would comprise representatives of trade unions business and in particular small, medium size enterprises together with government. It was seen by the court as preferable for a committee comprising of an expert chosen by SACCAWU, another by Wal-Mart and a third by government to be invited to produce a report within three months of the delivery of the judgment which would then allow the court to develop an investment remedy which was both rational, justifiable in terms of the evidence provided, as well as in terms of the challenges with which the South African economy is confronted as a result of this merger and the legitimate concerns which follow from the provisions of the statute, in particular the future of small and medium sized producers.

[169] The court considered that the parties would, in turn, be entitled to place further affidavits before the court, following the report, in order to assist the court in framing the precise nature of the particular condition. There was the option of referring the matter back to the Tribunal which could have held further hearings and gather evidence before reformulating the condition—although cognisant of the time already taken to resolve the disputes concerning the merger and the need to bring this matter to finality as expeditiously as possible, this was not done.

[170] On this basis, a dialogic model was seen as suitable in which the court could engage with the parties to resolve the outstanding disputes—justifying an order that the court benefit from expert advice and further responses from the parties.

The debate in Wal-Mart informs many of the provisions of the Guidelines. When assessing the effect of a merger on a particular industrial sector or region, the Commission will consider the effect of the merger on development, environmental sustainability and employment (reflecting the introduction of suitability considerations), with a key theme being localisation.

When it comes to employment, the Guidelines contemplate an onus on the merging parties to show that contemplated retrenchments (in particular those occurring in proximate timeframes to the merger) are not merger related and/or to justify any retrenchments related to the merger (such as where the merger is required for the parties to remain competitive or may have consumer welfare enhancing outcomes). The Constitutional Court in Coca-Cola Beverages Africa (Coca-Cola Beverages Africa (Pty) Ltd v Competition Commission and another CCT 192/22) has, contrary to the Guidelines, also clarified that legal causation involves identifying the proximate cause of job losses (considering reality, predominance and efficiency) when differentiating between job losses due to a merger or those attributable to operational reasons applying good business sense—finding that the retrenchments were related to the reduction of labour costs (and not the merger in question).

In line with the statute, the Guidelines note that the merger's impact on the ability of small and medium businesses, or firms controlled or owned by historically disadvantaged persons, to effectively enter into, participate in or expand within the market are required to be considered. Prior to the amendment in 2019, the section only required consideration of such businesses or persons becoming competitive implying a lower threshold for considering whether a merger will have a detrimental impact in this regard.

The Guidelines also deal with considering on the extent to which a merger may effect the ability of national industries to compete in international markets.

Contrast the South African Wal-Mart decision to the following US case. Was the federal court right to hold that Puerto Rico's Attorney General acted unconstitutionally in seeking to impose restrictions on a merger based on their effects on local jobs and supply opportunities?

WAL-MART STORES, INC. v. RODRIGUEZ

238 F. Supp. 2d 395 (United States District Court of Puerto Rico 2002)

(The opinion was vacated as part of a settlement; it is not precedent)

Wal-Mart sought to buy Supermercados Amigo, a supermarket chain in Puerto Rico. The parties notified both the federal and commonwealth antitrust authorities. The FTC approved the acquisition subject to divestiture of four stores at locations where there were competitive overlaps. Meanwhile, local interests were pressuring the Puerto Rico Department of Justice and Anabelle Rodriguez, Secretary of Justice, to stop the merger under the Puerto Rico Anti-Monopoly Act, or at least to protect the public interest in jobs and local sales. Rodriguez believed that she was at liberty to negotiate for concessions on these points for the good of the people of the Commonwealth of Puerto Rico. "[T]he protection and preservation of existing jobs, as well as the creation of new ones, [was] the highest priority of the current administration." Rodriguez demanded that Wal-Mart "will not reduce or suspend its current volume of local agricultural and/or food products" and that Wal-Mart guarantee the maintenance of the current work force. Wal-Mart was willing to commit to buy as much locally as "it could" and submitted evidence that its local purchases were increasing; and it was willing even to maintain the *level* of its current workforce, but not to retain all existing employees. When the negotiations faltered, Rodriguez (for Puerto Rico) sued to enjoin the "monopolistic" merger.

In turn, Wal-Mart sued Rodriguez to block her from prohibiting the merger. The court granted Wal-Mart a preliminary injunction on grounds that Rodriguez had evidenced a pattern of bad faith in the negotiations and that the imposition of the conditions guaranteeing jobs and local purchases violated the Commerce Clause and Equal Protection Clause of the US Constitution.

In the course of its analysis, the court noted these effects of the "public policy" clauses:

Labor

> The controversy in the language of the agreements with regards to [the] labor issue can be best summarized as follows: while the PRDOJ wanted to get Wal-Mart to agree not to alter the current labor force, that is, the employees that are currently working at the Amigo stores, Wal-Mart was willing to agree to maintain the current number of employees, leaving open the possibility that current employees could be terminated as long as their positions were not eliminated. But despite their lack of intention to downsize their current work force, Plaintiffs could not agree to maintain the current employees and forego the possibility of ever letting go of anyone who currently works at Amigo. Wal-Mart anticipated that just like in any other acquisition, there was a possibility that the integration process would reveal deficiencies in the labor force that would need to be remedied. Moreover, no layoffs in the stores were anticipated, but Wal-Mart could not make the same commitment with regards to positions in their administrative and home offices. The phenomenon of attrition, over which they have no control, was also raised as a concern for Wal-Mart. Finally, as with the levels of purchase condition, Wal-Mart would be at a disadvantage with competitors if forced to maintain the current labor work force.

Buy-local

> . . . Defendant suggested in her various press releases that the people of Puerto Rico would be negatively affected by the merger of Wal-Mart and Amigo since there was no guarantee that they would buy the same level of merchandise and agricultural goods from local suppliers and distributors as Amigo had in the past. But Wal-Mart understood that these requests were not only unfair but contrary to the interest of the people of Puerto Rico. Knowledge of imposed quotas on Wal-Mart would limit its bargaining power with suppliers, who would end up selling goods at higher prices in light of the quotas, and that increment would have to be passed on to consumers, of course, the people of Puerto Rico. * * *
>
> . . . In both its effect and purpose, the requirement differentiates between local Puerto Rico growers and out-of-state producers by mandating a quota of local products to be purchased annually. This differential treatment favors the interests of Puerto Rico growers, who are given a guaranteed market for the products sheltered from the usual perils of the market, while shutting out out-of-state growers from the potentially lucrative business relationship with Wal-Mart. Regardless of the quality of their products, the consistency of their supply, or the prices they offer, local growers would have a guaranteed and insurmountable advantage over out-of-state growers. This, in part, violates Wal-Mart's right to engage in interstate commerce, which is now reduced to "exclusivity contracts" with local growers, despite the myriad alternatives in interstate commerce.

In the face of this direct and discriminatory interference with interstate commerce, the Secretary of Justice offers no legitimate purpose. As has been suggested throughout this opinion, she invokes the public policy of the administration she currently works with as her source of authority that allows her to make these demands from Plaintiffs during their negotiations. She stated in a press release that "the public policy is directed at protecting the necessary balance that should exist between Puerto Rican and foreign capital and the benefits that it entails for the consumers." Whether or not Wal-Mart *should* attempt to strike that balance is not for this Court nor any other to determine for as long as it engages as a free market participant within the boundaries of the law, it is to make its own business decisions without governmental interference. But confronted with facially discriminatory remarks such as this one, we can and do determine that the Secretary is engaging in state protectionism prohibited by the federal constitution.

Many jurisdictions, prominently including developing countries, settle merger cases with consent orders that preserve factories, preserve jobs, or preserve brands. For example, the Competition and Tariff Commission of Zimbabwe vetted the acquisition of Portland Holdings Ltd. (Porthold), Zimbabwe's largest of only three cement manufacturers, by Pretoria Cement Company (PCC), a South African company. The number two producer had recently been acquired by Lafarge of France. It was suspected that PCC planned to close the to-be-acquired Zimbabwean plant and to supply the Zimbabwean market from South Africa. The Zimbabwean Commission welcomed the acquisition as a check against Lafarge's power. It approved the transaction on condition that PCC agree "to maintain Porthold's cement plant as a going concern and to continue producing cement in Zimbabwe." Alexander J. Kububa, *Anti-Competitive Practices and Their Adverse Effects on Consumer Welfare: The Zimbabwean Experience, in* THE EFFECTS OF ANTI-COMPETITIVE BUSINESS PRACTICES ON DEVELOPING COUNTRIES AND THEIR DEVELOPMENT PROSPECTS (H. Qaqaya and G. Lipimile eds., UNCTAD 2008), pp. 73,107. What is the probable effect on competition or efficiency of the order to continue operations of the Zimbabwean plant? Does it depend in part on whether PCC's reasons for its plan were anticompetitive; e.g., to close down a competitor?

China, one of the newest yet most visible antitrust jurisdictions, exercised its merger enforcement powers to block the proposed acquisition by Coca Cola of Huiyuan, a major maker and seller of juices. Huiyuan is a leading brand in China. MOFCOM, the Ministry of Commerce, which has charge of mergers, prohibited the merger on "competition grounds": that Coca Cola would leverage its power in the carbonated soft drink market, raise entry barriers, and cause "negative influences" on competition in the juice market in China. (MOFCOM, March 2009) To critics, the facts did not seem to reveal harm to competition that could hurt consumers. Some observers speculated that perhaps MOFCOM wished to preserve for China ownership of a leading brand, or to hold back inroads by a large Western multinational.

The financial crisis of 2008–09 threatened the viability of banks (whose failure, it was feared, would have a domino effect, undermining whole economies), and of auto producers, among others. US, European, and other jurisdictions sponsored mergers and bailouts and took government stakes in the supported businesses. In the UK, HBOS was in crisis. The UK government engineered a rescue by Lloyds, in the form of a merger. The Office of Fair Trading determined that the proposed merger would be anticompetitive, and that the failing firm defense would not be available in that case. The Secretary of State, however, decided that the public interest in "maintaining the stability of the UK financial system" outweighed the harm to competition, and the UK passed legislation to allow threat to the financial system to justify an anticompetitive merger. See Harshita Mathur, *UK Merger Control in Times of Financial Crisis: Rebutting the Justifications for Lloyds—HBOS*, Concurrences N° 4–2009, www.concurrences.com.

Consider the range of non-competition concerns that inform merger cases. Comment on the wisdom of incorporating the non-competition factors into merger review; on the wisdom of the institutional design (e.g., who decides), and on how likely it is that the specified public interests will be furthered by the merger law. Contrariwise, consider the legitimacy of the competition law if public interest considerations are out of bounds.

b. National Interest, National Champions and Merger Policy

Beyond the public interest in mergers, often expressed in terms of labor effects or distributive concerns, mergers sometimes raise questions of national interest. A national government may believe that a merger creates a dominant domestic company—a "national champion"—that will strengthen the government's own global position, or it may be concerned that a merger of foreign companies may adversely affect national interests. Although such considerations undoubtedly sometimes motivate competition policy decisions, should they?

US caselaw generally holds that there is no place in antitrust law for consideration of any public interest other than competition itself. Efficiency and technological progressiveness are deemed to be part of competition. The failing firm defense to mergers might be an exception; but it is usually rationalized as part of competition/market power analysis.

Boeing/McDonnell Douglas

Boeing was the largest manufacturer of commercial jet aircraft in the world, accounting for about 64% of world market sales. Its only competitors were McDonnell Douglas (its acquisition target), which accounted for about 5% of the market, and Airbus Industrie, with about 30%. Airbus was a consortium of manufacturers in Britain,

France, Germany and Spain. Those countries had helped to finance Airbus.

Boeing and McDonnell Douglas were US companies and had no production assets in Europe, although they regularly made sales there. McDonnell Douglas also produced military jets, and its technology portfolio included patents from research and development undertaken with US government financing. In the commercial jet market, McDonnell Douglas had failed to invest in important new-generation developments and was facing financial and competitive difficulties. Its market share was withering. Boeing, meanwhile, had recently concluded 20-year exclusive supply agreements with three big American airlines—Delta, American, and Continental. The exclusive supply agreements represented about 11% of all world purchases of big commercial jets.

Commercial jet airplanes are very complex and sell in the range of $32 million to $171 million each. An order from an airline is typically worth billions of dollars. In view of the fact that each sale to an airline is so significant, Airbus and Boeing were fierce competitors for sales around the world.

Boeing and McDonnell Douglas filed premerger notifications in the United States and in the European Union. EC Competition Commissioner Karel Van Miert immediately expressed concerns about the merger and the exclusive agreements. On the US side, the Federal Trade Commission opened an investigation. The European Commission and the FTC made notifications to one another under the 1991 cooperation agreement (see Chapter 9, infra), and the European and American officials shared their perspectives. They sharply disagreed on the analysis of anticompetitive effects.

Early on, politicians entered the fray, with Europeans declaring that the merger was blatantly anticompetitive and seriously harmful to competition and to Airbus, and Americans declaring that the merger was good for the American economy. Laura D'Andrea Tyson, former head of the Council of Economic Advisors, was quoted in the Washington Post (May 4, 1997, p. H6) as saying that this merger was good for America "even if consumers of airplane seats are somewhat worse off." Commissioner Van Miert threatened that, if the merger should be consummated without EC approval, the European Commission would impose prohibitive fines on Boeing and might seize Boeing planes flying into Europe.

On July 1, 1997, the US FTC issued a statement announcing the closing of its investigation.

MATTER OF THE BOEING COMPANY/McDONNELL DOUGLAS CORPORATION

U.S. Federal Trade Commission, Statement
[FTC File No. 971–0051, available at https://www.ftc.gov/public-statements/1997/07/statement-chairman-robert-pitofsky-commissioners-janet-d-steiger-roscoe-b]

After an extensive and exhaustive investigation, the Federal Trade Commission has decided to close the investigation of The Boeing Company's proposed acquisition of McDonnell Douglas Corporation. For reasons discussed below, we have concluded that the acquisition would not substantially lessen competition or tend to create a monopoly in either defense or commercial aircraft markets.

There has been speculation in the press and elsewhere that the United States antitrust authorities might allow this transaction to go forward—particularly the portion of the transaction dealing with the manufacture of commercial aircraft—because aircraft manufacturing occurs in a global market, and the United States, in order to compete in that market, needs a single powerful firm to serve as its "national champion." A powerful United States firm is all the more important, the argument proceeds, because that firm's success contributes much to improving the United States' balance of trade and to providing jobs for U.S. workers.

The national champion argument does not explain today's decision. Our task as enforcers, conferred in clear terms by Congress in enacting the antitrust statutes, is to ensure the vitality of the free market by preventing private actions that may substantially lessen competition or tend to create a monopoly. In the Boeing-McDonnell Douglas matter, the Commission's task was to review a merger between two direct competitors.

We do not have the discretion to authorize anticompetitive but "good" mergers because they may be thought to advance the United States' trade interests. If that were thought to be a wise approach, only Congress could implement it. In any event, the "national champion" argument is almost certainly a delusion. In reality, the best way to boost the United States' exports, address concerns about the balance of trade, and create jobs is to require United States' firms to compete vigorously at home and abroad. Judge Learned Hand put the matter well a half century ago in describing the reasons for the commitment in the United States to the protection of the free market:

"Many people believe that possession of unchallenged economic power deadens initiative, discourages thrift and depresses energy; that immunity from competition is a narcotic, and rivalry is a stimulant, to industrial progress; that the spur of constant stress is necessary to counteract inevitable disposition to let well enough alone." [citing United States v. Alcoa, 148 F.2d 416, 427 (2d Cir. 1945)]

On its face, the proposed merger appears to raise serious antitrust concerns. The transaction involves the acquisition by Boeing, a company that accounts for roughly 60% of the sales of large commercial aircraft, of a non-failing direct competitor in a market in which there is only one other significant rival, Airbus Industrie, and extremely high barriers to entry. The merger would also combine two firms in the US defense industry that develop fighter aircraft and other defense products. Nevertheless, for reasons we will now discuss, we do not find that this merger will substantially lessen competition in any relevant market. * * *

With respect to the commercial aircraft sector, our decision not to challenge the proposed merger was a result of evidence that (1) McDonnell Douglas, looking to the future, no longer constitutes a meaningful competitive force in the commercial aircraft market and (2) there is no economically plausible strategy that McDonnell Douglas could follow, either as a stand-alone concern or as part of another concern, that would change that grim prospect.

The evidence collected during the staff investigation, including the virtually unanimous testimony of forty airlines that staff interviewed, revealed that McDonnell Douglas's commercial aircraft division, Douglas Aircraft Company, can no longer exert a competitive influence in the worldwide market for commercial aircraft. Over the past several decades, McDonnell Douglas has not invested at nearly the rate of its competitors in new product lines, production facilities, company infrastructure, or research and development. As a result, Douglas Aircraft's product line is not only very limited, but lacks the state of the art technology and performance characteristics that Boeing and Airbus have developed. Moreover, Douglas Aircraft's line of aircraft do not have common features such as cockpit design or engine type, and thus cannot generate valuable efficiencies in interchangeable spare parts and pilot training that an airline may obtain from a family of aircraft, such as Boeing's 737 family or Airbus's A–320 family.

In short, the staff investigation revealed that the failure to improve the technology and efficiency of its commercial aircraft products has lead to a deterioration of Douglas Aircraft's product line to the point that the vast majority of airlines will no longer consider purchasing Douglas aircraft and that the company is no longer in a position to influence significantly the competitive dynamics of the commercial aircraft market.

Our decision not to challenge the proposed merger does not reflect a conclusion that McDonnell Douglas is a failing company or that Douglas Aircraft is a failing division. Nor does our decision not to challenge the proposed merger reflect a conclusion that Douglas Aircraft could maintain competitively significant sales, but has simply decided to redeploy or retire its assets. While McDonnell Douglas's prospects for future commercial aircraft sales are virtually non-existent, its commercial aircraft production assets are likely to remain in the market for the near future as a result of a modest backlog of aircraft orders. As a result, it is unlikely that the aircraft division would have been liquidated quickly. Moreover, the failing company defense comes into play only where the Commission first finds that the transaction is likely to be anticompetitive. Here, the absence of any prospect of significant commercial sales, combined with a dismal financial forecast, indicate that Douglas Aircraft is no longer an effective competitor, and there is no prospect that position could be reversed. * * *

While the merger seems to pose no threat to the competitive landscape in either the commercial aircraft or in various defense markets, we find the twenty year exclusive contracts Boeing recently entered with three major airlines potentially troubling. Boeing is the largest player in the global commercial aircraft market and though the contracts now foreclose only about 11% of that market, the airlines involved are prestigious. They represent a sizeable portion of airlines that can serve as "launch" customers for aircraft manufacturers, that is, airlines that can place orders large enough and have sufficient market prestige to serve as the first customer for a new airplane. We intend to monitor the potential anticompetitive effects of these, and any future, long term exclusive contracts.

Immediately after the FTC closed its investigation, the Clinton Administration began to take an active political role in defending the merger to Europe. Key White House officials, including the President of the United States, argued to key European officials, including the President of the European Commission, that the merger was not anticompetitive, that it was important to employment and to the defense interests of the United States (the military assets of McDonnell Douglas would be best preserved in the hands of Boeing), and that the United States was "considering how to retaliate against Europe if it makes good on its threat to try and undermine the merger of [the] US aerospace giants. . . ." The Washington Post, July 17, 1997, p. C1. Reportedly, the Administration officials were considering imposing tariffs on European planes, limiting flights between the United States and France (the most adamant objector to the merger), and filing a protest with the World Trade Organization in view of European subsidies to Airbus.

On July 30, 1997, the Commission issued its decision in the matter of Boeing/McDonnell Douglas. It found that the merger would increase Boeing's dominance but backed away from a plan to prohibit the merger, and imposed significant conditions.

Glencore/Xstrata

On 16 April 2013 the Ministry of Commerce of the People's Republic of China (MOFCOM) granted conditional approval to the acquisition by Glencore International plc. (Glencore) of all of the remaining shares of Xstrata plc. (Xstrata), in which Glencore already held a minority equity interest. MOFCOM's assessment focused on the markets for copper concentrate, zinc concentrate and lead concentrate—in particular copper concentrate—where Glencore and Xstrata had overlapping production. Although the merged entity held a relatively limited market share of China's copper concentrate market (17.8% of China's imports in 2011), MOFCOM imposed both structural and behavioral conditions on the merger, including the extraterritorial divestiture of the $5.7 billion Las Bambas copper mine in Peru.

MOFCOM explicitly acknowledged that its decision was based on the strategic importance of copper to China:

> China is the world's major importing country for copper concentrate, with China's present demand accounting for about 50% of the total global demand. China's imports of copper concentrate in 2011 accounted for 68.5% of total domestic supply, and the trend shows an upward trajectory. In 2011, Glencore's and Xstrata's exports of copper concentrate to China accounted for 13.3% and 4.5% respectively of China's total imports, or 17.8% on a combined basis. The Chinese market is a major market for the undertakings concerned in the concentration. In 2011, Glencore and Xstrata sold respectively 53.7% and 17% of their copper concentrate supplies to the Chinese market.

The Chinese decision stood out among the major jurisdictions reviewing the merger. Both the Australian Competition and Consumer Commission and the US Department of Justice cleared the deal unconditionally in 2012. The European Commission focused on the markets for the production and trading of zinc (ultimately requiring the divestment of Glencore's minority stake in the world's largest zinc smelter, Nyrstar), but found no concerns as to copper.

The South African Competition Tribunal gave clearance with conditions in January 2013, but its concerns did not relate to competition considerations but rather to public interest issues involving employment.

Was it right for MOFCOM to base its competition assessment on China's unique interest as a leading copper importer and the wider effects on China's economy?

Alstrom/Siemens

In 2018, Alstrom and Siemens, French and German suppliers in the rail market respectively, announced a merger plan. On February 6, 2019, the European Commission issued a prohibition decision, finding that "the merger would have harmed competition in markets for railway signalling systems and very high-speed trains."

The Commission decision proved politically controversial. Many European observers felt Alstrom-Siemens consolidation was necessary to create a counterweight to the growth of the Chinese competitor CRRC. The German and French finance ministers penned a joint *'Franco-German Manifesto for a European industrial policy fit for the 21st Century.'* The ministers advocated for a new approach to European industrial policy resting on three pillars: (1) "massive" joint investments in innovation and development; (2) adopting defensive measures, such as a European foreign investment screening framework and a reciprocity mechanism for public procurement with third countries; and, (3) changes to Europe's competition law framework "to take greater account of competition at the global level, potential future competition and the time frame when it comes to looking ahead to the development of competition to give the European Commission more flexibility when assessing relevant markets," and the right of appeal to the European Council to overrule Commission decisions.

Should Europe do what the French and German ministers suggest? Should national or regional security or economic development priorities be permitted to trump competition policy? If so, was the problem with the Commission's prohibition decision that it neglected European economic security concerns? Or was the Commission correct to rule just on the grounds of its mandate—competition law—but there should have been some mechanism for political overruling over the Commission's decision by another European institution?

In 2024, former Italian Prime Minister Mario Draghi issued a 400-page report to the European Commission on the future of European economic competitiveness. Without referencing the

Siemens-Alhstrom affair directly, Draghi made the following points about national champions policy:

> Raising the EU's competitiveness is necessary to reignite productivity and sustain growth in this changing world. The core focus of a competitiveness agenda should be to raise productivity growth, which is the most important driver of long-term growth and leads to rising standards of living over time. Promoting competitiveness should not be seen in a narrow sense of a zero-sum game focused on conquering global market shares and raising trade surpluses. It should also not lead to policies of defending "national champions" that can stifle competition and innovation, or using wage repression to lower relative costs. Competitiveness today is less about relative labour costs and more about knowledge and skills embodied in the labour force. Beyond this broad objective, a focus on sectoral or industrial competitiveness can be particularly useful in situations where otherwise productive companies are disadvantaged by an unlevel global playing field, be it asymmetries in regulation or large subsidies abroad. In such scenarios, levelling the playing field may be necessary for continued productivity growth. Finally, a modern competitiveness agenda must also encompass security. Security is a precondition for sustainable growth, as rising geopolitical risks can increase uncertainty and dampen investment, while major geopolitical shocks or sudden stops in trade can be extremely disruptive.

c. Executive and Legislative Measures That Trump Antitrust

Statements extolling the "purity" of US antitrust do not prove that US competition *policy* is pure. Political pressures make themselves felt in one way or another. Examples include the failure of Chinese CNOOC's bid for UNOCAL because of US Congressional opposition; the US government-driven big bank and big auto mergers; the "buy American" conditionality of the bailouts often accompanying the government-sponsored mergers; and the large US government stakes taken in bailout beneficiaries. See, e.g., Bruce Lyons, *Competition Policy, Bailouts and the Economic Crisis*, Working Paper 09–4, Centre for Competition Policy, ISSN 1745–9648. See also Chapter 6, The State, points E. and F.

Before the beginning of his first term, in of January 2017, president-elect Donald Trump met with executives from the German chemical company Bayer and the agriculture company Monsanto at a time when their proposed $66 billion merger was pending antitrust review. According to media reports, Bayer and Monsanto made a number of economic commitments, although the parties denied that these were specifically linked to antitrust review of the merger: $8 billion in new R&D spending in the US, retention of 100 percent of Monsanto's US workforce; creation of 3,000 new US high-tech jobs, and keeping Monsanto's headquarters in St. Louis. *Bayer, Monsanto tout jobs, investment pledge to Trump, but analysts question how much is new*, CNBC (Jan 17, 2017) http://www.cnbc.com/2017/01/17/bayers-pledge-to-trump-has-some-analysts-scratching-their-heads.html.

Is it appropriate for governments to use their prosecutorial discretion to negotiate for better deals for their citizens when parties propose to merge? Does such horse trading corrupt the ostensible objectivity of competition law?

D. COOPERATION AND CONFLICT

1. Convergence on Pre-Merger Notification and Process

By year 2000 there were some 50 premerger notification regimes around the world. (As of this writing, that number is approaching 100). Parties planning a multijurisdictional merger had to know the rules of all regimes, many of which were not transparent. Some regimes required pre-merger notification and accompanying large filing fees even when the merger had no significant nexus with the jurisdiction and it could not possibly have harmed competition in the jurisdiction. Jurisdictions required filings based on different triggering events, and many requested different information in different formats. The business community's felt need to rationalize the merger process was a major impetus to the formation of the International Competition Network.

The ICN has proved to be a productive forum for coordination and convergence on pre-merger notification and process. One of the first working groups formed in the ICN was the Merger Working Group. Beginning with the first annual ICN conference in 2002, guiding principles and recommended practices were proposed and adopted; additional recommended practices are continually added, and steps are taken to publicize and track their implementation. See www.internationalcompetitionnetwork.org. For a description and assessment of the ICN, See Eleanor Fox, *Linked-In: Antitrust and the Virtues of a Virtual Network*, 43 International Lawyer 151 (2009).

2. Cooperation in Vetting Mergers of Common Interest

Jurisdictions cooperate, often intensely, in vetting mergers of common interest. In a 2013 OECD study, 21 agencies reported international cooperation with other agencies and the number of cases for which those agencies reported cooperating with other international agencies rose from approximately 90 in 2007 to 120 in 2011. Organization for Economic Co-operation and Development Competition Committee, Report on the OECD/ICN Survey on International Enforcement Co-operation (Feb. 12, 2013).

Chapter 9, on Global Governance, contains further information on the procedures jurisdictions follow to engage in cooperative merger assessment, including measures employed to protect the confidentiality of information collected during the review process.

3. Conflict

As more countries become active in merger regulation, conflicts among the decisions of competition authorities are bound to increase. Some well-known conflicts involved the mergers of Boeing/ McDonnell Douglas and General Electric/Honeywell. We begin with those cases, and then turn to the conflicts surrounding the merger of Gencor/Lonhro, which involved the jurisdictions of South Africa and the European Union, and Eurotunnel's acquisition of SeaFrance, which French competition authorities approved but the UK Supreme Court ultimately prohibited.

See the outlines of the *Boeing* case earlier in this chapter. GE/ Honeywell was the first merger cleared by the United States and prohibited by the European Union.

General Electric/Honeywell

General Electric was the largest of the three leading manufacturers of engines for large commercial jet aircraft, the other two being Rolls Royce and Pratt & Whitney. Honeywell was the leading supplier of certain avionic and non-avionic equipment used in jet aircraft, and competed with Thales and Rockwell Collins (in avionics) and Hamilton Sundstrand (in non-avionics). Honeywell was the dominant maker of engine starters for jet engines, which was a necessary input. It, as well as GE, manufactured jet engines for certain large regional jet aircraft and corporate jet aircraft, and small marine gas turbines. GE had a financial subsidiary, GE Capital, which provided financial assistance to airframe manufacturers in the form of platform program development, and it had a leasing subsidiary, GECAS, which was the world's largest buyer of airplanes, representing nearly 10 percent of all purchases of new commercial jet aircraft. GECAS had a policy of buying only airplanes that were fitted with GE engines, and GE Capital had bailed out at least one major airline, which returned the favor with an exclusive purchase order of GE jet engines.

The US authorities cleared the merger subject to a spin-off of some overlapping jet engine assets. The European Commission found more serious problems and eventually issued a decision. COMP/M 2220, Commission Decision 2004/134/EC. The Commission found that GE was a dominant firm in the markets for jet engines for large commercial aircraft and large regional aircraft, and that the acquisition, through leveraging, bundling, and strategic behavior, would enhance GE's dominance and confer dominance on Honeywell in certain avionic and non-avionic products. It also found anticompetitive horizontal overlaps, but the more significant parts of the case were conglomerate. The finding of anticompetitive conglomerate effects was based on the prediction that GE would offer package and bundled deals and use its leverage to shift market share away from competitors until their business was no longer profitable and they abandoned competition with Honeywell.

When the Commission enjoined the merger, American officials denounced the decision. Treasury Secretary Paul O'Neil called the European Commission "the closest thing you can find to an autocratic organization that can successfully impose their will on things that one would think are outside their scope of attention."[3] US Justice Department officials announced that the decision protected competitors, not competition, and implied that the European Commission was less than proficient in economics. If the merged firm offered bundles at low prices, this was competition; let the competitors compete.

GE appealed to the European Court of First Instance. The Court upheld the decision of the European Commission, but only on grounds of residual horizontal engine overlaps. The Commission had not sufficiently proved that the merged firm would use leverage. Case T–210/01, [2005] ECR II–5575. By the time the Court judgment came down four-and-a-half years after the Commission decision, the tensions had dissipated. See Eleanor Fox, *GE/Honeywell: The U.S. Merger that Europe Stopped—A Story of the Politics of Convergence*, supra p. 382.

---

3 Tom Brown, Update 2—U.S. Treasury Chief Slaps at Europe Over GE Deal, Reuters, June 27, 2001.

Gencor/Lonrho

Two South African platinum and rhodium mining companies proposed to merge, combining Implats, a subsidiary of Gencor, having about 17% of world market sales, and LPD (a subsidiary of the UK firm, Lonrho, which had a principal sales office in Belgium), having about 15% of sales. The combined firm would have 32% of sales. The leading firm, Anglo American ("Amplats"), had about 43% of sales. Together the two remaining South African firms would hold about 89% of world reserves. Russia, through its firm Almaz, had a 22% share of sales and 10% of reserves. North American producers accounted for 5% of sales and had 1% reserves; and recycling firms accounted for 6% of sales. Russia was expected to dispose of its stocks in two years.

The South African Competition Board vetted the merger and found no competition problem. The European Commission vetted the merger and was concerned that, when the Russian stocks were depleted in a couple of years, Gencor/LPD (Lonrho) and Anglo American, the world market leader, would jointly exercise dominant market power (collective dominance).

While examining the proposed merger, the Competition Directorate of the European Commission invited comment from the South African authorities. The South African Deputy Minister of Foreign Affairs officially submitted his government's observations to the Commission. He stated in a letter to the European Commission that the South African Government favored the consolidation. As to competitive effects, the Minister noted that the two remaining platinum firms in South Africa were now more equally matched, and he conveyed the South African view that the market would work better with two equally matched competitors than under market domination by Anglo American. The Minister did not contest the intervention of the European Community. However, he wrote: "Having regard to the importance of mineral resources to the South African economy," South Africa favored allowing the consolidation and attacking any collusion between Anglo American and Gencor/LPD if and when it arose. (judgment, para. 3)

The European Commission proceeded to find that the merger would create a dominant duopoly and was therefore incompatible with the common market, and it prohibited it. Gencor appealed.

Gencor argued on appeal not only that the merger was procompetitive but that the Community had no jurisdiction since the merger involved economic activities conducted within the territory of a non-member country and had been approved by authorities of that country. Gencor contended that the European Merger Regulation applied only to concentrations carried out within the European Community. It based its construction on the language of the Merger Regulation (especially recitals), the Treaty articles on which the Regulation was based, and the international law principle of territoriality. Gencor addressed the one important extraterritorial European Court of Justice authority, *Wood Pulp*, [1988] ECR 5193, see Chapter 8 infra, wherein the Court had asserted jurisdiction over an offshore cartel designedly raising prices in Europe. Gencor distinguished *Wood Pulp* on grounds that the wood pulp cartel was implemented in Europe. Gencor said: While the high prices [of wood pulp] were agreed to offshore, the conspiracy to raise prices was implemented by selling at the conspiratorial prices into the Community. By contrast, the platinum merger was implemented in South Africa and "is thus primarily relevant to the industrial and competition policy of that non-member country." (para. 56)

The Court of First Instance rejected Gencor's construction of the Merger Regulation. Gencor Ltd. v. Commission, Case T–102/96, [1999] ECR II–753. The court said:

> According to *Wood pulp*, the criterion as to the implementation of an agreement is satisfied by mere sale within the Community, irrespective of the location of the sources of supply and the production plant. It is not disputed that Gencor and Lonrho carried out sales in the Community before the concentration and would have continued to do so thereafter. (para. 87)

The CFI proceeded to assess the legitimacy of jurisdiction under international law. Noting that the transaction entailed the merger of the firms' marketing operations throughout the world, including the Community, it said:

> Application of the Regulation is justified under public international law when it is foreseeable that a proposed concentration will have an immediate and substantial effect in the Community. (para. 90)

The CFI concluded that the merger's effect in the Community would be immediate, substantial and foreseeable. It construed "immediate" to include "medium term"—after Russian platinum stocks were exhausted and thus after a force that could be disruptive of Anglo and Gencor's duopoly behavior would have been removed. It concluded that an *abuse* (a price rise resulting from collective behavior) need not be immediate; it is enough that a transaction causes a lasting structural alteration, making abusive behavior economically rational.

As to substantiality of the effect, Gencor claimed that the merging parties' sales and market shares in Europe were too small to cause a substantial effect and that the merging parties' greater sales elsewhere—Japan and the United States—undermined "substantiality." The court rejected this claim. It said:

> The fact that, in a world market, other parts of the world are affected by the concentration cannot prevent the Community from exercising its control over a concentration which substantially affects competition within the common market by creating a dominant position.

Likewise, the court rejected the claim that the exercise of jurisdiction violated an international principle of non-interference, if there is such a principle, or the principle of proportionality. The court said that there was no conflict between the laws of the two jurisdictions and therefore no interference because South Africa did not require the firms to do what the European Community required them not to do. Nor was it shown how the completion of the merger would enhance South Africa's vital economic or commercial interests.

Moreover, as the European Commission had argued, the merger was like an export cartel. Only a small amount of platinum was sold in South Africa. South Africa stood to gain more by exploiting the world than it stood to lose by exploiting its own consumers.

Thus, the court held, it had jurisdiction.

South Africa did not further resist Europe's decision.

Eurotunnel/SeaFrance

SeaFrance, provided ferry service across the English Channel, went into liquidation in 2012 following years of heavy losses. The French Commercial Court overseeing the liquidation process received bids for SeaFrance and ultimately chose Eurotunnel's bid, finding that it offered the best outcome for creditors and was the only bid that would preserve the employment of former SeaFrance employees.

The French Autorité de la Concurrence and the UK Office of Fair Trading both opened investigations into the acquisition. By the end of 2012, the French authority had cleared the deal, but the OFT referred the matter to the UK Competition Commission, worried about a lessening of competition in the provision of short-sea cross-Channel transport services. In June of 2013, the Competition Commission issued a decision finding the acquisition unlawful and prohibiting Eurotunnel from operating ferry services at the port of Dover.

While agreeing on market definition and the potential for anticompetitive effects in the cross-Channel transport services market, the French and UK authorities differed in several important respects. The UK authority believed that, absent the acquisition by Eurotunnel, SeaFrance would have been acquired by another buyer whose acquisition would have been competitively preferable. The French authority found such possibilities too speculative to entertain. Additionally, the UK authority found that, given the existence of excess capacity in the market, the acquisition would likely lead to the exit of another rival—DFDS/LD—from Dover-Calais route, at least in the short term. By contrast, the French authority found that the existence of excess authority would constrain price increases.

What accounts for the difference in analysis of the two national authorities? Commentators have pointed out several distinctions in the statutory and procedural dimensions of merger review on the two sides of the Channel. The UK merger guidelines specifically call for a consideration of counterfactual scenarios in assessing whether a merger substantially lessens competition, whereas the French guidelines contain no analogous provision. Further, the Competition Commission's in-depth investigation following the referral from the OFT allowed it to uncover some troubling references in Eurotunnel documents, to the effect that Eurotunnel's motivation for the acquisition was to prevent DFDS/LD from acquiring SeaFrance's vessels at a low cost and driving down prices. The French authority did not have access to these documents when it made its decision. *See* Matt Evans & Marguerite Lavedan, *Eurotunnel/SeaFrance: Unbridgeable gap over the Channel?*, http://www.jonesday.com/euro tunnelseafrance-unbridgeable-gap-over-the-channel-mlex-ab-extra-07-02-2013/.

In 2015, the UK Supreme Court upheld the finding of illegality. Société Coopérative de Production SeaFrance SA (Respondent) v. The Competition and Markets Authority, [2015] UKSC 75.

In November of 2024, *Business at OECD* (BIAC) group released a report that highlighted a number of difficulties faced by companies navigating cross-border mergers. BIAC summarized the problem as follows:

> Cross-border mergers and acquisitions (M&A) spanning multiple jurisdictions face increasing—and often intense—complexity and challenges of managing parallel regulatory reviews. With the proliferation of diverse regulatory regimes, businesses are confronted with varying legal frameworks, substantive analyses, and timelines, making

the process of cross-border mergers very burdensome, lengthy, costly and in general difficult to predict. Navigating these challenges is further compounded by the rise of new regulatory mechanisms, such as foreign direct investment (FDI) screenings and the EU Foreign Subsidies Regulation (FSR), as well as industry-specific legislation, such as the Digital Markets Act (DMA), which introduce additional layers of scrutiny and complication to cross-border transactions, especially in sectors involving technology and operating within the digital markets/ industry.

These challenges are not necessarily limited to the largest corporations, which may have the knowledge and resources to navigate such hurdles. It is not uncommon for smaller businesses to engage in cross-border M&A and they can often face intense regulatory complexity for their deals. Anything that can be done to ensure consistency, streamline processes, align timelines and, crucially, improve legal certainty and predictability, can only be welcomed by businesses.

Among the specific obstacles to cross-border mergers highlighted by BIAC were "jurisdictional complexity and uncertainty," "digitalization and data protection," national security screenings, and increasing scrutiny of deals that may harm innovation. BIAC argued that the discrepancies in enforcement "and the challenges they pose for successfully navigating merger control reviews underscores the urgent need for a more harmonized approach to mergers reviewed across multiple jurisdictions." The report concluded with the following advice to competition authorities:

- Only assert jurisdiction over cross-border mergers with a strong connection to their jurisdiction.
- Use clear, objective criteria to determine when a merger must be notified or, in countries without mandatory notification or residual call in powers, when it qualifies for review.
- Set reasonable information requirements for effective merger review.
- Ensure that mergers with minimal competitive concerns are processed through an expedited review.
- Conduct merger reviews and make decisions within a reasonable, clear timeframe.

- Avoid contradictory remedies for businesses and work towards aligned remedies.

4. Resolution of Conflict

The forces of global competition combined with a high level of cooperation seem constantly to push towards convergence of substantive law and analysis, and to make it less likely that another *Boeing/McDonnell Douglas* or *GE/Honeywell* will occur. But still, conflicts arise. Not every nation applies the same mode of analysis or adopts the same platform or presumptions at the same time. When Oracle, the largest proprietary database company, proposed to take over Sun Microsystems, a leading open-source database company, the transaction was cleared by the US as not anticompetitive; but the European Commission proceeded with an investigation and a Statement of Objections. It expressed concern that Oracle would suppress Sun's popular open-source product, despite the insistence by both Oracle and the US Department of Justice that there were many other open-source and proprietary database companies. Ultimately, the EU cleared the acquisition with commitments from Oracle that it would maintain Sun's open-source database as a competitive force.

China, too, has asserted itself in merger clearances. Coca Cola proposed to acquire Huiyuan, the leading juice company in China and one with a strong brand name. The US and the EU approved the acquisition. China prohibited it. Likewise, the US and EU approved General Motors' acquisition of Delphi, a major automobile electronic parts supplier. China allowed but conditioned the deal.

What modus operandi should be in place for a next time when divergence on a major issue of common concern is brewing? As a beginning, the authorities of the potentially conflicting jurisdictions might adopt a protocol to confer intensively, pinpoint their differences, and attempt to resolve them. But they did this in *Boeing/McDonnell Douglas* and *GE/Honeywell.* Should there be protocols for deferring to the party with the greatest contacts and largest consumer market at least where there is a single world market or at least common competitive conditions in the different jurisdictions? Will developing countries—sometimes victims of increased buying power that is beyond the radar of developed countries—be part of the conversation?

For further discussion of conflict and its resolution, see Chapter 10, Global Governance.

Chapter 7

THE STATE

A. INTRODUCTION

Thus far we have spoken of restraints of competition by private firms. But market competition can be harmed just as well, sometimes more severely and enduringly, by acts of the state. The state may act at all levels—from local to national—in ways that keep the forces of competition from working or that bias its results in favor of cronies, ordained winners, or other favorites. In many cases the harms to competition are mere by-products of policies that are part of a legitimate governance system, such as rent control or utility regulation. In many other cases, the acts are "rogue" acts, such as misuse of power by an official to benefit his friends. In between are state acts or measures that suppress competition excessively in view of any proper government purpose.

In various jurisdictions, such as the United States, neither the state (of the Union) nor federal bodies are covered by the antitrust laws, although local government acts may be covered. The state is presumed to act in the public interest. The boundaries between legislatures and courts are an inherent part of the checks and balances of the system, and the boundaries between states and the federal government are an inherent part of U.S. federalism. If state government exceeds its proper bounds, the citizens of the state may resist politically within the institutions of the state. And if a state exceeds its federalist bounds and harms the country, it may be called to account through the commerce clause of the Constitution for unduly burdening interstate commerce, or the federal legislature can pass preemptive legislation. The United States was not and is not a statist society. Few firms are state-owned. Business has grown on its merits (or luck, or sometimes by misuse of business power), not by state command or privilege. Accordingly, the issue of anticompetitive state acts and measures has not surfaced as an antitrust issue in the United States, except to the extent that the antitrust agencies advocate against excessively restrictive government measures. In fact, in the United States, state action in the context of antitrust refers not to condemning anticompetitive state action but, contrariwise, to allowing private anticompetitive action when firms are acting in the shadow of state command or policy. Most nations have some form of this defense, as discussed below.

A critical mass of other jurisdictions embed state offenses within their antitrust laws. Most prominently and predictably, this is done in common markets, which have functions both of policing internal market "trade" restraints (member state laws may improperly impair free movement), as well as policing business restraints. European Union law is the most mature example and is a model for other common markets and nations, and this chapter therefore spends considerable time on this model.

In the European context, at the birth of the Treaty of Rome establishing the European Economic Community, parochial state restraints were the principal problem. Border barriers were high; high barriers fueled hatreds; they could undermine the project of a peaceful Europe. The principal effort of the founders of the European Community was to abolish Member State restraints that undermined free movement of goods, services, capital and people. Accordingly, Europe adopted its free-movement articles: states were enjoined not to impair free movement. See Articles 30–37, 45–66 of the Treaty on the Functioning of the European Union (TFEU). Read the selected articles in Appendix 1. It was foreseen that, when state barriers went down, the businesses within each nation would try to re-erect them (and they did try; see Chapter 2, Cartels). To protect the internal market as well as to protect the people from economic abuses, the drafters included the competition articles, now 101 and 102 of the TFEU. The drafters were also mindful of the statist tradition in most of the original six nations (France, Italy, Germany and the Benelux countries). Many state-owned firms procured their supplies only or at least preferentially from nationals; and many states conferred exclusive franchises and other privileges. The drafters knew that state firms and their privileged beneficiaries would claim exemptions from antitrust and try to continue their discriminatory operations in the manner to which they were accustomed, thus undermining the cause of market integration. Therefore they included in the Treaty Article 37—Member States must "adjust any State monopolies of a commercial character" to assure no discrimination in procurement or marketing; Article 4(3) of the Treaty on European Union (TEU)—Member States must "facilitate the achievement of the Union's tasks" and refrain from measures that could jeopardize the achievement of the Union's objectives; and Article 106 TFEU—"In the case of public undertakings, and undertakings to which Member States grant special or exclusive rights," Member States may not enact or maintain any measure contrary to the anti-discrimination (based on nationality) and competition articles; and undertakings entrusted with operation of services of general economic interest are subject to the competition rules insofar as application of those rules does not obstruct the performance of the tasks assigned to them.

Finally, the drafters were confronted with national governments that maintained their nationalism by giving large subsidies and other aids to their own firms, either creating national champions that would have state-backed muscle to outcompete businesses across the borders, or propping up firms that would otherwise close doors and jobs. The freedom of states to grant aids as they chose would also perpetuate economic nationalism and discrimination and undermine the mission of one common market. Therefore the drafters, in now Articles 107 and 108 TFEU, prohibited Member States from granting aids that may distort competition. Member States must file their intention to grant aids, which are subject to approval as specified in legislation.

Thus, the European Union centrally addresses state measures and restraints in its competition policy. It has developed a mature case law defining the contours.

Europe is not alone in pinpointing the state as a source of impairment of competition. A number of transitional and emerging economies include state restraints in their antitrust coverage, especially where an inherited "excessive state' is one of the most daunting problems they confront in moving to a functioning market system. Many developing countries also face the dilemma of corrupt governments that privilege cronies in various markets, and governments that freely grant economic privileges. Moreover, some jurisdictions such as Russia and China prohibit state and local measures that restrict the free flow of goods across provincial lines. China, which has no commerce clause in its constitution and has a history of provincial roadblocks against goods from other provinces, has included in its Anti-Monopoly Law very articulated prohibitions against "abuse[s] of administrative monopoly", i.e., abuses of power by government bodies. See Eleanor M. Fox and Debroah Healey, *When the State Harms Competition—The Role for Competition Law*, 79 Antitrust L.J. 769 (2014).

The subject of anticompetitive state restraints has gained an increasingly high profile in international antitrust fora such as the UNCTAD Competition and Consumer Branch and the International Competition Network (ICN). The ICN curriculum project has produced a training module on State Restraints, which you may want to watch. It is available at https://www.internationalcompetition network.org/training/state-restraints/.

This chapter presents the problem of competition and the state (which may be local, provincial, or national) in six parts. First, advocacy, which is competition *policy* to reduce state restraints. Second, state-owned enterprises' abuses of dominance. Third, abuse of dominance by state-privileged firms. Fourth, state measures and the scope of state action defenses as justification for private anticompetitive acts. Fifth, the relationship between competition law and sectoral regulation and the extent of regulatory preemption. Sixth, the status of hybrid state-and-private restraints, including a limited antitrust jurisdiction in the World Trade Organization.

Act of state, foreign sovereign immunity, and foreign sovereign compulsion are treated in Chapter 9 in our discussion of extraterritoriality and related questions. The problems treated in this chapter involve either state acts or measures that may harm competition within the state's own community, or such state acts or measures seen within a larger polity of which the state is a part.

B. ADVOCACY

One of the most important tasks of a competition agency, especially agencies that face powerful business lobbies and institutional structures built in pre-market eras, is competition advocacy. The advocacy may be addressed both to the government and to the people. The International Competition Network has highlighted the important role of advocacy since its foundation in 2001. Influential papers and remarks have been contributed by Allan Fels of Australia, Beatriz Boza of Peru, John Fingleton of Ireland and the UK, and Bill Kovacic of the United States, who have been among the most successful advocates of pro-competition solutions to complex economic problems and whose work has been a counter to private interest lobbying. The work of ICN's Advocacy Working Group is described at https://www.internationalcompetitionnetwork.org/working-groups/advocacy/.

Meanwhile, on the ground, competition officials of developing countries have highlighted problems and helped industries work for the benefit of the people, including by alleviation of poverty of exploited farmers. See Thulasoni Kaira, The Role of Competition Law and Policy in Alleviating Poverty—The Case of Zambia, in THE EFFECTS OF ANTI-COMPETITIVE BUSINESS PRACTICES ON DEVELOPING COUNTRIES AND THEIR DEVELOPMENT PROSPECTS, 133, 150–57 (cotton) (Qaqaya & Lipimile eds, UNCTAD 2008).

Here is one example of effective advocacy. Numerous others are continuously unfolding, as highlighted in an annual competition held by the World Bank in coordination with the ICN. We tell the story of cement in Tanzania, as relayed by Godfrey Mkocha, Director General of the Fair Competition Commission of Tanzania.

Cement is a basic commodity; a necessity for shelter and buildings. Cement markets are notoriously oligopolistic and perennially a breeding ground for cartels. In Tanzania, there are three significant cement companies: Tanzania Portland Cement, Tanga Cement, and Mbeya Cement. India and Pakistan are well positioned to ship their own higher quality, lower cost cement into Tanzania.

In 2005 the East African Community (EAC) signed a protocol classifying cement as a sensitive product, thereby warranting a protective duty of 55%, which was to be reduced to 35% by 2009. Meanwhile, a great shortage occurred, leading the EAC states to agree, in 2008, to reduce the duty to zero. Their effort succeeded; supply increased and prices fell.

But when the prices fell, the East African Cement Producers Association went into action. They lobbied the Government at the highest levels to reinstate the 35% duty. They took their case to the press, convincing reporters to sound the alarm that cheap cement imports from Pakistan and India were about to destroy thousands of jobs and undermine the Tanzanian economy. A headline in the Tanzanian Sunday Citizen read: "Cheap cement now threatens economy." (May 31, 2009) The article reported that citizens were celebrating the falling price of cement "little knowing the situation is precipitating their country's economic doom." It continued:

> "This situation is bound to affect the forthcoming budget, which has already suffered from the shrink in revenue due to the global financial crisis. * * *
>
> Cement industry is estimated to contribute about Sh30 billion as income tax only. The industry also contributes other billions to Government coffers through import duty and other taxes.
>
> There are fears that if the imports trend will continue at the current level, the Government might lose billions in revenue from the industry."

The Fair Competition Commission quickly sent a response to the press:

The Editor,
The Citizen

The Fair Competition Commission (FCC) wishes to address the messages contained in the articles which appeared in your esteemed newspaper on 25th May, 2009 written by George Sembony, headed *Import said to be hurting Tanga firm;* and 31st May, 2009 by Sunday Citizen Reporter headed *Decision on cement duty awaits new budget* and Mnaku Mbani headed *cheap cement now threatens economy.*

FCC commends the writer's efforts to report on the views of local manufactures on cement sub-sector which is very important to Tanzania industrial development. The writer reported that there is fear among local cement manufacturers, over the influx of cement imported from giant factories in Pakistan and India, likely to kill the country's cement industry due to the fact that Tanzania cement sector cannot compete with that of India and Pakistan since the costs of production in the country are 2.5% higher due to higher power tariffs. The cement manufacturers want the duty re-introduced in order to curb what they term oversupply, marked distortion and dumping.

Reading through the article, it is evident that the challenge to ensure the public understands fundamental principles of market economy particularly competition and its eventual benefits remains enormous across the citizenry. FCC as a market support institution whose role is to promote and protect competition in trade and commerce would like to put the issues in context.

For the past one year, consumers country-wide were concerned about the rise of retail prices and the scarcity of cement in the market. An analysis of the cement sub-sector was conducted in order to establish the underlying causes or price rises and scarcity in the cement market and the following were observed to be the issues undermining consumers of the benefits that they would have otherwise enjoyed.

(i) There are only three cement producers in the country who also own cement plants in other East African countries. This situation restrained competition in the country and within the East African sub region.

(ii) Cement being a bulky product, transportation cost is a significant factor in the determination of final prices to the consumer. In Tanzania, cement factories are sparsely and unevenly located (Tanga, Mbeya and Dar es Salaam). Also, most of the cement factories lack depots in different parts of the country; as a result they have left distribution and transportation in the hands of few private businesses. The foregoing, coupled with the current weak and limited transportation network alternatives, make the final cement price higher.

(iii) The contestability of Tanzania cement market through imports of cement from the world market was limited due to the then high protection rate set for cement in the East African market; therefore the internal producers were simply taking advantage of the protection without doing anything to the high prices caused by the rising demand.

A short term solution was then sought to lower substantially the protection rate for cement in order to discipline the internal industry through competition.

Generally, the rationale for governments to protect an industry is to maintain employment and the attendant benefits in their countries. However, in the case of the cement industry which is capital intensive, such intended benefits have to be weighed against the high construction costs such a policy introduces in the economy. This situation is worse where our country is developing and therefore construction is a must and where the Government itself is using a high proportion of its budget in construction. It means the country is increasing the costs to itself and limits the growth of the downstream construction industry thus curtailing the employment benefits which the country was purporting to protect in the first place.

We wish to recall that the cement industry has registered success particularly as a result of the ever booming construction industry in the country, and the profit enjoyed by manufacturers has never lower as evidenced by the dividends paid to their investors.

The Governments of the East African Community decision eventually to reduce the suspended duty should be commended. Also the decision of the Government of Tanzania to encourage the location of new cement plants to new areas in Tanzania is a smart decision.

It is against this background that The Fair Competition Commission would like to echo the Government move to ensure that the market remains open and contestable by allowing the interplays that discipline the market and lessen the consumer's burden. If cement produced thousands of miles from Tanzania can beat the production costs of our local cement industry, then the economists should think again on what we want to protect by re-introducing the suspended duty.

Michael Shilla
Ag. DIRECTOR GENERAL
FAIR COMPETITION
COMMISSION

The Citizen printed the FCC's letter, on June 6, 2009. The Business Times Economic & Financial Weekly also printed the letter (June 5–11 edition) but with one addition: a provocative headline (provocative because the industry was still importuning the Ministry of Industry and Trade to reinstate the duty): "As Cheaper cement from India, Pakistan floods market . . . Government tells local manufacturers 'NO' to protection."

The Ministry of Industry and Trade was angry with the message of the headline. It confronted the Fair Competition Commission. Why was the FCC pretending to speak for the Government? The FCC demurred; it had not spoken for the Government; it was speaking for competition, as it had the duty to do. The press, not the Commission, wrote the misleading headline: The Government says No.

Meanwhile, the FCC's procompetition arguments convinced Tanzanian President Jayaka Kikwete. Kikwete stood up for competition, not protection. In the midst of the controversy between the competition authority and the trade ministry, the President was the guest of honor at the inaugural ceremony of a new plant of Tanzania Portland Cement. He used the opportunity to announce that, indeed, the Government said no. The Government would not reinstate the protective duty.

On July 10, 2009, The Business Times Economic & Financial Weekly changed its tone. It carried a headline: "Locally manufactured cement: consumers' confidence wanes." The subhead said: "Kikwete cautions on high prices; Pakistan cement better—Experts." The article reported the experts' opinion that Pakistan produced a far higher quality cement than the Tanzanian producers, and it reported Kikwete's advice to the local producers to find the way to lower the price of cement.

Notes and Questions

The Tanzanian incident illustrates the tangled web produced when domestic competitors fight to protect their markets. Protection means less competition at home and higher prices. Protection of the domestic cement producers, in the Tanzania story, meant worse roads, neglected infrastructure, vulnerable buildings for schools and housing, and fewer jobs in these sectors, while protecting existing jobs (and profits) in the laggard domestic cement plants and removing a spur to make them better.

Competition advocacy can cover very wide ground. You may think of it as pro-market advocacy. Competition advocacy includes examination of and recommendations regarding existing and proposed legislation. In 2024 and 2025, China strengthened its Fair Competition

Review System in Market Development, according to which all proposed legislation is examined to avoid "excessive and inappropriate intervention in the market." In Peru, the competition authority INDECOPI is charged with challenging anticompetitive regulations via regulatory impact assessments (known as AIR Ex Ante). Since 2010, the Italian competition authority (AGCM) is also tasked with the review of national, regional and local legislative bills and administrative measures that may create restrictions of competition. The US agencies, while not having such a mandate, do extensive competition advocacy.

C. ABUSE OF DOMINANCE BY STATE-OWNED ENTERPRISE: PARADIGM CASES

Many jurisdictions that have recently adopted market systems and antitrust laws have been statist economies. The state owned and operated the businesses. Others were mixed economies: a mix of state and private ownership. Yet others reserved state ownership for specific services and goods of critical importance, often in regulated sectors, such as telecommunications, electricity, utilities, and transport. Even as state-owned entities were privatized, they sometimes retained historical privileges conferred by the state. Often the state, to maximize the revenues it would receive from the sale, sold the business with its monopoly intact, realizing a monopoly premium. The "people" did not feel the promised benefits of privatization, and sometimes felt more exploited under a market regime.

An initial question, often answered by the antitrust statute, is whether state-owned enterprises are covered by the antitrust laws and to what extent. In the European Union, the competition law applies to state-owned enterprises with an exception—SOEs are exempted to the extent necessary to provide "services of general economic interest". In China, SOEs in regulated sectors are answerable to sector regulation; the. Anti-Monopoly Law, Art. 7; but they are not exempt from the competition law.

In this section we deal with antitrust laws that cover state enterprises. We ask: In the application of the law against abuse of dominance or monopolization, are state-owned enterprises different from other enterprises? Is there reason to single them out?

In general, the legal analysis of SOE conduct is not differentiated, but there are characteristics of state enterprise and often its privatized successors that make them especially likely to restrain competition in ways that will not be cured by the market. Indeed, the drafters of the European Treaty of Rome were especially aware of the many state enterprises in Europe, their unique power to exploit, their habits of preferring to do business with their own nationals, and their incentives to preserve their own domains by their access to government privilege, when they drafted (now) Article 101 TFEU (abuse of dominance), and included (now) Article 106 TFEU.

For the problem of excessive pricing by state-owned and recently privatized-firms, see the South African cases, Chapter 5, supra. This section concerns exclusionary practices.

We begin here with two ports cases—cases in which state-owned ports used their power over the facility to block or disadvantage foreign shippers or competitors. The first, *Port of Genoa*, shows how European principles of free movement, non-discrimination, non-abuse of dominance, and the Member States' duty of loyalty to carry out the single market objective, interact. The second, *Rødby*, is a more traditional antitrust case that highlights the incentive of the state facility owner to keep adjacent markets for itself. Both are precursors to a number of the cases that you will read in the sections below on State Privilege and State Responsibility.

Ports Cases

Ports and ports authorities were principally owned by states. They were literally and figuratively gateways to markets. Typically, states adopted measures to bolster their ports' powers to exclude; and exclusion of competitors and exploitation of consumers were common. The ports cases are helpful illustrations 1) factually, of problems of state ownership and exclusive privilege, and 2) legally, of the interrelationship of the several Treaty articles applied to address the problems of abuse, to promote liberalization, and to assure non-discriminatory access.

Before reading the cases, read in Appendix 1 Articles 102 TFEU (abuse of dominance), Article 106 TFEU (application of antitrust to SOEs and holders of special or exclusive rights, and obligations of Member States not to legislate to the contrary effect), and Article 4(3) TEU (Member State's duty to facilitate the achievement of the Union's tasks and to "abstain from any measure which could jeopardize the attainment of the Union's objectives").

MERCI CONVENZIONALI PORTO DI GENOVA v. SIDERURGICA GABRIELLI SPA

Case C–179/90, ECLI:EU:C:1991:347 (Court of Justice of the European Union 1991)

The Italian Navigation Code established an exclusive right to organize dock work for third parties, and required retention of dock work companies that employed only registered workers of Italian nationality. Carriers coming to port were not permitted to use their crew to load and unload. The organizer of dock work was generally controlled by the port authority.

Merci and Compagnia enjoyed the exclusive right to organize dock work. Siderurgica Gabrielli SpA arrived in the Port of Genoa with goods, but Merci delayed in providing unloading services and Siderurgica Gabrielli suffered damages, for which it sought compensation. The Italian court asked the ECJ whether the Italian rules violated (now) Articles 4(3) TEU, 34 TFEU (free movement of goods), 45 (free movement of workers), 102 and 106, and whether Siderurgica Gabrielli had a remedy.

Advocate General Van Gerven identified the anticompetitive and discriminatory effects inherent in the Italian law:

22 [W]e must now consider whether these abuses of a dominant position within the meaning of Article [102]—in so far as the national court regards them as established—are imposed, or facilitated, or made inevitable by the relevant national legislation. I think there can be little doubt about this. In fact, the scale of charges and other, presumably unfair, contractual conditions applied by Merci and Compagnia are made possible, if not inevitable, by the national legislation applicable and are facilitated, if not made compulsory, by the port authorities under the powers conferred on them by national legislation. The other abuses too are made possible by that legislation. But for the monopoly for the performance of dock work conferred on it by the Italian legislation, Compagnia could certainly not have afforded to abstain from using modern technology, and it is clear also that the dissimilar treatment of trading parties was possible only as a result of the monopoly granted to Merci and the complexity and lack of transparency of the scale of charges devised by the authority.

The Court ruled:

19 [I]t appears from the circumstances described by the national court and discussed before the Court of Justice that the undertakings enjoying exclusive rights in accordance with the procedures laid down by the national rules in question are, as a result, induced either to demand payment for services which have not been requested, to charge disproportionate prices, to refuse to have recourse to modern technology, which involves an increase in the cost of the operations and a prolongation of the time required for their performance, or to grant price reductions to certain consumers and at the same time to offset such reductions by an increase in the charges to other consumers.

20 In these circumstances it must be held that a Member State creates a situation contrary to Article [102] of the Treaty where it adopts rules of such a kind as those at issue before the national court, which are capable of affecting trade between Member States as in the case of the main proceedings, regard being had to the factors mentioned in . . . this judgment relating to the importance of traffic in the Port of Genoa.

21 As regards the interpretation of Article [102] of the Treaty requested by the national court, it is sufficient to recall that a national measure which has the effect of facilitating the abuse of a dominant position capable of affecting trade between Member States will generally be incompatible with that article, which prohibits quantitative restrictions on imports and all measures having equivalent effect (see Case 13/77 GB–INNO–BM v ATAB [1977] ECR 2115, paragraph 35) in so far as such a measure has the effect of making more difficult and hence of impeding imports of goods from other Member States.

22 In the main proceedings it may be seen from the national court' s findings that the unloading of the goods could have been effected at a lesser cost by the ship' s crew, so that compulsory recourse to the services of the two undertakings enjoying exclusive rights involved extra expense and was therefore capable, by reason of its effect on the prices of the goods, of affecting imports.

23 It should be emphasized in the third place that even within the framework of Article [106], the provisions of Articles [34, 45 and 102] of the Treaty have direct effect* and give rise for interested parties to rights which the national courts must protect (see in particular, as regards Article [102] of the Treaty).

24 The answer to the first question, as reformulated, should therefore be that:

> Article [106(1) TFEU], in conjunction with Articles [34, 45 and 102 TFEU], precludes rules of a Member State which confer on an undertaking established in that State the exclusive right to organize dock work and require it for that purpose to have recourse to a dock-work company formed exclusively of national workers; Articles [34, 45 and 102] of the Treaty, in conjunction with Article [106], give rise to rights for individuals which the national courts must protect.

---

* Editors' note: This means that the specified Articles are positive law in the Member States. They do not need implementing legislation to become enforceable law.

Notes and Questions

1. Note how the law condemns national measures as affronting competition and free movement rules intertwined. While these are common market cases, the EU competition provisions have been incorporated into many national laws. Moreover, more and more nations are now part of free trade areas and common markets, and the European jurisprudence is a model of how the competition rules integrate with the internal market free movement rules.

2. Following the judgment, Italy revised its law to open up competition for port-handling. The Commission, however, was not satisfied. It found that local authorities systematically refused to grant operating licenses to potential competitors of long-established dock services companies. Italy, in response, issued licensees. XXVth Report on Competition Policy (1995), pp. 58–59. The Commission again found that the Italian reform was insufficient and indeed that it created new problems. It found additional infringements, by decision of 97/744, 21 October 1997.

PORT OF RØDBY

94/119/EC, Commission decision of 21 Dec. 1993, O.J. L 055
26 January 1994 at 0052

[DSB was a Danish public undertaking which operated as a department of the transport ministry. It held the exclusive right to organize railroad traffic in Denmark and the exclusive right to manage the Port of Rødby, and it operated ferry services between Denmark and neighboring countries. Stena was a Swedish shipping group which specialized in ferry services and wished to operate between Denmark and Germany (Puttgarden), which essentially links eastern Denmark with Germany and the rest of western Europe.

Stena requested permission from the Danish government to use the existing port facilities at Rødby or to build a port in the vicinity. The Danish government refused. Stena complained to the Commission.]

Abuse of dominant position

12 The refusal to allow 'Euro-Port A/S', a subsidiary of the Swedish group [Stena] to operate from Rødby has the effect of eliminating a potential competitor on the Rødby-Puttgarden route and hence of strengthening the joint dominant position of DSB and [its partner] DB on that route.

According to the case law of the Court, an abuse within the meaning of Article [102] is committed in cases where, without any objective necessity, an undertaking holding a dominant position on a particular market reserves to itself an ancillary activity which might be carried out by another undertaking as part of its activities on a neighbouring but separate market, with the possibility of eliminating all competition from such undertaking.

Thus an undertaking that owns or manages and uses itself an essential facility, i.e. a facility or infrastructure without which its competitors are unable to offer their services to customers, and refuses to grant them access to such facility is abusing its dominant position.

Consequently, an undertaking that owns or manages an essential port facility from which it provides a maritime transport service may not, without objective justification, refuse to grant a shipowner wishing to operate on the same maritime route access to that facility without infringing Article [102].

13 According to the case-law of the Court, Article [106] (1) prohibits Member States from placing, by law, regulation or administrative provision, public undertakings and undertakings to which they grant exclusive rights in a position in which those undertakings could not place themselves by their own conduct without infringing Article [102]. The Court added that, where the extension of the dominant position of a public undertaking or an undertaking to which the State has granted exclusive rights resulted from a State measure, such a measure constituted an infringement of Article [106], read in conjunction with Article [102] of the Treaty. . . .

Thus, for the reasons given above, any firm in the same position as DSB which refused to grant another shipping operator access to the port it controlled would be abusing a dominant position. Where, as in the present case, a Member State has refused such access and has strengthened the effects of the refusal by also refusing to authorize the construction of a new port, it constitutes a State measure in breach of Article [106], read in conjunction with Article [102].

14 The reasons given by the Danish Transport Ministry for rejecting both requests of 'Euro-Port A/S' . . . are the following:

> —the plan of 'Euro-Port A/S' . . . (Stena), to build a new terminal is not acceptable as that undertaking has allegedly 'not established that there is an unsatisfied demand for a ferry service' and it is 'most unlikely that such a demand would arise', . . .
>
> —'Euro-Port A/S' (Stena) could not operate from the existing port facilities as this would have the effect of

preventing the companies already operating in the port from expanding their activities. * * *

The Commission concludes . . . that:

—there was indeed an unsatisfied demand for ferry services in May 1990 since one year later DSB and DB had expanded their services,

—the increase in the activities of DB and DSB in 1991 confirms that the port of Rødby was not saturated.

15 The Commission also considers that there is no evidence that the existing facilities at Rødby would today be saturated or that, subject to alterations which Stena has informed the Commission it is prepared to finance, existing port capacity is unable to cope with an increase in trade.

The Commission also notes that the Swedish group (Stena) has acquired land adjacent to the port facilities of Rødby which is perfectly suitable for development as a terminal by Stena.

It therefore concludes that there are no technical constraints preventing the Stena group from sailing between Rødby and Puttgarden.

16 . . . [T]he Danish authorities . . . [stressed] that their refusals were justified under Community law. They stated that it would be impossible to allow Stena access to the existing facilities, giving technical reasons and referring for the first time, without any further details, to obligations incumbent upon DB and DSB in the general interest.

This would appear to indicate that, in the view of the Danish authorities, the technical feasibility of access to the port is not a problem or is not the only problem and that they also have a duty to protect the public undertaking DSB from a competitor on the market for ferry services.

Nor can the Commission share the view of the Danish authorities that the alleged saturation of the existing port facilities would make pointless any attempt to introduce competition since this could not in any event lead to an increase in the number of sailings between Rødby and Puttgarden.

Even on a saturated market, an improvement in the quality of products or services offered or a reduction in prices as a result of competition is a definite advantage for consumers; this could also lead to an increase in demand which, in the present case, could be met by expanding the port. * * *

Article [106](2)

18 The Commission considers that the application of the competition rules in the present case does not impede the particular task entrusted to the public undertaking DSB namely to organize rail services and manage the port facilities at Rødby. Therefore the exception provided for in Article [106](2) [where application would obstruct the performance of tasks assigned to them] does not apply.

Conclusion

19 In view of the foregoing, the Commission considers that the measures referred to in paragraphs 1 and 2 constitute infringements of Article [106](1) of the Treaty, read in conjunction with Article [102].

Notes and Questions

1. Does the Commission rule out the defense of market saturation in law as well as in fact? Does it suggest why DSB denied the permission? What does the case imply about incentives, and how can the incentives be aligned with competition values?

2. In the aftermath of the *Rødby* case, the Commission became concerned that construction of a new port would be inefficient. It adopted a revised remedy "legally separating the provision of the network from the commercial services using the network." http://www.eubusiness.com/topics/competition/liberalisation. Is this a superior remedy? Explain the difference.

3. How would the *Port of Genoa* problem be dealt with in the United States? In view of the synergies among the Treaty articles and the differences in US and EU competition law treatment, comment on the constitutional dimension of EU competition law.

4. How would the *Rødby* problem be dealt with under US law? Is the port an essential facility? Would the entity that both owned or managed the port and operated the ferry have a duty to license a competing ferry service? See Verizon Communications Inc. v. Law Offices of Curtis V. Trinko, 540 U.S. 398 (2004). Would insufficient demand be a defense?

5. In several important cases, the state-owned entities had tried, unsuccessfully, to use state ownership as a shield to Article 102 liability. In *British Telecom* (Italy v. Commission), the Court held that a state telecommunications monopoly abused its dominance by preventing private message-forwarding agencies from receiving and forwarding international telephone calls. Case 41/83, EU:C:1985:120. In *Telemarketing*, the Court stated that a broadcasting monopoly would abuse its dominant position by refusing to sell broadcasting time to a telemarketing firm that competed with the monopoly firm's subsidiary.

Case 311/84, Centre Belge d'Etudes de Marché-Télémarketing SA v. Compagnie Luxembourgeoise de Télédiffusion SA, EU:C:1985:394.

6. The port cases reflect principles and problems common to a range of infrastructure industries and regulated sectors, including transport, post, telecommunications and energy. The European law that applies to restrictive state measures and to abusive action by undertakings is intertwined. In some sectors, notably energy and telecommunications, the EU undertook major liberalization projects, aided by framework directives. The objective was to *improve* conditions of competition, not just to prevent its restriction. See Neelie Kroes, *Improving Competition in European Energy Markets through Effective Unbundling*, Chapter 9 in 2007 Fordham Competition Law Institute, INTERNATIONAL ANTITRUST LAW & POLICY, p. 247 (B. Hawk ed. 2007).

D. STATE PRIVILEGE OR LICENSE; LIMITS TO EXCLUSIVITY

Many states grant to a designated enterprise exclusive rights or privileges, such as the exclusive right to run an employment service, the exclusive right to deliver the mail, or, as we saw above, the exclusive right to run a port. What are the implications for competition of these exclusive grants?

Article 106(2) of the Treaty on the Functioning of the European Union, as we have just seen, prohibits public undertakings or undertakings to which special or exclusive rights are granted from violating the antitrust provisions and the anti-discrimination provisions of the Treaty. They are subject to these articles insofar as their application does not obstruct their performance of the particular tasks assigned to them.

HÖFNER v. MACROTRON GMBH

Case C–41/90, ECLI:EU:C:1991:161 (Court of Justice of the European Union 1991)

[German law, intended to achieve a high level of employment and to improve the distribution of jobs, conferred on the Bundesanstalt für Arbeit (Federal Employment Office) the exclusive right of placement; i.e. exclusivity as employment agent. The law required the Office to provide the service free of charge. Placement activities by others were punishable by fine. Messrs. Höfner and Elser contracted with Macrotron to present to Macrotron a suitable candidate for the post of sales manager, for a fee. They presented such a candidate, but Macrotron decided not to employ him and refused to pay the fee stipulated, alleging, inter alia, that the contract was void by reason of the German law. Höfner and Elser rejoined that the German law was void because it unnecessarily restrained their competition in violation of Article 106, and exclusion of their competition amounted to abuse of dominance under Article 102. The national court referred questions to the Court of Justice.]

16 In its fourth question, the national court asks more specifically whether the monopoly of employment procurement in respect of business executives granted to a public employment agency constitutes an abuse of a dominant position within the meaning of Article [102], having regard to Article [106](2). . . .

17 According to the appellants in the main proceedings, an agency such as the Bundesanstalt is both a public undertaking within the meaning of Article [106](1) and an undertaking entrusted with the operation of services of general economic interest within the meaning of Article [106](2) of the Treaty. The Bundesanstalt is therefore, they maintain, subject to the competition rules to the extent to which the application thereof does not obstruct the performance of the particular task assigned to it, and it does not in the present case. The appellants also claim that the action taken by the Bundesanstalt, which extended its statutory monopoly over employment procurement to activities for which the establishment of a monopoly is not in the public interest, constitutes an abuse within the meaning of Article [102] of the Treaty. They also consider that any Member State which makes such an abuse possible is in breach of Article [106](1) and of the general principle whereby the Member States must refrain from taking any measure which could destroy the effectiveness of the Community competition rules.

18 The Commission takes a somewhat different view. The maintenance of a monopoly on executive recruitment constitutes, in its view, an infringement of Article [106](1) read in conjunction with Article [102] of the Treaty where the grantee of the monopoly is not willing or able to carry out that task fully, according to the demand existing on the market, and provided that such conduct is liable to affect trade between Member States. * * *

21 It must be observed, in the context of competition law, first that the concept of an undertaking encompasses every entity engaged in an economic activity, regardless of the legal status of the entity and the way in which it is financed and, secondly, that employment procurement is an economic activity.

22 The fact that employment procurement activities are normally entrusted to public agencies cannot affect the economic nature of such activities. Employment procurement has not always been, and is not necessarily, carried out by public entities. That finding applies in particular to executive recruitment.

23 It follows that an entity such as a public employment agency engaged in the business of employment procurement may be classified as an undertaking for the purpose of applying the Community competition rules.

24 It must be pointed out that a public employment agency which is entrusted, under the legislation of a Member State, with the operation of services of general economic interest . . . remains subject to the competition rules pursuant to Article [106](2) of the Treaty unless and to the extent to which it is shown that their application is incompatible with the discharge of its duties.

25 As regards the manner in which a public employment agency enjoying an exclusive right of employment procurement conducts itself in relation to executive recruitment undertaken by private recruitment consultancy companies, it must be stated that the application of Article [102] of the Treaty cannot obstruct the performance of the particular task assigned to that agency in so far as the latter is manifestly not in a position to satisfy demand in that area of the market and in fact allows its exclusive rights to be encroached on by those companies.

26 Whilst it is true that Article [102] concerns undertakings and may be applied within the limits laid down by Article [106](2) to public undertakings or undertakings vested with exclusive rights or specific rights, the fact nevertheless remains that the Treaty requires the Member States not to take or maintain in force measures which could destroy the effectiveness of that provision. . . . * * *

29 . . . [T]he simple fact of creating a dominant position of that kind by granting an exclusive right within the meaning of Article [106](1) is not as such incompatible with Article [102] of the Treaty. A Member State is in breach of the prohibition contained in those two provisions only if the undertaking in question, merely by exercising the exclusive right granted to it, cannot avoid abusing its dominant position.

30 Pursuant to Article [102](b), such an abuse may in particular consist in limiting the provision of a service, to the prejudice of those seeking to avail themselves of it.

31 A Member State creates a situation in which the provision of a service is limited when the undertaking to which it grants an exclusive right extending to executive recruitment activities is manifestly not in a position to satisfy the demand prevailing on the market for activities of that kind and when the effective pursuit of such activities by private companies is rendered impossible by the maintenance in force of a statutory provision under which such

activities are prohibited and nonobservance of that prohibition renders the contracts concerned void. * * *

34 In view of the foregoing considerations, it must be stated in reply to the fourth question that a public employment agency engaged in employment procurement activities is subject to the prohibition contained in Article [102] of the Treaty, so long as the application of that provision does not obstruct the performance of the particular task assigned to it. A Member State which has conferred an exclusive right to carry on that activity upon the public employment agency is in breach of Article [106](1) of the Treaty where it creates a situation in which that agency cannot avoid infringing Article [102] of the Treaty. That is the case, in particular, where the following conditions are satisfied:

—the exclusive right extends to executive recruitment activities

—the public employment agency is manifestly incapable of satisfying demand prevailing on the market for such activities

—the actual pursuit of those activities by private recruitment consultants is rendered impossible by the maintenance in force of a statutory provision under which such activities are prohibited and non-observance of that prohibition renders the contracts concerned void

—the activities in question may extend to the nationals or to the territory of other Member States.

Notes and Questions

1. What is the standard for running afoul of Article 106(2) of the Treaty? How difficult will it be for Messrs. Höfner and Elser to win their argument before the national court?

2. Note the difference between plaintiffs' proposed formulation (para. 17) and the Commission's (para. 18). Which did the Court accept? Which is the more workable? Which is the better standard, given the Community's dual interests in respecting Member State regulation in the public interest and supporting freedom of competition?

3. Does the Court in effect require an efficiency audit of the Federal Employment Office to determine whether it manifestly cannot satisfy demand? Is the Office's ability to satisfy demand a function of the resources that the German government makes available to it? Do all dominant firms abuse their dominance by simply not providing enough goods or service (at what price level?), or is it critical that the

government-granted exclusive privilege prevents anyone else from serving the market?

4. In Case C–320/91, Régie des Postes v. Corbeau, EU:C:1993:198, a Belgian law—enacted before the development of courier service—gave exclusive mail delivery rights to the Belgian Post Office and prohibited private mail delivery. Mr. Corbeau set up a private mail delivery service in Liège. Corbeau collected mail from his clients and guaranteed delivery before noon the following day to all addressees within town limits. He delivered in-town mail and dispatched the out-of-town mail by post. When prosecuted, Corbeau asserted a violation of Article 106.

In answer to a question posed by the Belgian court (a procedure available under Article 267 TFEU), the European Court of Justice advised the Belgian court that an undertaking charged with the provision of universal service may not restrict competition more than necessary to achieve its public mission in view of contemporary market conditions. The Court of Justice left it to the national court to determine what was "more than necessary."

Was Corbeau skimming the cream from the Belgian Post's business? At some point, would cream-skimming compromise the economic stability of the post office and disable it from fulfilling its obligation to provide universal service? How can the national court determine how much competition is too much for the Belgian Post to fulfill its public mission?

Note the effect of the law: the holder of state-granted exclusive rights may forfeit exclusivity.

5. There is a gap in the coverage of Articles 101, 102 and 106 of the Treaty. Member State bodies are subject to those Treaty obligations only if they carry out economic activities. Bodies that regulate the market but do not participate in it are not covered. In Case C–205/03 P, FENIN v. Commission, EU:C:2006:453, the Court of Justice acknowledged that the public bodies that ran the Spanish national healthcare system and provided free services funded by social security contributions and other state funding were not "undertakings," and it held that a state body that is not an undertaking does not become so in its role as purchaser of goods—here, medical goods and equipment. The purchasing activity is not "dissociable from the service subsequently provided." The holding of *FENIN* means that suppliers to state bodies carrying out public functions are not protected by Article 102 from the state body's exploitative and discriminatory purchasing conduct. Does this holding shield too much activity from the antitrust provisions? Is it sufficient protection that the state is subject to Article 18 TFEU, which prohibits the state from discriminating based on nationality?

6. The United States Sherman Act imposes liability on "any person" who restrains trade or monopolizes. "Person" includes associations, corporations, and other entities. State and local government-owned entities may qualify as persons. See City of Lafayette v. Louisiana Power & Light Co., 435 U.S. 389 (1978). However, in U.S. Postal Service v. Flamingo Industries (USA) Ltd., 540 U.S. 736 (2004), the US Supreme Court held that the U.S. Postal Service, in view of its public characteristics and responsibilities, should be treated as part of the US Government and not as a market participant; therefore it was not a "person" within the meaning of the Sherman Act.

E. STATE MEASURES

1. State Measures—State Responsibility

State legislation is a frequent source of distortion of competition. Distortions may result from national laws on price control, sector regulation (e.g., oil, tobacco, transport), taxation, and various social and national industrial policies. But states, of course, must be empowered to take action in the public interest, meaning that some balance must be struck and the question is, what is that balance?

The answer may be context-dependent. While the US allows for the consideration of public interest justifications in granting immunity to the States for measures restraining commerce among States or distorting competition when acting in their sovereign capacity, the EU adopted a stricter view.

Consider the extent to which EU Article 4 TEU [duty of sincere cooperation], the competition provisions, and the freedoms of movement, suggest a generous overriding of anticompetitive state legislation? The Court of Justice bowed in the direction of a broad preemption in its judgment in Case 13/77, NV GB-INNO-BM v. Vereniging van de Kleinhandelaars in Tabak (*INNO/ATAB*), EU:C:1977:185. A Belgian law required, for tax collection purposes, that tobacco products be sold at a price affixed to the label by the manufacturer or importer. The Court of Justice said:

> [W]hile it is true that Article [102] is directed at undertakings, nonetheless it is also true that the Treaty [now Article 4 TEU] imposes a duty on Member States not to adopt or maintain in force any measure which could deprive that provision of its effectiveness. Id., para. 31.

In succeeding decades, the Court took a more modest (but still firm) view of Member State obligations. In 1993, amid concerns that the "center" had taken too much power for itself and was unduly eclipsing Member State prerogatives, the Court of Justice restruck the balance in cases involving national law with a by-product effect on free movement of goods, *Keck*, EU:C:1993:905. The shifted perspective, which would give greater regard to Member State prerogatives, bore its imprint in a trio of contemporaneous competition cases.

In this trio, the Court held: A Member State infringes Articles TEU4/TFEU101 if it "requires or favors the adoption of agreements, decisions or concerted practices contrary to Article [101], or reinforces such effects, or deprives its own legislation of its official character by delegating economic responsibility to private traders" (quoting from INNO/ATAB). Ohra Schadeverzekeringen NV v. Netherlands (Ohra), Case C–245/91, EU:1993:887; W. Meng v. Germany (Meng), Case C–2/91, EU:C:1993:885; Gebrüder Reiff GmbH & Co. KG v. Bundesanstalt für den Güterfernverkehr (Reiff), Case C–185/91, EU:C:1993:886. The cases exonerated Member State measures that had anticompetitive effects; namely, national law that forbade insurance agents from granting rebates, and national law that entrusted trucking tariffs to boards that included individuals recommended by the truckers, where the board members were obliged to act in the public interest and the Minister of Transport could intervene to set the tariff. In a recent case, the Court of justice interpreted Article 101 TFEU in combination with Article 4(3) TUE as meaning that a Bulgarian legislation prohibiting lawyer fees from being lower than the amount provided for by the professional association regulation constitutes a restriction on competition by object (Em akaunt BG EOOD, C-438/22, EU:C:2024:71).

Some questions remain. How broadly or narrowly would the Court construe its mandate that the State must not undermine the effectiveness of Articles 101 and 102? Would the analysis of States measures under internal market rules be more relevant to balance the public interest objectives and the impact of the measure on the market? See Damien Gerard, *EU Competition Policy After Lisbon: Time to Review the 'State Action Doctrine'*, 1 Journal of European Competition Law & Practice 202 (2010).

CONSORZIO INDUSTRIE FIAMMIFERI (*ITALIAN MATCHES*)

(responsibility of the state)

Case C–198/01, ECLI:EU:C:2003:430 (Court of Justice of the European Union 2003)

[In Consorzio Industrie Fiammiferi (Italian matches), Case C–198/01, EU:C:2003:8055, Italy, by an 80 year-old Royal Decree, organized a match cartel. Italy required the Italian match producers to join a consortium. The minister set the price for matches, and the consortium of competitors was required to allocate quotas. Government officials had the duty to oversee the quotas. A German match producer complained to the Italian Antitrust Authority that it was having difficulty entering the Italian market. Swedish producers later complained that they were denied a fair quota and could sell only to the Italian match consortium. The Italian Antitrust Authority opened proceedings. It found Treaty violations both by Italy and the Italian producers. An Italian Tribunal referred questions to the Court of Justice. Here is the response of the Court regarding Italy's responsibility.]

45 . . . [A]lthough Articles [101 and 102 TFEU] are, in themselves, concerned solely with the conduct of undertakings and not with laws or regulations emanating from Member States, those articles, read in conjunction with Article [4 TEU], which lays down a duty to cooperate, none the less require the Member States not to introduce or maintain in force measures, even of a legislative or regulatory nature, which may render ineffective the competition rules applicable to undertakings.

46 The Court has held in particular that Articles [4 TEU and 101 TFEU] are infringed where a Member State requires or favours the adoption of agreements, decisions or concerted practices contrary to Article [101 TFEU] or reinforces their effects, or where it divests its own rules of the character of legislation by delegating to private economic operators responsibility for taking decisions affecting the economic sphere.

47 Moreover, since the Treaty of Maastricht entered into force, the . . . Treaty has expressly provided that in the context of their economic policy the activities of the Member States must observe the principle of an open market economy with free competition. . . .

48 It is appropriate to bear in mind, second, that in accordance with settled case-law the primacy of Community law requires any provision of national law which contravenes a Community rule to be disapplied, regardless of whether it was adopted before or after that rule.

49 The duty to disapply national legislation which contravenes Community law applies not only to national courts but also to all organs of the State, including administrative authorities, which entails, if the circumstances so require, the obligation to take all appropriate measures to enable Community law to be fully applied.

50 Since a national competition authority such as the Authority is responsible for ensuring, *inter alia*, that Article [101 TFEU] is observed and that provision, in conjunction with Article [4 TEU], imposes a duty on Member States to refrain from introducing measures contrary to the Community competition rules, those rules

would be rendered less effective if, in the course of an investigation under Article [101 TFEU] into the conduct of undertakings, the authority were not able to declare a national measure contrary to the combined provisions of Articles [4 TEU] and [101 TFEU] and if, consequently, it failed to disapply it.

51 In that regard, it is of little significance that, where undertakings are required by national legislation to engage in anti-competitive conduct, they cannot also be held accountable for infringement of Articles [101 and 102 TFEU]. Member States' obligations under Articles 3(1)(g) EC,* [4 TEU, 101 TFEU and 102 TFEU], which are distinct from those to which undertakings are subject under Articles [101 and 102 TFEU], none the less continue to exist and therefore the national competition authority remains duty-bound to disapply the national measure at issue.

In the following case, legislation itself—which would have extended a postal monopoly to an adjacent market that had been developed by private firms, was impugned. By adopting the legislation, the Slovak Republic infringed the Treaty.

SLOVAKIAN POSTAL LEGISLATION RELATING TO HYBRID MAIL SERVICES

Commission Decision of 7 Oct. 2008, Case COMP/39.562, O J C322 (17 Dec. 2008, p. 10)

[The Postal Act of the Slovak Republic (2004) reserved to the government entity, Slovenská Pošta, the sole right and the duty to provide universal service for delivery of all collected mail. Hybrid mail (electronically transmitted to the service provider and printed, put into an envelope, and delivered by the provider) was not covered by the reservation. Slovak Telecom issued a call for tenders for sending its invoices by hybrid mail. Triggered by this event, two private companies answered the tender and entered the market for receipt, conversion and delivery of hybrid mail. They delivered hybrid mail within their areas, which covered about three-fourths of the Slovak population, and used the network of Slovenská Pošta for the rest. Three years later, with the state post office unhappy with the competition, the Slovak Parliament enacted an amendment to the Postal Act extending the state reservation to hybrid mail.

The European Commission brought proceedings alleging that the announcement breached (now) Article 106 in conjunction with

---

* Editors' Note: Article 3(1)(g) of the EC Treaty identified "undistorted competition" as an activity of the Community. The Treaty of Lisbon removed this provision and put a substitute into a protocol. The protocol states that the Treaty on European Union "includes a system ensuring that competition is not distorted . . . ."

Article 102. Slovenská Pošta argued in justification that the extension was necessary to maintain the provision of a service of general economic interest. It submitted studies on the cost of universal service, and projected losses in the future if it were not assured of a monopoly of the hybrid mail. The European Commission found the cost figures and projections unreliable and unrealistic. It found a violation. The General Court affirmed.]

3. COMMISSION ANALYSIS

3.1. Applicability of Article [106](1) of the Treaty

85 Article [106](1) reads as follows: *"In the case of public undertakings and undertakings to which Member States grant special or exclusive rights, Member States shall neither enact nor maintain in force any measure contrary to the rules contained in this Treaty, in particular to those rules provided for in Article [18] and Articles [101] to [109]."*
* * *

87 The Postal Act reserves to Slovenská Pošta the right to distribute certain postal items, as defined in Article 7 of the Act. Slovenská Pošta thus also enjoys exclusive rights within the meaning of Article [106] (1).

88 The Amendment constitutes a State measure within the meaning of Article [106](1) of the . . . Treaty as do the enforcement measures by the Slovak authorities against an alleged breach of the reserved area. The Postal Regulatory Office, notwithstanding the fact that it might enjoy independence with regard to the central government and administration of the Slovak Republic, is a public body under Slovak law, invested with public powers and is as such, as regards the application of the Treaty rules, to be regarded as bound by the rules incumbent on the Member States. Enforcement activities of the Postal Regulatory Office are state measures which must conform to the rules of the . . . Treaty.

* * *

3.1.3. Dominant Position on the market for traditional mail services

113 According to constant case law, an undertaking holding a statutory monopoly on a substantial part of the common market is considered to occupy a dominant position within the meaning of Article [102] of the Treaty. Slovakia is a substantial part of the common market within which, as demonstrated earlier, Slovenská Pošta has been granted an exclusive statutory licence to provide basic postal services.

3.1.4. Infringement of Article [106](1) in conjunction with Article [102] of the Treaty

114 In its 1998 Postal Notice, the Commission set out its approach as regards the respect of competition rules in the postal sector. The Notice stresses that ". . . *the Commission will ensure that monopoly power is not used for extending a protected dominant position into liberalized activities.*" The Notice further clarifies that ". . . *the use, without objective justification, of a dominant position on one market to obtain market power on related or neighboring markets which are distinct from the former, at the risk of eliminating competition on those markets*" would be contrary to Articles [106] in conjunction with Article [102]. More particularly, the use of a dominant position to extend the monopoly from the reserved market to a previously liberalized market would be ". . . *incompatible with the Treaty provisions, in the absence of specific justification, if the functioning of services in the general economic interest was not previously endangered. The Commission considers that it would be appropriate for Member States to inform the Commission of any extension of special or exclusive rights and of the justification therefore.*"

115 The Commission has come to the conclusion that the State measure at stake infringes Article [106](1) in conjunction with Article [102] of the Treaty in two ways:

3.1.4.1. Extension of Slovenská Pošta's exclusive right

116 According to the Court of Justice of the European Communities, an abuse within the meaning of Article [102] is committed where, without any objective justification, an undertaking holding a dominant position on a particular market reserves to itself other ancillary activities in neighbouring but distinct markets, although these activities could also be carried out by another undertaking as part of its activities on this neighbouring but separate market. With regard to Article [106](1) in conjunction with Article [102], it is settled case law that the extension by means of a measure adopted by the State, of a monopoly into a neighbouring and competitive market, without any objective justification, is prohibited as such by Article [106](1) in conjunction with Article [102].

117 . . . . The state measure in question . . . reserves a part of the value chain of the hybrid mail service (the distribution of such items) to the incumbent postal operator Slovenská Pošta, while it was liberalised before that state measure.

118 In their replies to the letter of formal notice as well as in subsequent submissions, the Slovak authorities and Slovenská Pošta argued that the legislative changes did not amount to an extension

of Slovenská Pošta's exclusive right to the activity of distributing hybrid mail items since this activity already fell within the reserved area before the Amendment. In their view, the purpose of the new law was merely to *"eliminate the possibility of incorrect interpretation of the postal service act"* and to *"confirm and maintain"* the current legal situation.

119 The Commission has carefully considered the arguments put forward by the Slovak government and Slovenská Pošta in support of their contention that the delivery of hybrid mail items was always part of the reserved area and that therefore the Amendment merely provides further clarification to the matter. For the reasons set out below, the Commission maintains its conclusion set out in the letter of formal notice that the delivery of hybrid mail items was an activity open to competition prior to the adoption of the state measure in question.

* * *

148 Consequently, the Commission considers that before the entry into force of the Amendment, hybrid mail delivery services were *de iure* and *de facto* open to competition in Slovakia. Thus, the Amendment extended the exclusive rights of Slovenská Pošta to the activity of distributing items of hybrid mail, an activity which, before the Amendment, was open to competition.

3.1.4.2. Limitation of the output to the end-user

149 It is settled case law that "*an abuse may in particular consist in limiting the provision of a service, to the prejudice of those seeking to avail themselves of it. A Member State creates a situation in which the provision of a service is limited when the undertaking to which it grants an exclusive right . . . is manifestly not in a position to satisfy the demand prevailing on the market for activities of that kind and when the effective pursuit of such activities by private companies is rendered impossible . . .*".[33]

150 To the extent that only private operators are able to offer additional services such as tracking services and seven day a week delivery together with their offer of hybrid mail services, the reservation of hybrid mail delivery would deprive customers of these services. These extra services, in particular track-and-trace services, appear to be one of the main criteria used by customers to select postal service providers. As has been explained above, hybrid mail is a particularly attractive form of postal services for customers such as banks, insurance and telecommunications companies which have

---

[33] Case C–41/90 *Höfner and Elser*, [1991] ECR p. I–1979.

regular invoices to send to end-users. For such customers of postal service operators, additional services such as track-and-trace are of particular importance as they allow them to avoid bad credit and to have precise information on whether a particular postal item has been distributed to the end user. Such information is valuable for companies sending invoices. In its reply to the letter of facts, whilst Slovenská Pošta contests the "other" additional services alleged by SMS, it does not contest that the track and trace services offered to Slovak Telekom by SMS are value-added services.

151 Slovenská Pošta is currently not offering such additional services for items of hybrid mail correspondence. In fact, insofar as the private competitors have to rely on the distribution network of Slovenská Pošta, they are themselves not able to offer their customers such services. After the reservation of the delivery of hybrid mail services, these additional services as offered by the private competitors (such as track-and-trace service and seven days a week delivery) will thus no longer be available to customers.

* * *

3.1.6. Conclusion

158 On the basis of the above, the Commission considers that the Slovak Republic has infringed Article [106](1) in conjunction with Article [102].

3.2. No justification under Article [106](2) of the Treaty

159 Under Article [106](2) of the Treaty, *"undertakings entrusted with the operation of services of general economic interest [. . .] shall be subject to [Treaty rules], in particular the rules on competition, in so far as the application of such rules does not obstruct the performance, in law or in fact of the particular task assigned to them. The development of trade must not be affected to such an extent as would be contrary to the interests of the Community"*.

3.2.1. Burden of proof

160 As the Court held in a number of cases, it is incumbent on a Member State which invokes Article [106](2), as a derogation from the fundamental rules of the Treaty, to show that the conditions for application of that provision are fulfilled.

* * *

3.2.2. No obstruction of the universal service in case hybrid mail remains open to competition

165 Even though there is a presumption of *prima facie* justification under Article [106](2) for services covered by the reserved area as

defined in the Postal Directive . . ., this is different if a service was already liberalised and if the functioning of the public service was not previously endangered. In such a case the extension of the monopoly in the previously liberalised activity would be incompatible, in the absence of a specific justification. . . .

166 Article 7 of the Postal Directive only allows such reservation *"to the extent necessary to ensure the maintenance of universal service"*. In *International Mail Spain*[39], the Court held that Member States may extend the postal monopoly if they "*establish that, in the absence of such a reservation, achievement of that universal service would be precluded, or that reservation is necessary to enable that service to be carried out under economically acceptable conditions*".

167 In light of this jurisprudence, the Member State has to demonstrate that, without the requested extension or reservation, the achievement of the universal service would be either precluded or could at least not be carried out under economically acceptable conditions. The Commission considers that the Slovak government has not met this standard.

* * *

3.2.3. Extension of the monopoly is not necessary to ensure the quality of postal service provided by Slovenská Pošta's competitors

195 The Slovak Authorities further submit that the *status quo "might impair the quality of the postal services provided in Slovakia"*. They argue that alternative postal operators have destroyed postal items: "*After 1 April 2008 it has been demonstrated that certain items of mail up to 50g have been distributed by alternative operators; some cases have been documented by the police. The mail items concerned were found in rubbish bins and did not bear the logo of Slovenská Pošta a.s., i.e. they were not distributed by means of the distribution network of Slovenská Pošta*".

196 The Commission cannot accept this line of argument. First, under competitive conditions postal service providers have an obvious incentive to ensure that mail items entrusted to them are delivered to the recipients. Contracts are concluded accordingly. In particular, postal operators commit themselves to achieve certain quality targets. If they do not reach these targets and do not satisfy their customers, they risk losing these customers to competitors featuring a higher quality performance.

197 Moreover, Article 9 of the Postal Directive allows Member States to condition the granting of authorisations to certain requirements

39 Case C–162/06, *International Mail Spain,* [2007] ECR p. I–9911.

in terms of quality, availability and performance of the postal services. To the extent that competitive forces are not sufficient to prevent postal items ending up in rubbish bins, this authorisation regime constitutes a much less intrusive and more flexible tool to ensure high quality standards. Against this background, the Commission considers that it is disproportionate to extend Slovenská Pošta's monopoly on the grounds that alternative postal operators have in some instances provided a service of bad quality. * * *

3.2.4. Conclusion

199 On the basis of the above, the Slovak government and Slovenská Pošta have failed to prove that the extension of the postal monopoly to hybrid mail services was necessary for the universal service to be provided under economically acceptable conditions.

Slovakia and its Post Office were enraged by the Commission's decision, refused to comply, and filed an appeal (which they lost). A local headline declared: "Slovakia to EC: 'The State is no Chicken to be Plucked.'" ePostal News, Dec. 1, 2008. The Commission ordered Slovakia to implement its order. It advised the competitors that they were free to compete. See Commission press release, 29 Oct. 2009, IP/09/1632. The General Court affirmed, in the judgment above, and appeal of the General Court. judgment is pending. Slovenská Pošta v. Commission, Case T–556/08, EU:T:2015:189.

DEI v. COMMISSION

(Greek lignite)
Case C–553/12 P, ECLI:EU:C:2014:2083
(Court of Justice of the European Union 2014)

[In Dimosia Epicheirisi Ilektrismou AE (DEI) v. Commission (Greek lignite), Greece granted its state-owned enterprise quasi-exclusive rights to deposits of lignite, the cheapest and most attractive source of electric energy, after the liberalization of the electricity market. The Commission found that this grant protected DEI's dominant position on the downstream market for the wholesale sale of electricity, creating inequality of opportunities between economic operators, in violation of Articles 102/106(1). The General Court annulled the decision on grounds that the Commission had not shown "that privileged access to lignite was capable of creating a situation in which, by the mere exercise of its exploitation rights, [DEI] could have been able to commit abuses of a dominant position on the wholesale electricity market or was led to commit such abuses on that market." para. 92. The Court of Justice annulled the General Court judgment, holding that it was not necessary for the Commission to demonstrate an abuse to which the measure could have led; it was sufficient that the challenged act created inequality of opportunity between economic operators and thus distorted competition. Thus:]

41 . . . [A] Member State is in breach of the prohibitions laid down by Article [106(1)] in conjunction with Article [102] if it adopts any law, regulation or administrative provision that creates a situation in which a public undertaking or an undertaking on which it has conferred special or exclusive rights, merely by exercising the preferential rights conferred upon it, is led to abuse its dominant position or when those rights are liable to create a situation in which that undertaking is led to commit such abuses. In that respect, it is not necessary that any abuse should actually occur. * * *

43 It is clear from the Court's case-law that a system of undistorted competition, such as that provided for by the Treaty, can be guaranteed only if equality of opportunity is secured as between the various economic operators.

44 It follows that if inequality of opportunity between economic operators, and thus distorted competition, is the result of a State measure, such a measure constitutes an infringement of Article [106(1)] read together with Article [102]. * * *

46 It follows from the matters addressed in paragraphs 41 to 45 above that, as the Advocate General states in point 55 of his Opinion, infringement of Article 86(1) EC in conjunction with Article 82 EC may be established irrespective of whether any abuse actually exists. All that is necessary is for the Commission to identify a potential or actual anti-competitive consequence liable to result from the State measure at issue. Such an infringement may thus be established where the State measures at issue affect the structure of the market by creating unequal conditions of competition between companies, by allowing the public undertaking or the undertaking which was granted special or exclusive rights to maintain (for example by hindering new entrants to the market), strengthen or extend its dominant position over another market, thereby restricting competition, without it being necessary to prove the existence of actual abuse.

47 In those circumstances, it follows that, contrary to the General Court's analysis . . . , it is sufficient to show that that potential or actual anti-competitive consequence is liable to result from the State measure at issue; it is not necessary to identify an abuse other than that which results from the situation brought about by the State measure at issue. It also follows that the General Court erred in law in holding that the Commission, by finding that DEI, a former

monopolistic undertaking, continued to maintain a dominant position on the wholesale electricity market by virtue of the advantage conferred upon it by its privileged access to lignite and that that situation created inequality of opportunity on that market between the applicant and other undertakings, had neither identified nor established to a sufficient legal standard the abuse to which . . . the State measure in question had led or could have led DEI.

Recently, a few more of these cases landed before the European Court of Justice. For example, the Court found a Romanian legislation incompatible with Article 106 and Article 102 TFEU as it granted a state-owned company the possibility of obtaining an extension of its exclusive right for the exploitation of mineral water resources for successive periods of five years, without having to face a competitive tender (Romaqua, C–510/22, EU:C:2023:694).

Are these holdings dramatic, in their limitation on Member States' power to grant privileges to their state-owned firms even if the SOE might do nothing to abuse dominance? The grant of such special privileges is sometimes referred to as a breach of the notional norm of competitive neutrality. Some jurisdictions such as Australia implement the norm as part of a regulatory process to determine whether legislation may give the state or state-owned entities unnecessary advantages.

Notes and Questions

1. Article 37 of the TFEU requires that Member States must "adjust any State monopolies of a commercial character so as to ensure that no discrimination regarding conditions under which goods are procured and marketed exists between nationals of Member States." Sweden maintained an alcohol monopoly for sales at retail, and provided a procedure for the grant of licenses to import, export, produce, and sell at wholesale. Mr. Franzen, without a license, imported wine from Denmark and sold it in Sweden. When he was prosecuted, he argued that the Swedish monopoly was itself illegal under Articles 34 and 37 and also that the system of licensing was illegal. The Court of Justice did not endorse the idea that monopolies are inconsistent with Article 37 of the Treaty. Merely, monopolies must be so organized and operated so as to exclude discrimination between nationals and non-nationals so that goods from other Member States are not put at a disadvantage. Case C–189/95, Franzen, EU:C:1997:504, paras. 39–41.

2. If monopolies are permissible under Article 37, can they be made impermissible under Article 106? Can they be made impermissible only if they constitute a new monopolization? Was Slovakia's only

mistake that it had not anticipated and thus reserved hybrid mail delivery from the start? If it had reserved this function from the start, what would have been the Commission's and (would-be) competitors' claims, and how likely would they have been to prevail?

Regulation of the Professions

In some jurisdictions, professions are exempt from the competition laws. In other jurisdictions they get special treatment, especially when the state restrains their competition. In Chapter 3, we saw that jurisdictions have widely varying perspectives on how to address anticompetitive restraints by members of learned professions. The following case regards an Italian law restraining the price competition of lawyers.

CIPOLLA V. FAZARI AND MACRINO v. MELONI

Cases C–94/04, C–202/04, ECLI:EU:C:2006:758
(Court of Justice of the European Union 2006)

[Pursuant to a 73-year old Italian law, Italy adopted maximum and minimum fee schedules for lawyers, from which there could be no derogation except in narrow circumstances. The schedules were based on a draft prepared by the National Lawyers' Council—a body of lawyers.

In connection with three fee disputes, an Italian court referred questions regarding the validity of the Italian law to the Court of Justice. First the Court held that the procedure did not encourage or require agreements or abuses contrary to Articles 4 TEU/101 TFEU or 102 TFEU.]

58 The prohibition of derogation, by agreement, from the minimum fees set by a scale such as that laid down by the Italian legislation is liable to render access to the Italian legal services market more difficult for lawyers established in a Member State other than the Italian Republic and therefore is likely to restrict the exercise of their activities providing services in that Member State. That prohibition therefore amounts to a restriction within the meaning of Article [56 TFEU].

59 That prohibition deprives lawyers established in a Member State other than the Italian Republic of the possibility, by requesting fees lower than those set by the scale, of competing more effectively with lawyers established on a stable basis in the Member State concerned and who therefore have greater opportunities for winning clients than lawyers established abroad.

60 Likewise, the prohibition thus laid down limits the choice of service recipients in Italy, because they cannot resort to the services of

lawyers established in other Member States who would offer their services in Italy at a lower rate than the minimum fees set by the scale.

61 However, such a prohibition may be justified where it serves overriding requirements relating to the public interest, is suitable for securing the attainment of the objective which it pursues and does not go beyond what is necessary in order to attain it.

62 In order to justify the restriction on freedom to provide services which stems from the prohibition at issue, the Italian Government submits that excessive competition between lawyers might lead to price competition which would result in a deterioration in the quality of the services provided to the detriment of consumers, in particular as individuals in need of quality advice in court proceedings.

63 According to the Commission, no causal link has been established between the setting of minimum levels of fees and a high qualitative standard of professional services provided by lawyers. In actual fact, quasi-legislative measures such as, inter alia, rules on access to the legal profession, disciplinary rules serving to ensure compliance with professional ethics and rules on civil liability have, by maintaining a high qualitative standard for the services provided by such professionals which those measures guarantee, a direct relationship of cause and effect with the protection of lawyers' clients and the proper working of the administration of justice.

64 In that respect, it must be pointed out that, first, the protection of consumers, in particular recipients of the legal services provided by persons concerned in the administration of justice and, secondly, the safeguarding of the proper administration of justice, are objectives to be included among those which may be regarded as overriding requirements relating to the public interest capable of justifying a restriction on freedom to provide services . . ., on condition, first, that the national measure at issue in the main proceedings is suitable for securing the attainment of the objective pursued and, secondly, it does not go beyond what is necessary in order to attain that objective.

65 It is a matter for the national court to decide whether, in the main proceedings, the restriction on freedom to provide services introduced by that national legislation fulfils those conditions. For that purpose, it is for that court to take account of the factors set out in the following paragraphs.

66 Thus, it must be determined, in particular, whether there is a correlation between the level of fees and the quality of the services provided by lawyers and whether, in particular, the setting of such minimum fees constitutes an appropriate measure for attaining the

objectives pursued, namely the protection of consumers and the proper administration of justice.

67 Although it is true that a scale imposing minimum fees cannot prevent members of the profession from offering services of mediocre quality, it is conceivable that such a scale does serve to prevent lawyers, in a context such as that of the Italian market which, as indicated in the decision making the reference, is characterised by an extremely large number of lawyers who are enrolled and practising, from being encouraged to compete against each other by possibly offering services at a discount, with the risk of deterioration in the quality of the services provided.

68 Account must also be taken of the specific features both of the market in question, as noted in the preceding paragraph, and the services in question and, in particular, of the fact that, in the field of lawyers' services, there is usually an asymmetry of information between "client-consumers" and lawyers. Lawyers display a high level of technical knowledge which consumers may not have and the latter therefore find it difficult to judge the quality of the services provided to them.

69 However, the national court will have to determine whether professional rules in respect of lawyers, in particular rules relating to organisation, qualifications, professional ethics, supervision and liability, suffice in themselves to attain the objectives of the protection of consumers and the proper administration of justice.

* * *

Notes and Questions

1. Doesn't the Italian law facilitate an anticompetitive agreement among lawyers on minimum fees? What is the best argument that state measures setting minimum lawyer fees harm free movement *and* consumers and should be caught at least presumptively by Articles 4 TEU/101 TFEU?

Note the Commission's argument that enforced price floors do not correlate with higher quality services. Note also that, in most jurisdictions, competitors have a right to combine to procure government action (the right to lobby)—a point relevant to Private Responsibility (the question of liability of the lawyers) below.

The main question of this section is the responsibility of the state not to solicit a minimum fee schedule from the lawyers and not to adopt such a schedule.

2. How will the national court determine whether the law "actually serves the objectives of the protection of consumers and the

proper administration of justice" and whether the restrictions are "disproportionate in light of those objectives?" Would a bright line (e.g., states may not adopt minimum fee schedules) have been superior? Did the Court miss two good opportunities for declaring the lawyers' fee schedules anticompetitive and inconsistent with the Treaties: Articles 4/101, and Article 56? In the aftermath of the case, Italy concluded that minimum lawyer fees are not in the public interest, and it abolished them.

3. The US Constitution protects free speech. Under First Amendment protections as incorporated in the Fourteenth Amendment, states of the United States may not prevent lawyers' truthful price-advertising of routine legal services. Bates v. State Bar of Arizona, 433 U.S. 350 (1977). But states may regulate lawyers and other professionals in the public interest. Id. For example, states may limit the number of lawyers in their state by requiring that they pass state bar examinations. See Hoover v. Ronwin, 466 U.S. 558 (1984).

In general, states of the United States *may* restrain competition unless they impose an undue burden on interstate commerce. Parker v. Brown, 317 U.S. 341 (1943). US law does not have an Article 4 TFEU or Article 106. The question in the United States centers almost entirely on whether private actors can hide behind an order or policy of the state; that is, whether they have a state action defense.

Can a state of the United States, through its courts, order lawyers to adhere to a minimum fee schedule as long as "the state" sets or supervises the fee level?

2. Private Responsibility and the State Action Defense

Private actors may disown responsibility on grounds that the anticompetitive act was not theirs; it was the act of the state.

Students of US law will know the progeny of *Parker v. Brown*, delineating when private actors who engage in anticompetitive acts can successfully attribute their acts to the state and accordingly be sheltered by the state action defense. In short, the state must have a clearly articulated and affirmatively expressed policy to replace competition, the anticompetitive effect must have been the foreseeable (i.e., inherent, logical or ordinary) result of what the state authorized and the private anticompetitive conduct must be actively supervised by the state. California Retail Liquor Dealers Association v. Midcal Aluminum, Inc., 445 U.S. 97 (1980). For a contemporary application, see FTC v. Phoebe Putney Health System, Inc., 568 U.S. 216 (2013). The European Union has a substantial body of law corresponding to the US state action defense.

COMMISSION AND FRANCE v. LADBROKE RACING LTD.

Cases C–359/95 P, C–379/95 P, ECLI:EU:C:1997:531
(Court of Justice of the European Union 1997)

[French law created Pari Mutuel Urbain (PMU) as a joint service of the authorized racing companies to manage their rights in off-track betting, and it granted PMU exclusive rights to run off-track betting on horse races held in France and horse race betting organized in France. French law prohibited anyone other than PMU to place or accept bets on horse races.

Ladbroke Racing Ltd., an operator of off-track betting, filed with the Commission a complaint against France under Article 106, and a complaint against the ten main racing companies in France and PMU under Articles 101 and 102.

Before taking a position on the Article 106 claim, which included allegations of illegal state aid, the Commission rejected the allegations of violation of Articles 101 and 102 on grounds that those articles did not apply. The General Court reversed. The Court of Justice upheld the Commission.]

33 Articles [101] and [102] of the Treaty apply only to anti-competitive conduct engaged in by undertakings on their own initiative. If anti-competitive conduct is required of undertakings by national legislation or if the latter creates a legal framework which itself eliminates any possibility of competitive activity on their part, Articles [101] and [102] do not apply. In such a situation, the restriction of competition is not attributable, as those provisions implicitly require, to the autonomous conduct of the undertakings.

34 Articles [101] and [102] may apply, however, if it is found that the national legislation does not preclude undertakings from engaging in autonomous conduct which prevents, restricts or distorts competition. * * *

CONSORZIO INDUSTRIE FIAMMIFERI (*ITALIAN MATCHES*)

(responsibility of producers; see supra for responsibility of the state)
Case C–198/01, ECLI:EU:C:2003:430 (Court of Justice of the European Union 2003)

[*Consorzio Industrie Fiammiferi* (*Italian matches*) (see facts supra) concerned a state-sponsored match cartel. Italian law required the Italian match producers to join a consortium and to set sellers' quotas. A minister set the prices, the match producers set the quotas, and government officials had the duty to oversee the quotas. The Italian Antitrust Authority brought proceedings. It observed that the producers had the autonomy to set the quotas in the most anticompetitive way, and they did so by substantially keeping the Germans and the Swedes out of the market. The Authority held, and the Court confirmed, that the Italian match producers violated the competition law to the extent that they took autonomous action, and (as we saw above) that the Italian law offended the Treaty and had to be disapplied. The consortium contested the decision in the Italian Administrative Tribunal, and the Tribunal referred questions to the Court of Justice.]

42 [The CIF (the consortium) argues] . . . that is inconceivable that the undertakings should be obliged not to apply the Italian legislation when faced with mandatory national rules. * * *

The first question * * *

52 As regards . . . the penalties which may be imposed on the undertakings concerned, it is appropriate to draw a two-fold distinction by reference to whether or not the national legislation precludes undertakings from engaging in autonomous conduct which might prevent, restrict or distort competition and, if it does, by reference to whether the facts at issue pre-dated or post-dated the national competition authority's decision to disapply the relevant national legislation.

53 First, if a national law precludes undertakings from engaging in autonomous conduct which prevents, restricts or distorts competition, it must be found that, if the general Community-law principle of legal certainty is not to be violated, the duty of national competition authorities to disapply such an anti-competitive law cannot expose the undertakings concerned to any penalties, either criminal or administrative, in respect of past conduct where the conduct was required by the law concerned.

54 The decision to disapply the law concerned does not alter the fact that the law set the framework for the undertakings' past conduct. The law thus continues to constitute, for the period prior to the decision to disapply it, a justification which shields the undertakings concerned from all the consequences of an infringement of Articles [101 and 102 TFEU] and does so vis-à-vis both public authorities and other economic operators.

55 As regards penalising the future conduct of undertakings which, prior to that time, were required by a national law to engage in anti-competitive conduct, it should be pointed out that, once the national competition authority's decision finding an infringement of Article [101 TFEU] and disapplying such an anti-competitive national law becomes definitive in their regard, the decision becomes binding on

the undertakings concerned. From that time onwards the undertakings can no longer claim that they are obliged by that law to act in breach of the Community competition rules. Their future conduct is therefore liable to be penalised.

56 Second, if a national law merely encourages, or makes it easier for undertakings to engage in autonomous anti-competitive conduct, those undertakings remain subject to Articles [101 and 102 TFEU] and may incur penalties, including in respect of conduct prior to the decision to disapply that national law.

57 It must none the less be made clear that, although such a situation cannot lead to acceptance of practices which are likely further to exacerbate the adverse effects on competition, it nevertheless means that when the level of the penalty is set the conduct of the undertakings concerned may be assessed in the light of the national legal framework, which is a mitigating factor.

58 In light of the foregoing considerations, the answer to be given to the first question referred for a preliminary ruling is that, where undertakings engage in conduct contrary to Article [101(1) TFEU] and where that conduct is required or facilitated by national legislation which legitimises or reinforces the effects of the conduct, specifically with regard to price-fixing or market-sharing arrangements, a national competition authority, one of whose responsibilities is to ensure that Article [101 TFEU] is observed:

—has a duty to disapply the national legislation;

—may not impose penalties in respect of past conduct on the undertakings concerned when the conduct was required by the national legislation;

—may impose penalties on the undertakings concerned in respect of conduct subsequent to the decision to disapply the national legislation, once the decision has become definitive in their regard;

—may impose penalties on the undertakings concerned in respect of past conduct where the conduct was merely facilitated or encouraged by the national legislation, whilst taking due account of the specific features of the legislative framework in which the undertakings acted.

The second question

59 By its second question, the referring court wishes to know whether national legislation, under which competence to fix the retail selling prices of a product is delegated to a ministry and power to allocate production between undertakings is entrusted to a consortium to

which the relevant producers are obliged to belong, may be regarded, for the purposes of Article [101(1) TFEU], as preventing those undertakings from engaging in autonomous conduct which hinders, restricts or distorts competition.

60 First, it should be noted that, in the Authority's submission, the CIF was a consortium of which membership was compulsory only until 1994. Decree-Law No 331/1993 made membership optional for the undertakings.

61 In those circumstances, it is for the referring court to decide whether its second question relates solely to the period prior to entry into force of Decree-Law No 331/1993 or whether it also relates to the subsequent period. * * *

63 The CIF submits that, by requiring it to allocate quotas between the member undertakings—regardless of the rules and criteria by reference to which the quotas are set—the Italian legislature eliminated *ab initio* any opportunity which those undertakings might have had to engage in competition in order to win larger market shares.

64 It explains that Article 4 of the 1992 agreement requires match production to be allocated between member undertakings by a committee, the quota allocation committee, composed of representatives from the industry and presided over by an official from the State Monopolies Board, appointed by the Finance Minister.

65 Therefore, quite apart from the quota actually awarded to each undertaking, the quota-allocation system imposed by the legislature eliminates in principle competition between the member undertakings, which must in any event comply with the production quota allocated. Consequently, any competitive effort intended to increase production is futile.

66 In order to answer the second question, it is appropriate to consider first whether national legislation of the kind at issue in the main proceedings precludes undertakings from engaging in autonomous conduct which remains capable of preventing, restricting or distorting competition and, if it does, to go on to ascertain whether any additional restrictions for which the undertakings are blamed are actually attributable to the Member State concerned.

67 First, it should be observed that the possibility of excluding particular anti-competitive conduct from the scope of Article [101(1) TFEU] on the ground that it has been required of the undertakings in question by existing national legislation or that the legislation has precluded all scope for any competitive conduct on their part has been only partially accepted by the Court of Justice.

68 It is appropriate to observe, second, that price competition does not constitute the only effective form of competition or that to which absolute priority must in all circumstances be given.

69 Consequently, pre-determination of the sales price of matches by the Italian State does not, on its own, rule out all scope for competitive conduct. Even if limited, competition may operate through other factors.

70 Third, although the Italian legislation at issue in the main proceedings confers on the CIF, a consortium membership of which is compulsory for manufacturers, power to allocate production between the member undertakings, it does not set out either the rules or the criteria by reference to which allocation is to be carried out. In addition, . . . it seems that the CIF's commercial monopoly was abolished as early as 1983 when the prohibition on non-members of the consortium manufacturing and selling matches was lifted.

71 In those circumstances, the remaining competition between the member undertakings is liable to distortion going beyond that already brought about by the legal obligation itself.

72 In that regard, the investigation carried out by the Authority revealed a system of ongoing and *ad hoc* transfers of production quotas and agreements on exchanges of quotas between the undertakings, that is to say agreements which were not provided for by the law.

73 In addition, the Commission referred to a fixed quota of about 15% set aside for imports. In its submission, that quota was not set by national law and thus the CIF enjoyed autonomous decision-making power in that regard.

74 The Commission also submits that the agreement concluded between the CIF and Swedish Match, which, as early as 1994, enabled Swedish Match to supply significant quantities of matches for the CIF to sell in Italy in return for Swedish Match's undertaking not to enter the Italian market directly, bears witness to the CIF's freedom of action as regards business decisions.

75 It is for the referring court to assess whether there are any grounds for such assertions.

76 Fourth and finally, the documents before the Court do not show that decisions of the CIF such as those mentioned in paragraphs 70 to 74 of this judgment fall outside the scope of Article [101(1) TFEU] as a result of a measure taken by a public authority.

77 On the one hand, four of the five members of the quota-allocation committee are representatives of the manufacturers, whom nothing

in the relevant national legislation prevents from acting exclusively in their own interests. The committee, which takes decision by simple majority, may adopt resolutions even if its chairman, the only person with public-interest duties, votes against them, and the committee can therefore act in accordance with the requirements of the member undertakings.

78 Furthermore, the public authorities do not have an effective means of controlling decisions taken by the quota-allocation committee.

79 On the other hand, the Authority's investigation showed that the task of allocating production between the member undertakings is actually carried out not by the quota-allocation committee but by the quota-compliance committee, which is composed solely of CIF members on the basis of agreements drawn up by the member undertakings.

80 The answer to be given to the second question referred for a preliminary ruling must therefore be that it is for the referring court to assess whether national legislation such as that at issue in the main proceedings, under which competence to fix the retail selling prices of a product is delegated to a ministry and power to allocate production between undertakings is entrusted to a consortium to which the relevant producers are obliged to belong, may be regarded, for the purposes of Article [101(1) TFEU], as precluding those undertakings from engaging in autonomous conduct which remains capable of preventing, restricting or distorting competition.

Notes and Questions

1. Since prices were set by the government official, what competition was left to harm?

2. A major precedent preceded Case C–35/96, *Italian matches*: Commission v. Italy (*CNSD*), EU:C:1998:303. In this case regarding customs agents, Italy had delegated to a competitors' association the legal responsibility to set the tariffs, and it required the customs agents to adhere to the tariffs their association had set. The Court of Justice held that, by this delegation and measure, Italy breached its obligations under Articles 4 TEU/101 TFEU. Italy had required the conclusion of an agreement contrary to Article 101, declined to influence its terms, and assisted in ensuring compliance. para. 55. By giving the tariffs an official character, it deterred customers from contesting the custom agents' prices. Moreover, the competitors' association violated Article 101. It set the maximum and minimum prices.

3. Comment on the scope, in Europe, for public and for private responsibility for anticompetitive acts in shadow of state policy. Compare and contrast *Parker v. Brown* and its progeny. Does Europe

appropriately limit state anticompetitive action, or does it interfere too much with the sovereignty of the Member States?

4. For a comparison of the *Italian matches* case with US law, see Eleanor Fox, *State Action in Comparative Context: What if* Parker v. Brown *were Italian*, Chap. 19 in Fordham Corp. L. Inst., INTERNATIONAL ANTITRUST LAW & POLICY (B. Hawk ed. 2004).

F. STATE AID: EU

1. Introduction

States are tempted to give money and other benefits to support local firms and to attract non-local firms. Frequently states are asked to favor one competitor, sector or region over another, often to save a failing business and to save jobs. At mid-twentieth century before adoption of the EC Treaty of Rome, extensive and undisciplined state support of industry was the norm in Europe. If trade barriers were removed but state aids flourished, Europe would never be one common market.

In order to contain state aid and provide transparency for permissible aid, the European Treaty includes (now) TFEU Articles 107–109. The United States, however, does not have state aid control.

In Europe, state aid is "any aid granted by a Member State or through state resources in any form whatsoever. . . ." Direct subsidy is the most common form of aid, but state aid also includes exemptions from fiscal or social charges, credit guarantees, credit at low interest, credit or equity investments that would not be available in the market, payment by the state of a higher price to domestic suppliers, sale by the state below the market price to domestic buyers, assumption by the state of part of an undertaking's risk, tax concessions (e.g., to encourage the takeover of an ailing firm), and virtually any other benefit conferred by the state on terms that would not be acceptable to a private investor.

Article 107(1) declares that any state aid that "distorts or threatens to distort competition by favouring certain undertakings or the production of certain goods shall, insofar as it affects trade between Member States, be incompatible with the common market." Paragraphs (2) and (3) are derogations from this general prohibition.

Paragraph (2) lists forms of aid that "shall be compatible" with the common market. Aid that shall be compatible under paragraph (2) is:

(a) aid of a social character granted to individual consumers without discrimination as to origin of products,

(b) damage relief in natural disasters or exceptional occurrences, and

(c) aid to the economy of certain areas of the Federal Republic of Germany affected by the division of Germany insofar as it is required to compensate for economic disadvantages caused by that division.

Paragraph (3) specifies aid that the Commission *may* declare compatible with the common market. Frequently invoked by Member States, this section empowers the Commission to declare compatible aid in the following five categories:

(a) "aid to promote the economic development of areas where the standard of living is abnormally low or where there is serious underemployment";

(b) "aid to promote the execution of an important project of common European interest or to remedy a serious disturbance in the economy of a Member State";

(c) "aid to facilitate the development of certain economic activities or of certain economic areas, where such aid does not adversely affect trading conditions to an extent contrary to the common interest";

(d) "aid to promote cultural and heritage conservation where such aid does not affect trading conditions and competition in the Community to an extent that is contrary to the common interest"; and

(e) other categories added by decision of the Council.

Article 108 sets forth a notification, waiting and adjudication procedure for state aids. Member States must notify to the Commission all proposed measures of state aid that may affect Member State commerce. The proposed measures must not be put into effect until clearance. The Commission may authorize the aid without conditions, authorize the aid after agreed modifications, or open formal proceedings. The Commission must give notice to concerned parties to submit their comments. See Regulation 2015/1589, laying down detailed rules for the application of Article 108 TFEU. [2015] O.J. L 248/9.

If the Commission finds that the proposed aid is not compatible with the common market or that aid is being misused, it must direct the state to abolish or alter the aid within a specified time period. If the Member State fails to comply, the Commission or an interested Member State may refer the matter to the Court of Justice. If a Member State grants illegal aid, it must recover it from the recipient.

To eliminate red tape and to concentrate on the cases that matter most, the Commission has enacted block exemption regulations that eliminate the need for notification if certain conditions are met. The General Block Exemption Regulation 651/2014 covers a wide array of state aid targets, including aid for environmental protection, risk capital, R&D and innovation, newly created small enterprises, and broadband rollout. The regulation on de minimis aid, 2023/2831, also exempts Member States from the notification requirement for small amounts of aid. Various horizontal and sector-specific rules and guidelines clarify the Commission's policy to approve different forms of aid. There is considerable case law on what is a state aid. An investment at market rates is not state aid. The Treaty does not prevent a state from participating in the economy as long as it acts as a "market economy operator." The state can therefore be a shareholder without breaching Article 107 TFEU if the transaction is at market rate.

In its progressive privatization of Electricité de France (EDF), the former electricity monopoly, France restructured EDF's accounts. It converted a debt it was owed by EDF into equity. The transaction had fiscal consequences; EDF avoided paying a tax by incorporating the debt into capital. France argued that this was neutral from a state aid perspective; it could have requested EDF to pay the tax and later make a capital injection to the amount of the tax. In other words, France argued, it acted as a market economy operator and provided no advantage to EDF.

The Commission disagreed. It found that it was not possible to apply the market economy operator test to a fiscal operation, since taxation is the exclusive province of the state and it is not possible to compare its fiscal policy with that of a hypothetical private investor.

The Court of Justice annulled the Commission decision. EDF v. Commission, Case C–124/10 P, EU:C:2012:318. It recalled that Article 107(1) TFEU covers state aid "in any form whatsoever." The form of the measure does not matter, only its effects do. Therefore, the Commission was required to take a global view of the measures and assess their overall effects. A Member State that wishes to rely on the market economy operator principle needs to demonstrate, using evidence prepared before or at the moment of its investment decision, that it was rational for it do so as an investor. Policy considerations such as social or environmental objectives cannot be taken into account (although they might be relevant in assessment of the compatibility of the aid).

Does a privatized transport receive state aid when the state continues to cover the costs of public service obligations? Altmark Trans sought to organize public transport in a new East German länder. In Altmark Trans GmbH, Regierungspräsidium Magdeburg, Case C–280/00, EU:C:2003:415, the Court of Justice held that public subsidies for transportation services are not state aids, and therefore do not require notification and justification, where they constitute compensation for the discharge of public service obligations. Such subsidies fall outside of Article 107 if the following conditions are satisfied: 1) the recipient must be required to discharge clearly defined public service obligations, 2) the formula for calculating the compensation must be established beforehand in an objective and transparent matter, 3) the compensation must not exceed what is necessary to discharge the public service, and 4) either the undertaking must be chosen in a public procurement procedure or the level of compensation needed to fulfill the public service obligation must have been determined on the basis of the costs of a typical, well-run undertaking.

The Commission has issued detailed rules based on the *Altmark* principles to enable states to assess their practices and increase legal certainty. A package regarding services of general economic interest (SGEI) includes Commission communications, a decision and a regulation setting forth de minimis thresholds for the compensation of public services. It is available at http://ec.europa.eu/competition/state_aid/legislation/sgei.html.

Earlier, Germany decided to promote windmill energy. German law obliged all regional public electricity suppliers to buy windmill power as a portion of their energy and to pay the wind-generated electricity at a price higher than the price of other energy; and it obliged upstream electricity suppliers to pay to the regional suppliers a part of the extra costs. PreussenElektra, an upstream supplier, tried to avoid paying part of the extra costs of windmill energy on grounds that its supplementary payment to the regional supplier (Schleswag, which happened to be Preussen's own subsidiary) would constitute an illegal subsidy of wind energy. The Court rejected the argument. It ruled that Preussen Elektra's supplementary payment, although commanded by the state, was merely a private payment and did not take the mantle of German aid. PreussenElektra, C–379/98, EU:C:2001:160.

Why wasn't the supplementary payment in fact a subsidy? Did this interpretation bless an end run around Article 107? Could

Preussen and Schleswag sue Germany for maintaining a state measure that restrained trade by putting them at a competitive disadvantage vis-à-vis Electricité de France and others in violation of Article 34 or 35 of the Treaty?

Although the European Union has developed the most advanced State aid control regime, it is not the sole regional organization to have adopted such a system. For example, Article 88 (c) of the treaty on the West African Economic and Monetary Union (WAEMU) prohibits "public aid to distort competition by favouring certain undertakings or the production of certain goods" since its conclusion in 1994.

2. State Aid Policy

State aid control is a major facet of European Community policy. It accounts for half of the enforcement activity of the Competition Directorate. Alexander Schaub, when Director General for Competition, described the system as follows:

General developments in State aid control

> . . . [T]he maintenance of a system of free and undistorted competition is one of the cornerstones of the European Union. It is undisputed that competition may be distorted by advantages given by public authorities to certain companies which compete with other companies in the Union. All efforts under the anti-trust rules to ensure that companies do not distort competition and trade within the Union would be to no avail if Member States were allowed to seek to outbid each other in offering subsidies to save firms in economic difficulties or to attract investment.
>
> Today, this applies more than ever. There are three major reasons for the increasing importance of State aid control:
>
> —First, as the Internal Market becomes a reality, the elimination of a vast number of trade barriers between Member States also progresses. This means that the more classical forms of distortion of competition by Member States have disappeared. If not properly controlled, state aid may be used to replace the barriers to trade that have already been dismantled.
>
> —Second, the single market in Europe and increased world-wide competition have led to widespread liberalisation of sectors where competition was or is still restricted or even excluded, such as telecommunications, postal services and energy. The consequence of this trend is obvious:

introducing competition necessarily means enlarging the scope of State aid control to these sectors.

—There is a third reason for the increasing importance of State aid control: in periods of serious economic difficulties with politically unsustainable levels of unemployment, Governments—not only in the EU, but also in other regions of the world—are tempted to use aid as an instrument to combat unemployment, often merely shifting the problem to another factory, another sector, another area, another country.

The characteristics of State aid control in the EU

One might, of course, at least in theory, advocate the simple ban of State aid to achieve free and undistorted competition throughout the European Union. However, experience has shown that in some cases there are valid reasons to grant aid.

Properly controlled, the granting of aid may contribute to the development of the Community as a whole, whilst potentially harmful or protectionist effects can be eliminated.

But who would be able to carry out this task in a neutral and well-balanced way? The Treaty of Rome solved this question by entrusting the Commission with the task of ensuring a level playing field of competition throughout Europe.

This is indeed the very centre-piece of State aid control in the European Union: the Treaty of Rome not only obliges the Member States to inform the Commission of subsidies granted to enterprises. The obligation goes an important step further and makes the award of aid subject to prior approval by the Commission.

The obligation of notification prior to implementation and, more than that, the fact that the implementation of a plan to grant or alter aid is subject to approval by an independent authority, is one of three key elements which make the control of State aid in the European Union unique both in international and national law. Only the Commission may find aid compatible by applying one of the exemption clauses provided for in the Treaty. Implementing new aid without having obtained the Commission's approval is illegal.

> The second element characterizing the State aid control system established by the European Union follows from the first: there are remedies against State aid decisions. Also private operators, in particular aid recipients and competitors, may seek judicial review before the European Courts.
>
> Third, the Commission is not only entrusted with the day-to-day application of the State aid rules, but is also empowered to develop the Community's State aid control policy. Within the wide margin of discretion entrusted to it, the Commission has gradually developed policy through cases and through a variety of policy frameworks, communications and notices. Furthermore, we have established a strict and consistent policy on recovery of incompatible aid in cases where a Member State has not fulfilled its obligation to await the Commission's decision before awarding aid.
>
> To sum up: what we have achieved during the past years is an increased notification discipline and a very high public awareness of the distortive effects of aid. In many sectors, industry is the Commission's best ally in combatting unlawfully granted aid—through complaints to the Commission and through an increasing number of cases brought to national Courts. I take this as an encouraging sign that industry widely supports a strict state aid discipline. . . .

Alexander Schaub, remarks to CIRFS General Assembly, European Competition Policy—in particular developments in policy on State aid control, Brussels, May 14, 1997.

In 2005, under Competition Commissioner Neelie Kroes, the Commission adopted a State Aid Action Plan. The plan put state aid on a more focused, economic basis. It was intended to improve competitiveness of European industry, create sustainable jobs, ensure social and regional cohesion, and improve public services—all of which were major objectives of the European Union's "Lisbon Strategy" of 2005.

* * *

The financial crisis hit Europe and most of the world in 2008. The 2008 Report on Competition Policy devoted the state aid control section to the crisis and the role of state aid policy in recovery.

REPORT ON COMPETITION POLICY (2008)

European Commission

* * *

1.4. State Aid Control

1.4.1. Shaping the rules and policy

32 At the beginning of 2008 the Commission's focus in the State aid field was to continue with the implementation of the State Aid Action Plan (SAAP). However, the onset of the financial and economic crisis shifted that focus and the Commission rapidly issued three Communications on the role of State aid policy in the context of the crises and the recovery process.

33 In the context of the financial crisis, the Commission first gave initial guidance on the application of State aid rules to measures taken in relation to financial institutions, which exceptionally were based on Article [107](3)(b) of the [TFEU] which allows for aid to remedy a serious disturbance in the economy of a Member State. Subsequently, the Commission supplemented and refined its guidance with a new Communication on how Member States can recapitalise banks in the current financial crisis to ensure adequate levels of lending to the rest of the economy and stabilise financial markets, whilst avoiding excessive distortions of competition. In addition, the Commission adopted a new temporary framework providing Member States with additional possibilities to tackle the effects of the credit squeeze on the real economy. All measures are time-limited until the end of 2010, although the Commission, based on Member States' reports, will evaluate whether the measures should be maintained beyond 2010, depending on whether the crisis continues.

34 As regards the implementation of the SAAP, the Commission adopted, as announced, a General Block Exemption Regulation (GBER) giving automatic approval for a range of aid measures and so allowing Member States to grant such aid without first notifying the Commission, provided that they fulfil all the requirements laid down in the Regulation. In the context of the Climate Change Package, the Commission adopted new guidelines on State aid for environmental protection which introduce a standard assessment for minor cases and a detailed assessment for cases that may involve significant distortions of competition. The Commission also prolonged the Framework on State aid rules for shipbuilding for a further three years, until 31 December 2011. A new Notice on State aid in the form of guarantees sets out clear and transparent methodologies to calculate the aid element in a guarantee and

provides simplified rules for SMEs, including predefined safe-harbour premiums and single premium rates for low-amount guarantees.

[35] In addition, public consultations were launched on new rules relating to public service broadcasting, the possible extension until 2012 of the Cinema Communication (scheduled for adoption in January 2009), the guidance documents on the in-depth assessment of regional aid to large investment projects and on criteria for the compatibility analysis in the field of training, as well as on disadvantaged and disabled workers for State aid cases subject to individual notification.

[36] The Commission also launched in 2008 a number of public consultations on procedural issues, such as a consultation on a draft Best Practice Code (BPC) on the conduct of State aid control proceedings and the draft notice on Simplified procedure (SP) for the treatment of certain types of State aid. The aim of both documents is to ensure greater transparency, predictability and efficiency of State aid procedures in line with the SAAP. The discussion with the Member States and other stakeholders regarding the BPC and SP will take place early 2009. The drafts are currently due to be adopted in the first half of 2009. The Commission also consulted on a draft Commission Notice on the enforcement of State aid law by national courts.

[37] In 2008, the Commission continued its efforts to improve the enforcement and monitoring of State aid decisions. The Commission is seeking to achieve, on the basis of the recovery notice adopted in 2007, a more effective and immediate execution of recovery decisions. Information submitted by the Member States concerned shows that good progress towards recovery was made during that period. This is also reflected in the amounts of aid recovered. Of the EUR 10.3 billion of illegal and incompatible aid to be recovered under decisions adopted since 2000, some EUR 9.3 billion (i.e. 90.7% of the total amount) had actually been recovered by the end of 2008. In addition, a further EUR 2.5 billion in recovery interest had been recovered.

[38] As announced in the SAAP, the Commission continued to take a strict line towards Member States that failed to effectively implement recovery decisions addressed to them. In 2008 the Commission initiated legal action under either Article [108(2) TFEU] or Article [260(2) TFEU] for failure by Member States to comply with recovery obligations. It decided to initiate Article [108(2) TFEU] in five cases involving Italy and Slovakia, as well as decisions to proceed with Article [260(2) TFEU] in eight cases involving Italy and Spain.

39 In the interest of increased transparency and better communication, DG Competition has published on its webpage a Vademecum on State aid rules summarizing the main rules applicable to State aid control.

1.4.2. Applying the rules

40 The update of the State aid Scoreboard in autumn 2008 shows that Member States are increasingly making use of the possibilities offered by the recently revised EU State aid rules to better target their aid. Member States awarded on average 80% of their aid to horizontal objectives in 2007, compared with around 50% in the mid-1990s, with increased spending on Research and Development (R&D) and environmental aid. In the face of the current financial crisis, coordinated action by Member States and the Commission has ensured that support schemes for the financial sector have been implemented promptly in compliance with State aid rules.

41 Over the last 25 years, the overall level of State aid has fallen from over 2% of GDP in the 1980s to around 0.5% in 2007. Whilst highlighting the continuing trend for Member States to focus their aid on horizontal objectives, the Scoreboard nevertheless showed that, following the recent financial crisis, the share of rescue and restructuring aid is likely to increase significantly for some countries in 2008.

42 In 2008, the Commission approved 88 notified schemes on the basis of the 2006 Community Framework for research and development and innovation; 66 of these were purely R&D schemes, nine were innovation-oriented aid schemes and 13 were mixed, pursuing both R&D and innovation objectives.

43 In addition, an important decision was adopted in several individual cases involving the Italian aeronautic sector, following an assessment on the basis of the Community frameworks for State aid for R&D of 1996 and 1986. The decision, adopted on 11 March, covers 17 individual R&D projects in the aeronautic sector supported by the Italian authorities during the 1990s. The decision requires the immediate reimbursement of the loans for most of the individual projects, plus interest on arrears in certain cases. The beneficiaries have reimbursed around EUR 350 million within the time limit of two months laid down by the decision.

44 In the area of risk capital financing for SMEs, the Commission approved 18 risk capital schemes under the Risk Capital Guidelines. Eleven schemes were assessed on the basis of Chapter 4 of the guidelines, since they complied with the safe harbour provisions allowing a light assessment; three schemes were assessed under

Chapter 5, following a detailed assessment. In three cases the Commission considered that the scheme did not involve State aid. One scheme was partly considered as no aid and partly assessed under Chapter 4 of the Guidelines.

45 In the field of industrial restructuring, the Commission adopted a decision requesting Romania to recover EUR 27 million unlawful aid in relation to the privatisation of Automobile Craiova, which had been sold on conditions aiming at ensuring a certain level of production and employment, accepting in exchange a lower sales price. Furthermore, following several years of investigation, the Commission concluded that the attempts of the Polish authorities to restructure the shipyards in Gdynia and Szczecin and to return them to viability had failed. As a result, the Commission required Poland to recover the illegal State aid from the shipyards through a controlled sale of the yards' assets and subsequent liquidation of the companies.

* * *

3. State Aid in Times of Crisis

3.1. Financial crisis

The financial crisis of 2008–09 prompted the establishment of an Economic Crisis Team and the adoption of a temporary framework. See https://competition-policy.ec.europa.eu/state-aid_en. The Commission urged the Member States to contact the Economic Crisis Team regarding all state aid related measures and national recovery plans. The Commission maintains a "scoreboard" of Member State action to fight the financial crisis, and summarizes the states' plans and actions and the Commission's responses in approving or disapproving the proposed aid. See https://competition-policy.ec.europa.eu/state-aid/publications_en under "Scoreboard, reports and studies."

Not surprisingly, the financial crisis of 2008–2009 gave rise to emergency calls for mergers and restructurings. Several Member States announced plans to pour state monies into their firms to keep them afloat. French President Sarkozy announced plans to lend Peugeot Citroen and Renault three billion euros each in exchange for a promise not to shut French plants or lay off French workers. Competition Commissioner Neelie Kroes responded that nationalistic measures violated Community law, and, working with the Directorate General for Competition, she offered community-wide plans to speed up the vetting of emergency mergers and state-aid approvals. Sarkozy withdrew the conditionality of his plan.

In several speeches, Commissioner Neelie Kroes described problems and solutions, and called for the Member States to resist a descent into nationalism that could threaten the single market. Her successors, Joaquin Almunia and Margrethe Vestager, have consistently followed suit.

3.2. Public health crisis

When the Coronavirus hit Europe in 2020, the European Commission adapted its State aid rulebook. In March 2020 it adopted a temporary framework to help Member States support their economies, which was subsequently updated several times. On the basis of this "temporary framework", the Commission approved €3.2 trillion in State aid, including a €7 billion package from the French government to Air France, "to provide urgently needed liquidity for companies, save jobs, enable research and development and ensure the supply of products to fight the coronavirus outbreak." The then Executive Vice-President and Competition Commissioner Margrethe Vestager said:

"We continue to work closely with Member States to ensure that European businesses have access to urgently needed liquidity. Our rules now also enable such support through subordinated debt. As the crisis evolves, many businesses will also need capital to stay afloat. If Member States decide to step in, we will apply today's rules to ensure that taxpayers are sufficiently remunerated and their support comes with strings attached, including a ban on dividends, bonus payments as well as further measures to limit distortions of competition. And for public transparency, large companies also have to report on the use of aid received and compliance with their responsibilities linked to the green and digital transitions. Because we have to uphold European values and the need for a level playing field to be able to bounce back strongly from this crisis.

That's also why much more is needed than State aid control. We need a European recovery plan that is green and digital and to the benefit of all European consumers. That's in the interest of all of Europe—to make sure that this global symmetric crisis does not transform into an asymmetric shock to the detriment of Member States with less possibility to help their industry and the EU's competitiveness as a whole."

* * *

The Temporary Framework to support the economy during the coronavirus outbreak expired in June 2022. The same year, another temporary crisis framework was adopted to enable EU Member

States to support the economy in the context of Russia's invasion of Ukraine.

3.3. Other crisis, including environment

In March 2023, the European Commission adopted a broader instrument called the "Temporary Crisis and Transition Framework" to enable Member States to foster support measures in sectors (such as environment, renewable energy and sustainable agriculture) that are key for the transition to a "net-zero" economy (see https://competition-policy.ec.europa.eu/state-aid/temporary-crisis-and-transition-framework_en).

While also amending and prolonging the measures adopted after Russia's invasion of Ukraine, this new crisis framework aims primarily to accelerate investments in key sectors for the transition towards a net-zero economy, such as batteries, solar panels, wind turbines, heat-pumps, electrolysers and carbon capture usage and storage, as well as the production and recycling of related critical raw materials. Further amendments to this framework are expected in the second semester of 2025.

4. State Aid and the Tax Cases

Since 2013, the European Commission has been investigating allegations of favorable tax treatment given to certain companies through tax rulings that give "advanced clarification." That overall investigation had led to the opening of formal proceedings against The Netherlands for aid granted to Starbucks, Luxembourg for aid granted to Fiat, McDonald's, Engie and Amazon, Belgium for operating an excess profit exemption scheme, the UK with respect to its tax scheme for multinationals and, most famously, Ireland for aid granted to Apple. The overall concern was that Member States artificially reduce certain companies' tax base and thus their overall tax burden by means of rulings that rely on transfer prices and do not reflect economic reality. The strategy artificially reduces taxable profits.

The Commission characterized its investigation into Member States' tax ruling practices as part of an overall plan for "fair and effective taxation" aimed at tackling tax avoidance (and, conversely, fiscal dumping). It has attracted criticism from the United States, which claims that the Commission is discriminating against American companies, depriving them of deals they have negotiated with host countries to invest in those countries; and that the Commission is challenging the deals illegitimately under the banner of state aid when it is really a matter of individual Member States' tax policy—a function reserved to the states under EU law.

The Court of Justice was petitioned to review many Commission decisions in relation to tax ruling cases. It undertook very refined assessments and sided in some cases with and in other against the Commission. The Apple case attracted most attention, notably as it required Ireland to recover illegal tax benefits from Apple worth up to EUR 13 billion. In September 2024, the Grand Chamber of the Court of Justice eventually upheld the Commission decision, thereby reversing the annulment that had previously been ordered by the EU General Court. In essence, the Court of Justice agreed with the Commission that, by excluding from the relevant tax base the profits generated by the use of intellectual property licenses held by Apple Sales International and Appel Operations Europe, the tax rulings issued by Ireland between 1991 and 2014 conferred unlawful and incompatible State aid to the Apple Group. Commission v. Ireland, C–465/20 P, EU:C:2024:724.

Director General of DG Competition Johannes Laitenberger gave the following explanation at the time about the initiative to crack down on unduly favorable tax treatments.

STATE AID TAX CASES: SINE TIMORE AUT FAVORE

Director General Johannes Laitenberger
Competition Directorate General, European Commission
St. Gallen, 20 May 2016

* * *

. . . EU competition law has a specific feature that does not exist in other jurisdictions. It is the complementarity of antitrust and merger control, on the one hand, and of State aid control, on the other, that makes for a comprehensive system to prevent and control distortions of competition in our Single Market. So I thought that it would be of interest to open a window on this area of the Commission's competition enforcement work.

Rationale of State aid law

It would have been impossible to build a common market in post-war Europe without a confidence-building, equitable, law-based framework for the working of such a market. Setting the rules to integrate the Member States' markets was the task of lawmakers. To make sure that the rules would have their intended effect on the ground through effective enforcement, they empowered the Commission as a supranational authority. And this included enforcing the principle of competitive neutrality.

For almost 60 years now, the Commission has protected what is today the Single Market against distortive practices of private businesses, state-owned enterprises and governments alike. The EU's competition rules are ultimately based on a double rationale:

- As an agreed set of rules, they build economic peace between nations and peoples.
- As rules against anti-competitive practices, they make markets work better and enhance consumer welfare.

In all likelihood, the EU's Single Market will always be work in progress. The financial and economic crisis has clearly shown that. But without its rules, it is difficult to imagine how the EU and its Member States would have been able to tackle this and other critical developments and build and restore prosperity together.

* * *

State aid modernisation

Over the last few years, the Commission has introduced a comprehensive programme to modernise the implementation of State aid rules. Building on a more economic approach, and in line with better regulation principles, it makes it easier for EU countries to grant aid that is unproblematic from a competition point of view.

The new rules allow Member States to further economic development and address equity issues while the Commission can scrutinise more rigorously measures with a significant potential to distort the Single Market. The new rules do so by extending the block exemption possibilities in such a way that nowadays some 90% of all aid measures need no longer be notified to the Commission. There's also a comprehensively new set of compatibility rules for notified aid anchored on the same economic principles.

Just yesterday, the Commission adopted a Notice on the Notion of State aid—a key policy document that completes the State aid modernisation process. This makes today a good day to take a look at one of the workstreams in State aid control that is often in the news these days—our State aid cases on aggressive corporate tax planning practices.

In the field of taxation, the Notice consolidates the Commission's practice and the Court's jurisprudence. As such, it is meant to give guidance on broad principles of State aid control in this field and thus can be useful to national policy makers. Against this background, let me say a few words about our approach to aggressive corporate tax planning practices that may result in selective advantages for some businesses over others.

State aid control and aggressive tax planning

A special Task Force was set up within DG Competition to look into the issue as early as 2013. This was motivated by the gradual emergence of market information suggesting that tax rulings were being exploited to grant selective advantages to certain multinational businesses. I would like to situate our work on aggressive corporate tax planning in a wider context.

Since the financial and economic crisis of 2007–2008, there has been sustained and multifaceted work on the root causes that have led to the instability and imbalances for which we're still paying the price. This is a vast agenda pursued at international, regional and national level.

Tackling tax evasion and tax avoidance is a key point in that agenda. A lot of the work done under this point is on the regulatory side. Think of the OECD's Base Erosion and Profit Shifting project. The organisation has worked on the project with G20 countries on an equal footing and over 80 more countries have been involved.

Within the EU, the Commission has put forward an Action Plan to reform corporate taxation, increase transparency and close loopholes. At the start of the year, the Anti-Tax Avoidance Package was adopted. It included—among other things—anti-abuse measures and better exchanges of information among national tax authorities. Just last month, new rules were proposed requiring multinational groups to report on profits made and taxes paid on a country by-country basis.

The underlying principle of these reforms is to have companies pay tax where they make their profits. Our work in State aid control does not substitute or replace this agenda by other means. But the Commission's special responsibility in the field of State aid control arises in this context as naturally as in others. Let me turn to how DG Competition approaches this task.

Fiscal aid is State aid

Since our aggressive corporate tax planning cases were formally opened, some commentators were surprised that the Commission would look into tax arrangements on the basis of State aid rules. I must say that they seem to have a rather short memory. Before this expert audience, the point that State aid can come in many forms—including fiscal aid—should nevertheless be obvious.

When government measures distort competition in the Single Market, it doesn't matter whether they come as direct subsidies or tax relief to certain economic operators. The European Court of

Justice confirmed this principle in 1974 with its seminal judgment in Case 173/73 Italy v Commission. It's the effect that counts—and the effect is not negligible. More than one third of non-crisis State aid is granted in the form of fiscal advantages.

In plain language, State aid control of tax practices and other fiscal arrangements is old hat for the Commission. I will give you a few examples.

As far back as 1998, the Commission found that an Irish 10% corporate tax rate for the manufacturing sector was incompatible aid and ordered its phase-out. In the same year, to give guidance to national authorities, it also issued a Communication on the application of State aid rules to direct business taxation.

In 2001, then Competition Commissioner Mario Monti announced the launch of a large scale investigation into business taxation schemes involving twelve Member States. The main competition concern at the time were preferential tax arrangements—the so-called 'coordination centres'—which multinational corporations used to determine their tax bills.

The Commission later closed the most significant cases and found incompatible fiscal aid in Belgium, Germany, Spain, France, the Netherlands, Finland, the UK, Ireland, Greece, Italy and Sweden. The Member States were requested to terminate the measures. The crux of the matter was that these practices were only benefitting a selected number of multinationals and many of them were not in compliance with the arm's length principle.

The idea behind this principle is quite straightforward. The terms of commercial transactions between two companies belonging to the same group should reflect conditions observed in the market for similar transactions between independent companies.

The European Court of Justice later confirmed the Commission's approach. The arm's length principle—the Court said—was the correct yardstick the Commission could use to ensure that multinationals would be taxed in the same way as non-integrated, standalone companies.

Fiscal aid today

Commissioner Monti's initiative came in the wake of efforts to tackle harmful tax competition among EU Member States in the late 1990s. For example, in 1997 the Council of Economy and Finance Ministers adopted a Code of Conduct for direct business taxation.

As I have mentioned, the context is different today. The financial and economic crisis has drawn attention to aggressive corporate tax planning practices, in particular those benefiting multinational corporations operating as groups. Some economic operators seem to have been pushing the limits of aggressive corporate tax planning very far. In doing so, a number of them have taken advantage of so-called tax rulings and other fiscal arrangements that are available in certain EU Member States.

Allegations about these instances were, for instance, the object of public hearings in the US Senate and the UK's House of Commons. The Commission regarded the media reports and the parliamentary debates of a few years back as market information. The Commission listened and decided to look deeper into the matter.

In response to this, the Task Force mentioned earlier was set up under Vice-President Joaquín Almunia. Its task was looking into aggressive corporate tax planning practices, with an emphasis on tax rulings. The Task Force set out to collect factual evidence by studying the tax ruling practices of Member States and analysing nearly 1,000 rulings.

Given that fiscal secrecy had barred scrutiny hitherto; this has allowed the Commission to gain an unprecedented insight into this matter. While certain practices in favour of businesses relying on tax rulings have always been at odds with State aid rules, their scale had never surfaced before. If the advantages granted to selected multinationals are significant, the need to restore the level playing field has become greater.

Member States' corporate taxation law as reference system

Let me address a criticism sometimes addressed to us that our State aid cases call into question existing corporate taxation law of EU Member States.

I believe that the claim is misguided. To establish whether a tax measure raises State aid concerns, we examine whether it gives a selective advantage to one or several economic operators over others. To that end, we compare the tax treatment of the companies that benefit from them to the ordinary tax treatment reserved to companies in comparable circumstances under national law.

So, the truth is that we take ordinary corporate-tax law in each Member State as the very reference against which we assess whether the tax treatment in individual cases departed from national law or practice. Let me make this even clearer using tax rulings as an example.

In general, granting tax rulings is a normal and justified practice in so far as they provide legal certainty to taxpayers. Provided the rulings do not grant selective advantages to specific companies, but clarify individual situations in line with tax rules as applied to everybody else in comparable factual and legal situations, they do not raise issues under EU State aid law.

The Commission is not in the business of second-guessing the work of national tax authorities with regard to every single tax ruling. The Commission has subjected to deeper scrutiny those rulings where taxation did not reflect actual economic reality—in particular regarding transactions between companies that belong to the same group.

Selective advantages and competition distortions

When determining selectivity we are comparing the tax treatment of the company benefitting from a tax ruling or a special tax regime to the ordinary tax treatment of companies under national law.

The profits made by standalone companies are taxed in the jurisdiction where they are recorded according to the rules and rates that apply in that jurisdiction. In contrast, a multinational group can record its profits in different entities and across multiple jurisdictions. What happens when the multinational needs to allocate profits between the companies it controls?

These internal allocations raise no concern when taxes are paid where profits are generated. Things can become problematic when profits are shifted from high-taxation to low-taxation jurisdictions—or even to jurisdictions where companies are allowed to pay almost no taxes. To be more precise, things become problematic when this is done by agreeing inflated prices for the transfer of goods and services between group companies that don't reflect market conditions—and with tax rulings that confirm these agreements.

Many rulings also determine a company's tax basis as a mark-up on performance indicators. Often, taxable profits are calculated as a percentage of operating expenses. In principle, this system could be justified when the value-added of a group company is closely linked to the type of expenses used in the calculation and when the contribution the company makes to the overall operations of the group is not substantial. However, concerns may arise when indicators like these are used in a way that fails to capture the company's actual commercial value and thus artificially reduce the group's taxable profits.

And here the matter goes beyond the mere mis-application of national tax law or discrimination between taxpayers. The matter becomes a distortion of competition. Subsidies—including selective forms of tax relief—have the potential to distort the ability of companies to compete on the merits.

Moreover, economic activity generated on the back of such arrangements may lack a sound economic rationale and be unsustainable. Activity created in this fashion in one EU Member State could come at the expense of another EU Member State which is not in a position to offer tax advantages. Benefits granted to selected operators can harm their rivals.

These distortions eventually translate into economic inefficiencies and, possibly, even into macroeconomic imbalances because activities and capital flows are displaced. Many factors influence companies' investment and expansion decisions, such as infrastructure, labour skills and costs, and proximity to customers. Of course, tax rates can also be a legitimate consideration. However, these decisions should not be driven by the possibility for specific, selected operators to artificially lower their tax bases and effective taxation. And there should be no financial-capacity distortion between economic operators by allowing a few to build up war chests thanks to untaxed profits.

Let me add that standalone companies are not the only ones that are harmed by these practices. Large integrated companies that pay their taxes in different countries following the arm's length principle are also at a disadvantage.

By analysing the situations that give rise to these concerns with a view of restoring level competition conditions, the Commission therefore fulfils the classic State aid mission—that is, identifying and correcting competition distortions that are not justified. If a company has received undue advantages, State aid law specifies in which cases it should return them in order to restore competitive conditions in the markets.

The rules are clear. Here, this means recovering unpaid taxes—up to a period of ten years—and making sure that taxes are paid correctly in the future. Obviously, the rules specify that the company cannot be asked to return the money if it has legitimate expectations—that is, if the Commission has previously expressed a different view or assessment. Also, there is no recovery when the legal certainty principle can be invoked. A typical example is when the Commission takes a decision on a novel case. However—as we will see presently—neither of these conditions applied in the State aid decisions the Commission has taken so far.

Decisions taken so far

So far, formal proceedings were opened on tax arrangements in Luxembourg, the Netherlands, Ireland and Belgium between 2014 and 2015. In the meantime, following the proposals of Competition Commissioner Margrethe Vestager, the Commission has taken three decisions.

The first two came in October last year, when the Commission found that the tax rulings offered to Fiat Finance & Trade in Luxembourg and to Starbucks in the Netherlands were illegal forms of State aid. To level the playing field, each of the two groups was ordered to return an estimated €20–30 million—broadly equivalent to the tax rebates they had unduly received. Let me tell you what we have found in these cases in a nutshell.

With a tax ruling, a tax authority tells a company in advance the amount of tax it will pay given certain conditions. In principle—as I said—there is nothing wrong with tax rulings. They need not pose competition concerns. In fact, they are useful to companies, which can better predict their costs. In contrast, the rulings that were sanctioned in our decisions endorsed artificial systems that did not reflect economic reality and granted selective advantages.

In the cases of Starbucks and Fiat, the systems worked on the basis of transfer prices. These are the prices that a company within a group pays for things such as a loan or royalties to another company belonging to the same group. Once again, transfer prices are fine as long as they follow the arm's length principle. But the transfer prices of Starbucks and Fiat did not meet these requirements.

The Dutch Starbucks roaster paid a substantial royalty to another group company for coffee roasting know-how, although no other Starbucks or independent roaster in a similar situation paid such royalty. The end result was that—because of this royalty payments—Starbucks ended up paying little tax in the Netherlands.

Fiat Finance & Trade is based in Luxembourg and provides financial services, such as intra-group loans, to other Fiat Group companies. As these activities can be compared to those of a bank, the taxable profit can also be determined similarly to that of a bank. However, here the tax ruling endorsed an artificial method lowering both the capital basis and its remuneration. As a result, Fiat Finance & Trade has only paid taxes on a small portion of its actual capital at a very low remuneration that is not in line with market rate.

The decisions the Commission took last year will offer guidance to tax administrations in the EU. They must make sure that the transfer prices they accept are credible and in line with market terms.

The third and latest decision taken by the Commission is from last January and involves Belgium's so-called Excess Profit scheme, where we found a different method to reduce the tax burden. The scheme was open only to multinational groups and their actual profits were compared to a notional profit they would have made if they had been standalone companies.

The excess profit that resulted from this hypothetical comparison was not taxed. As a result, the multinationals that were part of the scheme—and only them—got tax discounts of more than 50% and in some cases of up to 90%. To bring things back to balance, the Commission ordered Belgium to recover from the more than 30 companies that had received the undue rebates an estimated €700 million in total.

Cases in the pipeline

These are the three decisions the Commission has taken. There are ongoing investigations as well, with openings so far involving Apple in Ireland, and Amazon and McDonald's in Luxembourg.

Moreover, the Task Force has been reviewing over a thousand tax rulings from the LuxLeaks files and from EU countries, which we requested a few years ago. The review reveals that the majority of rulings are not used for aggressive corporate tax planning. Most are well documented and aim at allocating profits between companies with genuine economic activities.

The rule that tax be paid where profit is made seems to be respected more often than not. So, most rulings don't seem to grant a selective advantage. But there seem to be outliers. Our ongoing review is looking for rulings that may grant individual companies terms that are not available to others in comparable circumstances. . . .

As you can see, what is sometimes depicted as an extraordinary and unprecedented initiative is in fact deeply rooted in the Commission's enforcement work. The extraordinary part are the practices the Commission has to correct—not the fact that the Commission is correcting them.

As far as the Commission is concerned, all cases are equal and none is more equal than others. Every case—regardless of its visibility—is investigated and assessed on its own merits. We try to obtain the best possible information; we look at the facts; and we reach a decision based on evidence and the law.

Our assessment is based at all times on applicable State aid rules and the jurisprudence of the European Court of Justice. Finally—and perhaps most importantly—we take great care to respect due process and the right of defence of the administrations and companies involved. There's a Latin phrase that sums up our approach: sine timore aut favore. We will continue to enforce the rules without fear or favour.

This is a message that I would like to send to the law-abiding competitors of the corporations that receive illegal aid, which end up sustaining higher costs. The message also goes to tax authorities in EU countries, which must check the final result of the arrangements they make with corporations.

But above all the message goes out to the people, who expect businesses to play by the rules—more so since each and every citizen is expected to play by the rules. In this sense, State aid rules are part of good governance. The financial and economic crisis has shaken the people's belief in economic governance. Our work can help restore that belief.

Notes and Questions

1. Article 107(1) prohibits state aid that "distorts or threatens to distort competition by favoring certain [firms or goods]. . . ." What does "distort[ing] competition" mean? Does the phrase mean the same thing in Article 107(1) as in Article 101(1) TFEU?

2. Do you agree that state aid normally "distorts competition"? In what sense? Does it harm competition from the viewpoint of consumers? from the viewpoint of competitors? from the vantage of protecting the competition process and the right to compete on the merits? Can state aid intensify competition? How can or should the Commission and Court deal with procompetitive effects (lower prices, more business formation) of state aid?

3. The United States, in contrast with the EU, has no national subsidy control, except as required by the GATT/WTO, and except for prohibition of discriminatory subsidies that impose an undue burden on interstate commerce. See West Lynn Creamery v. Healy, 512 U.S. 186 (1994). US law reflects the belief that freedom of state and local governments to grant subsidies or other benefits, whether to compete for business establishment or to prop up business in financial difficulty, is a healthy form of state autonomy and competition. See Camps Newfound/Owatonna, Inc. v. Town of Harrison, 520 U.S. 564, 589 (1997); and see Justice Scalia, dissenting, at 605–08. Are there good reasons why Europe has state aid control and the United States does not?

4. Firms in Europe frequently challenge a grant of state aid to their rivals, and typically they are accorded standing to do so. Thus, when Ford and Volkswagen set up a joint venture in Portugal to make multi-purpose vehicles—a new endeavor for both joint venture partners—Matra, the dominant maker of MPVs, complained that Portugal's grant of infrastructure aid to the new entrant violated Article 107 TFEU, and that the joint venture agreement itself violated Articles 101 and 102 TFEU in part because the aid distorted competition. (How would Matra argue this point?) Matra lost on the merits; both the aid and the joint venture were allowed. See Case T–17/93, Matra Hachette SA v. Commission, EU:T:1994:89.

Why would a firm challenge a grant of aid to its rival? Why, in particular, would a dominant firm challenge a grant of aid to a new entrant? Is the complainant likely to be complaining about harm to competition, about unfair advantages, or about competition itself? Would buyers of the products produced by a subsidized firm ever have an interest in challenging a state aid? Would it be accurate to view rivals' complaints about grants of state aid as complaints about unfair competition?

5. Explain the relationship between the state aid body of law and the antitrust (Articles 101 and 102 TFEU) and merger control bodies of law. While there are many differences, Europe took advantage of the synergies of its laws in the financial crisis of 2008, using its combined powers of subsidy control, merger control and restructuring, and doing so on an emergency basis. See Neelie Kroes, Competition Law in an Economic Crisis, Opening address at the 13th Annual Competition Conference of the International Bar Association, Fiesole, 11 September 2009 (SPEECH/09/385).

6. Are the deep tax breaks offered by certain Member States to certain multinational firms to induce investment in their countries better viewed under the lens of Member State tax policy or EU state aid policy? For developments on state aid and tax rulings, see http://ec.europa.eu/competition/state_aid/tax_rulings/index_en. html. See also Case T–755/15, Luxembourg v. Commission, pending; and Case T–759/15, Fiat Chrysler Finance Europe v. Commission, pending.

7. European Commission officials take pride in what they view as a coherent and holistic competition system in Europe. Are they right to extol the virtues of the European system? Does US competition policy need more coherence? Should the US Attorney General in Charge of Antitrust have a seat at the economic-policy table? Would the US be served or disserved by a state (or federal) aid policy, requiring notification and justification of significant state, local, or federal aid to enterprises?

5. Extending Control to Foreign State Aid: The Foreign Subsidies Regulation (FSR)

Over time, the EU has grown concerned that subsidies from non-EU governments may have distorted competition within the EU internal market, especially by giving recipients an unfair advantage in acquiring companies or winning contracts for public procurement in the EU. To address this problem and close this perceived regulatory gap, the Foreign Subsidies Regulation (FSR) was enacted and entered into force on 12 July 2023 (Regulation 2022/2560 on foreign subsidies distorting the internal market, [2022] O.J. L 330/1).

Under the FSR Regulation, a prior notification to the Commission is required by (i) parties to a merger, acquisition or joint venture generating an EU turnover of at least €500 million, when the transaction in question involves a foreign financial contribution of at least €50 million, and (ii) bidders in public procurements with a contract value of at least €250 million involving a financial contribution by a non-EU government of at least €4 million. In addition, the Commission may request notifications for smaller amounts where it suspects that a subsidy has had market distortive effects.

In assessing the distortive effects of foreign subsidies, the Commission balances the possible distortive effects with possible positive effects, such as aid to the environment, to determine the net effects thereof and consider whether remedies are required. Remedies may range from the divestment of certain assets or mandatory access to particular infrastructure, for example, to the outright prohibition of a particular transaction or disqualification of subsidized procurement bids.

In September 2024, the European Commission adopted its first decision pursuant to the FSR Regulation, whereby it conditionally approved the acquisition of parts of PPF Telecom, a telecommunication operator based in the Netherlands, by Emirates Telecommunications Group, a telecommunications operator based in the United Arab Emirates and controlled by the Emirates Investment Authority (see https://ec.europa.eu/commission/presscorner/detail/en/ip_24_4842).

Guidance on the substantive assessment carried out by the Commission under the FSR Regulation is expected by January 2026. In the meantime, a register of notified cases is available on the website of DG COMP at https://competition-policy.ec.europa.eu/foreign-subsidies-regulation_en.

G. THE RELATIONSHIP BETWEEN REGULATION AND COMPETITION: US/EU

Every antitrust jurisdiction must make decisions on the relationship between sector regulation and competition law. Does regulation oust the competition law regime, or do the two regimes co-exist where co-existence is possible?

The answer can depend on a jurisdiction's system of federalism and hierarchy of laws. For example, in the United States, an exemption from antitrust law may be implied where sector regulation covers the same set of practices as those sought to be challenged under antitrust law. See Credit Suisse Securities v. Billing, 551 U.S. 264 (2007). Also see *Trinko*, supra, 540 U.S. 398 (2004), suggesting deferral of antitrust to a regulatory regime. In Europe, the perspective is quite different. In *Deutsche Telekom*, concerned with a price squeeze that the German regulator allowed and virtually ordered, the General Court said: If the firm is caught in such a bind between the regulator and EU law, the firm should go back to the regulator and request a price change that would dissipate the price squeeze. Case T–271/03, Deutsche Telekom AG v. Commission, EU:T:2008:101, paras. 261–271, affirmed on other grounds; the Court of Justice believed that Deutsche Telekom could cure the price squeeze without a modification of the regulator's orders. C–280/08 P, EU:C:2010:603.

The design of the two systems can produce different outcomes. In the United States, federal regulation is on a hierarchical par the antitrust system. Congress can privilege one or the other. In the EU, the antitrust system is Treaty law, and the sector regulation derives from the Member State.

Which system, US or EU, is more protective of competition? of efficiency? In which case or regime do consumers get the better deal? Does it matter whether Deutsche Telekom would lower its wholesale price or raise its retail price to avoid an illegal price squeeze?

H. CHINA: ABUSE OF ADMINISTRATIVE MONOPOLY

On the eve of adoption of China's Anti-Monopoly Law in 2008, distinguished Professor Huang Yong, a consultant to the drafters, wrote Pursuing the Second Best: The History, Momentum and Remaining Issues of China's Anti-Monopoly Law, 75 Antitrust L.J. 117 (2008). In this article Professor Huang says:

. . . . China which has a culture thousands of years old, with an ideology that is extremely conservative and even feudalistic, is a country undergoing a painful transition from command economy to market orientation. . . .

* * *

The Desire to Contain Abusive State Power

"The abuse of executive power to distort or restrict competition is a phenomenon that exists among state agencies and organizations which are authorized by the law and regulations to control public affairs, albeit to a various degree. The AML needs to tackle this problem seriously."

—Cao Kangtai, Notes to the Draft PRC Anti-Monopoly Law

As provided by Article 10 of the AML, the so-called administrative monopoly generally refers to abusive conduct committed by state agencies and organizations, which are authorized by the law and regulations to control public affairs, to the extent that they distort or restrict competition. Two factors account for the widespread and intractable existence of administrative monopoly in the Chinese economic system. The first is the tradition, hundreds of years old, that "state power comes first"; in other words, a tradition that state power controls every single aspect of the society's economic life. The second is the current political and economic structure, which has closely linked monopoly enterprises to the government since the 1949 revolution.

In today's China, people have agreed upon two conclusions with respect to the corrosive effects caused by intrusive State power upon economic development and even upon the political system. First, ever expanding abusive State power is the biggest threat to a functioning competitive market system; second, the problem of administrative monopoly stems from the social structure, which is beyond any single statute to resolve. The ultimate solution relies on both economic and political reform. However, for China, the process of reform can take a long time, longer than competition could afford. Therefore, a second best option would be to adopt some technical restraints against certain State powers within the AML framework, which might be an unsatisfactory but realistic approach. This is a reflection of the "doctrine of the golden mean" in the Confucian school, an equivalent to pragmatism.

In accordance with this line of thoughts, the AML was revised in 2022 to increase the anti-monopoly oversight over State authorities. It now requires public authorities to carry out fair competition reviews when adopting rules that may affect economic activities (article 5), and prohibits them from obstructing market entry or to apply unequal treatments (article 40).

* * *

Responding to its unique problem, China has a unique provision in its Anti-Monopoly Law. Chapter V prohibits abuse of administrative powers to restrict competition, known as abuse of administrative monopoly. Although the 2008 AML did not give the antitrust authorities the power to enforce the provision directly, Article 54 of the 2022 AML now empowers them to investigate suspected administrative abuses by administrative monopolies. Generally, the AML was revised in 2022 to increase the anti-monopoly oversight over State authorities by requiring public authorities to carry out fair competition reviews when adopting rules that may affect economic activities (article 5), and prohibits them from obstructing market entry or to apply unequal treatments (article 40). In order to make the oversight more operational, China's State Council issued a Regulation on Fair Competition Review in June 2024, and introduced a set of measures in March 2025 to enhance the implementation of the Regulation on Fair Competition Review in an effort to ensure a level playing field for all market players and free markets from regional protectionist practices. Matters initiated under the 2008 AML by the enforcement agency National Development and Resources Commission in 2014 include: In Yunan Province, the Provincial Communication Administration organized a cartel among the Yunan branches of China Mobile, China Telecom, China Unicom and China Railcom restricting refunds to customers. The NDRC reported the suspected violation to the superior authority, the National Communication Administration, and the superior authority ordered the local authority to cease the practice. The cartel members were fined.

In Shandong Province, the Department of Transport adopted policies for vehicles, including those carrying hazardous chemicals, to be monitored and required that they use a designated company for platform services and testing. The NDRC found that designating the supplier of services deprived road transport companies of freedom to choose their supplier and elevated fees. It suggested to the Shandong provincial government to order the Shangdong DOT to allow the users free choice.

In Hebei Province, the NDRC found that the Department of Transportation, the Department of Finance and the Price Bureau jointly gave local passenger transport companies a 50% discount on road tolls. The NDRC found that the discount was a subsidy giving the local firms an unfair competitive advantage over their out-of-province competitors, and requested the Hebei provincial government to withdraw the policy. See Susan Ning, China's Anti-monopoly Law and Its Enforcement against State Monopolies: Achievements and Limitations, in Antitrust in Emerging and Developing Countries (Fox, First, Charbit, Ramundo eds., Concurrences Review 2016), at 9.

Meanwhile, SAIC (State Administration for Industry & Commerce, the agency in charge of non-price restraints) took action in Inner Mongolia, finding that the local Safety Supervision and Administration Bureau was responsible for an illegal division of geographic markets among fireworks wholesale companies, which the Bureau claimed would prevent accidents caused by fireworks of poor quality induced by aggressive competition. The local SAIC branch fined the wholesalers 7% of their annual revenue for the prior year, and imposed a fine of 8% on those wholesalers who, taking advantage of their monopoly, imposed unreasonable conditions on retailers.

Private parties may also sue to enforce Chapter V, and litigation is pending.

In their article, "Fair Competition Review—key step in competition policy," in King & Wood Mallesons' China Law Insight, Susan Ning, Kate Peng and Gong Ting describe China's establishment of its Fair Competition Review Mechanism for all draft laws, regulations, administrative policies, practices and instruments to ensure against (for example) state and local discriminations on entry and exit, preferential treatments including tax exemptions, and designation of who shall provide goods and services. They then outline the scope of Chapter V and show the connection between the AML enforcement, the Fair Competition Review Mechanism, and other mechanisms to attack obstructions of competition by government bodies. The authors write:

> Another latest effort made by China's top government to fight against administrative monopoly to elevate the deterring effects for such potential violations is in the NDRC's latest draft (for public consultation) guidelines on determining the illegal gains generated from monopoly conduct and on setting fines ("Fining Guidelines"). The Fining Guidelines stipulate that when determining the aggravating circumstances on setting fines, if certain undertakings take the initiative to impel the administrative authorities to eliminate or restrict competition through abusing their administrative powers, the AMEAs (Anti-Monopoly Enforcement Authorities) may deem it as aggravating circumstance when setting fines.

b) In the context of Administrative Litigation Law * * *

Another effort was made to reduce the legal barrier to prevent private individuals and enterprises from initiating administrative litigation against administrative monopoly. The previous Administrative Litigation Law ("ALL") makes a distinction between "abstract administrative act" and "concrete (individualized) administrative act." A private individual or entity can only bring to court cases against concrete administrative acts or administrative acts specifically issued against an individual or company. This approach is similar to the EU's direct effect principle, which enables a private individual or entity to bring a competition law case before a national court. In contrast, administrative litigation against "abstract administrative activity" (i.e., a legislative measure issued by a government agency) was explicitly excluded by the previous ALL. The abuses of administrative monopolies, in practice, are usually carried out in the form of legislative or other similar measures, and therefore are categorized as "abstract administrative act". At such, if these measures are not concrete or addressed to individuals, under the previous Administrative Litigation Law, no administrative litigation could be successfully initiated. The revised ALL, however, has removed such limitations.

c) Achievements and Limitations

There is no doubt that significant achievements were made by the AML and the ALL to fight against administrative monopoly. Recent intensified enforcement decisions underline the point that the AMEAs have targeted abuses by administrative monopolies as their enforcement priority.

There are, however, certain limitations such as the ex post nature of the assessment. These controls over administrative monopoly are carried out on a case by case basis and therefore require a relatively long time to realize such deterring effects and thus remedy such infringements. Against such backdrop, such mechanism provides a comprehensive review of all the government measures in place (or in future) by the prescribed competition standards. This review will not only remove the very roots of administrative monopoly, but also promote the awareness of all the government officials at different levels to fully recognize the importance of competition policy in a market economy.

Conclusion

The importance of market competition is increasingly well understood in China. As mentioned above, two features of China's systemic and policy environment raise issues for market competition:

abuse of the administrative powers of government agencies, and policies to promote the development of particular sectors and firms. While these features exist in all modern economies, their extent in China is exceptional. Alongside the current enforcement of the AML and the ALL, the introduction of fair competition review, conceived by the highest level of the Chinese government, represent a significant change in the government's thinking about the role of the state and its relationship with the economy. In view of the above, the establishment of the fair competition review mechanism is indeed a milestone in China's efforts to fully transform into a market economy.

Available at: http://www.chinalawinsight.com/2016/06/articles/antitrust-international-trade/fair-competition-review-key-step-in-competition-policy/.

Notes and Questions

1. Comment on the Chinese law against abuse of administrative monopoly and China's project to identify and correct unnecessarily anticompetitive legislation and regulations. Are these provisions likely to make a significant contribution to China's (socialist) market economy?

2. What will it take to make these laws successful?

3. Are other jurisdictions that are faced with extensive state restraints likely to take lessons from China?

4. Would separation-of-powers issues counsel against administrative monopoly law in some jurisdictions?

I. TRADE INSTRUMENTS

1. The WTO: Hybrid State and Private Restraints

Combinations of state and private action may pose serious anticompetitive restraints. But the private action might be shielded from challenge by state action, and the state action, even if anticompetitive and excessive, may not be proscribed. This was a problem in *Kodak/Fuji Film.** Kodak, in its attempts to contest the Japanese film market, alleged that it was severely handicapped by the combination of Japanese state and private restraints that, cumulatively, blocked all efficient ways to get to market in Japan. Rules of the World Trade Organization provided no recourse—even if one accepts the facts as argued by Kodak.

* Panel Report, *Japan-Measures Affecting Consumer Photographic Film and Paper*, WT/DS44/R (Mar. 31, 1998) (adopted Apr. 22, 1998). Since this was a WTO case, it was limited to Japan's trade-restraining laws or acts.

The World Trade Organization has few antitrust rules, but it does have a set of rules applicable to telecommunications companies and the state measures that regulate them. Telecoms companies have historically been state-owned. Many were newly privatized. The modus operandi of the telecoms firms has frequently been nationalistic, undermining the promise of an open and competitive world telecommunications system. This combination of factors led to the adoption of antitrust rules accompanying the Telecommunications Agreement in the WTO. Only one antitrust case has arisen under the antitrust rules accompanying the Telecommunications Agreement. The case demonstrates the potential for analyzing intertwined public and private restraints as a coherent whole.

MEXICAN TELECOMS**

Telmex is the dominant telecommunications company in Mexico. It was state-owned then privatized. Telmex is regulated by COFETEL, the Mexican telecommunications regulatory agency. Telmex is also subject to the Mexican Federal Competition Law, but it has been notoriously successful in maneuvering around control by the Mexican Federal Competition Commission.

COFETEL regulates the sector through rulemaking. COFETEL rules conferred on Telmex the power to fix the rate to be paid by all foreign carriers (e.g., AT&T and MCI) terminating calls in Mexico. Mexico had licensed several Mexican firms (the "concessionaires") in addition to Telmex to terminate calls in Mexico. COFETEL rules required these firms to charge no less than the Telmex fee for termination, and the rules decreed a market-sharing system in support of the high price. This, according to the United States, was an anticompetitive, incumbent-protecting strategy that amounted to a cartel. It was a strategy carried out by and for the benefit of Mexican firms, and one that Mexico was bound to prevent by its WTO commitment in the General Agreement on Trade in Services (GATS), the Telecommunications Annex to the GATS, and the accompanying Reference Paper. The United States filed a claim before the WTO alleging that Mexico had failed to open its telecommunications market, as promised. The claim included an antitrust charge.[1]

Mexico was among 69 member states of the WTO that signed the GATS Annex on Telecommunications and the Reference Paper. The Reference Paper contains the antitrust obligation that lay at the

** Based on Eleanor Fox, *Mexican Telecoms*: Modest World Antitrust, 21 Antitrust 74 (ABA Antitrust Law Section, fall 2006).

1 See Panel Report, Mexico—Measures Affecting Telecommunications Services, WT/DS204/R (Apr. 2, 2004) (adopted June 1, 2004), ¶¶ 7.222–.224.

center of the dispute. The Reference Paper requires signatories to maintain "appropriate measures" to prevent major suppliers "from engaging in or continuing anti-competitive practices." The relevant provisions are as follows:

(1) *Competitive safeguards*

(1.1) *Prevention of anti-competitive practices in telecommunications*

Appropriate measures shall be maintained for the purpose of preventing suppliers who, alone or together, are a major supplier from engaging in or continuing anti-competitive practices.

(1.2) *Safeguards*

The anti-competitive practices referred to in the above paragraph shall include in particular:

(a) engaging in anti-competitive cross-subsidization;

(b) using information obtained from competitors with anti-competitive results; and

(c) not making available to other services suppliers on a timely basis technical information about essential facilities and commercially relevant information which are necessary for them to provide services.

Based on this language, the WTO panel was called upon to decide a series of difficult questions: Was it an anticompetitive practice for Telmex to set an excessive termination fee and for all Mexican rivals to accede to charging no less than the fee Telmex would set? Was this behavior a contemplated "anti-competitive practice," in view of the fact that the conduct was ordered by rules of the nation's regulatory agency? Were Mexico's antitrust law and regulatory rules "appropriate measures" to prevent anticompetitive practices, obviating any violation? Indeed, were the regulatory rules procompetitive (as Mexico improbably maintained)? If they were anticompetitive, were the Mexican rules and practices a justified form of industrial policy (if so, Mexico did not fail to maintain "appropriate" measures) on the theory that the monopoly border-charge was meant to be used by the Mexican telecommunication firms to fund infrastructure in the poorest parts of Mexico and thus to enhance Mexico's economic development?

The questions for the panel were difficult in light of the wording of the main document at issue, the Reference Paper. The antitrust obligation clearly was not drafted by antitrust lawyers. Its wording and context gave fodder to Mexico's strategy of playing with the meaning of "anti-competitive." It also gave Mexico cover to claim that measures protecting Mexican carriers from being played off one another by foreign carriers, preventing new entrants from triggering a price war and preventing large carriers from undercutting new entrants, were procompetitive measures.

Construing the Reference Paper

The Meaning of "anti-competitive." Mexico argued for a narrow construction of Section 1 of the Reference Paper. It relied heavily on the three stated examples of "anti-competitive" practices in Section 1.2. The examples are: unfair low prices because of cross-subsidization, unfair use of information, and unfair withholding of information. Mexico contended that the examples demonstrated the meaning of "anti-competitive" in the Reference Paper. The word referred, said Mexico, to: "actions taken by private companies to gain an advantage over their competitors." Thus cartels were not "anti-competitive practices."

The heading "*Safeguards*" over the text of the antitrust obligations tended to support Mexico's narrow interpretation. The GATS obliges nations to open their markets. Safeguards are protections against a surge of trade that may result from openness. The antitrust clause could be seen as a check against the inflow of unfair (e.g., low-priced) competition.

This argument did not convince the panel. Cartels, it pointed out, are the paradigmatic anticompetitive practice. The anti-cartel principle is well recognized around the world. It is well documented in the Havana Charter, the OECD Hard Core Cartel Recommendation, and the UNCTAD Set of Multilateral Rules. It is unthinkable (the panel implied) that the phrase "anti-competitive practices" does not include cartels.

State action. Mexico further argued that "anti-competitive practices" at least means no more than practices illegal under antitrust laws, and the conduct in question was ordered by COFETEL's rules. It was protected by the state action doctrine, said Mexico, and therefore was not legally an "anti-competitive practice." The European Union joined Mexico in arguing that the state action doctrine and the nature of the rules as a regulatory choice defeated the United States's case.

Again, the panel was not convinced. It said: "The Panel is aware that, pursuant to doctrines applicable under the competition laws of some Members, a firm complying with a specific legislative requirement of such a Member . . . may be immunized . . . ." But in most of these jurisdictions, domestic legislatures have the power to limit the scope of competition law. GATS commitments, by contrast, are international; they are designed to limit the regulatory powers of WTO members. A member "cannot unilaterally erode its international commitments."

The panel said that a state action defense should be particularly disfavored in an international context. The use of state power to insulate a national champion at the expense of outsiders is a discrimination of the sort that, conceptually, trade law does not tolerate. A state should not be permitted to *order* trade-harming anticompetitive conduct to evade its burden to prohibit just such conduct.

The panel might also have noted the limits to the state action defense, in both the United States and the European Union. US law holds that a state of the United States may not order price fixing and then immunize the price fixers from violating the federal antitrust laws.[2] A Member State of the European Union may not order "its" firms to fix quotas and then insulate them from EU competition law when they decline to allocate quotas to outsiders.[3] If a Mexican antitrust action had been brought against the Mexican firms, they may not have had a successful state action defense.

A "right" to industrial policy? Mexico had a third string to its bow. Regardless of a state action or immunity defense, said Mexico, the Reference Paper obligation is limited. It says only that "*appropriate* measures shall be maintained for the purpose of preventing [major] suppliers . . . from engaging in or continuing anti-competitive practices." Mexico said it maintained appropriate measures: it had an antitrust law and enforced it. Moreover, Mexico was required to take only *appropriate* measures. It was appropriate for Mexico to adopt cartel-organizing rules as a matter of regulatory sovereignty to protect and promote Mexican investment in domestic infrastructure and thereby to advance its economic development.

There are two convincing answers to Mexico's claim of right to design its own industrial policy. First, Mexico itself had undertaken in its WTO obligations not to charge an excessive termination fee. COFETEL's rules authorized private firms to do what Mexico could not do. Nations have the power to contract away the right to adopt regulation that handicaps foreign traders. Second, Mexico's regulation was clearly not likely to achieve its putative object: help the Mexican poor. Extra private profits for national firms do not translate into infrastructure investment. Moreover, lower prices of

---

[2] Schwegmann Bros. v. Calvert Distillers Corp., 341 U.S. 384, 71 S.Ct. 745, 95 L.Ed. 1035 (1951).

[3] Case C–198/01, *Italian Matches*, EU:C:2003:430.

the incoming calls were good for poor Mexicans. Large numbers of the callers into Mexico are Mexicans who have come to the United States for work to support their families, and they need to be in touch with the families they left behind.[4]

Because Mexico's means were so unlikely to achieve its putative ends, one might suspect a different driving force behind the COFETEL rules. Perhaps the aim was to continue the privileges of a former state-owned monopoly and its legendarily powerful, politically well-connected owner, Carlos Slim. As EU policy makers often observe, it may take a supranational law to give a nation the will to say no; the will to deny advantages to a powerful player.[5]

Conclusion

Mexican Telecoms was a hard case. It was hard because it was not clear that the nations meant to limit their regulatory powers by agreeing to Section 1 of the Reference Paper. It was hard because Mexico had a credible argument at every fork in the road. (Did "anti-competitive" practice mean only unfair competition? Was there a state-action shield? Was there a national regulatory policy defense?)

But *Mexican Telecoms* was a wise decision. In this first WTO antitrust case,[6] the panel gave a victory to markets over nationalism.

---

4 *See* Mary Anastasia O'Grady, *Americas: A Telecom Monopoly Cripples Mexico*, WALL ST. J., Feb. 10, 2006, at A19 ("Telmex has 95% of the country's fixedline market," leading to high prices and sub-optimal use. TELMEX—through its powerful owner Carlos Slim, and successive presidents (Zedillo, Fox) who are beholden to Mr. Slim—suppresses the growth of wireless and voice-over-Internet. The Minister for Communication and Transportation, Pedro Cerisola, is a former TELMEX district manager. Cerisola "has actively engaged in protecting Telmex against competition." Not only do the poor suffer from prices that are too high, but they suffer from suppressed growth. "[T]he rest of the country suffered from [TELMEX's] favored position. In a modern age when businesses need low-priced, high-quality telecommunications to compete in a global economy, Mexican growth has borne the cost of Mr. Slim's privilege. Any genuine effort to help the poor necessarily requires more healthy competition, starting in the telecom market.").

5 See Rafael del Villar, Competition and Equity in Telecommunications, Chapter 9 in NO GROWTH WITHOUT EQUITY? INEQUALITY, INTERESTS, AND COMPETITION IN MEXICO (S. Levy and M. Walton eds. 2009), at 321. Del Villar describes how Mexico privatized Telmex while continuing its monopolistic privileges, and argues that:

> Mexico could achieve a good deal simply by complying with the provisions of the Federal Telecommunications Act and the reference paper, as well as by ensuring clear separation between the major carriers and the regulatory agency.

6 In a prior matter, *Kodak/Fuji Film*, the United States complained that Japan tolerated private anticompetitive restraints; but when the United States brought its case in the GATT, it challenged only Japan's trade-restraining laws. The United States lost. See Panel Report, Japan—Measures Affecting Consumer Photographic Film and Paper, WT/DS44/R (Mar. 31, 1998) (adopted Apr. 22, 1998).

The panel report was a first step towards integrating trade and competition.

2. Regional Agreements

The new generation of regional free trade agreements may include a chapter on state-owned enterprises and designated monopolies. These chapters would approximate competitive neutrality for state and state-owned enterprises and monopolies designated by the state and provide transparency as to the identities of these enterprises. The chapter negotiated for the Trans-Pacific Partnership, which is in abeyance since the US withdrawal, may be a guide for such chapters in the future. Here is a relevant excerpt from the chapter in TPP:

TRANS-PACIFIC PARTNERSHIP

(2016, not adopted)

Chapter 17

State-Owned Enterprises and Designated Monopolies

(footnotes deleted)

Article 17.3: Delegated Authority

Each Party shall ensure that when its state-owned enterprises, state enterprises and designated monopolies exercise any regulatory, administrative or other governmental authority that the Party has directed or delegated to such entities to carry out, those entities act in a manner that is not inconsistent with that Party's obligations under this Agreement.

Article 17.4: Non-discriminatory Treatment and Commercial Considerations

1. Each Party shall ensure that each of its state-owned enterprises, when engaging in commercial activities:

(a) acts in accordance with commercial considerations in its purchase or sale of a good or service, except to fulfil any terms of its public service mandate that are not inconsistent with subparagraph (c)(ii);

(b) in its purchase of a good or service:

(i) accords to a good or service supplied by an enterprise of another Party treatment no less favourable than it accords to a like good or a like service supplied by enterprises of the Party, of any other Party or of any non-Party; and

(ii) accords to a good or service supplied by an enterprise that is a covered investment in the Party's territory treatment no less favourable than it accords to a like good or a like service supplied by enterprises in the relevant market in the Party's territory that are investments of investors of the Party, of any other Party or of any non-Party; and

(c) in its sale of a good or service:

(i) accords to an enterprise of another Party treatment no less favourable than it accords to enterprises of the Party, of any other Party or of any non-Party; and

(ii) accords to an enterprise that is a covered investment in the Party's territory treatment no less favourable than it accords to enterprises in the relevant market in the Party's territory that are investments of investors of the Party, of any other Party or of any non-Party.

2. Each Party shall ensure that each of its designated monopolies:

(a) acts in accordance with commercial considerations in its purchase or sale of the monopoly good or service in the relevant market, except to fulfil any terms of its designation that are not inconsistent with subparagraph (b), (c) or (d);

(b) in its purchase of the monopoly good or service:

(i) accords to a good or service supplied by an enterprise of another Party treatment no less favourable than it accords to a like good or a like service supplied by enterprises of the Party, of any other Party or of any non-Party; and

(ii) accords to a good or service supplied by an enterprise that is a covered investment in the Party's territory treatment no less favourable than it accords to a like good or a like service supplied by enterprises in the relevant market in the Party's territory that are investments of investors of the Party, of any other Party or of any non-Party; and

(c) in its sale of the monopoly good or service:

(i) accords to an enterprise of another Party treatment no less favourable than it accords to enterprises of the Party, of any other Party or of any non-Party; and

(ii) accords to an enterprise that is a covered investment in the Party's territory treatment no less favourable than it accords to enterprises in the relevant market in the Party's territory that are investments of investors of the Party, of any other Party or of any non-Party; and

(d) does not use its monopoly position to engage in, either directly or indirectly, including through its dealings with its parent, subsidiaries or other entities the Party or the designated monopoly owns, anticompetitive practices in a non-monopolised market in its territory that negatively affect trade or investment between the Parties.

3. Paragraphs 1(b) and 1(c) and paragraphs 2(b) and 2(c) do not preclude a state-owned enterprise or designated monopoly from:

(a) purchasing or selling goods or services on different terms or conditions including those relating to price; or

(b) refusing to purchase or sell goods or services, provided that such differential treatment or refusal is undertaken in accordance with commercial considerations.

Article 17.5: Courts and Administrative Bodies

1. Each Party shall provide its courts with jurisdiction over civil claims against an enterprise owned or controlled through ownership interests by a foreign government based on a commercial activity carried on in its territory. This shall not be construed to require a Party to provide jurisdiction over such claims if it does not provide jurisdiction over similar claims against enterprises that are not owned or controlled through ownership interests by a foreign government.

2. Each Party shall ensure that any administrative body that the Party establishes or maintains that regulates a state-owned enterprise exercises its regulatory discretion in an impartial manner with respect to enterprises that it regulates, including enterprises that are not state-owned enterprises.

Notes and Questions

1. What advances are made by these provisions? How significant do you expect them to be, if they are enforced?

2. China was not party to the TPP negotiations, but the agreement would have been open to non-founding nations to join. Would China be likely to see the excerpted provisions as in China's interests?

Would the US see China's acceptance of these provisions as good for the US?

3. Why is the antitrust clause (Article 17.4 2(d)) only in paragraph 2 (re designated monopolies) and not in paragraph 1 (re SOEs)? Why is the antitrust clause limited to leveraging a monopoly position into a non-monopolized market in its territory rather than inclusive of all monopolistic restraints? Would greater coverage in each case be good for competition? a step too far for sovereignty?

4. Does EU law, for the internal market, prohibit all conduct addressed in TPP Chapter 17? Does it go further? See sections C through H above.

J. CONCLUSION

US antitrust law disciplines private power and private restraints. Other jurisdictions, trying to create markets, face an additional challenge: the state. State restraints, including acts and measures that privilege favored firms, are serious barriers. The European Union led the way in integrating the law against undue public and private restraints. China's young antitrust law significantly targets state restraints. In virtually all jurisdictions, whether or not their law covers state restraints, the competition agencies commonly engage in advocacy against disproportionate competition-harming state and local measures. Increasingly, nations are part of free trade areas that may integrate trade and competition disciplines. The World Trade Organization is, notionally, a logical forum to integrate the disciplines on a world level, but it does so only exceptionally, as in telecoms. The challenge is left to national and regional agendas.

Chapter 8

ENFORCEMENT: SYSTEMS AND INSTITUTIONS

A. INTRODUCTION

As new jurisdictions join the antitrust community, they must not only adopt substantive antitrust rules but also create institutional apparatuses for the enforcement of antitrust law. Usually, the choice of institutional structure is heavily influenced by preexisting constitutional, statutory, administrative, cultural, and historical opportunities and constraints. A variety of institutional systems are emerging around the world. In this chapter, we cannot describe all of the different models. Rather, we introduce some of the standard institutional questions that antitrust regimes must frequently decide.

At the outset, it may be useful to take a quick look at the two most significant institutional models—those of the US and the EU. In the US, antitrust enforcement is both public and private (meaning that both governmental prosecutors and agencies and private litigants may seek to enforce the antitrust laws). On the public side, there are two separate antitrust agencies—the Department of Justice Antitrust Division and the Federal Trade Commission—with much concurrent and overlapping jurisdiction. Every state may also enforce federal antitrust law, as well as its own antitrust laws, through civil actions by the state Attorney General. The Justice Department alone can bring federal criminal enforcement actions. In order to sue civilly, it must bring injunctive actions in federal court. The Federal Trade Commission has a choice of suing in federal district court and hence subjecting itself to ordinary civil litigation rules and procedures or else bringing an administrative action within the agency. However, even when administrative actions are brought within the agency, they are essentially adversarial in nature, with administrative law judges playing the judicial role, agency prosecutorial teams playing the prosecutorial function, and the defendants entitled to a full evidentiary hearing on the record. The full Commission sits as a quasi-appellate court, reviewing administrative law judge decisions, and from Commission decisions the losing defendant may take an appeal to a federal appellate court.

Private enforcement for treble damages is authorized by statute, and in recent years has far outstripped public enforcement (at least in terms of the number of cases filed). Private enforcement can occur in state or federal court and follows ordinary civil litigation rules. Both parties theoretically have a right to demand a jury trial in damages actions, although in practice there are fewer than 10 civil antitrust jury trials a year in the federal system. Prevailing plaintiffs are entitled to automatic trebling of their damages and to collect their attorneys' fees—often in the tens of millions of dollars—from defendants. Defendants are exposed to joint and several liability and members of class actions can usually opt out of the class and pursue individual actions against the defendant.

Federal antitrust law generally does not preempt state regulatory schemes that displace competition with some other regulatory framework. So long as the state clearly and affirmatively articulates a policy to suppress competition in favor of some other objective and actively supervises the anticompetitive scheme, state law prevails over federal law.

The EU system is quite different in many respects. At a European Union level (as opposed to the institutional arrangements within each Member State), the institutions most critical to competition law and policy are the Commission, the Council, and the General Court and the Court of Justice of the European Union. The Commission acts as a collegial body for the good of the whole Union. The members are expected not to pursue national interests. The Commission is often referred to as the executive body of the European Union. It initiates legislative process by drafting legislation in the form of Council Regulation, such as for merger control, Commission Regulation, such as for group exemptions for certain common forms of agreement, and Commission Notices, such as safe harbors for de minimis restraints. Also, and very importantly for competition law, the Commission has adjudicative powers. It decides competition law cases that originate with the Commission.

The Council, or Council of Ministers, is comprised of ministers from the government of each Member State. The constituency changes according to the subject matter at hand, so, for example, the economic ministers sit on economic matters. The Council exercises primary legislative power in the Union. Increasingly in fields other than competition law, it shares power with the European Parliament.

Competition cases may be initiated in the Competition Directorate General of the Commission (Directorate General for Competition or "DG COMP" for short). The Commission has powers to investigate and to obtain documents. The Commission may file a Statement of Objections, which describes the conduct involved and contains a preliminary assessment. If a compromise is reached at this point, the Commission issues a decision making commitments binding on the entities involved (called "undertakings"). Otherwise, the firms involved may file a written defense, submit documents, and request a hearing, which is held before a hearing examiner. The case handlers within the Competition Directorate General draft a preliminary decision. The draft is vetted by the Legal Service (lawyers' lawyers to the various directorates of the Commission and to the other institutions) and by an advisory committee of the Member State representatives. The resulting revised draft decision is submitted to and ordinarily adopted by the College of Commissioners. The firms involved or other persons with a special interest can seek (full or partial) annulment or modification of the decision in the General Court, which is comprised of judges from all Member State. Either party can appeal the court judgment to the highest court of the European Union, the Court of Justice ("CJEU"), which is comprised of a judge from each Member State. When an appeal is taken to the CJEU, an advocate general is often assigned to the case. The advocate general—who has the standing of a judge and acts as an adviser to the Court—hears the case along with the panel of judges and writes a usually learned opinion, analyzing the facts and law and expressing his or her opinion as to the appropriate outcome. In a high percentage of cases, the Court of Justice follows the opinion of the advocate general. The judgments of both courts must be by consensus; there are no dissents.

Parties may choose to settle investigations by proposing "commitments" to resolve the Commission's investigation. The Commission will not accept proposed commitments without first "market testing" them by seeking public comment. In cartel cases, the Commission or the parties may propose a settlement—essentially, a fine level. If the parties agree on a settlement, the defendants must accept the Commission's objections and acknowledge their liability.

The Commission cannot enforce the Treaty's competition law provisions criminally, nor can private litigants seek redress before the Commission. The process is strictly civil and administrative. The Commission's essential coercive power is to order fines, which may be quite large (up to 10% of the defendant corporations' annual worldwide revenue).

Competition law cases may also be initiated by national competition authorities or by private litigants, in national courts. However, for reasons that will be discussed shortly, private antitrust litigation has historically been far less common in Europe than in the US. If an issue of EU competition law arises in a national court and the interpretation of EU law is not clear, the national court may (and the national court of last resort must) refer the issue to the Court of Justice under Article 267 TFEU. This is called a preliminary reference. In these cases, too, an advocate general provides his or her opinion to the Court.

B. PUBLIC ENFORCEMENT MODELS AND DISTINCTIVE ISSUES

1. Single Agency or Multiple Agencies?

The US's dual agency system (FTC and Department of Justice) has long been a curiosity. Why would you have two different federal agencies with largely concurrent and overlapping jurisdiction? Every few years some group studies this question and recommends leaving the existing system largely intact. In 2007, the bi-partisan, Congressionally appointed Antitrust Modernization Commission released an evaluative report on the entire gambit of modern US antitrust law. Among other things, the twelve members of the Commission considered whether dual federal enforcement should continue. Three of the twelve—including two former heads of the Antitrust Division—voted to recommend abolishing the FTC's antitrust enforcement authority and vesting responsibility for all antitrust enforcement with the Justice Department. But the majority recommended retaining the dual enforcement structure. With the benefit of nearly 100 years of dual-agency history, the Commissioners asserted that the real justification for continuing with dual enforcement is not any theoretical or practical advantage to having multiple agencies, but rather path dependence: "Although concentrating enforcement authority in a single agency generally would be a superior institutional structure, the significant costs and disruption of moving to a single-agency system at this point in time would likely exceed the benefits." The Commissioners noted further practical difficulties with such a switch: "there is no consensus as to which agency would preferably retain antitrust enforcement authority" and any such move "would likely be politically very difficult."

Initially, China's Anti-Monopoly law went even further than the US and granted antitrust authority to three agencies: the National Development and Reform Commission ("NDRC") with jurisdiction over price-related offenses, the State Administration of Industry and Commerce ("SAIC") with jurisdiction over other non-merger offenses, and the Ministry of Commerce ("MOFCOM") with jurisdiction over merger review. However, in 2018, China consolidated antitrust enforcement into a single agency—the State Administration for Market Regulation ("SAMR").

In most emerging antitrust jurisdictions, the recent trends have similarly been in the direction of consolidating rather than dispersing antitrust enforcement. In 2014, the United Kingdom moved from two agencies—the Office of Fair Trading and the Competition Commission—to a single agency—the Competition and Markets Authority ("CMA"). Brazil consolidated three agencies into a single independent agency: the Brazilian Antitrust Authority—CADE—in 2012. India's 2002 Anti-Monopoly Law created a single Competition Commission. In 2003, Portugal migrated from a two-agency system to a single Competition Authority (Autoridade da Concorrência) consisting of a council (Conselho) and the sole supervisor (Fiscal Único). In 2008, France consolidated its merger and general competition enforcement functions in a new competition authority, although the Economics Minister reserves significant powers to intervene in merger cases based on "industrial development, competitiveness of the undertakings concerned relative to international competition or the creation and preservation of jobs."

Is the handwriting on the wall for the US's multiple-agency system? Probably not. The Antitrust Division and FTC have been around too long and have too many constituencies in high places. Still, for younger antitrust regimes that are open to experimenting with different models, single agency models seem to be the most popular.

2. Administrative vs. Judicial Enforcement

As new antitrust jurisdictions design their own institutions, a fundamental question is whether to prefer an administrative model in which first-instance decisions are handled by a board or agency, or whether instead to make the public enforcer an executive or prosecutorial entity that brings cases before a court or tribunal. A common argument for the administrative model is that it permits competition law experts to handle the matter more efficiently and thoroughly and saves judicial review for appellate courts that can resolve any purely legal questions rather than muddling through complex and contested factual records and obtuse economic questions. On the other hand, proponents of the executive model argue that separation between the investigatory/prosecutorial and adjudicative functions advances the legitimacy of competition law enforcement and increases the quality of decision-making by sharpening the executive's preparation of its case.

Both models—and, sometimes, hybrid models—can be seen in emerging antitrust jurisdictions.

India's 2002 Competition Act creates a Competition Commission consisting of no more than ten members. The Commission has the power to investigate violations of the Act, impose injunctive remedies, and mete out monetary penalties. Article 36 of the Act gives the Commission the right to regulate its own procedures. Appeals may be taken to the National Company Law Appellate Tribunal.

In China, SAMR acts as an administrative body with the power to investigate and issue binding decisions. Affected parties may apply for administrative review or file suit in a Chinese court to annul the administrative decision. (Seeking administrative review does not impair the right to see subsequent judicial review). In the case of merger decisions, administrative practice holds that the parties may first seek administrative review before seeking judicial review.

In contrast to the administrative approach in China and India, South Africa and Chile follow an executive/prosecutorial model. In South Africa, the Competition Commission investigates potential violations of the Competition Act and decides whether to bring a case If the investigation reveals a violation of the Act, the Commission may bring an enforcement action before the Competition Tribunal—a court. From decisions of the Tribunal, appeals can be taken to the Competition Appeal Court.

In Chile, Fiscalía Nacional Económica ("FNE") is an executive department similar to the US Justice Department's Antitrust Division. When it decides to bring a case, it sues before the Tribunal for the Defense of Free Competition (TDLC) and acts as a prosecutor in the proceedings.

3. Due Process, Procedural Fairness, and Rule of Law

Systems that rely primarily on administrative enforcement have been challenged in recent years by critics claiming that administrative processes often deprive them of procedural rights necessary to fair administration of justice and due process of law. As noted, before the European Commission, defendants are accorded certain rights of defense, including access to the file (excluding business secrets), a right of written reply, and a hearing before an independent hearing officer. Despite these allowances, there have been calls for reforms to provide greater checks on administrative processes, particularly as European fines for violations of competition law have swelled to over 1 billion € in some cases.

In A. Menarini Diagnostics S.R.L. v. Italy, 43509 Eur. Ct. H.R. 08 (2011), the European Court of Human Rights ("ECtHR") held that Article 6(1) of the European Convention on Human Rights, which guarantees the right to a fair trial in criminal cases, applies in competition cases. In 2001, the Autorità Garante della Concorrenza e del Mercato (AGCM), the Italian competition authority, investigated Menarini, an Italian pharmaceutical company, for price fixing and market division and imposed a € 6 million fine. Menarini brought an action before the ECtHR, arguing that although the enforcement action was classified as administrative under Italian law, it was functionally criminal under the Convention. The ECtHR agreed, holding that whether Article 6 applied could not be predicated on the designation of a particular process as administrative rather than criminal as a matter of domestic law. But despite finding Article 6 applicable, the court held the Article not infringed since the administrative decision had been reviewed by a juridical court with plenary power of review over the administrative decision.

The moral of *Menarini* remains unclear. Some commentators view the decision's precedent as significantly expanding the availability of due process arguments for European defendants charged with competition law violations. In a decision issued shortly after Menarini, Posten Norge v. EFTA Surveillance Authority, Case E–15/10 EFTA (April 18, 2012), the European Free Trade Area Court held that Article 6 requires that antitrust defendants be afforded a presumption of innocence. On the other hand, officials at the European Commission lauded *Menarini* as vindicating the Commission's administrative procedures, since the Italian system upheld in *Menarini* was closely predicated on EU procedure.

Questions continue to be raised concerning the adequacy of judicial review of administrative processes. Some critics have argued that the standard of judicial review is too lax. European courts have historically accorded the European Commission a broad "margin of discretion," whereby judicial review is limited "to an examination of the relevance of the facts and of the legal consequences which the Commission deduces therefrom" which limits judicial review to "verifying whether the relevant procedural rules have been complied with, whether the facts have been accurately stated and whether there has been any manifest error of assessment or a misuse of powers." Consten and Grundig v. Commission, Case C–56/64, EU:C:1966:41; Remia v. Commission, Case 42/84, EU:C:1985:327. Is such a standard of review sufficient in light of the severe consequences of an administrative finding of violation of the TFEU?

After years of criticism from some corners that the European system fails to sufficiently protect defendants' procedural rights, the CJEU responded. In a stream of cases starting in the 2010's, the CJEU embraced a full review standard whereby "not only must the EU judicature establish, among other things, whether the evidence relied on is factually accurate, reliable and consistent but also whether that evidence contains all the relevant information which must be taken into account in order to assess a complex situation and whether it is capable of substantiating the conclusions drawn from it." Chalkor v. Commission, Case C-386/10 P, EU:C:2011:815; *CB v Commission,* C-67/13 P, EU:C:2014:2204. Subsequently, the CJEU annulled a number of Commission decisions on due process grounds. For example, in March of 2017, in United Parcel Service, Inc. v. Commission, the General Court annulled a 2013 Commission decision prohibiting UPS from acquiring TNT Express NV. The General Court held that that the Commission had violated UPS's due process rights by failing to communicate to UPS a final version of its econometric analysis—which contained substantive changes to the models discussed during the administrative procedure—and therefore had failed to give UPS an opportunity to express its views before adopting its decision. Although acknowledging the need for speed in merger review, the General Court held that at least the essential elements of the Commission's revised econometric analysis should have been communicated to UPS. In 2019, the European Court of Justice upheld the General Court decision. C–265/17 P. It held that rights of defense is a general principle of EU law and that, in the context of merger investigations, this requires that, before the adoption of a final decision, the Commission put the merging parties in a position from which they can effectively present their views and arguments. However, on 21 December 2023, the European Court of Justice upheld the General Court's dismissal of UPS' €1.7 billion claim for damages allegedly suffered due to the Commission's prohibition of the proposed concentration between UPS and TNT, essentially because UPS failed to demonstrate that it would have secured approval for the TNT transaction absent the procedural breach. Case T–834/17, as confirmed by the ECJ in Case C–297/22 P.

C. SPECIALIZED ANTITRUST COURTS

The US has no specialized antitrust court. When the Department of Justice sues, it must do so in the generalist Article III federal district courts. Review from FTC decisions goes to the generalist Article III federal appellate courts. Although there has occasionally been talk about the possibility of creating a specialized antitrust court, the experience with the specialized patent court (the

Court of Appeals for the Federal Circuit) has been mixed and a specialized antitrust court is nowhere on the horizon.

Similarly, review from European Commission decisions are to the General Court and then to the CJEU, neither of which is a specialized antitrust court. The General Court and CJEU may be expected to acquire more antitrust expertise than their sister courts in the US since a higher percentage of their docket is probably competition law cases, but they are still not antitrust specialists.

A number of jurisdictions, however, have experimented with specialized antitrust courts. The Canada Competition Tribunal, created in 1986, is one of the oldest specialized antitrust tribunals. The Tribunal is composed of up to six judicial members appointed from among the judges of the Canadian Federal Court and not more than eight lay members. Appeals from the Competition Tribunal are to the Federal Court of Appeal and from there to the Canadian Supreme Court. Other jurisdictions with specialized antitrust courts include the UK, China, India, and South Africa.

As the complexity of antitrust increases, perhaps we should expect that more jurisdictions will migrate toward specialized antitrust courts. One of the major issues that many developing countries face in implementing an effective antitrust system is a lack of training and economic sophistication in the judiciary. Creating an antitrust court can alleviate some of these concerns, although there may be constitutional or administrative law reasons why this may be difficult or impossible in some jurisdictions.

On the other hand, there are reasons to be skeptical that specialized antitrust courts are better than generalist courts. Generalist courts may be better at seeing the big picture of economic and social consequences of particular decisions, more deferential to agency decision-makers, and less likely to develop "tunnel vision." With the development of more specialized antitrust courts around the world, it will be interesting to compare the performance of generalist and specialized judges and see what lessons can be drawn about their comparative performance.

D. FEDERALISM AND ENFORCEMENT BY MULTIPLE SOVEREIGNS

1. Division of Authority

An issue that arises in federal or quasi-federal systems like the US, Australia, Canada, and the EU is how best to divide authority between the national (or regional) authority and the states, territories, or Member States. The US follows a model of essentially concurrent and equal authority for the federal government (whether FTC or Department of Justice) and the states to bring antitrust enforcement actions. Usually, the state Attorneys General have focused on local or regional issues whereas the Federal Government has pursued large matters of national importance.

The US system has occasionally generated some friction between the federal and state governments. The one high-profile case where some commentators perceived such friction was the *Microsoft* case. In addition to the Department of Justice, a number of states participated in the case as plaintiffs. Judge Richard Posner, who acted as a mediator in the case, complained afterwards that the state Attorneys General were an obstacle to settling the case and proposed a federal statute that would allow the Justice Department to settle cases in a way that would preempt state hold-outs. Needless to say, Judge Posner's proposal generated some controversy. The state antitrust personnel that participated in *Microsoft* have a very different view of their role in the case, viewing their own contributions as important to the development of the legal theories and the evidence and denying that there was friction between federal and state personnel.

The EU has faced its own "federalism" issues." Like the US, the EU system includes a trans-state (indeed, trans-national) authority, the European Commission, trans-state (indeed, trans-national) courts, General Court and CJEU, and national competition authorities and courts in each state. The relationships between these different institutions on a European and national level naturally create complex legal, political, and regulatory policy issues.

One of the major moves in the EU in recent years has been an effort to decentralize competition law decision making and grant increased authority and responsibility to national competition authorities and courts. This has particularly been manifested with respect to the treatment of anticompetitive agreements—what in the US would be analyzed under Section 1 of the Sherman Act and what in the EU is analyzed under Article 101 of the TFEU. Article 101 sets forth a two-stage process for assessing possible anticompetitive effects of such agreements. Article 101(1) catches agreements that prevent, restrict, or distort competition. Article 101(2) declares such agreements void. Article 101(3) states that Article 101(1) may be declared inapplicable [later translated as "an exemption may be given"] if four conditions are met. In essence, the conditions are that the agreement must be on balance procompetitive, efficient or technologically progressive, that competition must be restrained no more than necessary to fulfill these objectives, and consumers must get a fair share of these benefits.

Article 101 needed legislative implementation, and was implemented in 1962 by Regulation 17, which declared that the Commission alone could give Article 101(3) exemptions. Regulation 17 set out a structure for clearing and exempting agreements. Under this structure, if parties notified an agreement, the provision declaring the agreement void was stayed until the Commission ruled on the entitlement to the exemption.

The centralized notification/exemption system required a huge amount of paperwork and analysis, but the process was important for the young European Community. The Competition Directorate General had to get acquainted with the types of restraints business imposed, and to develop policies and rules based on the facts. By the 1990s, however, the balance had shifted. The paperwork and time and effort it took to analyze the thousands of filed agreements were extraordinary, and the workload increased geometrically with the admission of new accession states. Delays were long. The bureaucratic and reactive work drained resources, to the marginalization of major proactive work. Moreover, the structure of the system had resulted in highly rigid and regulatory rules that were out of step with increasingly well accepted modes of economic analysis.

In 2003, the Commission undertook a program of modernization and adopted Council Regulation (EC) No 1/2003. Regulation 1/2003 is printed in Appendix 3. The introduction of Regulation 1 was a dramatic event. It reflected significant procedural reform whereby powers would devolve to Member States but Member States would be obliged to carry out EU law and policy, and a new network of national authorities, combined with continuing sharing of information about all relevant national court judgments, would assure consistency and coherence.

The core of Regulation 1 was the abolition of the requirement that agreements that fall within Article 101(1) must be notified. It makes Article 101(3) directly effective, so that national competition authorities and national courts, as well as the Commission, may decide whether agreements fulfill the requirements of Article 101(3). This sharing of power lightens the Commission's workload, giving it more time to consider more serious restraints of Union-wide interest.

Regulation 1 established the following procedures, among others:

(1) Article 3 imposes two fundamental obligations on the courts and competition authorities of the Member States, to preserve the realm of EU law. First, where national competition law is applied to agreements and

abusive practices that may affect trade between Member States, Article 3(1) imposes the obligation on national authorities and courts to apply Articles 101 and/or 102 concurrently with the national law. Second, Article 3(2) obliges the competition authorities and courts of the Member States not to invoke national law to prohibit agreements or concerted practices that may affect trade between Member States but that are not prohibited by Community competition law. Member States may, however, be more aggressive than Article 102 in applying national laws against abuse of dominance.

(2) The Commission retains the ability to deal with any case affecting trade between Member States, thereby relieving national authorities of their competence to apply EU law in a particular case. In addition, Article 10 equips the Commission with the sole power to adopt, on its own initiative and when the Community public interest so requires, ex ante decisions finding that a particular agreement or practice does not infringe Articles 101 or 102. An exercise of Article 10 power precludes national courts and competition authorities from adopting decisions in the same case that would run counter to the Commission's decision.

(3) In order to ensure the consistent application of EU competition law throughout the Community, Regulation 1 creates mechanisms for information sharing and consultation among national competition authorities and the center through the creation of the European Competition Network (ECN)—a robust and well-functioning network that has encouraged cooperation in handling cases, facilitated case allocation, and produced soft convergence of national laws and procedures. Also, national courts are entitled to ask the Commission for its support in the application of Articles 101 and 102, and both national competition authorities and the Commission are empowered to make amicus curiae submissions before the national courts. The Commission is entitled to publish opinions on any particular novel or unresolved questions for the application of Article 101 or 102.

Read Regulation 1/2003 in Appendix 3. Consider its virtues in terms of devolution, empowerment, shared deliberation, cross-fertilization, coherence, and networking. What lessons might

Regulation 1 hold for other communities of nations facing multiple and sometimes overlapping systems of law? Although the EU has now withdrawn the notification and exemption system, a large number of jurisdictions have adopted the procedural framework and substance of EU law, and a number of notification and exemption systems remain in place.

Regulation 1/2003's devolution of enforcement authority required new efforts to ensure homogenous application of Articles 101 and 102 TFEU by separate national competition authorities. As noted the ECN serves this function by creating a framework for competition authorities to exchange information and cooperate on cases. In order to ensure successful interaction at the right personnel level, the ECN has created a variety of working groups. There is a Heads of Authorities' working group for the highest level policy-making, topical expertise working groups (101, 102, Cartels, Vertical Mergers, Fines, Chief Economists, Cooperation and Due Process, Digital Investigations and AI, International, and Advocacy & Communication), and sectoral working groups (Basic Industries & Raw Materials, Energy, Environment, Digital/DMA, Food & FMCG, Pharmaceuticals, Banking and Financial Services, Insurance, Sports, Telecommunications, and Transportation). In many significant cases, national competition authorities have used these processes successfully to coordinate and strengthen their enforcement efforts. As noted in Chapter 4, for example, multiple member states took action to prevent anticompetitive restrictions in the hotel booking sector. Information about these efforts was shared through the ECN.

By most accounts, the ECN has been successful at achieving a high degree of homogeneity and cooperation among national competition authorities in the wake of 1/2003. To further improve cooperation within the ECN and level the enforcement playing field across the EU, a dedicated instrument known as the "ECN+ Directive" was adopted in 2019. This Directive 2019/1 aims to ensure that national competition authorities have the appropriate enforcement means and tools in order to bring about a genuine common competition enforcement area across the EU. To that end, the ECN+ Directive endowed national competition authorities with a minimum set of independence guarantees and of investigative, decision-making, and fining powers, while also harmonizing leniency programs and enhancing cooperation between national competition authorities. By the end of 2024, all Member States but one had transposed the ECN+ Directive's main provisions.

2. Competition Law Preemption of Anticompetitive Local Regulations

One set of issues that often come up in federal systems is whether anticompetitive regulations adopted by local or national governments should be preempted by competition law principles. The US and the EU have developed extensive bodies of law about when state or national laws or regulatory schemes are repugnant to federal or European competition law norms. The issues are complicated, and we will not try to deal with them substantively here. We dealt with aspects of these issues in Chapter 7 on the State.

Focusing on the institutional aspects, it may be of interest to briefly survey a model that was successfully implemented by the Australian Government between 1994 and 2007. In 1994, the Australian government launched a National Competition Policy ("NCP") in order to remedy a relative decline in Australia's economic performance. The NCP committed Australia to a national policy of competition as the key driver of economic performance. A Competition Principles Agreement of 1996 between the federal and state governments contained a "guiding legislative principle" that competition should not be restricted unless the restriction creates some net public benefit that could not be achieved in some way less restrictive of competition. This is called the competitive neutrality principle.

Acting in tandem with the states and territories, the government identified 1,800 pieces of legislation extending across a range of industries and sectors, for competition impact review. The competitive impact reviews were to be undertaken by the governments and bureaucracies of the states and territories. A federal entity—the National Competition Council ("NCC") was assigned a supervisory and consolidating function with respect to the competition impact review effort. The NCC published detailed guidelines for review of the legislation. It listed the following as examples of the types of restrictions that may restrict competition: legislatively created monopolies to provide or operate infrastructure, marketing schemes (particularly in agriculture) or special government-backed initiatives; licensing schemes which restrict entry to particular businesses such as taxi licenses and airline agreements; regulations which restrict entry to particular professions such as the medical profession; quota restrictions to preserve natural resources; regulations which specify strict technical standards for products or services; and administratively determined pricing arrangements for nominated goods and services. The guidelines called for three principal phases of review: (1)

establishment of review, determining scope and structure, appointing the review team, ascertaining terms of reference, and ensuring stakeholder involvement; (2) undertaking the review, by clarifying objectives, identifying any restrictions, analyzing costs and benefits, and reviewing alternatives; and (3) implementing the review and recommendations, by promulgating changes to the legislation, ensuring adequate means to facilitate the adjustment, and making a public explanation of the changes.

During the course of the competitive impact review, the states and territories reported their findings and actions to the NCC. The NCC, in turn, consolidated and reviewed the information reported by the states and territories and transmitted the information to the Ministry of the Treasury. An important aspect of the competition review framework was that the federal government committed to make specified payments to the states and territories if they met certain benchmark goals in regulatory reform. The NCC made recommendations to the Treasury about whether the relevant goals had been met and the Treasury made final decisions about deductions from the incentive payments for unmet goals.

The NCP review and incentive payment process ended in the 2005–2006 period. Overall, however, the NCP process appears to have been a success. In February of 2005, the Australian Productivity Commission (another independent commission) released a report largely praising the effect of the NCP. Among the Commission's findings were that the NCP contributed to the productivity surge that underpinned 13 years of consecutive economic growth and associated strong growth in household incomes, directly reduced the prices of goods and services such as electricity and milk, stimulated business innovation, customer responsiveness, and choice, and helped meet some environmental goals, including the more efficient use of water. One particular area of success was in agricultural marketing. Examples include Queensland ending its export marketing monopoly for barley; Victoria deregulating its monopoly barley marketing arrangements; Western Australia and Tasmania removing supply and marketing restrictions on eggs; Western Australia and South Australia removing entry and pricing restrictions on bulk handling; and all jurisdictions removing centralized price fixing for poultry growing services. PRODUCT COMMISSION, REVIEW OF NATIONAL COMPETITION POLICY REFORMS, PRODUCTIVITY COMMISSION INQUIRY REPORT, NO. 33, February 2005 (Austl.).

The Australian example is interesting because it shows how much progress can be made to increase the competitiveness of markets in a federal system when the federal and local governments commit themselves to a reform process and the federal government doles out payments to the local governments as incentives to achieve specified goals. Instead of using a "stick" to coerce local adherence to national competition norms, Australia very successfully relied on a "carrot" approach instead. You have seen other examples in 7.

The need for national competition law to play a role in preempting anticompetitive local regulations is particularly acute in countries that are transitioning from state-owned and operated to market economies. However, there are often very significant impediments to antitrust law playing this role. For example, China's Anti-Monopoly Law (AML) prohibits abuse of "administrative powers to restrict competition." Administrative abuses include, and the law targets, measures of provincial and local governments that discriminate against and burden the flow of goods from one province or locality into another. The enforcement powers against these abuses are weak, but the competition authorities have had some modest success in rolling back abuses. The law does not exclude from its coverage state-owned enterprises, but the most important and dominant SOEs are in strategic sectors. Enterprises in strategic sectors remain under the supervision of the Chinese state and in some cases they seem as a practical matter to be immune from enforcement by the antitrust authorities.

In June 2016, China's State Council issued its *Opinions of the State Council on Establishing a Fair Competition Review System During the Development of Market-oriented Review System*. The Fair Competition Review System ("FCRS") is designed to prevent actions by state agencies that unduly distort competition. FCRS has three facets: (i) public education and awareness campaigns; (ii) development of implementation regulations and mechanisms; and (iii) FCRS reviews of state regulations. Early indications suggest that the measure could be successful in limiting governmental distortions of competition.

E. MARKET STUDIES

Many competition authorities have statutory power to conduct market studies that may inform their future enforcement actions, new legislation, regulation, or deregulation, or other aspects of public policy. For instance, the United States Federal Trade Commission has authority "to gather and compile information concerning, and to investigate from time to time the organization, business, conduct, practices, and management of any person, partnership, or corporation engaged in or whose business affects commerce." Importantly, the Commission can use compulsory process (i.e., subpoenas) to gather information for these market studies. The

Commission has used these Section 6(b) investigative powers to study various significant competition issues and lay the groundwork for future action. For example, in 2021 the Commission staff reported findings from a 6(b) study of acquisition activities by Alphabet Inc., Amazon.com, Inc., Apple Inc., Facebook, Inc., and Microsoft Corp. between Jan. 1, 2010 and Dec. 31, 2019. The staff reported on 616 transactions, many of which did not meet the reporting requirements under the Hart Scott Rodino Act, and hence escaped ex ante regulatory review. FTC Chair Lina Khan remarked, "this study underscores the need for us to closely examine reporting requirements under the Hart-Scott-Rodino Act and to identify areas where the FTC may have created loopholes that are unjustifiably enabling deals to fly under the radar." https://www.ftc.gov/system/files/documents/public_statements/1596332/remarks_of_chair_lina_m_khan_regarding_non-hsr_reported_acquisitions_by_select_technology_platforms.pdf.

The European Commission has similar powers to conduct market studies, and they need not be directly tied to competition or consumer protection issues as the FTC's studies should be. For example, since 2013, the Commission has been tracking the progression of the "European Data Economy" and issuing a series of reports. It has highlighted "big data's disruptive potential and highlighted the socio-economic importance of innovative data-driven transformative processes," and noted that "[t]he emergence of Artificial Intelligence tools and services powered by data also underlines the crucial role of data." https://digital-strategy.ec.europa.eu/en/library/european-data-market-study-2024-2026.

A 2020 OECD report highlights the importance of market studies to competition authority work, particularly as to dynamic markets where novel competition issues may arise: "Market studies can play a key preventive role in identifying and diagnosing emerging competition issues by exploring the different drivers and clarifying the options available to tackle them from a competition policy, enforcement, regulatory, or other policy perspective. As a result, market studies can initiate solutions to mitigate consumer harm before it becomes significant, promote further competition, and reduce the likelihood of (or opportunities) for violations of competition rules." OECD (2020), Using market studies to tackle emerging competition issues, https://www.oecd.org/en/topics/competition.html.

F. PRIVATE ENFORCEMENT

In most jurisdictions, antitrust enforcement largely means enforcement by the government—usually a competition commission or public prosecutor. In some jurisdictions, injured persons can sue for compensation only if the government first gets a judgment or order. In the US, however, enforcement has come to be as much or more a private enterprise as a governmental one. Indeed, in raw numerical terms, private lawsuits (those initiated by private plaintiffs) far outnumber public ones. In the federal courts, there are roughly 800–1000 new private lawsuits filed every year compared to fewer than 80 antitrust actions by the Department of Justice Antitrust Division and Federal Trade Commission. The incidence of case filings can be misleading, since the antitrust agencies are involved in many enforcement activities that do not result in the filing of a lawsuit and some private actions are follow-ons to government cases or strategic counterclaims in contract or intellectual property suits. Still, it is clear that private enforcement is an essential part of the US enforcement system. In recent years, almost all of the Supreme Court's antitrust decisions have involved only private parties.

Should the rest of the world follow the US example and open up their enforcement system to private litigants? It's a complicated question. The US private antitrust litigation system is part of a much larger system of private enforcement of law. Culturally, the US has tended to be individualistic, decentralized, and adversarial in its view of rights and wrongs, thus allowing many aspects of society to be governed by private litigation rather than governmental regulation. The US has far more advanced and complex systems and institutions of private litigation than do most other countries. Even if other countries wanted to follow the US model, building the necessary systems would take time.

Still, in many countries there is a growing sense that the government should not be the only antitrust enforcer and that an effective system of private enforcement is necessary for detection and deterrence and is important for compensation. Indeed, many countries have theoretically had a right of private enforcement for a long time, and the move now is to make the theoretical right a practical right.

Unlike in the US's federal system where private antitrust claims can be asserted in both state and federal court, in the EU system there is no procedural vehicle for injured parties to sue antitrust violators in a European court. Private enforcement can take place only within the courts of the Member States. However, European Union law requires that the Member States provide remedies for persons whose rights under EU law are violated. *See Marshall*, Case C–271/91, EU:C:1993:335. In the *Crehan* case, Case C–453/99, EU:C:2001:465, the European Court of Justice applied these principles to competition law: "*The full effectiveness of Article [101] of the Treaty and, in particular, the practical effect of the prohibition laid down in Article [101(1)] would be put at risk if it were not open to any individual to claim damages for loss caused to him by a contract or by conduct liable to restrict or distort competition*" (para. 26). The European Court of Justice further clarified that claiming damages for breach of the EU antitrust principles was indeed "*a right*" and went on to formulate a policy rationale in support of actions for damages before national courts inasmuch as they "*strengthen[. . .] the working of the Community competition rules and discourage[. . .] agreements or practices . . . liable to restrict or distort competition*".

However, European litigants have historically faced considerable obstacles to effect private redress for violations of the competition provisions of the TFEU. Among these are the absence of procedural rights enjoyed by US litigants. Collective redress mechanisms (such as class actions) are not generally available, contingency fee arrangements are often prohibited, discovery is unavailable or tightly controlled, and only single damages are allowed. In addition, many European jurisdictions follow the English rule on fee-shifting in which the loser pays the winner's attorney's fees. Such a rule can discourage the initiation of private litigation. Hence, a 2004 study commissioned by DG COMP on the conditions of claims for damages in case of infringement of EU competition rules famously concluded that "[t]*he picture that emerges . . . is one of astonishing diversity and total underdevelopment*", with a mere 28 damage awards identified in the contemporary judicial practice of national courts across the continent. Yet, twenty years later, that picture is unrecognizable due to a combination of (i) the formal recognition by Regulation 1/2003 of the full direct effect of Articles 101 and 102 TFEU and of the essential complementary role played by private enforcement in safeguarding competition and (ii) the adoption of a dedicated legal instrument, combined with soft law tools on the quantification of antitrust harms.

Indeed, on December 5, 2014, after a ten-year period of study and political engagement, a "Directive on Antitrust Damages Actions" (or "Damages Directive") became effective in the European Union. Compliance was required by the end of 2016 and by early 2019 all Member States had transposed it in domestic law. Because of the importance of the Directive, we include most of the document below.

Since the enactment of the Damages Directive, competition damages actions and, by extension, the private enforcement of EU competition law, have become much more widespread in the EU. The 2014–2019 period witnessed a fivefold increase in the number of cases brought annually before national courts from 50 to 239, while damages claims were filed in thirteen Member-States. These numbers have further increased since then, notably as a result of thousands of follow-on damages claims brought across the EU against members of the so-called "trucks cartel" that consisted of collusive arrangements on medium- and heavy-trucks pricing and gross price increases for over 15 years (see Case AT.39824—Trucks). In parallel, national courts have referred an increasing number of questions to the European Court of Justice on points of law relevant to competition damages actions, including on the determination of the competent courts and applicable law, on the interplay between public and private enforcement, and on the interpretation of substantive provisions of the Damages Directive.

DIRECTIVE 2014/104/EU OF THE EUROPEAN PARLIAMENT AND OF THE COUNCIL

of 26 November 2014 on certain rules governing actions for damages under national law for infringements of the competition law provisions of the Member States and of the European Union

(Text with EEA relevance)

[Preamble Omitted]

CHAPTER I

SUBJECT MATTER, SCOPE AND DEFINITIONS

Article 1

SUBJECT MATTER AND SCOPE

1. This Directive sets out certain rules necessary to ensure that anyone who has suffered harm caused by an infringement of competition law by an undertaking or by an association of undertakings can effectively exercise the right to claim full compensation for that harm from that undertaking or association. It sets out rules fostering undistorted competition in the internal market and removing obstacles to its proper functioning, by ensuring equivalent protection throughout the Union for anyone who has suffered such harm.

2. This Directive sets out rules coordinating the enforcement of the competition rules by competition authorities and the enforcement of those rules in damages actions before national courts.

Article 2

DEFINITIONS [OMITTED]

Article 3

RIGHT TO FULL COMPENSATION

1. Member States shall ensure that any natural or legal person who has suffered harm caused by an infringement of competition law is able to claim and to obtain full compensation for that harm.

2. Full compensation shall place a person who has suffered harm in the position in which that person would have been had the infringement of competition law not been committed. It shall therefore cover the right to compensation for actual loss and for loss of profit, plus the payment of interest.

3. Full compensation under this Directive shall not lead to overcompensation, whether by means of punitive, multiple or other types of damages.

Article 4

PRINCIPLES OF EFFECTIVENESS AND EQUIVALENCE

In accordance with the principle of effectiveness, Member States shall ensure that all national rules and procedures relating to the exercise of claims for damages are designed and applied in such a way that they do not render practically impossible or excessively difficult the exercise of the Union right to full compensation for harm caused by an infringement of competition law. In accordance with the principle of equivalence, national rules and procedures relating to actions for damages resulting from infringements of Article 101 or 102 TFEU shall not be less favourable to the alleged injured parties than those governing similar actions for damages resulting from infringements of national law.

CHAPTER II

DISCLOSURE OF EVIDENCE

Article 5

DISCLOSURE OF EVIDENCE

1. Member States shall ensure that in proceedings relating to an action for damages in the Union, upon request of a claimant who has presented a reasoned justification containing reasonably available facts and evidence sufficient to support the plausibility of its claim for damages, national courts are able to order the defendant or a

third party to disclose relevant evidence which lies in their control, subject to the conditions set out in this Chapter. Member States shall ensure that national courts are able, upon request of the defendant, to order the claimant or a third party to disclose relevant evidence.

This paragraph is without prejudice to the rights and obligations of national courts under Regulation (EC) No 1206/2001.

2. Member States shall ensure that national courts are able to order the disclosure of specified items of evidence or relevant categories of evidence circumscribed as precisely and as narrowly as possible on the basis of reasonably available facts in the reasoned justification.

3. Member States shall ensure that national courts limit the disclosure of evidence to that which is proportionate. In determining whether any disclosure requested by a party is proportionate, national courts shall consider the legitimate interests of all parties and third parties concerned. They shall, in particular, consider:

(a) the extent to which the claim or defence is supported by available facts and evidence justifying the request to disclose evidence;

(b) the scope and cost of disclosure, especially for any third parties concerned, including preventing non-specific searches for information which is unlikely to be of relevance for the parties in the procedure;

(c) whether the evidence the disclosure of which is sought contains confidential information, especially concerning any third parties, and what arrangements are in place for protecting such confidential information.

4. Member States shall ensure that national courts have the power to order the disclosure of evidence containing confidential information where they consider it relevant to the action for damages. Member States shall ensure that, when ordering the disclosure of such information, national courts have at their disposal effective measures to protect such information.

5. The interest of undertakings to avoid actions for damages following an infringement of competition law shall not constitute an interest that warrants protection.

6. Member States shall ensure that national courts give full effect to applicable legal professional privilege under Union or national law when ordering the disclosure of evidence.

7. Member States shall ensure that those from whom disclosure is sought are provided with an opportunity to be heard before a national court orders disclosure under this Article.

8. Without prejudice to paragraphs 4 and 7 and to Article 6, this Article shall not prevent Member States from maintaining or introducing rules which would lead to wider disclosure of evidence.

Article 6

DISCLOSURE OF EVIDENCE INCLUDED IN THE FILE OF A COMPETITION AUTHORITY

1. Member States shall ensure that, for the purpose of actions for damages, where national courts order the disclosure of evidence included in the file of a competition authority, this Article applies in addition to Article 5.

2. This Article is without prejudice to the rules and practices on public access to documents under Regulation (EC) No 1049/2001.

3. This Article is without prejudice to the rules and practices under Union or national law on the protection of internal documents of competition authorities and of correspondence between competition authorities.

4. When assessing, in accordance with Article 5(3), the proportionality of an order to disclose information, national courts shall, in addition, consider the following:

(a) whether the request has been formulated specifically with regard to the nature, subject matter or contents of documents submitted to a competition authority or held in the file thereof, rather than by a non-specific application concerning documents submitted to a competition authority;

(b) whether the party requesting disclosure is doing so in relation to an action for damages before a national court; and

(c) in relation to paragraphs 5 and 10, or upon request of a competition authority pursuant to paragraph 11, the need to safeguard the effectiveness of the public enforcement of competition law.

5. National courts may order the disclosure of the following categories of evidence only after a competition authority, by adopting a decision or otherwise, has closed its proceedings:

(a) information that was prepared by a natural or legal person specifically for the proceedings of a competition authority;

(b) information that the competition authority has drawn up and sent to the parties in the course of its proceedings; and

(c) settlement submissions that have been withdrawn.

6. Member States shall ensure that, for the purpose of actions for damages, national courts cannot at any time order a party or a third party to disclose any of the following categories of evidence:

(a) leniency statements; and

(b) settlement submissions.

7. A claimant may present a reasoned request that a national court access the evidence referred to in point (a) or (b) of paragraph 6 for the sole purpose of ensuring that their contents correspond to the definitions in points (16) and (18) of Article 2. In that assessment, national courts may request assistance only from the competent competition authority. The authors of the evidence in question may also have the possibility to be heard. In no case shall the national court permit other parties or third parties access to that evidence.

8. If only parts of the evidence requested are covered by paragraph 6, the remaining parts thereof shall, depending on the category under which they fall, be released in accordance with the relevant paragraphs of this Article.

9. The disclosure of evidence in the file of a competition authority that does not fall into any of the categories listed in this Article may be ordered in actions for damages at any time, without prejudice to this Article.

10. Member States shall ensure that national courts request the disclosure from a competition authority of evidence included in its file only where no party or third party is reasonably able to provide that evidence.

11. To the extent that a competition authority is willing to state its views on the proportionality of disclosure requests, it may, acting on its own initiative, submit observations to the national court before which a disclosure order is sought.

Article 7

LIMITS ON THE USE OF EVIDENCE OBTAINED SOLELY THROUGH ACCESS TO THE FILE OF A COMPETITION AUTHORITY

1. Member States shall ensure that evidence in the categories listed in Article 6(6) which is obtained by a natural or legal person solely through access to the file of a competition authority is either deemed to be inadmissible in actions for damages or is otherwise protected under the applicable national rules to ensure the full effect of the limits on the disclosure of evidence set out in Article 6.

2. Member States shall ensure that, until a competition authority has closed its proceedings by adopting a decision or otherwise, evidence in the categories listed in Article 6(5) which is obtained by a natural or legal person solely through access to the file of that competition authority is either deemed to be inadmissible in actions for damages or is otherwise protected under the applicable national rules to ensure the full effect of the limits on the disclosure of evidence set out in Article 6.

3. Member States shall ensure that evidence which is obtained by a natural or legal person solely through access to the file of a competition authority and which does not fall under paragraph 1 or 2, can be used in an action for damages only by that person or by a natural or legal person that succeeded to that person's rights, including a person that acquired that person's claim.

Article 8

PENALTIES

1. Member States shall ensure that national courts are able effectively to impose penalties on parties, third parties and their legal representatives in the event of any of the following:

(a) their failure or refusal to comply with the disclosure order of any national court;

(b) their destruction of relevant evidence;

(c) their failure or refusal to comply with the obligations imposed by a national court order protecting confidential information;

(d) their breach of the limits on the use of evidence provided for in this Chapter.

2. Member States shall ensure that the penalties that can be imposed by national courts are effective, proportionate and

dissuasive. The penalties available to national courts shall include, with regard to the behaviour of a party to proceedings for an action for damages, the possibility to draw adverse inferences, such as presuming the relevant issue to be proven or dismissing claims and defences in whole or in part, and the possibility to order the payment of costs.

CHAPTER III

EFFECT OF NATIONAL DECISIONS, LIMITATION PERIODS, JOINT AND SEVERAL LIABILITY

Article 9

EFFECT OF NATIONAL DECISIONS

1. Member States shall ensure that an infringement of competition law found by a final decision of a national competition authority or by a review court is deemed to be irrefutably established for the purposes of an action for damages brought before their national courts under Article 101 or 102 TFEU or under national competition law.

2. Member States shall ensure that where a final decision referred to in paragraph 1 is taken in another Member State, that final decision may, in accordance with national law, be presented before their national courts as at least prima facie evidence that an infringement of competition law has occurred and, as appropriate, may be assessed along with any other evidence adduced by the parties.

3. This Article is without prejudice to the rights and obligations of national courts under Article 267 TFEU.

Article 10

LIMITATION PERIODS

1. Member States shall, in accordance with this Article, lay down rules applicable to limitation periods for bringing actions for damages. Those rules shall determine when the limitation period begins to run, the duration thereof and the circumstances under which it is interrupted or suspended.

2. Limitation periods shall not begin to run before the infringement of competition law has ceased and the claimant knows, or can reasonably be expected to know:

(a) of the behaviour and the fact that it constitutes an infringement of competition law;

(b) of the fact that the infringement of competition law caused harm to it; and

(c) the identity of the infringer.

3. Member States shall ensure that the limitation periods for bringing actions for damages are at least five years.

4. Member States shall ensure that a limitation period is suspended or, depending on national law, interrupted, if a competition authority takes action for the purpose of the investigation or its proceedings in respect of an infringement of competition law to which the action for damages relates. The suspension shall end at the earliest one year after the infringement decision has become final or after the proceedings are otherwise terminated.

Article 11

JOINT AND SEVERAL LIABILITY

1. Member States shall ensure that undertakings which have infringed competition law through joint behaviour are jointly and severally liable for the harm caused by the infringement of competition law; with the effect that each of those undertakings is bound to compensate for the harm in full, and the injured party has the right to require full compensation from any of them until he has been fully compensated.

2. By way of derogation from paragraph 1, Member States shall ensure that, without prejudice to the right of full compensation as laid down in Article 3, where the infringer is a small or medium-sized enterprise (SME) as defined in Commission Recommendation 2003/361/EC (8), the infringer is liable only to its own direct and indirect purchasers where:

(a) its market share in the relevant market was below 5 % at any time during the infringement of competition law; and

(b) the application of the normal rules of joint and several liability would irretrievably jeopardise its economic viability and cause its assets to lose all their value.

3. The derogation laid down in paragraph 2 shall not apply where:

(a) the SME has led the infringement of competition law or has coerced other undertakings to participate therein; or

(b) the SME has previously been found to have infringed competition law.

4. By way of derogation from paragraph 1, Member States shall ensure that an immunity recipient is jointly and severally liable as follows:

(a) to its direct or indirect purchasers or providers; and

(b) to other injured parties only where full compensation cannot be obtained from the other undertakings that were involved in the same infringement of competition law.

Member States shall ensure that any limitation period applicable to cases under this paragraph is reasonable and sufficient to allow injured parties to bring such actions.

5. Member States shall ensure that an infringer may recover a contribution from any other infringer, the amount of which shall be determined in the light of their relative responsibility for the harm caused by the infringement of competition law. The amount of contribution of an infringer which has been granted immunity from fines under a leniency programme shall not exceed the amount of the harm it caused to its own direct or indirect purchasers or providers.

6. Member States shall ensure that, to the extent the infringement of competition law caused harm to injured parties other than the direct or indirect purchasers or providers of the infringers, the amount of any contribution from an immunity recipient to other infringers shall be determined in the light of its relative responsibility for that harm.

CHAPTER IV

THE PASSING-ON OF OVERCHARGES

Article 12

PASSING-ON OF OVERCHARGES AND THE RIGHT TO FULL COMPENSATION

1. To ensure the full effectiveness of the right to full compensation as laid down in Article 3, Member States shall ensure that, in accordance with the rules laid down in this Chapter, compensation of harm can be claimed by anyone who suffered it, irrespective of whether they are direct or indirect purchasers from an infringer, and that compensation of harm exceeding that caused by the infringement of competition law to the claimant, as well as the absence of liability of the infringer, are avoided.

2. In order to avoid overcompensation, Member States shall lay down procedural rules appropriate to ensure that compensation for actual loss at any level of the supply chain does not exceed the overcharge harm suffered at that level.

3. This Chapter shall be without prejudice to the right of an injured party to claim and obtain compensation for loss of profits due to a full or partial passing-on of the overcharge.

4. Member States shall ensure that the rules laid down in this Chapter apply accordingly where the infringement of competition law relates to a supply to the infringer.

5. Member States shall ensure that the national courts have the power to estimate, in accordance with national procedures, the share of any overcharge that was passed on.

Article 13

PASSING-ON DEFENCE

Member States shall ensure that the defendant in an action for damages can invoke as a defence against a claim for damages the fact that the claimant passed on the whole or part of the overcharge resulting from the infringement of competition law. The burden of proving that the overcharge was passed on shall be on the defendant, who may reasonably require disclosure from the claimant or from third parties.

Article 14

INDIRECT PURCHASERS

1. Member States shall ensure that, where in an action for damages the existence of a claim for damages or the amount of compensation to be awarded depends on whether, or to what degree, an overcharge was passed on to the claimant, taking into account the commercial practice that price increases are passed on down the supply chain, the burden of proving the existence and scope of such a passing-on shall rest with the claimant, who may reasonably require disclosure from the defendant or from third parties.

2. In the situation referred to in paragraph 1, the indirect purchaser shall be deemed to have proven that a passing-on to that indirect purchaser occurred where that indirect purchaser has shown that:

(a) the defendant has committed an infringement of competition law;

(b) the infringement of competition law has resulted in an overcharge for the direct purchaser of the defendant; and

(c) the indirect purchaser has purchased the goods or services that were the object of the infringement of competition law, or has purchased goods or services derived from or containing them.

This paragraph shall not apply where the defendant can demonstrate credibly to the satisfaction of the court that the overcharge was not, or was not entirely, passed on to the indirect purchaser.

Article 15

ACTIONS FOR DAMAGES BY CLAIMANTS FROM DIFFERENT LEVELS IN THE SUPPLY CHAIN

1. To avoid that actions for damages by claimants from different levels in the supply chain lead to a multiple liability or to an absence of liability of the infringer, Member States shall ensure that in assessing whether the burden of proof resulting from the application of Articles 13 and 14 is satisfied, national courts seized of an action for damages are able, by means available under Union or national law, to take due account of any of the following:

(a) actions for damages that are related to the same infringement of competition law, but that are brought by claimants from other levels in the supply chain;

(b) judgments resulting from actions for damages as referred to in point (a);

(c) relevant information in the public domain resulting from the public enforcement of competition law.

2. This Article shall be without prejudice to the rights and obligations of national courts under Article 30 of Regulation (EU) No 1215/2012.

Article 16

GUIDELINES FOR NATIONAL COURTS

The Commission shall issue guidelines for national courts on how to estimate the share of the overcharge which was passed on to the indirect purchaser.

CHAPTER V

QUANTIFICATION OF HARM

Article 17

QUANTIFICATION OF HARM

1. Member States shall ensure that neither the burden nor the standard of proof required for the quantification of harm renders the exercise of the right to damages practically impossible or excessively difficult. Member States shall ensure that the national courts are empowered, in accordance with national procedures, to estimate the amount of harm if it is established that a claimant suffered harm but it is practically impossible or excessively difficult precisely to quantify the harm suffered on the basis of the evidence available.

2. It shall be presumed that cartel infringements cause harm. The infringer shall have the right to rebut that presumption.

3. Member States shall ensure that, in proceedings relating to an action for damages, a national competition authority may, upon request of a national court, assist that national court with respect to the determination of the quantum of damages where that national competition authority considers such assistance to be appropriate.

CHAPTER VI

CONSENSUAL DISPUTE RESOLUTION

Article 18

SUSPENSIVE AND OTHER EFFECTS OF CONSENSUAL DISPUTE RESOLUTION

1. Member States shall ensure that the limitation period for bringing an action for damages is suspended for the duration of any consensual dispute resolution process. The suspension of the limitation period shall apply only with regard to those parties that are or that were involved or represented in the consensual dispute resolution.

2. Without prejudice to provisions of national law in matters of arbitration, Member States shall ensure that national courts seized of an action for damages may suspend their proceedings for up to two years where the parties thereto are involved in consensual dispute resolution concerning the claim covered by that action for damages.

3. A competition authority may consider compensation paid as a result of a consensual settlement and prior to its decision imposing a fine to be a mitigating factor.

Article 19

EFFECT OF CONSENSUAL SETTLEMENTS ON SUBSEQUENT ACTIONS FOR DAMAGES

1. Member States shall ensure that, following a consensual settlement, the claim of the settling injured party is reduced by the settling co-infringer's share of the harm that the infringement of competition law inflicted upon the injured party.

2. Any remaining claim of the settling injured party shall be exercised only against non-settling co-infringers. Non-settling co-infringers shall not be permitted to recover contribution for the remaining claim from the settling co-infringer.

3. By way of derogation from paragraph 2, Member States shall ensure that where the non-settling co-infringers cannot pay the damages that correspond to the remaining claim of the settling injured party, the settling injured party may exercise the remaining claim against the settling co-infringer.

The derogation referred to in the first subparagraph may be expressly excluded under the terms of the consensual settlement.

4. When determining the amount of contribution that a co-infringer may recover from any other co-infringer in accordance with their relative responsibility for the harm caused by the infringement of competition law, national courts shall take due account of any damages paid pursuant to a prior consensual settlement involving the relevant co-infringer.

Notes and Questions

1. The EU Damages Directive innovates in many respects but also rejects US law in a number of important ways. Among others, it rejects treble or punitive damages (although it allows for prejudgment interest), allows for standing by indirect purchasers, the pass-on defense (i.e., that a particular plaintiff's damages should be reduced because that plaintiff passed on some of the monopoly overcharge to downstream purchasers), and permits a right of contribution against co-defendants. US law rejects these positions. *See* Hanover Shoe, Inc. v. United Shoe Machinery Corp., 392 U.S. 481 (1968) (rejected pass-on defense); Illinois Brick Co. v. Illinois, 431 U.S. 720 (1977) (rejecting indirect purchaser standing); Texas Indus., Inc. v. Radcliff Mat., Inc., 451 U.S. 630 (1981) (rejecting right of contribution). One way to understand these differences is based on the differing objectives of private enforcement in the two systems. Article 2 of the Damages Directive places compensation of injured parties as the overriding objective of private enforcement in Europe. By contrast, US law tends to treat private litigants as "private attorneys general" who serve the public interest in deterrence. Is it

possible for a private litigation system to serve both the compensation and deterrence objectives simultaneously, or must trade-off decisions be made? If so, then which objective should be prioritized?

2. How much weight should other jurisdictions place on the American experience with private enforcement? In Chadha v. Bayer Inc. (2003), 63 O.R. (3d) (C.A.), leave to appeal refused [2003] S.C.C.A. No 106, the Ontario Court of Appeal stated the following: "[W]hile the decisions of the Supreme Court of the United States [particularly *Hanover Shoe* (no pass-on defense) and *Illinois Brick* (no indirect purchaser standing)] deserve serious consideration by this court, they plainly are not binding. Moreover, it appears that the two decisions relied on are based significantly upon policy considerations relating to the enforcement of American antitrust law. These policy considerations may well differ from the values underlying Canadian competition law. One need look no further than the treble damages remedy which played a significant role in the Supreme Court decisions referred to above." On September 28, 2009, the Ontario Superior Court of Justice issued the first decision by a Canadian court in a contested case certifying a price-fixing class action on behalf of a class including indirect purchasers. In Irving Paper Limited et al. v. Atofina Chemicals Inc., [2009] O.J. No. 4021. Courts in British Columbia and other Canadian provinces have refused similar requests, influenced in part by the US precedents. *See, e.g.*, Pro-Sys Consultants Ltd. v. Infineon Technologies AG, 2008 BCSC 575.

3. Is it a good idea to limit private suits to only those cases in which the government has already established liability in a private suit? Certainly, this diminishes the amount of frivolous litigation. But it also means that private enforcement will not be a robust addition to public enforcement in ferreting out wrong-doing, serving as a counterweight to politically motivated refusals to bring meritorious cases, or bringing additional resources to antitrust enforcement. In 2005, South Korea legislatively abolished its requirement that a prior suit by the Korea Fair Trade Commission (KFTC) must be brought to a successful conclusion before a private suit could be brought and is currently considering other measures to liberalize private enforcement. Private antitrust filings in Korea appear to be growing, with up to 30 cases pending in recent years. COMPETITION POLICY INTERNATIONAL, OVERVIEW OF CURRENT ANTITRUST ENFORCEMENT IN KOREA (2014), https://www.competitionpolicyinternational.com/overview-of-current-antitrust-enforcement-in-korea/.

Private Enforcement in China and Chile: A Comparative Note

Chile is one of the most active competition law jurisdictions in Latin America. As in much of the world, private antitrust has been slowly developing in Chile in recent years. *See generally* Nicolás Lewin & Francisco Borquez, *The Development of Private Enforcement Regarding*

Damages Actions in Chile (CPI Antitrust Chronicle, January 2016). Private litigants seeking damages typically await a final decision in the Chilean Competition Defense Tribunal ("TDLC")—Chile's specialized antitrust court, in favor of the National Economic Prosecutor's Office ("FNE") before pressing their damages claim in a civil court as a follow-on action. However, as of this writing there is a division of authority among the lower Chilean courts as to whether a stand-alone action in civil court can be brought. Consumer associations have begun to test the possibility of stand-alone cases.

The Chilean competition statute does not provide directly for class actions, but class actions are allowed under the consumer protection act, and consumers have been allowed to use the consumer protection act to seek damages for violations of the competition act. Chilean courts have not yet resolved the possibility of the pass-on defense and direct purchaser rules, although this has been subject to intensive academic commentary and among the Chilean competition law bar.

Chile does not allow for punitive damages or damages multipliers, and attorney fee shifting is only allowed in rare cases. All defendants are jointly and severally liable and contribution is allowed. The statute of limitations for competition law violations is four years. Significantly, Chile does not recognize a right of compulsory discovery, which impairs the ability of private plaintiffs to obtain evidence to substantiate their claims if the FNE has not already established all of the relevant facts.

Despite procedural and institutional obstacles, private plaintiffs have seen some significant victories. In 2015, for example, a telecom company that was in the business of converting landline calls to cellular calls won a $20 million judgment against Telefonica, a Spanish telecommunications company, on refusal to deal, margin squeeze, and price discrimination claim. Many Chilean observers expect a significant growth in private competition law enforcement in coming years. NICOLAS LEWIN & FRANCISCO BORQUEZ, COMPETITION POLICY INTERNATIONAL, THE DEVELOPMENT OF PRIVATE ENFORCEMENT REGARDING DAMAGES ACTIONS IN CHILE (2016), https://www.competitionpolicyinternational.com/wp-content/uploads/2016/01/Lewin.pdf.

China, like Chile, has seen the gradual expansion of private antitrust litigation since the adoption of China's Antimonopoly Law ("AML") in 2007. Article 60 of the amended AML provides that "[w]here the monopolistic conduct of an undertaking has caused losses to another person, it shall bear civil liabilities according to law," hence creating a private right of action for damages.

Like Chile, China has granted jurisdiction over antitrust cases to designated courts. The Intermediate People's Courts, which are ordinarily appellate courts, hear private antitrust cases in most jurisdictions. The apparent rationale for lodging original jurisdiction in an appellate court was the complexity of antitrust cases. Also, in 2014 China established Intellectual Property Courts in Beijing, Shanghai, and Guangzhou, and those courts hear private antitrust cases in their districts.

The Civil Procedure Law permits any plaintiff with a "direct interest" in a case to sue. "Direct" here does not have the "direct injury" sense of US law—indirect purchasers apparently have standing to sue for overcharges. Class actions or group actions brought by public interest associations are in principle permitted, but to date no such actions have been brought.

Chinese law permits private standalone cases, i.e., the private plaintiff need not await a successful public enforcement action. Most private cases to date have been standalone proceedings. However, there remains an open question as to whether the People's Courts would permit a private case to proceed if there were an ongoing administrative investigation on the same subject. The Supreme People's Court has empowered lower courts to terminate a private action when there is an ongoing administrative investigation. Further, a finding of liability by the administrative agency does not guarantee success in a private follow-on action. The courts will still scrutinize whether the facts upon which the enforcement authority relies are sufficient to substantiate an infringement in the private litigation. In a widely watched decision in November of 2016, Junwei Tian v. Beijing Carrefour Shuangjing Store, the Beijing High Court rejected a private follow-on case on grounds of insufficiency of evidence. The plaintiff purchased a tin of Abbott's infant formula in February of 2013. A few months later, China's National Development and Reform Commission ("NDRC") fined six infant formula suppliers, including Abbott, for engaging in resale price maintenance. The High Court held that the plaintiff could not rely on the NDRC decision, since the Commission had not identified the particular retailers with which Abbott had agreed to RPM. Further, the only contract between Abbott and the retailer admitted into evidence contained only non-binding pricing recommendations, which did not permit an inference of actual RPM.

Despite many obstacles, private enforcement in China is growing. In 2024, the Supreme People's Court issued new guidance on private litigation for violations of the Antimonopoly Law that are intended to ease the burdens on private plaintiffs. Among other things, the new guidance suggests mechanisms to facilitate follow-on litigation through reliance on administrative findings and adjusts burdens of proof in cases involving claims for abuse of dominance, concerted conduct, and resale price maintenance.

G. CRIMINAL ENFORCEMENT

1. Justifications for Criminal Enforcement

Most countries treat antitrust as a civil and administrative matter and do not impose criminal penalties. The historical exception to this rule is the United States, which aggressively prosecutes cartels and imposes substantial prison sentences on the ring-leaders. Other jurisdictions have adopted criminal enforcement over the years, and more recently, the notion increasingly has gained popularity. In Korea, the Monopoly Regulation and Fair Trade Act was revised in 2013 to facilitate increased criminal prosecutions of individuals who now face a substantial fine and three year prison sentence. In August of 2016, the Parliament of Chile adopted a new criminal provision applicable to hard-core cartels, with the possibility of imprisonment up to ten years. Similarly, in 2016 South Africa introduced individual criminal liability for "knowing acquiescence" in a cartel, with a maximum prison sentence of six months.

Why should a regime consider criminalization of cartel behavior? Consider the following succinct explanation from the Australian Competition & Consumer Commission, which added a criminal component to its cartel law in 2008: "Cartel activity will not be deterred if the potential penalties are perceived by firms and their executives to be outweighed by the potential rewards. Under Australia's existing penalty regime, there was a real danger that, at least for some of the bigger international cartels, the penalties were simply not a deterrent. Imprisonment has no such qualifications—it is a penalty for which no company or shareholder can be forced to pick up the cost."

Consider also the following 2001 statement from the Director General of the British Chambers of Commerce: "If there is a guiding principle that dictates the way we do business in the UK it is that it should be conducted fairly. Anti-competitive practices create weak markets, protect the inefficient, deprive us of choice, stifle innovation and support bad practice. They defraud consumers and break the will of those business people who work hard to pursue their ambitions—the kinds of business people who are my members. . . . It is right that managers should also face sanctions, because they can gain significantly if the companies they work for make excess profits—it feeds through into executive bonuses and share options. Those operating a cartel are engaging in theft and should face a similar sanction. . . ."

Another argument commonly made in favor of criminalizing cartel behavior is that antitrust sanctions need to be applied to individuals, and not merely to corporations, in order to achieve optimal deterrence. Although corporate fines may contribute to deterrence, corporate fines are only effective in changing managerial behavior if corporations are able adequately to police their managers, which is not always the case. Further, a corporate fine has little effect on a culpable manager who has left the corporation since the time of the violation and does not own many of the corporate defendant's shares. Hence, individual criminal liability—including jail time—may be necessary to change business culture and behavior.

Assuming that individuals are criminally prosecuted for antitrust violations, what remedies should be imposed upon convicted defendants that achieve not only general deterrence, but also ameliorate competitive conditions in the future? In recent years, there has been an increasingly vibrant conversation in white collar criminal law circles about suspension and debarment of cartel ringleaders as devices to reform corporate culture and reduce recidivism. For example, under UK law a director involved in a cartel conspiracy may be debarred from continuing to serve as a director. Proponents of debarment argue that it more effectively changes future behavior than fines; skeptics worry that it may detract from criminal fines, which have the potential of deterring violations in the first place.

Even assuming that criminal enforcement against individuals is necessary for adequate deterrence, there remains a fairness question: Is it just to impose criminal penalties for non-fraudulent, non-coercive business agreements that are still legal, or at least culturally accepted, in parts of the world? Consider this fundamental question as you read about leniency programs next.

2. Leniency

Even beyond the basic question of whether criminal enforcement is appropriate, there is a further question about whether the methods used to "crack" cartel cases are fair. The US has long used various "leniency" tools to encourage cartel members to "rat out" their co-conspirators. The US offers two different forms of leniency. The first, complete amnesty from prosecution, is only available to cartel participants (whether corporate or individual) who are the first to come forward with information about the cartel. The requirements for obtaining amnesty are strict. In the case of a corporation, for example, the cooperator must satisfy six criteria: (1) at the time the corporation came forward, the Antitrust Division had not yet received information about the cartel; (2) the corporation, upon discovering the cartel, took prompt and effective action to terminate its part in the conspiracy; (3) the corporation reports its wrongdoing with candor and completeness and provides continuing cooperation throughout the investigation; (4) the confession is truly a corporate act; (5) where possible, the corporation makes restitution to injured parties; and (6) the corporation did not coerce another party to participate in the illegal activity and was not the leader or originator of the cartel.

If a party does not qualify for amnesty, it may still seek the additional kind of leniency—a reduction in their penalty. In the case of a corporation, this means a lower fine and in the case of an individual, usually a reduced prison sentence. Such a reduction in the fine is available in exchange for "substantial assistance" with an ongoing cartel investigation. As with the amnesty program, there is an incentive to get in earlier, since the fine reduction diminishes the later a defendant comes forward to cooperate.

The European Commission follows a similar amnesty program and fine reduction program, although all of the Commission's enforcement powers are administrative and benefits are not reserved for the first in. The following is the Commission's description of its amnesty and leniency program:

> In essence, the leniency policy offers companies involved in a cartel—which self-report and hand over evidence—either total immunity from fines or a reduction of fines which the Commission would have otherwise imposed on them. It also benefits the Commission, allowing it not only to pierce the cloak of secrecy in which cartels operate but also to obtain insider evidence of the cartel infringement. The leniency policy also has a very deterrent effect on cartel formation and it destabilizes the operation of existing cartels as it seeds distrust and suspicion among cartel members.
>
> In order to obtain total immunity under the leniency policy, a company which participated in a cartel must be the first one to inform the Commission of an undetected cartel by providing sufficient information to allow the Commission to launch an inspection at the premises of the companies allegedly involved in the cartel. If the Commission is already in possession of enough information to launch an inspection or has already undertaken one, the company must provide evidence that enables the Commission to prove the cartel infringement. In all cases, the company must also fully cooperate with the Commission throughout its procedure, provide it with all evidence in its possession and put an end to the infringement immediately. The cooperation with the Commission implies that the existence

> and the content of the application cannot be disclosed to any other company. The company may not benefit from immunity if it took steps to coerce other undertakings to participate in the cartel.
>
> Companies which do not qualify for immunity may benefit from a reduction of fines if they provide evidence that represents "significant added value" to that already in the Commission's possession and have terminated their participation in the cartel. Evidence is considered to be of a "significant added value" for the Commission when it reinforces its ability to prove the infringement. The first company to meet these conditions is granted 30 to 50% reduction, the second 20 to 30% and subsequent companies up to 20%.
>
> The Commission considers that any statement submitted to it within the context of its leniency policy forms part of the Commission's file and may therefore not be disclosed or used for any other purpose than the Commission's own cartel proceedings.[33]

Corporate leniency programs have proven so effective at catching cartels (think of the familiar Prisoner's Dilemma to see why) that they have spread quickly around the world. Most jurisdictions with an anti-cartel law also offer some sort of leniency or amnesty to incentivize cartel defections and obtain necessary information to convict other participants. For example, in 2014—ten years into its modern antitrust regime—Egypt amended its competition law to add a cartel leniency provision. In the following year, 2015, Egypt was reportedly able to crack a cartel much more quickly than before—obtaining hard evidence and wrapping up the case quickly through the use of its new leniency tool. http://globalcompetitionreview.com/insight/the-european-middle-eastern-and-african-antitrust-review-2017/1067875/egypt-competition-authority.

Undoubtedly, leniency can be effective, but some critics claim that it diverts agencies from detection efforts and creates undue complexity. Further, should it bother us that two very similarly situated cartel participants receive very different legal treatment? Does leniency get in the way of other important values, such as compensation and compliance? With the widespread popularity of leniency tools leading to record fines around the world, academics and enforcers have begun increasingly to pose these questions. For a comprehensive look, see ANTI-CARTEL ENFORCEMENT IN A

---

33 https://competition-policy.ec.europa.eu/antitrust-and-cartels/leniency_en.

CONTEMPORARY AGE: LENIENCY RELIGION (Caron Beaton-Wells & Christopher Tran, eds., 2015). As you ponder this question, you may want to revisit a question lurking at the foundations of antitrust law—are the purposes of antitrust law only economic, or are they moral as well?

3. Double Jeopardy and Extradition

In previous times, when the US was virtually alone in vigorously prosecuting cartels, US and foreign executives involved in the same price-fixing conspiracy often received vastly different treatment. The US executives might serve serious prison time while the foreign executives got off scott free. This happened because the foreign executives (unless they happen to be present in the US) were beyond the jurisdiction of the US courts and foreign governments refused to extradite to the US for antitrust violations.

The US still had some leverage with foreign executives, since for professional reasons many of them needed to be able to travel in the US. So the prevailing practice was for the Justice Department to negotiate a plea deal that had the foreign executives paying a fine but not serving prison time.

In the last decade, this has all begun to change. In 1999, the Justice Department announced a shift in policy, stating that it would no longer allow foreign executives a free pass from jail time. Then, as other jurisdictions began shifting toward criminal enforcement themselves, they began to revisit their traditional reluctance to extradite on antitrust charges. The United Kingdom had long been the leader in resisting extradition to the US for antitrust violations, but has now come to cooperate with US extradition requests. Other countries are now joining suit. In April 2014, Romano Pisciotti, an Italian national, was extradited from Germany to the United States on charges of conspiring to rig bids, fix prices, and allocate market shares for marine hose. According to a US Justice Department press release, this marked the first successfully litigated extradition on an antitrust charge. https://www.justice.gov/opa/pr/first-ever-extradition-antitrust-charge.

Although extradition for antitrust offenses remains unlikely in many parts of the world, the arm of criminal justice has certainly grown longer in recent years.

The increasing possibility that international business executives will not only be extradited to the US but also be prosecuted in another jurisdiction raises the possibility of double jeopardy—prosecution twice for the same crime. Formally, successive prosecutions by separate sovereign governments does not count as double jeopardy especially when each suit is based on effects in separate jurisdictions, but one might still worry that in a world of overlapping jurisdiction, multiple layers of criminal and civil enforcement, and aggressive amnesty and leniency programs, the potential for vastly disparate treatment of different members of the same cartel will be aggravated. And this is on top of treble damages in private enforcement actions.

At the same time, antitrust regimes around the world are increasingly cooperating not only to share information leading to the detection and successful prosecution of cartels, but also to coordinate penalties. For example, in 2008 the US Justice Department and several European competition agencies uncovered an international cartel to allocate markets, rig bids, and fix prices for marine hose (a flexible rubber hose used to transfer oil between tankers and storage facilities) that operated in the US, Europe, and Japan. As a result of coordinated prosecutions and plea deals, several defendants were sentenced to concurrent prison terms both in the US and in the UK, which meant that they only ended up serving prison time in the UK where the court imposed the longer sentence. For example, Bryan Allison of Dunlop, Oil & Marine Ltd., a marine hose manufacturer located in Grimsby, UK, was sentenced to pay a $100,000 criminal fine and serve a 24 month prison sentence in the US. However, the UK Crown Court sentenced him to serve 36 months in jail in the UK and, given the concurrent nature of the sentences, he is serving jail time in the UK only.

H. MERGER ENFORCEMENT

An important procedural issue in modern competition law enforcement is the requirement of filing notification of mergers and large acquisitions with governmental antitrust enforcers. In the US, the Hart-Scott-Rodino Act ("HSR") requires firms that meet specified dollar thresholds to file a premerger notification 30 days (or 15 days for an all-cash transaction) prior to closing their merger. The HSR filing goes to both federal antitrust agencies—Department of Justice and FTC—who then decide among themselves which will review the merger. If the 30 days expire without any further action from the government, the parties may close the transaction. However, prior to the expiration of the 30 days, the agencies can issue a "second request" for documents that extends the prohibition on closing the transaction until the parties have substantially completed the document production requested.

The practical effect of the HSR is to transform merger control from an adjudicatory process in the courts, as it was prior to HSR's adoption in 1976, into a largely administrative process where decisions on mergers and compromises over divestiture packages or conduct remedies are made internally within the agencies in a dialogue with the merging parties. Although parties may sometimes comply with second requests and then litigate if the agencies sue for a preliminary injunction, parties often cannot afford the delay and uncertainty inherent in fully satisfying a second request and then waiting for the government to sue, if it's still unhappy with the merger. Hence, parties have a strong incentive to cooperate with the government in order to assuage its concerns or, failing that, to walk away from problematic mergers.

Although people often speak of HSR "clearance," HSR is not a clearance process. The statute does not affect the substance of merger legality under Section 7 of the Clayton Act, nor do the agencies formally "clear" a merger when it goes through the HSR process. Formally, the only legal requirement is that all notifiable mergers be notified and not closed until the various disclosure requirements are satisfied and the waiting period expires. Neither the government nor private parties are formally barred from suing the merging parties after the closure of a merger that the government did not challenge during the HSR review process. There have been a small number of private challenges to such mergers, some by state Attorneys General, and even some by federal agencies. Still, the practical effect of HSR has been to transform merger review into a largely public and largely administrative process in the US.

The EU also has a premerger notification requirement, but it differs from HSR in some important respects. Subject to various exceptions, parties to a "concentration" (the relevant term of art) with a Union dimension (as specified, similarly to HSR, using complex monetary thresholds) must file premerger notification forms and wait for a final decision before closing the transaction. The Commission has exclusive power, vis-à-vis the Member State authorities, to allow or disallow these transactions. The Member States have ceded authority to prevent or authorize such transactions, except when legitimate national interests such as security, plurality of media, or prudential concerns are at stake, and except in certain circumstances when a distinct State market is affected.

In some cases, a concentration even with a Union dimension threatens competition in a distinct market within one Member State. In such cases the Member State authority may ask the Commission to refer the concentration to it, and the Commission *may* grant the reference. But if the affected territory is not a substantial part of the common market, the Commission *must* grant the reference. The

Commission may also investigate mergers not of Union dimension at the request of one or more Member States.

Unlike under HSR, some joint ventures—those that are created to "perform[ ] on a lasting basis all of the functions of an autonomous economic entity"—are concentrations that require notification. These joint ventures are called "full-function" joint ventures, and get the benefits of one-stop Merger Regulation if they meet the thresholds.

Despite their differences, the US and the EU share one very important feature—they both require that notification be given *before* the merger closes. Not so in all parts of the world. Some jurisdictions have adopted post-merger notification provisions where the merging parties cannot notify certain categories of merger until they have already closed. For example, South Korea requires pre-merger notification of mergers exceeding certain monetary thresholds and post-merger notification for mergers with lower monetary values. Japan had long followed a post-merger notification system, but in 2009 adopted a new pre-merger notification system for securities acquisitions exceeding the prescribed thresholds.

Premerger notification regulations must specify a number of criteria, including the types of transactions covered, the economic threshold of the transaction, the amount of filing fee, what information must be supplied with the notification, and the required nexus of the transaction to the domestic economy. Consider, for example, Brazil's 2012 introduction of a new mandatory pre-merger notification for all mergers meeting the statutory thresholds. Law No. 12 529/2011. Mergers of foreign companies are included in the statute's coverage if (1) the companies directly operate in Brazil; (2) a vertical or horizontal relationship between the parties could directly affect Brazilian commerce; or (3) the companies export goods or services to Brazil or perform any activities in Brazil. The filing fee is about $26,000 and a substantial amount of information, including a 500-word description of the transaction, corporate financial documents, all agreements involved in the merger, the parties' definition of the relevant market, a description of the business or service of the parties, the structure of demand, an assessment of monopoly purchasing power, an assessment of entry and rivalry conditions, and an assessment of oligopolistic coordination. Plenty to keep lawyers busy!

Premerger notification regimes are now the norm. The increasing number of regimes with merger notification requirements and the variety of the requirements themselves is increasing the complexity and costs of large international mergers. Merger filing fees can be in the tens or hundreds of thousands of dollars, which adds up quickly for the merging parties if exacted in scores of jurisdictions but merger filing fees have become an attractive revenue source for jurisdictions. Should we be concerned about excessive global taxation of mergers? Further, the uncoordinated nature of merger notification and review procedures and timing creates the possibility that national authorities could use their power to delay mergers to exact concessions from the merging parties that have little to do with any anticompetitive effects of a merger. Suppose, for example, that a merger could result in the closure of a plant in a particular jurisdiction or the elimination of local suppliers to the merger companies, even though the merging parties would not obtain any market power from the merger. One could imagine the national competition authority in the affected jurisdiction using its power over the merger process to hold up the merger until it had exacted a promise from the merging parties not to eliminate local jobs or suppliers.

Concerns such as these have led some commentators to call for a unified international merger notification system and the harmonization of procedures for merger review. We return to such issues in Chapter 10 when we consider the possibility of global antitrust governance. In the meantime, it may be useful to consider a list of eight guiding principles for merger review recommended by the International Competition Network ("ICN"), an international network of competition enforcement agencies:

GUIDING PRINCIPLES FOR MERGER NOTIFICATION AND REVIEW PROCEDURES

1. Sovereignty. Jurisdictions are sovereign with respect to the application of their own laws to mergers.

2. Transparency. In order to foster consistency, predictability, and fairness, the merger review process should be transparent with respect to the policies, practices, and procedures involved in the review, the identity of the decision-maker(s), the substantive standard of review, and the bases of any adverse enforcement decisions on the merits.

3. Non-discrimination on the basis of nationality. In the merger review process, jurisdictions should not discriminate in the application of competition laws and regulations on the basis of nationality.

4. Procedural fairness. Prior to a final adverse decision on the merits, merging parties should be informed of the competitive concerns that form the basis for the proposed adverse decision and the factual basis upon which such concerns are based, and should

have an opportunity to express their views in relation to those concerns. Reviewing jurisdictions should provide an opportunity for review of such decisions before a separate adjudicative body. Third parties that believe they would be harmed by potential anticompetitive effects of a proposed transaction should be allowed to express their views in the course of the merger review process.

5. Efficient, timely, and effective review. The merger review process should provide enforcement agencies with information needed to review the competitive effects of transactions and should not impose unnecessary costs on transactions. The review of transactions should be conducted, and any resulting enforcement decision should be made, within a reasonable and determinable time frame.

6. Coordination. Jurisdictions reviewing the same transaction should engage in such coordination as would, without compromising enforcement of domestic laws, enhance the efficiency and effectiveness of the review process and reduce transaction costs.

7. Convergence. Jurisdictions should seek convergence of merger review processes toward agreed best practices.

8. Protection of confidential information. The merger review process should provide for the protection of confidential information.

* * *

Understanding antitrust institutions and procedures is critical to understanding the operation of antitrust law. Two different jurisdictions may have identical-sounding substantive laws that operate very differently in practice because of the institutional mechanisms by which they are enforced. Conversely, two different jurisdictions may have very different sounding substantive rules that tend to converge in practice because they are mediated by institutions that wish to bring their national competition law into conformity with comparative or international standards. In this chapter, we have surveyed some of the chief institutional attributes of competition law systems. When studying a new country's competition law, it is always important to be aware not only of what the laws are, but *how* and *by whom* they are enforced.

Chapter 9

EXTRATERRITORIALITY

A. INTRODUCTION

The economy is global. Suppliers and buyers participate in global markets, and cartels, mergers, and dominant firm abuses cross many borders. When does the competition law of one nation reach conduct or transactions launched on foreign shores? These are questions of subject matter jurisdiction or (more accurately) prescriptive jurisdiction.[1] How far did the legislature intend for the competition law to reach? Are constraints imposed by international law or soft norms?

Over the last centuries, nations began to approach the issue cautiously, staying within bounds of nationality and territoriality. Assertions of jurisdiction over offshore acts were called "extraterritorial," with a pejorative connotation. A presumption against extraterritoriality applies to statutory interpretation in some nations, including the United States,[2] suggesting a possible illegitimate stepping out of bounds and treading on the territory of another sovereign, which would have to be justified to preserve the harmony among nations. But eventually, with the lowering of trade barriers, the integration of markets, and the springing up of markets without territorial roots (the Internet), it came to be recognized that nations have the right to protect themselves from the anticompetitive effects of conduct and transactions launched abroad or remotely. If the nation's legislature has authorized the enforcement against acts or actors abroad that threaten harm to the nation, the question is not—Is the enforcement extraterritorial?, but rather, Is it sufficiently connected with potential harm in the enforcing jurisdiction?, and, if it conflicts with the law and policy of another interested jurisdiction, has it gone beyond bounds of proportionality? Personal jurisdiction must always be established, and defenses related to foreign government action or involvement authorizing or approving the conduct or transaction may be applicable.

This chapter covers history and evolution of the effects doctrine in the United States and of the implementation/qualified effects

1 Morrison v. National Australia Bank, 561 U.S. 247 (2010).

2 E.g., RJR Nabisco, Inc. v. European Community, 579 U.S. 325 (2016).

doctrines in the EU; recent expansions of the doctrines in the EU and the UK; reception by developing countries; and the defenses: comity, foreign sovereign immunity, foreign sovereign compulsion, and immunity for petitioning the sovereign.

B. UNITED STATES AND THE DEVELOPMENT OF THE EFFECTS DOCTRINE

The United States led the world in developing principles of jurisdiction over foreign acts and actors that threatened anticompetitive harm in the United States. The first big, and lasting landmark case, was United States v. Aluminum Co. of America, 148 F.2d 416 (2d Cir. 1945) ("Alcoa"). The United States sued non-US firms for an offshore cartel targeted at the United States. The court famously held the Sherman Act applicable if the defendants intended to affect and did affect US commerce; dubbed the effects test. This was a time before many nations had anti-cartel laws; and some nations, such as the UK, prohibited cartels only if they were against the public interest. US effects jurisdiction angered United States' trading partners, especially the UK, which claimed that their citizens had the right to do on their territory what was legal on their territory.

Limits developed. Under the Swiss Watchmakers precedent, US courts may not require foreign firms acting in their home territory to do what their home governments forbid, or to abstain from doing what the home government requires, for such an order would interfere impermissibly with the sovereignty of the foreign state. United States v. Watchmakers of Switzerland Info. Center, 1963 (CCH) Trade Cas. ¶ 70,600 (S.D.N.Y. 1962); 1965 (CCH) Trade Cas. ¶ 71,352 (S.D.N.Y. 1965) (judgment revised to apply only to conduct that operated outside of Switzerland).

In the 1960s and 1970s, a number of US antitrust suits, public and private, targeted foreign nationals. In the private cases, British and other nationals were sued for treble damages as members of world cartels that targeted American buyers. One prominent case involved the Rio Tinto Zinc uranium cartel. After the US government imposed an embargo against sales of enriched uranium, the big world suppliers of uranium boycotted (jointly refused to sell to) Westinghouse, the biggest user of enriched uranium which it needed in its electricity generators. Westinghouse and others sued the boycotters. At about the same time US plaintiffs sued the members of a shipping "conference"—a long-standing consortium of shippers who claimed immunity from antitrust. The suits caused an outcry by the British and led to Britain's enactment of a blocking and clawback statute, the British Protection of Trading Interests Act, 1980, ch. 11. The blocking provisions blocked the production of UK-based documents for purposes of foreign litigation. The clawback provisions allowed a British firm to recover (to "claw back") in Great Britain penal damages paid pursuant to a foreign judgment. Hence, two-thirds of treble damages awards could be retrieved. Various other nations, including France, Germany, Australia, and Canada, also adopted blocking or clawback statutes. See Restatement (Third) of Foreign Relations Law of the United States § 442, Reporters' Note No. 4 (1987). (Restatement (Third) has been superseded by Restatement (Fourth). In response to threats of retaliation by trading partners, US courts developed balancing principles, premised on the proposition that the courts either lack jurisdiction or should refrain from exercising jurisdiction if foreign nations' and foreign nationals' interests outweighed the US interests in enforcement of the antitrust laws. Timberlane Lumber Co. v. Bank of America, 549 F.2d 597 (9th Cir. 1976); Mannington Mills, Inc. v. Congoleum Corp., 595 F.2d 1287 (3d Cir. 1979). Contrariwise, a third American court held that courts cannot balance incommensurables (i.e., American interests in antitrust enforcement against British interests against it); the court declared that it had concurrent jurisdiction with UK courts over a conspiracy among American, British, and other airlines to destroy maverick Freddie Laker's no-frills low-priced "sky train" between London and New York. Laker Airways Ltd. v. Sabena, Belgian World Airlines, 731 F.2d 909 (D.C. Cir. 1984). Many US courts premised jurisdiction on direct, substantial and foreseeable effects in the United States, and this was the test used by the US antitrust agencies.

Meanwhile, not only were US trading partners angry about application of US antitrust law to their citizens, but American businesses were aggrieved by precedents holding them bound by US antitrust rules (then, the strictest in the world) in their business abroad. The US Congress responded with the Foreign Trade Antitrust Improvements Act of 1982 ("FTAIA"), which made clear that the Sherman Act did not follow American firms in foreign markets (export cartels were fine). Second, for commerce other than import commerce (which was set to one side as still covered by the pre-existing rules, the FTAIA provided that the Sherman Act would not apply unless the conduct has a direct, substantial and reasonably foreseeable effect on US domestic commerce or export trade and that effect gives rise to a Sherman Act claim under another section of the Sherman Act.

This latter clause is convoluted but that was of no significance for nearly two decades when the Supreme Court took up a case called *Empagran,* which we cover in due course. First, we turn to the EU's adoption of a form of the effects test, and to refinements in the US.

After *Empagran*, we turn to a modern series of cases involving input cartels abroad, assembly of the inputs into finished devices abroad, and then sale of the finished product into the regulating jurisdiction. Are the effects in the jurisdiction sufficiently direct, or too remote?

C. FURTHER DEVELOPMENT OF EFFECTS TESTS

Up until the late 1980s, influenced by the strong opposition of the UK, the EU resisted an effects test. Then Europe was confronted with an offshore wood pulp cartel, allegedly agreed to in the United States, Canada and Finland. The conspirators had no offices in the EU and some had no parents or subsidiaries doing business there.

Å. ÅHLSTRÖM OSAKEYHTIÖ v. COMMISSION (*WOOD PULP*)

Cases C–89, 104, 114, 116, 117, 125–129/85, ECLI:EU:C:1988:447 (Court of Justice of the European Union 1988)

[The Commission brought proceedings against 41 wood pulp producers from the United States, Canada, and Finland and two of their trade associations for allegedly making concerted price announcements and fixing prices. The Commission found infringements and imposed fines. The firms sued for annulment both for lack of agreement and lack of jurisdiction. The jurisdictional issue came before the Court first. The Court found jurisdiction (but later found that there was insufficient evidence to infer that defendants had a cartel agreement). In the portions of the opinion that appear below, the court established the existence of jurisdiction over conduct that occurred outside the territorial boundaries of the European Union as long as it was "implemented" in the EU.]

[3] [T]he Commission set out the grounds which in its view justify the Community's jurisdiction to apply Article [101 of the Treaty on the Functioning of the European Union] of the Treaty to the concertation in question. It stated first that all the addressees of the decision were either exporting directly to purchasers within the Community or were doing business within the Community through branches, subsidiaries, agencies or other establishments in the Community. It further pointed out that the concertation applied to the vast majority of the sales of those undertakings to and in the Community. Finally it stated that two-thirds of total shipments and 60 per cent of consumption of the product in question in the Community had been affected by such concertation. The Commission concluded that 'the effect of the agreements and practices on prices announced and/or charged to customers and on resale of pulp within the EEC was

therefore not only substantial but intended, and was the primary and direct result of the agreements and practices'. * * *

6 All the applicants which have made submissions regarding jurisdiction maintain first of all that by applying the competition rules of the Treaty to them the Commission has misconstrued the territorial scope of Article [101]. They note that in its judgment of 14 July 1972 (Case 48/69, ICI v. EC: [1972] ECR 619) the Court did not adopt the 'effects doctrine' but emphasized that the case involved conduct restricting competition within the Common Market because of the activities of subsidiaries which could be imputed to the parent companies. The applicants add that even if there is a basis in Community law for applying Article [101] to them, the action of applying the rule interpreted in that way would be contrary to public international law which precludes any claim by the Community to regulate conduct restricting competition adopted outside the territory of the Community merely by reason of the economic repercussions which that conduct produces within the Community.

7 The applicants which are members of the [trade association] KEA further submit that the application of Community competition rules to them is contrary to public international law in so far as it is in breach of the principle of non-interference. They maintain that in this case the application of Article [101] harmed the interest of the United States in promoting exports by United States undertakings as recognized in the Webb-Pomerene Act of 1918 under which export associations, like the KEA, are exempt from United States antitrust laws.

8 Certain Canadian applicants also maintain that by imposing fines on them and making reduction of those fines conditional on the producers giving undertakings as to their future conduct the Commission has infringed Canada's sovereignty and thus breached the principle of international comity. * * *

Incorrect assessment of the territorial scope of Article [101] of the Treaty and incompatibility of the decision with public international law

(a) The individual undertakings

11 In so far as the submission concerning the infringement of Article [101] of the Treaty itself is concerned, it should be recalled that that provision prohibits all agreements between undertakings and concerted practices which may affect trade between member-States and which have as their object or effect the restriction of competition within the Common Market are prohibited.

12 It should be noted that the main sources of supply of wood pulp are outside the Community, in Canada, the United States, Sweden and Finland and that the market therefore has global dimensions. Where wood pulp producers established in those countries sell directly to purchasers established in the Community and engage in price competition in order to win orders from those customers, that constitutes competition within the Common Market.

13 It follows that where those producers concert on the prices to be charged to their customers in the Community and put that concertation into effect by selling at prices which are actually coordinated, they are taking part in concertation which has the object and effect of restricting competition within the Common Market within the meaning of Article [101] of the Treaty.

14 Accordingly, it must be concluded that by applying the competition rules in the Treaty in the circumstances of this case to undertakings whose registered offices are situated outside the Community, the Commission has not made an incorrect assessment of the territorial scope of Article [101].

15 The applicants have submitted that the decision is incompatible with public international law on the grounds that the application of the competition rules in this case was founded exclusively on the economic repercussions within the Common Market of conduct restricting competition which was adopted outside the Community.

16 It should be observed that an infringement of Article [101], such as the conclusion of an agreement which has had the effect of restricting competition within the Common Market, consists of conduct made up of two elements, the formation of the agreement, decision or concerted practice and the implementation thereof. If the applicability of prohibitions laid down under competition law were made to depend on the place where the agreement, decision or concerted practice was formed, the result would obviously be to give undertakings an easy means of evading those prohibitions. The decisive factor is therefore the place where it is implemented.

17 The producers in this case implemented their pricing agreement within the Common Market. It is immaterial in that respect whether or not they had recourse to subsidiaries, agents, sub-agents, or branches within the Community in order to make their contacts with purchasers within the Community.

18 Accordingly the Community's jurisdiction to apply its competition rules to such conduct is covered by the territoriality principle as universally recognized in public international law.

19 As regards the argument based on the Infringement of the principle of non-interference, it should be pointed out that the applicants who are members of KEA have referred to a rule according to which where two States have jurisdiction to lay down and enforce rules and the effect of those rules is that a person finds himself subject to contradictory orders as to the conduct he must adopt, each State is obliged to exercise its jurisdiction with moderation. The applicants have concluded that by disregarding that rule in applying its competition rules the Community has infringed the principle of non-interference.

20 There is no need to enquire into the existence in international law of such a rule since it suffices to observe that the conditions for its application are in any event not satisfied. There is not, in this case, any contradiction between the conduct required by the United States and that required by the Community since the Webb-Pomerene Act merely exempts the conclusion of export cartels from the application of United States antitrust laws but does not require such cartels to be concluded.

21 It should further be pointed out that the United States authorities raised no objections regarding any conflict of jurisdiction when consulted by the Commission . . . .

22 As regards the argument relating to disregard of international comity, it suffices to observe that it amounts to calling in question the Community's jurisdiction to apply its competition rules to conduct such as that found to exist in this case and that, as such, that argument has already been rejected.

23 Accordingly it must be concluded that the Commission's decision is not contrary to Article [101] of the Treaty or to the rules of public international law relied on by the applicants.

* * *

Notes and Questions

Wood Pulp established a form of effects jurisdiction for Europe: "implementation." The test was later to be applied to off-shore mergers the effects of which were sufficiently linked to Europe to allow a conclusion that the merger was implemented in Europe. Gencor (Lonrho) v. Commission, Case T–102/96 999 E.C.R. II–753. (The merger was equivalent to an export cartel, and one merger partner had sales offices in the EU.)

The broad reading of "implementation" was confirmed in *InnoLux.* InnoLux, located in Taiwan, was a member of a conspiracy in Korea and Taiwan to fix liquid crystal display panels. InnoLux sold the price-fixed panels to its subsidiaries, also outside of the EEA. The subsidiaries incorporated the panels into TVs, computer monitors, notebooks and smartphones and sold the finished products throughout the world, including into the EEA. The Court of Justice gave short shrift to the claim that the conspiracy was not implemented in the EEA:

> 62 It should also be pointed out that excluding those sales would have the effect of artificially minimizing the economic significance of the infringement committed by a particular undertaking, since the mere fact such sales genuinely affected by the cartel in the EEA are excluded from being taken into account would lead to the imposition of a fine which bore no actual relation to the scope of application of that cartel in that territory . . . .

Case C–231/14P, InnoLux v. Commission, EU:C:2015:451.

Note on Intel v. Commission

Case C–413/14 P, ECLI:EU:C:2017:632
(Court of Justice of the European Union

The next big step in Europe came in the *Intel* case. Intel, as American company, was the dominant supplier of a critical chip in laptop computers and notebooks. It accounted for approximately 70% of the European market. AMD, an American company and the only significant competitor, finally developed a superior chip. Intel went into action to derail AMD. It introduced loyalty rebates. For big-buyer customers who had already signed contracts with AMD, Intel tried to buy them off; to pay them to breach the contracts with AMD and thereby, with the loyalty rebates, to prevent the good new chip from getting traction in its critical first few months. Intel, from Silicon Valley, had conversations with officials of Lenovo in China, to the following effect: Do not buy AMD's new chip. I will pay you to break your contract with AMD. Lenovo broke its contract with AMD, continued to use Intel's chip in its laptops, and sold the finished products in the European Economic Area and the rest of the world.

The European Commission found that Intel had abused its dominance in violation of Article 102 TFEU. Intel sought to sever and exclude the Lenovo segment of the case. It argued that the Intel-Lenovo acts were not implemented in the EEA and that EU did not have an effects test. Advocate General Wahl agreed with Intel that the Lenovo episode was not implemented in the EEA. He urged the Court to adopt a qualified effects test, but opined that this test was not met either. He wrote that the test required the Commission to prove that Intel's Lenovo related conduct had foreseeable, direct and immediate effects in the EEA but that the effects appeared "hypothetical, speculative and unsubstantiated." ECLI:EU:C:2016:788, para. 324.

The Court summarily rejected Intel's challenge to jurisdiction as unfounded. The court held that public international law allows jurisdiction "when it is *foreseeable* that the conduct in question will have an *immediate* and *substantial* effect in the European Union."

Regarding foreseeability of immediate effects, the Court said: "[I]t is sufficient to take account of the probable effects of conduct on competition in order for the foreseeability criterion to be satisfied." Further, "Intel's conduct vis-à-vis Lenovo formed part of an overall strategy intended to ensure that no Lenovo notebook equipped with an AMD CPU would be available on the market, including in the EEA . . . ." Thus, "the General Court did not err in considering . . . that Intel's conduct was capable of producing an immediate effect in the EEA."

As to substantiality, the Court said: "It suffices . . . that the General Court held that Intel's conduct vis-à-vis Lenovo formed part of an overall strategy aimed at foreclosing AMD's access to the most important sales channels . . . ." "[F]aced with [such] . . . strategy . . ., it was appropriate to take into consideration the conduct of the undertaking viewed as a whole in order to assess the substantial nature of its effects on the market of the EU and of the EEA." "[T]o do otherwise would lead to an artificial fragmentation of comprehensive anticompetitive conduct, capable of affecting the market structure within the EEA, into a collection of separate forms of conduct which might escape the European Union's jurisdiction."

Intel v. Commission, Case C–413/14P, 6 Sept. 2017, ECLI:EU:C:2017:808, [paras. 49–57 of judgment, quoted from Eleanor Fox, Extraterritorial Jurisdiction, Antitrust, and the EU Intel Case: Implementation, Qualified Effects, and the Third Kind, 42 Fordham Int'l L.J. 981, 986 (2019).

Was the Court right to (adopt and) expand the qualified effects test to include conduct integrally part of a strategy (merely) *capable* of having a substantial and foreseeable effect in EU markets? Is it important for enforcement to have such breadth in view of abuses in global commerce?

* * *

Back in the United States, not long after *Wood Pulp* and thus before *Intel*, the US Supreme Court took *its* next step in the spirit of emphasizing effects and avoiding unpredictable balancing, While *Hartford Fire*, immediately below, is in the spirit, like *Intel*, of expansive jurisdiction, read with caution, for you will see more reserve in the succeeding US benchmark—*Empagran*.

HARTFORD FIRE INS. CO. v. CALIFORNIA

509 U.S. 764 (United States Supreme Court 1993)

[Lloyds of London reinsurers had allegedly collaborated with US insurers and also among themselves in London to limit reinsurance in the US market. Their agreements not to supply certain high risk coverage, and therefore to "boycott" the forums that included such coverage, were specifically directed at the US market. When sued, the British reinsurers moved to dismiss, arguing that comity required dismissal. In the passage that follows, the Supreme Court rejected the British reinsurers' argument.]

JUSTICE SOUTER: * * *

Finally, we take up the question presented, whether certain claims against the London reinsurers should have been dismissed as improper applications of the Sherman Act to foreign conduct. The Fifth Claim for Relief in the California Complaint alleges a violation of § 1 of the Sherman Act by certain London reinsurers who conspired to coerce primary insurers in the United States to offer CGL [commercial general liability] coverage on a claims-made basis, thereby making "occurrence CGL coverage . . . unavailable in the State of California for many risks." The Sixth Claim for Relief in the California Complaint alleges that the London reinsurers violated § 1 by a conspiracy to limit coverage of pollution risks in North America, thereby rendering "pollution liability coverage . . . almost entirely unavailable for the vast majority of casualty insurance purchasers in the State of California." The Eighth Claim for Relief in the California Complaint alleges a further § 1 violation by the London reinsurers who, along with domestic retrocessional reinsurers, conspired to limit coverage of seepage, pollution, and property contamination risks in North America, thereby eliminating such coverage in the State of California.

At the outset, we note that the District Court undoubtedly had jurisdiction of these Sherman Act claims, as the London reinsurers apparently concede. . . . Although the proposition was perhaps not always free from doubt, see American Banana Co. v. United Fruit Co., 213 US 347 (1909), it is well established by now that the Sherman Act applies to foreign conduct that was meant to produce and did in fact produce some substantial effect in the United States. . . . Such is the conduct alleged here: that the London reinsurers engaged in unlawful conspiracies to affect the market for insurance in the United States and that their conduct in fact produced substantial effect.

According to the London reinsurers, the District Court should have declined to exercise such jurisdiction under the principle of international comity. The Court of Appeals agreed that courts should look to that principle in deciding whether to exercise jurisdiction under the Sherman Act. This availed the London reinsurers nothing, however. To be sure, the Court of Appeals believed that "application of [American] antitrust laws to the London reinsurance market 'would lead to significant conflict with English law and policy,'" and that "[s]uch a conflict, unless outweighed by other factors, would by itself be reason to decline exercise of jurisdiction." But other factors, in the court's view, including the London reinsurers' express purpose to affect United States commerce and the substantial nature of the effect produced, outweighed the supposed conflict and required the exercise of jurisdiction in this litigation.

When it enacted the FTAIA [the Foreign Trade Antitrust Improvements Act of 1982], Congress expressed no view on the question whether a court with Sherman Act jurisdiction should ever decline to exercise such jurisdiction on grounds of international comity. . . . We need not decide that question here, however, for even assuming that in a proper case a court may decline to exercise Sherman Act jurisdiction over foreign conduct (or, as Justice Scalia would put it, may conclude by the employment of comity analysis in the first instance that there is no jurisdiction), international comity would not counsel against exercising jurisdiction in the circumstances alleged here.

The only substantial question in this litigation is whether "there is in fact a true conflict between domestic and foreign law." Société Nationale Industrielle Aérospatiale v. United States Dist. Court for Southern Dist. of Iowa, 482 US 522, 555 (1987) (Blackmun, J., . . .). The London reinsurers contend that applying the Act to their conduct would conflict significantly with British law, and the British Government, appearing before us as *amicus curiae,* concurs. They assert that Parliament has established a comprehensive regulatory regime over the London reinsurance market and that the conduct alleged here was perfectly consistent with British law and policy. But this is not to state a conflict. "[T]he fact that conduct is lawful in the state in which it took place will not, of itself, bar application of the United States antitrust laws," even where the foreign state has a strong policy to permit or encourage such conduct. Restatement (Third) Foreign Relations Law § 415, Comment *j;* see *Continental Ore Co.,* supra, 370 US, at 706–707. No conflict exists, for these purposes, "where a person subject to regulation by two states can comply with the laws of both." Restatement (Third) Foreign Relations Law § 403, Comment *e.* Since the London reinsurers do not argue that British law requires them to act in some fashion prohibited by the law of the United States, or claim that their compliance with the laws of both countries is otherwise impossible, we see no conflict with British law. . . .

* * *

JUSTICE SCALIA, dissenting in part, joined by JUSTICES O'CONNOR, KENNEDY, and THOMAS:

Petitioners, various British corporations and other British subjects, argue that certain of the claims against them constitute an inappropriate extraterritorial application of the Sherman Act. It is important to distinguish two distinct questions raised by this petition: whether the District Court had jurisdiction, and whether the Sherman Act reaches the extraterritorial conduct alleged here. On the first question, I believe that the District Court had subject-matter jurisdiction over the Sherman Act claims against all the defendants (personal jurisdiction is not contested). Respondents asserted nonfrivolous claims under the Sherman Act, and 28 U.S.C. § 1331 vests district courts with subject-matter jurisdiction over cases "arising under" federal statutes.

The second question—the extraterritorial reach of the Sherman Act—has nothing to do with the jurisdiction of the courts. It is a question of substantive law turning on whether, in enacting the Sherman Act, Congress asserted regulatory power over the challenged conduct. If a plaintiff fails to prevail on this issue, the court does not dismiss the claim for want of subject-matter jurisdiction—want of power to adjudicate; rather, it decides the claim, ruling on the merits that the plaintiff has failed to state a cause of action under the relevant statute.

There is, however, a type of "jurisdiction" relevant to determining the extraterritorial reach of a statute; it is known as "legislative jurisdiction," "jurisdiction to prescribe." This refers to "the authority of a state to make its law applicable to persons or activities," and is quite a separate matter from "jurisdiction to adjudicate." There is no doubt, of course, that Congress possesses legislative jurisdiction over the acts alleged in this complaint. But the question in this litigation is whether, and to what extent, Congress *has* exercised that undoubted legislative jurisdiction in enacting the Sherman Act.

Two canons of statutory construction are relevant in this inquiry. The first is the "longstanding principle of American law 'that legislation of Congress, unless a contrary intent appears, is meant to apply only within the territorial jurisdiction of the United States.' "

. . . The Sherman Act contains . . . "boilerplate language," [coverage of foreign commerce] and if the question were not governed by precedent, it would be worth considering whether that presumption controls the outcome here. We have, however, found the presumption to be overcome with respect to our antitrust laws; it is now well established that the Sherman Act applies extraterritorially.

But if the presumption against extraterritoriality has been overcome or is otherwise inapplicable, a second canon of statutory construction becomes relevant: "[A]n act of congress ought never to be construed to violate the law of nations if any other possible construction remains." Murray v. Schooner Charming Betsy, 2 Cranch 64 (1804) (Marshall, C.J.). This canon . . . is relevant to determining the substantive reach of a statute because "the law of nations," or customary international law, includes limitations on a nation's exercise of its jurisdiction to prescribe. See Restatement (Third) §§ 401–416. Though it clearly has constitutional authority to do so, Congress is generally presumed not to have exceeded those customary international-law limits on jurisdiction to prescribe.

Consistent with that presumption, this and other courts have frequently recognized that, even where the presumption against extraterritoriality does not apply, statutes should not be interpreted to regulate foreign persons or conduct if that regulation would conflict with principles of international law.

* * *

. . . [P]recedent has also tempered the extraterritorial application of the Sherman Act with considerations of "international comity.". . . The "comity" they refer to is not the comity of courts, whereby judges decline to exercise jurisdiction over matters more appropriately adjudged elsewhere, but rather what might be termed "prescriptive comity": the respect sovereign nations afford each other by limiting the reach of their laws. That comity is exercised by legislatures when they enact laws, and courts assume it has been exercised when they come to interpreting the scope of laws their legislatures have enacted. . . . Considering comity in this way is just part of determining whether the Sherman Act prohibits the conduct at issue.

. . . Rarely would these factors [relevant to the reasonableness of Congress' reach] point more clearly against application of United States law. The activity relevant to the counts at issue here took place primarily in the United Kingdom, and the defendants in these counts are British corporations and British subjects having their principal place of business or residence outside the United States. Great Britain has established a comprehensive regulatory scheme governing the London reinsurance markets, and clearly has a heavy "interest in regulating the activity. . .". Finally, § 2(b) of the McCarran-Ferguson Act allows state regulatory statutes to override the Sherman Act in the insurance field, subject only to the narrow "boycott" exception set forth in § 3(b)—suggesting that "the importance of regulation to the [United States]," Restatement (Third) § 403(2)(c), is slight. Considering these factors, I think it unimaginable that an assertion of legislative jurisdiction by the United States would be considered reasonable, and therefore it is inappropriate to assume, in the absence of statutory indication to the contrary, that Congress has made such an assertion.

* * *

Notes and Questions

1. We have included substantial excerpts from Justice Scalia's dissent because of the extent to which Justice Scalia's perspective has gained greater currency. How does Scalia's dissent differ from the opinion of the Court? Consider in particular what is a "true conflict?"

2. Note, however, that Justice Scalia accepted Restatement of Foreign Relations Law (Third)'s understanding that customary international law prohibits extraterritorial applications of law that go beyond the bounds of "reasonableness." Restatement (Fourth), which replaces Restatement (Third), states that customary international law imposes no such case-by-case limitation. Merely, it requires a "genuine connection" of the offense with the regulating jurisdiction, and recognizes that States seek to reduce conflicts by limiting the reach of their rules as a matter of domestic law. Restatement Fourth, Sec. 407.

THE EMPAGRAN LITIGATION

After *Hartford Fire* and for much of the next decade, US courts applied the US antitrust laws broadly as usual. Then, the worldwide vitamins cartel was uncovered. Authorities in a number of jurisdictions successfully prosecuted the conspirators. Many private actions followed in the United States.

The defendant price-fixers—mostly foreign—pressed their plea for a narrow construction of the US statute (The Foreign Trade Antitrust Improvements Act of 1982, or FTAIA) that clarified and limited extraterritorial antitrust.

During the 1990s, a global vitamins cartel—self-styled "Vitamins, Inc."—fixed the prices of vitamins sold around the world. The conspirators included multinational corporations located in Belgium, France, Germany, Japan, the Netherlands, Switzerland, and the US (US subsidiaries of Japanese firms). Total sales affected by the cartel were estimated at $34 billion. Primarily as the result of enforcement actions of the US Justice Department, the cartel was cracked in the late 1990s. Competition authorities in Australia, Canada, the EU, Japan, and South Korea also imposed penalties. Then private class actions were filed, all in the US, with its plaintiff-friendly incentives for class actions, broad discovery, contingent lawyer fees, cost rules, and treble damages. One class comprised solely non-US plaintiffs, who hailed from Australia, Ecuador, Panama, and Ukraine. By the time this litigation reached the US Supreme Court on preliminary motions, the legal dispute had crystallized into a single question: Does a US court have jurisdiction over the claims of foreign purchasers from foreign sellers who were members of a global cartel that also fixed prices in the US? Seven foreign governments (Germany, Belgium, Canada, Japan, Great Britain and Northern Ireland, Ireland, and the Netherlands) submitted a total of four amicus curiae briefs (several filed together), all of them urging the Court to deny jurisdiction. The various national governments made different kinds of arguments. The British, for example, argued that the UK was trying to build its own private enforcement system and that allowing British purchasers to sue in US courts would undermine that effort; and the Japanese argued that excessive damages awards would bankrupt Japanese companies. We print below excerpts from three of numerous amicus briefs filed in the Supreme Court following lower court denial of the motions to dismiss.

AMICUS BRIEF OF GERMANY AND BELGIUM IN SUPPORT OF DEFENDANTS

The court of appeals' decision incorrectly interprets the FTAIA in a manner that will do grave harm to the antitrust enforcement efforts of the international community. The court's interpretation drastically expands the extraterritorial reach of the United States' antitrust laws to situations in which the conduct and the alleged anticompetitive effects suffered by foreign plaintiffs occur only in foreign countries. Yet, in those situations, other nations have a significant interest in the transaction and its effects and have jurisdiction to regulate or prohibit that conduct. The court's holding thus directly conflicts with the well-established principle that United States statutes are to be construed to avoid conflict with other nations' laws and to avoid unreasonableness in the exercise of U.S. courts' jurisdiction.

The court of appeals' expansive interpretation of the United States' antitrust laws will permit foreign civil litigants to use United States lawsuits to circumvent the choices made by foreign governments about the most appropriate remedies available for anticompetitive behavior. The court's interpretation of the FTAIA also threatens to undermine international antitrust cooperation and enforcement, contrary to the "underlying policies of deterrence" upon which the court relied. For example, foreign governments use leniency programs similar to the one utilized by the Department of Justice ("DOJ") to obtain information about violations; they then use that information to deter other abuses. Yet private suits, such as respondents', create strong disincentives for companies to participate in such programs because to do so increases the risk that the information they disclose to governments will subject them to private civil liability and treble damages.

* * *

... [T]he theory and application of the competition laws of Belgium, Germany, the EU, and the U.S. differ in important ways. For example, in the U.S., agency practice and courts decide whether certain agreements restraining competition are illegal by applying a "rule of reason" analysis. By contrast, German law provides for a very broad-reaching prohibition of agreements between competitors, with enumerated exceptions. So, too, for the Belgian regime, which prohibits cartels under the Belgian Act, and then provides for exemptions ...

Sometimes those varying approaches may result in different decisions as to the method of enforcement or whether a prohibition is appropriate at all. And, irrespective of whether a different outcome may result under the various systems, U.S. law should not trump Germany's and Belgium's sovereign rights to make their own choices about how to structure and apply their competition laws in determining liability and imposing remedies.

* * *

Historically, other nations have bristled at extraterritorial applications of United States antitrust laws. These concerns have resulted in foreign governments taking a number of measures to counter what they perceive to be an illegitimate encroachment into their sovereignty. Such encroachments by U.S. courts invariably will alter the relationships between nations. The effectiveness of international treaties is threatened when other nations conclude that the U.S. has overreached in the application of its domestic laws to foreign conduct.

German officials already have expressed concern about the court of appeals' expansive application of U.S. jurisdiction in this case. In a recent lecture given at an antitrust conference in Bonn and attended by United States and EU officials, former German Economic Minister (and recent chief German negotiator of the

German-U.S. forced labor settlement) Otto Graf Lambsdorff commented on the *Empagran* decision. Mr. Lambsdorff opined that "American antitrust laws were created to protect the American consumer and not to regulate the competitive conditions in foreign countries," and he observed that "[a] German court—as well as every other European—would obviously deny jurisdiction" were the roles reversed, because "[a]ny other decision would rightly provoke protest by both US companies and the US government."

One consequence of foreign disapproval with U.S. encroachments on other nation-states' antitrust enforcement efforts will be a refusal to enforce judgments obtained in U.S. lawsuits. . . .

These and other international reactions to the extraterritorial application of U.S. law should make apparent the high stakes of this case.

AMICUS BRIEF OF UK, IRELAND, AND THE NETHERLANDS IN SUPPORT OF DEFENDANTS

The decision below would permit United States courts to hear private claims by foreign plaintiffs seeking redress for antitrust injuries allegedly suffered by them in Australia, Ecuador, Panama and Ukraine from sales of vitamins there and in other foreign countries by foreign sellers. These injuries do not arise from any contacts or relationships with plaintiffs in the United States. The argument that treble damages for foreign injuries can be recovered in a United States court because the conduct at issue also resulted in injuries to *other* parties who made purchases in the United States is a complete *non sequitur*. These unrelated injuries were the basis for other private actions in United States courts and have been fully compensated. In addition, such a rule potentially would permit virtually any significant commercial transaction to be the basis for private United States treble damage claims, usurping the enforcement systems of other countries to United States private actions.

This decision would provide substantial encouragement for widespread forum shopping, might impede competition law enforcement programs in the United Kingdom, Ireland and the Netherlands as well as the European Community, and would undermine respect for national sovereignty. The court of appeals' ruling has the potential for generating needless friction between foreign and United States legal systems and could lead to less, not more, cooperation and coordination of competition laws by all nations. It would wrongly expand the extraterritorial reach of the United States antitrust laws beyond this Court's or, to our knowledge, any foreign court's exercise of jurisdiction. International law principles recognize that a nation may prescribe laws and adjudicate claims beyond its own territory only where its assertion of jurisdiction does not infringe the rights of other nations to determine the law applicable to conduct within their own territories.

* * *

The international convergence of amnesty programs has become effective because it is "much easier and far more attractive for companies to simultaneously seek and obtain leniency in the United States, Europe, Canada, and in other jurisdictions where the applicants have exposure." The Governments, however, are concerned about any policy or action that would make the programs less attractive to whistle-blowers. Competition authorities in the United Kingdom, Ireland and the Netherlands have all concluded that the proposed expansion of United States jurisdiction over private treble damages claims could have an adverse effect on international cartel enforcement. Enforcement officials from Germany and the United States agree. The issue here is that participants in leniency programs receive no immunity from private damage actions. The expansion of United States jurisdiction and the accompanying availability of private treble damages may discourage potential whistle-blowers from providing evidence. When coming forward to expose secret agreements, they may be required to pay much greater damages than if the cartel otherwise would have not have been detected. If these forecasts are borne out by experience, cartel detection and deterrence will be diminished and consumer welfare will not be served. * * *

No other country has adopted the United States' unique "bounty hunter" approach that permits a private plaintiff to "recover threefold the damages by him sustained, and the cost of suit, including a reasonable attorney's fee." The rules governing United States treble damage actions strongly favor private antitrust plaintiffs. They provide for generous class action certifications, broad discovery rules, virtually irrebuttable presumptions of liability based on successful government actions, jury trials, subsidized contingency fee arrangements, asymmetrical rules on payment of attorneys' fees, and no contribution among defendants. The parliaments of the United Kingdom, Ireland and the Netherlands all recently enacted statutes allowing private actions for competition law violations, but have chosen to do so on a more limited basis.

Expanding the jurisdiction of this generous United States private claim system could skew enforcement and increase international business risks. It makes United States courts the forum of choice without regard to whose laws are applied, where the injuries occurred or even if there is any connection to the court except the ability to get *in personam* jurisdiction over the defendants. Lord Denning best captured these anomalies when he observed: "As a moth is drawn to the light, so is a litigant drawn to the United States. If he can only get his case into their courts, he stands to win a fortune." Smith Kline & French Labs Ltd. v. Bloch, [1983] 1 W.L.R. 730 (C.A. 1982). Enlarging the prescriptive jurisdiction of the United States to provide a US antitrust remedy to foreign buyers with no cognizable US nexus will attract even more litigants and will increase the number of private antitrust claims filed in United States courts. There is no apparent justification for such a shift. While additional penalties could marginally increase deterrence, in this circumstance where international public enforcement is diminished, the likely effect may be to lessen overall detection.

* * *

AMICUS BRIEF OF CERTAIN PROFESSORS IN SUPPORT OF PLAINTIFFS IN F. HOFFMANN-LA ROCHE LTD. V. EMPAGRAN S.A.

(excerpt from)

Brief of Professors Darren Bush, John M. Connor, John J. Flynn, Shubha Ghosh, Warren Grimes, Joseph E. Harrington, Jr., Norman Hawker, Robert Lande, William G. Shepherd and Steven Semeraro

The past decade has witnessed nothing less than an explosion in the discovery of private international cartels with global price-fixing ambitions. This brief presents two major economic arguments in support of the decision below. First, in the context of international price-fixing conspiracies conduct relating to "wholly foreign" purchases necessarily affects domestic commerce. This is because international cartels must prevent international geographic arbitrage in order to succeed in controlling prices in any targeted national market.

Second, this brief assembles empirical evidence that, in the absence of affirmance of the judgment below, the global aspirations of contemporary cartels offer an insuperable challenge to a core aim of the antitrust laws: Deterrence. The broad geographic harm generated by the scores of modern global price-fixing conspiracies has overwhelmed the ability of corporate antitrust sanctions to provide enough financial disincentives to discourage the formation of similar cartels in the future. These sanctions have been inadequate to deter cartel formation because the probability of being caught by one or more of the world's antitrust authorities remains well below 100% and because the *expected* illegal monopoly profits made worldwide are more than sufficient to compensate would-be conspirators for their *expected* liabilities in jurisdictions with effective antitrust laws and enforcement. Permitting foreign buyers who purchased the products of international cartels abroad to pursue civil antitrust damages actions in U.S. courts is necessary to produce the level of damages needed to protect the U.S. economy and its consumers from future cartel injuries. Affirmance will also enhance the probability of discovery of clandestine cartels by multiplying the number of jurisdictions in which private parties have an incentive to investigate collusive behavior. * * *

[T]he international vitamin cartel generated the largest total of antitrust fines and penalties in history, which are calculated to be between $4.4 and $5.6 billion. But the cartel's monopoly profits in all areas of the world were $9 to $13 billion. Thus, the criminal and civil justice systems of the globe produced fines and damages that amounted to only about half of this cartel's illegal profits. These sanctions are much less than the amount needed to discourage future cartel formation. One of the best ways to discourage cartels is to increase the expected costs in the event the participants are caught, in order that the expected penalties exceed the expected benefits. As a practical matter, this deterrence benefit to the United States' consumers and its economy—something surely intended by Congress—is likely to be achieved only if federal law is construed to give injured foreign customers like Respondents the power to sue in the courts of the United States under American antitrust laws. * * *

[The cartel impacted the US market. If the US prices had been competitive, arbitrage would have destroyed the cartel.]

* * *

Even assuming prosecutorial conditions will resemble recent historical patterns of punishment, a judgment of affirmance will greatly improve international cartel deterrence and will lead it to approach optimal deterrence. The precise degree of deterrence will depend on the perceived probability that international cartels will be detected, investigated, and convicted. It is widely believed that the probability of detecting clandestine cartels is less than one-third. The degree of deterrence will also depend on the proportion of the price-fixing overcharges awarded to plaintiffs in civil suits, which on average has been less than 100% and in individual cases never exceeds double damages. If these estimates are correct and conditions remain unchanged, permitting wholly foreign buyers to seek redress for antitrust injury in U.S. courts, will mean that typical would-be cartelists will face, if not an optimal level of deterrence, the likelihood of a much smaller degree of underdeterrence than exists today.

* * *

Who is right? Would US' hosting this action in US courts be an unreasonable intrusion into the policy space of trading partners? Would it increase or lessen deterrence?

Note that the *Empagran* issue as framed by the Court is different from the problem treated in the cases above (e.g. *Alcoa, Wood Pulp, Hartford Fire.* In those cases, and perhaps some 95% of antitrust extraterritoriality cases, the question is whether the jurisdiction can protect itself from conduct abroad that harms the jurisdiction's citizens; not whether remote plaintiffs can use the jurisdiction's courts to condemn antitrust wrongs with effects elsewhere.

F. HOFFMANN-LA ROCHE LTD. V. EMPAGRAN S.A.

542 U.S. 155 (United States Supreme Court 2004)

JUSTICE BREYER:

The Foreign Trade Antitrust Improvements Act of 1982 (FTAIA) excludes from the Sherman Act's reach much anticompetitive conduct that causes only foreign injury. It does so by setting forth a general rule stating that the Sherman Act "shall not apply to conduct involving trade or commerce . . . with foreign nations." 15 U.S.C. § 6a. It then creates exceptions to the general rule, applicable where (roughly speaking) that conduct significantly harms imports, domestic commerce, or American exporters.* * *

To clarify: The issue before us concerns (1) significant foreign anticompetitive conduct with (2) an adverse domestic effect and (3) an independent foreign effect giving rise to the claim. In more concrete terms, this case involves vitamin sellers around the world that agreed to fix prices, leading to higher vitamin prices in the United States and independently leading to higher vitamin prices in other countries such as Ecuador. We conclude that, in this scenario, a purchaser in the United States could bring a Sherman Act claim under the FTAIA based on domestic injury, but a purchaser in Ecuador could not bring a Sherman Act claim based on foreign harm.

I.

The plaintiffs in this case originally filed a class-action suit on behalf of foreign and domestic purchasers of vitamins under, inter alia, § 1 of the Sherman Act and §§ 4 and 16 of the Clayton Act. Their complaint alleged that petitioners, foreign and domestic vitamin manufacturers and distributors, had engaged in a price-fixing conspiracy, raising the price of vitamin products to customers in the United States and to customers in foreign countries.

As relevant here, petitioners moved to dismiss the suit as to the foreign purchasers (the respondents here), five foreign vitamin distributors located in Ukraine, Australia, Ecuador, and Panama, each of which bought vitamins from petitioners for delivery outside the United States. Respondents have never asserted that they purchased any vitamins in the United States or in transactions in United States commerce, and the question presented assumes that the relevant "transactions occur[red] entirely outside US commerce." The District Court dismissed their claims. It applied the FTAIA and found none of the exceptions applicable. Thereafter, the domestic purchasers transferred their claims to another pending suit and did not take part in the subsequent appeal.

A divided panel of the Court of Appeals reversed. The panel concluded that the FTAIA's general exclusionary rule applied to the case, but that its domestic-injury exception also applied. It basically read the plaintiffs' complaint to allege that the vitamin manufacturers' price-fixing conspiracy (1) had "a direct, substantial, and reasonably foreseeable effect" on ordinary domestic trade or commerce, i.e., the conspiracy brought about higher domestic vitamin prices, and (2) "such effect" gave "rise to a [Sherman Act] claim," i.e., an injured domestic customer could have brought a Sherman Act suit, 15 U.S.C. §§ 6a(1), (2). Those allegations, the court held, are sufficient to meet the exception's requirements.

The court assumed that the foreign effect, i.e., higher prices in Ukraine, Panama, Australia, and Ecuador, was independent of the domestic effect, i.e., higher domestic prices. But it concluded that, in light of the FTAIA's text, legislative history, and the policy goal of deterring harmful price-fixing activity, this lack of connection does not matter.

We granted certiorari to resolve a split among the Courts of Appeals about the exception's application. . . .

II.

The FTAIA seeks to make clear to American exporters (and to firms doing business abroad) that the Sherman Act does not prevent them from entering into business arrangements (say, joint-selling arrangements), however anticompetitive, as long as those arrangements adversely affect only foreign markets. It does so by removing from the Sherman Act's reach, (1) export activities and (2) other commercial activities taking place abroad, unless those activities adversely affect domestic commerce, imports to the United States, or exporting activities of one engaged in such activities within the United States.

The FTAIA says:

> "Sections 1 to 7 of this title [the Sherman Act] shall not apply to conduct involving trade or commerce (other than import trade or import commerce) with foreign nations unless—
>
> "(1) such conduct has a direct, substantial, and reasonably foreseeable effect—
>
> "(A) on trade or commerce which is not trade or commerce with foreign nations [i.e., domestic trade or commerce], or on import trade or import commerce with foreign nations; or
>
> "(B) on export trade or export commerce with foreign nations, of a person engaged in such trade or commerce in the United States [i.e., on an American export competitor]; and
>
> "(2) such effect gives rise to a claim under the provisions of sections 1 to 7 of this title, other than this section.
>
> "If sections 1 to 7 of this title apply to such conduct only because of the operation of paragraph (1)(B), then sections 1 to 7 of this title shall apply to such conduct only for injury to export business in the United States."

This technical language initially lays down a general rule placing all (non-import) activity involving foreign commerce outside the Sherman Act's reach. It then brings such conduct back within the Sherman Act's reach provided that the conduct both (1) sufficiently affects American commerce, i.e., it has a "direct, substantial, and reasonably foreseeable effect" on American domestic, import, or (certain) export commerce, and (2) has an effect of a kind that antitrust law considers harmful, i.e., the "effect" must "giv[e] rise to a [Sherman Act] claim." §§ 6a(1), (2).

We ask here how this language applies to price-fixing activity that is in significant part foreign, that has the requisite domestic effect, and that also has independent foreign effects giving rise to the plaintiff's claim.

* * *

IV.

We turn now to the basic question presented, that of the exception's application. Because the underlying antitrust action is complex, potentially raising questions not directly at issue here, we reemphasize that we base our decision upon the following: The price-fixing conduct significantly and adversely affects both customers outside the United States and customers within the United States, but the adverse foreign effect is independent of any adverse domestic effect. In these circumstances, we find that the FTAIA exception does not apply (and thus the Sherman Act does not apply) for two main reasons.

First, this Court ordinarily construes ambiguous statutes to avoid unreasonable interference with the sovereign authority of other nations. . . . This rule of construction reflects principles of customary international law-law that (we must assume) Congress ordinarily seeks to follow. See . . . Hartford Fire Ins. Co. v. California, 509 US 764, 817 (1993) (Scalia, J., dissenting) (identifying rule of construction as derived from the principle of " 'prescriptive comity' ").

This rule of statutory construction cautions courts to assume that legislators take account of the legitimate sovereign interests of other nations when they write American laws. It thereby helps the potentially conflicting laws of different nations work together in harmony-a harmony particularly needed in today's highly interdependent commercial world.

No one denies that America's antitrust laws, when applied to foreign conduct, can interfere with a foreign nation's ability independently to regulate its own commercial affairs. But our courts have long held that application of our antitrust laws to foreign anticompetitive conduct is nonetheless reasonable, and hence consistent with principles of prescriptive comity, insofar as they reflect a legislative effort to redress domestic antitrust injury that foreign anticompetitive conduct has caused. See United States v. Aluminum Co. of America, 148 F.2d 416, 443–444 (C.A.2 1945) (L. Hand, J.) . . . .

But why is it reasonable to apply those laws to foreign conduct insofar as that conduct causes independent foreign harm and that foreign harm alone gives rise to the plaintiff's claim? Like the former case, application of those laws creates a serious risk of interference with a foreign nation's ability independently to regulate its own commercial affairs. But, unlike the former case, the justification for that interference seems insubstantial. See Restatement § 403(2) (determining reasonableness on basis of such factors as connections with regulating nation, harm to that nation's interests, extent to which other nations regulate, and the potential for conflict). Why should American law supplant, for example, Canada's or Great Britain's or Japan's own determination about how best to protect Canadian or British or Japanese customers from anticompetitive conduct engaged in significant part by Canadian or British or Japanese or other foreign companies? * * *

The Areeda and Hovenkamp treatise [1978] notes that under the Court of Appeals' interpretation of the statute

> "a Malaysian customer could . . . maintain an action under United States law in a United States court against its own Malaysian supplier, another cartel member, simply by noting that unnamed third parties injured [in the United States] by the American [cartel member's] conduct would also have a cause of action. Effectively, the United States courts would provide worldwide subject matter jurisdiction to any foreign suitor wishing to sue its own local supplier, but unhappy with its own sovereign's provisions for private antitrust enforcement, provided that a different plaintiff had a cause of action against a different firm for injuries that were within US [other-than-import] commerce. It does not seem excessively rigid to infer that Congress would not have intended that result." * * *

Respondents reply that many nations have adopted antitrust laws similar to our own, to the point where the practical likelihood of interference with the relevant interests of other nations is minimal. Leaving price fixing to the side, however, this Court has found to the contrary. See, e.g., *Hartford Fire*, 509 US, at 797–799 (noting that the alleged conduct in the London reinsurance market, while illegal under United States antitrust laws, was assumed to be perfectly consistent with British law and policy). * * *

Regardless, even where nations agree about primary conduct, say, price fixing, they disagree dramatically about appropriate remedies. The application, for example, of American private treble-damages remedies to anticompetitive conduct taking place abroad has generated considerable controversy. And several foreign nations have filed briefs here arguing that to apply our remedies would unjustifiably permit their citizens to bypass their own less generous remedial schemes, thereby upsetting a balance of competing considerations that their own domestic antitrust laws embody. . . .

These briefs add that a decision permitting independently injured foreign plaintiffs to pursue private treble-damages remedies would undermine foreign nations' own antitrust enforcement policies by diminishing foreign firms' incentive to cooperate with antitrust authorities in return for prosecutorial amnesty. * * *

Respondents alternatively argue that comity does not demand an interpretation of the FTAIA that would exclude independent foreign injury cases across the board. Rather, courts can take (and sometimes have taken) account of comity considerations case by case, abstaining where comity considerations so dictate.

In our view, however, this approach is too complex to prove workable. The Sherman Act covers many different kinds of anticompetitive agreements. Courts would have to examine how foreign law, compared with American law, treats not only price fixing but also, say, information-sharing agreements, patent-licensing price conditions, territorial product resale limitations, and various forms of joint venture, in respect to both primary conduct and remedy. The legally and economically technical nature of that enterprise means lengthier proceedings, appeals, and more proceedings—to the point where procedural costs and delays could themselves threaten interference with a foreign nation's ability to maintain the integrity of its own antitrust enforcement system. Even in this relatively simple price-fixing case, for example, competing briefs tell us (1) that potential treble-damages liability would help enforce widespread anti-price-fixing norms (through added deterrence) and (2) the opposite, namely, that such liability would hinder antitrust enforcement (by reducing incentives to enter amnesty programs). How could a court seriously interested in resolving so empirical a matter—a matter potentially related to impact on foreign interests—do so simply and expeditiously?

We conclude that principles of prescriptive comity counsel against the Court of Appeals' interpretation of the FTAIA. Where foreign anticompetitive conduct plays a significant role and where foreign injury is independent of domestic effects, Congress might have hoped that America's antitrust laws, so fundamental a component of our own economic system, would commend themselves to other nations as well. But, if America's antitrust policies could not win their own way in the international marketplace for such ideas, Congress, we must assume, would not have tried to impose them, in an act of legal imperialism, through legislative fiat.

* * *

Taken together, these two sets of considerations, the one derived from comity and the other reflecting history, convince us that Congress would not have intended the FTAIA's exception to bring independently caused foreign injury within the Sherman Act's reach.

* * *

Notes and Questions

1. Did the Court properly construe FTAIA subparagraph (2) to require, for jurisdiction over foreign conduct other than import commerce, that the US effect must give rise to *the plaintiff's claim* rather than, as the statute says, must "give[ ] rise to a claim under the provisions of [the Sherman Act] other than this section"? The clause might have meant that the conduct must give rise to a Sherman Act claim, rather than merely impose an effect unrelated to competition on US commerce. By that construction, there would still be a serious standing question: Did the foreign plaintiffs have standing to challenge the vitamins cartel under the Sherman Act? However, under the latter construction, the court would not have lacked jurisdiction over the subject matter of the lawsuit challenging the cartel.

2. The Court repeatedly assumed that the vitamin cartel's US effects had nothing to do with the effects that harmed plaintiffs. Thus the Court assumed a wholly foreign cartel that hurt foreign plaintiffs only. Injury from a cartel that had no effects in the US would not be covered by the Sherman Act in any event, with or without the FTAIA.

3. On remand, the Supreme Court's assumption of an independent cartel was proved wrong. The lower court clarified that the plaintiffs were complaining about the same global cartel that hurt Americans. To determine whether plaintiffs' harms were sufficiently connected to the US effects, the lower court announced a rule of proximate cause—Did the US effects proximately cause plaintiffs' injury? The court answered No and dismissed the case. 417 F.3d 1267, 1271 (D.C. Cir. 2005).

4. Would all foreign nations want to disqualify the US as a forum for hosting their citizens' claims for harms from a world cartel? Might Ecuador—which did not yet have an antitrust law—have been happy for its citizens to recover damages in US courts?

5. Does *Empagran* limit the scope of the conduct that an American plaintiff suing an American defendant can challenge under the Sherman Act? In Advanced Micro Devices, Inc. v. Intel Corporation, 452 F. Supp. 2d 555 (D. Del. 2006), AMD argued that there was a single global market for microprocessors and that Intel's anticompetitive conduct around the world marginalized AMD both in Europe and in the US. The court ruled that AMD could not assert a monopolization claim regarding AMD's sale of microprocessors manufactured in Germany and sold to foreign customers, even though it could assert a monopolization claim as to microprocessors sold in the US. Does this approach balkanize individual litigations, requiring different parts of the same case to be litigated in different jurisdictions?

6. Note that *Empagran*, as framed by the Court, is different from the typical antitrust extraterritoriality case. In the typical case, there is a clear link between the offense and the effect in the jurisdiction—e.g., price-fixing and price rise. The question concerns the length of the chain. How far can a court go to protect its nation's own markets and citizens from anticompetitive acts abroad? *Empagran* fits more within the genre of using US courts to do good in the world.

Along latter lines, in Kruman v. Christie's Intern., 129 F. Supp. 2d 620 (S.D.N.Y. 2001), plaintiffs sought to invoke the Alien Tort Claims Act as a basis for federal court jurisdiction over claims by foreign purchasers and sellers in the London art auction houses Christie's and Sotheby's. The theory was that the norm against price-fixing is now a world norm and its violation is a tort committed in violation of the law of nations. The court rejected this argument. The Supreme Court later held that the Alien Torts Claims Act does not apply extraterritorially—even to heinous civil rights violations—occurring abroad. Kiobel v. Royal Dutch Petroleum Co., 569 U.S. 108 (2013).

D. EVOLVING MODERN LITIGATION: SUBJECT MATTER JURISDICTION ACROSS THE WORLD

We deal here with current issues of jurisdiction over foreign defendants, both subject matter and personal jurisdiction, and with conduct sometimes involving long chains of causation. In a later section we treat government involvement: comity and defenses, as in the US Chinese Vitamin C litigation and the so far unsuccessful attempts to challenge the world oil cartel—OPEC.

US. For subject matter jurisdiction, the world has in general converged around the test of whether the anticompetitive effects in the enforcing jurisdiction are direct, substantial, and reasonably foreseeable, or a variation on these terms. This is the US test subject to the extra screen of *Empagran*. The input cartel cases often involve the question whether the harm to plaintiffs is sufficiently direct. A US court dismissed the case of a private plaintiff, Motorola Mobility, alleging overpricing of a smartphone embedding LDC panels price-fixed in Korea and Taiwan and sold to Motorola Mobility's Chinese subsidiaries, which incorporated the panels in smartphones in China and sold the smartphones to Motorola Mobility in the US. Motorola Mobility LLC v. AU Optronics Corp., 775 F.3d 816 (2014) (finding that the Chinese subsidiaries were the direct victims and the ones who could sue) (reminiscent of the facts in the EU's *InnoLux* case, supra at 586, but InnoLux was not a private case). But another US court upheld the criminal conviction of a Korean executive who was one of the price fixers in the same cartel in Korea, despite the fact that the bulk of the products were sold into international commerce and not into the US, and despite the FTAIA. United States v. Hsiung, 758 F.3d 1074 (9th Cir. 2014), amended by 778 F.3d 738 (9th Cir. 2015). See also Minn-Chem, Inc. v. Agrium, Inc., 683 F.3d 845, 853–54 (7th Cir. 2012), taking a flexible view of directness of effects where the effects are substantial and foreseeable.

EU. In Europe, a series of cases arose from the air cargo cartel, in which air carriers jointly set levels of fuel and security surcharges, which themselves constituted about a quarter of freight service charges. The carriers sold their air cargo services to freight forwarders, who sold their services to shippers. The carriers alleged lack of EU jurisdiction for inflation of the price of inbound flight services. The General Court found jurisdiction on the basis of qualified effects, taking the conduct both in isolation and as a part of a single, continuous infringement. Shippers were charged higher prices, leading, probably, to higher prices of the shipped goods in the EU. Effects in the EU were foreseeable, substantial, and sufficiently immediate. Martinair Holland v. Commission, Case T–323/17, ECLI:EU:T:2022:174, and sister cases, on appeal.

The *iiyama* case, also a long-chain case with third party intervention, was a private follow-on damages action in the courts of the UK (then still a member of the EU) after the EU found and fined the LCD (liquid crystal display) and CRT (cathode ray tube) cartels. Computer and TV monitors were price-fixed in Asia. Iiyama, a Japanese company, bought the monitors in Asia, incorporated them into electronic products in Asia, and distributed them to its subsidiaries in the EU. It sought damages in the UK. The UK Court of Appeals denied dismissal for lack of jurisdiction. The court said:

> 95. For all these reasons, we agree with the claimants that Intel is an important decision in the context of the present cases, and that it provides substantial support for the argument that a worldwide cartel which was intended to produce substantial indirect effects on the EU internal market may satisfy the qualified effects test for jurisdiction. Whether or not the test is satisfied will depend on a full examination of the intended and actual operation of the cartel as a whole. Such an examination can only take place in light of the full facts as they emerge and are assessed at trial. The exercise is not one suitable for summary determination on the basis of assumed facts.
>
> 96. We should say a little more about the elusive concept of "indirect" effects. Mr Beard submitted that the purchase of cartelised goods by the claimants within the EU had to be characterised as indirect effects in every instance where the supply chain included a prior sale by a cartel member outside the EU at an inflated price to

an innocent third party (typically an OEM in Asia), and that the existence of such a prior sale precluded EU law from taking account of subsequent indirect effects in the EU, even if the inflated price had been passed on down the chain to the claimants. Such indirect effects, he said, were merely knock-on or ripple effects, and fell outside the territorial scope of EU competition law.

97. The only remedy open to the claimants in such a situation, submitted Mr Beard, was to bring proceedings under the local competition law in whichever Asian country the first sale outside the cartel had taken place. The fact that such claims might now be time-barred, because they would be subject to a shorter limitation period than the six-year period applicable to the present claims brought in England, was irrelevant. Furthermore, unless the territorial reach of EU law were curtailed in this way, there would be a risk of multiple proceedings in different jurisdictions, double recovery by those who had suffered from the cartel, and double jeopardy for the defendants.

98. While there may be force in some of these points when the position is fully examined at trial, we are unable to agree with Mr Beard that the legal position is as stark as he would have us accept. The European case law which we have reviewed shows it to be at least arguable with a real prospect of success that intended effects within the EU internal market of a worldwide cartel fall within the scope of Article 101, and that the production of such effects on the EU market, if substantial and of a systemic nature, may properly be characterised as immediate effects of the offending agreements. The test is one of substance rather than terminology, and in the context of the qualified effects test we do not consider that directness of effect should be treated as an additional requirement to immediacy of effect. The relevant criterion is that the effects produced in the EU should be immediate, and the European Court has now given authoritative guidance on how that concept should be understood. We are unable to accept the proposition that the mere existence of even one prior sale to an innocent third party outside the EU at an early stage of the supply chain must, without more, lead to the conclusion that the test of immediacy cannot be satisfied. Like the other criteria, it requires an overall assessment in light of the offending conduct viewed as a whole.

99. Nor are we impressed by arguments based on the possible multiplicity of proceedings, or the risk of double jeopardy to the defendants. Those who participate in a worldwide cartel cannot complain if their conduct gives rise to proceedings in different jurisdictions, or if they have to meet possibly overlapping claims. Any developed legal system will have mechanisms in place to deal with problems of this nature, and so far as the present proceedings are

concerned, no realistic risk of double recovery has been drawn to our attention. Furthermore, it is axiomatic that no claimant can recover more than the loss which it can show it has actually suffered as a result of the offending agreements. If the present claims were to remain struck out, there would instead be a very real risk of the "artificial fragmentation of comprehensive anti-competitive conduct" which, as the Court warned . . . in Intel, might thereby escape the European Union's jurisdiction.

100. Similarly, we are unimpressed by the point that the purchases by the claimants within the EU come at the end of an intermediate series of intra-group transactions. It is true that sales or transfers within an undertaking do not normally have independent significance for the purposes of EU competition law, but that is not the point. What matters is that the cartel was always intended to have worldwide effect, including in the EU, and it must have been contemplated that the supply chains whereby cartelised goods ended up being purchased within the EU might include intra-group transactions. The important point is that purchases are ultimately made, at an inflated cartel price, within the territory of the EU. The existence of such purchases, on any substantial scale, must therefore have an effect on the operation of the internal market.

iiyama (UK) et al. v. Samsung et al., The LCD Appeals [2018] EWCA Civ. 220.

Japan. Japan seems also to enjoy a wide reach of its law, also tested in the CRT cartel case, but with a different articulation of the controlling principle. The cartel members were CRT manufacturers located in Malaysia, Indonesia and Thailand. Their parent companies sold the price-fixed tubes to Southeast Asian subsidiaries of Japanese TV manufacturers. The Japanese TV manufacturers ordered their subsidiaries to purchase from chosen suppliers—who turned out to be price fixers—and directly negotiated the key terms of the purchase on behalf of their Southeast Asian subsidiaries. The subsidiaries incorporated the price-fixed parts into TV sets, and then sold most of them to the Japanese TV manufacturers. The Japanese TV manufacturers then resold the TVs, some in Japan but mostly internationally outside of Japan. The JFTC fined the foreign price fixers. (This was the first time that it fined foreign price fixers.) The case went up to the Japanese Supreme Court.

The Japanese Supreme Court held that the Japanese Anti-Monopoly law would apply as long as all substantive elements of the violation are met. "Extraterritoriality" was not a relevant concept.

An article from Japan's Library of Congress article describes the case: "The Court's decision was based on article 1 of the Act [of the

Japanese Anti-Monopoly Act, or "JAMA"], which states the purpose of the Act is to "promote democratic and wholesome development of the national economy as well as secure the interests of general consumers" by promoting fair and free competition. (Sup. Ct., Dec. 12, 2017 (translation by author).) Therefore, the location where the acts were committed does not affect the application of the Act, as long as they resulted in impairing the free competition of the Japanese market. (Id.)" https://www.loc.gov/item/global-legal-monitor/2017-12-19/japan-supreme-court-affirms-extraterritoriality-of-antimonopoly-act/

The Court explained:

Therefore, the JFTC may issue such orders against enterprises engaged in a cartel as long as all the requirements in the JAMA are met. The expression 'causing substantial restraint of competition in any particular field of trade' in Article 2(6) of the JAMA, which defines unreasonable restraint of trade, means to impair the competitive function of the market of the trade in question .... Accordingly, even if a price-fixing cartel as in this case (i.e., unreasonable restraint of trade) is concluded outside Japan, the cartel disturbs Japan's free competition economic order if the Japanese market is one of the markets whose competitive function the price-fixing cartel may impair—for instance, if the price-fixing cartel impairs competition in which a counterparty to a transaction is situated in Japan.

* * *

[After stressing that the Japanese TV manufacturers were the principal parties in selecting the sellers of the tubes and negotiating and dictating the terms on which the subsidiaries would buy . . .]

We therefore find on the facts that the Japanese TV manufacturers and their local manufacturers together carried out the transactions for the purchase of the CRTs in question as part of their economic activity. We thus hold that the Agreement impaired the competitive function of the market for the transactions to which the Japanese TV manufacturers situated in Japan appeared as counterparties.

Japan Sup. Ct., Dec. 12, 2017, 2016 (Gyo-hi) No. 233.

See Kazuaki Nishioka, International scope of the Japanese Anti-monopoly Act in cross-border cartel cases: a Japanese approach to 'extraterritorial application,' 8 Journal of Antitrust Enforcement 590 (2020), quoting the Court.

How would you describe the basis for the exercise of jurisdiction, apart from meeting the requirements of the substantive offense? If the Japanese TV manufacturers had not controlled the transactions of the subsidiaries, what result? If the Japanese TV manufacturers had resold all of the TV sets outside of Japan, would that have mattered?

China

The Anti-Monopoly Law of the People's Republic of China provides:

"Article 2 This Law is applicable to monopolistic conducts in economic activities within the territory of the People's Republic of China; and it is applicable to monopolistic conducts outside the territory of the People's Republic of China, which serve to eliminate or restrict competition on the domestic market of China."

Here are excerpts from a blog, from the law firm Winston & Strawn, reporting on the suit brought by the Chinese e-commerce firm Mengbian against Amazon Europe (which does not do business in China) for violating the Chinese Anti-Monopoly Law by dropping Mengbian's online store from Amazon Marketplace thereby impairing its competition in the Chinese market. The suit has subsequently been withdrawn, perhaps by reason of settlement.

CHINESE E-COMMERCE COMPANY SUES AMAZON EUROPE UNDER CHINA'S ANTI-MONOPOLY LAW

October 2, 2023

On August 22, 2023, the Guangzhou Intellectual Property Court announced that it has accepted a case brought by Mengbian, a Chinese e-commerce firm that operates an online store on the Amazon marketplace, against Amazon Europe for violation of China's Anti-Monopoly Law. . . .

According to the announcement, Mengbian alleges that Amazon Europe has a dominant position in the e-commerce market within Europe, and Amazon Europe abused that position by closing Mengbian's online store, blocking its account, and refusing to trade with it without justifiable reasons. . . .

Background

It has been widely publicized that Amazon has removed a number of Chinese sellers from its platform in recent years. The Shenzhen Cross-Border E-Commerce Association estimates that at least 50,000 Chinese vendors' accounts have been negatively impacted and Chinese e-commerce firms had suffered losses of over 100 billion yuan (approximately US$13B).

As a result, affected Chinese companies have been exploring various avenues to obtain remedies, including utilizing Chinese courts, often despite choice-of-law and choice-of-forum provisions in the contract. In such circumstances, arguments typically include invalidity of contract or some sort of tort. Mengbian's approach against Amazon Europe could be the first attempt to use China's Anti-Monopoly Law. . . .

Jurisdiction of China Courts

Chinese courts may assert jurisdiction over a cross-border antitrust matter based on (i) the general provisions of jurisdiction applicable to contract or tort claims, or (ii) the extra-territoriality provision of the Anti-Monopoly Law. For tort claims, jurisdiction can be established either where the defendant is located or at the location of the infringing conduct. The latter can include the place where the violation was committed and the place where the results of the violation occurred. Here, the court explicitly identified Mengbian's domicile in Guangzhou as "the place where the results of the violation occurred," and, therefore, the court asserted jurisdiction.

The Anti-Monopoly Law has an independent basis to assert extraterritorial jurisdiction, which applies when the monopolistic behavior outside of China has an "exclusionary or restrictive effect on competition in the domestic market." Based on this provision, Chinese courts may assert subject matter jurisdiction over companies located outside of China. * * *

Notes and Questions

1. What are the claims for and against subject matter jurisdiction by the Chinese courts in the suit by Mengbian? What should Mengbian be required to prove to establish jurisdiction?

2. Assertions of China's long-arm jurisdiction are not entirely new. A decade earlier, Huawei, the Chinese technology and device firm, sued InterDigital Corporation, the US firm with a suite of standard essential patents, for abusing dominance by violating FRAND obligations to license its SEPs on fair, reasonable and non-discriminatory terms. Huawei claimed that IDC abused its dominance in both the US and Chinese markets. Huawei exported devices using the SEPs to the US market but its competition allegedly was impaired because it was under the (illegal) handicap of having to pay a monopoly price for the licenses; thus the abuse of dominance in the US market could eliminate or restrict competition in China. The Chinese court stated that the AML applies when the conduct "directly has a major,

substantial and reasonably foreseeable effect of impairing and restricting the domestic production activities, export opportunity and export trade of domestic enterprises," and held for Huawei on both jurisdiction and substance.

Huawei Jishu Youxian Gongsi Su Jiaohu Shuzi Tongxin Youxian Gongsi (华为技术有限公司诉交互数字通信有限公司) [Huawei Tech. Co. v. InterDigital Communications, Inc.], 2013 Yue Gao Fa Min San Zhong Zi No. 306 (Guangdong High People's Ct. 2013) pp. 38–39.

Comment on the exercise of jurisdiction. The point of violation was failure to license on FRAND terms in the US. Trace this to the harm alleged to Huawei and the Chinese market for the products embedding the SEPs. What was the antitrust harm, and was it (sufficiently) direct?

SOUTH AFRICA

The Foreign Exchange Rate Litigation: Subject matter and personal jurisdiction

For subject matter jurisdiction, South Africa has long applied the test of whether the conduct complained of has direct, foreseeable, and substantial consequences in the country. For personal jurisdiction, presence in the country was normally required. The jurisdictional requirements were tested when traders for some 28 mostly international banks, many with no presence or office in South Africa, fixed the Rand/dollar exchange rates over many years at least until the conspiracy was discovered.

COMMISSION v. BANK OF AMERICA, ET AL.

215/CAC/APR23) [2024] ZACAC 1

[Following convictions in the United States for manipulations of the Rand/dollar exchange rates, the Competition Commission of South Africa referred to the Tribunal 28 local and international banks for price-fixing and market division in violation of the South African Competition Law. Many of the banks were peregrini (foreign). Some were pure peregrini—they were not domiciled and they did not carry on business in South Africa. Others were local peregrini—they had a local branch or office in South Africa. Defendants sought to dismiss for lack of subject matter jurisdiction, and the pure peregrini sought to dismiss for lack, also, of personal jurisdiction. The motions raised difficult fact-based questions; jurisdiction was dependent on links of the conduct and of the defendants to South Africa and links of the conduct to an alleged overall conspiracy harming South Africa. Here are excerpts from the judgment of the Court of Appeal, examining whether the Commission's referral affidavit to the Tribunal had supplied sufficient facts with respect to each of the defendants.]

Judge Dennis Davis: * * *

The question of personal and subject matter jurisdiction

[79] Before dealing with the role of each of these banks and whether the Commission made out a sufficient case for each of these banks to be referred to the Tribunal, it is necessary, albeit briefly, to again emphasize the question of subject matter and personal jurisdiction. . . .

[80] Section 3 (1) of the Act which provides that the Act applies to all economic activity within or having an effect within the Republic sets out the terms of subject matter jurisdiction. It was described by this Court in American Soda Ash Corporation CHC Global (Pty) v Competition Commission of South Africa and others [2003] ZACAC 6 at para 18 as follows:

'The question is not whether the consequences of the conduct is criminal or, for that matter anti-competitive, but whether the conduct complained of has, direct and foreseeable' substantial consequences within the regulating country. In other words, 'the effects' in the present case must be such that they fall within the regulatory framework of the Act whether they are uncompetitive or not.' * * *

[82] The referral affidavit seeks to describe the manner in which the Commission establishes subject matter jurisdiction thus:

'The conspiracy had a direct or immediate and substantial effect in the Republic and it was foreseeable that impugned conduct would, or had the potential, to have such an effect.

The common manner in which the effect of the impugned conduct [is] felt is that the buyers of ZAR pay artificially inflated prices for buying the currency and sell at artificially reduced prices when selling the currency.'

[83] So much for subject matter jurisdiction. In respect of personal jurisdiction as it pertained to peregrini banks, the Court in its 2020 decision said the following as it was applicable to peregrini banks.

'Given the very objective of the cartelists was to manipulate the USD/ZAR exchange rate so that they could make a higher profit, common sense and logic tell us that it would be foreseeable that customers would suffer as a result, either directly as investors in a given transaction or in the prices of goods and services for export and import purposes.' * * *

[85] [The case] . . . requires an examination as to whether there was an SOC [single overall conspiracy, which was used to link defendants] between the respondent banks of a kind that reveals not simply that the Rand was the subject of the trades but that the conspiracy was sufficiently connected to South Africa because by virtue of it being an overall conspiracy, foreign banks had effectively entered into "business with South African banks". This provided sufficient connection between these respondent banks and South African jurisdiction to sustain a finding of personal jurisdiction in the circumstances of the case. This concept of personal jurisdiction as developed by this Court was predicated on an economy where business is no longer based on bricks and mortar but rather on modern technology which has created the conditions for a global economy where national borders are transcended by virtue of technological development. It follows that to sustain an argument that there [were] sufficient connecting factors the need is to provide clear evidence of linkages to the South African banks as part of an overall conspiracy and which thus linked the incolae banks [foreign but resident] with the peregrini banks.

* * *

Conclusion [after sorting through the facts alleged as to each defendant and requiring dismissal of 23 of 28]

[175] The Commission based its entire case on a SOC in which all of the respondent banks were said to be participants. As set out in the discussion on the jurisprudence derived from the European courts and which was the basis of the Commission's own employment of the concept of a SOC, it was necessary for the Commission to meet the core requirements thereof.

[176] To repeat, on the Commission's own version, it was required to show a common anti-competitive objective, that is an overall plan in which all of the respondent banks participated to pursue a common economic objective. It was required to show that each firm had made an intentional contribution by its own conduct to the common objectives pursued by all of the participants to the SOC. It further was required to show that each respondent bank was aware of the actual conduct planned or put into effect by the other undertakings in pursuit of these objectives; that is to perpetuate a SOC or that each respondent bank could reasonably have foreseen that it participated in the SOC and that it was prepared to take the risk. As is evident from 2020 Court order it behoved the Commission to provide significant further details in the referral affidavit over and above its initiation referral affidavit to show that this overall conspiracy could be proved to include all the respondent banks.

[177] Compounding the difficulty of this ambitious cause of action as developed by the Commission was the fact that a number of the banks were peregrini as a result of which the Commissions was required to make a showing of both personal and subject matter jurisdiction. As is evident from the 2020 judgment, this Court was prepared to extend the concept of personal jurisdiction beyond the strictures of the existing common law position; that is beyond the requirements of a local presence in South Africa or a party prepared to consent to jurisdiction. It found that in an appropriate case personal jurisdiction could be extended if there was a case in which peregrini were part of a conspiracy in which they participated with South African banks directly such that peregrini banks could be considered to be participants in the cartel. . . .

[178] Manifestly, evidence to that effect is designed to meet the requirement of personal jurisdiction. It is an onerous requirement because by so developing the law, this Court was prepared to extend the concept of personal jurisdiction to meet the demands of a global economy in circumstances where this development was suitably circumscribed by means of the evidence required. In addition, the Commission was required to make a showing of subject matter jurisdiction which in essence is encapsulated in s3 (1) of the Act. The Tribunal, unfortunately, conflated these two requirements. The Tribunal's treatment reduced the personal jurisdiction component to an almost meaningless exercise. It is important to distinguish these two requirements to ensure that both are adequately shown by the Commission in seeking to hold peregrini banks accountable for their conduct.

[179] It is for this reason that an occasional participation in a chatroom or unspecified conduct which is tenuously inferred as being part of the overall conspiracy is insufficient to meet these jurisdictional requirements.

[180] While subject matter jurisdiction is widely couched in the words employed in s 3 (1) the basis of subject matter jurisdiction was set out expressly in the referral affidavit as follows:

'The conspiracy had a direct or immediate, and substantial effect in the Republic and it was foreseeable that the impugned conduct would, or had the potential to, have such an effect.

The common manner in which the effects of the impugned conduct are felt is that buyers of ZAR pay artificially inflated prices for buying the currency and sell at artificially reduced prices when selling the currency.'

[181] It should be noted that the manner in which 'the effect of the conduct' is set out in the referral affidavit has significant implications. As pointed out in argument by counsel for the third and fourth respondents, between 2007 and 2013, the relevant period for the case brought about the existence of the SOC, daily trades in the South African domestic forex market increased from USD10.7b to USD18b. The daily ZAR foreign exchange on the spot markets amounted to approximately USD 26.28b with USD 6.6b daily on the outright forwards market. The largest single transaction pleaded by the Commission in respect of the alleged SOC was USD 25m.

[182] It may well be that the effect that various trades documented by the Commission had on the Rand was so insignificant as to have had no material effect thereon. But that is a matter which is better dealt with at trial where the respondent banks, which have a case to answer, can provide evidence to gainsay the case made by out by the Commission.

Notes and Questions

1. Note the difference between personal and subject matter jurisdiction. Both must be present in all cases. Personal jurisdiction is closely associated with due process of law. The defendant must have minimum contacts with the jurisdiction, such that it is fair for the jurisdiction to take action that affect its rights. Was the court's flexible—but nonetheless demanding—treatment of personal jurisdiction important "to meet the demands of a global economy" in which harms are easily inflicted from distant locations?

2. Note the court's concluding observations about the need for an effect within the jurisdiction. This is a hugely important caveat. The traders were making extra profits by manipulating the Rand/dollar exchange rates. They may not have cared whether South Africa or the US came out ahead. It is possible that there was no effect or no (perceptible) negative effect on the South African currency market. "Effect" in the case has yet to be litigated. Does this mean that rogue traders can sit in their offices in New York, London, Sao Paulo, and other financial centers of the world, manipulate the Rand/dollar rate by conduct that violates the South African law, and be effectively immune from South African law? Should there be an easier path to jurisdiction over foreign acts that substantially and foreseeably intrude on another nation's important interests—such as the integrity of its currency including exchange rates? If so, what should the principle be?

E. EXTRATERRITORIALITY IN DEVELOPING COUNTRIES AND SMALL ECONOMIES

Global abuses can harm competition most directly in the global commons. Price-elevated products placed on the global market may quickly find their way to national/regional markets in proportion to the usual purchasing patterns; e.g., 30% to the EU, 30% to the US. The big jurisdictions purchases are substantial and the imports into those jurisdictions is foreseeable to the offenders at the time of the offense. "Directness" and "immediacy" are flexible enough to admit of third party interventions if the effects in the nation are foreseeable and likely to be substantial. Thus, in cases like Intel or InnoLux, subject matter jurisdiction is not likely to be an obstacle. But what about small jurisdictions, in Africa or South America or the Caribbean?

Professor Marek Martyniszyn points out that broad principles of extraterritoriality might be of no advantage to them. He writes:

"In more general terms Intel also points to existing power imbalances affecting capacity of different systems to safeguard their markets and deal with foreign anticompetitive conduct. . . . [E]xtraterritoriality does not offer the same potential to all. In this case, EU law applied because the EU market constituted a significant part of the world market and indeed the non-EU Intel duly paid the fine initially imposed of 1.06 billion euro, back then the largest such fine ever imposed. Authorities of a much less significant market might not have a similar possibility. Even if discontinued thanks to enforcement in other systems, domestic harm would often remain unaddressed. That is, there would be no retrospective transfer of extracted wealth (by means of fines) and no deterrence would be generated, potentially leaving the market open for anticompetitively exploits."

Marek Martyniszyn, *Intel, iiyama* and *Air Cargo*: Far-Reaching Extraterritorial Application of EU Competition Law, 43(11) European Competition Law Review 505–512 (2022).

At the same time that developing countries' and small economies' practical powers to catch anticompetitive restraints are small compared with the powers of the developed world, the needs of developing and small economies to protect and to grow competition are likely to be greater. The South African digital market study has recommended that Google has an antitrust duty to provide friendly interfaces of a sort that small South African businesses are able to manage, and to do and not do in South Africa what it must do and not do in the EU under the Digital Markets Act. Online

Intermediation Platforms Market Inquiry, Final Report and Decision, July 2023, Sec. 3

Wang'ombe Kariuki and Rafe Mazer have written a report on digital platforms in continental Africa: The need for a new competition policy approach in digital economies, Concurrences, May 2024, https:// www.concurrences.com/en/review/issues/no-2-2024/international/africa-the-need-for-a-new-competition-policy-approach-in-digital-economies. The Report documents the immense opportunity but also the immense challenges facing small business in Africa, and proposes recommendations for gatekeepers' obligations to reach out to small African businesses and modalities for operationalizing their recommendations under the new African competition protocol within the African Continental Free Trade Agreement. Obligations would include those specified in the EU Digital Markets Act and go further.

How should competition law/policy respond to the problem of disparity of power between the developed and developing world? If the South African Competition Commission should sue Google (US) for failure to provide an appropriate interface for South African businesses and Google should move to dismiss on grounds of no subject matter jurisdiction, what are South African courts likely to hold? What are US and EU courts likely to hold in a similar situation? If South African courts should find jurisdiction, find a violation, and order Google's compliance with EU DMA rules, how is Google likely to respond? If, when the African competition protocol is operational, the new African Competition Commission should make similar rulings, is Google more likely to comply? Is there a case that African jurisdiction would violate customary international law? What is the principle limiting its jurisdiction? What would be the practical effect if US and EU courts would find the prescription (interpretation of the statutes) or the enforcement excessively extraterritorial?

Mergers

Mergers famously have extraterritorial effects. Large multinational mergers tend to affect the world. Scores of jurisdictions may require pre-transaction filings for the same merger, and competition authorities of several countries may clear the merger with conditions that may or may not be consistent. Nations may prohibit mergers that other jurisdictions clear. See discussion in Chapter 6, Mergers.

Today, many nations' competition authorities coordinate intensely on mergers of common concern, and they may try to reach common results or compatible remedies. Still, divergences occur.

It is well accepted that every nation likely to be affected by a merger has a right to merger control; lack of subject matter jurisdiction is not normally invoked. But is there or should there be a duty of nations to seek coherence? Should there be a duty of comity not to prohibit a merger that a home jurisdiction clears and supports? Is there a comity obligation to make remedies compatible? Remember, however, that mergers can affect different markets differently. Moreover, some jurisdictions are more risk-taking or more precautionary than others. What problems are posed by comity obligations of coherence?

* * *

Should it be fair game for all nations' laws to reach offshore acts that harm them? Would a world vision to protect the global competition commons demand no less? Or do sovereign interests, combined with concerns of double counting, cumulative remedies, substantive disagreements, and procedural differences, counsel significant limits? While the questions are playing out in courts and agencies around the world, jurisdictions seem bolder than ever to control offshore acts that threaten them.

Even if cases pass the "substantial, foreseeable, directness" test, defenses may be available. We turn to them now.

F. COMITY AND FOREIGN GOVERNMENT DEFENSES

Cases might get dismissed on grounds of comity or on grounds of Act of State, foreign sovereign immunity, foreign sovereign compulsion, political question, or the right to petition a sovereign. Formulations of these doctrines may vary from jurisdiction to jurisdiction. Comity is a doctrine of mutual respect and deference to greater interests to preserve the harmony of nations. It is used frequently in the exercise of prosecutorial discretion whether to sue, or to devise relief. It is seldom invoked to dismiss a case, but this has recently been done in the case of the vitamins C cartel among Chinese manufacturers that China claimed to have ordered. The Act of State doctrine holds that no one may sue the state for official acts within its own territory, nor question the validity of such acts. Foreign sovereign immunity means that states are immune from challenge to their sovereign acts. Immunity does not apply to commercial acts. Foreign sovereign compulsion means that the foreign sovereign compelled the act; the defense may require a showing of both true compulsion and significant punishment for disobeying the order. Petitioning a foreign sovereign—to get anticompetitive measures by anticompetitive means—is normally not an offense in democracies because of the right to petition. Political questions are questions that only the government can resolve and would do so as a matter of politics, not law; there are no judicially manageable standards for courts to resolve them.

United States has the largest body of law on these issues. We include here US agency guidelines; a recent US case that was (unusually) dismissed on grounds of prescriptive comity; and material on the world oil cartel—OPEC—which is a consortium of the oil-producing nations and their corporate entities; the OPEC "exemption" or claim of it is regarded by some as the biggest "hole" in the antitrust laws.

1. US Agency Guidelines

ANTITRUST GUIDELINES FOR INTERNATIONAL ENFORCEMENT AND COOPERATION US DEPARTMENT OF JUSTICE AND FEDERAL TRADE COMMISSION (2017)

(excerpts; footnotes omitted)

4. Agencies' Consideration of Foreign Jurisdictions

4.1. Comity

In enforcing the federal antitrust laws, the Agencies consider international comity. Comity itself reflects the broad concept of respect among co-equal sovereign nations and plays a role in determining "the recognition which one nation allows within its territory to the legislative, executive or judicial acts of another nation." In determining whether to investigate or bring an action, or to seek particular remedies in a given case, the Agencies take into account whether significant interests of any foreign sovereign would be affected.

A decision to take an investigative step or to prosecute an antitrust action under the federal antitrust laws represents a determination that the importance of antitrust enforcement outweighs any relevant foreign policy concerns. That determination is entitled to deference. Some courts have undertaken a comity analysis in disputes between private parties.

In performing this comity analysis, the Agencies consider a number of relevant factors. The relative weight given to each factor depends on the facts and circumstances of each case. Among other things, the Agencies weigh: the existence of a purpose to affect or an actual effect on U.S. commerce; the significance and foreseeability of the effects of the anticompetitive conduct on the United States; the degree of conflict with a foreign jurisdiction's law or articulated policy; the extent to which the enforcement activities of another jurisdiction, including remedies resulting from those enforcement activities, may be affected; and the effectiveness of foreign enforcement as compared to U.S. enforcement.

An investigation or enforcement action by a foreign authority will not preclude an investigation or enforcement action by either the Department or the Commission. Rather, the Agency will determine whether, in light of actions by the foreign authority, investigation or enforcement is warranted to address harm or threatened harm to U.S. commerce and consumers from anticompetitive conduct. In cases in which an Agency opens an investigation or brings an enforcement action concerning conduct under investigation by a foreign authority, it may coordinate with that authority.

Several of the comity factors considered by the Agencies warrant further discussion.

First, when considering the degree of conflict with foreign laws, the Agencies review the relevant laws of the interested foreign sovereigns. In the context of the Agencies' enforcement, conflicts of law are rare. As more jurisdictions have adopted and enforce antitrust laws that are compatible with those of the United States, it has become increasingly common that no conflict exists between U.S. antitrust enforcement interests and the laws or policies of a foreign sovereign. Further, no conflict of law exists if a person subject to the laws of two sovereigns can comply with both. Moreover, no conflict exists in cases where foreign law is neutral as to particular conduct, because it remains possible for the parties in question to comply with the U.S. antitrust laws without violating foreign law. In situations where a conflict of law exists, however, comity may counsel in favor of declining enforcement.

Second, the Agencies will assess the articulated interests and policies of a foreign sovereign beyond whether there is a conflict with foreign law. In determining whether to investigate or bring an enforcement action regarding an alleged antitrust violation, the Agencies consider the extent to which a foreign sovereign encourages or discourages certain courses of conduct or leaves parties free to choose among different courses of conduct.

Third, the Agencies consider whether the objectives sought to be obtained by U.S. enforcement could be achieved by foreign enforcement. The Agencies may consult with interested foreign authorities with the purpose of working to understand and address harm or threatened harm to U.S. commerce and consumers from anticompetitive conduct.

4.2. Consideration of Foreign Government Involvement

In some instances, a foreign government may be involved in anticompetitive conduct that involves or affects U.S. commerce. In determining whether to conduct an investigation or to file an enforcement action in cases in which foreign government involvement is known or suspected, the Agencies consider four legal doctrines that lie at the intersection of government action and the antitrust laws: (1) foreign sovereign immunity; (2) foreign sovereign compulsion; (3) act of state; and (4) petitioning of sovereigns.

4.2.1 Foreign Sovereign Immunity

In civil cases, the Foreign Sovereign Immunities Act of 1976 ("FSIA") provides the "sole basis for obtaining jurisdiction over a foreign state in the courts of this country." The FSIA shields foreign states from the civil jurisdiction of the courts of the United States, subject to certain enumerated exceptions and to treaties in place at the time of the FSIA's enactment. Under the FSIA, federal courts have jurisdiction over foreign states in certain cases in which the foreign state has:

a. waived immunity explicitly or by implication;

b. engaged in commercial activity;

c. expropriated property in violation of international law;

d. acquired rights to property in the United States;

e. committed certain torts within the United States; or

f. agreed to arbitration of the dispute.

The "commercial activity" exception is the most relevant exception for antitrust purposes. The FSIA provides that a foreign state is not immune from jurisdiction of U.S. courts when:

> the action is based upon a commercial activity carried on in the United States by the foreign state; or upon an act performed in the United States in connection with a commercial activity of the foreign state elsewhere; or upon an act outside the territory of the United States in connection with a commercial activity of the foreign state elsewhere and that act causes a direct effect in the United States.

"Commercial activity" is defined to include "either a regular course of commercial conduct or a particular commercial transaction or act," and the FSIA provides that "the commercial character of an activity shall be determined by reference to the nature of the course of conduct or particular transaction or act, rather than by reference to its purpose." Commercial activity is distinct from sovereign activity inasmuch as the former is understood to include "those powers that can also be exercised by private citizens," while the latter is understood to include "powers peculiar to sovereigns." In other words, the principal question is whether the government is acting "not as a regulator of a market, but in the manner of a private player within it."

To determine whether an action is "based upon" a commercial activity, a court must focus on "the particular conduct on which the plaintiff's action is based," i.e., "those elements that, if proven, would entitle a plaintiff to relief and the gravamen of the complaint."

As a practical matter, most activities of foreign state-owned enterprises operating in the commercial marketplace are "commercial" and, therefore, such enterprises are not immune from the jurisdiction of the U.S. courts in actions to enforce the antitrust laws by virtue of the FSIA. The commercial activities of these enterprises are subject to the U.S. antitrust laws to the same extent as the activities of privately owned foreign firms.

4.2.2 Foreign Sovereign Compulsion

Because U.S. antitrust laws can extend to foreign persons and conduct with a sufficient connection to the United States, some persons may find themselves subject to foreign legal requirements that conflict with the laws of the United States. In these circumstances, courts have recognized a limited defense against application of the U.S. antitrust laws when a foreign sovereign compels the very conduct that the U.S. antitrust law would prohibit. If it is possible, however, for a party to comply with both the foreign law and the U.S. antitrust laws, the existence of the foreign law does not provide any legal excuse for actions that do not comply with U.S. law. Similarly, that conduct may be lawful, approved, or encouraged in a foreign jurisdiction does not, in and of itself, bar application of the U.S. antitrust laws—even when the foreign jurisdiction has a strong policy in favor of the conduct in question.

Two rationales underlie the limited defense of foreign sovereign compulsion. First, Congress enacted the U.S. antitrust laws against the background of well-recognized principles of international law and comity, pursuant to which U.S. authorities give due deference to the official acts of foreign governments. A defense for actions compelled by foreign sovereigns under certain circumstances serves to accommodate equal sovereigns. Second, fairness considerations require a mechanism to provide a predictable rule of decision for those seeking to conform their behavior to all applicable laws.

The Agencies recognize and consider this foreign sovereign compulsion defense when determining whether to bring an enforcement action. Because of the limited scope of the defense, however, the Agencies will refrain from bringing an enforcement action based on considerations of foreign sovereign compulsion only when certain criteria are satisfied.

First, the foreign government must have compelled the anticompetitive conduct under circumstances in which a refusal to comply with the foreign government's command would give rise to the imposition of penal or other severe sanctions. As a general matter, the Agencies regard the foreign government's formal representation that refusal to comply with its command would have such a result as being sufficient to establish that the conduct in question has been compelled. To be sufficient, however, the representation must contain enough detail to enable the Agencies to see precisely how the compulsion would be accomplished under foreign law. Foreign government measures short of compulsion do not suffice for this defense, although they may be a relevant comity consideration if, for example, the measures reflect an articulated policy of the foreign government.

Second, the defense generally applies only when the compelled conduct can be accomplished entirely within the foreign sovereign's own territory. If the compelled conduct occurs in the United States, the Agencies will not recognize the defense. For example, the defense would not apply if a foreign government required the U.S. subsidiaries of several firms to organize a cartel in the United States to fix the price at which products would be sold in the United States.

Third, the order must come from the foreign government acting in its governmental capacity. The defense does not arise from conduct that would fall within the FSIA commercial activity exception.

* * *

Illustrative Example E

Situation:

Increased quantities of Commodity X have flooded the world market over the last several years, including substantial amounts coming into the United States. The officials of Countries Alpha, Beta, and Gamma meet with their respective domestic firms and urge them to "rationalize" production of Commodity X by cooperatively cutting back. Going one step further, the government of Country Gamma orders cutbacks from its domestic firms, subject to substantial penalties for non-compliance. Producers from Countries Alpha and Beta agree among themselves to institute comparable cutbacks, but their governments do not require them to do so. The overseas production cutbacks have sufficient effects on U.S. commerce for the antitrust laws to apply.

Discussion:

The Agencies would not find that foreign sovereign compulsion precludes prosecution of the agreement in restraint of trade entered into by the participants from Countries Alpha and Beta. The Agencies would acknowledge a defense of sovereign compulsion, however, for the participants from Country Gamma.

4.2.3 Act of State Doctrine

The act of state doctrine prevents courts from "declar[ing] invalid the official act of a foreign sovereign performed within its own territory." Applying this doctrine, courts decline to adjudicate claims or issues that would require the court to judge the validity of the sovereign act of a foreign state in its own territory. This doctrine is rooted in considerations of international comity and the separation of powers.

The doctrine does not apply to every act taken by an individual or entity affiliated with a sovereign state. For instance, it does not apply to the acts of individual government officials acting outside their official capacity. Nor does it apply to private actors, even when those acts are approved or condoned by the foreign government in question.

Accordingly, when a restraint on competition arises directly from the act of a foreign sovereign, such as the grant of a license, award of a contract, or expropriation of property, the Agencies may refrain from bringing an enforcement action based on the principles animating the act of state doctrine. More specifically, the Agencies may exercise enforcement discretion and decline to challenge foreign acts of state if the facts and circumstances indicate that: (1) the specific conduct complained of is a public act of the sovereign, (2) the act was taken within the territorial jurisdiction of the sovereign, and (3) the conduct relates to a matter that is governmental, rather than commercial.

4.2.4 Petitioning of Sovereigns

Under the *Noerr-Pennington* doctrine, a genuine effort to obtain or influence action by governmental entities in the United States falls outside the scope of the Sherman Act, even if the intent or effect of that effort is to restrain or monopolize trade. It is the view of the Agencies that the principles undergirding this doctrine apply to the petitioning of foreign governments. The Agencies, therefore, will not challenge under the antitrust laws genuine efforts to obtain or influence action by foreign government entities. But as with *Noerr-Pennington*, the Agencies will not exercise this discretion when faced with "sham" activities, in which petitioning "ostensibly directed toward influencing governmental action, is a mere sham to cover . . . an attempt to interfere directly with the business relationships of a competitor," or when Noerr-Pennington would otherwise not apply.

Illustrative Example F

Situation:

Corporation 1 and Corporation 2 have mines in Country Alpha where they extract Mineral X. Corporation 1 and Corporation 2 use different techniques to extract Mineral X. Corporation 1 launches a campaign designed to foster the adoption and retention of regulations that would effectively outlaw Corporation 2's mining technique. As part of this broader campaign, Corporation 1 files a complaint with Country Alpha's Ministry of Mines alleging severe health and safety concerns stemming from Corporation 2's mining technique and demanding the permanent closure of Corporation 2's mine. If successful, Corporation 1 would have an effective monopoly on the U.S. market for Mineral X. The Country Alpha Ministry of Mines decides to investigate the complaint, leading to the temporary shutdown of Corporation 2's operations.

Discussion:

Had Corporation 1's activities been directed at a U.S. government entity and the *Noerr-Pennington* doctrine applied, the Agencies would not take action against Corporation 1. Applying like principles here, the Agencies would not institute enforcement action against Corporation 1 for lodging a complaint with the Country Alpha Ministry of Mines.

Notes and Questions

1. Note the differences among the concepts. Act of State and foreign sovereign immunity are sovereignty defenses that do not allow consideration of the merits of a case against the sovereign. The petitioning right means that the jurisdiction values the right of petition; it is akin to free speech and is not an offense; and in any event it is the State, not private defendants, that would take the anticompetitive act. Foreign sovereign compulsion is more nuanced. It entails deference to a foreign sovereign taking action on its own territory; but there are certain things that the foreign sovereign may not compel (without accountability), such as ordering its nationals to fix prices on US territory. Moreover, "compulsion" and "order" is construed narrowly. Foreign sovereign encouragement and approval are not enough. The

political question doctrine holds that courts may not decide foreign policy questions; political questions are not justiciable.

2. Comity has been an ambiguous concept. At one time it was given wide scope and was considered a doctrine of deference for courts to apply, especially in cases by private plaintiffs. As you see above, the US antitrust authorities do their own comity balancing before initiating a proceeding, and they expect the courts to respect their judgment that deference to a foreign government is not required. In the caselaw above in which comity has been asserted, the courts have pivoted from comity as a rule of judicial discretion to a concept of Congressional proscription: Did Congress intend for the Sherman Act to reach so far under circumstances like these?—prescriptive comity. Thus, comity is now presented as a matter of implied statutory interpretation on the assumption that Congress would not have intended for its law to intrude unreasonably into the affairs of other nations. In US law, there is a pending question whether comity balancing is ever appropriate where defendants' conduct foreseeably harmed competition in the US and no true conflict prevented defendants from following the law of both home and host jurisdictions. Reconsider the *Hartford Fire Insurance* case, supra at 588, and compare the majority with the dissenting opinions in *Animal Science (*Vitamin C*)* (dismissing on comity grounds), of which you will read excerpts below. What was the right result, in both cases?

2. US Caselaw

ANIMAL SCIENCE PRODUCTS, INC. (IN RE VITAMIN C LITIGATION)

8 F.4th 136 (United States Court of Appeals for the Second Circuit 2021)

[In the 1990s and early 2000s, just before China's modern competition law was adopted and spanning the period of China's entry into the WTO, the Chinese producers of vitamin C agreed to fix their export prices into the US and elsewhere. By their price-fixing, they raised prices significantly—about 28% to 80%. They did so in the context of meetings of their trade association, which in China includes significant government presence. Pursuant to the agreement, the government allegedly set minimum export prices. The Chinese manufacturers charged various prices above the minimum. When the US buyers sued, the Chinese firms defended that the Chinese government had ordered them to agree to the export prices, and that the trade association was effectively a government body. The Chinese Ministry MOFCOM came to the support of the Chinese manufacturers. MOFCOM stated in an amicus brief in the case that it ordered the price-fix.

The district court, dealing with conflicting evidence, denied the Chinese manufacturers' motion for summary judgment. At trial, the jury found as a fact that China had not ordered the price fix and that none of the other defenses applied. It returned a verdict for plaintiffs which, after trebling, was $147 million. Defendants appealed. The appellate court reversed, holding that it was bound to accept MOFCOM's interpretation that it ordered the price-fix and that comity required deference to China. The Supreme Court reversed and remanded, holding that the US courts were not bound by a foreign government's interpretation of its own documents and law but rather owed sympathetic deference. On remand, the appellate court found that defendants were faced with a true conflict, and that the other comity balancing factors were still relevant to deciding "prescriptive comity"—whether Congress "intended" the Sherman Act to reach so far. It balanced the factors and dismissed, in a two-to-one decision, on grounds of prescriptive comity.

Here are excerpts from the majority and dissenting opinions.]

Judge Nardini: * * *

E. International Comity Principles Favor Dismissal

Balancing these factors [—conflict, nationality of defendants and site of conduct, effectiveness of enforcement and alternative remedies, foreseeable harms to American consumers, expected reciprocity, and effect on foreign relations—], we decline to construe U.S. antitrust law as reaching defendants' conduct in the circumstances presented here, and we conclude that principles of international comity warrant dismissal. The existence of a true conflict between Chinese and U.S. antitrust law, Chinese nationality of all of the defendants, extraterritorial nature of the anticompetitive conduct, and potential impact upon foreign relations together strongly favor dismissal. While the efficacy of enforcing a judgment is unclear, we acknowledge that enforcement could be salutary for the international Vitamin C market, especially given that economic harm to American consumers was foreseeable. The United States undoubtedly has a substantial interest in the uniform enforcement of its antitrust laws, including the deterrence value of treble damages against foreign companies whose anticompetitive conduct causes substantial and foreseeable economic injury to American consumers. Yet the U.S. Department of Justice has not brought criminal antitrust enforcement actions against these defendants, and the Department of State has not weighed in as an amicus curiae on either side of the issue. There are also alternate means for the United States to vindicate those interests, such as through bilateral diplomatic efforts, multilateral discussions, trade proceedings in the WTO, or dispute resolution in another international forum. While the stakes are high for both countries, we conclude that the United

States' concern with extraterritorial enforcement of a private civil judgment under its antitrust laws is substantially diminished in these circumstances. In light of these considerations of international comity, we do not construe the Sherman and Clayton Acts to reach the present controversy.

JUDGE WESLEY, dissenting:

. . . [T]he defendants were not legally required to engage in any concerted action. They could have complied with Chinese law without violating the Sherman Act by resigning from the Subcommittee and thereby independently setting their prices at or above the industry-coordinated minimum price, abstaining from any "meeting of the minds" to agree on price. . . . The Ministry and defendants do not dispute this conclusion. . . . [T]he Ministry did not argue vitamin C exporters who were not members of the Subcommittee still needed to coordinate prices. In fact, both the Ministry and the majority emphasize that price coordination occurred through the Vitamin C Subcommittee. . . . * * *

Moreover, the record makes clear that Chinese law did not require the defendants to agree on prices above the minimum of $3.35/kg, which is what the defendants did. . . . * * *

. . . Wang Qi, an executive of one of the original defendants that settled before trial, testified: Question: And when the minimum price for verification and chop [seal of approval for export] was $3.35, the Chamber of Commerce did not care if your company sold Vitamin C at a price higher than $3.35; isn't that right? Answer (Qi): Correct. That is like a minimum price. Question: You were free to decide about prices above $3.35 when that was the minimum price? Answer (Qi): Yes, when it's over they don't care. . . . * * *

International comity is a careful balancing act [noting in footnote the claim that the Supreme Court has rejected balancing as unworkable]. It requires "tak[ing] into account the interests of the United States, the interests of the foreign state, and those mutual interests the family of nations have in just and efficiently functioning rules of international law." .In re Maxwell Commc'n Corp, 93 F.3d 1036, 1048 (2d Cir. 1996). Accordingly, "[w]hen there is a conflict, a court should seek a reasonable accommodation that reconciles the central concerns of both sets of laws." Societe Nationale Industrielle Aerospatiale v. U.S. Dist. Ct. for S. Dist. of Iowa, 482 U.S. 522, 555 (1987) (Blackmun, J., concurring). China's purpose in enacting the PVC regime, as characterized by the Ministry, was to "transition from a State-controlled economy" as it entered the WTO and to avoid anti-dumping sanctions. . . . Even accepting for argument's sake that Chinese law required the defendants to coordinate on a minimum price to achieve its concern about anti-dumping claims, applying comity for agreements above the minimum goes above and beyond accommodating the central interests of the foreign state.

Nothing in the international comity precedents implies a true conflict exists where only part of the defendants' conduct was required under foreign law. As the Supreme Court held in *Hartford Fire*, there is no true conflict if foreign law did not "require[ ] [defendants] to act in some fashion prohibited by the law of the United States" or if the defendants' "compliance with the laws of both countries" was possible. 509 U.S. at 799. . . .

The defendants could have complied with Chinese law and the Sherman Act by: (1) exercising their legal right to resign from the Subcommittee and not participating in any conspiracy to set prices, or (2) not colluding on prices above the minimum, the only price needed to receive a chop. Given the "virtually unflagging obligation of the federal courts to exercise the jurisdiction given them," Colorado River Water Conservation Dist. v. United States, 424 U.S. 800, 817 (1976), this is not the "rare" case presenting "extraordinary circumstances" that warrants dismissal on the basis of comity . . . .
* * *

Notes and Questions

1. Critique both opinions. Which is the better approach? Which is a better fit with the current US law, considering both *Hartford Fire* and *Empagran*?

2. Is it obvious how the balance of the factors comes out? Is it a question of discretion, requiring deference to the judges who do the balancing? Is it fair to call the exercise "prescriptive comity"—this is what Congress must have meant—rather than judicial balancing?

3. The Chinese manufacturers agreed to fix prices, and raised them as much as 80%. There is a soft world norm that price-fixing is illegal, and the strong US anti-cartel law is well known. Should China be able to immunize its firms from US antitrust law by ordering its firms to fix prices into the US? By saying in court: I ordered them to do it?

4. Suppose that, in the heyday of US car manufacturing, Michigan ordered General Motors, Ford and Chrysler to agree on the prices they would charge for out-of-state sales, and the car companies did so. They would soon discover that their price fixing was illegal, for a state of the United States cannot order its firms to fix prices and free them from application of the federal antitrust laws. California Retail Liquor Dealers Ass'n v. Midcal Aluminum, Inc., 445 U.S. 97 (1980); Schwegmann Bros. v. Calvert Distillers Corp., 341 U.S. 384 (1951). Should a foreign government have more power than the states of the

United States to confer immunity on price-fixers into the US? Explain the differences.

Within the EU, the rule is similar to the rule within the US. An Italian official set the price for matches in Italy and an Italian law required the Italian match producers to set quotas. The producers set the quotas, slighting the Germans and Swedes, who wanted to sell matches in Italy. EU law has a counterpart to the US state action doctrine—if acts of a private party are compelled by the state and thus are not autonomous, the acts are attributable to the state and the private parties do not violate the competition law. But, in the *Italian matches* case, the court said: the Italian match producers did not have to set the quotas in so anticompetitive a way. In the discretionary space, the quota-setting was an act of the producers. The producers as well as Italy violated the competition law. Consorzio Industrie Fiammiferi v. Autoria Garante della Concorrenza, EU:C:2003:430.

3. OPEC: Foreign Sovereign Immunity, Act of State, and Political Question

The big oil producing nations of the world, centered in the Middle East, have had an oil producers' cartel since 1960. OPEC accounts for some three quarters of the world's oil reserves, and it has been blamed for several oil crises and about a trillion dollars of oil overcharges to Americans alone.

On several occasions the US government has considered suit against OPEC or its member countries or companies; but—for diplomatic reasons—has not sued. A private action was brought against OPEC in the 1970s in the wake of an oil crisis, but the suit was dismissed as raising a political question and as barred by the Act of State doctrine. International Association of Machinists v. OPEC, 649 F.2d 1354 (9th Cir. 1981).

In later years, in the face of rising oil prices, Congress has repeatedly vetted its ire against OPEC. It perennially introduces—but has never passed—a bill that would authorize the Justice Department to sue OPEC. The colloquial name of the bill is NOPEC—No Oil Producing and Exporting Cartels.

The few US judicial opinions have differed on whether the US antitrust laws prohibit OPEC. In Prewitt Enterprises, Inc. v. OPEC, 2001 WL 624789; 2001–2 Trade Cas. (CCH) ¶ 73,246 (N.D. Ala. 2001) (opinion vacated and case dismissed for failure of service, 353 F.3d 916 (11th Cir. 2003), the district court would have permitted a class action by oil buyers against OPEC. The then member states of OPEC (Iraq, Libya, Iran, Saudi Arabia, United Arab Emirates, Qatar, Kuwait, Algeria, Nigeria, Indonesia, and Venezuela) and non-member cooperating states (Norway, Mexico, Russia, and Oman) were not named as defendants; thus there was no suit against a sovereign. The court found it "beyond dispute that OPEC was created and exists for the express purpose of coordinating, limiting, stabilizing and otherwise controlling crude oil production and export in order to increase its members' revenues." It further found that "the Sherman Act plainly reaches agreements in restraint of trade entered into by foreign entities such as OPEC acting abroad that have a substantial and adverse impact in the United States." Turning to the sovereign immunity question, the court found that neither OPEC nor the state co-conspirators (non-defendants) could claim immunity given that they were engaging in conduct "plainly commercial in nature," as evidenced by the fact that the illegal acts "can be performed by private persons as well as sovereign states." Finding OPEC's conduct to be a per se violation of Section 1 of the Sherman Act, the district court entered a permanent injunction against its continued price fixing. But, as noted above, the decision was vacated and the case dismissed for failure of service.

By contrast, in a case against a Venezuelan-based oil company and related corporate entities that allegedly colluded with OPEC to fix oil prices, the Federal Court of Appeals for the 5th Circuit declared that the courts had no subject matter jurisdiction. The court said:

> . . . Appellants, retailers of gasoline products in the United States, have asked the federal courts to adjudicate the merits of their antitrust claims against oil production companies that have allegedly participated in a conspiracy to fix prices. . . . Appellants allege a conspiracy that is orchestrated by the sovereign member nations of OPEC. We hold today that Article III courts lack subject matter jurisdiction over Appellants' claims because they present nonjusticiable political questions that are constitutionally committed to the political branches responsible for the conduct of United States foreign relations and national security policy. Any ruling on the merits of this case would, by its core essence, impermissibly interfere with the Executive Branch's longstanding policy of engaging with OPEC nations regarding the global supply of oil through diplomacy instead of private litigation. The constitutional concerns that inform our declination of jurisdiction under the political question doctrine similarly persuade us that adjudication of Appellants' claims is precluded by the act of state doctrine.

Spectrum Stores Inc. v. Citgo Petroleum Corp., 632 F.3d 938 (5th Cir.), cert. denied (Sup. Ct. 2011). See, similarly, D'Augusta v. American Petroleum Institute, 117 F.4th 1094 (9th Cir. 2024); International Association of Machinists and Aerospace Workers v. OPEC, 649 F.2d 1354 (9th Cir. 1981).

Congress, meanwhile, at various times, has introduced the NOPEC bill—No Oil Producing and Exporting Cartels. Here is the text of the NOPEC bill introduced in the Senate term 2023–2024.

NOPEC

Senate, 118th CONGRESS, 2023–24, S. 678

To amend the Sherman Act to make oil-producing and exporting cartels illegal.

IN THE SENATE OF THE UNITED STATES

A BILL

To amend the Sherman Act to make oil-producing and exporting cartels illegal.

Be it enacted by the Senate and House of Representatives of the United States of America in Congress assembled,

SECTION 1. SHORT TITLE.

This Act may be cited as the 'No Oil Producing and Exporting Cartels Act of 2023' or 'NOPEC'.

SEC. 2. SHERMAN ACT.

The Sherman Act (15 U.S.C. 1 et seq.) is amended by adding after section 7 the following:

'SEC. 7A. OIL PRODUCING CARTELS.

'(a) In General—It shall be illegal and a violation of this Act for any foreign state, or any instrumentality or agent of any foreign state, to act collectively or in combination with any other foreign state, any instrumentality or agent of any other foreign state, or any other person, whether by cartel or any other association or form of cooperation or joint action—

'(1) to limit the production or distribution of oil, natural gas, or any other petroleum product;

'(2) to set or maintain the price of oil, natural gas, or any petroleum product; or

'(3) to otherwise take any action in restraint of trade for oil, natural gas, or any petroleum product;

when such action, combination, or collective action has a direct, substantial, and reasonably foreseeable effect on the market, supply, price, or distribution of oil, natural gas, or other petroleum product in the United States.

(b) Inapplicability of defenses.—No court of the United States shall decline, based on the act of state, foreign sovereign compulsion, or political question doctrine to make a determination on the merits in an action brought under this section.

"(c) Enforcement.—The Attorney General of the United States shall have the sole authority to bring an action to enforce this section. Any such action shall be brought in any district court of the United States as provided under the antitrust laws.".

SEC. 3. No sovereign immunity in oil cartel cases. . . .

Notes and Questions

1. Should the US Congress pass NOPEC? Should the world tolerate the oil cartel? Or must it, as a practical question of political power and international relations?

2. If NOPEC should pass, will world oil prices go down? What are the difficulties in implementation? How would a court order against OPEC or its members be formulated? (Consider imposing obligations on the commercial entities versus imposing obligations on the States.) How could it be enforced?

CONCLUSION

This chapter has worked through the reach of national/ regional (EU) competition laws to cover actors and acts performed abroad. It has highlighted regulation and litigation at national/regional level to control acts launched outside of the jurisdiction and transactions consummated by firms domiciled abroad. Is this outreach inevitable, given global commerce, new technologies, integration of the world, and the global dispersion of effects of conduct and transactions of large corporations? The chapter has also reviewed defenses and norms of deference, especially in view of conflicting foreign sovereign interests. As of this writing, the flexibility of national/regional jurisdictions to control offshore conduct and transactions that affect them seems to have the upper hand. Will this norm continue in light of the current tide of nationalism?

Chapter 10

GLOBAL GOVERNANCE

A. INTRODUCTION

For most of a century the wisdom of an international antitrust regime has been debated. At the close of World War II, the free nations of the world began negotiating a global trading system to control transnational restrictive business practices. The Havana Charter, negotiated in 1947 to 1948, would have required nations to take measures against transborder business practices such as price-fixing, market divisions, and restraints limiting market access and fostering monopolistic conduct. The Havana Charter was never adopted, but it was the precursor to the General Agreement on Tariffs and Trade.

Also in the 1940s, in the wake of world cartels that harmed America in its war effort, the United States pioneered the effects doctrine to protect itself from offshore cartels. United States v. Aluminum Co. of America ("Alcoa"), 148 F.2d 416 (2d Cir. 1945). Although resisted for years, effects jurisdiction is now well accepted in world-wide. See generally Chapter 9.

Effects jurisdiction is unilateral. It protects nations' citizens even in the absence of global cooperation or an international framework. This chapter is about the next step: community rather than unilateralism. It is about a possible international framework or norms, regional law, grass-roots level cooperation, and convergence of law.

While ambitions for a world regime began as early as the 1940s, concerns for sovereignty dictated caution and defeated the earliest world initiatives. Extraterritorial jurisdiction filled the slack in some measure but also triggered conflicts and generated the need for comity if not convergence. Globalization exposed the limits of national law and led to a renewed call for a global vision. Then, once again, sovereignty concerns and national interests overwhelmed cosmopolitan thinking. These concerns and interests have produced robust efforts, which continue today, to nurture roots-up convergence, most prominently through the vehicle of the International Competition Network, discussed below.

This Chapter continues, in Part B, with an overview essay on the ups and downs in the project for a global antitrust framework. Continuing with the subject of "higher law"—that is, law that is higher than national, it provides excerpts from a United Nations set of principles—the only world competition code in existence, albeit drafted in a different era. The Chapter then turns to the newly adopted and ambitious competition law for continental Africa, and references other and growing regional law. Part C shifts to the other end of the continuum—grassroots and bi-lateral cooperation; long a mainstay of attempts to deal with conflicts and, in more recent years, to maximize joint interests in common enforcement. Part D fleshes out regional cooperation through regional economic communities (RECs) and free trade agreements (FTAs). Part E treats the three major international institutions for research, cooperation, and convergence—the Organization for Economic Cooperation and Development (OECD), the United Nations Conference on Trade and Development (UNCTAD), and the International Competition Network (ICN), which are three vibrant organizations working for coherence, better standards, and better understanding in competition law.

B. HIGHER LAW

1. The Project of World Antitrust

WORLD ANTITRUST—A GLOBAL FRAMEWORK FOR GLOBAL PROBLEMS?

by Eleanor Fox, edited and reprinted with permission, originally published in International Antitrust Law & Policy: Fordham Competition Law 50th Anniversary Volume (Juris Publishing 2025)

I. Introduction

We have seen three inflection points in the quest for world antitrust. These are: the UNCTAD Set of Principles (1980), the proposals of the European Union for a competition regime within the World Trade Organization (1995–2001), and the birth of the International Competition Network (ICN, 2001). The birth of ICN was seen by some as putting to rest a world antitrust project, and by others as a foundational step for adopting a world system. The flames of the project have simmered. Is there unfinished business? Is the lack of a world framework for megamergers, export and world cartels, global abuses of dominant market power, and the interface of trade and competition, a problem to be reckoned with? Is there a practical formulation or vision fit for the 21st century?

This essay begins with the UNCTAD Set of Principles and Rules on Competition (and background from some years before). It then sprints forward to the 1990s, a decade in which we saw a plethora of cross-border private restraints and conflicting national solutions, potentially undermining the newly liberalized international economic order. We include the debate throughout the 1990s on the virtues and costs of a system of international antitrust law, envisioned within the framework of the World Trade Organization.

In the new millennium, antitrust as an agenda item for the WTO was jettisoned in view of higher trade priorities. Independently, the debate on what to do about cross-border antitrust problems shifted to the newly born ICN, which was conceived to be a virtual, roots-up project on "antitrust all of the time"—i.e., not antitrust and trade. As ICN took root, critics of a world antitrust project declared the project laid to rest; the end of history. But was it? The new millennium has spawned new technologies and with them new global abuses and yet larger megamergers. Analysis is fragmented by national boundaries. Developing country antitrust is coming into its own and developing countries have a new awareness of restraints launched in the Global North that impair competition in the Global South. Is there a path for higher than national law for solving the competition problems that are bigger than nations?

II. The UNCTAD Set

In the 1970s, the industrialized countries, the developing countries, and the communist bloc negotiated a corporate code of conduct. Even then, the idea for an international code governing private business conduct was not new. Just after World War II, the world was beginning to realize the harmful effects of the cartels of the 1930s, including their support for authoritarian regimes. There were negotiations in Havana to create an international trading system which would have included obligations to protect free competition. But the Havana Charter was rejected. Very few countries then had competition laws and many even opposed a market economy. The Truman administration's failure to submit the Treaty to the US Senate, reportedly because of concerns of loss of sovereignty and the desire of US industry to get protective legislation, was a decisive blow.

By the 1970s, some 33 countries had competition laws; US multinationals were expanding, and developing countries were aggrieved by restrictive practices of the multinational enterprises (MNEs), such as joint venture agreements that limited the developing-country-partner's exports, and discriminatory low pricing. For their part, the industrialized countries were aggrieved by developing country preferences for their state-owned businesses, and they wanted a path for consultation on disputes. Even countries that rejected a market economy were interested in an agreement—in order to rein in the MNEs. The nations reached agreement in 1980. The UNCTAD Set prohibits anticompetitive agreements (prominently cartels), predatory and discriminatory behavior and other abuses of dominance including certain unfair trade practices, and anticompetitive mergers. It covers state actors in their commercial capacity. It provides for consultations and information sharing. It is voluntary; that is, there is no enforcement mechanism.

What has come of the UNCTAD Set? Developed countries hear relatively little of it, but it is an important document for the developing world and it—along with the Model Code developed to accompany it—has influenced and continues to influence developing countries in adopting and applying their competition laws. Every five years, UNCTAD reviews and readopts the Set in principle.

After adoption of the UNCTAD Set, a decade elapsed before the next serious debate on a global antitrust agenda.

III. The Debate of the 1990s—an Antitrust Agenda in the WTO

The 1980s were a busy decade. Trade barriers fell at the end of the Tokyo Round (1979). Cross-border deals and conduct accelerated. Nations or their competition authorities signed numerous, significant bi-lateral arrangements, promising to notify one another when antitrust action was to be taken affecting the significant interests of the other, to share information, to meet periodically, and ultimately, to embrace positive comity—whereby the competition authority of a country suffering injury abroad—such as by denial of market access, would request the authority of the excluding country to bring suit, and where appropriate the requesting nation would stand back to await the outcome. The Berlin Wall fell at the end of 1989. Central and Eastern European nations embraced democracy, markets, and antitrust, and some requested technical assistance. With the now growing competition law family, harmonization and convergence became key objectives.

Was the next step needed—a competition law for the world?

The 1990s saw another significant fall in the barriers to trade, culminating at the end of the Uruguay Trade Round in 1994 and in the formation of the World Trade Organization, along with assimilation of the post-Soviet democracies and their new antitrust regimes. The European Union's new merger competence was coming into its own. The EU's challenge, and then clearance with tough conditions, of Boeing's acquisition of McDonnell Douglas, highlighted the divergences in substantive law. Eastman Kodak's inability to penetrate the Japanese market, allegedly because of private restraints supported by Japan, fueled the argument that we needed to lift our gaze from national law, national borders, and national interests, and take a holistic, world-regarding view.

A number of proposals were put forward for an international antitrust law or framework. The most prominent of these was suggested by the European Community.

The European Community commissioned a group of experts to consider how to devise a world regime to control private firm restraints in world commerce. In 1995, the Group of Experts submitted their report. The Report recommended a global project within the WTO, beginning modestly and working up to a full competition regime. It would begin with basic building blocks of bans against cartels and boycotts, bilateral arrangements, agreement on core principles such as nondiscrimination and due process, technical assistance, and the requirement that nations adopt an antitrust law. It would build up to a complete antitrust law, with dispute resolution. It was contemplated as a plurilateral agreement—thus, nations could choose to sign. The Experts' Report became the basis for proposals by the European Commission to the European Council and then the European Union to the WTO.

The EU proposal gathered momentum in the mid-1990s. In December 1996, the WTO established a Working Group on the Interaction between Trade and Competition Policy. Under the leadership of Frederic Jenny, it produced excellent work product, highlighting the competition and trade-and-competition problems that rose to world level and had no home.

However, the United States and developing countries were opposed to the European proposal. The United States pled that it would lead to bad principles of law (for example, too expansive an abuse of dominance law) and to unaccountable bureaucracy. Developing countries opposed on nearly opposite grounds—that the competition principles likely to be negotiated would open their markets wide to efficient Western giants and would deprive the developing countries of the policy space they needed to grow their own firms. They stressed again that most developing countries did not have antitrust laws at the time, and they did not have the experience necessary to negotiate wisely on their own behalf.

Responding to the criticism by the United States, the EU continually contracted its proposal, eliminating dispute resolution except for nations' failing to adopt or enforce an antitrust law. It eliminated substantive rules except for a rule against hard core cartels. In light of the EU revisions, the United States agreed not to oppose an antitrust agenda item for the next trade round, and the antitrust item was placed on the agenda of the then new Doha Development Trade Round. At the ministerial meeting of the Doha round in Cancun in 2003, however, the antitrust item was dropped along with other new issues; the new issues detracted from pressing core trade issues such as reducing cotton subsidies. Indeed, little progress has been made on the core trade issues and the Doha Round has all but failed.

IV. The New Millennium

If world antitrust had momentum in the 1990s, history had a different path in store. From the developing country perspective, too few countries had operative antitrust laws (although the number was growing fast). More experience was needed. From the industrialized countryside, there was increased skepticism that there could be a manageable world antitrust project. The attraction of world-level vision to solve world problems fell by the wayside.

Policy makers sought other paths for convergence and conflict reduction. An alternative route was embraced—a roots-up network with no binding rules. The International Competition Network (ICN), a virtual network of antitrust authorities with non-governmental advisors, was formed in 2001. ICN was to be, in effect, the converse of the WTO project: jurisdictions would collaborate informally to tease out their commonalities of law and procedure. ICN would be all and only antitrust; no trade; no trade and competition. And nothing would be binding.

The ICN had its first of now 24 annual conferences in spring 2002. It has succeeded beyond expectations in bringing together the antitrust/competition authorities of the world and in developing networks of cooperation, collaboration, and the sharing of information. It is, however, essentially limited to enhancing and, through more knowledge, converging national competition laws and procedures and practices. It does not cross borders and seas or provide a trade-and-competition interface; nor does it nudge towards a holistic view of outcomes such as megamergers or export/regional cartels.

On the virtues of a global framework for antitrust, the first two decades of the new millennium were quiet. Businesses and their lawyers sometimes expressed annoyance with the scores of merger regimes, their duplicative filings, and the sometimes inconsistent outcomes. Policymakers, enforcers and scholars sometimes expressed the value of a more holistic picture. Regional and export cartels continued to exist, given the practical inability of smaller and poorer jurisdictions to control them. Meanwhile, developing countries increasingly adopted competition laws and gained experience in enforcing them. Then came the birth of Big Tech—companies bigger than nations, truly global, challenging national authorities to control their global abuses. National authorities are inventing and reinventing the wheel to control Big Tech Gatekeeper and similar abuses; publishing guidelines and adopting regulation; specifying prohibited or presumptively prohibited conduct, each in their own slightly different ways; with smaller, poorer nations worried, with cause, that the most powerful gatekeepers would withdraw from business in their country if the agencies flexed their regulatory muscles.

As a world regime has been written off by many observers as impractical, unworkable, or simply unwise, regional solutions and even a continental solution are flourishing. In Africa, a Competition Protocol for all Africa has been approved and is pending ratification. The African Continental Free Trade Agreement (AfCFTA) competition policy was adopted on 19 February 2023, providing for the establishment of a continental competition regulator. It aims to adopt a hard law approach to competition law enforcement on the continent focusing on collusive conduct, minimum resale price maintenance, restrictions on passive sales, abuses of dominance that prevent, restrict or distort competition, and the notification of mergers of continental dimension.

The document introduces concepts such as gatekeepers, and prohibiting core platforms from engaging in certain restraints.

The protocol provides a vehicle for Africa to engage with continent-wide and world restraints, including megamergers and global giants' conduct that hurt Africa.

Meanwhile, Big Tech world-wide abuses have led to conversations among antitrust authorities to try to develop plurality norms to counter global wrongs.

V. Conclusion

It is no longer the case that so few countries have competition laws, or so few developing countries have the relevant experience, that a world antitrust project is premature. As of 2024, approximately 140 countries have antitrust/competition laws. Most are developing countries. Most have had experience enforcing their competition laws and collaborating with neighbors and others. Even so, the time for world antitrust has not come.

This is so for two reasons. One, not having a world regime, nations and their competition authorities have taken steps that fill some gaps or otherwise make a world regime less urgent. National-agency-to-national-agency cooperation has deepened. Fora for collaboration and experience-sharing have multiplied from OECD, UNCTAD and ICN to the BRICS, the African Competition Forum, APEC, COMPAL, and the Arab Competition Network, with some of the above tailored to geography, language, and level of development. Direct interactions between competition authorities have also increased in the context of specific matters. Confidentiality waivers have become a practice in this context and facilitate engagement between regulators on matters. Higher-than-national law is a feature of some regional free trade agreements and common markets; and now with the AfCFTA Competition Protocol, even for the whole African continent. Convergence where amenable and informed divergence are at a reasonably high level, thanks mostly to ICN and OECD, eliminating some conflicts while revealing but softening others.

Two, as developing and emerging economies have gained expertise in enforcing their competition laws and charting their competition policies, they have discovered their own voice, and it is not the same as the West's. The best rules for the most powerful nations with the most robust markets are not always the best rules for the most vulnerable. Apart from some very general principles, it is probably the case that developing and emerging economies will not want the West to write their competition laws for them; and they will not want or need to negotiate the differences.

Still, is there unfinished business in the global antitrust space? The absence of a world regime facilitates parochialism—which is on the rise today. The world lacks a trade/competition interface, and it lacks a vision from the top, obscuring the dimensions of the global problems. There are unnecessary externalities, conflicts, and duplications. There is no global "bite" to deter global abuses. Global giants can replicate, across jurisdictions, conduct that contravenes guidelines in a growing number of nations. The global gatekeepers put each plaintiff in each litigation to proof, not only that specific abusive conduct is anticompetitive but that the gatekeeper has market power sufficient even to trigger antitrust control.

Jurisdictions are trying to create solutions. South Africa is en route to requiring Global Gatekeepers to do in South Africa what they must do in the European Union. Professor Michal Gal proposes free movement of judgments, which would allow one jurisdiction to take advantage of judgments entered (with due process) abroad against international cartels. For megamergers, this author has proposed elsewhere a collaboration of nations to mimic world welfare: Imagine the next megamerger with significant harms in Africa, after the African Continental Competition Protocol is operational and when the head of the African competition commission sits at the international table with the heads of the competition authorities of the US, EU, Latin America, and Asia together representing the interests of the world. If the (net) harms to the world are substantial, the enforcers agree that the best remedy is a prohibition, and they go home with the courage of their convictions to enjoin the merger under their national laws.

But the gaps in the trade and competition interface, and within antitrust itself, will never be closed or overcome by national-competition-authority-to-national-competition-authority collaboration. For example, the potash export cartel is now worsened from the shocks of the Russia-Ukraine war. Professor Jenny stated in 2012 (and continues to stress in contemporary remarks):

> A multilateral trade negotiation could limit the ability of countries to sponsor or tolerate the participation of their domestic firms in exploitative export cartels and/or provide for a mechanism to compensate countries victims of such cartels.

Robert Anderson, William Kovacic, Anna Caroline Müller and Nadezhda Sporysheva have highlighted items of unfinished business, including issues related to state owned enterprises, industrial policy, intellectual property interface, digital markets, and due process, in a paper intended "to serve as a resource for reflection on related issues, if and/or when WTO Members decide to undertake such an exercise."

World antitrust is not likely to be on the antitrust agenda again for a long time, although agency collaboration and cooperation, and regional efforts, are sure to appear regularly. Momentum for a world regime for world issues has long since evaporated. But the intensity of global problems is increasing. The next surge of interest may come in a new shape to fit new exigencies. The chapter on world norms has not been closed.

Notes and Questions

1. Comment on the state of international competition law. Do we need international competition law or world competition norms? In what form—soft or hard law? In what venue? Should it be selective (e.g. no export cartels) or comprehensive? Is it a realistic aspiration?

2. While the WTO has no general antitrust rules, a few sector-specific agreements contain antitrust obligations. For example, the Telecommunications Agreement, which is part of the General Agreement on Trade in Services (GATS), includes an optional agreement called a Reference Paper. Signatories to the Reference Paper agree to have and enforce a competition law. A WTO panel held that Mexico violated the

Reference Paper by ordering its companies that terminate calls incoming from other nations to form a cartel. The panel held that Mexico violated its obligation to enforce the law against cartels by ordering a cartel. Mexico—Measures Affecting Telecommunications Services—Report of the Panel, 02/04/2004, Doc #: 04–1211.

2. The UNCTAD Set of Principles: Voluntary Rules for the World

We have described above the background of the adoption of the UNCTAD Set of Principles, previously called restrictive business practices (RBPs) and now called competition principles. Also as noted, most nations have signed on to the Set, which was adopted in 1980. Compliance is voluntary. While the Set could be called, in theory, a soft competition law for the world, it is not so regarded, but it is used as a document to guide developing countries, both in substantive law and in cooperation and dispute resolution. It is treated as a recommendation to the UNCTAD Member States to maintain transparent and sound principles and processes of competition law and to provide a foundation for best practices.

As will be seen, the substantive rules and principles are sometimes quite general, and in some cases (abuse of dominance) they would reach unfair trade practices and not necessarily anticompetitive conduct. Nonetheless, the Set is reaffirmed by the UN every five years. The UNCTAD Competition and Consumer Branch offers a Model Competition Law based on the Set, including annotations compiled from submissions by Member States giving examples of their applications of the law. https://unctad.org/publication/model-law-competition.

Here are excerpts from the UNCTAD Set of Principles, which is now called a multilateral agreement on competition policy:

THE SET OF MULTILATERALLY AGREED EQUITABLE PRINCIPLES FOR THE CONTROL OF RESTRICTIVE BUSINESS PRACTICES

(excerpts, UNCTAD 1980)

* * *

A. Objectives

Taking into account the interests of all countries, particularly those of developing countries, the Set of Multilaterally Agreed Equitable Principles and Rules are framed in order to achieve the following objectives:

1. To ensure that restrictive business practices do not impede or negate the realization of benefits that should arise from the liberalization of tariff and non-tariff barriers affecting world trade, particularly those affecting the trade and development of developing countries;

2. To attain greater efficiency in international trade and development, particularly that of developing countries, in accordance with national aims of economic and social development and existing economic structures, such as through:

(*a*) The creation, encouragement and protection of competition;

(*b*) Control of the concentration of capital and/or economic power;

(*c*) Encouragement of innovation;

3. To protect and promote social welfare in general and, in particular, the interests of consumers in both developed and developing countries;

4. To eliminate the disadvantages to trade and development which may result from the restrictive business practices of transnational corporations or other enterprises, and thus help to maximize benefits to international trade and particularly the trade and development of developing countries;

5. To provide a Set of Multilaterally Agreed Equitable Principles and Rules for the control of restrictive business practices for adoption at the international level and thereby to facilitate the adoption and strengthening of laws and policies in this area at the national and regional levels.

* * *

B. Multilaterally agreed equitable principles for the control of restrictive business practices

In line with the objectives set forth, the following principles are to apply:

(i) *General principles*

1. Appropriate action should be taken in a mutually reinforcing manner at national, regional and international levels to eliminate, or effectively deal with, restrictive business practices, including those of transnational corporations, adversely affecting international trade, particularly that of developing countries and the economic development of these countries.

2. Collaboration between Governments at bilateral and multilateral levels should be established and, where such collaboration has been established, it should be improved to facilitate the control of restrictive business practices.

3. Appropriate mechanisms should be devised at the international level and/or the use of existing international machinery improved to facilitate exchange and dissemination of information among Governments with respect to restrictive business practices.

4. Appropriate means should be devised to facilitate the holding of multilateral consultations with regard to policy issues relating to the control of restrictive business practices.

5. The provisions of the Set of Principles and Rules should not be construed as justifying conduct by enterprises which is unlawful under applicable national or regional legislation.

* * *

(ii) *Preferential or differential treatment for developing countries*

7. In order to ensure the equitable application of the Set of Principles and Rules, States, particularly developed countries, should take into account in their control of restrictive business practices the development, financial and trade needs of developing countries, in particular of the least developed countries, for the purposes especially of developing countries in:

(*a*) Promoting the establishment or development of domestic industries and the economic development of other sectors of the economy, and

(*b*) Encouraging their economic development through regional or global arrangements among developing countries.

* * *

C. Principles and Rules for enterprises, including transnational corporations

1. Enterprises should conform to the restrictive business practices laws, and the provisions concerning restrictive business practices in other laws, of the countries in which they operate, and, in the event of proceedings under these laws, should be subject to the competence of the courts and relevant administrative bodies therein.

2. Enterprises should consult and co-operate with competent authorities of countries directly affected in controlling restrictive

business practices adversely affecting the interests of those countries. In this regard, enterprises should also provide information, in particular details of restrictive arrangements, required for this purpose, including that which may be located in foreign countries, to the extent that in the latter event such production or disclosure is not prevented by applicable law or established public policy. Whenever the provision of information is on a voluntary basis, its provisions should be in accordance with safeguards normally applicable in this field.

3. Enterprises, except when dealing with each other in the context of an economic entity wherein they are under common control, including through ownership, or otherwise not able to act independently of each other, engaged on the market in rival or potentially rival activities, should refrain from practices such as the following when, through formal, informal, written or unwritten agreements or arrangements, they limit access to markets or otherwise unduly restrain competition, having or being likely to have adverse effects on international trade, particularly that of developing countries, and on the economic development of these countries:

(*a*) Agreements fixing prices, including as to exports and imports;

(*b*) Collusive tendering;

(*c*) Market or customer allocation arrangements;

(*d*) Allocation by quota as to sales and production;

(*e*) Collective action to enforce arrangements, e.g. by concerted refusals to deal;

(*f*) Concerted refusal of supplies to potential importers;

(*g*) Collective denial of access to an arrangement, or association, which is crucial to competition.

4. Enterprises should refrain from the following acts or behavior in a relevant market when, through an abuse* or acquisition and abuse of a dominant position of market power, they limit access to markets or otherwise unduly restrain competition, having or being likely to have adverse effects on international trade, particularly that

---

* Whether acts or behavior are abusive or not should be examined in terms of their purpose and effects in the actual situation, in particular with reference to whether they limit access to markets or otherwise unduly restrain competition, having or being likely to have adverse effects on international trade, particularly that of developing countries, and on the economic development of these countries, and to whether they are [appropriate, and consistent with the purposes of the Set].

of developing countries, and on the economic development of these countries:

(*a*) Predatory behavior towards competitors, such as using below cost pricing to eliminate competitors;

(*b*) Discriminatory (i.e. unjustifiably differentiated) pricing or terms or conditions in the supply or purchase of goods and services, including by means of the use of pricing policies in transactions between affiliated enterprises which overcharge or undercharge for goods or services purchased or supplied as compared with prices for similar or comparable transactions outside the affiliated enterprises;

(*c*) Mergers, takeovers, joint ventures or other acquisitions of control, whether of a horizontal, vertical or a conglomerate nature;

(*d*) Fixing the prices at which goods exported can be resold in importing countries;

(*e*) Restrictions on the importation of goods which have been legitimately marked abroad with a trademark identical with or similar to the trademark protected as to identical or similar goods in the importing country where the trademarks in question are of the same origin . . . ;

(*f*) When not for ensuring the achievement of legitimate business purposes, such as quality, safety, adequate distribution or service:

(i) Partial or complete refusals to deal on the enterprise's customary commercial terms;

(ii) Making the supply of particular goods or services dependent upon the acceptance of restrictions on the distribution or manufacture of competing or other goods;

(iii) Imposing restrictions concerning where, or to whom, or in what form or quantities, goods supplied or other goods may be resold or exported;

(iv) Making the supply of particular goods or services dependent upon the purchase of other goods or services from the supplier or his designee.

* * *

D. International measures

Collaboration at the international level should aim at eliminating or effectively dealing with restrictive business practices, including those of transnational corporations, through strengthening and improving controls over restrictive business practices adversely affecting international trade, particularly that of developing countries, and the economic development of these countries. In this regard, action should include [work to achieve common approaches, communications, publications, and consultations to find mutually acceptable solutions]. . .

* * *

Notes and Questions

1. The UNCTAD rules and principles were intended to be sympathetic to developing countries, whose businesses were generally not as efficient and of the same scale as the major business enterprises in the developed world. Businesses in developing countries were fearful of being crushed by Western giants' use of unfair tactics into and within developing countries. Is this still a concern today? Does contemporary law reflect the extent to which countries were subject to colonial and other oppressive regimes?

2. To what extent do the rules and principles (part C and D) correspond with or differ from the competition laws of the most mature jurisdictions, e.g. the US and EU?

3. If you were called upon to modernize the Set's rules and principles, continuing its special regard for the needs of developing countries, how would you change it?

3. Regional Higher Competition Law

a. The European Union

The European Union is the most successful common market with higher-level competition law. It operates under principles of supremacy of law and subsidiarity. The Treaties contain both free movement law and competition law, contemplating a high level of market integration. While most common markets, and surely agreements within the WTO, do not contemplate that level of market integration, the EU institutions provide a helpful notional model; and indeed EU competition law is itself probably the most emulated model for new competition regimes.

b. *The African Continental Competition Protocol*

In 2023, the African Union adopted a Competition Protocol for the Continent. It is subject to ratification, which is expected, and it is en route to becoming operational.

The Competition Protocol is a part of the African Continental Free Trade Agreement. AfCFTA contemplated the adoption of a competition protocol to help create an integrated Africa, support and not undermine trade liberalization, and manage the competition regimes and sectoral regulation of national, regional and continental authorities.

Through the process of conception and negotiation at the end of the 1990s and in the early 2020s, there was much discussion and debate on whether the Protocol should be a full-fledged competition law for Africa, with prohibitions and a system of enforcement, as well as a center for coordination of national and regional law; or whether it should be only the latter. The former vision won out. The Protocol contains the full panoply of the usual competition law rules and principles, and more—in the interests of equity, fairness, inclusiveness, and empowerment of African business. It prohibits the abuse of economic dependence and it contains specific rules to control the conduct of digital gatekeepers.

The Protocol establishes the AfCFTA Competition Authority. Decisions taken by a Board can be appealed to a Tribunal. The Protocol applies to all economic activities having a significant effect on competition in the AfCFTA market; conduct of continental dimension does have a significant effect in the AfCFTA market. The Protocol does not apply to matters within national or regional jurisdiction.

Here are the substantive rules and standards, as in the final published protocol (Jan. 2023):

PART II

ANTI-COMPETITIVE BUSINESS PRACTICES AND CONDUCT

* * *

Article 5

Anti-competitive Practices

State Parties agree that the following practices contemplated in Article 3(1) of this Protocol are incompatible with the proper functioning of the Market:

a) agreements between undertakings, decisions by associations of undertakings and concerted practices between undertakings which have, as their object or effect, the prevention, restriction or distortion of competition in the Market;

b) abuse by one or more undertakings of a dominant position in the Market;

c) mergers or acquisitions that are likely to prevent, restrict or distort competition in the Market, in particular, by giving rise to the creation or strengthening of a dominant position; and

d) abuse of economic dependence and any other anti-competitive practices.

Article 6

Prohibited Horizontal Business practices

1. All Agreements, decisions by associations of undertakings or concerted practices by undertakings that are engaged in the Market as competitors or potential competitors, involving the following restrictive horizontal practices, are prohibited:

a) agreements directly or indirectly fixing prices and trading conditions;

b) restraints on production or sale, including by quota or output restriction;

c) collusive tendering or bid-rigging;

d) agreements, which result in market or customer allocation;

e) concerted refusal to purchase or supply; or

f) collective denial of access to an arrangement, or association, which is crucial to competition.

2. Any Agreement, decision by associations of undertakings or concerted practice between undertakings in a horizontal relationship other than those contemplated in paragraph 1 of the article is prohibited if it has the effect of distorting, preventing or restricting competition in the Market, unless a party to the Agreement, concerted practice, or decision can prove that any technological, efficiency or other pro-competitive gain resulting from it outweighs that effect.

This Article shall not apply where undertakings belong to a common undertaking and those undertakings are under joint control or where they are otherwise not able to act independently of each other.

Article 7

Prohibited Vertical Business Practices

1. The practice of minimum resale price maintenance is prohibited.

2. Notwithstanding paragraph 1, a supplier or producer may recommend the minimum resale price to the reseller of a good or service provided that:

a) the supplier or producer makes it clear to the reseller that the recommendation is not binding; and

b) if the product has its price stated on it, the words "recommended price" appear next to the stated price.

3. Any Agreement, decision by associations of undertakings or concerted practice between undertakings in a vertical relationship restricting passive sales is prohibited.

4. Any Agreement, decision by associations of undertakings or concerted practice between undertakings in a vertical relationship other than those contemplated under Article 7.1 and 7.3 is prohibited if it has the effect of distorting, preventing or restricting competition in the Market, unless a party to the Agreement, decision and/or concerted practice, can prove that any technological, efficiency or other pro-competitive, gain resulting from it outweighs that effect.

Article 8

Exemptions

1. Any Agreement, decision by associations of undertakings or concerted practice between undertakings specified in Article 6.2 and 7.4 may, upon application, be exempted from the application of this Protocol for a prescribed period, provided that parties can demonstrate that such is necessary to pursue certain legitimate goals for the public benefit and development of the Market. The exempted Agreements or conduct may include, but are not limited to:

a) cooperation on research and development;

b) joint-ventures intended to achieve economic development;

c) measures to promote sustainable development, growth, transformation, or stability of any industry;

d) measures fostering competitiveness and efficiency gains that promote employment or industrial expansion; and

e) activities of professional associations designed to develop or enforce professional standards of competence reasonably necessary for the protection of the public.

2. Upon application for exemption by an undertaking(s) or an association of undertakings, the Authority shall:

a) grant the exemption;

b) grant the exemption with such conditions as considered appropriate; or

c) deny the exemption application.

Article 9

Abuse of a dominant position

1. The determination for dominance in a market may be based on:

a) market share to be determined in a regulation and level of concentration; or

b) market power considerations including barriers to entry, countervailing power, the level of actual or potential competition in terms of number of competitors, production capacity and product demand or the history of competition and rivalry between competitors.

2. Any abuse by an undertaking or a group of undertakings of a dominant position within the Market shall be prohibited insofar as it prevents, restricts or distorts competition or likely prevents, restricts and distorts competition in the Market if it, among others:

a) eliminates or restricts or is likely to eliminate or restrict any other undertaking(s) from the Market;

b) directly or indirectly imposes unfair purchase or selling prices or other restrictive terms or conditions;

c) sets prices below cost;

d) limits the production of goods or services for the Market to the detriment of consumers;

e) makes the conclusion of an Agreement subject to acceptance by another party of supplementary obligations which, by their nature or according to commercial usage, have no connection with the subject of such Agreement;

f) refuses to give a competitor or customer access to an essential facility or input when it is economically feasible to do so;

g) applies dissimilar conditions to equivalent transactions with other trading parties, thereby placing them at a competitive disadvantage.

Article 10

Mergers and Acquisitions

1. The provisions of this Article shall apply to mergers and acquisitions with continental dimension in the Market where:

a) both the acquiring undertaking and target undertaking or either the acquiring undertakings or target undertakings operate, directly or indirectly, in the Market; and

b) the combined annual turnover and/or assets of the undertakings concerned equals to or exceeds the thresholds to be determined by a Regulation.

2. Threshold for notification and merger notification fees shall be calculated based on the combined annual continental turnover or combined value of assets as provided in paragraph 1.b of this Article.

3. Undertakings falling within the scope of this Article that seeks to enter a merger of continental dimension shall notify the Authority and no merger shall come into effect before the written approval of the Authority.

4. A merger shall be deemed to exist when a change of control on a lasting basis, results from:

a) the amalgamation of two or more previously independent undertakings or parts of these undertakings;

b) acquisition of the ability of one or more undertakings to exercise control, directly or indirectly, over the whole or parts of one or more other undertakings, whether by the purchase of securities or assets, by contract or by any other means; or

c) the establishment or acquisition of a joint venture by two or several other undertakings, performing on a lasting basis all the functions of an autonomous economic entity.

5. Control shall be constituted by rights, contracts or any other means which, either separately or in combination, and considering all factual and legal considerations, confer the possibility of exercising decisive influence on the whole or parts of one or more undertakings, in particular by:

a) acquisition of the majority of the total voting rights or total capital contributions of another undertaking, either separately or in combination;

b) the constitution of a minority with a veto power;

c) ownership or the right to use all or part of the assets of another person;

d) rights or contracts which confer decisive influence on the composition, voting or decisions of the organs of another person on the appointment of the majority of the members of the Board of directors or on the decisions of the Board of directors or the shareholders' meetings;

e) more than half of the members of the Board of directors or the members of the shareholders' meetings are the same between the concerned undertakings;

f) having the ability to materially influence the policy of the undertaking or undertakings in a manner comparable to a person who, in ordinary commercial practice, can exercise an element of control referred to above.

6. A merger that is likely to substantially lessen, prevent, restrict, or distort competition in the Market or in a substantial part of it, including by giving rise to the creation or strengthening of a dominant position, shall be declared incompatible with the Protocol.

7. In determining whether a merger is likely to substantially lessen, prevent, restrict, or distort competition within the Market, the Authority shall consider all relevant competitive factors, including:

a) the competitive structure of all markets affected by the merger;

b) barriers to entry including consideration of the ease of entry, including tariff and regulatory barriers;

c) the level and trends of concentration;

d) the history of collusion;

e) the degree of countervailing power;

f) the dynamic characteristics including growth, innovation, and product differentiation;

g) the nature and extent of vertical integration including the undertakings likely to be affected by the merger, the merging undertakings' control of essential facilities and financial resources;

h) whether the business or part of the business of a party to the merger or proposed merger has failed or is likely to fail, the burden of proof falls upon the concerned undertakings;

i) whether the merger will result in the removal of an effective competitor; or

j) any pro-competitive effects of the merger, which may outweigh the harmful effects on competition, the burden of proof falls upon the concerned undertakings.

8. In determining whether a merger is likely to substantially lessen, prevent, restrict, or distort competition within the Market or a substantial part of it, the Authority shall also consider all relevant public interest factors, including:

a) the potential to promote sustainable and inclusive socio-economic and industrial development;

b) employment;

c) the ability of small and medium-sized businesses to become competitive; or

d) the ability of industries in the Market to compete in other international markets.

9. Upon notification of a merger by an undertaking or undertakings and following a merger review process, the Authority shall:

a) approve the merger without conditions;

b) approve the merger with conditions; or

c) deny the merger.

10. The Authority may revoke its decision to approve or conditionally approve the merger or, in respect of a conditional approval, make any appropriate decision regarding any conditions relating to the merger, if;

a) the decision was based on incorrect information for which a party to the merger is responsible;

b) the approval was obtained by deceit; or

c) an undertaking concerned has breached an obligation attached to the decision.

Article 11

Abuse of economic dependence and any other anti-competitive practices

1. Economic dependence is deemed to exist where undertakings as suppliers or purchasers of a certain type of goods or services are dependent on another undertaking or a group of

undertakings in such a way that sufficient and reasonable possibilities for switching to third parties do not exist and there is a significant imbalance between the power of such undertakings or group of undertakings and the countervailing power of other undertakings.

2. The determination of economic dependence shall be based on:

a) the market share of the undertaking in the Market;

b) the relative strength of the undertaking;

c) the existence or not of alternative solutions;

d) the factors that led to the situation of dependence.

3. It is prohibited for an undertaking or a group of undertakings or gatekeepers to abuse the relative position of economic dependence over a customer or supplier if the conduct substantially affects the functioning and structure of competition in the Market.

4. Undertakings that are designated as gatekeepers or core platforms are prohibited from engaging in any of the following conduct:

a) imposing price or service parity clauses on business users;

b) imposing anti-steering provisions, or otherwise preventing business users from engaging consumers directly outside of a core platform;

c) using business user data to compete against the business user;

d) self-preferencing of services or products offered by the gatekeeper on a core platform;

e) differentiation in fees or treatment against small and medium enterprises;

f) placing restrictions on the portability of data or other actions that inhibit switching platforms for business and end-users;

g) failing to identify paid ranking as advertising in search results and to allow paid results to exceed organic results on the first results page;

h) combining personal data sourced from different services offered by the gatekeeper; or

i) requiring the pre-installation of gatekeeper applications or services on devices.

5. The Council of Ministers shall develop a Regulation designating Undertakings as gatekeepers or core platforms.

Notes and Questions

1. Compare the African Competition Protocol with US antitrust law and with EU competition law. In particular, note that US antitrust law does not prohibit exploitation; it privileges the freedom of even monopoly firms to charge as high a price as they like and to deal with whom they like and on terms they choose; and it opposes duties (of even monopoly firms) to lend a helping hand to smaller rivals. Contrast provisions of the African Protocol. What might explain the differences in perspective?

2. Comment on the extent to which the Protocol goes beyond consumer welfare or efficiency-based competition law. To what extent do characteristics of developing countries, with majority very poor populations, poor—infrastructure, and challenges from corruption, cronyism, and firm inefficiency, support the differences?

3. To what extent is public interest or national interest a defense? Comment on how these issues are handled and what are the trade-offs.

4. Is the Protocol applicable to multinational firms, such as the Big Tech giants? What defenses or narrative would you expect, e.g., Google to assert if and when it is sued in Africa under Article 11 for denying to African SMEs fair access to its platform?

c. The Common Market for Eastern and Southern Africa (COMESA)

There are many regional common markets in the world. Most do not have a common competition law. Many require their member states to have and enforce a competition law.

In Africa, the Common Market for Eastern and Southern Africa (COMESA) is the leading jurisdiction with a common competition law. It has a well-developed system of merger control and has begun to enforce in the areas of cartels and abuse of dominance. It has well developed rules and regulations.

The design of the African Competition Protocol contemplates that the "center" will be supported by regional pillars, which in turn may be supported by national authorities. COMESA is now the strongest regional pillar. In view of the coming continental enforcement, other regional economic communities in Africa are building capacity for common regional competition law.

C. GRASS ROOTS EFFORTS AND BI-LATERAL COOPERATION

We turn now to the other end of the spectrum from higher level law—national and bi-national efforts to solve problems of conflicts, and, in some cases, to explore ways to advance joint interests in enforcement. This is the bread-and-butter of agencies' "international antitrust."

The United States and the EU were pioneers in these efforts, and the EU/US collaboration and cooperation is at an advanced stage. Many other nations and groups are increasing their cooperation and coordination, formally and informally. We treat regional groups in Part D.

The international institutions—ICN, OECD, and UNCTAD—are major facilitators of cooperation, convergence, informed divergence, and documentation of better and best practices. We treat them specially in Part E.

The US Antitrust Guidelines for International Enforcement and Cooperation (2017) provide guidance on the principles that, according to the US agencies, will guide them. The guidance focuses on the tools available, transparency, engagement, information sharing and confidentiality, and for mergers, aligning timetables, and cooperation in substantive assessment and remedies. Here are excerpts.

US ANTITRUST GUIDELINES FOR INTERNATIONAL ENFORCEMENT AND COOPERATION

(2017) (footnotes omitted)

* * *

5. International Cooperation

Effective enforcement of the U.S. antitrust laws in a global economy benefits from cooperation with foreign authorities. The Agencies are committed to cooperating with foreign authorities on both policy and investigative matters. This cooperation contributes to convergence on substantive enforcement standards that seek to advance consumer welfare, based on sound economics, procedural fairness, transparency, and non-discriminatory treatment of parties. The Agencies' international policy work and case cooperation are closely connected. As noted above, consistent approaches to competition law, policy, and procedures across jurisdictions facilitate case cooperation among competition authorities. Moreover, through case cooperation, the Agencies and cooperating authorities often raise important substantive and procedural issues as they arise in practice, which can lead to greater convergence in substantive analysis and procedures. In keeping with these Guidelines' focus on international enforcement and practice, this Chapter focuses on investigations and case cooperation.

International case cooperation helps agencies investigating a particular matter to identify issues of common interest, gain a better understanding of relevant facts, and achieve consistent outcomes. Cooperation can yield better results for competition and promote efficiency for both cooperating agencies and subjects of an investigation. It can improve substantive analyses and procedures, and ensure that investigations and remedies are as consistent and predictable as possible, which improves outcomes, and reduces uncertainty and expense to firms doing business across borders. When either Agency reviews a case that raises possible competitive concerns in jurisdictions outside of the United States, it may consult with the relevant foreign authorities about the matter and coordinate and cooperate with those authorities conducting parallel investigations. As described in greater detail throughout this chapter, cooperation can include a broad range of practices, from initiating informal discussions and informing cooperating authorities of the different stages of their investigations, to engaging in detailed discussions of substantive issues, exchanging information, conducting interviews at which two or more agencies may be present, and coordinating remedy design and implementation, as relevant and appropriate.

5.1 Investigations and Cooperation

Increasingly, the Agencies' investigations involve conduct, entities, individuals, and information located outside the United States. The Agencies employ a combination of their own investigative tools and cooperation with foreign authorities in investigating and seeking appropriate remedies in certain international matters.

5.1.1 Investigative Tools

When practical and consistent with enforcement objectives, the Agencies may request that parties and third parties voluntarily: provide documents; submit to interviews; or provide other information related to an investigation. These requests may seek documents or information located outside the United States. The Agencies also may use compulsory measures to obtain documents and information. Specifically, the Agencies may compel production of documents or information via civil investigative demand ("CID") or subpoena. U.S. law provides authority for such compulsory measures directed to persons over whom the courts have personal jurisdiction.

The Agencies may compel the production of documents or information, including documents or information located outside the United States, when the documents or information sought are within the "possession, custody, or control" of an individual or entity subject to the jurisdiction of the United States and are not protected by the attorney-client privilege or the work-product doctrine.

When one of the Agencies investigates a transaction notified under the HSR Act, it may issue a request for additional documents or information, typically called a "Second Request." Compliance with a Second Request requires production of all responsive documents and information, no matter where located.

Conflicts can arise where foreign statutes purport to prevent individuals or entities from disclosing documents or information for use in U.S. proceedings. The mere existence of such statutes, however, does not excuse noncompliance with a request for documents or information from one of the Agencies.

Because unilaterally collecting documents or information from individuals or entities located abroad can adversely affect law enforcement relationships with foreign countries, the Agencies use compulsory measures after carefully considering the importance of the documents or information to the investigation or prosecution and the availability of other means to obtain them. When such compulsory measures are warranted, the Agencies may seek to work with the foreign authority involved as appropriate.

5.1.2 Confidentiality

The Agencies' enforcement activities benefit greatly from access to sensitive, nonpublic information from businesses and consumers. The Agencies recognize the importance of protecting the confidentiality of sensitive, nonpublic information received from parties and foreign authorities. The Agencies protect the confidentiality of all such information received, be it from businesses or consumers located domestically or abroad, or from foreign authorities, under applicable provisions of U.S. law.

Several statutes require the Agencies to treat as confidential certain information obtained in the course of an investigation. The HSR Act prohibits the Agencies from disclosing information obtained pursuant to the act, including the fact that the parties filed notice of a proposed transaction and confidential business information provided in a filing or in response to a document or information request. The FTC Act restricts disclosure of information that the Commission receives pursuant to compulsory process, or produced voluntarily in lieu of process, in a law enforcement investigation. The

FTC Act also prohibits the Commission from making public any trade secret or any commercial or financial information it obtains that is privileged or confidential, except in limited circumstances. The Antitrust Civil Process Act prohibits the Department from disclosing documents or testimony obtained pursuant to a CID without the consent of the person that produced the materials, except in limited circumstances. Other federal laws also require the Agencies to treat specific types of information as confidential, without regard to the manner in which the information is obtained. For example, laws governing privacy, national security information, and trade secrets require that the Agencies treat certain information as confidential.

There are certain, discrete circumstances in which the Agencies may disclose a person's confidential information for a specific use. The HSR Act, the FTC Act, and the Antitrust Civil Process Act do not bar the Agencies' use of a person's confidential information in judicial and administrative proceedings. However, the Federal Rules of Civil Procedure and FTC Rules of Practice include procedures to protect confidential information used in judicial proceedings or FTC administrative proceedings.

The Agencies also are subject to the Freedom of Information Act ("FOIA"), which provides the public with a right of access to certain agency records. This statute, however, contains several exemptions that protect information provided to the Agencies. It permits the Agencies to withhold certain categories of documents from requesters, including information protected by statute (such as the HSR Act or FTC Act), "commercial or financial information obtained from a person [that is] privileged or confidential," inter- or intra-agency memoranda or letters that would be routinely privileged in civil discovery, and "files the disclosure of which would constitute a clearly unwarranted invasion of personal privacy." In addition, an exemption from FOIA's disclosure regime applies to certain information compiled for law enforcement purposes, including when disclosure could interfere with enforcement proceedings or disclose the identity of a confidential source.

5.1.3 Legal Bases for Cooperation

The Agencies' authority to cooperate with foreign authorities is inherent in their ability to act in furtherance of their mandates. The Department and FTC, therefore, each has the discretion to cooperate, including when it furthers its enforcement interests. Cooperation can be facilitated by bilateral and multilateral arrangements. The Agencies have also developed best practices and guidance documents on cooperation for specific types of investigations. These arrangements and guidance documents can serve as a catalyst for cooperation and provide useful guidance to coordinate and facilitate enforcement activities. They are not necessary for cooperation to take place, and the Agencies may cooperate with relevant foreign authorities in the absence of any formal arrangement. These bilateral and multilateral arrangements do not change the signatories' laws, including laws concerning the treatment of confidential information.

The IAEAA authorizes the Agencies to enter into antitrust-specific mutual assistance agreements with foreign authorities that allow the Agencies to share evidence relating to antitrust violations already in their possession and provide each other with investigatory assistance in obtaining evidence, subject to certain limitations. As noted in Section 2.6, the IAEAA does not apply to materials submitted pursuant to the HSR Act.

5.1.4 Types of Information Exchanged and Waivers of Confidentiality

If a transaction or conduct under antitrust investigation in the United States is also being investigated by a foreign authority, the Department or the Commission may contact the authority. The Agencies may share with these foreign authorities relevant publicly available information. Similarly, it remains in the Agencies' discretion whether to share with cooperating foreign authorities agency non-public information, which is information that the Agencies are not statutorily prohibited from disclosing, but that the Agencies normally treat as non-public and withhold from public disclosure. Examples of agency non-public information include the existence of an open investigation and the Agencies' staff views as to the merits of a case, market definition, competitive effects, substantive theories of harm, and remedies. Before exchanging agency non-public information, the Agencies will have reached an understanding that the foreign authority will maintain the information in confidence and in accordance with that authority's laws and rules. This may be through bilateral or multilateral cooperation agreements or arrangements, or other means.

While confidentiality obligations generally prohibit the Agencies from disclosing to foreign authorities confidential information submitted by a person, that person can enable the Agencies to engage in more meaningful cooperation with foreign authorities by granting the Agencies a waiver of confidentiality as to information that may be otherwise protected from disclosure. The Agencies issued a joint model waiver of confidentiality for use in civil matters, which serves to streamline the waiver process and published explanatory materials that provide further details on waivers of confidentiality, applicable confidentiality rules, and the process for providing a waiver of confidentiality.

A waiver identifies the terms under which a person agrees to waive statutory confidentiality protections vis-à-vis the agency that originally received the person's confidential information. A waiver also describes an agency's policy regarding how it will treat the information it receives from another agency pursuant to a waiver, although it is not an agreement signed by the agency. Waivers are limited in scope to a specific, named matter and designate the agencies that may share the waiving person's confidential information. Waivers generally allow the cooperating authorities to share documents, statements, data, and other information.

Waivers enable deeper communication, cooperation, and coordination among competition authorities concurrently reviewing a matter. They can lead to more effective, efficient investigations and better-informed, more consistent enforcement decisions based on the Agencies' increased ability to share information.

The Agencies will protect information received from a foreign authority pursuant to a waiver under applicable provisions of U.S. law. The Agencies will not seek information that is privileged under U.S. law from foreign authorities through waivers or other cooperative activities.

Similarly, the Agencies will provide information to foreign authorities pursuant to a waiver when they have reached an understanding with the recipient agency that it will maintain the confidentiality of such information consistent with its laws and rules. Generally, a person that has waived the confidentiality of its information as to one of the Agencies also will provide a separate waiver of confidentiality to the relevant foreign authority, based on the waiving person's understanding of the foreign authority's confidentiality protections.

The Agencies may request a waiver of confidentiality, but the decision whether to provide one rests solely with the producing person. Refusal to provide a waiver will not prejudice the outcome of an investigation, though, in some cases, the absence of a waiver may have practical effects such as increasing the risk of inconsistent outcomes between jurisdictions. Further, declining to grant a waiver will not preclude the Agencies from sharing publicly available or agency non-public information with foreign authorities.

Illustrative Example G

Situation: Corporation 1 and Corporation 2 each manufacture Product X and Product Y. Corporation 1 and Corporation 2 enter into an agreement to merge. The proposed merger meets the threshold for premerger notification in the United States under the HSR Act and the thresholds for premerger notification in several other jurisdictions. Corporation 1 and Corporation 2 inform the U.S. Agency reviewing the merger as well as reviewing foreign authorities that the merger will be notified or reviewed in multiple jurisdictions. Pre-notification consultations and pre-merger filings are timed to facilitate communication and cooperation among reviewing authorities at key decision-making stages of their respective investigations.

Discussion: After learning that the merger will be notified or reviewed in more than one jurisdiction, the U.S. Agency contacts the foreign reviewing authorities to discuss review timetables and assess the potential for cooperation. The extent of cooperation with each foreign authority reviewing the matter will vary depending on factors including the depth of that authority's investigation, the competitive conditions in that authority's jurisdiction, and the scope of potential remedies likely to be considered. The U.S. Agency requests a waiver of confidentiality from Corporation 1 and Corporation 2 to allow for the exchange of confidential information with the reviewing authorities in Countries Alpha, Beta, and Gamma, given the nature of the competitive concerns raised by the merger in these jurisdictions. Corporation 1 and Corporation 2 voluntarily grant these waivers, as well as the waivers of confidentiality requested by each of these reviewing authorities. The U.S. Agency cooperates with the reviewing authorities in Countries Delta and Epsilon on the basis of publicly available and agency non-public information, without exchanging confidential business information.

As reviews of the merger proceed, the U.S. Agency and the other reviewing authorities arrange communications between and among themselves as appropriate to their investigations. The U.S. Agency and authorities of Alpha, Beta, and Gamma each arrange regular, bilateral calls and, in some instances, certain of these agencies conduct interviews together, facilitated by waivers. These reviewing agencies, as well as the reviewing authorities of Delta and Epsilon, also conduct status calls, based on publicly available and agency non-public information to update each other on the timing of reviews and theories of harm. The reviewing authorities of Delta and Epsilon identify that the merger's effects in their jurisdictions are likely to be insignificant, and that they will close their investigations accordingly.

5.1.5 Remedies

The Agencies seek remedies that effectively address harm or threatened harm to U.S. commerce and consumers, while attempting to avoid conflicts with remedies contemplated by their foreign counterparts. An Agency will seek a remedy that includes conduct or assets outside the United States only to the extent that including them is needed to effectively redress harm or threatened harm to U.S. commerce and consumers and is consistent with the Agency's international comity analysis.

When multiple authorities are investigating the same transaction or same conduct, the Agencies may cooperate with other authorities, to the extent permitted under U.S. law, to facilitate obtaining effective and non-conflicting remedies. Cooperation also may facilitate the development of a proposed remedies package that comprehensively addresses the concerns of multiple authorities. In some circumstances, cooperation may result in one authority closing an investigation without remedies after taking another authority's remedies into account.

Illustrative Example H

Situation: After investigating the merger as outlined in Illustrative Example G, the U.S. Agency finds that the merger is likely to substantially lessen competition in the U.S. market for Product X, and therefore that the merger would violate Section 7 of the Clayton Act. The U.S. Agency determines that these competitive concerns likely can be addressed through a divestiture of Corporation 1's assets related to Product X. Countries Alpha, Beta, and Gamma also find that the merger will harm competition in their markets for Product X, and Country Gamma has additional concerns about a reduction of competition in Gamma's market for Product Y.

Discussion: The U.S. Agency and the authorities in Alpha, Beta, and Gamma discuss, among themselves and with Corporation 1 and Corporation 2, a proposed remedy for the competitive concerns regarding Product X, in an effort to identify a package of assets for divesture that addresses the reviewing agencies' competitive concerns.

In this instance, the U.S. Agency and the foreign reviewing authorities agree that the same divestiture remedy for Product X will effectively address the competitive concerns in their respective jurisdictions. Corporation 1 and Corporation 2 enter into a consent decree in the United States that includes divestiture of specified assets of Corporation 1's related to Product X, and the authority in Alpha seeks the same divestiture remedy to ensure enforceability of the remedy in its jurisdiction. Country Beta concludes that the remedies secured in the United States and in Country Alpha are sufficient to address its competitive concerns and closes its investigation. Country Gamma seeks a remedy identical to that entered into in the United States and Country Alpha regarding Product X, coupled with an additional remedy to address the competitive harm in its jurisdiction regarding Product Y.

5.2 Special Considerations in Criminal Investigations

Among the Department's top priorities is the criminal investigation and prosecution of international price-fixing cartels. Because these cartels often involve foreign located defendants, witnesses, and evidence, antitrust enforcement in this context can present not only an investigatory challenge but also a special need for international cooperation and coordination. Mutual Legal Assistance Treaties ("MLATs") are an important basis for international cooperation in the Department's criminal antitrust enforcement. MLATs are used often in criminal investigations to gather evidence located outside the United States. Parties to these agreements have agreed to assist one another in criminal law enforcement matters. The specific provisions of MLATs vary, but they generally provide for assistance in obtaining evidence and in serving documents in one jurisdiction at the request of the other.

The Department also coordinates with foreign authorities when they are conducting cartel investigations parallel with the Department's own. The Department sometimes shares information to coordinate investigative steps. For example, to minimize the risk of document destruction, the Department and foreign authorities can time dawn raids and searches to coincide in multiple jurisdictions. And the Department and foreign authorities may also coordinate on logistical aspects of their parallel investigations to help minimize overlapping and inconsistent demands placed on cooperating individuals and firms. The Department recognizes that such coordination has the benefit of decreasing the costs to cooperators and increasing the pace of the investigations and is committed to engaging in such coordination where practicable.

The Department's ability to share information with foreign authorities is not unlimited, however. An essential component in the investigation and enforcement of the criminal antitrust laws is the grand jury, which is subject to the grand jury secrecy rule. Through its subpoenas, a grand jury can "compel the production of evidence or the testimony of witnesses as it considers appropriate, and its operation generally is unrestrained by the technical procedural and evidentiary rules governing the conduct of criminal trials." The

Department is prohibited, however, from disclosing matters occurring before the grand jury absent an applicable exception. This prohibition cannot be waived by a subject of the investigation, a grand jury witness, or a recipient of a grand jury subpoena. The prohibition, however, does not apply to these persons and therefore does not generally prohibit disclosures by them.

In addition, a criminal investigation can gather information through the assistance of an applicant under the Department's Corporate and Individual Leniency Policies for antitrust crimes. To qualify for leniency under those policies, the applicant is required, among other things, to report the wrongdoing with candor and completeness and provide full, continuing, and complete cooperation. That required cooperation includes the production of all documents, information, or other materials in the applicant's possession, custody, or control, wherever located, that are requested by the Department in connection with the criminal antitrust investigation and are not protected by the attorney-client privilege or the work product doctrine.

Notes and Questions

1. Comment on the extent of cooperation between the US agencies and their counterparts in other jurisdictions, as envisioned by the US agencies. What should be the next step?

2. Is agency cooperation of the sort envisioned by the US authorities likely to advance the cause of efficiency in enforcement throughout the world? How? Is it likely to advance other goals? E.g., convergence of law and analysis? fairness in treatment (due process)?

3. Note the considerable attention, and deference, given to parties' claims of confidentiality. Is it important for authorities to respect these claims despite the greater ease in enforcement when documents are shared? Business firms may over-claim confidentiality. What happens or should happen if firms over-claim confidentiality of documents that are key to an enforcement action?

4. What is the rule of restraint that the U.S. agencies impose on themselves in seeking remedies? (See § 5.1.5.) Revisit also the comity section of the Guidelines, § 4.1 (see Chapter 9, supra). Can you derive from these self-restraining declarations notional world norms to reconcile conflicting sovereign interests? If all competition authorities of the world followed these norms, would problems of conflict be solved? Would the norms of restraint affect deterrence?

5. The Guidelines are about agency-to-agency cooperation. They do not tell courts what to do. Are there aspects of the Guidelines that the courts could and should apply to themselves?

Bilateral cooperation agreements

The US Guidelines refer to and cite the numerous bilateral cooperation agreements and best practices agreements to which the US is a party. These include agreements with China, India, Canada, Brazil, Mexico, Japan, and many others. The EU is party to even more such agreements. See https://competition-policy.ec.europa.eu/international-relations/bilateral-relations_en.

These agreements are generally about sharing information and avoiding conflicts. To give you an idea of the coverage of such agreements, we include excerpts from the US/EU agreements of 1991 and 1998. Together, they establish procedures for both negative and positive comity. Negative, or traditional, comity involves deferring to a trading partner when the first party's enforcement would adversely affect the important interests of the other party. Positive comity contemplates situations in which both parties have an interest in the antitrust enforcement and one is better placed to bring the proceedings. The first party may request and await the better-placed party's investigation and enforcement before taking action itself.

Here are excerpts from the US/EU 1991 and 1998 agreements. The second agreement, while further elaborating on positive comity, excludes mergers from its scope.

US/EU ANTITRUST COOPERATION AGREEMENT OF 1991

* * *

Article II
NOTIFICATION

1. Each Party shall notify the other whenever its competition authorities become aware that their enforcement activities may affect important interests of the other Party.

2. Enforcement activities as to which notification ordinarily will be appropriate include those that:

a) Are relevant to enforcement activities of the other Party;

b) Involve anticompetitive activities (other than a merger or acquisition) carried out in significant part in the other Party's territory;

c) Involve a merger or acquisition in which one or more of the parties to the transaction, or a company controlling one or more of the parties to the transaction, is a company incorporated or organized under the laws of the other Party or one of its states or member states;

d) Involve conduct believed to have been required, encouraged or approved by the other Party; or

e) Involve remedies that would, in significant respects, require or prohibit conduct in the other Party's territory.

3. With respect to mergers or acquisitions required by law to be reported to the competition authorities, notification under this Article shall be made:

a) In the case of the Government of the United States of America,

(i) not later than the time its competition authorities request, pursuant to 15 U.S.C. § 18a(e), additional information or documentary material concerning the proposed transaction,

(ii) when its competition authorities decide to file a complaint challenging the transaction, and

(iii) where this is possible, far enough in advance of the entry of a consent decree to enable the other Party's views to be taken into account; and

b) In the case of the Commission of the European Communities,

(i) when notice of the transaction is published in the Official Journal, pursuant to Article 4(3) of Council Regulation no. 4064/89, or when notice of the transaction is received under Article 66 of the ECSC Treaty and a prior authorization from the Commission is required under that provision,

(ii) when its competition authorities decide to initiate proceedings with respect to the proposed transaction, pursuant to Article 6(1)(c) of Council Regulation no. 4064/89, and

(iii) far enough in advance of the adoption of a decision in the case to enable the other Party's views to be taken into account.

4. With respect to other matters, notification shall ordinarily be provided at the stage in an investigation when it becomes evident that notifiable circumstances are present, and in any event far enough in advance of

a) the issuance of a statement of objections in the case of the Commission of the European Communities, or a complaint or indictment in the case of the Government of the United States of America, and

b) the adoption of a decision or settlement in the case of the Commission of the European Communities, or the entry of a consent decree in the case of the Government of the United States of America, to enable the other Party's views to be taken into account.

5. Each Party shall also notify the other whenever its competition authorities intervene or otherwise participate in a regulatory or judicial proceeding that does not arise from its enforcement activities, if the issues addressed in the intervention or participation may affect the other Party's important interests. Notification under this paragraph shall apply only to

a) regulatory or judicial proceedings that are public,

b) intervention or participation that is public and pursuant to formal procedures, and

c) in the case of regulatory proceedings in the United States, only proceedings before federal agencies.

Notification shall be made at the time of the intervention or participation or as soon thereafter as possible.

6. Notifications under this Article shall include sufficient information to permit an initial evaluation by the recipient Party of any effects on its interests.

Article III
Exchange of Information

1. The Parties agree that it is in their common interest to share information that will (a) facilitate effective application of their respective competition laws, or (b) promote better understanding by them of economic conditions and theories relevant to their competition authorities' enforcement activities and interventions or participation of the kind described in Article II, paragraph 5.

2. In furtherance of this common interest, appropriate officials from the competition authorities of each Party shall meet at least twice each year, unless otherwise agreed, to

a) exchange information on their current enforcement activities and priorities, (b) exchange information on economic sectors of common interest, (c) discuss policy changes which they are considering, and (d) discuss other matters of mutual interest relating to the application of competition laws.

3. Each Party will provide the other Party with any significant information that comes to the attention of its competition authorities about anticompetitive activities that its competition authorities believe is relevant to, or may warrant, enforcement activity by the other Party's competition authorities.

4. Upon receiving a request from the other Party, and within the limits of Articles VIII and IX, a Party will provide to the requesting Party such information within its possession as the requesting Party may describe that is relevant to an enforcement activity being considered or conducted by the requesting Party's competition authorities.

Article IV
COOPERATION AND COORDINATION IN ENFORCEMENT ACTIVITIES

1. The competition authorities of each Party will render assistance to the competition authorities of the other Party in their enforcement activities, to the extent compatible with the assisting Party's laws and important interests, and within its reasonably available resources.

2. In cases where both Parties have an interest in pursuing enforcement activities with regard to related situations, they may agree that it is in their mutual interest to coordinate their enforcement activities. In considering whether particular enforcement activities should be coordinated, the Parties shall take account of the following factors, among others:

a) the opportunity to make more efficient use of their resources devoted to the enforcement activities;

b) the relative abilities of the Parties' competition authorities to obtain information necessary to conduct the enforcement activities;

c) the effect of such coordination on the ability of both Parties to achieve the objectives of their enforcement activities; and

d) the possibility of reducing costs incurred by persons subject to the enforcement activities.

3. In any coordination arrangement, each Party shall conduct its enforcement activities expeditiously and, insofar as possible, consistently with the enforcement objectives of the other Party.

4. Subject to appropriate notice to the other Party, the competition authorities of either Party may limit or terminate their participation in a coordination arrangement and pursue their enforcement activities independently.

Article V

COOPERATION REGARDING ANTICOMPETITIVE ACTIVITIES IN THE TERRITORY OF ONE PARTY THAT ADVERSELY AFFECT THE INTERESTS OF THE OTHER PARTY

1. The Parties note that anticompetitive activities may occur within the territory of one Party that, in addition to violating that Party's competition laws, adversely affect important interests of the other Party. The Parties agree that it is in both their interests to address anticompetitive activities of this nature.

2. If a Party believes that anticompetitive activities carried out on the territory of the other Party are adversely affecting its important interests, the first Party may notify the other Party and may request that the other Party's competition authorities initiate appropriate enforcement activities. The notification shall be as specific as possible about the nature of the anticompetitive activities and their effects on the interests of the notifying Party, and shall include an offer of such further information and other cooperation as the notifying Party is able to provide.

3. Upon receipt of a notification under paragraph 2, and after such other discussion between the Parties as may be appropriate and useful in the circumstances, the competition authorities of the notified Party will consider whether or not to initiate enforcement activities, or to expand ongoing enforcement activities, with respect to the anticompetitive activities identified in the notification. The notified Party will advise the notifying Party of its decision. If enforcement activities are initiated, the notified Party will advise the notifying Party of their outcome and, to the extent possible, of significant interim developments.

4. Nothing in this Article limits the discretion of the notified Party under its competition laws and enforcement policies as to whether or not to undertake enforcement activities with respect to the notified anticompetitive activities, or precludes the notifying Party from undertaking enforcement activities with respect to such anticompetitive activities.

Article VI

AVOIDANCE OF CONFLICTS OVER ENFORCEMENT ACTIVITIES

Within the framework of its own laws and to the extent compatible with its important interests, each Party will seek, at all stages in its enforcement activities, to take into account the important interests of the other Party. Each Party shall consider important interests of the other Party in decisions as to whether or not to initiate an investigation or proceeding, the scope of an investigation or proceeding, the nature of the remedies or penalties sought, and in other ways, as appropriate. In considering one another's important interests in the course of their enforcement activities, the Parties will take account of, but will not be limited to, the following principles:

1. While an important interest of a Party may exist in the absence of official involvement by the Party with the activity in question, it is recognized that such interests would normally be reflected in antecedent laws, decisions or statements of policy by its competent authorities.

2. A Party's important interests may be affected at any stage of enforcement activity by the other Party. The Parties recognize, however, that as a general matter the potential for adverse impact on one Party's important interests arising from enforcement activity by the other Party is less at the investigative stage and greater at the stage at which conduct is prohibited or penalized, or at which other forms of remedial orders are imposed.

3. Where it appears that one Party's enforcement activities may adversely affect important interests of the other Party, the Parties will consider the following factors, in addition to any other factors that appear relevant in the circumstances, in seeking an appropriate accommodation of the competing interests:

a) the relative significance to the anticompetitive activities involved of conduct within the enforcing Party's territory as compared to conduct within the other Party's territory;

b) the presence or absence of a purpose on the part of those engaged in the anticompetitive activities to affect consumers, suppliers, or competitors within the enforcing Party's territory;

c) the relative significance of the effects of the anticompetitive activities on the enforcing Party's interests as compared to the effects on the other Party's interests;

d) the existence or absence of reasonable expectations that would be furthered or defeated by the enforcement activities;

e) the degree of conflict or consistency between the enforcement activities and the other Party's laws or articulated economic policies; and

f) the extent to which enforcement activities of the other Party with respect to the same persons, including judgments or undertakings resulting from such activities, may be affected.

Article VII
CONSULTATION

[Parties shall consult on request.]

* * *

Article VIII
CONFIDENTIALITY OF INFORMATION

* * *

The 1991 cooperation agreement was an advance over the earlier agreements in criminal matters (MLATs), which merely require each party to notify the other party when an action is being brought that might affect the other's important interests and suggest refraining from suit in appropriate cases. The 1998 agreement further articulates positive comity. Here are excerpts.

US/EU ANTITRUST COOPERATION AGREEMENT OF 1998 . . . ON THE APPLICATION OF POSITIVE COMITY PRINCIPLES IN THE ENFORCEMENT OF THEIR COMPETITION LAWS

* * *

Article I
SCOPE AND PURPOSE OF THIS AGREEMENT

1. This Agreement applies where a Party satisfies the other that there is reason to believe that the following circumstances are present:

a. Anticompetitive activities are occurring in whole or in substantial part in the territory of one of the Parties and are adversely affecting the interests of the other Party; and

b. The activities in question are impermissible under the competition laws of the Party in the territory of which the activities are occurring.

2. The purposes of this Agreement are to:

a. Help ensure that trade and investment flows between the Parties and competition and consumer welfare within the territories of the Parties are not impeded by anticompetitive activities for which the competition laws of one or both Parties can provide a remedy, and

b. Establish cooperative procedures to achieve the most effective and efficient enforcement of competition law, whereby the competition authorities of each Party will normally avoid allocating enforcement resources to dealing with anticompetitive activities that occur principally in and are directed principally towards the other Party's territory, where the competition authorities of the other Party are able and prepared to examine and take effective sanctions under their law to deal with those activities.

* * *

Article III
POSITIVE COMITY

The competition authorities of a Requesting Party may request the competition authorities of a Requested Party to investigate and, if warranted, to remedy anticompetitive activities in accordance with the Requested Party's competition laws. Such a request may be made regardless of whether the activities also violate the Requesting Party's competition laws, and regardless of whether the competition authorities of the Requesting Party have commenced or contemplate taking enforcement activities under their own competition laws.

Article IV
DEFERRAL OR SUSPENSION OF INVESTIGATIONS IN RELIANCE ON ENFORCEMENT ACTIVITY BY THE REQUESTED PARTY

1. The competition authorities of the Parties may agree that the competition authorities of the Requesting Party will defer or suspend pending or contemplated enforcement activities during the pendency of enforcement activities of the Requested Party.

2. The competition authorities of a Requesting Party will normally defer or suspend their own enforcement activities in favor of enforcement activities by the competition authorities of the Requested Party when the following conditions are satisfied:

a. The anticompetitive activities at issue:

i. do not have a direct, substantial and reasonably foreseeable impact on consumers in the Requesting Party's territory, or

ii. where the anticompetitive activities do have such an impact on the Requesting Party's consumers, they occur principally in and are directed principally towards the other Party's territory;

b. The adverse effects on the interests of the Requesting Party can be and are likely to be fully and adequately investigated and, as appropriate, eliminated or adequately remedied pursuant to the laws, procedures, and available remedies of the Requested Party. The Parties recognize that it may be appropriate to pursue separate enforcement activities where anticompetitive activities affecting both territories justify the imposition of penalties within both jurisdictions; and

c. The competition authorities of the Requested Party agree that in conducting their own enforcement activities, they will:

i. devote adequate resources to investigate the anticompetitive activities and, where appropriate, promptly pursue adequate enforcement activities;

ii. use their best efforts to pursue all reasonably available sources of information, including such sources of information as may be suggested by the competition authorities of the Requesting Party;

iii. inform the competition authorities of the Requesting Party, on request or at reasonable intervals, of the status of their enforcement activities and intentions, and where appropriate provide to the competition authorities of the Requesting Party relevant confidential information if consent has been obtained from the source concerned. The use and disclosure of such information shall be governed by Article V;

iv. promptly notify the competition authorities of the Requesting Party of any change in their intentions with respect to investigation or enforcement;

v. use their best efforts to complete their investigation and to obtain a remedy or initiate proceedings within six months, or such other time as agreed to by the competition authorities of the Parties, of the deferral or suspension of enforcement activities by the competition authorities of the Requesting Party;

vi. fully inform the competition authorities of the Requesting Party of the results of their investigation, and take into account the views of the competition authorities of the Requesting Party, prior to any settlement, initiation of proceedings, adoption of remedies, or termination of the investigation; and

vii. comply with any reasonable request that may be made by the competition authorities of the Requesting Party.

When the above conditions are satisfied, a Requesting Party which chooses not to defer or suspend its enforcement activities shall inform the competition authorities of the Requested Party of its reasons.

3. The competition authorities of the Requesting Party may defer or suspend their own enforcement activities if fewer than all of the conditions set out in paragraph 2 are satisfied.

4. Nothing in this Agreement precludes the competition authorities of a Requesting Party that choose to defer or suspend independent enforcement activities from later initiating or reinstituting such activities. In such circumstances, the competition authorities of the Requesting Party will promptly inform the competition authorities of the Requested Party of their intentions and reasons. If the competition authorities of the Requested Party continue with their own investigation, the competition authorities of the two Parties shall, where appropriate, coordinate their respective investigations under the criteria and procedures of Article IV of the 1991 Agreement.

Article V
CONFIDENTIALITY AND USE OF INFORMATION

* * *

Article VI
RELATIONSHIP TO THE 1991 AGREEMENT

This Agreement shall supplement and be interpreted consistently with the 1991 Agreement, which remains fully in force.

* * *

Notes and Questions

1. The US and EU competition officials and staffs have a deeply cooperative relationship. In addition to the two bilateral agreements excerpted above, which are the basis for much sharing of information and other cooperation, the EU and US entered an agreement in 2011 on best practices in cooperation in merger investigations; and in 2021 they launched the EU-US Joint Technology Competition Policy Dialogue for developing common approaches and strengthening cooperation in the technology sector. https://competition-policy.ec.europa.eu/international-relations/bilateral-relations/usa_en.

2. Comment on negative comity and positive comity in the 1991 and 1998 US/EU agreements and the potential contributions of each. Why does the 1998 agreement exclude mergers from positive comity?

3. The adoption of a track for positive comity was an important conceptual advance, but it has seldom been formally invoked. Nonetheless, the cooperation agreements and innumerable other ongoing interactions have fostered a spirit of cooperation, and the antitrust authorities—not just of US and EU, but of the world, are in fact deeply cooperative and mutually supportive.

4. Nonetheless, conflicts and implicit conflicts occur. The EU and the UK have sometimes prohibited mergers that the US authorities or courts clear. EU, UK, German and other law is often tougher on the Big Tech firms than is US law. (Are these conflicts? even if the US agencies applaud the tougher enforcement, which they may not be able to secure at home, given more conservative law?) Is it to be expected that analyses will sometimes conflict, or effects in different markets may lead to different results? Does it matter if the home country of the merging or allegedly abusing firms is the US? Does it matter if few or no assets of the merging firms are in the enforcing jurisdiction?

D. REGIONAL COOPERATION IN RECs AND FTAs

1. Introduction

Regional economic communities (RECs) and free trade agreements are significant vehicles for cooperation and convergence. Some of the RECs are common markets and custom unions. Some are looser vehicles for cooperation. We have spoken above of common markets that have a common competition law. More often, RECs have no common competition law but, as noted, require their member states to have and enforce a competition law. This undertaking is mirrored in many free trade agreements. Here is a sampling of the arrangements.

2. Australia-New Zealand Closer Economic Relations

One of the most successful longstanding cooperations is that between Australia and New Zealand. A protocol in the Australia-New Zealand Closer Economic Relations Trade Agreement (ANZCERTA) provided for abolition of the anti-dumping laws between the two countries and extension of competition laws to trade in goods affecting trans-Tasman trade. Pursuant thereto, in 1990, both Australia and New Zealand amended their competition laws to prohibit misuse of market power in trans-Tasman trade and to provide for trans-Tasman jurisdiction. In particular, a person who has a dominant position in Australia, New Zealand, or Australia and New Zealand must not take advantage of that power to restrict entry or prevent or deter competition. In addition, the competition commission of each jurisdiction may use its discovery powers in the other country, and the two countries agree to give mutual assistance in investigations. See New Zealand Commerce Act 1986 as amended, section 36A; Australian Trade Practices Act 1974 as amended, section 46A.

3. The United States-Mexico-Canada Agreement

The United States-Mexico-Canada Agreement (2020) supersedes and updates the North American Free Trade Agreement (NAFTA, 1994). While NAFTA, during the days its negotiation, held promise for adopting a regional competition law, this did not happen, in large part because of the asymmetries of the countries. The three parties, the US, Canada and Mexico, have cooperated on competition enforcement in deep and successful ways, but often outside of the FTA through bilateral cooperation agreements, nurturing personal relations in devotion to the task and opportunity to cooperate.

USMCA includes competition provisions in Chapter 21. Article 21.1 provides that "Each Party shall maintain national competition laws that proscribe anticompetitive business conduct to promote competition in order to increase economic efficiency and consumer welfare, and shall take appropriate action with respect to that conduct." The Chapter provides for cooperation and coordination between Members' competition authorities in issues of competition and enforcement policy. It mandates transparency and due process. Issues covered by Chapter 21 are not subject to arbitration (the authorized dispute settlement) under the USCMA.

Chapter 22 of USMCA states that the parties have the right to designate monopolies. The Monopolies must act in accordance with commercial considerations.

Article 22.4 requires the parties to ensure that the designated monopoly will not engage in "anticompetitive practices in a non-monopolized market in its territory that negatively affect trade or investment between the Parties". Only one proceeding arose under the parallel section in NAFTA—a claim by United Parcel Service of America against Canada Post, a state-owned company, for anticompetitive cross-subsidies and price predation. The case was dismissed as not subject to dispute resolution under the FTA.[1]

NAFTA Article 1504 had established a Working Group on Trade and Competition "to report, and to make recommendations on further work as appropriate, to the Commission within five years of the date of entry into force of this Agreement on relevant issues concerning the relationship between competition laws and policies and trade in the free trade area." The working group, comprising officials of the three nations, met a number of times but it did not file a report and did not make recommendations; it could not reach agreement even on subjects as basic as treatment of export cartels from one FTA country into another. Accordingly, there is no common US-Canada-Mexico antitrust regime or framework; although the competition authorities of all three nations frequently and even intensively consult and coordinate under bilateral agreements. Prohibiting export cartel exemptions, limiting antidumping laws, and limiting state action immunity, all within the FTA, were lost opportunities. See Antitrust Law Section, American Bar Association, Task Force Report on the Competition Dimensions of NAFTA (1994).

4. Trans-Pacific Partnership (CPTPP)

The Comprehensive and Progressive Agreement for Trans-Pacific Partnership agreement is an example of a mega-regional agreement. It comprises an original 11 nations from Australia, Japan and Singapore to Brunei and Vietnam, and later saw the accession of the UK. The United States was one of the original 12, but withdrew. The competition chapter (Chapter 16) might be regarded as state-of-the-art for competition chapters in free trade agreements. The chapter does not contain an integrated competition law for the collaborating nations but rather a mandate for members to have and maintain a national competition law "with the objective of promoting economic efficiency and consumer welfare." The nations would undertake to ensure procedural fairness (due process) and to provide private rights of action, and to cooperate. Adjacent Chapter 17 is a

---

1 United States Parcel Service of America, Inc. v. Government of Canada, Award on Jurisdiction (NAFTA Arbitration Tribunal, November 22, 2002), https://2009-2017.state.gov/s/l/c3749.htm.

state-of-the-art provision requiring state-owned enterprises to act in accordance with commercial considerations and not to engage in anticompetitive practices, and to compete on a level playing field without unfair advantages from their governments.

5. Southeast Asia

The 10 southeast Asian countries established the ASEAN Community on the last day of 2015. They aim at an integrated single market and full regional integration. ASEAN includes the ASEAN Economic Community, with Blueprint 2025 to accomplish integration and create a level playing field. ASEAN does not contemplate a central competition law but rather functioning national competition laws of each of the member states, with harmonization and cooperation. The harmonization and integration objectives pose challenges in view of "the ASEAN way"—recognition of the autonomy of each nation to design its own competition law, which may include the industrial policy and SOE privileges of each.

Other cooperations of or including Asian Pacific countries include APEC (Asia-Pacific Economic Cooperation) and RCEP (Regional Comprehensive Economic Partnership, including Indo-Pacific countries).

6. Africa

Developing countries and small jurisdictions have additional reasons to form FTAs with competition competences. They may lack size and resources to run effective competition agencies. Collaborating with neighbors can enhance their effectiveness. Collaborating with neighbors who are at relatively equal levels of development can eliminate a fear of being exploited and can produce a community of common interests. Several such FTAs are in Africa, and in Latin America (below).

In Africa there are a number of regional economic communities, most of them overlapping in their membership. In view of the coming African Continental competition competence, the RECs are preparing for their enhanced roles as pillars to support the center.

COMESA—the Common Market for Eastern and Southern Africa—(mentioned above) is the largest and most mature common market in Africa. It has been a customs union since 2008 and has built up a higher-law competition jurisprudence, of which merger control is the most advanced. It promises to be a solid pillar for the African Continental Competition Protocol when it becomes operational.

The West African Economic and Monetary Union (WAEMU) comprises principally the French-speaking countries. The WAEMU Commission has jurisdiction in relation to merger control within its Member States over mergers which could lead to an abuse of a dominant position. Premerger notification is not mandatory, but it is necessary if the parties wish to obtain an exemption or a negative clearance.

The Economic Community of West African States (ECOWAS) comprises 12 West African states, including the large nation of Nigeria and many smaller states. French and English are both official languages, and both heritages inform the law. Some members have common law traditions; some, civil law. Language and cultural divides are among the challenges.

The ECOWAS competition authority deals with regional issues. Domestic matters are left to the member states. The ECOWAS Community Competition Rules, which are modeled on the EU Treaty, cover agreements, abuse of dominance, public enterprises, and state aids. An Executive Board of the ECOWAS Competition Regulatory Authority is operative, and the Council (Board) responsible for making determinations was constituted in October 2024. A mandatory merger notification is in effect.

The East African Community (EAC) is a customs union comprising Burundi, Democratic Republic of the Congo, Kenya, Rwanda, Somalia, South Sudan, Uganda, and Tanzania. The EAC Competition Authority (EACCA) has jurisdiction over all conduct and transactions with cross-border effects within the community. The member countries are geographically close and have strong links in common ports and transportation systems. The challenges include institutional and resource needs and asymmetry of the nations. Trade flows among the countries are increasing. Merger notification thresholds and merger filing fees are specified, and the EAC has adopted merger control guidelines. The merger control regime came into effect November 1, 2025. The authority aspires to be an active, functioning regional enforcer.

Africa also has significant grass-roots collaboration. The African Competition Forum is an informal network of African national and regional authorities, like a little ICN for Africa. Launched in 2011, it supports adoption of competition laws by those nations still without them, it helps build capacities of new authorities, supports advocacy, and assists in implementing reforms. A prime example of their work is an ambitious research project studying three sectors in five nations—cement, sugar and poultry, in Botswana, Kenya, Namibia, South Africa and Tanzania. The study identifies important linkages between trade and competition, agricultural regulatory policy, and firm behavior. The data indicate where competition is obstructed, and have been continuingly useful in enforcement policy and advocacy. See Simon Roberts, ed., Competition in Africa: Insights from Key Industries (2016).

7. Latin America

Latin American countries have several overlapping regional trade agreements. These include the Andean Community, which is modeled after the European Union and has aspirations to become a Latin American common market. The competition rules of the Andean Community forbid anticompetitive practices that may affect trade among the member states. The Secretary General of the community may impose sanctions for violations. Member states without competition laws (Bolivia and until 2009 Ecuador) can apply the Andean rules to restraints within their own jurisdictions until the nations adopt their own laws.

The Andean Community, formed in 1969, originally consisted of Bolivia, Colombia, Ecuador, Peru, and Chile; Venezuela joined but withdrew. Chile withdrew. The Andean Community was formed to facilitate cooperation in industry, agriculture and trade. It nominally protects free competition across borders. It issues few decisions, and has been hampered by extreme ideological differences among its member states regarding their trust or not for free markets.

Mercosur is the Common Market of the Southern Cone. Its full members are Brazil, Argentina, Paraguay, Uruguay, and Bolivia. Chile, Colombia, Ecuador, Peru, Guyana and Suriname are associate members, Venezuela was suspended as a member. This is the largest trading group in South America. Mercosur aspires to integrate all of South America in a trading bloc. However, it faces many internal divisions including disputes on political economy—the importance, or the dangers, of free markets. The controlling Fortaleza Protocol, signed in December 1996, lists 17 forbidden, anticompetitive practices. The members are required to adopt national competition laws, set up competition authorities, and deal with restraints at national level. Member states may refer national rulings to the Mercosur institutions. The national authorities are tasked with enforcing Mercosur's orders.

CARICOM, the free trade area of the Caribbean Community, comprises a number of small and isolated states. In 2008, it set up an Anti-Monopoly Commission, modeled after the European single market. The CARICOM Commission is empowered to operate both on community level and within its member states on matters with cross-border effects. CARICOM has 15 member states and 5 associate states. Of its members, only Barbados, Guyana, Jamaica, Trinidad & Tobago, and St. Vincent have competition laws, and not all of these laws are operational.

* * *

8. The BRICS Countries

The original five BRICS countries are Brazil, Russia, India, China and South Africa. They have been joined by newly admitted Egypt, Ethiopia, Iran, and the United Arab Emirates. While neither a common market nor an FTA, nor clustered within one discreet region, this set of remarkably growing economies is closely cooperating on competition policy. The competition authorities signed a Memorandum of Understanding for closer cooperation in 2016. They hold bi-annual competition conferences. They share information and learn from one another on common challenges of institutional design, awareness of the law, the growth of competition concerns surrounding global value chains, integrity of agriculture and food systems, and relationship of inclusiveness goals to competition, among others. They have established a Digital Competition Forum. They contemplate significant coordination on merger reviews of global economic concentrations, and may launch a "merger radar" that would allow them to monitor mergers in all BRICS countries.

* * *

Thus, we see a slice of the many cooperations, at different levels, different speeds, and different degrees of commitment.

E. THE INTERNATIONAL ORGANIZATIONS

There are three principal international competition organizations (or subdivisions of them), all of which have been mentioned above and all of which are devoted to advancing cooperation, coordination, knowledge and capacity building, and development of sound principles and best practices in competition law and policy. None of them is a rule-making or law-enforcing body.

The Organization of Economic Cooperation and Development (OECD), founded in 1961, is an organization of largely developed countries that researches social and economic problems, organizes fora to share ideas and practices, and sometimes issues recommendations. It has a Competition Committee.

OECD Competition Committee has a dynamic work program, with excellent research papers by the secretariat and submissions from its members on topics of evolving interest. It does peer reviews of competition authorities. One of its most important recommendations is a recommendation against hard core cartels, first adopted in 1998 and replaced by an updated recommendation in 2019. The document "RECOMMENDS that Adherents make hard core cartels illegal regardless of the existence of proof of actual adverse effects on markets, and design their anti-cartel laws, policies and enforcement practices with a view to ensuring that they halt and deter hard core cartels and provide effective compensation for cartel victims, in accordance with their legal frameworks, institutional set up and procedural safeguards." OECD/LEGAL/0452, July 2, 2019. The OECD competition website is worth consulting. https://www.oecd.org/en/topics/competition.html.

The United Nations Conference on Trade and Development (UNCTAD), now called UN Trade and Development, was formed in 1964 as an intergovernmental organization within the United Nations. It caters largely to the Global South and promotes their interests in world trade and development. It has a Competition and Consumer Branch, which facilitates research in competition and consumer law, presents programs and discussions, and facilitates networking of its members. It too peer reviews competition authorities of members.

We presented above the main founding document of UNCTAD Competition—the Set of Multilaterally Agreed Equitable Principles and Rules for the Control of Restrictive Business Practices Principles.

The International Competition Network was founded in 2001. It was intended to fill a gap that could not be filled by the OECD, UNCTAD, or the WTO. The OECD is an organization of developed countries. The UNCTAD is an organization devoted to developing countries. The WTO is a trade organization; the competition authorities take a back seat to the trade representative. Moreover, the WTO jurisdictions negotiate trade rules and trade rule violations are subject to dispute resolution. The competition authorities wanted a "room" of their own,—an inclusive, virtual organization without rule-making or administrative or adjudicatory power, in an informal and sharing environment conducive to solving actual problems and to converging law "on the ground."

ICN has passed its 25th anniversary. It now has approximately 140 members. It has generated an immense and immensely useful work product. It hosts annual conferences. It convenes working groups of volunteers—including non-governmental advisors—from numerous jurisdictions, whose work ranges from coordination of jurisdictions' rules on pre-merger process to informal technical assistance, to attempts to understand the abuse of dominance laws of all of the members and to tease out the common principles on which recommended practices or guidelines can be built.

Spend time on the website of the ICN, www.internationalcompetitionnetwork.org. Comment on the scope and usefulness of its work.

The ICN is generally regarded as a notable success. Has it alleviated the need for an antitrust regime in the WTO? Is there still a need to rationalize law on export cartels or a need for rules to integrate trade and competition? Are developing country voices sufficiently heard? What should be next steps to advance the coherence, effectiveness, suitability, and legitimacy of competition law and policy in the nations and in the world?

F. CONCLUSION

Global power and transnational effects are a hallmark of twenty-first century competition. National competition law leaves gaps, overlaps, nationalism, and conflicts. Higher level law promises greater coherence but poses problems of sovereignty and administrability.

Comment on the state of the international competition order and what you would do to improve it.

APPENDICES

App. **Page**

Appendix 1

EUROPEAN UNION

TREATY ON EUROPEAN UNION

(1992, as amended by Treaty of Lisbon, effective December 1, 2009)

TITLE I

* * *

Article 4

* * *

3. Pursuant to the principle of sincere cooperation, the Union and the Member States shall, in full mutual respect, assist each other in carrying out tasks which flow from the Treaties.

The Member States shall take any appropriate measure, general or particular, to ensure fulfilment of the obligations arising out of the Treaties or resulting from the acts of the institutions of the Union.

The Member States shall facilitate the achievement of the Union's tasks and refrain from any measure which could jeopardise the attainment of the Union's objectives.

* * *

TREATY ON THE FUNCTIONING OF THE EUROPEAN UNION

(1957, as amended and renamed by Treaty of Lisbon, effective as of December 1, 2009)

PART ONE

PRINCIPLES

Article 1

1. This Treaty organises the functioning of the Union and determines the areas of, delimitation of, and arrangements for exercising its competences.

2. This Treaty and the Treaty on European Union constitute the Treaties on which the Union is founded. These two Treaties, which have the same legal value, shall be referred to as 'the Treaties'.

TITLE I

CATEGORIES AND AREAS OF UNION COMPETENCE

Article 2

1. When the Treaties confer on the Union exclusive competence in a specific area, only the Union may legislate and adopt legally binding acts, the Member States being able to do so themselves only if so empowered by the Union or for the implementation of Union acts.

2. When the Treaties confer on the Union a competence shared with the Member States in a specific area, the Union and the Member States may legislate and adopt legally binding acts in that area. The Member States shall exercise their competence to the extent that the Union has not exercised its competence. The Member States shall again exercise their competence to the extent that the Union has decided to cease exercising its competence.

3. The Member States shall coordinate their economic and employment policies within arrangements as determined by this Treaty, which the Union shall have competence to provide.

4. The Union shall have competence, in accordance with the provisions of the Treaty on European Union, to define and implement a common foreign and security policy, including the progressive framing of a common defence policy.

5. In certain areas and under the conditions laid down in the Treaties, the Union shall have competence to carry out actions to support, coordinate or supplement the actions of the Member States, without thereby superseding their competence in these areas. Legally binding acts of the Union adopted on the basis of the provisions of the Treaties relating to these areas shall not entail harmonisation of Member States' laws or regulations.

6. The scope of and arrangements for exercising the Union's competences shall be determined by the provisions of the Treaties relating to each area.

Article 3

1. The Union shall have exclusive competence in the following areas:

(a) customs union;

(b) the establishing of the competition rules necessary for the functioning of the internal market;

(c) monetary policy for the Member States whose currency is the euro;

(d) the conservation of marine biological resources under the common fisheries policy;

(e) common commercial policy.

2. The Union shall also have exclusive competence for the conclusion of an international agreement when its conclusion is provided for in a legislative act of the Union or is necessary to enable the Union to exercise its internal competence, or in so far as its conclusion may affect common rules or alter their scope.

Article 4

1. The Union shall share competence with the Member States where the Treaties confer on it a competence which does not relate to the areas referred to in Articles 3 and 6.

2. Shared competence between the Union and the Member States applies in the following principal areas:

(a) internal market;

(b) social policy, for the aspects defined in this Treaty;

(c) economic, social and territorial cohesion;

(d) agriculture and fisheries, excluding the conservation of marine biological resources;

(e) environment;

(f) consumer protection;

(g) transport;

(h) trans-European networks;

(i) energy;

(j) area of freedom, security and justice;

(k) common safety concerns in public health matters, for the aspects defined in this Treaty.

3. In the areas of research, technological development and space, the Union shall have competence to carry out activities, in particular to define and implement programmes; however, the exercise of that competence shall not result in Member States being prevented from exercising theirs.

4. In the areas of development cooperation and humanitarian aid, the Union shall have competence to carry out activities and

conduct a common policy; however, the exercise of that competence shall not result in Member States being prevented from exercising theirs.

* * *

PART THREE

UNION POLICIES AND INTERNAL ACTIONS

* * *

TITLE II

FREE MOVEMENT OF GOODS

Article 28

1. The Union shall comprise a customs union which shall cover all trade in goods and which shall involve the prohibition between Member States of customs duties on imports and exports and of all charges having equivalent effect, and the adoption of a common customs tariff in their relations with third countries.

2. The provisions of Article 30 and of Chapter 2 of this Title shall apply to products originating in Member States and to products coming from third countries which are in free circulation in Member States.

* * *

CHAPTER 1

THE CUSTOMS UNION

Article 30

Customs duties on imports and exports and charges having equivalent effect shall be prohibited between Member States. This prohibition shall also apply to customs duties of a fiscal nature.

* * *

CHAPTER 3

PROHIBITION OF QUANTITATIVE RESTRICTIONS BETWEEN MEMBER STATES

Article 34

Quantitative restrictions on imports and all measures having equivalent effect shall be prohibited between Member States.

Article 35

Quantitative restrictions on exports, and all measures having equivalent effect, shall be prohibited between Member States.

Article 36

The provisions of Articles 34 and 35 shall not preclude prohibitions or restrictions on imports, exports or goods in transit justified on grounds of public morality, public policy or public security; the protection of health and life of humans, animals or plants; the protection of national treasures possessing artistic, historic or archaeological value; or the protection of industrial and commercial property. Such prohibitions or restrictions shall not, however, constitute a means of arbitrary discrimination or a disguised restriction on trade between Member States.

Article 37

1. Member States shall adjust any State monopolies of a commercial character so as to ensure that no discrimination regarding the conditions under which goods are procured and marketed exists between nationals of Member States.

The provisions of this Article shall apply to any body through which a Member State, in law or in fact, either directly or indirectly supervises, determines or appreciably influences imports or exports between Member States. These provisions shall likewise apply to monopolies delegated by the State to others.

2. Member States shall refrain from introducing any new measure which is contrary to the principles laid down in paragraph 1 or which restricts the scope of the articles dealing with the prohibition of customs duties and quantitative restrictions between Member States.

3. If a State monopoly of a commercial character has rules which are designed to make it easier to dispose of agricultural products or obtain for them the best return, steps should be taken in applying the rules contained in this Article to ensure equivalent safeguards for the employment and standard of living of the producers concerned.

* * *

TITLE IV

FREE MOVEMENT OF PERSONS, SERVICES AND CAPITAL

CHAPTER 1

WORKERS

Article 45

1. Freedom of movement for workers shall be secured within the Union.

2. Such freedom of movement shall entail the abolition of any discrimination based on nationality between workers of the Member States as regards employment, remuneration and other conditions of work and employment.

3. It shall entail the right, subject to limitations justified on grounds of public policy, public security or public health:

(a) to accept offers of employment actually made;

(b) to move freely within the territory of Member States for this purpose;

(c) to stay in a Member State for the purpose of employment in accordance with the provisions governing the employment of nationals of that State laid down by law, regulation or administrative action;

(d) to remain in the territory of a Member State after having been employed in that State, subject to conditions which shall be embodied in regulations to be drawn up by the Commission.

4. The provisions of this Article shall not apply to employment in the public service.

* * *

CHAPTER 2

RIGHT OF ESTABLISHMENT

Article 49

Within the framework of the provisions set out below, restrictions on the freedom of establishment of nationals of a Member State in the territory of another Member State shall be prohibited. Such prohibition shall also apply to restrictions on the setting-up of agencies, branches or subsidiaries by nationals of any Member State established in the territory of any Member State.

Freedom of establishment shall include the right to take up and pursue activities as self-employed persons and to set up and manage undertakings, in particular companies or firms . . . , under the conditions laid down for its own nationals by the law of the country where such establishment is effected, subject to the provisions of the Chapter relating to capital.

* * *

Article 52

1. The provisions of this Chapter and measures taken in pursuance thereof shall not prejudice the applicability of provisions laid down by law, regulation or administrative action providing for special treatment for foreign nationals on grounds of public policy, public security or public health.

2. The European Parliament and the Council shall, acting in accordance with the ordinary legislative procedure, issue directives for the coordination of the abovementioned provisions.

* * *

CHAPTER 3

SERVICES

Article 56

Within the framework of the provisions set out below, restrictions on freedom to provide services within the Union shall be prohibited in respect of nationals of Member States who are established in a Member State other than that of the person for whom the services are intended.

The European Parliament and the Council, acting in accordance with the ordinary legislative procedure, may extend the provisions of the Chapter to nationals of a third country who provide services and who are established within the Union.

* * *

Article 61

As long as restrictions on freedom to provide services have not been abolished, each Member State shall apply such restrictions without distinction on grounds of nationality or residence to all persons providing services. . . .

* * *

TITLE VII

COMMON RULES ON COMPETITION, TAXATION AND APPROXIMATION OF LAWS

CHAPTER 1

RULES ON COMPETITION

SECTION 1

RULES APPLYING TO UNDERTAKINGS

*Article **101***

1. The following shall be prohibited as incompatible with the internal market: all agreements between undertakings, decisions by associations of undertakings and concerted practices which may affect trade between Member States and which have as their object or effect the prevention, restriction or distortion of competition within the internal market, and in particular those which:

(a) directly or indirectly fix purchase or selling prices or any other trading conditions;

(b) limit or control production, markets, technical development, or investment;

(c) share markets or sources of supply;

(d) apply dissimilar conditions to equivalent transactions with other trading parties, thereby placing them at a competitive disadvantage;

(e) make the conclusion of contracts subject to acceptance by the other parties of supplementary obligations which, by their nature or according to commercial usage, have no connection with the subject of such contracts.

2. Any agreements or decisions prohibited pursuant to this Article shall be automatically void.

3. The provisions of paragraph 1 may, however, be declared inapplicable in the case of:

—any agreement or category of agreements between undertakings,

—any decision or category of decisions by associations of undertakings,

—any concerted practice or category of concerted practices,

which contributes to improving the production or distribution of goods or to promoting technical or economic progress, while allowing consumers a fair share of the resulting benefit, and which does not:

(a) impose on the undertakings concerned restrictions which are not indispensable to the attainment of these objectives;

(b) afford such undertakings the possibility of eliminating competition in respect of a substantial part of the products in question.

Article 102

Any abuse by one or more undertakings of a dominant position within the internal market or in a substantial part of it shall be prohibited as incompatible with the internal market in so far as it may affect trade between Member States.

Such abuse may, in particular, consist in:

(a) directly or indirectly imposing unfair purchase or selling prices or other unfair trading conditions;

(b) limiting production, markets or technical development to the prejudice of consumers;

(c) applying dissimilar conditions to equivalent transactions with other trading parties, thereby placing them at a competitive disadvantage;

(d) making the conclusion of contracts subject to acceptance by the other parties of supplementary obligations which, by their nature or according to commercial usage, have no connection with the subject of such contracts.

* * *

Article 106

1. In the case of public undertakings and undertakings to which Member States grant special or exclusive rights, Member States shall neither enact nor maintain in force any measure contrary to the rules contained in the Treaties, in particular to those rules provided for in Article 18 [prohibiting discrimination based on nationality] and Articles 101 to 109.

2. Undertakings entrusted with the operation of services of general economic interest or having the character of a revenue-producing monopoly shall be subject to the rules contained in the Treaties, in particular to the rules on competition, in so far as the application of such rules does not obstruct the performance, in law or in fact, of the particular tasks assigned to them. The development of

trade must not be affected to such an extent as would be contrary to the interests of the Union.

3. The Commission shall ensure the application of the provisions of this Article and shall, where necessary, address appropriate directives or decisions to Member States.

SECTION 2

AIDS GRANTED BY STATES

Article 107

1. Save as otherwise provided in the Treaties, any aid granted by a Member State or through State resources in any form whatsoever which distorts or threatens to distort competition by favouring certain undertakings or the production of certain goods shall, in so far as it affects trade between Member States, be incompatible with the internal market.

2. The following shall be compatible with the internal market:

(a) aid having a social character, granted to individual consumers, provided that such aid is granted without discrimination related to the origin of the products concerned;

(b) aid to make good the damage caused by natural disasters or exceptional occurrences;

(c) aid granted to the economy of certain areas of the Federal Republic of Germany affected by the division of Germany, in so far as such aid is required in order to compensate for the economic disadvantages caused by that division. Five years after the entry into force of the Treaty of Lisbon, the Council, acting on a proposal from the Commission, may adopt a decision repealing this point.

3. The following may be considered to be compatible with the internal market:

(a) aid to promote the economic development of areas where the standard of living is abnormally low or where there is serious underemployment, and of the regions referred to in Article 349, in view of their structural, economic and social situation;

(b) aid to promote the execution of an important project of common European interest or to remedy a serious disturbance in the economy of a Member State;

(c) aid to facilitate the development of certain economic activities or of certain economic areas, where such aid does not adversely affect trading conditions to an extent contrary to the common interest;

(d) aid to promote culture and heritage conservation where such aid does not affect trading conditions and competition in the Union to an extent that is contrary to the common interest;

(e) such other categories of aid as may be specified by decision of the Council on a proposal from the Commission.

Article 108

1. The Commission shall, in cooperation with Member States, keep under constant review all systems of aid existing in those States. It shall propose to the latter any appropriate measures required by the progressive development or by the functioning of the internal market.

2. If, after giving notice to the parties concerned to submit their comments, the Commission finds that aid granted by a State or through State resources is not compatible with the internal market having regard to Article 107, or that such aid is being misused, it shall decide that the State concerned shall abolish or alter such aid within a period of time to be determined by the Commission.

If the State concerned does not comply with this decision within the prescribed time, the Commission or any other interested State may, in derogation from the provisions of Articles 258 and 259, refer the matter to the Court of Justice of the European Union direct.

On application by a Member State, the Council may, acting unanimously, decide that aid which that State is granting or intends to grant shall be considered to be compatible with the internal market, in derogation from the provisions of Article 107 or from the regulations provided for in Article 109, if such a decision is justified by exceptional circumstances. If, as regards the aid in question, the Commission has already initiated the procedure provided for in the first subparagraph of this paragraph, the fact that the State concerned has made its application to the Council shall have the effect of suspending that procedure until the Council has made its attitude known.

If, however, the Council has not made its attitude known within three months of the said application being made, the Commission shall give its decision on the case.

3. The Commission shall be informed, in sufficient time to enable it to submit its comments, of any plans to grant or alter aid. If it considers that any such plan is not compatible with the internal market having regard to Article 107, it shall without delay initiate

the procedure provided for in paragraph 2. The Member State concerned shall not put its proposed measures into effect until this procedure has resulted in a final decision.

4. The Commission may adopt regulations relating to the categories of State aid that the Council has, pursuant to Article 109, determined may be exempted from the procedure provided for by paragraph 3 of this Article.

Article 109

The Council, on a proposal from the Commission and after consulting the European Parliament, may make any appropriate regulations for the application of Articles 107 and 108 and may in particular determine the conditions in which Article 108(3) shall apply and the categories of aid exempted from this procedure.

* * *

PART SEVEN

GENERAL AND FINAL PROVISIONS

* * *

Article 352

1. If action by the Union should prove necessary, within the framework of the policies defined in the Treaties, to attain one of the objectives set out in the Treaties, and the Treaties have not provided the necessary powers, the Council, acting unanimously on a proposal from the Commission and after obtaining the consent of the European Parliament, shall adopt the appropriate measures. Where the measures in question are adopted by the Council in accordance with a special legislative procedure, it shall also act unanimously on a proposal from the Commission and after obtaining the consent of the European Parliament.

2. Using the procedure for monitoring the subsidiarity principle referred to in Article 5(3) of the Treaty on European Union, the Commission shall draw national Parliaments' attention to proposals based on this Article.

3. Measures based on this Article shall not entail harmonisation of Member States' laws or regulations in cases where the Treaties exclude such harmonisation.

4. This Article cannot serve as a basis for attaining objectives pertaining to the common foreign and security policy and any acts adopted pursuant to this Article shall respect the limits set out in Article 40, second paragraph, of the Treaty on European Union.

* * *

PROTOCOL (NO 27)

ON THE INTERNAL MARKET AND COMPETITION

THE HIGH CONTRACTING PARTIES,

CONSIDERING that the internal market as set out in Article 3 of the Treaty on European Union includes a system ensuring that competition is not distorted,

HAVE AGREED that:

To this end, the Union shall, if necessary, take action under the provision of the Treaties, including under Article 352 of the Treaty on the Functioning of the European Union.

This protocol shall be annexed to the Treaty on European Union and to the Treaty on the Functioning of the European Union.

Appendix 2

EUROPEAN UNION COUNCIL REGULATION NO. 1/2003

OF 16 DECEMBER 2002 ON THE IMPLEMENTATION OF THE RULES ON COMPETITION, ARTICLES 81 AND 82 OF THE TREATY

O. J. L1/1 (4 Jan. 2003)

[This regulation references the article numbers of the Treaty establishing the European Community (TEC). These articles have been renumbered. Article 81 TEC is now Article 101 of the Treaty on Functioning of the European Union (TFEU). Article 82 TEC is now Article 102 TFEU. Article 83 TEC is now Article 103 TFEU. A revision of Regulation 1/2003 is expected in September 2026.]

THE COUNCIL OF THE EUROPEAN UNION,

Having regard to the Treaty establishing the European Community, and in particular Article 83 thereof,

Having regard to the proposal from the Commission,

Having regard to the opinion of the European Parliament,

Having regard to the opinion of the European Economic and Social Committee,

Whereas:

(1) In order to establish a system which ensures that competition in the common market is not distorted, Articles 81 and 82 of the Treaty must be applied effectively and uniformly in the Community. Council Regulation No 17 of 6 February 1962, First Regulation implementing Articles 81 and 82 of the Treaty, has allowed a Community competition policy to develop that has helped to disseminate a competition culture within the Community. In the light of experience, however, that Regulation should now be replaced by legislation designed to meet the challenges of an integrated market and a future enlargement of the Community.

(2) In particular, there is a need to rethink the arrangements for applying the exception from the prohibition on agreements, which

restrict competition, laid down in Article 81(3) of the Treaty. Under Article 83(2)(b) of the Treaty, account must be taken in this regard of the need to ensure effective supervision, on the one hand, and to simplify administration to the greatest possible extent, on the other.

(3) The centralised scheme set up by Regulation No 17 no longer secures a balance between those two objectives. It hampers application of the Community competition rules by the courts and competition authorities of the Member States, and the system of notification it involves prevents the Commission from concentrating its resources on curbing the most serious infringements. It also imposes considerable costs on undertakings.

(4) The present system should therefore be replaced by a directly applicable exception system in which the competition authorities and courts of the Member States have the power to apply not only Article 81(1) and Article 82 of the Treaty, which have direct applicability by virtue of the case-law of the Court of Justice of the European Communities, but also Article 81(3) of the Treaty.

(5) In order to ensure an effective enforcement of the Community competition rules and at the same time the respect of fundamental rights of defence, this Regulation should regulate the burden of proof under Articles 81 and 82 of the Treaty. It should be for the party or the authority alleging an infringement of Article 81(1) and Article 82 of the Treaty to prove the existence thereof to the required legal standard. It should be for the undertaking or association of undertakings invoking the benefit of a defence against a finding of an infringement to demonstrate to the required legal standard that the conditions for applying such defence are satisfied. This Regulation affects neither national rules on the standard of proof nor obligations of competition authorities and courts of the Member States to ascertain the relevant facts of a case, provided that such rules and obligations are compatible with general principles of Community law.

(6) In order to ensure that the Community competition rules are applied effectively, the competition authorities of the Member States should be associated more closely with their application. To this end, they should be empowered to apply Community law.

(7) National courts have an essential part to play in applying the Community competition rules. When deciding disputes between private individuals, they protect the subjective rights under Community law, for example by awarding damages to the victims of infringements. The role of the national courts here complements that of the competition authorities of the Member States. They should therefore be allowed to apply Articles 81 and 82 of the Treaty in full.

(8) In order to ensure the effective enforcement of the Community competition rules and the proper functioning of the cooperation mechanisms contained in this Regulation, it is necessary to oblige the competition authorities and courts of the Member States to also apply Articles 81 and 82 of the Treaty where they apply national competition law to agreements and practices which may affect trade between Member States. In order to create a level playing field for agreements, decisions by associations of undertakings and concerted practices within the internal market, it is also necessary to determine pursuant to Article 83(2)(e) of the Treaty the relationship between national laws and Community competition law. To that effect it is necessary to provide that the application of national competition laws to agreements, decisions or concerted practices within the meaning of Article 81(1) of the Treaty may not lead to the prohibition of such agreements, decisions and concerted practices if they are not also prohibited under Community competition law. The notions of agreements, decisions and concerted practices are autonomous concepts of Community competition law covering the coordination of behaviour of undertakings on the market as interpreted by the Community Courts. Member States should not under this Regulation be precluded from adopting and applying on their territory stricter national competition laws which prohibit or impose sanctions on unilateral conduct engaged in by undertakings. These stricter national laws may include provisions which prohibit or impose sanctions on abusive behaviour toward economically dependent undertakings. Furthermore, this Regulation does not apply to national laws which impose criminal sanctions on natural persons except to the extent that such sanctions are the means whereby competition rules applying to undertakings are enforced.

(9) Articles 81 and 82 of the Treaty have as their objective the protection of competition on the market. This Regulation, which is adopted for the implementation of these Treaty provisions, does not preclude Member States from implementing on their territory national legislation, which protects other legitimate interests provided that such legislation is compatible with general principles and other provisions of Community law. In so far as such national legislation pursues predominantly an objective different from that of protecting competition on the market, the competition authorities and courts of the Member States may apply such legislation on their territory. Accordingly, Member States may under this Regulation implement on their territory national legislation that prohibits or imposes sanctions on acts of unfair trading practice, be they unilateral or contractual. Such legislation pursues a specific objective, irrespective of the actual or presumed effects of such acts on competition on the market. This is particularly the case of

legislation which prohibits undertakings from imposing on their trading partners, obtaining or attempting to obtain from them terms and conditions that are unjustified, disproportionate or without consideration.

(10) Regulations such as 19/65/EEC, (EEC) No 2821/71, (EEC) No 3976/87, (EEC) No 1534/91, or (EEC) No 479/92 empower the Commission to apply Article 81(3) of the Treaty by Regulation to certain categories of agreements, decisions by associations of undertakings and concerted practices. In the areas defined by such Regulations, the Commission has adopted and may continue to adopt so called "block" exemption Regulations by which it declares Article 81(1) of the Treaty inapplicable to categories of agreements, decisions and concerted practices. Where agreements, decisions and concerted practices to which such Regulations apply nonetheless have effects that are incompatible with Article 81(3) of the Treaty, the Commission and the competition authorities of the Member States should have the power to withdraw in a particular case the benefit of the block exemption Regulation.

(11) For it to ensure that the provisions of the Treaty are applied, the Commission should be able to address decisions to undertakings or associations of undertakings for the purpose of bringing to an end infringements of Articles 81 and 82 of the Treaty. Provided there is a legitimate interest in doing so, the Commission should also be able to adopt decisions which find that an infringement has been committed in the past even if it does not impose a fine. This Regulation should also make explicit provision for the Commission's power to adopt decisions ordering interim measures, which has been acknowledged by the Court of Justice.

(12) This Regulation should make explicit provision for the Commission's power to impose any remedy, whether behavioural or structural, which is necessary to bring the infringement effectively to an end, having regard to the principle of proportionality. Structural remedies should only be imposed either where there is no equally effective behavioural remedy or where any equally effective behavioural remedy would be more burdensome for the undertaking concerned than the structural remedy. Changes to the structure of an undertaking as it existed before the infringement was committed would only be proportionate where there is a substantial risk of a lasting or repeated infringement that derives from the very structure of the undertaking.

(13) Where, in the course of proceedings which might lead to an agreement or practice being prohibited, undertakings offer the Commission commitments such as to meet its concerns, the Commission should be able to adopt decisions which make those

commitments binding on the undertakings concerned. Commitment decisions should find that there are no longer grounds for action by the Commission without concluding whether or not there has been or still is an infringement. Commitment decisions are without prejudice to the powers of competition authorities and courts of the Member States to make such a finding and decide upon the case. Commitment decisions are not appropriate in cases where the Commission intends to impose a fine.

(14) In exceptional cases where the public interest of the Community so requires, it may also be expedient for the Commission to adopt a decision of a declaratory nature finding that the prohibition in Article 81 or Article 82 of the Treaty does not apply, with a view to clarifying the law and ensuring its consistent application throughout the Community, in particular with regard to new types of agreements or practices that have not been settled in the existing case-law and administrative practice.

(15) The Commission and the competition authorities of the Member States should form together a network of public authorities applying the Community competition rules in close cooperation. For that purpose it is necessary to set up arrangements for information and consultation. Further modalities for the cooperation within the network will be laid down and revised by the Commission, in close cooperation with the Member States.

(16) Notwithstanding any national provision to the contrary, the exchange of information and the use of such information in evidence should be allowed between the members of the network even where the information is confidential. This information may be used for the application of Articles 81 and 82 of the Treaty as well as for the parallel application of national competition law, provided that the latter application relates to the same case and does not lead to a different outcome. When the information exchanged is used by the receiving authority to impose sanctions on undertakings, there should be no other limit to the use of the information than the obligation to use it for the purpose for which it was collected given the fact that the sanctions imposed on undertakings are of the same type in all systems. The rights of defence enjoyed by undertakings in the various systems can be considered as sufficiently equivalent. However, as regards natural persons, they may be subject to substantially different types of sanctions across the various systems. Where that is the case, it is necessary to ensure that information can only be used if it has been collected in a way which respects the same level of protection of the rights of defence of natural persons as provided for under the national rules of the receiving authority.

(17) If the competition rules are to be applied consistently and, at the same time, the network is to be managed in the best possible way, it is essential to retain the rule that the competition authorities of the Member States are automatically relieved of their competence if the Commission initiates its own proceedings. Where a competition authority of a Member State is already acting on a case and the Commission intends to initiate proceedings, it should endeavour to do so as soon as possible. Before initiating proceedings, the Commission should consult the national authority concerned.

(18) To ensure that cases are dealt with by the most appropriate authorities within the network, a general provision should be laid down allowing a competition authority to suspend or close a case on the ground that another authority is dealing with it or has already dealt with it, the objective being that each case should be handled by a single authority. This provision should not prevent the Commission from rejecting a complaint for lack of Community interest, as the case-law of the Court of Justice has acknowledged it may do, even if no other competition authority has indicated its intention of dealing with the case.

(19) The Advisory Committee on Restrictive Practices and Dominant Positions set up by Regulation No 17 has functioned in a very satisfactory manner. It will fit well into the new system of decentralised application. It is necessary, therefore, to build upon the rules laid down by Regulation No 17, while improving the effectiveness of the organisational arrangements. To this end, it would be expedient to allow opinions to be delivered by written procedure. The Advisory Committee should also be able to act as a forum for discussing cases that are being handled by the competition authorities of the Member States, so as to help safeguard the consistent application of the Community competition rules.

(20) The Advisory Committee should be composed of representatives of the competition authorities of the Member States. For meetings in which general issues are being discussed, Member States should be able to appoint an additional representative. This is without prejudice to members of the Committee being assisted by other experts from the Member States.

(21) Consistency in the application of the competition rules also requires that arrangements be established for cooperation between the courts of the Member States and the Commission. This is relevant for all courts of the Member States that apply Articles 81 and 82 of the Treaty, whether applying these rules in lawsuits between private parties, acting as public enforcers or as review courts. In particular, national courts should be able to ask the Commission for information or for its opinion on points concerning

the application of Community competition law. The Commission and the competition authorities of the Member States should also be able to submit written or oral observations to courts called upon to apply Article 81 or Article 82 of the Treaty. These observations should be submitted within the framework of national procedural rules and practices including those safeguarding the rights of the parties. Steps should therefore be taken to ensure that the Commission and the competition authorities of the Member States are kept sufficiently well informed of proceedings before national courts.

(22) In order to ensure compliance with the principles of legal certainty and the uniform application of the Community competition rules in a system of parallel powers, conflicting decisions must be avoided. It is therefore necessary to clarify, in accordance with the case-law of the Court of Justice, the effects of Commission decisions and proceedings on courts and competition authorities of the Member States. Commitment decisions adopted by the Commission do not affect the power of the courts and the competition authorities of the Member States to apply Articles 81 and 82 of the Treaty.

(23) The Commission should be empowered throughout the Community to require such information to be supplied as is necessary to detect any agreement, decision or concerted practice prohibited by Article 81 of the Treaty or any abuse of a dominant position prohibited by Article 82 of the Treaty. When complying with a decision of the Commission, undertakings cannot be forced to admit that they have committed an infringement, but they are in any event obliged to answer factual questions and to provide documents, even if this information may be used to establish against them or against another undertaking the existence of an infringement.

(24) The Commission should also be empowered to undertake such inspections as are necessary to detect any agreement, decision or concerted practice prohibited by Article 81 of the Treaty or any abuse of a dominant position prohibited by Article 82 of the Treaty. The competition authorities of the Member States should cooperate actively in the exercise of these powers.

(25) The detection of infringements of the competition rules is growing ever more difficult, and, in order to protect competition effectively, the Commission's powers of investigation need to be supplemented. The Commission should in particular be empowered to interview any persons who may be in possession of useful information and to record the statements made. In the course of an inspection, officials authorised by the Commission should be empowered to affix seals for the period of time necessary for the inspection. Seals should normally not be affixed for more than 72 hours. Officials authorised by the Commission should also be

empowered to ask for any information relevant to the subject matter and purpose of the inspection.

(26) Experience has shown that there are cases where business records are kept in the homes of directors or other people working for an undertaking. In order to safeguard the effectiveness of inspections, therefore, officials and other persons authorised by the Commission should be empowered to enter any premises where business records may be kept, including private homes. However, the exercise of this latter power should be subject to the authorisation of the judicial authority.

(27) Without prejudice to the case-law of the Court of Justice, it is useful to set out the scope of the control that the national judicial authority may carry out when it authorises, as foreseen by national law including as a precautionary measure, assistance from law enforcement authorities in order to overcome possible opposition on the part of the undertaking or the execution of the decision to carry out inspections in non-business premises. It results from the case-law that the national judicial authority may in particular ask the Commission for further information which it needs to carry out its control and in the absence of which it could refuse the authorisation. The case-law also confirms the competence of the national courts to control the application of national rules governing the implementation of coercive measures.

(28) In order to help the competition authorities of the Member States to apply Articles 81 and 82 of the Treaty effectively, it is expedient to enable them to assist one another by carrying out inspections and other fact-finding measures.

(29) Compliance with Articles 81 and 82 of the Treaty and the fulfilment of the obligations imposed on undertakings and associations of undertakings under this Regulation should be enforceable by means of fines and periodic penalty payments. To that end, appropriate levels of fine should also be laid down for infringements of the procedural rules.

(30) In order to ensure effective recovery of fines imposed on associations of undertakings for infringements that they have committed, it is necessary to lay down the conditions on which the Commission may require payment of the fine from the members of the association where the association is not solvent. In doing so, the Commission should have regard to the relative size of the undertakings belonging to the association and in particular to the situation of small and medium-sized enterprises. Payment of the fine by one or several members of an association is without prejudice to

rules of national law that provide for recovery of the amount paid from other members of the association.

(31) The rules on periods of limitation for the imposition of fines and periodic penalty payments were laid down in Council Regulation (EEC) No 2988/74, which also concerns penalties in the field of transport. In a system of parallel powers, the acts, which may interrupt a limitation period, should include procedural steps taken independently by the competition authority of a Member State. To clarify the legal framework, Regulation (EEC) No 2988/74 should therefore be amended to prevent it applying to matters covered by this Regulation, and this Regulation should include provisions on periods of limitation.

(32) The undertakings concerned should be accorded the right to be heard by the Commission, third parties whose interests may be affected by a decision should be given the opportunity of submitting their observations beforehand, and the decisions taken should be widely publicised. While ensuring the rights of defence of the undertakings concerned, in particular, the right of access to the file, it is essential that business secrets be protected. The confidentiality of information exchanged in the network should likewise be safeguarded.

(33) Since all decisions taken by the Commission under this Regulation are subject to review by the Court of Justice in accordance with the Treaty, the Court of Justice should, in accordance with Article 229 thereof be given unlimited jurisdiction in respect of decisions by which the Commission imposes fines or periodic penalty payments.

(34) The principles laid down in Articles 81 and 82 of the Treaty, as they have been applied by Regulation No 17, have given a central role to the Community bodies. This central role should be retained, whilst associating the Member States more closely with the application of the Community competition rules. In accordance with the principles of subsidiarity and proportionality as set out in Article 5 of the Treaty, this Regulation does not go beyond what is necessary in order to achieve its objective, which is to allow the Community competition rules to be applied effectively.

(35) In order to attain a proper enforcement of Community competition law, Member States should designate and empower authorities to apply Articles 81 and 82 of the Treaty as public enforcers. They should be able to designate administrative as well as judicial authorities to carry out the various functions conferred upon competition authorities in this Regulation. This Regulation recognises the wide variation which exists in the public enforcement

systems of Member States. The effects of Article 11(6) of this Regulation should apply to all competition authorities. As an exception to this general rule, where a prosecuting authority brings a case before a separate judicial authority, Article 11(6) should apply to the prosecuting authority subject to the conditions in Article 35(4) of this Regulation. Where these conditions are not fulfilled, the general rule should apply. In any case, Article 11(6) should not apply to courts insofar as they are acting as review courts.

(36) As the case-law has made it clear that the competition rules apply to transport, that sector should be made subject to the procedural provisions of this Regulation. Council Regulation No 141 of 26 November 1962 exempting transport from the application of Regulation No 17 should therefore be repealed and Regulations (EEC) No 1017/68, (EEC) No 4056/86 and (EEC) No 3975/87 should be amended in order to delete the specific procedural provisions they contain.

(37) This Regulation respects the fundamental rights and observes the principles recognised in particular by the Charter of Fundamental Rights of the European Union. Accordingly, this Regulation should be interpreted and applied with respect to those rights and principles.

(38) Legal certainty for undertakings operating under the Community competition rules contributes to the promotion of innovation and investment. Where cases give rise to genuine uncertainty because they present novel or unresolved questions for the application of these rules, individual undertakings may wish to seek informal guidance from the Commission. This Regulation is without prejudice to the ability of the Commission to issue such informal guidance,

HAS ADOPTED THIS REGULATION:

CHAPTER I

PRINCIPLES

Article 1

APPLICATION OF ARTICLES 81 AND 82 OF THE TREATY

1. Agreements, decisions and concerted practices caught by Article 81(1) of the Treaty which do not satisfy the conditions of Article 81(3) of the Treaty shall be prohibited, no prior decision to that effect being required.

2. Agreements, decisions and concerted practices caught by Article 81(1) of the Treaty which satisfy the conditions of Article 81(3)

of the Treaty shall not be prohibited, no prior decision to that effect being required.

3. The abuse of a dominant position referred to in Article 82 of the Treaty shall be prohibited, no prior decision to that effect being required.

Article 2

BURDEN OF PROOF

In any national or Community proceedings for the application of Articles 81 and 82 of the Treaty, the burden of proving an infringement of Article 81(1) or of Article 82 of the Treaty shall rest on the party or the authority alleging the infringement. The undertaking or association of undertakings claiming the benefit of Article 81(3) of the Treaty shall bear the burden of proving that the conditions of that paragraph are fulfilled.

Article 3

RELATIONSHIP BETWEEN ARTICLES 81 AND 82 OF THE TREATY AND NATIONAL COMPETITION LAWS

1. Where the competition authorities of the Member States or national courts apply national competition law to agreements, decisions by associations of undertakings or concerted practices within the meaning of Article 81(1) of the Treaty which may affect trade between Member States within the meaning of that provision, they shall also apply Article 81 of the Treaty to such agreements, decisions or concerted practices. Where the competition authorities of the Member States or national courts apply national competition law to any abuse prohibited by Article 82 of the Treaty, they shall also apply Article 82 of the Treaty.

2. The application of national competition law may not lead to the prohibition of agreements, decisions by associations of undertakings or concerted practices which may affect trade between Member States but which do not restrict competition within the meaning of Article 81(1) of the Treaty, or which fulfil the conditions of Article 81(3) of the Treaty or which are covered by a Regulation for the application of Article 81(3) of the Treaty. Member States shall not under this Regulation be precluded from adopting and applying on their territory stricter national laws which prohibit or sanction unilateral conduct engaged in by undertakings.

3. Without prejudice to general principles and other provisions of Community law, paragraphs 1 and 2 do not apply when the competition authorities and the courts of the Member States apply national merger control laws nor do they preclude the

application of provisions of national law that predominantly pursue an objective different from that pursued by Articles 81 and 82 of the Treaty.

CHAPTER II

POWERS

Article 4

POWERS OF THE COMMISSION

For the purpose of applying Articles 81 and 82 of the Treaty, the Commission shall have the powers provided for by this Regulation.

Article 5

POWERS OF THE COMPETITION AUTHORITIES OF THE MEMBER STATES

The competition authorities of the Member States shall have the power to apply Articles 81 and 82 of the Treaty in individual cases. For this purpose, acting on their own initiative or on a complaint, they may take the following decisions:

—requiring that an infringement be brought to an end,

—ordering interim measures,

—accepting commitments,

—imposing fines, periodic penalty payments or any other penalty provided for in their national law.

Where on the basis of the information in their possession the conditions for prohibition are not met they may likewise decide that there are no grounds for action on their part.

Article 6

POWERS OF THE NATIONAL COURTS

National courts shall have the power to apply Articles 81 and 82 of the Treaty.

CHAPTER III

COMMISSION DECISIONS

Article 7

FINDING AND TERMINATION OF INFRINGEMENT

1. Where the Commission, acting on a complaint or on its own initiative, finds that there is an infringement of Article 81 or of Article 82 of the Treaty, it may by decision require the undertakings

and associations of undertakings concerned to bring such infringement to an end. For this purpose, it may impose on them any behavioural or structural remedies which are proportionate to the infringement committed and necessary to bring the infringement effectively to an end. Structural remedies can only be imposed either where there is no equally effective behavioural remedy or where any equally effective behavioural remedy would be more burdensome for the undertaking concerned than the structural remedy. If the Commission has a legitimate interest in doing so, it may also find that an infringement has been committed in the past.

2. Those entitled to lodge a complaint for the purposes of paragraph 1 are natural or legal persons who can show a legitimate interest and Member States.

Article 8

INTERIM MEASURES

1. In cases of urgency due to the risk of serious and irreparable damage to competition, the Commission, acting on its own initiative may by decision, on the basis of a prima facie finding of infringement, order interim measures.

2. A decision under paragraph 1 shall apply for a specified period of time and may be renewed in so far this is necessary and appropriate.

Article 9

COMMITMENTS

1. Where the Commission intends to adopt a decision requiring that an infringement be brought to an end and the undertakings concerned offer commitments to meet the concerns expressed to them by the Commission in its preliminary assessment, the Commission may by decision make those commitments binding on the undertakings. Such a decision may be adopted for a specified period and shall conclude that there are no longer grounds for action by the Commission.

2. The Commission may, upon request or on its own initiative, reopen the proceedings:

(a) where there has been a material change in any of the facts on which the decision was based;

(b) where the undertakings concerned act contrary to their commitments; or

(c) where the decision was based on incomplete, incorrect or misleading information provided by the parties.

Article 10

FINDING OF INAPPLICABILITY

Where the Community public interest relating to the application of Articles 81 and 82 of the Treaty so requires, the Commission, acting on its own initiative, may by decision find that Article 81 of the Treaty is not applicable to an agreement, a decision by an association of undertakings or a concerted practice, either because the conditions of Article 81(1) of the Treaty are not fulfilled, or because the conditions of Article 81(3) of the Treaty are satisfied.

The Commission may likewise make such a finding with reference to Article 82 of the Treaty.

CHAPTER IV

COOPERATION

Article 11

COOPERATION BETWEEN THE COMMISSION AND THE COMPETITION AUTHORITIES OF THE MEMBER STATES

1. The Commission and the competition authorities of the Member States shall apply the Community competition rules in close cooperation.

2. The Commission shall transmit to the competition authorities of the Member States copies of the most important documents it has collected with a view to applying Articles 7, 8, 9, 10 and Article 29(1). At the request of the competition authority of a Member State, the Commission shall provide it with a copy of other existing documents necessary for the assessment of the case.

3. The competition authorities of the Member States shall, when acting under Article 81 or Article 82 of the Treaty, inform the Commission in writing before or without delay after commencing the first formal investigative measure. This information may also be made available to the competition authorities of the other Member States.

4. No later than 30 days before the adoption of a decision requiring that an infringement be brought to an end, accepting commitments or withdrawing the benefit of a block exemption Regulation, the competition authorities of the Member States shall inform the Commission. To that effect, they shall provide the Commission with a summary of the case, the envisaged decision or, in the absence thereof, any other document indicating the proposed course of action. This information may also be made available to the

competition authorities of the other Member States. At the request of the Commission, the acting competition authority shall make available to the Commission other documents it holds which are necessary for the assessment of the case. The information supplied to the Commission may be made available to the competition authorities of the other Member States. National competition authorities may also exchange between themselves information necessary for the assessment of a case that they are dealing with under Article 81 or Article 82 of the Treaty.

5. The competition authorities of the Member States may consult the Commission on any case involving the application of Community law.

6. The initiation by the Commission of proceedings for the adoption of a decision under Chapter III shall relieve the competition authorities of the Member States of their competence to apply Articles 81 and 82 of the Treaty. If a competition authority of a Member State is already acting on a case, the Commission shall only initiate proceedings after consulting with that national competition authority.

Article 12

EXCHANGE OF INFORMATION

1. For the purpose of applying Articles 81 and 82 of the Treaty the Commission and the competition authorities of the Member States shall have the power to provide one another with and use in evidence any matter of fact or of law, including confidential information.

2. Information exchanged shall only be used in evidence for the purpose of applying Article 81 or Article 82 of the Treaty and in respect of the subject-matter for which it was collected by the transmitting authority. However, where national competition law is applied in the same case and in parallel to Community competition law and does not lead to a different outcome, information exchanged under this Article may also be used for the application of national competition law.

3. Information exchanged pursuant to paragraph 1 can only be used in evidence to impose sanctions on natural persons where:

—the law of the transmitting authority foresees sanctions of a similar kind in relation to an infringement of Article 81 or Article 82 of the Treaty or, in the absence thereof,

—the information has been collected in a way which respects the same level of protection of the rights of defence of natural persons as provided for under the national rules of the receiving authority. However, in this case, the information exchanged cannot be used by the receiving authority to impose custodial sanctions.

Article 13

SUSPENSION OR TERMINATION OF PROCEEDINGS

1. Where competition authorities of two or more Member States have received a complaint or are acting on their own initiative under Article 81 or Article 82 of the Treaty against the same agreement, decision of an association or practice, the fact that one authority is dealing with the case shall be sufficient grounds for the others to suspend the proceedings before them or to reject the complaint. The Commission may likewise reject a complaint on the ground that a competition authority of a Member State is dealing with the case.

2. Where a competition authority of a Member State or the Commission has received a complaint against an agreement, decision of an association or practice which has already been dealt with by another competition authority, it may reject it.

Article 14

ADVISORY COMMITTEE

1. The Commission shall consult an Advisory Committee on Restrictive Practices and Dominant Positions prior to the taking of any decision under Articles 7, 8, 9, 10, 23, Article 24(2) and Article 29(1).

2. For the discussion of individual cases, the Advisory Committee shall be composed of representatives of the competition authorities of the Member States. For meetings in which issues other than individual cases are being discussed, an additional Member State representative competent in competition matters may be appointed. Representatives may, if unable to attend, be replaced by other representatives.

3. The consultation may take place at a meeting convened and chaired by the Commission, held not earlier than 14 days after dispatch of the notice convening it, together with a summary of the case, an indication of the most important documents and a preliminary draft decision. In respect of decisions pursuant to Article 8, the meeting may be held seven days after the dispatch of the operative part of a draft decision. Where the Commission dispatches a notice convening the meeting which gives a shorter period of notice than those specified above, the meeting may take place on the

proposed date in the absence of an objection by any Member State. The Advisory Committee shall deliver a written opinion on the Commission's preliminary draft decision. It may deliver an opinion even if some members are absent and are not represented. At the request of one or several members, the positions stated in the opinion shall be reasoned.

4. Consultation may also take place by written procedure. However, if any Member State so requests, the Commission shall convene a meeting. In case of written procedure, the Commission shall determine a time-limit of not less than 14 days within which the Member States are to put forward their observations for circulation to all other Member States. In case of decisions to be taken pursuant to Article 8, the time-limit of 14 days is replaced by seven days. Where the Commission determines a time-limit for the written procedure which is shorter than those specified above, the proposed time-limit shall be applicable in the absence of an objection by any Member State.

5. The Commission shall take the utmost account of the opinion delivered by the Advisory Committee. It shall inform the Committee of the manner in which its opinion has been taken into account.

6. Where the Advisory Committee delivers a written opinion, this opinion shall be appended to the draft decision. If the Advisory Committee recommends publication of the opinion, the Commission shall carry out such publication taking into account the legitimate interest of undertakings in the protection of their business secrets.

7. At the request of a competition authority of a Member State, the Commission shall include on the agenda of the Advisory Committee cases that are being dealt with by a competition authority of a Member State under Article 81 or Article 82 of the Treaty. The Commission may also do so on its own initiative. In either case, the Commission shall inform the competition authority concerned.

A request may in particular be made by a competition authority of a Member State in respect of a case where the Commission intends to initiate proceedings with the effect of Article 11(6).

The Advisory Committee shall not issue opinions on cases dealt with by competition authorities of the Member States. The Advisory Committee may also discuss general issues of Community competition law.

Article 15

COOPERATION WITH NATIONAL COURTS

1. In proceedings for the application of Article 81 or Article 82 of the Treaty, courts of the Member States may ask the Commission to transmit to them information in its possession or its opinion on questions concerning the application of the Community competition rules.

2. Member States shall forward to the Commission a copy of any written judgment of national courts deciding on the application of Article 81 or Article 82 of the Treaty. Such copy shall be forwarded without delay after the full written judgment is notified to the parties.

3. Competition authorities of the Member States, acting on their own initiative, may submit written observations to the national courts of their Member State on issues relating to the application of Article 81 or Article 82 of the Treaty. With the permission of the court in question, they may also submit oral observations to the national courts of their Member State. Where the coherent application of Article 81 or Article 82 of the Treaty so requires, the Commission, acting on its own initiative, may submit written observations to courts of the Member States. With the permission of the court in question, it may also make oral observations.

For the purpose of the preparation of their observations only, the competition authorities of the Member States and the Commission may request the relevant court of the Member State to transmit or ensure the transmission to them of any documents necessary for the assessment of the case.

4. This Article is without prejudice to wider powers to make observations before courts conferred on competition authorities of the Member States under the law of their Member State.

Article 16

UNIFORM APPLICATION OF COMMUNITY COMPETITION LAW

1. When national courts rule on agreements, decisions or practices under Article 81 or Article 82 of the Treaty which are already the subject of a Commission decision, they cannot take decisions running counter to the decision adopted by the Commission. They must also avoid giving decisions which would conflict with a decision contemplated by the Commission in proceedings it has initiated. To that effect, the national court may assess whether it is necessary to stay its proceedings. This obligation

is without prejudice to the rights and obligations under Article 234 of the Treaty.

2. When competition authorities of the Member States rule on agreements, decisions or practices under Article 81 or Article 82 of the Treaty which are already the subject of a Commission decision, they cannot take decisions which would run counter to the decision adopted by the Commission.

CHAPTER V

POWERS OF INVESTIGATION

Article 17

INVESTIGATIONS INTO SECTORS OF THE ECONOMY AND INTO TYPES OF AGREEMENTS

1. Where the trend of trade between Member States, the rigidity of prices or other circumstances suggest that competition may be restricted or distorted within the common market, the Commission may conduct its inquiry into a particular sector of the economy or into a particular type of agreements across various sectors. In the course of that inquiry, the Commission may request the undertakings or associations of undertakings concerned to supply the information necessary for giving effect to Articles 81 and 82 of the Treaty and may carry out any inspections necessary for that purpose.

The Commission may in particular request the undertakings or associations of undertakings concerned to communicate to it all agreements, decisions and concerted practices.

The Commission may publish a report on the results of its inquiry into particular sectors of the economy or particular types of agreements across various sectors and invite comments from interested parties.

2. Articles 14, 18, 19, 20, 22, 23 and 24 shall apply mutatis mutandis.

Article 18

REQUESTS FOR INFORMATION

1. In order to carry out the duties assigned to it by this Regulation, the Commission may, by simple request or by decision, require undertakings and associations of undertakings to provide all necessary information.

2. When sending a simple request for information to an undertaking or association of undertakings, the Commission shall

state the legal basis and the purpose of the request, specify what information is required and fix the time-limit within which the information is to be provided, and the penalties provided for in Article 23 for supplying incorrect or misleading information.

3. Where the Commission requires undertakings and associations of undertakings to supply information by decision, it shall state the legal basis and the purpose of the request, specify what information is required and fix the time-limit within which it is to be provided. It shall also indicate the penalties provided for in Article 23 and indicate or impose the penalties provided for in Article 24. It shall further indicate the right to have the decision reviewed by the Court of Justice.

4. The owners of the undertakings or their representatives and, in the case of legal persons, companies or firms, or associations having no legal personality, the persons authorised to represent them by law or by their constitution shall supply the information requested on behalf of the undertaking or the association of undertakings concerned. Lawyers duly authorised to act may supply the information on behalf of their clients. The latter shall remain fully responsible if the information supplied is incomplete, incorrect or misleading.

5. The Commission shall without delay forward a copy of the simple request or of the decision to the competition authority of the Member State in whose territory the seat of the undertaking or association of undertakings is situated and the competition authority of the Member State whose territory is affected.

6. At the request of the Commission the governments and competition authorities of the Member States shall provide the Commission with all necessary information to carry out the duties assigned to it by this Regulation.

Article 19

POWER TO TAKE STATEMENTS

1. In order to carry out the duties assigned to it by this Regulation, the Commission may interview any natural or legal person who consents to be interviewed for the purpose of collecting information relating to the subject-matter of an investigation.

2. Where an interview pursuant to paragraph 1 is conducted in the premises of an undertaking, the Commission shall inform the competition authority of the Member State in whose territory the interview takes place. If so requested by the competition authority of that Member State, its officials may assist the officials and other

accompanying persons authorised by the Commission to conduct the interview.

Article 20

THE COMMISSION'S POWERS OF INSPECTION

1. In order to carry out the duties assigned to it by this Regulation, the Commission may conduct all necessary inspections of undertakings and associations of undertakings.

2. The officials and other accompanying persons authorised by the Commission to conduct an inspection are empowered:

(a) to enter any premises, land and means of transport of undertakings and associations of undertakings;

(b) to examine the books and other records related to the business, irrespective of the medium on which they are stored;

(c) to take or obtain in any form copies of or extracts from such books or records;

(d) to seal any business premises and books or records for the period and to the extent necessary for the inspection;

(e) to ask any representative or member of staff of the undertaking or association of undertakings for explanations on facts or documents relating to the subject-matter and purpose of the inspection and to record the answers.

3. The officials and other accompanying persons authorised by the Commission to conduct an inspection shall exercise their powers upon production of a written authorisation specifying the subject matter and purpose of the inspection and the penalties provided for in Article 23 in case the production of the required books or other records related to the business is incomplete or where the answers to questions asked under paragraph 2 of the present Article are incorrect or misleading. In good time before the inspection, the Commission shall give notice of the inspection to the competition authority of the Member State in whose territory it is to be conducted.

4. Undertakings and associations of undertakings are required to submit to inspections ordered by decision of the Commission. The decision shall specify the subject matter and purpose of the inspection, appoint the date on which it is to begin and indicate the penalties provided for in Articles 23 and 24 and the right to have the decision reviewed by the Court of Justice. The Commission shall take such decisions after consulting the

competition authority of the Member State in whose territory the inspection is to be conducted.

5. Officials of as well as those authorised or appointed by the competition authority of the Member State in whose territory the inspection is to be conducted shall, at the request of that authority or of the Commission, actively assist the officials and other accompanying persons authorised by the Commission. To this end, they shall enjoy the powers specified in paragraph 2.

6. Where the officials and other accompanying persons authorised by the Commission find that an undertaking opposes an inspection ordered pursuant to this Article, the Member State concerned shall afford them the necessary assistance, requesting where appropriate the assistance of the police or of an equivalent enforcement authority, so as to enable them to conduct their inspection.

7. If the assistance provided for in paragraph 6 requires authorisation from a judicial authority according to national rules, such authorisation shall be applied for. Such authorisation may also be applied for as a precautionary measure.

8. Where authorisation as referred to in paragraph 7 is applied for, the national judicial authority shall control that the Commission decision is authentic and that the coercive measures envisaged are neither arbitrary nor excessive having regard to the subject matter of the inspection. In its control of the proportionality of the coercive measures, the national judicial authority may ask the Commission, directly or through the Member State competition authority, for detailed explanations in particular on the grounds the Commission has for suspecting infringement of Articles 81 and 82 of the Treaty, as well as on the seriousness of the suspected infringement and on the nature of the involvement of the undertaking concerned. However, the national judicial authority may not call into question the necessity for the inspection nor demand that it be provided with the information in the Commission's file. The lawfulness of the Commission decision shall be subject to review only by the Court of Justice.

Article 21

INSPECTION OF OTHER PREMISES

1. If a reasonable suspicion exists that books or other records related to the business and to the subject-matter of the inspection, which may be relevant to prove a serious violation of Article 81 or Article 82 of the Treaty, are being kept in any other premises, land and means of transport, including the homes of directors, managers

and other members of staff of the undertakings and associations of undertakings concerned, the Commission can by decision order an inspection to be conducted in such other premises, land and means of transport.

2. The decision shall specify the subject matter and purpose of the inspection, appoint the date on which it is to begin and indicate the right to have the decision reviewed by the Court of Justice. It shall in particular state the reasons that have led the Commission to conclude that a suspicion in the sense of paragraph 1 exists. The Commission shall take such decisions after consulting the competition authority of the Member State in whose territory the inspection is to be conducted.

3. A decision adopted pursuant to paragraph 1 cannot be executed without prior authorisation from the national judicial authority of the Member State concerned. The national judicial authority shall control that the Commission decision is authentic and that the coercive measures envisaged are neither arbitrary nor excessive having regard in particular to the seriousness of the suspected infringement, to the importance of the evidence sought, to the involvement of the undertaking concerned and to the reasonable likelihood that business books and records relating to the subject matter of the inspection are kept in the premises for which the authorisation is requested. The national judicial authority may ask the Commission, directly or through the Member State competition authority, for detailed explanations on those elements which are necessary to allow its control of the proportionality of the coercive measures envisaged.

However, the national judicial authority may not call into question the necessity for the inspection nor demand that it be provided with information in the Commission's file. The lawfulness of the Commission decision shall be subject to review only by the Court of Justice.

4. The officials and other accompanying persons authorised by the Commission to conduct an inspection ordered in accordance with paragraph 1 of this Article shall have the powers set out in Article 20(2)(a), (b) and (c). Article 20(5) and (6) shall apply mutatis mutandis.

Article 22

INVESTIGATIONS BY COMPETITION AUTHORITIES OF MEMBER STATES

1. The competition authority of a Member State may in its own territory carry out any inspection or other fact-finding measure

under its national law on behalf and for the account of the competition authority of another Member State in order to establish whether there has been an infringement of Article 81 or Article 82 of the Treaty. Any exchange and use of the information collected shall be carried out in accordance with Article 12.

2. At the request of the Commission, the competition authorities of the Member States shall undertake the inspections which the Commission considers to be necessary under Article 20(1) or which it has ordered by decision pursuant to Article 20(4). The officials of the competition authorities of the Member States who are responsible for conducting these inspections as well as those authorised or appointed by them shall exercise their powers in accordance with their national law.

If so requested by the Commission or by the competition authority of the Member State in whose territory the inspection is to be conducted, officials and other accompanying persons authorised by the Commission may assist the officials of the authority concerned.

CHAPTER VI

PENALTIES

Article 23

FINES

1. The Commission may by decision impose on undertakings and associations of undertakings fines not exceeding 1% of the total turnover in the preceding business year where, intentionally or negligently:

(a) they supply incorrect or misleading information in response to a request made pursuant to Article 17 or Article 18(2);

(b) in response to a request made by decision adopted pursuant to Article 17 or Article 18(3), they supply incorrect, incomplete or misleading information or do not supply information within the required time-limit;

(c) they produce the required books or other records related to the business in incomplete form during inspections under Article 20 or refuse to submit to inspections ordered by a decision adopted pursuant to Article 20(4);

(d) in response to a question asked in accordance with Article 20(2)(e),

—they give an incorrect or misleading answer,

—they fail to rectify within a time-limit set by the Commission an incorrect, incomplete or misleading answer given by a member of staff, or

—they fail or refuse to provide a complete answer on facts relating to the subject-matter and purpose of an inspection ordered by a decision adopted pursuant to Article 20(4);

(e) seals affixed in accordance with Article 20(2)(d) by officials or other accompanying persons authorised by the Commission have been broken.

2. The Commission may by decision impose fines on undertakings and associations of undertakings where, either intentionally or negligently:

(a) they infringe Article 81 or Article 82 of the Treaty; or

(b) they contravene a decision ordering interim measures under Article 8; or

(c) they fail to comply with a commitment made binding by a decision pursuant to Article 9.

For each undertaking and association of undertakings participating in the infringement, the fine shall not exceed 10% of its total turnover in the preceding business year.

Where the infringement of an association relates to the activities of its members, the fine shall not exceed 10% of the sum of the total turnover of each member active on the market affected by the infringement of the association.

3. In fixing the amount of the fine, regard shall be had both to the gravity and to the duration of the infringement.

4. When a fine is imposed on an association of undertakings taking account of the turnover of its members and the association is not solvent, the association is obliged to call for contributions from its members to cover the amount of the fine.

Where such contributions have not been made to the association within a time-limit fixed by the Commission, the Commission may require payment of the fine directly by any of the undertakings whose representatives were members of the decision-making bodies concerned of the association.

After the Commission has required payment under the second subparagraph, where necessary to ensure full payment of the fine, the Commission may require payment of the balance by any of the members of the association which were active on the market on which the infringement occurred.

However, the Commission shall not require payment under the second or the third subparagraph from undertakings which show that they have not implemented the infringing decision of the association and either were not aware of its existence or have actively distanced themselves from it before the Commission started investigating the case.

The financial liability of each undertaking in respect of the payment of the fine shall not exceed 10% of its total turnover in the preceding business year.

5. Decisions taken pursuant to paragraphs 1 and 2 shall not be of a criminal law nature.

Article 24

PERIODIC PENALTY PAYMENTS

1. The Commission may, by decision, impose on undertakings or associations of undertakings periodic penalty payments not exceeding 5% of the average daily turnover in the preceding business year per day and calculated from the date appointed by the decision, in order to compel them:

(a) to put an end to an infringement of Article 81 or Article 82 of the Treaty, in accordance with a decision taken pursuant to Article 7;

(b) to comply with a decision ordering interim measures taken pursuant to Article 8;

(c) to comply with a commitment made binding by a decision pursuant to Article 9;

(d) to supply complete and correct information which it has requested by decision taken pursuant to Article 17 or Article 18(3);

(e) to submit to an inspection which it has ordered by decision taken pursuant to Article 20(4).

2. Where the undertakings or associations of undertakings have satisfied the obligation which the periodic penalty payment was intended to enforce, the Commission may fix the definitive amount of the periodic penalty payment at a figure lower than that which would arise under the original decision. Article 23(4) shall apply correspondingly.

CHAPTER VII

LIMITATION PERIODS

Article 25

LIMITATION PERIODS FOR THE IMPOSITION OF PENALTIES

1. The powers conferred on the Commission by Articles 23 and 24 shall be subject to the following limitation periods:

(a) three years in the case of infringements of provisions concerning requests for information or the conduct of inspections;

(b) five years in the case of all other infringements.

2. Time shall begin to run on the day on which the infringement is committed. However, in the case of continuing or repeated infringements, time shall begin to run on the day on which the infringement ceases.

3. Any action taken by the Commission or by the competition authority of a Member State for the purpose of the investigation or proceedings in respect of an infringement shall interrupt the limitation period for the imposition of fines or periodic penalty payments. The limitation period shall be interrupted with effect from the date on which the action is notified to at least one undertaking or association of undertakings which has participated in the infringement. Actions which interrupt the running of the period shall include in particular the following:

(a) written requests for information by the Commission or by the competition authority of a Member State;

(b) written authorisations to conduct inspections issued to its officials by the Commission or by the competition authority of a Member State;

(c) the initiation of proceedings by the Commission or by the competition authority of a Member State;

(d) notification of the statement of objections of the Commission or of the competition authority of a Member State.

4. The interruption of the limitation period shall apply for all the undertakings or associations of undertakings which have participated in the infringement.

5. Each interruption shall start time running afresh. However, the limitation period shall expire at the latest on the day on which a period equal to twice the limitation period has elapsed

without the Commission having imposed a fine or a periodic penalty payment. That period shall be extended by the time during which limitation is suspended pursuant to paragraph 6.

6. The limitation period for the imposition of fines or periodic penalty payments shall be suspended for as long as the decision of the Commission is the subject of proceedings pending before the Court of Justice.

Article 26

LIMITATION PERIOD FOR THE ENFORCEMENT OF PENALTIES

1. The power of the Commission to enforce decisions taken pursuant to Articles 23 and 24 shall be subject to a limitation period of five years.

2. Time shall begin to run on the day on which the decision becomes final.

3. The limitation period for the enforcement of penalties shall be interrupted:

(a) by notification of a decision varying the original amount of the fine or periodic penalty payment or refusing an application for variation;

(b) by any action of the Commission or of a Member State, acting at the request of the Commission, designed to enforce payment of the fine or periodic penalty payment.

4. Each interruption shall start time running afresh.

5. The limitation period for the enforcement of penalties shall be suspended for so long as:

(a) time to pay is allowed;

(b) enforcement of payment is suspended pursuant to a decision of the Court of Justice.

CHAPTER VIII

HEARINGS AND PROFESSIONAL SECRECY

Article 27

HEARING OF THE PARTIES, COMPLAINANTS AND OTHERS

1. Before taking decisions as provided for in Articles 7, 8, 23 and Article 24(2), the Commission shall give the undertakings or associations of undertakings which are the subject of the proceedings

conducted by the Commission the opportunity of being heard on the matters to which the Commission has taken objection. The Commission shall base its decisions only on objections on which the parties concerned have been able to comment. Complainants shall be associated closely with the proceedings.

2. The rights of defence of the parties concerned shall be fully respected in the proceedings. They shall be entitled to have access to the Commission's file, subject to the legitimate interest of undertakings in the protection of their business secrets. The right of access to the file shall not extend to confidential information and internal documents of the Commission or the competition authorities of the Member States. In particular, the right of access shall not extend to correspondence between the Commission and the competition authorities of the Member States, or between the latter, including documents drawn up pursuant to Articles 11 and 14. Nothing in this paragraph shall prevent the Commission from disclosing and using information necessary to prove an infringement.

3. If the Commission considers it necessary, it may also hear other natural or legal persons. Applications to be heard on the part of such persons shall, where they show a sufficient interest, be granted. The competition authorities of the Member States may also ask the Commission to hear other natural or legal persons.

4. Where the Commission intends to adopt a decision pursuant to Article 9 or Article 10, it shall publish a concise summary of the case and the main content of the commitments or of the proposed course of action. Interested third parties may submit their observations within a time limit which is fixed by the Commission in its publication and which may not be less than one month. Publication shall have regard to the legitimate interest of undertakings in the protection of their business secrets.

Article 28

PROFESSIONAL SECRECY

1. Without prejudice to Articles 12 and 15, information collected pursuant to Articles 17 to 22 shall be used only for the purpose for which it was acquired.

2. Without prejudice to the exchange and to the use of information foreseen in Articles 11, 12, 14, 15 and 27, the Commission and the competition authorities of the Member States, their officials, servants and other persons working under the supervision of these authorities as well as officials and civil servants of other authorities of the Member States shall not disclose information acquired or exchanged by them pursuant to this

Regulation and of the kind covered by the obligation of professional secrecy. This obligation also applies to all representatives and experts of Member States attending meetings of the Advisory Committee pursuant to Article 14.

CHAPTER IX

EXEMPTION REGULATIONS

Article 29

WITHDRAWAL IN INDIVIDUAL CASES

1. Where the Commission, empowered by a Council Regulation, such as Regulations 19/65/EEC, (EEC) No 2821/71, (EEC) No 3976/87, (EEC) No 1534/91 or (EEC) No 479/92, to apply Article 81(3) of the Treaty by regulation, has declared Article 81(1) of the Treaty inapplicable to certain categories of agreements, decisions by associations of undertakings or concerted practices, it may, acting on its own initiative or on a complaint, withdraw the benefit of such an exemption Regulation when it finds that in any particular case an agreement, decision or concerted practice to which the exemption Regulation applies has certain effects which are incompatible with Article 81(3) of the Treaty.

2. Where, in any particular case, agreements, decisions by associations of undertakings or concerted practices to which a Commission Regulation referred to in paragraph 1 applies have effects which are incompatible with Article 81(3) of the Treaty in the territory of a Member State, or in a part thereof, which has all the characteristics of a distinct geographic market, the competition authority of that Member State may withdraw the benefit of the Regulation in question in respect of that territory.

CHAPTER X

GENERAL PROVISIONS

Article 30

PUBLICATION OF DECISIONS

1. The Commission shall publish the decisions, which it takes pursuant to Articles 7 to 10, 23 and 24.

2. The publication shall state the names of the parties and the main content of the decision, including any penalties imposed. It shall have regard to the legitimate interest of undertakings in the protection of their business secrets.

Article 31

REVIEW BY THE COURT OF JUSTICE

The Court of Justice shall have unlimited jurisdiction to review decisions whereby the Commission has fixed a fine or periodic penalty payment. It may cancel, reduce or increase the fine or periodic penalty payment imposed.

Article 32

EXCLUSIONS

This Regulation shall not apply to:

(a) international tramp vessel services as defined in Article 1(3)(a) of Regulation (EEC) No 4056/86;

(b) a maritime transport service that takes place exclusively between ports in one and the same Member State as foreseen in Article 1(2) of Regulation (EEC) No 4056/86;

(c) air transport between Community airports and third countries.

* * *

Article 44

REPORT ON THE APPLICATION OF THE PRESENT REGULATION

Five years from the date of application of this Regulation, the Commission shall report to the European Parliament and the Council on the functioning of this Regulation, in particular on the application of Article 11(6) and Article 17.

On the basis of this report, the Commission shall assess whether it is appropriate to propose to the Council a revision of this Regulation.

Article 45

ENTRY INTO FORCE

This Regulation shall enter into force on the 20th day following that of its publication in the Official Journal of the European Communities.

It shall apply from 1 May 2004.

This Regulation shall be binding in its entirety and directly applicable in all Member States.

Done at Brussels, 16 December 2002.

[footnotes omitted]

Appendix 3

UNITED STATES STATUTES

THE SHERMAN ANTITRUST ACT

(1890 as amended)

§ 1. Trusts and combinations in restraint of trade illegal

Every contract, combination in the form of trust or otherwise, or conspiracy, in restraint of trade or commerce among the several States, or with foreign nations, is declared to be illegal. Every person who shall make any contract or engage in any combination or conspiracy hereby declared to be illegal shall be deemed guilty of a felony, and, on conviction thereof, shall be punished by fine not exceeding $100,000,000 if a corporation, or, if any other person, $1,000,000, or by imprisonment not exceeding 10 years, or by both said punishments, in the discretion of the court.

§ 2. Monopolizing trade illegal

Every person who shall monopolize, or attempt to monopolize, or combine or conspire with any other person or persons, to monopolize any part of the trade or commerce among the several States, or with foreign nations, shall be deemed guilty of a felony, and, on conviction thereof, shall be punished by fine not exceeding $100,000,000 if a corporation, or, if any other person, $1,000,000, or by imprisonment not exceeding 10 years, or by both said punishments, in the discretion of the court.

* * *

§ 7. Conduct involving trade or commerce with foreign nations

FOREIGN TRADE ANTITRUST IMPROVEMENTS ACT OF 1982, TITLE IV

This Act shall not apply to conduct involving trade or commerce (other than import trade or import commerce) with foreign nations unless—

(1) such conduct has a direct, substantial, and reasonably foreseeable effect—

(A) on trade or commerce which is not trade or commerce with foreign nations, or on import trade or import commerce with foreign nations; or

(B) on export trade or export commerce with foreign nations, of a person engaged in such trade or commerce in the United States; and

(2) such effect gives rise to a claim under the provisions of sections 1 to 7 of this Act, other than this section.

If this Act applies to such conduct only because of the operation of paragraph (1)(B), then this Act shall apply to such conduct only for injury to export business in the United States.

THE CLAYTON ACT

(1914 as amended, principally in 1936 and 1950)

§ 3. Sale or lease on condition not to use goods of competitor

It shall be unlawful for any person engaged in commerce, in the course of such commerce, to lease or make a sale or contract for sale of goods, wares, merchandise, machinery, supplies, or other commodities, whether patented or unpatented, for use, consumption, or resale within the United States or any Territory thereof or the District of Columbia or any insular possession or other place under the jurisdiction of the United States, or fix a price charged therefor, or discount from, or rebate upon, such price, on the condition, agreement, or understanding that the lessee or purchaser thereof shall not use or deal in the goods, wares, merchandise, machinery, supplies, or other commodities of a competitor or competitors of the lessor or seller, where the effect of such lease, sale, or contract for sale or such condition, agreement, or understanding may be to substantially lessen competition or tend to create a monopoly in any line of commerce.

* * *

§ 4. Suits by persons injured

(a) Amount of recovery; prejudgment interest

Except as provided in subsection (b) of this section, any person who shall be injured in his business or property by reason of anything forbidden in the antitrust laws may sue therefor in any district court of the United States in the district in which the defendant resides or is found or has an agent, without respect to the amount in controversy, and shall recover threefold the damages by him sustained, and the cost of suit, including a reasonable attorney's fee. The court may award under this section, pursuant to a motion by such person promptly made, simple interest on actual damages for the period beginning on the date of service of such person's pleading setting forth a claim under the antitrust laws and ending on the date of judgment, or for any shorter period therein, if the court finds that the award of such interest for such period is just in the circumstances. In determining whether an award of interest under this section for any period is just in the circumstances, the court shall consider only—

1) whether such person or the opposing party, or either party's representative, made motions or asserted claims or defenses so lacking in merit as to show that such party or representative acted intentionally for delay, or otherwise acted in bad faith;

2) whether, in the course of the action involved, such person or the opposing party, or either party's representative, violated any applicable rule, statute, or court order providing for sanctions for dilatory behavior or otherwise providing for expeditious proceedings; and

3) whether such person or the opposing party, or either party's representative, engaged in conduct primarily for the purpose of delaying the litigation or increasing the cost thereof.

(b) Amount of damages payable to foreign states and instrumentalities of foreign states

1) Except as provided in paragraph (2), any person who is a foreign state may not recover under subsection (a) of this section an amount in excess of the actual damages sustained by it and the cost of suit, including a reasonable attorney's fee.

2) Paragraph (1) shall not apply to a foreign state if—

A) such foreign state would be denied, under section 1605 (a)(2) of title 28, immunity in a case in which the action is based upon a commercial activity, or an act, that is the subject matter of its claim under this section;

B) such foreign state waives all defenses based upon or arising out of its status as a foreign state, to any claims brought against it in the same action;

C) such foreign state engages primarily in commercial activities; and

D) such foreign state does not function, with respect to the commercial activity, or the act, that is the subject matter of its claim under this section as a procurement entity for itself or for another foreign state.

* * *

§ 4A. Suits by United States; amount of recovery; prejudgment interest

Whenever the United States is hereafter injured in its business or property by reason of anything forbidden in the antitrust laws it may sue therefor in the United States district court for the district in which the defendant resides or is found or has an agent, without respect to the amount in controversy, and shall recover threefold the damages by it sustained and the cost of suit. The court may award under this section, pursuant to a motion by the United States promptly made, simple interest on actual damages for the period beginning on the date of service of the pleading of the United States setting forth a claim under the antitrust laws and ending on the date of judgment, or for any shorter period therein, if the court finds that the award of such interest for such period is just in the circumstances. In determining whether an award of interest under this section for any period is just in the circumstances, the court shall consider only—

(1) whether the United States or the opposing party, or either party's representative, made motions or asserted claims or defenses so lacking in merit as to show that such party or representative acted intentionally for delay or otherwise acted in bad faith;

(2) whether, in the course of the action involved, the United States or the opposing party, or either party's representative, violated any applicable rule, statute, or court order providing for sanctions for dilatory behavior or otherwise providing for expeditious proceedings;

(3) whether the United States or the opposing party, or either party's representative, engaged in conduct primarily for the purpose of delaying the litigation or increasing the cost thereof; and

(4) whether the award of such interest is necessary to compensate the United States adequately for the injury sustained by the United States.

* * *

§ 4C. Actions by state attorneys general

(a) Parens patriae; monetary relief; damages; prejudgment interest

(1) Any attorney general of a State may bring a civil action in the name of such State, as parens patriae on behalf of natural persons residing in such State, in any district court of the United

States having jurisdiction of the defendant, to secure monetary relief as provided in this section for injury sustained by such natural persons to their property by reason of any violation of sections 1 to 7 of this title. The court shall exclude from the amount of monetary relief awarded in such action any amount of monetary relief

(A) which duplicates amounts which have been awarded for the same injury, or

(B) which is properly allocable to

(i) natural persons who have excluded their claims pursuant to subsection (b)(2) of this section, and

(ii) any business entity.

(2) The court shall award the State as monetary relief threefold the total damage sustained as described in paragraph (1) of this subsection, and the cost of suit, including a reasonable attorney's fee. The court may award under this paragraph, pursuant to a motion by such State promptly made, simple interest on the total damage for the period beginning on the date of service of such State's pleading setting forth a claim under the antitrust laws and ending on the date of judgment, or for any shorter period therein, if the court finds that the award of such interest for such period is just in the circumstances. In determining whether an award of interest under this paragraph for any period is just in the circumstances, the court shall consider only—

(A) whether such State or the opposing party, or either party's representative, made motions or asserted claims or defenses so lacking in merit as to show that such party or representative acted intentionally for delay or otherwise acted in bad faith;

(B) whether, in the course of the action involved, such State or the opposing party, or either party's representative, violated any applicable rule, statute, or court order providing for sanctions for dilatory behavior or other wise providing for expeditious proceedings; and

(C) whether such State or the opposing party, or either party's representative, engaged in conduct primarily for the purpose of delaying the litigation or increasing the cost thereof.

(b) Notice; exclusion election; final judgment

(1) In any action brought under subsection (a)(1) of this section, the State attorney general shall, at such times, in such manner, and with such content as the court may direct, cause notice thereof to be given by publication. If the court finds that notice given solely by publication would deny due process of law to any person or persons, the court may direct further notice to such person or persons according to the circumstances of the case.

(2) Any person on whose behalf an action is brought under subsection (a)(1) of this section may elect to exclude from adjudication the portion of the State claim for monetary relief attributable to him by filing notice of such election with the court within such time as specified in the notice given pursuant to paragraph (1) of this subsection.

(3) The final judgment in an action under subsection (a)(1) of this section shall be res judicata as to any claim under section 15 of this title by any person on behalf of whom such action was brought and who fails to give such notice within the period specified in the notice given pursuant to paragraph (1) of this subsection.

(c) Dismissal or compromise of action

An action under subsection (a)(1) of this section shall not be dismissed or compromised without the approval of the court, and notice of any proposed dismissal or compromise shall be given in such manner as the court directs.

(d) Attorneys' fees

In any action under subsection (a) of this section—

(1) the amount of the plaintiffs' attorney's fee, if any, shall be determined by the court; and

(2) the court may, in its discretion, award a reasonable attorney's fee to a prevailing defendant upon a finding that the State attorney general has acted in bad faith, vexatiously, wantonly, or for oppressive reasons.

* * *

§ 7. Acquisition by one corporation of stock of another

No person engaged in commerce or in any activity affecting commerce shall acquire, directly or indirectly, the whole or any part of the stock or other share capital and no person subject to the jurisdiction of the Federal Trade Commission shall acquire the whole or any part of the assets of another person engaged also in commerce or in any activity affecting commerce, where in any line of commerce or in any activity affecting commerce in any section of the country, the effect of such acquisition may be substantially to lessen competition, or to tend to create a monopoly.

No person shall acquire, directly or indirectly, the whole or any part of the stock or other share capital and no person subject to the jurisdiction of the Federal Trade Commission shall acquire the whole or any part of the assets of one or more persons engaged in commerce or in any activity affecting commerce, where in any line of commerce or in any activity affecting commerce in any section of the country, the effect of such acquisition, of such stocks or assets, or of the use of such stock by the voting or granting of proxies or otherwise, may be substantially to lessen competition, or to tend to create a monopoly.

* * *

§ 7A. [Hart-Scott-Rodino premerger notification and reporting omitted]

* * *

WEBB-POMERENE ACT (EXPORT TRADE ACT)

(1918 as amended)

§ 1. Terms defined

The words "export trade" wherever used in this Act mean solely trade or commerce in goods, wares, or merchandise exported, or in the course of being exported from the United States or any Territory thereof to any foreign nation; but the words "export trade" shall not be deemed to include the production, manufacture, or selling for consumption or for resale, within the United States or any Territory thereof, of such goods, wares, or merchandise, or any act in the course of such production, manufacture, or selling for consumption or for resale.

The words "trade within the United States" wherever used in this Act mean trade or commerce among the several States or in any Territory of the United States, or in the District of Columbia, or between any such Territory and another, or between any such Territory or Territories and any State or States or the District of Columbia, or between the District of Columbia and any State or States.

The word "association" wherever used in this subchapter means any corporation or combination, by contract or otherwise, of two or more persons, partnerships, or corporations.

§ 2. Export trade and antitrust legislation

Nothing contained in the Sherman Act shall be construed as declaring to be illegal an association entered into for the sole purpose of engaging in export trade and actually engaged solely in such export trade, or an agreement made or act done in the course of export trade by such association, provided such association, agreement, or act is not in restraint of trade within the United States, and is not in restraint of the export trade of any domestic competitor of such association: Provided, That such association does not, either in the United States or elsewhere, enter into any agreement, understanding, or conspiracy, or do any act which artificially or intentionally enhances or depresses prices within the United States of commodities of the class exported by such association, or which substantially lessens competition within the United States or otherwise restrains trade therein.

* * *

§ 4. Unfair methods of competition in export trade

The prohibition against "unfair methods of competition" and the remedies provided for enforcing said prohibition contained in the Federal Trade Commission Act shall be construed as extending to unfair methods of competition used in export trade against competitors engaged in export trade, even though the acts constituting such unfair methods are done without the territorial jurisdiction of the United States.

§ 5. Information required; powers of Federal Trade Commission

Every association which engages solely in export trade, within thirty days after its creation, shall file with the Federal Trade Commission a verified written statement setting forth the location of its offices or places of business and the names and addresses of all its officers and of all its stockholders or members, and if a corporation, a copy of its certificate or articles of incorporation and bylaws, and if unincorporated, a copy of its articles or contract of association, and on the 1st day of January of each year every association engaged solely in export trade shall make a like statement of the location of its offices or places of business and the names and addresses of all its officers and of all its stockholders or members and of all amendments to and changes in its articles or certificate of incorporation or in its articles or contract of association. It shall also furnish to the Commission such information as the Commission may require as to its organization business, conduct, practices, management, and relation to other associations, corporations, partnerships, and individuals. Any association which shall fail so to do shall not have the benefit of the provisions of section two and section three of this Act, and it shall also forfeit to the United States the sum of $100 for each and every day of the continuance of such failure, which forfeiture shall be payable into the Treasury of the United States, and shall be recoverable in a civil suit in the name of the United States brought in the district where the association has its principal office, or in any district in which it shall do business. It shall be the duty of the various United States attorneys, under the direction of the Attorney General of the United States, to prosecute for the recovery of the forfeiture. The costs and expenses of such prosecution shall be paid out of the appropriation for the expenses of the courts of the United States.

Whenever the Federal Trade Commission shall have reason to believe that an association or any agreement made or act done by such association is in restraint of trade within the United States or in restraint of the export trade of any domestic competitor of such association, or that an association either in the United States or elsewhere has entered into any agreement, understanding, or conspiracy, or done any act which artificially or intentionally enhances or depresses prices within the United States of commodities of the class exported by such association, or which substantially lessens competition within the United States or otherwise restrains trade therein, it shall summon such association, its officers, and agents to appear before it, and thereafter conduct an investigation into the alleged violations of law. Upon investigation, if it shall conclude that the law has been violated, it may make to such association recommendations for the readjustment of its business, in order that it may thereafter maintain its organization and management and conduct its business in accordance with law. If such association fails to comply with the recommendations of the Federal Trade Commission, said Commission shall refer its findings and recommendations to the Attorney General of the United States for such action thereon as he may deem proper.

For the purpose of enforcing these provisions the Federal Trade Commission shall have all the powers, so far as applicable, given it in the Federal Trade Commission Act.

EXPORT TRADING COMPANY ACT OF 1982

An act to encourage exports by facilitating the formation and operation of export trading companies, export trade associations, and the expansion of export trade services generally.

TITLE I—GENERAL PROVISIONS

SHORT TITLE

Sec. 101. This title may be cited as the "Export Trading Company Act of 1982".

FINDINGS; DECLARATION OF PURPOSE

Sec. 102. (a) The Congress finds that—

(1) United States exports are responsible for creating and maintaining one out of every nine manufacturing jobs in the United States and for generating one out of every seven dollars of total United States goods produced;

(2) the rapidly growing service-related industries are vital to the well-being of the United States economy inasmuch as they create jobs for seven out of every ten Americans, provide 65 per centum of the Nation's gross national product, and offer the greatest potential for significantly increased industrial trade involving finished products;

(3) trade deficits contribute to the decline of the dollar on international currency markets and have an inflationary impact on the United States economy;

(4) tens of thousands of small-and medium-sized United States businesses produce exportable goods or services but do not engage in exporting;

(5) although the United States is the world's leading agricultural exporting nation, many farm products are not marketed as widely and effectively abroad as they could be through export trading companies;

(6) export trade services in the United States are fragmented into a multitude of separate functions, and companies attempting to offer export trade services lack financial leverage to reach a significant number of potential United States exporters;

(7) the United States needs well-developed export trade intermediaries which can achieve economies of scale and acquire expertise enabling them to export goods and services profitably, at low per unit cost to producers;

(8) the development of export trading companies in the United States has been hampered by business attitudes and by government regulations;

(9) those activities of State and local governmental authorities which initiate, facilitate, or expand exports of goods and services can be an important source for expansion of total United States exports,

as well as for experimentation in the development of innovative export programs keyed to local, State, and regional economic needs;

(10) if United States trading companies are to be successful in promoting United States exports and in competing with foreign trading companies, they should be able to draw on the resources, expertise, and knowledge of the United States banking system, both in the United States and abroad; and

(11) the Department of Commerce is responsible for the development and promotion of United States exports, and especially for facilitating the export of finished products by United States manufacturers.

(b) It is the purpose of this Act to increase United States exports of products and services by encouraging more efficient provisions of export trade services to United States producers and suppliers, in particular by establishing an office within the Department of Commerce to promote the formation of export trade associations and export trading companies, by permitting bank holding companies, bankers' banks, and Edge Act corporations and agreement corporations that are subsidiaries of bank holding companies to invest in export trading companies, by reducing restrictions on trade finance provided by financial institutions, and by modifying the application of the antitrust laws to certain export trade.

* * *

TITLE III—EXPORT TRADE CERTIFICATES OF REVIEW

EXPORT TRADE PROMOTION DUTIES OF SECRETARY OF COMMERCE

SEC. 301. To promote and encourage export of trade, the Secretary may issue certificates of review and advise and assist any person with respect to applying for certificates of review.

APPLICATION FOR ISSUANCE OF CERTIFICATE OF REVIEW

SEC. 302. (a) To apply for a certificate of review, a person shall submit to the Secretary a written application which—

(1) specifies conduct limited to export trade, and

(2) is in a form and contains any information, including information pertaining to the overall market in which the applicant operates, required by rule or regulation promulgated under section 310.

(b)(1) Within ten days after an application submitted under subsection (a) is received by the Secretary, the Secretary shall publish in the Federal Register a notice that announces that an application for a certificate of review has been submitted, identifies each person submitting the application, and describes the conduct for which the application is submitted.

(2) Not later than seven days after an application submitted under subsection (a) is received by the Secretary, the Secretary shall transmit to the Attorney General—

(A) a copy of the application—

(B) any information submitted to the Secretary in connection with the application, and

(C) any other relevant information (as determined by the Secretary) in the possession of the Secretary, including information regarding the market share of the applicant in the line of commerce to which the conduct specified in the application relates.

ISSUANCE OF CERTIFICATE

SEC. 303. (a) A certificate of review shall be issued to any applicant that establishes that its specified export trade, export trade activities, and methods of operation will—

(1) result in neither a substantial lessening of competition or restraint of trade within the United States nor a substantial restraint of the export trade of any competitor of the applicant,

(2) not unreasonably enhance, stabilize, or depress, prices within the United States of the goods, wares, merchandise, or services of the class exported by the applicant,

(3) not constitute unfair methods of competition against competitors engaged in the export of goods, wares, merchandise or services of the class exported by the applicant, and

(4) not include any act that may reasonably be expected to result in the sale for consumption or resale within the United States of the goods, wares, merchandise, or services exported by the applicant.

(b) Within ninety days after the Secretary receives an application for a certificate of review, the Secretary shall determine whether the applicant's export trade, export trade activities, and methods of operation meet the standards of subsection (a). If the Secretary, with the concurrence of the Attorney General, determines that such standards are met, the Secretary shall issue to the applicant a certificate of review. The certificate of review shall specify—

(1) the export trade, export trade activities, and methods of operation to which the certificate applies,

(2) the persons to whom the certificate of review is issued, and

(3) any terms and conditions the Secretary or the Attorney General deems necessary to assure compliance with the standards of subsection (a)

(c) If the applicant indicates a special need for prompt disposition, the Secretary and the Attorney General may expedite action on the application, except that no certificate of review may be issued within thirty days of publication of notice in the Federal Register under section 302(b)(1).

(d)(1) If the Secretary denies in whole or in part an application for a certificate, he shall notify the applicant of his determination and the reasons for it.

(2) An applicant may, within thirty days of receipt of notification that the application has been denied in whole or in part, request the Secretary to reconsider the determination. The Secretary, with the concurrence of the Attorney General, shall notify the applicant of the determination upon reconsideration within thirty days of receipt of the request.

(e) If the Secretary denies an application for the issuance of a certificate of review and thereafter receives from the applicant a request for the return of documents submitted by the applicant in connection with the application for the certificate, the Secretary and the Attorney General shall return to the applicant, not later than thirty days after receipt of the request, the documents and all copies of the documents available to the Secretary and the Attorney General, except to the extent that the information contained in a document has been made available to the public.

(f) A certificate shall be void ab initio with respect to any export trade, export trade activities, or methods of operation for which a certificate was procured by fraud.

REPORTING REQUIREMENT; AMENDMENT OF CERTIFICATE; REVOCATION OF CERTIFICATE

SEC. 304. (a)(1) Any applicant who receives a certificate of review—

(A) shall promptly report to the Secretary any change relevant to the matter specified in the certificate, and

(B) may submit to the Secretary an application to amend the certificate to reflect the effect of the change on the conduct specified in the certificate.

(2) An application for an amendment to a certificate of review shall be treated as an application for the issuance of a certificate. The effective date of an amendment shall be the date on which the application for the amendment is submitted to the Secretary.

(b)(1) If the Secretary or the Attorney General has reason to believe that the export trade, export trade activities, or methods of operation of a person holding a certificate of review no longer comply with the standards of section 303(a), the Secretary shall request such information from such persons as the Secretary or the Attorney General deems necessary to resolve the matter of compliance. Failure to comply with such request shall be grounds for revocation of the certificate under paragraph (2).

(2) If the Secretary or the Attorney General determines that the export trade activities, or methods of operation of a person holding a certificate no longer comply with the standards of section 303 (a), or that such person has failed to comply with a request made under paragraph (1), the Secretary shall give written notice of the determination to such person. The notice shall include a statement of the circumstances underlying, and the reasons in support of, the determination. In the 60-day period beginning 30 days after the notice is given, the Secretary shall revoke the certificate or modify it as the Secretary or the Attorney General deems necessary to cause the certificate to apply only to the export trade, export trade activities, or methods of operation which are in compliance with the standards of section 303(a).

(3) For purposes of carrying out this subsection, the Attorney General, and the Assistant Attorney General in charge of the antitrust division of the Department of Justice, may conduct investigations in the same manner as the Attorney General and the Assistant Attorney General conduct investigations under section 3 of the Antitrust Civil Process Act, except that no civil investigative demand may be issued to a person to whom a certificate of review is issued if such a person is the target of such investigation.

JUDICIAL REVIEW; ADMISSIBILITY

SEC.305. (a) If the Secretary grants or denies, in whole or in part, an application for a certificate of review or for an amendment to a certificate, or revokes or modifies a certificate pursuant to section 304(b), any person aggrieved by such determination may, within 30 days of the determination, bring an action in any appropriate district court of the United States to set aside the determination on the ground that such determination is erroneous.

(b) Except as provided in subsection (a), no action by the Secretary or the Attorney General pursuant to this title shall be subject to judicial review.

(c) If the Secretary denies, in whole or in part, an application for a certificate of review or for an amendment to a certificate, or revokes or amends a certificate, neither the negative determination nor the statement of reasons therefor shall be admissible in evidence, in any administrative or judicial proceeding, in support of any claim under the antitrust laws.

PROTECTION CONFERRED BY CERTIFICATE OF REVIEW

SEC. 306. (a) Except as provided in subsection (b), no criminal or civil action may be brought under the antitrust laws against a person to whom a certificate of review is issued which is based on conduct which is specified in, and complies with the terms of, a certificate issued under section 303 which certificate was in effect when the conduct occurred.

(b)(1) Any person who has been injured as a result of conduct engaged in under a certificate of review may bring a civil action for injunctive relief, actual damages, the loss of interest on actual damages, and the cost of the suit (including a reasonable attorney's fee) for the failure to comply with the standards of section 303(a). Any action commenced under this title shall proceed as if it were an action commenced under section 4 or section 16 of the Clayton Act, except that the standards of section 303(a) of this title and the remedies provided in this paragraph shall be the exclusive standards and remedies applicable to such action.

(2) Any action brought under paragraph (1), there shall be filed within two years of the date the plaintiff has notice of the failure to comply with the standards of section 303(a) but in any event within four years after the accuse of action accrues.

(3) In any action brought under paragraph (1), there shall be a presumption that conduct which is specified in and complies with a certificate of review does comply with the standards of section 303 (a).

(4) In any action brought under paragraph (1), if the court finds that the conduct does comply with the standards of section 303(a), the court shall award to the person against whom the claim is brought the cost of suit attributable to defending against the claim (including a reasonable attorney's fee).

(5) The Attorney General may file suit pursuant to section 15 of the Clayton Act (15 U.S.C.25) to enjoin conduct threatening clear and irreparable harm to the national interest.

* * *

Editors' note: Title IV of the Export Trading Company Act is the Foreign Antitrust Improvements Act of 1982, which amends the Sherman and Federal Trade Commission Acts. The amendment to the Sherman Act is Section 7 of the Sherman Act, supra.

Index

References are to Pages